W9-DBQ-529

THIRD EDITION

The BUSINESS CORNERSTONE

Building a Solid Foundation

A CUSTOM TEXT FOR THE UNIVERSITY OF HOUSTON DOWNTOWN COLLEGE OF BUSINESS

With material from:

Exploring Research, Fourth Edition
by Neil J. Salkind

International Business: E-Business, Updated Edition
by John J. Wild, Kenneth L. Wild and Jerry C.Y. Han

Diversity Consciousness
by Richard D. Bucher

Critical Thinking: Tools for Taking Charge of Your Learning and Your Life
by Richard Paul and Linda Elder

Ethics and the Conduct of Business, Fourth Edition
by John R. Boatright

Critical Thinking: A Casebook
by Madeleine Picciotto

Learning Team Skills
by Arthur H. Bell and Dayle M. Smith

Making the Team: A Guide for Managers
by Leigh L. Thompson

The Ethical Process: An Approach to Disagreements and Controversial Issues, Third Edition
by Marvin T. Brown

Debating Points: Race and Ethnic Relations
by Henry L. Tischler

Taken from:

Exploring Research, Fourth Edition
by Neil J. Salkind
Copyright © 2000, 1997, 1994, 1991 by Prentice-Hall, Inc.
A Pearson Education Company
Upper Saddle River, New Jersey 07458

International Business: E-Business, Updated Edition
by John J. Wild, Kenneth L. Wild and Jerry C.Y. Han
Copyright © 2001 by Prentice-Hall, Inc.

Diversity Consciousness
by Richard D. Bucher
Copyright © 2000 by Prentice-Hall, Inc.

Critical Thinking: Tools for Taking Charge of Your Learning and Your Life
by Richard Paul and Linda Elder
Copyright © 2001 by Richard Paul and Linda Elder
Published by Prentice-Hall, Inc.

Ethics and the Conduct of Business, Fourth Edition
by John R. Boatright
Copyright © 2003, 2000, 1997, 1993 by Pearson Education, Inc.
Published by Prentice-Hall, Inc.

Critical Thinking: A Casebook
by Madeleine Picciotto
Copyright © 2000 by Prentice-Hall, Inc.

Learning Team Skills
by Arthur H. Bell and Dayle M. Smith
Copyright © 2003 by Pearson Education, Inc.
Published by Prentice-Hall, Inc.

Making the Team: A Guide for Managers
by Leigh L. Thompson
Copyright © 2000 by Prentice-Hall, Inc.

The Ethical Process: An Approach to Disagreements and Controversial Issues, Third Edition
by Marvin T. Brown
Copyright © 2003, 1999, 1996 by Marvin T. Brown
Published by Pearson Education, Inc.

Debating Points: Race and Ethnic Relations
by Henry L. Tischler
Copyright © 2000 by Prentice-Hall, Inc.

All rights reserved. No part of this book may be reproduced, in any form or by any means, without permission in writing from the publisher.

This special edition published in cooperation with Pearson Custom Publishing.

Printed in the United States of America

10 9 8 7 6 5 4 3 2

Please visit our web site at www.pearsoncustom.com

ISBN 0-536-84628-6

2004160131

LW

PEARSON CUSTOM PUBLISHING
75 Arlington Street, Suite 300, Boston, MA 02116
A Pearson Education Company

Contents

Module C

Critical Thinking and Business Ethics. 297

Module A

Research and International Business

Chapter 1

Research

Chapter 1a

The Role and Importance of Research

What You'll Learn About in This Chapter

- Who does research and why
- How research is defined, and what some of its purposes are
- What a model of scientific inquiry is and how it guides research activities
- What research is and what it isn't
- What researchers do and how they do it
- The characteristics of good research
- How a method of scientific inquiry guides research activity
- The different types of research methods and examples of each

Say Hello to Research!

Walk down the hall in any building on your campus where social science professors have their offices, to departments such as psychology, sociology, and human development. Do you see any bearded, disheveled, white-coated men wearing rumpled pants and smoking pipes, hunched over their computers and mumbling to themselves? How about disheveled, white-coated women wearing rumpled skirts, smoking pipes, hunched over their computers and mumbling to themselves?

Researchers hard at work? No. Stereotypes of what scientists look like and do? Yes. What you are more likely to see in the halls of your classroom building or in your adviser's office are men and women of all ages who are hard at work. They are committed to finding the answer to just one more piece of the great puzzle that helps us understand human behavior just a little better than the previous generation of scientists.

Just as everyone else, these people go to work in the morning, but unlike many others these researchers have a passion for understanding what they study and for coming as close as possible to finding the truth. While elusive and sometimes even unobtainable, researchers work toward these truths for the satisfaction of answering important questions and then using this new information to help others. Early intervention programs, treatments of psychopathology, conflict resolution techniques, effective drug programs, and even changes in policy and law have resulted from evidence that researchers collected. While not always perfect, each little bit of evidence from a new study or a new idea for a study contributes to a vast legacy of knowledge for the next generation of researchers, such as yourself.

You might already know and appreciate something about the world of research. The purpose of this book is to provide the tools you need to do even more, such as to

- Develop an understanding of the research process.
- Prepare you to conduct research of your own.
- Learn how to judge the quality of research.
- Learn how to read, search through, and summarize other research.
- Learn what the Internet is all about and how it can be used in everyday research activities.
- Reveal the mysteries of basic statistics, and show you how easy they can actually be.
- Measure the behaviors, traits, or attributes that interest you.
- Collect the type of data that relate to your area of interest.
- Use a leading statistical package (SPSS) to analyze data.
- Design research studies that answer the question you want answered.
- Write the type of research proposal that puts you in control—one that shows you have command of the content of the research as well as command of the way that the research should be done.

Sound ambitious? A bit terrifying? Exciting? Maybe those and more, but boring is one thing this research endeavor is not. That statement is especially true when you consider that the work you might be doing in this class as well as the research proposal that you might write could hold the key to expanding our knowledge and understanding of human behavior and indirectly, eventually helping others.

So here you are, beginning what is probably your first course in the area of research methods and wondering about everything from what researchers do to what your topic will be for your thesis. Relax. Thousands of students have been here before you and almost all of them have left with a working knowledge of what research is, how you do it, and what distinguishes a good research project from one that is doomed. Hold on and let's go. This trip will be exciting.

What Research Is and What It Isn't

Perhaps it is best to begin by looking at what researchers really do for a living. To do so, why not look at some of the best? Here are some researchers, the awards they won, and the focus of their work. These various awards were given in 1998 by the American Psychological Association in recognition of outstanding work. All of these people started out in a class just like the one you are in, reading a book similar to the one you are reading. Their interest in research and a particular issue continued to grow until it became their life's work.

The award of all awards, the Gold Medal Award for Lifetime Achievement, was received by Mary D. Alter Ainsworth for her breakthrough research in the relationship between young children and their caretakers. Harold Stevenson received the Distinguished Scientific Award for the Applications of Psychology for his contributions to the way children learn. His citation from the American Psychological Association states that he "took the study of children's learning from the laboratory into the arena of schools, culture and society." For her contributions to public policy and her work on the behalf of children and adolescents in the areas of cognitive, educational, and health aspects of their development, Rubi Takanishi received an Award for Distinguished Contribution to Research in Public Policy. Ellen S. Bersheid received a Distinguished Scientific Contribution Award in 1997 for her contributions to the understanding of attraction, affiliation, and relationships. And to help recognize excellence in research in new researchers, a Distinguished Scientific Award for an Early Career Contribution to Psychology was given to Mark S. Blumberg.

What all these people have in common is that at one time or another during their professional careers (even for the early career award), they were active participants in the process of doing research. Research is a process through which new knowledge is discovered. A **theory,** such as a theory of motivation or development or learning, for example, helps us organize this new information into a coherent body, a set of related ideas that explain events that have occurred and predict events that will happen. Theories are an important part of science. It is at the ground-floor level, however, that the researcher works to get the ball rolling, adding a bit of new insight here and a new speculation there, until they come together to form a corpus of knowledge.

High-quality research is characterized by many different attributes, many of which tend to be related to one another and also tend to overlap:

1. It is based on the work of others.
2. It can be replicated.
3. It is generalizable to other settings.
4. It is based on some logical rationale and tied to theory.
5. It is doable!
6. It generates new questions or is cyclical in nature.
7. It is incremental.
8. It is an apolitical activity that should be undertaken for the betterment of society.

First, *research is an activity based on the work of others.* No, this does not mean that you copy the work of others (that's plagiarism), but you always look to the work that has already been done to provide a basis for what and how you might conduct your own work. For example, if there have been 200 studies on the relationship between the number of children in a family and the average level of IQ scores, the results of those studies should not be ignored. You may not want to replicate any one of these studies, but you certainly should take methodologies that were used and the results into consideration when you plan your own research in that area.

A good example of this principle is the tremendous intellectual and scientific effort that went into the creation of the atomic bomb. Hundreds of top scientists from all over the world were organized at different locations in an intense and highly charged effort to combine their knowledge to create this horrible weapon. What was unique about this effort is that it was compressed in time; many people who would probably share each other's work in any case did so in days rather than months because of the military and political urgency of the times. What was discovered one day literally became the basis for the next day's experiments.

Second, while we're talking about other studies, *research is an activity that can be replicated.* If someone conducts a research study that examines the relationship between problem-solving ability and musical talent, the results of the experiment should be replicable to other groups for two reasons. First, one of the hallmarks of any credible scientific finding is that it can be replicated. If you can spin gold from straw, you should be able to do it every time, right? How about using a new method to teach children to read? Or developing early intervention programs that produce similar results when repeated? Second, if the results of an experiment can be replicated, they can serve as a basis for further research in the same area.

Third, *good research is generalizable to other settings.* This means, for example, that if adolescent boys are found to be particularly susceptible to peer pressure in one setting, the results would probably stand up (or be generalizable) in a different, but related, setting. While some research has limited generalizability since it is difficult to replicate the exact conditions under which the research was carried out, the results of most research can lend at least something to another setting.

Fourth, *research is based on some logical rationale and tied to theory.* Research ideas do not stand alone as just interesting questions. Rather, research activity provides answers to questions that help fill in pieces to what can be a large and complicated puzzle. No one could be expected to understand, through one grand research project, the entire process of intellectual development in children or the reason why adolescents form cliques or what actually happens during a midlife crisis. All these major areas of research need to be broken into smaller elements, and all these elements need to be tied together with a common theme, which more often than not is some underlying, guiding theory.

Fifth, and by all means, *research is doable!* Too often, especially for the young or inexperienced scientist (such as yourself), the challenge to come up with a feasible idea is so pressing that almost anything will do as a research topic. So your professor sometimes sees statements from students such as, The purpose of this research is to see if the use of drugs can be reduced through exposure to television commercials. This level of ambiguity and lack of a conceptual framework makes the statement almost useless and certainly not doable. Good research poses a question that can be answered, and then answers it in a timely fashion.

Sixth, *research generates new questions or is cyclical in nature.* Yes, what goes around comes around. The answers to today's research questions provide the foundation for research questions that will be asked tomorrow. You will learn more about this process later in this chapter when a method of scientific inquiry is described.

Seventh, *research is incremental.* No one scientist stands alone, instead they stand on the shoulders of others. Contributions that are made usually take place in small, easily definable chunks. The first study ever done on the development of language did not answer all the questions about language acquisition, nor did the last study that was done put the icing on the cake. Rather, all the studies in a particular area come together to produce a body of knowledge shared by different researchers and providing the basis for further research. The whole, or all the knowledge about a particular area, is more than the sum of the parts, because each new research advance not only informs us, but it also helps to place other findings in a different and often fruitful perspective.

Finally, at its best, *research is an apolitical activity that should be undertaken for the betterment of society.* I'm stressing at its best, since too often this or that special interest group dictates how research funding should be spent. Finding a vaccine for AIDS should not depend upon one's attitudes toward individual lifestyles. Similarly, whether early intervention programs should be supported is independent of one's personal or political views. And should research on cloning be abandoned because of its potential misuse? Of course not. It's how the discovery of new knowledge is used that results in its misuse, not the new knowledge itself.

While being apolitical, research should have as its ultimate goal the betterment of society. Researchers or practitioners do not withhold food from pregnant women to study the effects of malnutrition on children. To examine the stress-nutrition link, researchers do not force adults to eat particular diets that might be unhealthy. These unethical practices would not lead to a greater end, especially since there are other ways to answer such questions without resorting to possibly harmful practices.

If these attributes make for good research, what is bad research? It takes the opposite approach of all the things stated above and even more. In sum, bad research is the fishing trip you take looking for something important when it simply is not to be found. It is plagiarizing other people's work. Falsifying data to prove a point. Misrepresenting information and misleading participants. Unfortunately, there are researchers whose work is characterized by these practices, but they are in the minority.

A Model of Scientific Inquiry

In the past 20 years, the public has been exposed to the trials and tribulations of the research process as described through hundreds of books by and about the everyday work of scientists around the world. Some of the best of these books are listed in the Want to Know More? section at the end of this chapter.

Regardless of the specific content of these books, they all have one thing in common: The work was accomplished through adherence to guidelines that allowed these researchers to progress from point A to point Z while remaining confident that they were on the trail of finding (what they hoped was) an adequate answer to the questions they had posed.

Their methods and their conclusions are not helter-skelter because of one important practice: They share the same general philosophy about how questions about human behavior should be answered. In addition, for scientists to be able to trust their colleagues, in the sense of having confidence in the results produced by their studies, scientists must have something in common besides good intentions. As it turns out, what they share is a standard sequence of steps in formulating and answering a question.

When you read in a journal article that Method A is more effective than Method B for improving retention or memory, you can be pretty sure that the steps described next were followed, in one form or another. Because there is agreement about the general method used to answer the question, the results of this comparison of Method A to Method B can be applied to the next study. That perhaps would investigate variations of Method A and how and why they work. The research efforts of developmental psychologists, gerontologists (specialists in aging), linguists, and psychophysiologists all depend on the integrity of the process.

Figure 1.1 shows a set of such steps as part of a model of scientific inquiry. The goal of this model is to find the truth (whatever that means!) or, in other words, to use a **scientific method** that results in a reasonable and sound answer to important questions that will further our understanding of human behavior.

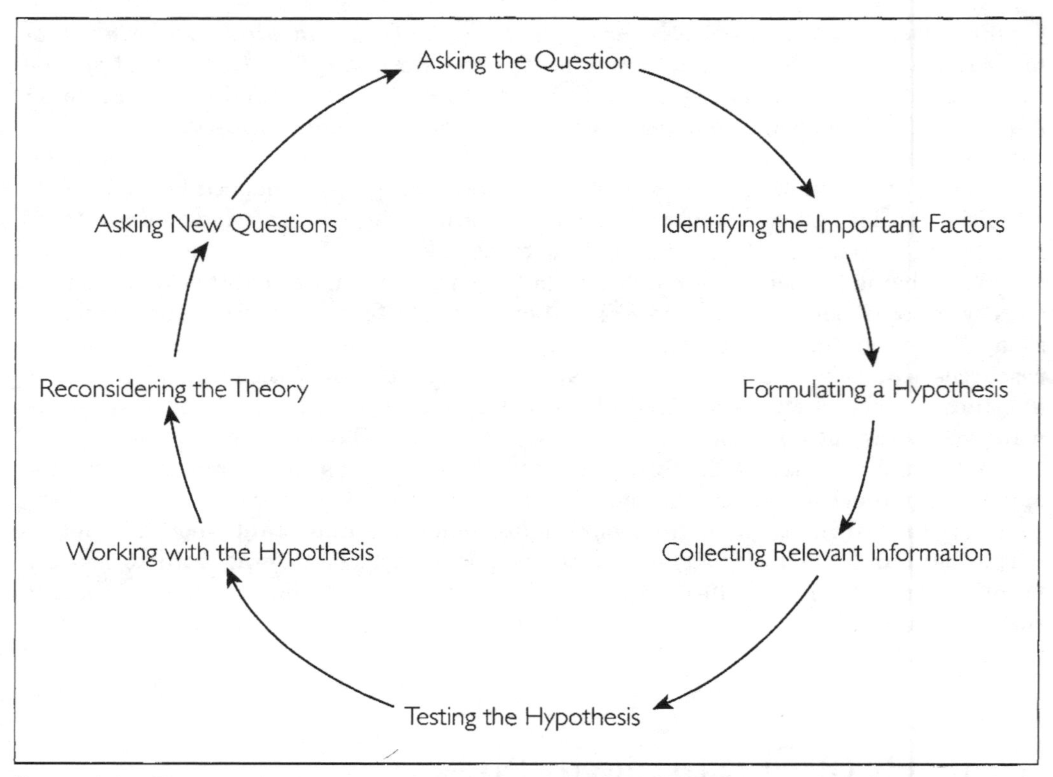

Figure 1.1 The steps in the research process, where each step sets the stage for the next.

An interesting and exciting topic, the effects of television on children, will be used as an example of the different steps in this model.

Asking the Question

Remember the story of the Wizard of Oz? When Dorothy realized her need to get to the Emerald City, she asked Glinda, the good witch, *But where do I begin?* Glinda's response: *Most people begin at the beginning, my dear, as is the case in almost any scientific endeavor.*

Our first and most important step is asking a question (I wonder what would happen if . . .) or identifying a need (We have to find a way to . . .) that arises as the result of curiosity, and it becomes necessary to find an answer. For example, you might be curious about how watching television affects the development of children's language skills. You also might feel an urgency to find out how to use television most effectively for educating children and adults about the dangers of drugs.

Such questions are informally stated and often intended as a source of discussion and stimulation about what direction the specific research topic should take. Where do such questions come from? They rarely come from the confines of a classroom or a laboratory. Rather, questions spring (in the fullest sense of the word) from our imagination and our own experiences, enriched by the worlds of science, art, music, and literature. It is no coincidence that many works of fiction (including science fiction) have a basis in fact. The truly creative scientist is always thinking about everything from solutions to existing questions to the next important question to ask. When Louis Pasteur said that chance favors the prepared mind, he was really saying, take advantage of all the experiences you can, both in and out of school. Only then can you be well prepared to recognize the importance of certain events, which will act as a stimulus for more rigorous research activity.

Questions can be as broad as inquiring about the effects of television on language development, or as specific as the relationship between the content of certain television commercials and teenagers' buying habits. Whatever their content or depth of inquiry, questions are the first step in any scientific endeavor.

Identifying the Important Factors

Once the question has been asked, the next step is to identify the factors that have to be examined to answer the question. They might range from the most simple, such as the child's age or socioeconomic status, to more complicated measures such as the effects of violent cartoons on the child's behavior.

The following list of factors have been investigated over the past 10 years by various researchers who have been interested in the effects of television on children:

- Age of the child
- Degree of violence in programs
- Stage of the child's cognitive growth
- Producer's attitude
- Facial expression
- Decision making
- Mother's description of viewing patterns
- Emotional arousal
- Ethnic differences in response to television programs
- Family communication patterns

And that is only 10 of hundreds of topics that could be explored. But of all the factors that could be important and that help us understand more about the effects of television, which ones should be selected as a focus? In general, you want to select factors that

- Have not been investigated before,
- Will contribute to the understanding of the question you are asking,
- Are available to investigate,
- Hold some interest for you personally or professionally, and
- Lead to another question!

It is hard enough to define the nature of the problem you want to study (see Chapter 3), let alone generate questions that lead to more questions, but once you begin the journey of becoming a scientist, you are a member of an elite group who has the responsibility to contribute to the scientific literature not only by what you do, but by what you see that needs to be done as well.

Formulating a Hypothesis

When asked what she thought a **hypothesis** was, a 9-year-old girl said it best: "An educated guess." A hypothesis results when the questions are transformed into statements that express the relationships between variables as an "if . . . then . . ." statement.

For example, if the question is: What effects does viewing violence on television have on boys? then the hypothesis could be: Boys who view aggressive acts during prime time cartoon shows are more likely to exhibit aggressive behaviors right after the television viewing session than boys who watch nonaggressive acts during prime time shows. Several characteristics make some hypotheses better than others, and we will talk about those in Chapter 2.

For now, you should realize that a hypothesis is an objective extension of the question that was originally posed. While all questions might not be answerable because of the way they are posed—which is fine for the question stage—a good hypothesis poses a question in a testable form. Good questions lead to good hypotheses, which in turn lead to good studies.

Collecting Relevant Information

Hypotheses should posit a clear relationship between different factors such as television viewing and aggressive behavior in males. That is the hypothesis' job. Once a hypothesis is formulated, the next step is the collection of information or empirical data that will confirm or refute the hypothesis. So if you are interested in whether or not viewing aggressive television programs leads to aggressive behavior, the kind of data that allow the hypothesis to be tested need to be collected.

For example, you might collect two types of data to test the hypothesis mentioned above. The first might be the number of violent acts in a 1-hour segment of prime time television. The second would be the number of aggressive behaviors observed in children who watched the program and the number of such acts in children who did not watch the program.

An important point about testing hypotheses is that you set out to test them, not to prove them. As a good scientist, you should be intent on collecting data that reveal as much of the truth about the world as possible and let the chips fall where they may, whether right or wrong or whether you agree or disagree with the outcomes. Setting out to prove a hypothesis can place scientists in the unattractive position of biasing the methods for collecting data or the way in which results are interpreted. If bias occurs, then the entire sequence of steps can fall apart. Besides, there's no really being wrong in science. Not having hypotheses supported means only that there are additional questions to ask or that the ones asked need to be reformulated. That is the beauty of good science—there is always another question to ask on the same topic that can shed just a bit more light. And who can tell? That bit more light might be just the amount needed to uncover an entirely new and significant finding, by you or someone else.

Testing the Hypothesis

Is it enough to simply collect data that relate to the phenomena being studied? Not quite. What if you have finished collecting data and find that boys who watched aggressive prime time television programs show 4.8 aggressive acts in the 1-hour period following exposure and that boys who watched a nonaggressive program exhibited an average of 2.4 acts? What would your conclusion be?

On the one hand, you could say that the boys who watched the aggressive programs were more than twice as aggressive. On the other hand, you might argue that the difference between the two averages is not large enough for you to reach any conclusion. To be able to say that watching the aggressive television segment really made a difference, you would have to see a much bigger difference, you might say. An unsolvable dilemma? Not at all.

Say hello to inferential statistics (and see Chapter 8 for more!), a set of tools that allows researchers to separate the effects of an isolated factor (such as aggressive or nonaggressive television viewing) from differences between groups that might be due to some other factor or to nothing other than **chance.** Yes, luck, fate, destiny, the wheels of fortune, or whatever you want to call what you cannot control, sometimes can be responsible for differences between groups. For example, what if one of the boys who did not watch the aggressive segment feels a bit crabby that day and decides to whack his playmate? Or if one of the boys who did watch the aggressive segment is tired and just does not feel like playing at all? The job of these tools is to help you separate the effects of the factors being studied from other, unrelated factors. What these statistical tools do is assign a probability level to an outcome so you can decide whether what you see is really due to what you think it is or is it due to something else that you will have to leave for the next study.

Working with the Hypothesis

Once you have collected the data that your question requires and have tested the hypothesis, as a good scientist you sit down, put up the old feet, look intellectual, and examine the results. The results may confirm or refute the hypothesis. In either case, it is off to the races. If it is a confirmation, then the importance of the factors that were hypothesized to be related and conceptually important were borne out, and you can go your merry way as the next scientific experiment is planned. If the hypothesis is not confirmed, it can very well be a time for learning something that was not known previously. In the example used earlier, it may mean that watching television segments with aggressive models does not alone result in aggressive behavior on the part of the boy. Although the researcher might be a bit disappointed that the initial hunch (formally called a hypothesis) was not supported, the results of a well-run study always provide valuable information, regardless of the outcome.

Reconsidering the Theory

Finally, it is time to take stock and relate all these research efforts to what guides our work in the first place: theory. Earlier in this chapter, a theory was defined as a set of statements that predict things that will occur in the future and explain things that have occurred in the past. But the very nature of theories is that they can be modified according to the results of research based on the same assumptions on which the theory is based.

For example, a particular approach to understanding the development of children and adults is known as social learning theory, which places special importance on the role of modeling and vicarious, or indirect, learning. According to this theory, exposure to aggressive behavior would lead to aggressive behavior, once the environment contains the same kinds of cues that were present when the initial aggressive model (such as aggressive cartoon characters) was observed.

If the hypothesis that observing such models increases aggression is confirmed, another building block, or piece of evidence, has been added to the house called social learning theory. Good scientists are always trying to see what type of brick (new information) fits where, or if it fits at all. In this way, new knowledge can change or modify the way the theory appears and what it has to say about human behavior. In this way, new questions might be generated from the theory that will help contribute further to the way the house is structured.

Asking New Questions

In any case, the last step in this simplified model of scientific inquiry is to ask a new question. It might be a simple variation on a theme (Do males react differently than females to aggressive models?) or a refinement of the original question (How much exposure to aggressive models is necessary before children begin modeling the behavior?). No matter if the hypothesis is supported or not, good research leaves you farther along the trail to answering the original question. You just might be at a different place than you thought or intended to be.

Different Types of Research

By now, you have a good idea what research is and how the research process works. Now it is time to turn your attention to a description and examples of different types of research methods and the type of questions they pose.

The types of research methods that will be discussed differ mostly on two dimensions: the nature of the question asked and the method used to answer it. One way in which these methods do not necessarily differ, however, is in the content or the focus of the research. In other words, if you are interested in the effects of television on children, your research can be nonexperimental, where you survey watching habits, or experimental, where you expose children to certain models and look at the effect of the exposure on their behavior.

A summary of the three general categories of research methods that will be discussed in *Exploring Research* is shown in Table 1.1. In this table you can see the purpose of each, the time frame that each encompasses, the degree of control the different method has over competing factors, "code" words that appear in research articles that can tip you off as to the type of research being conducted, and an example of each. Chapters 9, 10, and 11 go into greater detail about each of these research methods.

Nonexperimental Research

Nonexperimental research includes a variety of different methods that describe relationships between variables. The important distinction between nonexperimental methods and the others you will learn about later is that nonexperimental research methods do not set out, nor can they test, any causal relationships between variables. For example, if you wanted to survey the television-watching behavior of adolescents, you could do so by having them maintain a diary where they record what they watch and whom they watch it with. This descriptive study provides information about their television-watching habits but says nothing about why they watch what they do. You are not in any way trying to have an impact on their television-watching behavior or investigate why they might watch particular shows. This is nonexperimental in nature since no cause-and-effect relationships of any type are being hypothesized or investigated.

Nonexperimental research methods that will be covered in *Exploring Research* are descriptive, historical, and correlational. All three will be covered in Chapter 9. Here is a brief overview of each.

Type of Research	Purpose	Time Frame	Degree of Control over Factors	Code Words to Look for in Research Articles	Example
Nonexperimental (Descriptive)	Describe the characteristics of an existing phenomenon.	Current	None or low	"describe" "interview" "review literature"	A survey of dating practices of adolescent females.
Nonexperimental (Historical)	Relate events that have occurred in the past to current events.	Past	None or low	"past" "describe"	An analysis of Freud's use of hypnosis as it relates to current psychotherapy practices.
Nonexperimental (Correlational)	Examine the relationships between variables.	Current or past (correlation) future (prediction)	Low to medium spatial and verbal	"relationship" "related to" "associated with" "predicts"	An investigation that focuses on the relationship between the number of hours of television watching and grade point average.
Experimental	Test for true cause-and-effect relationships.	Current	High	"function of" "cause of" "comparison between" "effects of"	The effect of a preschool language program on the language skills of inner city children.
Quasi-Experimental	Test for causal relationships without having full control.	Current or past	Moderate to high	"function of" "cause of" "comparison between" "effects of"	Gender differences in abilities.

Table 1.1 Different types of research you will read about in *Exploring Research.*

Descriptive Research

Descriptive research describes the characteristics of an existing phenomenon. The U.S. Census is descriptive research as is any survey that assesses the current status of anything from the number of faucets in a house to the number of adults over the age of 60 who have grandchildren.

What can be done with this information? First, it provides a broad picture of a phenomenon you might be interested in exploring. For example, if you are interested in learning more about the reading process in children, you might want to consult *The Reading Report Card,* published by the Educational Testing Service in Princeton, New Jersey. This annual publication summarizes information about the reading achievement of children 9, 13, and 17 years of age. Or you might want to consult a publication of the Center for Disease Control, the *Morbidity and Mortality Weekly,* to find out what the current rate of measles cases might be in the Midwest, or the Bureau of Labor Statistics to determine the current unemployment rate and how many working single parents there are who have children under the age of 5 years (about 60%). If you want to know it, there is a place to find it. Descriptive research demands this type of information.

Another example is where Peter O. Peretti and Kris G. Majecen (1992) interviewed 58 elderly individuals, from 68 to 87 years of age, using a structured interview to investigate the variables that affect emotional abuse among the elderly. As a result of the interviews (a type of survey research), they found nine variables are common to elderly abuse, including lack of affection, threats of violence, and confinement.

Not only can descriptive research stand on its own, it can also serve as a basis for other types of research, in that a group's characteristics often need to be described before the meaningfulness of any differences can be addressed.

Historical Research

Historical research relates past events to one another or to current events. Basically, historical research (or **historiography**) answers the question: What is the nature of events that have happened in the past? For example, one might want to examine trends in the way mental illness has been treated or how attitudes toward work and families have changed. All these require the detective work of a historian: finding and collecting relevant data and then, just as with any other research endeavor, testing a hypothesis. In fact, like any other researcher, the historian collects data, analyzes them, and then comes to conclusions about the tenability of his or her hypothesis. One significant difference between historical research and other types of research is the type of data collected and the method of collection.

Researchers who do historical research often accomplish this goal through the use of primary sources (original documents or information from people who have personally experienced an event) and secondary sources (secondhand documents or information from people who may have some knowledge about the event but did not experience it firsthand). Even if these sources are readily available, however, one of the greatest challenges in doing such research is in knowing how much faith the researcher can put in the accuracy of the sources.

An example of historical research is a study by Nancy Burton and Lyle Jones (1982) which examined trends in achievement levels of African American versus white children. Burton and Jones examined high school graduation rates for African Americans versus whites who were born before 1913, between 1913 and 1922, 1923 and 1932, 1933 and 1942, 1943 and 1947, and 1948 and 1952 for people who were 25 years or older in 1977. They also examined a variety of other historical indicators in more recent groups of African American and white children and concluded that differences in achievement between groups are decreasing. To complete their analysis, Burton and Jones obtained data from the National Assessment of Educational Progress. With today's sophisticated data retrieval tools, historical researchers can use their computers (see Chapter 3) to tap into almost any database they need and save trips to the library.

Correlational Research

Descriptive and historical research provide a picture of events that are currently happening or have occurred in the past. Researchers often want to go beyond mere description and begin discussing the relationship that certain events might have with one another. The most likely type of research to answer questions about the relationship among variables or events is called **correlational research.**

What correlational research does, which neither descriptive nor historical research does, is provide some indication as to how two or more things are related to one another, or how well a specific outcome might be predicted by one or more pieces of information. Correlational research uses a numerical index called the correlation coefficient (see Chapter 9 for a complete discussion) as a measure of the strength of this relationship. Most correlational studies report such an index.

If you were interested in finding out the relationship between the number of hours that freshmen study and their grade-point averages, you would be doing correlational research because you are interested in the relationship between these two factors. If you were interested in finding out the best set of predictors of success in graduate school, you would be doing a type of correlational research that includes prediction.

For example, in a study of the relationship between temperament and attachment behavior in infants (Vaughn, Lefever, Seifer, & Barglow, 1989), the correlation among different types of attachment behaviors, how securely attached the infants were to their mothers, and the infant's general temperament (a term often used to discuss an infant's personality) were examined. The researchers found that an infant's temperament does not predict how securely attached the child is to his or her mother.

One of the most important points about correlational research is that it examines relationships between variables but in no way implies that one causes another. In other words, correlation and prediction examine associations but not causal relationships, where a change in one factor directly influences a change in another.

For example, it is a well-established fact that as the number of crimes in a community increases, so does the level of ice cream consumption! What is going on? Certainly, no thinking person would conclude that the two are causally related such that if you banned ice cream, there would be no more crimes. Rather, another variable, temperature, better explains the amount of ice cream consumed and crime rate (they both go up when it gets warm). It might seem ridiculous that people would identify causality just because events are related, but you do not have to read far in the daily newspaper to see politicians reaching such unwise conclusions.

Experimental Research

You already know that correlational research can help establish the presence of a relationship among variables but not give us any reason to believe that variables are causally related to one another. How does one find out if characteristics or behaviors or events are related in such a way that the relationship is a causal one? There are two types of research that can answer that question for us. The first is quasi-experimental research, and the second is experimental research. For now, let's briefly discuss experimental research.

The only way to establish a true cause-and-effect relationship in any study is to isolate and eliminate all the factors that might be responsible for a particular outcome and test only those that you directly want to measure.

Experimental research is where participants are assigned to groups based on some selected criterion often called the treatment variable. For example, let us say that you are interested in comparing the effects of two different techniques for reducing obsessive compulsive disorder behavior in adults. The first technique includes behavioral therapy, and the second does not. Once adults are assigned to groups and the programs are completed, you will want to look for any differences between the two groups as to the effects of the therapy on the number of obsessive compulsive behaviors. Because assignment to the groups is determined by the researcher, he or she has complete control over what the adults are exposed to.

This is the ideal model for establishing a cause-and-effect relationship since you have clearly defined the possible cause (if indeed it results in some effect) and can keep very close tabs on what is happening. Most important, however, you have complete control over the treatment.

In a quasi-experimental study, you do not have such a high degree of control because people have already been indirectly assigned to those groups (such as social class, abuse, gender, and type of injury) for which you are testing the effects.

The distinction between experimental and other methods of research does boil down to a matter of control. True experimental research designs, of which you will learn about in Chapter 10, isolate and control all the factors that could be responsible for any effects except the one of most interest.

For example, Fleming, Klein, and Corter (1992) examined the effects of participation in a social support group on depression, maternal attitudes, and behavior in new mothers. As part of the experimental design, the researchers divided a total of 142 mothers into three groups. Group 1 received the intervention, Group 2 received the no-intervention condition, and Group 3 received a special group-by-mail intervention. The key point here is the manipulation (the key word in experimental designs) of the condition for each of the three groups.

This research is experimental, since the researcher determined group membership participation in the social support group as a function of the treatment itself. As you will learn, in a quasi-experimental study the researcher has no control over group membership.

The primary difference between quasi-experimental and experimental research is that in quasi-experimental research the researcher does not have complete control over the criterion used to assign participants to groups, but in experimental research he or she does have that control, and what a difference that makes.

Quasi-Experimental Research

Quasi-experimental research is where participants are preassigned to groups based on some characteristic or quality these people bring to the study. Differences in sex, race, age, class in school, neighborhood of residence, type of job, and even experiences are examples. These group assignments have already taken place before the experiment begins, and the researcher has no control as to what people will belong to each group.

Let us say you are interested in examining voting patterns as a function of neighborhood. You can't change the neighborhood people live in, but you can use the quasi-experimental method to establish a causal link between residence and voting patterns. In other words, if you find that voting pattern and residence are related, you can say with some degree of confidence (but not as much as with an experimental study) that where one resides has some causal relationship as to how one votes.

The most important use of the quasi-experimental method is where researchers cannot, in good conscience, assign people to groups and test the effects of group membership on some other outcome. For example, researchers interested in the effects of parental unemployment on children could not very well encourage mothers or fathers to quit work. Rather, they would seek out families where parents are already unemployed and then conduct the research. Norma Radin and Rena Harold-Goldsmith (1989) did exactly that. They compared the involvement of 17 jobless fathers and 31 employed fathers with their children. They also looked at other factors, including the father's view of the male role in the family, maternal employment, and the child's age.

Quasi-experimental research is also called **post hoc** research or after-the-fact research since the actual research takes place after the assignment of groups such as employed versus unemployed, malnourished versus nonmalnourished, male versus female. Because assignment has already taken place, the researcher has a high degree, but not the highest degree, of control over the cause of whatever effects are being examined. For the highest degree of control to occur, the experimental model needs to be followed.

Applied Versus Basic Research

Sometimes in the research world, distinctions need to be made not only about the type of research but also about the most general category into which the implications or utility of the research might fall. This is where the distinction between basic and applied research comes in. But beware! This distinction is sometimes used as a convenient way to classify research activity rather than to shed light on the intent or purpose of the researcher and the importance of the study.

The most basic distinction between the two is that **basic research** (sometimes called pure research) is research that has no immediate application at the time it is completed, whereas **applied research** is research that does. If this appears to be a somewhat ambiguous distinction, it is, because almost all basic research eventually results in some worthwhile application over the long term.

For example, for every dollar spent on the basic research that supported the lunar missions during the 1960s and 1970s, six dollars were returned in economic impact. Data from basic research that hypothesizes a relationship between Alzheimer's disease in older people and Down syndrome (a genetic disorder) in younger people in time could prove to be the critical finding that leads to a cure for both diseases. Another example: Who cares if some children have a more difficult time than others in distinguishing between two very similar stimuli? You do, if you want to teach them how to read. Many different reading programs have grown directly from such basic research efforts.

Therefore, do not judge the quality of either the finished product or the worth of supporting a research project by branding it as basic or applied research. Rather, look closely at its content, and judge it on its merit. This approach obviously has been happening, since more and more reports about basic research (at one time beyond the interests of everyday practitioners) show up in such practitioner-oriented professional journals as *Phi Delta Kappan* and the American Psychological Association Monitor as well as the *Sunday New York Times Magazine, Newsweek, Science News,* and the *American Scientist.*

Summary

Great! You have finished the first chapter of *Exploring Research,* and I hope you have a good idea as to what research is (and isn't), what the purpose of research is, and some of the different ways in which research can be carried out. With this new information under your belt, let's turn to the next chapter, which focuses on some researchese, or the language that researchers use, and how these new terms fit together with what you have learned here.

Exercises

1. The process of research never stands independently from the content of what the research is about. As a student new to the field of research, and perhaps even to your own discipline (such as psychology or sociology or nursing), answer the following questions:
   (a) What areas within your discipline especially interest you?
   (b) Who are some of the outstanding researchers in your field, and what is the focus of their work?
   (c) Of the different types of research described and discussed in this chapter, which one do you think best fits the type of research that is done in your discipline?

2. Visit your college or university library, and locate an article from a professional journal that describes a research study. From the description of how scientific inquiry takes place (which you read about in this chapter), answer the following:
   (a) What is the primary question posed by the study?
   (b) What important factors are identified?
   (c) Is there a hypothesis stated? If so, what is it?

(d) Describe the way the information was collected.
(e) How could the results of the study affect the originally posed hypothesis?

3. Interview an active researcher on your campus and ask about his or her research activities including:
   (a) The focus of his or her research interests.
   (b) Why he or she is interested in this area.
   (c) What the most exciting part of the research is.
   (d) What the least exciting part of the research is.
   (e) What impact the results of the research may have on his or her particular discipline.

4. Select a discipline within the social and behavioral sciences, such as child development, social psychology, higher education, or health psychology. For the discipline you select, find a representative study that is quasi-experimental or experimental in nature. Write a one-paragraph description of the study. Do the same for an historical study as well.

5. In a fictitious correlational study, the results showed that age was related to strength. That is, as children get older, their strength increases. What is the problem with the statement that increased strength is caused by increasing age or that the stronger you get the older you get?

6. Write down your definition of science. How would your definition of science differ from a student's in a similar class 25 years ago? How would your definition differ from that put forth by a physical (e.g., physics, chemistry) scientist, if it differs at all?

7. Look for examples of editorials or research articles that present correlational evidence. Do the authors infer a cause-and-effect relationship in the correlation? Why might it be difficult for even seasoned researchers to keep from making this mistake?

8. Research often replicates findings made by others. What is the value in this process?

9. Identify five attributes that characterize high quality research.

10. Explain the difference between historical, correlational, and quasi-experimental research.

Want to Know More?

Further Readings

Bond, D. (1990). Economics and critical thinking. *Social Studies Review, 29*(3), 42–46.

Advocates the critical thinking approach including problem solving and hypothesis testing to help secondary teachers teach economic concepts to secondary students.

Dillenger, A.M. (1983). Experimentation in the classroom: Use of public school students as research subjects. *Journal of Law and Education, 12*(3), 347–78.
Reviews the history of research using students as subjects in public schools and the legal responsibilities involved in the approval and supervision of such research.

Dormen, L., & Edidin, P. (1989, July/August). Original spin. *Psychology Today, 23,* 47–51.
Discusses ways to stimulate your creative thought processes, including brainstorming by computer. Has some excellent suggestions for you to use to find ideas for research that may be personally interesting to you.

Kuhn, T.S. (1970). *The structure of the scientific revolution.* Chicago: The University of Chicago Press.
The book to read if you want to know more about how science is done and how different cultural and political forces influence the creation and revision of theories.

Wallen, N.E. (1989). A comparison of quantitative and qualitative research. *School of Education Review, 1*(1), 6–10.
Discusses important differences in the theory and practice of quantitative and qualitative research methodologies and suggests that each of these methodologies can be improved by utilizing key ingredients of the other.

Readings of Other Interest

Burke, J. (1978). *Connections.* Boston: Little Brown.
A companion book to the acclaimed PBS television series. Traces the development of modern technology back thousands of years. Shows how scientific innovation, need, and coincidence often work together to advance civilization.

Downey, M.T., & Levstik, L.S. (1988). Teaching and learning history: The research base. *Social Education, 52*(5), 336–338.
Presents a review of research literature that was undertaken to determine the extent to which research about teaching and learning history supports the current reform movement.

Evered, D., & Harnett, S. (Eds.). (1989). *The evaluation of scientific research.* New York: Wiley.
An accumulation of presentations at the Ciba Foundation Conference held in London in 1988 that discuss research trends, problems, methods, and evaluations. An overview for the new student to see how professionals in the research field view the techniques currently used.

Jackson, D., & Philippe, R.J. (Eds.). (1987). *Scientific excellence: Origins and assessment.* Newbury Park, CA: Sage.
Presentation of a group of papers that define the qualities of competent, successful scientists. Spends a great deal of time describing the behavior of psychologists. Gives the reader a flavor of what science is, and how it relates to research.

Chapter 1b

The Research Process: Coming to Terms

What You'll Learn About in This Chapter

- The path from formulating questions to seeking and finding solutions
- The difference between dependent and independent variables
- What a hypothesis is and how it works
- The importance of the null hypothesis
- The difference between the null and the research hypothesis
- The characteristics of a good hypothesis
- The importance of samples and populations in the research process
- What statistical significance means
- What criteria you should use to evaluate a research article
- How ethical research practices are the responsibility of all researchers
- Why confidentiality is among the most important of ethical criteria to maintain
- The ethical standards published by different professional organizations
- The importance of internal research practice review committees

From Problem to Solution

All you need is to identify an interesting question, collect some data, and poof! Instant research! Not quite. The model of scientific inquiry discussed in Chapter 1 does a nice job of specifying the steps in the research process, but there is quite a bit more to the process than that.

At the beginning of this chapter, we will provide a "real-life" example of how the process actually takes place and how researchers begin with what they see as a problem (to be solved) and end up with a solution (or the results) to that problem. Keep in mind, however, that the meanings of the words *problem* and *solution* go beyond solving a simple problem of the $2 + 2 = 4$ variety. Rather, the questions that researchers ask often reflect a more pressing social concern or economic issue. In addition, the results from a research study often provide the foundation for the next research endeavor.

We will look at an interesting study titled "Maternal Employment and Young Adolescents' Daily Experiences in Single-Mother Families" (Duckett & Richards, 1989) that examines the impact of maternal employment on adolescent development. One of the most creative things about this study is the way these researchers went about collecting the data they needed. They did not sit down and ask adolescents how they felt about this or that but instead tried to get an overall picture of their feelings outside of the laboratory setting.

The researchers who conducted this study with 436 fifth- through ninth-graders and their mothers were interested in a combination of issues that have received considerable attention in the print and electronic media. The general goal of the research (and the problem) was to better understand some of the factors and consequences that surround the increasingly large number of working mothers with adolescent children.

To narrow their investigation, they set out to learn about the general nature of the children's experiences as a function of having a mother who works as well as about the quality of time that the adolescents spent with their mothers. Given that so many mothers (more than 50% of those with children under 18 years of age) from both single- and dual-parent families are now working outside the home, answers to questions like those posed by this study are becoming increasingly important in the formation of social and economic policies.

To get their answers, the researchers had to compare adolescents living with two parents (382, or 88% of the total) with those adolescents who live with only their mothers (54, or 12% of the total). But to fully reach their goal of better understanding the effects of maternal employment, the researchers had to break down the group of children and parents even further, into those children whose mothers worked part-time, full-time, or were unemployed. When separated into groups based on these two factors (family configuration and employment status), the researchers can make a comparison within and between the six groups (all combinations of single- and two-parent families, with employed part-time, employed full-time, and unemployed mothers) and get the information they need to answer the general questions posed.

Now comes the really creative part of the study. They used a method called the *Experience Sampling Method* first developed by two other researchers (Csikszentmihalyi & Larson, 1987). According to this method, the adolescents participating in the study would carry electronic beepers. On an unpredictable schedule, they would receive a beep from beep central(!) and would then stop what they were doing and complete a self-report form. They would do this for one week.

A signal telling the participant to stop and complete the form was sent on an average of every two hours between the hours of 7:30 A.M. and 9:30 P.M., with a total of 49 signals sent for the week for each participant. This means that in the course of one week, 49 separate forms were completed providing information about how participants felt at any particular moment. For 436 participants at 49 forms each, a total of 21,364 forms was completed, which is a hefty sample of kids' behavior!

What was contained on these self-report forms? The adolescents had to report on what the researchers call affect (happy-sad, cheerful-irritable, friendly-angry) and arousal (alert-drowsy, strong-weak, excited-bored). Each of these six items was rated along a 1-to-7 scale. For example, they might indicate a 4, meaning they feel "right in the middle of happy and sad at that moment in time." These six items could be completed in a short period of time, and an accurate picture of the adolescent's daily life could then be formed. Adolescents also had to respond to "What were you doing?" and "Whom were you with?" as well as to some questions about their perceptions of their parents' friendliness and their feelings while with their parents.

Duckett and Richards have an interesting comparison (single-parent versus dual-parent moms, who are unemployed or employed part-time or full-time) and a nice-sized set of reactions from adolescents on which to base the researchers' analysis and discussion. To make sense of all this information, they compiled and then applied some statistical tests (you will learn more about these later) to reach their conclusions, including:

- Children of working single mothers benefit in ways other than just in the provision of income.
- Maternal employment is related to positive parent-child interactions.
- Children of single mothers employed full-time felt friendliest toward their fathers.

This was a well-designed and straightforward study that examined a question that bears on many issues that everyone from schoolteachers to employers needs answered. The study was done with a more than adequate number of participants and used methods that directly get at the type of information the researchers wanted. Although they did not answer every question about the relationship between maternal employment and adolescent development, the researchers did provide an important piece to the puzzle of understanding employment's effects on growing children and changing families. The researchers seemed to take a logical approach of going from a question that has some import for many groups in today's society and articulating it in such a way that it can be answered in a reasonable and efficient manner.

The issue of how children are affected by working parents is certainly still here, but the results of research such as that summarized above bring us closer to a solution to some of the questions posed by such work arrangements. To be the kind of researcher you want to be, you need to know the rules of the game and follow them as did Duckett and Richards. This knowledge begins with an understanding of some basic vocabulary and ideas.

The Language of Research

Significance levels? Null hypotheses? Independent variables? Factorial designs? Research hypotheses? Samples? Populations? These and other new words and terms form the basis for much of the communication that takes place in the research world. As with any endeavor, it is difficult to play the game unless you learn the rules. The rules begin here, with a basic understanding of the terminology that researchers use in their everyday activities. This chapter offers a language lesson of sorts. Once you become familiar with these terms, everything that follows in *Exploring Research* will be easier to understand and more useful. Each of the terms described and defined here will be used again throughout the book.

All About Variables

The word variable has several synonyms, such as changeable or unsteady. Our set of rules tells us that a variable is a noun, not an adjective, and represents a class of outcomes that can take on more than one value.

For example, hair color is a **variable** that can take on the values of red, brown, black, blond, and these days green, orange, and (I swear) puce. (I saw it outside my office this morning!) Other variables would be height (tall or short), weight (128 pounds or 150 pounds), age at immunization (6 weeks or 18 months), number of words remembered, time off work, party affiliation, and so on. The one thing these traits have in common is that the variable (such as party affiliation) can take on any one of several values (such as Republican, Democrat, or Independent).

Interestingly, variables that might go by the same name can take on different values—you could measure height in inches (60 inches) or in rank (the tallest), for example—or be defined differently, depending upon a host of factors such as the purpose of the research or the characteristics of the participants. For example, consider the variable called intelligence. For one researcher, the definition might be scores on the Stanford-Binet Intelligence Test, while for another it might be scores on the Kaufmann Assessment Battery. For Howard Gardner (1983), who believes in the existence of multiple intelligences, the definition might be performance in mathematics, music, or some physical activity. All these variables represent the same general construct of intelligence, assessed in different ways.

In the following few paragraphs, I describe several types of variables and summarize these types and what they do in Table 2.1.

Dependent Variables

A **dependent variable** represents the outcomes of a research study. For example, if you measure the difference between two groups of adults on how well they can remember a set of 10 single digits after a 5-hour period, the number of digits remembered is the dependent variable. Another example: If you are looking at the effect of parental

Method of Teaching Reading (Independent Variable)		
Method A (with Tutoring)	Method B (with Tutoring and Rewards)	Method C (No Tutoring and No Rewards)
Reading Scores	Reading Scores	Reading Scores

Table 2.1 Different types of variables.

involvement in school on children's grades, the grades that the children received would be considered a dependent variable.

You can think of a dependent variable as the outcome that may depend on the experimental treatment or on what the researcher changes or manipulates.

Independent Variables

An **independent variable** represents the treatments or conditions that the researcher controls to test their effects on some outcome. An independent variable is also known as a treatment variable, and it is within this context that the term is most often used. An independent variable is manipulated in the course of an experiment to understand the effects of this manipulation on the dependent variable.

For example, you might want to test the effectiveness of three different reading programs on children's reading skills. This design is illustrated in Figure 2.1. Method A includes tutoring. Method B includes tutoring and rewards, and Method C includes neither tutoring nor rewards (these kids just spend some time with the teacher). In this example, method of reading instruction is manipulated, and it is the independent variable. Reading scores are the outcome, or dependent, variable. This experiment includes three levels of one independent variable and one dependent variable.

What if you wanted to investigate whether there is a difference between males and females in their mathematics scores on some standardized test? In this example, the independent variable is gender (male or female) and the outcome or dependent variable is mathematics score.

Or, you could look at the effects of the number of hours of weekly TV watching time (less than 25 for group A or 25 or more for group B) on language skills. Here, the amount of time watching television is the independent variable, and language skills is the dependent variable.

The general rule to follow is that when the researcher is manipulating anything or assigning participants to groups based on some characteristic, such as age or ethnicity or treatment, that variable is the independent variable. When the researcher looks to some outcome to determine if the grouping had an effect, he or she looks to the dependent variable.

In some cases, when researchers are not interested in looking at the effects of one thing on another, but only in how variables may be related, there are no independent variables. For example, if you are interested only in the relationship between the amount of time a father spends with his children and his job performance, nothing is manipulated.

Independent variables must take on at least two levels or values (since they are variables). For example, if a researcher was studying the effects of gender differences (the independent variable) on language development (the dependent variable), the independent variable would have two levels, male and female. Similarly, if a researcher

Method of Teaching Reading (Independent Variable)		
Method A (with Tutoring)	Method B (with Tutoring and Rewards)	Method C (No Tutoring and No Rewards)
Reading Scores	Reading Scores	Reading Scores

Figure 2.1 Research designs can take on many different forms. Here, the researcher is examining the effects of three different methods or levels of teaching reading on reading scores. Notice that in the last method (C), neither treatment is implemented. This is the control condition.

Method of Teaching Reading (Independent Variable)		
Method A (with Tutoring)	Method B (with Tutoring and Rewards)	Method C (No Tutoring and No Rewards)
Reading Scores	Reading Scores	Reading Scores

Figure 2.2 Many experiments use more than one independent variable. In this example, there are three; gender, social class, and age.

was investigating age differences in stress for people ages 30–39, 40–49, and 50–59 years, the independent variable would be age, and it would have three levels.

What happens if you have more than one independent variable? Look at Figure 2.2, which represents a **factorial design** where gender, age, and social class are independent variables. Factorial designs are experiments that include more than one independent variable. Here are two levels of gender, three levels of age, and three levels of social class, accounting for a 2 by 3 by 3 design for a total of 18 (!) separate combinations, or cells, of levels of independent variables. You can see that as independent variables are added to a research design, the total number of cells increases rapidly.

The Relationship Between Independent and Dependent Variables

The best independent variable is independent of any other variable in the same study. In this way the independent variable can contribute the maximum amount of understanding beyond what other independent variables can offer.

The best dependent variable is one that is sensitive to changes in the different levels of the independent variable. Otherwise, even if the treatment had an effect, you would never know it.

Other Important Types of Variables

Independent and dependent variables are the two kinds of variables that you will deal with most often throughout *Exploring Research.* There are other variables that are important for you to know about as well, however, because an understanding of what they are and how they fit into the research process is essential for you to be an intelligent consumer and to have a good foundation as a beginning producer of research. Here are three more types of variables that you should be familiar with (see Table 2.1).

A **control variable** is a variable that has a potential influence on the dependent variable. Consequently, the influence has to be removed or controlled. For example, if you are interested in examining the relationship between reading speed and reading comprehension, you may want to control for differences in intelligence since intelligence is related both to reading speed and reading comprehension. Intelligence, then, needs to be held constant for you to get a good idea of the nature of the relationship between the variables of interest.

An **extraneous variable** is a variable that has an unpredictable impact upon the dependent variable. For example, if you are interested in examining the effects of television watching on achievement, you might find that the type of television programs watched is an extraneous variable that might affect achievement, since programs such as "Discovery," "Nova," "Sesame Street," and "3-2-1 Contact" might have a positive impact on achievement, and other programs might have a negative impact.

A **moderator variable** is a variable that is related to the variables of interest (such as the dependent and independent variable), masking the true relationship between the independent and dependent variable. For example, if you are examining the relationship between crime rate and ice cream consumption, you need to include temperature because it moderates that relationship. Otherwise, your conclusions will be inaccurate.

Hypotheses

In the last chapter, a **hypothesis** was defined as "an educated guess." While a hypothesis reflects many other things, perhaps its most important role is to reflect the general problem statement or question that was the motivation for undertaking the research study. That is why taking care and time with that initial question is so important. It can guide you through the creation of an hypothesis which in turn helps you determine the types of techniques you will use to test the hypothesis and answer the original question.

The "I wonder . . ." stage becomes the problem statement stage, which then leads to the study's hypothesis. Here is an example of each of these.

The Stage	**An Example**
"I wonder . . ."	It seems to me that several things could be done to help our employees lower their high absentee rate. Talking with some of them tells me that they are concerned about after school care for their children. I wonder what would happen if a program were started right here in the factory that could provide child supervision and activities?
The hypothesis	Parents who enroll their children in after school programs will miss fewer days of work in one year and will have a more positive attitude toward work as measured by the Attitude Toward Work survey (ATW) than parents who do not enroll their children in such programs.

A good hypothesis provides a transition from a problem statement into a form that is more amenable to testing using the research methods discussed in this book. We will talk about what makes a good hypothesis after defining the two types of hypotheses, the null hypothesis and research hypothesis, and how they are used.

The Null Hypothesis

The null hypothesis is an interesting little creature. If it could talk, it would say something like, "I represent no relationship between the variables that you are studying." In other words, **null hypotheses** are statements of equality such as:

- There will be no difference in the average score of ninth-graders and the average score of twelfth-graders on the ABC memory test.
- There is no relationship between personality type and job success.
- There is no difference in voting patterns as a function of political party.
- The brand of ice cream preferred is independent of the buyer's age, gender, and income.

A null hypothesis such as the ones described here would be represented by the following equation:

$$H_o: \mu_9 = \mu_{12}$$

where H_0 = the symbol for the null hypothesis
μ_9 = the symbol for the theoretical average for the population of ninth-graders
μ_{12} = the symbol for the theoretical average for the population of twelfth-graders

The four null hypotheses listed above all have in common a statement of two or more things being equal or unrelated to each other.

What are the basic purposes of the null hypothesis? The null acts as both a starting point and as a benchmark against which the actual outcomes of a study will be measured. Let's examine each of these purposes.

First, the null hypothesis acts as a *starting point* since it is the state of affairs that is accepted as true in the absence of other information. For example, let's look at the first null hypothesis stated above: There will be no difference in the average score of ninth-graders and the average score of twelfth-graders on the ABC memory test. Given no other knowledge of ninth- and twelfth-graders' memory skills, you have no reason to believe there will be differences between the two groups. You might speculate as to why one group might outperform another, but if you have no evidence *a priori* (before the fact), then what choice do you have but to assume that they are equal? This lack of a relationship, unless proven otherwise, is a hallmark of the method being discussed. In other words, until you prove that there is a difference, you have to assume that there is no difference.

Furthermore, if there are any differences between these two groups, you have to assume that the differences are due to the most attractive explanation for differences between any groups on any variable, chance! That's right; given no other information, chance is always the most likely explanation for differences between two groups. And what is chance? It is the random variability introduced into every study as a function of the individuals participating as well as many unforeseen factors. For example, you could take a group of soccer players and a group of football players and compare their running speeds. But who is to know whether some soccer players practice more, or if some football players are stronger, or if both groups are receiving additional training? What is more, perhaps the way their speed is being measured leaves room for chance; a faulty stopwatch or a windy day can contribute to differences unrelated to true running speed.

As good researchers, our job is to eliminate chance as a factor and to evaluate other factors that might contribute to group differences such as those that are identified as independent variables.

The second purpose of the null hypothesis is to provide a *benchmark* against which observed outcomes can be compared to see if these differences are due to chance or some other factor. The null hypothesis helps to define a range within which any observed differences between groups can be attributed to chance (which is the null hypothesis' contention) or due to something other than chance (which perhaps would be the result of the manipulation of the independent variable).

Most correlational, quasi-experimental, and experimental studies have an implied null hypothesis. Historical and descriptive studies may not. For example, if you are interested in the growth of immunization during the last 70 years (historical) or how people feel about school vouchers (descriptive), you are probably not concerned with positing a null hypothesis.

The Research Hypothesis

While a null hypothesis is a statement of no relationship between variables, a **research hypothesis** is a definite statement of the relationship between two variables. For example, for each of the null hypotheses stated earlier, here is a corresponding research hypothesis. Notice that I said "a" and not "the" corresponding research hypothesis, since there can certainly be more than one research hypothesis for any one null hypothesis. Here are some research hypotheses that correspond with the null hypotheses mentioned earlier.

- The average score of ninth-graders is different from the average score of twelfth-graders on the ABC memory test.
- There is a relationship between personality type and job success.
- Voting patterns are a function of political party.
- The brand of ice cream preferred is related to the buyer's age, gender, and income.

Each of these four research hypotheses has one thing in common. They are all statements of *inequality*. They posit a relationship between variables and not an equality, as the null hypothesis does. The nature of this inequality can take two different forms—*directional* and *nondirectional*. If the research hypothesis posits no direction to the inequality (such as different from), the research hypothesis is a nondirectional research hypothesis. If the research hypothesis posits a direction to the inequality (such as more than or less than), the research hypothesis is a directional research hypothesis.

The Nondirectional Research Hypothesis

Nondirectional research hypotheses reflect a difference between groups, but the direction of the difference is not specified. For example, the research hypothesis *The average score of ninth-graders is different from the average score of twelfth-graders on the ABC memory test* is nondirectional in that the direction of the difference between the two groups is not specified. The hypothesis states only that there is a difference and says nothing about the direction of that difference. It is a research hypothesis because a difference is hypothesized, but the nature of the difference is not specified.

A nondirectional research hypothesis such as the one described here would be represented by the following equation:

$$H_1: \overline{X}_9 \neq \overline{X}_{12}$$

where H_1 = the symbol for the first (of several possible) research hypothesis

$\overline{X}_9$ = the average memory score for the sample of ninth-graders

$\overline{X}_{12}$ = the average memory score for the sample of twelfth-graders

$\neq$ = not equal

The Directional Research Hypothesis

Directional research hypotheses reflect a difference between groups, and the direction of the difference is specified. For example, the research hypothesis: *The average score of twelfth-graders is greater than the average score of ninth-graders on the ABC memory test* is directional, since the direction of the difference between the two groups is specified. One is hypothesized to be greater than the other.

Directional hypotheses can take the form of

- A greater than B (or A > B), or
- B greater than A (or A < B).

These all represent inequalities. A directional research hypothesis such as the one described above, where twelfth-graders are hypothesized to score better than ninth-graders, would be represented by the following equation:

$$H_1: \overline{X}_{12} > \overline{X}_9$$

where H_1: = the symbol for the first (of possible several) research hypothesis

$\overline{X}_9$ = the average memory score for the sample of ninth-graders

$\overline{X}_{12}$ = the average memory score for the sample of twelth-graders

$>$ = greater or better or more than

What is the purpose of the research hypothesis? It is this hypothesis that is tested directly as one step in the research process. The results of this test are compared with what you expect by chance alone (reflecting the null hypothesis) to see which of the two explanations is the more attractive one for observed differences between groups.

Differences Between the Null Hypothesis and the Research Hypothesis

Besides the null hypothesis representing an equality and the research hypothesis representing an inequality, there are several other important differences between the two types of hypotheses. First, the two differ in that one (the null hypothesis) states there is no relationship between variables (an equality) while the other (the research hypothesis) states there is a relationship (an inequality). This is the primary difference.

Second, null hypotheses always refer to the population whereas research hypotheses always refer to the sample. As you will read later in this chapter, researchers select a sample of participants from a much larger population. It is too expensive and often impossible to work with the entire population.

Third, since the entire population cannot be directly tested (again, it is impractical, uneconomical, and often impossible), you can never really say that there is actually no difference between groups on a specified dependent variable (if you accept the null hypothesis). Rather, you have to infer it (indirectly) from the results of the test of the research hypothesis, which is based on the sample. Hence, the null hypothesis must be indirectly tested while the research hypothesis is directly tested.

Fourth, null hypotheses are always stated using Greek symbols, while research hypotheses are always stated using Roman symbols. For example, the null hypothesis that the average score for ninth-graders is equal to that of twelfth-graders is represented as:

$$H_o: \mu_9 = \mu_{12}$$

And, the research hypothesis that the average score for a sample of ninth-graders is different from the average score for a sample of twelfth-graders would be represented by the following equation:

$$H_1: \overline{X}_{12} \neq \overline{X}_9$$

Finally, because you cannot directly test the null hypothesis, it is an *implied* hypothesis. The research hypothesis is explicit. It is for this reason that you rarely see null hypotheses stated in research reports, whereas you almost always (at least stated in words) see a statement of the research hypothesis.

What Makes a Good Hypothesis?

Hypotheses are educated guesses. As with any guess, some are better than others right from the start. I cannot stress enough how important it is to ask the question you want answered and to keep in mind that any hypothesis you present is a direct extension of the original question you asked. This question will reflect your own personal interests and what research has been previously done.

With that in mind, here are some criteria you might use to decide whether an hypothesis you read in a research report or the ones you formulate are acceptable. Let's use an example of a study that examines the effects of after-school child care programs for employees who work late on the parents' adjustment to work. Here is a well-written hypothesis:

> Parents who enroll their children in after-school programs will miss fewer days of work in one year and will have a more positive attitude toward work as measured by the Attitude Toward Work Survey (ATW) than parents who do not enroll their children in such programs.

Here are the criteria:

1. A good hypothesis is stated in declarative form and not as a question. Hypotheses are most effective when they make a clear and forceful statement.
2. A good hypothesis posits an expected relationship between variables. The hypothesis that is being used as an example clearly describes the relationship between after-school child care, parents' attitude, and absentee rate. These variables are being tested to see if one (enrollment in the after school program) has an effect upon the others (absentee rate and attitude).

Notice the word expected in the above criterion? Defining an expected relationship is intended to prevent the "fishing trip approach" (sometimes called the "shotgun approach") that may be tempting to take but is not very productive. The fishing trip approach is where you throw out your line and take anything that bites. You collect data on as many things as you can regardless of your interest or even whether collecting the data is a reasonable part of a scientific investigation. Or you load up them guns and blast away at anything that moves. You are bound to hit something. The problem is you may not want what you hit, and, worse, you may miss what you want to hit, and even worse (if possible) you may not know what you hit!

Good researchers do not want just anything they can catch or shoot. They want specific results. To get them, researchers need their opening questions and hypotheses to be clear, forceful, and easily understood.

3. Hypotheses reflect the theory or literature they are based on. As you read in Chapter 1, the accomplishments of scientists can rarely be attributed to their

hard work alone. Their accomplishments also are due to many other researchers who have come before them and laid a framework for later explorations. A good hypothesis reflects this; it has a substantive link to existing literature and theory. In the above example, let's assume there is literature indicating that parents who know their children are being cared for in a structured environment can be more productive at work. Knowing this would allow one to hypothesize that an after-school program would provide parents the security they are looking for, which in turn allows them to concentrate on work rather than on the telephone to find out whether Rachel or Gregory got home safely.

4. A hypothesis should be brief and to the point. You want your hypothesis to describe the relationship between variables in a declarative form and to be as to the point as possible. The more to the point, the easier it will be for others (such as your master's thesis committee members!) to read your research and understand exactly what you are hypothesizing and what the important variables are. In fact, when people read and evaluate research (as you will learn more about later in this chapter), the first thing many of them do is find the hypotheses to get a good idea of the general purpose of the research and how things will be done. A good hypothesis tells you both these things.
5. Good hypotheses are testable hypotheses. This means that you can actually carry out the intent of the question reflected in the hypothesis. You can see from the sample hypothesis that the important comparison is between parents who have enrolled their child in an after-school program with those who have not. Then, such things as attitude and work days missed will be measured. These are both reasonable objectives. Attitude is measured by the Attitude Toward Work Survey (a fictitious title, but you get the idea), and absenteeism (the number of days away from work) is an easily recorded and unambiguous measure. Think how much harder things would be if the hypothesis were stated as *Parents who enroll their children in after-school care feel better about their job.* While you might get the same message, the results might be more difficult to interpret given the ambiguous nature of words such as feel better.

In sum, complete and well-written hypotheses should:

- Be stated in declarative form,
- Posit a relationship between variables,
- Reflect a theory or a body of literature that they are based on,
- Be brief and to the point, and
- Be testable.

When an hypothesis meets each of these five criteria, you know that it is good enough to continue with a study that will accurately test the general question from which the hypothesis was derived.

Samples and Populations

As a good scientist, you would like to be able to say that if Method A is better than Method B, this is true forever and always and for all people. Indeed, if you do enough research on the relative merits of Methods A and B and test enough people, you may someday be able to say that, but it is unlikely. It takes too much money and too much time (all those people!) to do all that research.

However, given the constraints of never enough time and never enough research funds that almost all scientists live with, the next best strategy is to take a portion of a larger group of participants and do the research with that smaller group. In this context, the larger group is referred to as a **population,** and the smaller group selected from a population is referred to as a **sample.**

Samples should be selected from populations in such a way that you maximize the likelihood that the sample represents the population as closely as possible. The goal is to have the sample as much like the population as possible. The most important implication of ensuring similarity between the two is that once the research is finished, the results based on the sample can be generalized to the population. When the sample does represent the population, the results of the study are said to be generalizable or to have generalizability.

The various types of sampling procedures are discussed in Chapter 4.

The Concept of Significance

There is probably no term or concept that represents more confusion for the beginning student than that of statistical significance. It is explained in detail in Chapter 8, but it is important to be exposed to the term early in *Exploring Research* since it is a basic and major component of understanding the research process.

At the beginning of this chapter, you read a simple overview of a study where two researchers examined the differences between adolescents whose mothers work and adolescents whose mothers do not (as well as family status, but for this example let's stick with the work and don't work groups).

Let's modify the meaning of the word differences to include the adjective, significant. What I mean by significant differences is that the differences observed between adolescents of mothers who work and of those who do not are due to some influence and do not appear just by chance. In this example, that factor is whether mothers work. Let's assume that other factors that might account for any differences were controlled for. Thus, the only thing left to account for the differences between adolescents is whether or not mothers work. Right? Yes. Finished? Not quite.

Since the world and you and I and the research process are not perfect, one must allow for some leeway. In other words, you need to be able to say that while you are pretty sure the difference between the two groups of adolescents is due to mothers' working, you cannot be absolutely, 100%, positively, unequivocally, indisputably (get the picture?) sure.

Why? For many different reasons. For example, you could just be (horrors!) wrong. Maybe during this one experiment, differences were not due to the group the adolescents were in but to some other factor that was inadvertently not accounted for, such as out-of-home experiences. How about if the people in one group were mostly adolescent males and reacted quite differently than the people in the other group, mostly adolescent females? If you are a good researcher and do your homework, such differences between groups are unlikely outcomes but possible nonetheless. This factor (gender) and others could certainly have an impact on the outcome or dependent variable and in turn have an impact on the final results and conclusion you reach.

So what to do? In most scientific endeavors that involve proposing hypotheses and examining differences between groups, there is bound to be a certain amount of error that cannot be controlled. Significance level is the risk associated with not being 100% confident that the difference is due to what you think and may be due to some unforeseen factor. If you see that a study resulted in significant findings at the .05 level, the translation is that a chance of 1 in 20 (or .05 or 5%) exists that any differences found were not due to the hypothesized reason (the independent variable is the case of a comparison between two groups) but to some other, unknown reason or reasons. Your job as a good scientist is to reduce this likelihood as much as possible by accounting for all the competing reasons, other than the one you are testing, for any differences that you observed. Since you cannot fully eliminate the likelihood, you deal with it by assigning a level of probability and report your results with that caveat. There is a technical side to determining specific levels of significance, and you will read more about that in Chapter 8.

That wraps up some vocabulary and provides you with a basic knowledge for understanding most of the important terms used in the research process. Being familiar with them will provide a foundation to continue to the next section of this chapter which deals with how to read and evaluate research articles.

Reading and Evaluating Research

Almost any research activity that you participate in involves the reading of research articles that appear in journals and textbooks. In fact, one of the most common faults of beginning researchers is not being sufficiently familiar with the wealth of research reports in their specific area of interest. It is indeed rare to find a research topic where nothing or nothing related has been done. You may not be able to find something that is exactly on the topic you wish to pursue (such as changes in adolescent behavior in Australian children who live in the outback), but there is plenty of information on adolescent behavior and plenty on children who live in Australia. Part of your job as a good scientist is to make the argument why these factors might be important to study. You can do that by reading and evaluating research that has been done in various disciplines on the same topic.

What Does a Research Article Look Like?

The only way to gain expertise in understanding the results of research studies is to read and practice understanding what they mean. Begin with one of the journals in your own area. Don't know of any? Then do one of two things.

- Visit your adviser or some faculty member in the area in which you are interested and ask the question, "What is the best research journal in my area?"
- Visit the library and look through the index of periodicals. You are bound to find tens if not hundreds of journals.

For example, for those of you interested in education and psychology and related areas, here is a sample of 10 research journals that were rated by 700 people as those they would most like to publish in and those that they would find the most useful for reporting important research findings (Terrance & Johnson, 1978). If these 700 other accomplished researchers find these valuable as sources of information, wouldn't they be a great place for you to start?

- *American Educational Research Journal*
- *American Psychologist*
- *Educational Researcher*
- *Educational and Psychological Measurement*
- *Harvard Educational Review*
- *Journal of Educational Research*
- *Journal of Educational Psychology*

- *Journal of Educational Measurement*
- *Phi Delta Kappan*
- *Review of Educational Research*

Here are 10 more that focus primarily on psychology:

- *Child Development*
- *Cognition*
- *Human Development*
- *Journal of Applied Developmental Psychology*
- *Journal of Experimental Psychology*
- *Journal of Personality and Social Psychology*
- *Journal of School Psychology*
- *Perceptual and Motor Skills*
- *Psychological Bulletin*
- *Sex Roles*

You will find a much more extensive list of journals in the next chapter.

Criteria for Judging a Research Study

Judging anyone else's work is never an easy task. A good place to start might be the following checklist organized to help you focus on the most important characteristics of any journal article. These eight areas can give you a good start in better understanding the general format of such a report and how well the author(s) communicated to you what they did, why they did it, how they did it, and what it all means.

1. *The Review of Previous Research.* How closely is the literature cited in the study related to previous literature? Is the review recent? Are there any seminal or outstanding references you know of that were left out?
2. *The Problem and Purpose.* Can you understand the statement of the problem? Is the purpose of the study clearly stated? Does the purpose seem to be tied to the literature that is reviewed? Is the objective of the study clearly stated? Is there a conceptual rationale to which the hypotheses are grounded? Is there a rationale for why the study is an important one to do?
3. *The Hypothesis.* Are the research hypotheses clearly stated? Are the research hypotheses explicitly stated? Do the hypotheses state a clear association between variables? Are the hypotheses grounded in theory or in a review and presentation of relevant literature? Are the hypotheses testable?
4. *The Method.* Are both the independent and dependent variables clearly defined? Are the definition and description of the variables complete? Is it clear how the study was conducted?
5. *The Sample.* Was the sample selected in such a way that you think it is representative of the population? Is it clear where the sample comes from and how it was selected? How similar are the participants in the study to those that have been used in similar studies?
6. *Results and Discussion.* Does the author relate the results to the review of literature? Are the results related to the hypothesis? Is the discussion of the results consistent with the results? Does the discussion provide closure to the initial hypothesis that the author presents?

7. *References.* Is the list of references current? Are they consistent in their format? Are the references complete? Does the list of references reflect some of the most important reference sources in the field?
8. *General Comments About the Report.* Is it clearly written and understandable? Is the language biased? What are the strengths and weaknesses of the research? What are the primary implications of the research? What would you do to improve the research?

Basic Principles of Ethical Research

Although researchers should be excited and enthusiastic about their work, the most important thing to remember is that human beings are serving as participants. These individuals need to be treated so that their dignity is maintained in spite of the research or the outcomes. Easier said than done? You bet.

The challenges that ethical behavioral research demands have created a whole field of study, called *ethics.* As long as researchers continue to use humans and animals as participants, the way these people and animals are treated and how they benefit, even indirectly, from participation are critical issues that must be kept in the forefront of all our considerations.

Later in this chapter, the specific guidelines published by professional groups for their members are listed. But first, let's address the general issues that arise in any discussion of ethical behavior.

Protection from Harm

Above all, subjects must be prevented from physical or psychological harm. If there is any doubt at the onset that there is a significant risk involved (relative to the payoffs), then the experiment should not be approved. Notice risks and benefits are the focus. In the case of a terminally ill child, the most dramatic and even unconfirmed techniques that may save the child's life (but may also hasten his or her death) may have a high risk, but the potential benefits may be just as important to consider.

Maintenance of Privacy

Maintenance of privacy speaks to several concerns, but most directly to anonymity. Being anonymous within a research context means that there is no way that anyone except the principal investigator (usually the director) can match the results of an experiment with the individual associated with these results.

Anonymity is most often maintained through the use of a single master sheet that contains both the names of the participants and their subject number. Then, on scoring sheets, code sheets, or other testing materials, only the number is placed. The list of corresponding names and numbers is kept in a secure place out of the public eye and often under lock and key.

A second concern regarding privacy is that one does not invade another's private space to observe behavior and collect data. For example, it would be unethical to secretly record the verbal interaction between therapists and their clients. While this might be a rich source of information, it would not be legitimate unless the client and therapist agree.

Coercion

People should not be forced, for whatever reason, into participation. College students and especially those in introductory psychology classes are often the most used population for many different research studies. Is it ethical to require these students to participate in an experiment? Probably not, yet many students must participate as a course requirement. Similarly, people in the workplace are often required to complete surveys, answer questionnaires, and provide other types of information for research purposes as a part of their job-related duties.

The key here is never *force* people to participate. If they do not want to participate, an alternative way to fulfill a course or job requirement should be provided.

Informed Consent

This may be the most important requirement, and the informed consent form might be the one tool to ensure ethical behavior. Without question, every research project that uses human participants should have an informed consent form read and signed by each participant or the person granting participation (in the case of a child with the parent signing off).

What does such a consent form look like? You can see one in Figure 2.3. These are not just invitations to participate (although they may be that as well), but a description of what will happen throughout the course of the research.

As you can see, such a letter contains at least the following information:

- The purpose of the research
- Who you are
- What you are doing
- How long the participant will be involved
- An offer to withdraw from the experiment at any time for any reason
- Potential benefits to the individual as well as to society
- Potential harm or risks for discomfort to the individual
- An assurance that the results will be kept in strictest confidence
- How to get a copy of the results
- How you can be reached should anyone have questions
- A place for prospective subjects (or parent of) to sign indicating that they agree to participate and that they understand the purpose of the research

The letter in Figure 2.3 is printed on official stationery and illustrates all of these points. It is not written in scientific mumbo-jumbo, but it is as straightforward as possible. The goal here is to inform, not to coerce or cajole people into participating.

Informed Consent with Children

There is an obvious problem when it comes to ensuring informed consent with children. An example is any investigation where the child is too young to give consent of any kind. It is left to the judgment of the parents whether they will allow their child to participate. The letter shown in Figure 2.3 was used in a study that included the participation of children.

But there are issues galore when it comes to ethics and children, far beyond the difficult process of ensuring that children will not be placed in any danger, either of

University of Kansas

Department of Educational Psychology & Research
213 Bailey Hall
Lawrence, KS 66045

December 15, 1999

Dear Mr. and Mrs. Prum:

The Department of Educational Psychology and Research at the University of Kansas supports the practice of informed consent and protection for human subjects participating in research. The following information is provided for you to decide whether you will allow Gus to participate in the present study. You are free to withdraw either or both of them at any time.

Gus will be asked to play a game with another child with a disability in a room that has toys and books and your child's behavior will be recorded on video tape. One session will last approximately 25 minutes. We are interested in studying the interaction between children who have a handicap and children who do not. This information is important since it will help us develop methods for increasing the effectiveness of efforts to integrate children with handicaps into the regular education classroom.

Your child's participation is solicited but strictly voluntary. We assure you that your child's name will not in any way be associated with the research findings. The information will be identified only through a code number.

If you would like additional information concerning this study before or after it is completed, please contact one of us by phone or mail. Thank you very much for your time and we appreciate your interest and cooperation.

Sincerely,

Bruce Saxon	Sam Fine
Graduate Student	Professor
(785) 555-3931	(785) 555-4526

Figure 2.3 A typical informed consent letter where the participants (or his or her parents) are informed as to the content of the study and the partcipant's rights.

a physical or psychological nature. For example, are 6-year-old children old enough to make a decision about withdrawing as the consent form should clearly state is an option for them? Can they understand the long-range implications of the research in which they are participating? The potential risks?

This is where the good judgment and personal ethics of the researcher comes into play. If a child feels strongly about not participating, you may lose that subject and those data, but his or her wishes need to be respected just as those of any adult would be. Additionally, forcing participation may result in an unhappy or angry child and untrustworthy data.

As children grow older, however, the issue becomes more complex. For example, what about the 12-year-old who is old enough to understand the purpose of the experiment? Should he or she sign the consent form as well as the parent(s)? No researcher in his or her right mind would not first obtain permission from the parent(s). Additionally, when school-age children are used in research, more and more school districts require that the proposal be reviewed by a schoolwide research committee. More researchers than ever now have liability insurance to cover themselves if an angry parent sues or some unintended injury occurs.

The best advice? Make any experimental session or treatment with children as pleasant as possible. One way to do that is to encourage them, make the activities pleasant, and reward them when you have finished (as long as the promise of a reward does not interfere with what you are studying). But above all, remember that children are physically, emotionally, and socially different from adults, and those differences must be taken into account when they are used as subjects. And finally get all the institution clearances you need to proceed. Make sure your adviser or professor knows what you are doing. More about this later in the chapter.

Confidentiality

Whereas anonymity means that records cannot be linked with names, confidentiality is maintained when anything that is learned about the participant is held in the strictest of confidence. This means that information is disguised when necessary (which touches on anonymity as well), but, more important, all the data are kept in a controlled situation.

The best way to maintain confidentiality is by minimizing the number of people who see or handle the data. There is no better example of this than recent concerns about AIDS and the results of screening tests. People are reluctant to be tested for HIV (the virus associated with AIDS) since they are concerned that insurance companies and potential employers will have access to the results of the tests and use them against the individual when he or she applies for a job or health or life insurance.

Sharing Results

Scientific knowledge belongs in the public domain, and, although there have been some heated arguments about when to tell whom, most researchers agree that it is important to bring new discoveries to the public as soon as practical and possible. When you complete your research and write up a final report, you should be willing to share your results with others.

Some of the most important of these others are the people who participated in your experiment. In practical terms, you can offer to send them a summary of the final report or have a meeting where they can be informed as to the outcomes.

Debriefing

Another component of sharing the results of an experiment is when a particular group of subjects needs to be debriefed. For example, you design an experiment where you tell one group of subjects a lie as part of the experiment. You might tell young children not to play with a particularly attractive toy and then videotape their behavior without their knowledge. Once the experiment is completed, it is your responsibility to inform them that they have been deceived to some extent for the purposes of the experiment. Most people will take that just fine (as do the contestants on "Candid Camera"), but some will get upset when they learn that they have been manipulated.

If they remain angry, it is difficult to do anything other than apologize and try to set the record straight. The easiest way to debrief participants is to talk with them immediately following the session or to send a newsletter telling participants the general intent and results of the study but leaving out specifics such as names.

Sharing Benefits

The last principle may be the most often violated. Here is the scenario. In an experiment, a treatment was used to increase the memory of older people in the early stages of Alzheimer's disease, a devastating and almost always fatal illness. Let's say that the researcher uses two groups, one that receives the training (the experimental group) and one that does not (the control group). Much to the researcher's pleasure, the treatment group learns faster and remembers much more for much longer. Success!

What is the concern? Simply that the group that did not receive the treatment should now be exposed to it. It is the right thing to do. When one group benefits from participation in a study, any other groups that participated in the study should benefit as well. This does not mean that it is possible that all elderly people can be helped. That may not be feasible. But all direct participants in the experiment should benefit equally.

All of these ethical issues apply to the different types of research methods described in Chapters 9, 10, and 11 with differing degrees of importance. For example, one need not be concerned about debriefings when conducting a case study since no treatment and no deception is involved. Nor would one be concerned with sharing of benefits in that situation.

Ensuring High Ethical Standards

There are several steps that even the beginning researcher can take to ensure that ethical principles are maintained. Here are some of the most important.

1. Do a computer simulation, where data are constructed and subjected to the effects of various treatments. For example, mathematical psychologists and statisticians often use Monte Carlo studies to examine the effects of a change in one variable (such as sample size) upon another (such as accuracy of measurement). Elaborate models of human behavior can be constructed, and different assumptions can be tested and conclusions drawn about human behavior. While this is somewhat advanced work, it does give you an idea of how certain experiments can be conducted with the "participants" being nothing more than values generated by a computer.
2. When the treatment is deemed harmful, do not give up. Rather, try to locate a population that has already been exposed to the harmful effects of some variable. For example, the thousands of children and pregnant women who were malnourished during World War II provided an invaluable sample for estimating the effects of malnourishment on fetal and neonatal development as well as the long-range effects of malnourishment on young children. While not pleasant, this is about the only way that such research is possible. This type of research is called quasi-experimental and will be covered in greater detail in Chapter 11.
3. Always secure informed consent. If the treatment includes risk, be absolutely sure that the risks are clear to the participant and other interested parties (parents, other family members).

4. When possible, publish all reports using group rather than individual data. This measure maintains confidentiality.
5. If you suspect that the treatment may have negative side effects, use a small, well-informed sample until you can expand the sample size and the ambitiousness of the project. Also, be sure to check with your institutional review board (more about that in a moment).
6. Use your colleagues to review your proposal and especially your experimental procedures before you begin. Ask them the question, "Would you participate without any fear of being harmed?" If they say "no," go back to the drawing board.
7. Almost every public institution (such as public universities) and every private agency (such as some hospitals and private universities) have what is called an **institutional review board.** Such boards consist of a group of people from several disciplines (including representatives from the community) who render a judgment as to whether participation in the experiment is free from harm. At the University of Kansas, the group is called the Advisory Committee on Human Experimentation (ACHE). There is a separate review board for experiments using animals.

The groups usually meet and then approve or disapprove the procedure (but not necessarily the content of research) and take into consideration the issues already discussed. These committees usually meet about once a month, and if a proposal that they review is not acceptable, they invite the researcher to resubmit according to their recommendations. Figure 2.4 is a sample of the form used by the ACHE at the University of Kansas.

The Role of Professional Organizations

It is unquestionably the role of the researcher to ensure that ethical standards are always kept in mind when conducting any type of research. There are more formalized sets of guidelines published by professional organizations such as the American Psychological Association (APA), the Society for Research in Child Development (SRCD), the American Sociological Association (ASA), the American Educational Research Association (AERA), and just about every other social or behavioral science professional group. To illustrate just what these guidelines suggest, here is a summary of those presented by the American Psychological Association (a group of about 25,000 professionals) and the Society for Research in Children Development (a group of about 6,000 professionals).

APA Ethical Guidelines

The guidelines formulated by an APA committee were first presented in 1953. Here is a summary of the latest guidelines:

1. When a study is planned, the researcher must be the first and most important judge of its ethical acceptability.
2. Subjects must be judged to be "at no risk" or "at minimal risk."
3. The researcher is responsible for ensuring ethical practices, including the behavior of assistants, students, employees, collaborators, and anyone else involved in the process.
4. A fair and reasonable agreement must be reached between the researcher and the subjects, prior to the beginning of the research.

#________

APPLICATION FOR PROJECT APPROVAL
ADVISORY COMMITTEE ON HUMAN EXPERIMENTATION

PLEASE USE A TYPEWRITER TO COMPLETE THIS FORM

1. Name of investigator(s) ________________________________
2. Department affiliation ________________________________
3. Campus mailing address ________________________________
4. Phone number(s): (a) Campus ____________ (b) Home ____________
5. Name of faculty member responsible for project ________________
6. Type of investigator and nature of activity. (Check appropriate categories.)

   ______ Faculty or staff of Kansas University

      ______ Project to be submitted for extramural funding; Agency ______

      ______ Project to be submitted for intramural funding; Source ______

      ______ Project unfunded

      ______ Other

   ______ Student at Kansas University

      ______ Graduate ______ Undergraduate ______ Special

      ______ Thesis ______ Dissertation

      ______ Class project (number and title of class) ________________

      ______ Independent study (name of faculty supervisor) ____________

      ______ Other (please explain)

7. Title of investigation ________________________________

____

ALL STUDENT APPLICATIONS SUBMITTED TO THE ACHE FOR REVIEW MUST BE SIGNED BY ALL INVESTIGATORS INCLUDING THE FACULTY MEMBER SUPERVISING THE RESEARCH ACTIVITY.

8. Individuals other than faculty, staff, or students at Kansas University. Please identify investigators and research group ________________________________

   ____

9. Certifications ________________________________

   ____

Figure 2.4 A sample form used in the institutional review for a research project.

I am familiar with the policies and procedures of the University of Kansas regarding human subjects in research. I subscribe to the standards and will adhere to the policies and procedures of the ACHE and . . .

I am familiar with the published guidelines for the ethical treatment of subjects associated with my particular field of study (e.g., as published by the American Psychological Association, American Sociological Association, etc.).

Date ____________________ Date ____________________

Signature ____________________ Signature ____________________

First Investigator ____________________ Faculty Supervisor ____________________

Signature ____________________ Signature ____________________

Second Investigator ____________________ Third Investigator ____________________

Principal Investigator ____________________ ACHE# ____________________

Title ____

10. Please answer the following questions with regard to the research activity proposed. Does the research involve:

	Yes	No
a. Drugs or other controlled substances?	_____	_____
b. Payment of subjects for participation?	_____	_____
c. Access to subjects through a cooperating institution?	_____	_____
d. Substances taken internally by or applied externally to the subjects?	_____	_____
e. Mechanical or electrical devices (e.g., electrodes) applied to the subjects?	_____	_____
f. Fluids (e.g., blood) or tissues removed from the subjects?	_____	_____
g. Subjects experiencing stress (physiological or psychological)?	_____	_____
h. Deception of subjects concerning any aspect of purposes or procedures?	_____	_____
i. Subjects who would be judged to have limited freedom of consent?	_____	_____
j. Any procedure or activities that might place the subjects at risk (psychological, physical, or social)?	_____	_____
k. Use of interviews, survey, questionnaires, audio or video recordings?	_____	_____
l. Data collection over a period greater than one year?	_____	_____
m. A copy of the consent form will be given to the subjects	_____	_____

(continued)

Figure 2.4 (Continued)

11. Approximate number of subjects to be involved in research ______ .

Complete the following questions on this page. Please do not use continuation sheets. ACHE will not process applications that do not stay within the page limitations. See instructions.

12. Project purpose(s)

13. Describe the proposed subjects (age, sex, race, or other special characteristics)

14. Describe how the subjects are to be selected

Figure 2.4 (Continued)

5. If deception is necessary, the researcher must be sure it is justified and a mechanism must be built in to ensure that subjects are debriefed when the research is concluded.
6. Researchers must respect the subject's choice to withdraw and must not practice coercion to get the subject back into participating.
7. Every possible effort should be made to protect participants from physical and psychological harm.
8. Once the research is complete, should the participant so indicate, the results should be shared and the participant should be given a chance to clarify any discrepancies she or he might be aware of.
9. If the research should result in harm of any kind, the researcher has the responsibility to correct the harm.
10. All the information obtained in a research study is confidential.

SRCD Ethical Guidelines

Because this is a group committed to learning more about the development of children, you will notice how precisely these guidelines are written to consider children's well-being:

1. The rights of the child supersede the rights of the investigator no matter what the age of the child.
2. All ethical issues surrounding the research project are the responsibility of the head investigator.
3. If there are changes in approved procedures that might affect the ethical conduct of the research, consultation with colleagues or experts should be undertaken.

4. The child should be fully informed as to the research process, and all questions should be answered in a way that can be understood.
5. Children are free to withdraw from the research at any time.
6. Informed consent from parents, teachers, or whoever is legally responsible for the child's welfare must be obtained in writing.
7. Informed consent must also be obtained from others who are involved in the experiment (such as parents, etc.), besides the individual child.
8. The responsibilities of the child and of the investigator must be made clear.
9. When the potential for harm is present, the investigator must either find an alternative way to collect the necessary information or abandon the research.
10. When deception is necessary, a committee of the investigator's peers should approve the planned methods.
11. All information is confidential.
12. If institutional records are to be used as a source of information, permission must be obtained from all affected parties.
13. The findings from any study should be reported to the participants in a way that is comprehensible to them.
14. Investigators should be especially careful about the way they report results to children and should not present the results in the form of advice.
15. If during the course of the investigation information arises that is important to the child's welfare, the investigator has an obligation to report the information to parents, teachers, or other appropriate parties.
16. All undesirable consequences should be corrected.
17. Investigators should be aware that research can have political, social, and human implications, and they should be mindful of this when results are reported and shared.
18. If treatments are effective, control groups should be offered similar opportunities to receive the treatment.
19. These ethical standards should be presented to students in the course of their training.
20. All investigators have the responsibility of maintaining their own ethical conduct and that of their colleagues as well.
21. Editors of journals that report investigations of children should provide authors space to summarize the steps they took to ensure these standards. If it is not clear such standards were followed, editors should request additional information.
22. These standards are always open to discussion and amendment.

Do the ethical standards of the APA and the SRCD work? In general, the answer is probably yes, but if they do, it's because of the individuals who make up the research community and follow these rules.

Summary

In order to play the research game, you have to know the rules. This chapter introduced you to some of the most important terms and concepts about the research process and those that will be mentioned again and again throughout this book. As you begin to review literature either in preparation of a proposal or for some related research activity, you will see these terms being used. You will also want to keep the important basic principles of ethics foremost in your mind as you plan your research activities.

Exercises

1. In the following examples, identify the independent and dependent variable(s).
   (a) Two groups of children were given different types of physical fitness programs to see if the programs had an effect on their strength.
   (b) A group of 100 heavy smokers was divided into five groups, and each group participated in a different stop-smoking program. After six months of program participation, the number of cigarettes each participant smoked each day was counted.
   (c) A university professor was interested in determining the best way to teach introductory psychology and assure that his students learn the material.

2. Why is the null hypothesis always a statement of equality? Why can the research hypothesis take on many different forms?

3. Write the null and research hypotheses for the following paragraph:

   A group of middle-aged men was asked to complete a questionnaire on their attitudes toward work and family. These men are married and have at least two children each. Another group of men, who have no children, also completed the same survey.

4. No one would argue that defining variables clearly and in an unambiguous manner is critical to good research. With that in mind, work as a group and define the following variables. Keep track of how different people's definitions reflect their personal view of what the variable represents, and note how easy it is to define some variables and how difficult it is to define others.
   (a) Intelligence
   (b) Height
   (c) Social skills
   (d) Age
   (e) Aggressiveness
   (f) Conservatism
   (g) Alcohol consumption
   (h) Street smarts
   (i) Personality

   Be sure to note that even those that appear to be easy to define, such as height, can take on different meanings and definitions (tall, 5′1″, awesome) as well.

5. A researcher spent five years on a project, and the majority of the results were not significant. How can the lack of significant results still make an important contribution to the field?

6. Indicate which of the following are variables and which are constants:
   (a) Lew's hair color
   (b) Age in years
   (c) Number of windows in your residence
   (d) The color of a late-model car
   (e) Time of day
   (f) Number of correct answers on this week's quiz
   (g) The number of signers of the Declaration of Independence
   (h) The name of the fifth girl in the third row

(i) Today's date
(j) Number of words remembered on a memory test

7. Go to the library and locate three journal articles in your area of interest. Do the following:
   (a) Identify the independent and dependent variables.
   (b) For each dependent variable, specify how it is going to be measured and whether it is clearly defined.
   (c) For each independent variable, identify the number of levels of that variable. What other independent variables would you find of interest to study?

8. What makes a good hypothesis?

9. What purpose does reading and evaluating research articles serve?

10. What are two of the basic principles of ethical research? Why are they important?

Want to Know More?

Further Readings

Jones, P. (1988). On-line research at the secondary level: Access to a world of information. *Tech Trends, 33*(3), 22–23.

Discusses the development of research skills through on-line searching by secondary students and compares on-line and optical data disk systems. Compares factors including cost, currency, subject areas, number of uses, search time, preparation needed, search methods, help needed, and alternative use of the equipment.

Keith, T.Z. (1995). Best practice in applied research. In A. Thomas & J. Grimes (Eds.), *Best practice in school psychology* (3rd ed.). Washington, DC: NASP, 143–153.

Looks into the factors of becoming an effective consumer of research. Investigates issues such as the quality of research questions, the appropriateness of the research sample, the statistical analysis used, and the generalizability of the research. Uses good examples to aid the reader in becoming a better consumer of research.

St. James, J.D. (1989). The MEL library in the undergraduate research methods course. *Behavior Research Methods, 21,* 245–247.

A library reference teaching tool for undergraduates to learn how to do research. Provides practical experiences in experimental design, data representation, and integration of results.

Readings of Other Interest

Callahan, D. (1989). *What kind of life.* New York: Simon & Schuster.

Discusses problems with our health care system from both a cultural and moral view. A good example of how to use a source to discover relevant and current potential research problems.

Cordell, B.J. (1991). A study of learning styles and computer assisted instruction. *Computers and Education, 16*(2), 175–183.

Investigates whether learning styles affect outcomes of learning with two computer assisted instruction design strategies, linear and branching.

James, P.D. (1990). *Devices and desires.* New York: Knopf.

A good example of the process of research used in detective work. Shows how problems are identified and how they lead to other problems until finally a solution is determined. Adam Dalgliesh, Scotland Yard commander, once again shows his intellectual abilities through sleuthing the solution by observation and interview techniques.

Winn, W., Li, T., & Shill, D. (1991). Diagrams as aids to problem solving: Their role in facilitating search and computation. *Educational Technology, Research and Development, 39*(1), 17–29.

Views two experiments conducted with graduate students to test hypotheses regarding the effectiveness of diagrams in which concepts were shown spatially. Compares response latencies for problems applying kinship rules to information presented in family trees and in lists of statements, and examines the use of rules to computer responses.

Chapter 1c

Selecting a Problem and Reviewing the Research

What You'll Learn About in This Chapter

- How to select a research problem
- Sorting out idea after idea until one fits your interests
- The importance of personal experience in selecting a problem
- The steps in reviewing the literature
- Different sources of information, and how to use them
- How to use journals, abstracts, and indexes
- The difference between primary and secondary resources
- Using a synthesis of literature
- How scholarly journals work
- All about computerized literature searches

So here you are, in the early part of a course that focuses on research methods, and now you have to come up with a problem that you are supposed to be interested in! You are probably so anxious about learning the material contained in your professor's lectures and what is in *Exploring Research* that you barely have time to think about anything else.

But if you stop for a moment and let your mind explore some of the issues in the behavioral and social sciences that have piqued your interest, you will surely find something that you want to know more about. That is what the research process is all about—finding out more about something that is, in part, already known.

Once you select an area of interest, you are only part of the way there. Next comes the statement of this interest in the form of a research question and then a formal hypothesis. Then it is on to reviewing the literature, a sort of fancy phrase that sounds like you will be very busy! A literature review involves library time and note taking and organizational skills, but it provides a perspective on your question that you cannot get without knowing what other work has been done as well as what new work needs to be done.

But hold on a minute! How is someone supposed to have a broad enough understanding of the field and spew forth well-formed hypotheses before the literature is reviewed and then become familiar with what is out there? As poet John Ciardi said, therein "lies the rub."

The traditional philosophers and historians of science would have us believe that the sequence of events leading up to a review of what has been done before (as revealed in the literature) is as shown in Figure 3.1a.

This sequence of steps as shown here is fine in theory. As you will find out, the actual process does not go exactly in the manner shown here.

The research question and research hypothesis are more an outgrowth of an interaction between the scientist's original idea and an ongoing, thorough review of the literature (good scientists are always reading!) as you see in Figure 3.1b. This means that once you formulate a hypothesis, it is not carved in stone but can be altered to fit what the review of literature may reflect, as well as any change in ideas you may have.

For example, you might be interested in the effects of extended after-school care programs on the socialization skills of children. That is the kernel of the idea you want to investigate. A research question might ask what the effects of after-school programs are on how well children get along with one another. As a hypothesis, you

Idea ⟶ Research Question ⟶ Research Hypothesis ⟶ Literature Review

Figure 3.1a From idea to literature review (with the research hypothesis on the way).

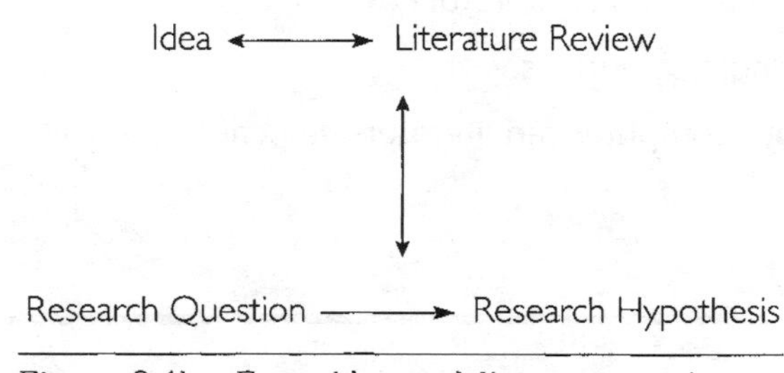

Figure 3.1b From idea and literature review to hypothesis.

predict that children who participate in extended after-school programs will have an increased level of social skills as measured by the XYZ test of socialization.

Use the results of previous studies to fine-tune your research ideas and hypothesis.

You might consider the hypothesis to be finished at this point, but in reality your ongoing review of the literature and your changing ideas about the relationship between the variables influences the direction your research will take. For example, what if you find out that a similar study has been done suggesting you add an interesting dimension (such as single- or dual-parent families) to your study, since the addition is consistent with the intent of the study? You should not have to restrict your creative thinking or your efforts to help you understand the effects of these after-school programs just because you have already formulated an hypothesis and completed a literature review. Indeed, the reason for completing the review is to see what new directions your work might take. The literature review and the idea play off one another to help you form a relevant and conceptually sound research question and research hypothesis.

In sum, you will almost always find that your first shot at an hypothesis might need revision, given the content of the literature you review. Remember, it is your idea that you will pursue. The way that you execute it as a research study will be determined by the way you state the research question and the way you test the research hypothesis. It is doubtful that a review of the relevant literature would not shed some light on this matter.

This chapter begins with some pointers on selecting a problem worth studying, and then the focus moves on to a description of the tools and the steps involved in preparing a review of the literature.

Selecting a Problem

People go to undergraduate and graduate school for a variety of reasons, including preparing for a career, the financial advantages that an education can ensure, and even to expand their personal horizons and experience the sheer joy of learning (what a radical thought!). Many of you are in this specific course for one or more of these reasons.

Select a problem that you are genuinely interested in.

The great commonality among your course work and activities is that you are exposed to a wealth of information you would not otherwise experience. That is the primary purpose of taking the time to select a research problem that makes sense to you and that interests you, while at the same time the project can make a contribution to your specific discipline. The selection of the area you want to work on is terribly important for two reasons. First, research takes a great deal of time and energy, and you want to be sure the area you select interests you. You will work so hard throughout this project that continuing to work on it, even if it's the most interesting project, may at times become too much. Just think of what it would be like if you were not interested! Second, the area you select is only the first step in the research process. If this goes well, the remaining steps, which are no more or less important, have a good chance of going well also.

Just as there are many different ways to go about selecting a research problem, there are also some hazards you can run into. To start you off on the right foot, here is a brief review of some of these almost fatal errors.

It is not hard to do, but *falling in love with your idea can be fatal.* This happens when you become so infatuated with an idea and the project and invest so much energy in it that you cannot bear to change anything about it. Right away someone is going to say, "What's wrong with being enthusiastic about your project?" My response is a strong "Nothing at all." As does your professor, most researchers encourage and look for enthusiasm in students (and scientists) as an important and essential quality. But enthusiasm is not incompatible with being objective and dispassionate about the actual research process (not the content). Sometimes, and this is especially true for beginning research students, researchers see their question as one of such magnitude and importance that they fail to listen to those around them, including their adviser, who is trying to help them formulate their problem in such a way as to make it more precise and, in the long run, easier to address. Be committed to your ideas and really like your topic a lot but not so much that it clouds your judgment as to the practical and right way to do things.

Next, *sticking with the first idea that comes to mind isn't always wise.* Some of you might remember the cartoon character Betty Boop and her inventor grandfather. Every time Betty had a problem, Grandpa would sit on his stool, cross his legs (taking a Rodin-like pose) and think about a solution. Like a bolt from the blue, the light bulb above his head would go on, and he would exclaim, "I've got it!," but it wouldn't be it quite yet. Another flash would occur, but once again not perfect. Invariably, it was the third time the light went on that he struck gold. Do you like your first idea for a research study? Great, but don't run out and place an advertisement for research subjects in the paper quite yet. Give it a few days and think about it, and by no means should you stop talking to other students and your adviser during this thinking stage. Second and third ideas are usually much more refined, easier to do, and more manageable than first ones. As you work, rewrite and rethink your work . . . constantly.

Want to guarantee an unsuccessful project that excites no one (but perhaps yourself)? *Doing something trivial* by selecting a problem that has no conceptual basis or has no apparent importance in the field can lead to a frustrating experience and one that provides no closure. Beginning students who make this mistake sometimes over intellectualize the importance of their research plans and don't stop for the moment it takes to ask themselves, "Where does this study fit in with all that has been done before?" Any scientific endeavor has as its highest goal the contribution of information that will help us better understand the world in general and the specific topic being studied in particular. If you find what has been done by reading previous studies and use that information as a foundation, you will surely come up with a research problem of significance and value.

Be realistic and attempt only what you can finish, given other demands on your time and energy.

Ah, then there is the *bites off more than he or she can chew researcher.* Silly? Not to the thousands of advisers who sit day after day in their offices trying to convince very well-intentioned beginning students that their ideas are interesting but that (for example) asking all the adults in New York City their attitudes toward increasing taxes for education may be a bit ambitious. Grand schemes are fine, but unless you can reduce a question to a manageable size, you might as well forget about starting. If these giant studies by first-timers ever do get done (most of the time they don't in their original form), it is usually a more negative than positive experience. Sometimes these students end up as ABDs (all but dissertation). While you may not be seeking a doctorate right now, the lesson is still a good one. Give yourself a break from the beginning, and choose a research question that is doable.

Finally, *do something that has already been done,* and you could be wasting your time. There is a fine line between what has been done and what is important to do next based on what has been done. Part of your job is to learn how to build and elaborate on the results of previous research without duplicating previous efforts. You might remember from the beginning of this chapter that we stressed how replication is an important component of the scientific process and good research? Your adviser can clearly guide you as to what is redundant (doing the same thing over without any sound rationale) and what is an important contribution (doing the same thing over but exploring an aspect of the previous research or even asking the same question while eliminating possibly confounding sources of variance present in the first study).

Defining Your Interests

It might be easy for an accomplished researcher to come up with additional ideas for research, but that is what he or she gets paid for (in part, anyway). Besides, experienced researchers can put all that experience to work for themselves and one thing (a study) usually leads to another (another study).

But what about the beginning student like yourself? Where do you get your ideas for research? Even if you have a burning desire to be an experimental psychologist, a teacher, a counselor, or a clinical social worker, where do you begin to find hints about ideas that you might want to pursue?

Don't disregard personal experience as an important source of ideas.

In some relatively rare cases, students know from the beginning what they want to select as a research area and what research questions they want to ask. But for many others, there is more anxiety and doubt than confidence. Before you begin the all-important literature review, first take a look at these suggestions for where you might find interesting questions that are well worth considering as research topics.

First, *personal experiences and firsthand knowledge* more often than not can be the catalyst for starting research. For example, perhaps you worked at a summer camp with disabled children and are interested in knowing more about the most effective way to teach these children. Or, through your own personal reading you have become curious about the aging process and how the process of learning changes with aging. At least three of my colleagues are special educators because they have siblings who were not offered the special services they needed as children to reach their potential. Your own experiences shape the type of person you are. It would be a shame to ignore your past when considering the general area and content of a research question, even if you cannot see an immediate link between these experiences and possible research activities. Keep reading, and you will see ways that you can create that link.

You may want to take complete responsibility for coming up with a research question. On the other hand, there is absolutely nothing wrong with going to your adviser or some other faculty member who is working on some interesting topic and asking, "What's next?" *Using ideas from your mentor or instructor* will probably make you very current with whatever is happening in your field. Doing so also will help to establish and nurture the important relationship between you and your adviser (or some other faculty member) that is necessary for an enjoyable and successful experience. These are the people doing the research, and it would be surprising not to find that they have more ideas than time to do them and would welcome an energetic and bright student (like you) who wants to help extend their research activities.

Next, you might *look for a research question that reflects the next step in the research process.* Perhaps A, B, and C have already been done, and D is next in line. For example, your special interest might be understanding the lifestyle factors that contribute to heart disease, and you already know that factors such as personality type (for example, Type A and Type B) and health habits (for example, social drinking) have been well studied and their effects documented. The next logical step might be to look at factors such as work habits (including occupation and attitude) or some component of family life (such as relationships with a spouse). As with research activities in almost all disciplines and within almost all topics, there is always that next logical step that needs to be taken.

Last, but never least, is that *you may have to come up with a research question because of this class.* Now that is not all that bad either, if you look at it this way: People who come up with ideas on their own are all set and need not worry about coming up with an idea by the deadline. Those people who have trouble coming up with ideas need a deadline, otherwise they would not get anything done. So while there are loftier reasons for coming up with research questions, sometimes it is just required by the powers that be.

Even so, work very hard at selecting a topic that you can formulate as a research question so that your interest is held throughout the duration of the activity.

Ideas, Ideas, Ideas (and What to Do with Them)

Even if you are sure what your interest might be, it is still difficult sometimes to come up with a specific idea for a research project. For better or worse, you are really the only one who can do this for yourself, but here is a list of possible research topics. For each of these topics, there is a wealth of associated literature. If one topic piques your interest, go to that literature (described in the second part of this chapter) and start reading. Here are 61 topics, one of which might strike a chord!

aggression
AIDS
bilingual education
biofeedback
biology of memory
birth control
body image
central nervous system
child care
circadian rhythms
classical conditioning
cognitive development
color vision
competition
compliance
computer applications
conflict
creativity
déja vu
delusions
depression
development of drawing
diets
divorce
dreams
drug abuse
early intervention
egocentrism
endocrine system
epilepsy
ethics
fat
fetal alcohol syndrome
fluid intelligence
gender differences
Head Start
identity
imagery
intelligence
language development
learning disabilities
mediation
memory
menarche
mental sets
middle adulthood
motivation
narcolepsy
neural development
nightmares
nutrition
optimism
pain
parenting
perception
prejudice
racial integration
reinforcement
relaxation
REM sleep
self-esteem

From Idea to Research Question to Hypothesis

Once you have determined what your specific interest might be, you should move as quickly as possible to formulate a research question that you want to investigate and begin your review of literature.

There is a major, important difference between your expressing an interest in a particular idea and the statement of a research question. Ideas are full of those products of luxurious thinking; beliefs, conceptions, suppositions, assumptions, what ifs, guesses, and more. Research questions are the articulation, best done in writing, of those ideas that at the least imply a relationship between variables. Why is it best done in writing? Because it is too easy to "get away" with spoken words. It is only when one has to write things down and live with them (spoken words seem to mysteriously vanish) that you face up to what has been said, make a commitment, and work to make sense out of the statement.

Research questions lead the way to hypotheses.

A research question is not a declarative statement like a hypothesis, but a clearly stated expression of interest and intent. In the pay-me-now or pay-me-later tradition, the more easily understood and clearer the research question, the easier your statement of an hypothesis and review of the literature will be. Why? Because from the beginning, a clear idea of what you want to do allows you to make much more efficient use of your time when it comes to searching for references and doing other literature review activities.

Finally, it is time to formulate an hypothesis or a set of hypotheses that reflects the research question. Remember in Chapter 2 how a set of five criteria that apply to the statement of any hypothesis was documented? To refresh your memory, here they are again. A well-written hypothesis:

1. Is stated in declarative form.
2. Posits a relationship between variables.
3. Reflects a theory or body of literature it is based on.
4. Is brief and to the point.
5. Is testable.

When you derive your hypothesis from the research question, you should look to these criteria as a test of whether what you are saying is easily communicated to others and easily understood. Remember, the sources for ideas can be anything from a passage that you read in a novel last night to your own unique and creative thoughts. When you get to the research question stage, however, you need to be more scientific and clearly state what your interest is and what variables will be considered.

Table 3.1 lists five research interests, the research questions that were generated from those ideas, and the final hypotheses. These hypotheses are only final in the sense that they more or less fit the five hypothesis criteria. Your literature review and more detailed discussion may mean that variables have to be further defined and perhaps even that new ones will need to be introduced. A good hypothesis tells what you are going to do, not how you will do it.

Research Interest or Ideas	Research Problem or Questions	Hypothesis
Open Classroom and Academic Success	What is the effect of open versus traditional classrooms on reading level?	Children taught reading in open classroom settings will read at a higher grade level than children taught reading in a traditional setting.
Test-Taking Skills and Grades	Will students who know how to "take" a test improve their scores?	Students who receive training in the "Here Today—Gone Tomorrow" method will score higher on the SATs than students who do not receive the training.
Television and Consumer Behavior	How does watching television commercial, affect the buying behavior of adolescents?	Adolescent boys buy more of the products advertised on television than do adolescent girls.
Drug Abuse and Child Abuse	Is drug abuse related to child abuse?	There is a positive relationship between drug abuse among adults and their physical and psychological abuse as children.
Adult Care	How have many adults adjusted to the responsibility of caring for their aged parents?	The number of children who are caring for their parents in the child's own home has increased over the past 10 years.

Table 3.1 Ideas, questions, and hypotheses. You never know where they will come from, so read widely and keep an open mind.

Reviewing the Literature

Here it comes again. Today's research is built on a foundation of the hard work and dedication of past researchers and their productive efforts. Where does one find the actual results of these efforts? In scholarly journals and books, which are located (that is right) in the library.

The review of literature provides a framework for the research proposal.

While all stages in the research process are important, a logical and systematic review of the literature often sets the stage for the completion of a successful research proposal and a successful study. Remember one of the fatal mistakes mentioned at the beginning of the chapter about selecting a research question that has been done before? Or one that is trivial? You find out about all these things and more when you see what has already been done and how it has been done. A complete review provides a framework within which you can answer the important question(s) that you pose. A review takes you chronologically through the development of ideas, shows how some ideas were left by the wayside for lack of support, and how some were confirmed as being truths. Extensive and complete reviews of the literature give you that important perspective to see what has been done and where you are going—crucial to a well-written, well-documented, and well-planned report.

So get your yellow (or recyclable white) pads, index cards, #2 pencil, laptop computer ready, and let's get started. Also, don't forget your school ID card so you can check out books.

The literature review process consists of the steps that you see in Figure 3.2. You begin with as clear an idea as possible about what you want to do, either in the form of a clear and general statement about the variables you want to study or as a research hypothesis. You should end with a well-written and clear document that details the rationale for why you chose the topic you did, how it fits into what has been done before, what needs to be done in the future, and its relative importance to the discipline.

General, secondary, and primary resources are all important, but very different, parts of the literature review.

There are basically three types of sources that you will consult throughout your review of the literature (as you can see in Table 3.2). The first are **general sources,** which provide clues to the location of references of a general nature on a topic. While they certainly have their limitations (which you will get to in a moment), they can be a real asset because they provide a general overview of, and introduction to, a topic. For example, let's say you are interested in the general area of sports psychology but

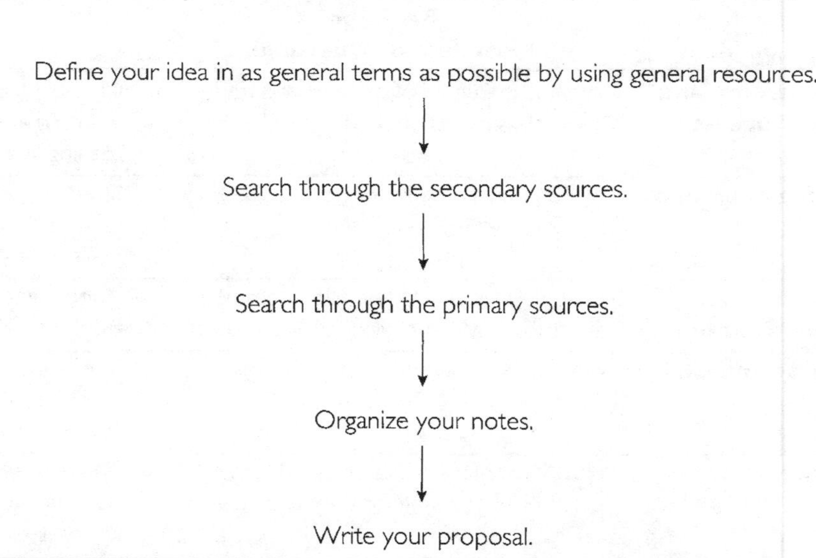

Figure 3.2 The steps in reviewing the literature. It is a formidable task, but when broken down step by step, it is well within your reach.

Information Source	What They Do	Example
General Sources	Provide an overview of a topic and provide leads to where more information can be found.	Daily newspapers, news weeklies, popular periodicals and magazines, trade books, *Reader's Guide to Periodical Literature, New York Times Index.*
Secondary Sources	Provide a level of information "once removed" from the original work.	Books on specific subjects and reviews of research.
Primary Sources	The original reports of the original work or experience.	Journals, abstracts, and scholarly books, ERIC, movies.

Table 3.2 Different types of information and what they do.

have absolutely no idea where to turn to find more information. You could start with the recent article that appeared in the *New York Times* and find the name of the foremost sports psychologist and then go to more detailed secondary or primary sources to find more about his or her work.

The second source type is called **secondary sources.** These sources are "once removed" from the actual research and are review papers, anthologies of readings, syntheses of other work in the area, textbooks, and encyclopedias.

Finally, the last and most important sources are **primary sources.** These are accounts of the actual research that has been done. They appear as journal articles or as other original works including abstracts. You can see a summary of what general, secondary, and primary resources do and some examples in Table 3.2. We also talk about these three different types of sources later in Chapter 9 when we discuss historical methods of doing research.

But before you get started, let me share my own particular bias. There is no substitute for using every resource that your library has to offer. And that means lots of time turning to old fashioned books and journals and reading their contents. But, in many cases, there's also no substitute for exploring and using electronic resources such as online databases, the World Wide Web and more. You'll learn about both here, but I want you always to remember that you won't find everything you need online (and much of it is not verifiable), yet online is where the most recent material shows up. And while hard copies of journals and books may be dated, they are ultimately more reliable, and a collection of such "hard" copies has a longer life span and is much more comprehensive than anything you can find (at least today) online.

Using General Sources

General sources of information provide two things: a general introduction to areas in which you might be interested and some clues as to where you should go for the more valuable or useful (in a scientific sense, anyway) information about your topic. They are also just great browsing material.

Any of the references we discuss below, especially the indexes of national newspapers and such, can offer you 5, 10, or 50 articles in a specific area. In these articles, you will often find a nice introduction to the subject area and a mention of some of the people doing research and where they are located. From there, you can look through other reference materials to find out what other work that person has done or even contact him or her directly.

There are loads of general sources in your college or university library as well as in the public library. Here is a brief description of just a few of the most often used sources and a listing of several others you might want to consult. Remember, use general sources only to orient yourself to what is out there and to familiarize yourself with the topic. While the articles in the *New York Times* are always interesting, well written, and informative, they do not take the place of reading and understanding the original research. And make sure you check to see if any of these sources are online and free, so they can be searched and printed out for your further examination. More about that later.

The Reader's Guide to Periodical Literature is far and away the most comprehensive available guide to general literature. It is organized by topic and is published monthly, covering hundreds of journals (such as the *New England Journal of Medicine*) and periodicals or magazines (such as *Scientific American*). Since the topics are alphabetically listed, you are bound to be able to find reading sources on a selected topic easily and quickly. Part of a page from *The Reader's Guide* is shown in Figure 3.3. As you can see, this page shows available entries on the topic of teenage pregnancy. Notice that there is a general heading, Teenage Pregnancy, and underneath is a listing of specific articles by title and where they appear.

Another valuable general source is *Facts on File (FOF),* published in New York since 1941. *FOF* summarizes news that is reported in more than 50 foreign and domestic newspapers and magazines, a great place to find out whether anything has appeared in these outlets in your particular area of interest. *FOF* is published weekly, and its index is cumulative for the current year, so it should not take you more than a few minutes to find out if there is information available.

The New York Times Index goes back to 1851 and lists all the articles published in the *Times* by subject. Once you find reference to an article that might be of interest, you then go to the stacks and select a copy of the actual issue or view it on microfilm. The originals are seldom available because they are printed on thin paper designed to hold up only for the few days that a newspaper might be passed around.

Instead, contents are recorded on microfilm or some other medium and are available through your library. Many libraries now offer microfilm readers that allow you to copy directly from the microfilm image and make a print or hard copy of what you are viewing. The full text of many newspapers is also now available electronically, which you will read about later in this chapter.

Nobody should take what is printed as the absolute gospel, but weekly news magazines such as *Time, Newsweek,* and *U.S. News and World Report* offer general information and keep you well informed about other related events as well. You may not

TEENAGE PREGNANCY

Family dysfunction [Hispanics' ascending teen birthrate] *National Review* v50 p 20 Mr 9 '98

His way out [B. Peterson's manslaughter plea bargin in case of Death of his and A. Grossberg's newborn son] M. Grant and E. McNeil. Il pors *People Weekly* v49 p44–9 Mr 23 '98

A secret birth: a baby's death: what went wrong? C.K. Binswanger, il *Glamour* v95 p 302–5+ S '97

Where have all the babies gone? [Infanticide] B. Ehrenreich. Il *Life* V21 p68–74+ Ja'98.

Figure 3.3 An entry from *The Reader's Guide to Periodical Literature.*

even know that you have an interest in a particular topic (such as ethical questions in research). A story on that topic might be in this week's issue, catch your eye, and before you know it you will be using that information to seek out other sources.

There are also some specialty magazines that you might want to know about. *Science News* (published weekly) and *Science Digest* (a monthly publication) provide summaries of important news from the world of science. They are current and informative.

Finally, there is the wealth of information you can dig out of everyday sources such as your local newspaper, company newsletters, and other publications. Local newspapers often carry the same Associated Press articles as major papers such as the *New York Times* and the *Washington Post.* And please do not forget the U.S. government and U.S. Government Printing Office (GPO). They regularly publish thousands of documents on everything from baseball to bees, and a large majority of them are free. (Don't worry—your parents have already paid.)

One especially useful source that you should not overlook is *The Statistical Abstract of the United States,* published yearly by the U.S. Department of Commerce. This is the national data book about the United States, including valuable and easily accessible information on demographics and much more. Want to know more about the GPO? Write to the Government Printing Office, North Capitol and H Streets, NW, Washington, DC 20401 for a catalog of what is available.

Not all of the general resources that we have mentioned above are currently online, but they probably will be soon. So, if you don't have access to the Internet at home, find out where you can gain access at school and use it! More about using the Internet for research purposes later in this chapter.

Using Secondary Sources

Secondary sources are those that you seek out if you are looking for a scholarly summary of the research that has been done in a particular area or if you are looking for further sources of references.

Reviews and Syntheses of Literature

These are the BIG books you often find in the reference section of the library (not on the stack shelves). Since so many people want to use them, they always have to be available. Here is a summary of some of the most useful.

Major syntheses of information such as reviews, can be a terrific foundation for your review.

Review of Research in Education first appeared in 1973 and is still published by the American Educational Research Association. The *Review* offers a collection of critical reviews of research in a specific area such as minimum competency testing or changing conceptions of intelligence. While the *Review* might not offer exactly what you want, it will give you a very good perspective on that subject if you hit upon the topic you are interested in.

There is also *The Encyclopedia of Educational Research,* last published in 1992, that consists of four volumes including 257 articles written by experts and stands as the standard general reference. Each of these articles contains an extensive bibliography, so it is a good place to start finding information about a particular topic.

A general secondary source of literature reviews is the *Annual Review of Psychology* (published by Annual Reviews) containing about 20 chapters and focusing on a wide range of topics. Just think of it: you can go through the last 10 years of these volumes and be very up to date on a wide range of general topics in psychology. If you happen to find one chapter on exactly what you want to do, you are way ahead of the game.

Another annual review that is well worth considering is *The National Society for the Study of Education* (or NSSE) Yearbooks. Each year since 1902, this society has published a two-volume annual that focuses on a particular topic such as adolescence, microcomputers in the classroom, gifted and talented children, or classroom management. The area of focus is usually some contemporary topic, and if you are interested in what is being covered, the information can be invaluable to you.

Interested in child development? Seek out the four-volume *Handbook of Child Psychology* (published in 1997 by John Wiley) or the *Handbook of Parenting* (published in 1995 by Larry Erlbaum Associates). The fourth edition of the *Handbook of Child Psychology* (edited by William Damon) is often used as the starting point (for ideas) by developmental and child psychology students, early childhood education students, medical and nursing students, and others across a wide field. The four individual volumes are

- History, Theory, and Methods,
- Infancy and Developmental Psychobiology,
- Cognitive Development, and
- Socialization, Personality, and Social Development

A more later life span approach is offered by the *Handbook of the Psychology of Aging* by James E. Birren and K. Warner Schaie (published by Academic Press in 1996). This large paperback deals with just about everything related to aging.

Also, do not forget the large number of scholarly books that sometimes have multiple authors and are edited by one individual or that are written entirely by one person (which in the latter case is sometimes considered a primary resource, depending upon its content). Use the good old card catalog (or your library's computerized search system) to find the title or author you need.

Using Primary Sources

Primary sources are the meat and potatoes of the literature review. While you will get some good ideas and a good deal of information from reading the secondary sources, you have to go to the real thing to get the specific information to make your points and to make your points stick!

In fact, your best bet is to include mostly primary sources in your literature review, with some secondary sources to help make your case, and do not even think about including general sources. It is not that the information in *Redbook* or the *St. Louis Dispatch* is not useful or valuable. It is secondhand, and you do not want to build an argument based on someone else's interpretation of a concept.

Using Journals

Journals? You want journals? Just take a look at the list in Table 3.3 arranged by category. This should be enough for you to answer your professor when he asks, "Who can tell me some of the important journals in your own field?" This list is only a small selection of what is out there.

Get to know your library and where you can find journals in your field—they are the history of your question.

Journals are by far the most important and valuable primary sources of information about a topic since they represent the most direct link between the researcher, the work of other researchers, and your own interests.

What actually is a journal, and how does it work? A journal is a collection (most often) of research articles published in a particular area by some professional group. For example, the American Psychological Association publishes journals including *The Journal of Experimental Psychology* and *The Journal of Counseling Psychology*

Psychology

Adolescence
American Journal of Family Therapy
American Journal of Orthopsychiatry
American Psychologist
Behavioral Disorders
Child Development
Child Study Journal
Developmental Psychology
Contemporary Educational Psychology
Educational and Psychological Measurement
Journal of Abnormal Child Psychology
Journal of Applied Behavioral Analysis
Journal of Autism and Developmental Disorders
Journal of Child Psychology and Psychiatry and Allied Disciplines
Journal of Consulting and Clinical Psychology
Journal of Counseling Psychology
Journal of Educational Psychology
Journal of Experimental Child Psychology
Journal of Experimental Psychology: Human Perception and Performance
Journal of Experimental Psychology: Learning, Memory, and Cognition
Journal of Genetic Psychology
Journal of Humanistic Psychology
Journal of Personality and Social Psychology
Journal of Psychology
Journal of Research in Personality
Journal of School Psychology
Perceptual and Motor Skills
Psychological Bulletin
Psychological Review
Psychology in the Schools
Psychology of Women Quarterly
Small Group Behavior
Transactional Analysis Journal

Special Education and Exceptional Children

Academic Therapy
American Annals of the Deaf
American Journal of Mental Deficiency
Behavioral Disorders
Education and Training of the Mentally Retarded
Education of the Visually Handicapped
Exceptional Children
Exceptional Education Quarterly
Exceptional Parent
Focus on the Exceptional Child
Gifted Child Quarterly
Hearing and Speech Action
International Journal for the Education of the Blind
Journal for the Education of the Gifted
Journal of The Association for the Severely Handicapped
Journal of Learning Disabilities
Journal of Mental Deficiency Research
Journal of Special Education
Journal of Special Education Technology
Journal of Speech and Hearing Disorders
Journal of Speech and Hearing Research
Journal of Visual Impairment and Blindness
Learning Disability Quarterly
Mental Retardation
Sightsaving Review
Teaching Exceptional Children
Teacher Education and Special Education
Teacher of the Blind
Topics in Early Childhood Special Education
Volta Review

Health and Physical Education

Journal of Health and Educational
Journal of Health Education
Journal of Alcohol and Drug Education
Journal of Leisure Research
Journal of Motor Learning
Journal of Nutrition Education
Journal of Outdoor Education
Journal of Physical Education, Recreation and Dance
Journal of School Health
Journal of Sport History
Physical Educator
Research Quarterly of the American Alliance for Health, Physical Education, Recreation and Dance
School Health Review

(continued)

Table 3.3 Selection of journals.

Guidance and Counseling

American Mental Health Counselors Association Journal
Counselor Education and Supervision
Elementary School Guidance and Counseling
Humanistic Education and Development
Measurement and Evaluation in Counseling and Development
Personnel and Guidance Journal
School Counselor
School Guidance Worker
Vocational Guidance Quarterly

Reading, Language Arts, English

English Education
English Journal
Journal of Linguistics
Journal of Reading
Journal of Reading Behavior
Journal of Research in Reading
Language Learning
Reading Horizons
Reading Improvement
Reading Psychology
Reading Research Quarterly
Reading Teacher
Reading World
Research in the Teaching of English

Education

Administrative Science Quarterly
Administrator's Notebook
Adult Education
Alberta Journal of Educational Research
American Biology Teacher
American Education
American Educational Research Journal
American Journal of Education
American School Board Journal
Arithmetic Teacher
Art Education
Black Scholar Bulletin of the National Association of Secondary Schools Principals
Business Education Forum
Business Education World
Career Education
Clearing House College Board Review
College Quarterly of Research and Practice
College Research Quarterly
Computers and Education
Educational Administration Quarterly
Educational Communication and Technology: A Journal of Theory, Research, and Development
Educational Evaluation and Policy Analysis
Educational Gerontology
Educational Leadership
Educational Record
Educational Research Quarterly
Educational Researcher
Elementary School Journal
Evaluation Review
High School Journal
Home Economics Research
Journal Integrated Education
Journal for Research in Mathematics Education
Journal of Aesthetic Education
Journal of Biological Education
Journal of Block Studies
Journal of Business Education
Journal of Career Education
Journal of Computer-Based Instruction
Journal of Computers in Mathematics and Science Teaching
Journal of Drug Education
Journal of Economics Education
Journal of Educational Measurement
Journal of Educational Research
Journal of Educational Statistics
Journal of Experimental Education
Journal of Instructional Development
Journal of Negro Education
Journal of Research and Development in Education
Journal of Research in Mathematics Education
Journal of Research in Music Education
Journal of Research in Science Teaching
Journal of Social Studies Research
Journal of Teacher Education
Journal of Vocational Educational Research
Kappa Delta Pi Record
Library Quarterly

Table 3.3 (Continued)

Education (continued)

Library Research
Lifelong Learning: The Adult Years
Mathematics and Computer Education
Mathematics Teacher
Modern Language Journal
Music Education Journal
National Education Association Research Bulletin
National Elementary Principal
Negro Education Review
Peabody Journal of Education
Phi Delta Kappan
Review of Educational Research
School Library Media Quarterly
School Psychology Review
School Science and Mathematics
School Science Review
Science and Children
Science Education
Science Teacher
Secondary School Theatre Journal
Social Education
Studies in Art Education
Studies in Educational Evaluation
Teachers College Record
Theory and Research in Social Education
Theory into Practice
Today's Education
Voc Ed
Young Children

Sociology and Anthropology

American Anthropologist
American Behavioral Scientist
American Journal of Sociology
American Sociological Review
Anthropology and Education Quarterly
Child Welfare
Family Relations
Group and Organization Studies
Human Organization
Human Services in the Rural Environment
Journal of Correctional Education
Journal of Marriage and the Family
Rural Sociology
Sex Roles: A Journal of Research
Social Work
Sociology and Social Research
Sociology of Education
Urban Anthropology
Urban Education
Urban Review
Youth and Society

Analytical Research

Administration and Society
American Historical Review
American Political Science Review
Annals of the American Academy of Political and Social Science
Comparative Education Review
Daedalus
Economics of Education Review
Education and Urban Society
Educational Forum
Educational Studies
Educational Theory
Harvard Civil Rights
Civil Liberties Law

Table 3.3 (Continued)

(among many others). The Society for Research in Child Development publishes *Child Development* and *Child Development Monographs,* among others. Membership in these groups gets you the journals as part of the package, or you can subscribe separately for just the journals.

Most respectable journals work something like this. First, a researcher writes an article according to a specific format (such as the one shown in Chapter 13) and then sends in as many copies as the journal editor requires (usually three). Guidelines for preparing manuscripts are usually found at the front of each issue.

Second, once the article has been received by the editor, who is usually an acknowledged expert in that particular field, the article is sent to at least three reviewers who are also experts in the field. These reviewers participate in a process called blind review, where they do not know the author(s) of the paper. The authors' names appear only on a cover sheet that is torn off by the editor, and the social security number or some other coded number is used for identification. This makes the process quite fair where there is no possibility that personalities get in the way of what can be a highly competitive goal: publishing in the best journals. The reviewers each make a recommendation. The options from which the reviewers can select are usually something like:

- *Accept outright,* meaning that this is an outstanding article and can be accepted for publication as is.
- *Accept with revisions,* meaning that some changes need to be made by the author(s) before it is accepted.
- *Reject with suggestions for revisions,* meaning that the article is not acceptable as of now, but after changes are made the author(s) should be invited to resubmit it.
- *Reject outright,* meaning that the article is completely unacceptable.

The peer review process of reviewing journals ensures that the expert reviewers see the research before it is published.

Finally, if a consensus is reached by the reviewers, the editor of the journal conveys that decision to the author(s). If not, it is the editor's job to make a decision or to send the article to another reviewer for additional comments. Editors work very hard to ensure that the review process and the journal publication process are fair. Editors' terms usually are four to six years.

By the way, you might be interested to know that the average rejection rate for the top journals is about 80%. Yes, 80% of the articles submitted never get in, but those rejected by the top journals usually find their way into other journals. Just because they are not accepted by the journals with the highest rejection rate does not mean they are not useful reports. In fact, several studies have shown that there is little consistency among reviewers, and what one might rank high, another might rank quite low. However, in general, it's safe to say that the better scientific reports are published by the better journals.

One more note about primary sources in general. If you know of a journal or a book that you might need and your library does not have it, do not despair. First, check other libraries within driving distance or check with some of the professors in your department. They might have it available for loan. If all else fails, use the interlibrary loan system, which your reference librarian will be glad to help you with. This service helps you locate and physically secure the reference materials you want for a limited amount of time from another library. The system usually works fast and is efficient.

Using Abstracts

If journals are the workhorses of the literature review, collections of abstracts cannot be very far behind in their convenience and usefulness. An **abstract** is a one- (or at most two-) paragraph summary of a journal article. It contains all the information readers should need to decide whether to read the entire journal article.

By perusing collections of abstracts, researchers can save a significant amount of time compared with leafing through the journals that these abstracts are drawn from. Most abstracts also include subject and author indexes to help readers find what they are looking for, and abstracts of articles routinely appear in more than one abstract resource. For example, a study on how to deal with disruptive children might appear in *PsychInfo (formerly PsychAbstracts-* from a journal such as *Perceptual and Motor Skills)* as well as in the *Current Index to Journals in Education* (from a journal such as *Psychology in the Schools*). Do not be concerned if there is overlap. Actually, it means you are covering all the bases.

Abstracts help you save the time it would take to locate potentially important sources of information.

Here is a brief description of some abstract collections you might find useful.

The granddaddy (grandmommy?) of all the abstracts is *PsychInfo,* published by the American Psychological Association. *PsychInfo* regularly reviews and abstracts over 1,000 journals in the following 23 different areas:

- General psychology
- Psychometrics and statistics and methodology
- Human experimental psychology
- Animal experimental and comparative psychology
- Physiological psychology and neuroscience
- Psychology and the humanities
- Physiological intervention
- Communications systems
- Developmental psychology
- Social processes and social issues
- Social psychology
- Personality psychology
- Psychological and physical disorders
- Health and mental health treatment and prevention
- Professional personnel and health personnel issues
- Educational psychology
- Industrial and organizational psychology
- Sport psychology and leisure
- Military psychology
- Consumer psychology
- Engineering and environmental psychology
- Intelligent systems
- Forensic psychology and legal issues

There is unlimited information in *PsychInfo,* and the online nature lets you search electronically. Figure 3.4 shows the first abstract that was returned when the search term "teenage pregnancy" was entered.

One other way to use *PsychInfo* is by looking up the key word bibliography. Under this heading you will find a list of bibliographies that have already been published. Maybe you will be lucky and find the one that focuses on your area of interest. Two indexes that are especially useful (published by the Educational Resources Information Center or ERIC) are *Resources in Education* and *Current Index to Journals in Education,* each of which performs a separate function.

Resources in Education (RIE) presents the abstracts of papers that have been presented at conferences, the results of "in-house" investigations including progress reports while a project continues, and other documents that do not readily appear in formal journals. Many of these papers are eventually published and are then contained in abstracts such as *PsychInfo.*

Current Index to Journals in Education (*CIJE*) is not really an index but a set of abstracts from more than 750 journals focusing on the broadly defined field of education. Once again, you can expect these journal abstracts to appear elsewhere as well.

As with *PsychInfo,* the ERIC system works with a set of descriptive terms found in a thesaurus, the *Thesaurus of ERIC Descriptors,* which is always your first stop on the way to using *RIE* or *CIJE.* Once you find the search words or descriptors, you then use the subject index (published monthly) until you find the number of a reference that sounds like what you want. Finally, you are off to the actual description of the reference. If you want a hard copy of the entire document represented by this abstract (ERIC calls abstracts resumes), you can order either a hard copy or a microfilm copy

Record 1 of 1 - PsycINFO 1996-1998/12

AN: 1998-06383-008SEE PREVIOUS CHAPTER SEE NEXT CHAPTER

TI: Betwixt and between: Sexuality in the context of adolescent transitions.

AU: Graber,-Julia-A.; Brooks-Gunn,-Jeanne; Galen,-Britt-R.

BK: Jessor, Richard (Ed); et-al. (1998). New perspectives on adolescent risk behavior. (pp. 270–316). New York, NY, USA: Cambridge University Press. xii, 564 pp. SEE BOOK

AB: (from the book) Changes occurring during adolescence are inherently defined by an individual's social context and by the roles and expectations for behavior based on an individual's identification with or membership in a group. Adolescents' experiences, as they develop a sexual identity or sense of self as a sexual being, fit the notion of "betwixt and between," as adolescents' behavior frequently does not match the expectations for their behavior as expressed by the adults around them. This chapter focuses on several themes that have been prevalent in the study of adolescent sexuality, and, to a lesser extent, in the study of teenage pregnancy, focusing on the notion of transition-based turning points in characterizing sexual initiation. The concepts of role transitions and their potential importance in the life course are reviewed, and a survey of recent reorientations in the study of adolescent sexuality is offered. ((c) 1998 APA/PsycINFO, all rights reserved)

Figure 3.4 A *PsychInfo* entry.

(smaller and cheaper) through the ERIC Document Reproduction Service using forms available at your library. It usually takes about two weeks to receive the document. But you may not need to order a copy. If you have a government documents department in your library, it might already have the document on hand. Also, you might be able to contact the original author as listed in the resume. Better yet, it may be available online. Check ERIC out at http://ericae.net/scripts/ewiz/amain2.asp where you can use the search wizard to create a query.

ERIC has been in business since 1981 and has 18 regional clearinghouses that archive, abstract, and disseminate educational articles and documents. Education is broadly defined, so many disciplines in the social and behavioral sciences are covered quite adequately. You can see how broad ERIC's reach is by examining the list of subject areas covered by these 18 clearinghouses:

- Adult, career, and vocational education
- Assessment and evaluation
- Community colleges
- Counseling and student services
- Disabilities and gifted education
- Educational management
- Elementary and early childhood education
- National parent information network

- Higher education
- Information and technology
- AskERIC
- Languages and linguistics
- Reading, English, and communication
- Rural education and small schools
- Science, mathematics, and environmental education
- Social studies/social science education
- Teaching and teacher education
- Urban education

Think that is enough to get started? *PsychInfo* and the ERIC sets of abstracts are major resources, but there are others that are a bit more specialized and also very useful.

Figure 3.5 shows you an abstract from a recent issue of *Child Development Abstracts & Bibliography.* You can see that it contains the complete reference for the article and a one-paragraph summary of the article's contents including:

- An introductory sentence about the article's contents.
- A description of the participants by age and other factors of interest.
- A statement of the results.

Child Development Abstracts & Bibliography abstracts more than 300 journals and provides reviews of books about children and families including coverage in six different areas:

- Biology, health, and medicine
- Cognition, learning, and perception
- Social psychology and personality studies
- Education
- Psychiatry and clinical psychology
- History, theory, and methodology

Titles of other abstracts such as *Sociological Abstracts, Exceptional Child Education Resources, Research Related to Children,* and *Dissertation Abstracts* reveal the wide variety of available reference material.

486. Kingery, Paul M.; Coggeshall, Mark B.; & Alford, Aaron A. (1998). **Violence at school: Recent evidence from four national surveys.** Psychology in the Schools, 35, 247-258.

Four surveys (the Youth Risk Behavior Survey, the Monitoring the Future Survey, the National Longitudinal Study of Adolescent Health, and the National Victimization Survey School Crime Supplement) using nationally representative samples that include questions about violence are administered among school-aged youth. The data from those four databases are reviewed in this article to assess risk factors for weapon carrying and the level of the school violence problem. The percentage of youths in grades 9-12 who were involved in a single fight in a given year declined in recent years while the prevalence of more frequent fighting has not. The most important risk factors identified for carrying weapons at school dealt with the student's involvement with violence in the broader community context both as perpetrator and victim.

Figure 3.5 An entry from Child Development Abstracts & Bibliography, which surveys more than 300 different journals.

Using Indexes

Journals and abstracts provide the substance of an article, a conference presentation, or a report. If you want a quick overview of where things might be located, turn to an **index,** an alphabetical listing of entries by topic, author, or both.

Indexes help you locate the source of important information.

A good starting point in any literature review is to look at the work of people in the same position as you are in, master's or doctoral students. First, there is the *Comprehensive Dissertation Index,* published by the University of Michigan, listing dissertations for which abstracts are available.

Other similar indexes are *American Doctoral Dissertations* published by the University of Michigan and *Master's Theses Directories (for a variety of disciplines).* While not as current as the *Comprehensive Dissertation Index* mentioned above, *American Doctoral Dissertations* lists dissertation titles by subject and year as gleaned from commencement programs.

The widely used and popular *Social Sciences Citation Index (SSCI)* and *Science Citation Index (SCI)* work in an interesting and creative way. *SCI* deals with the fields of medicine, agriculture, and technology. *SSCI* deals with the fields of social and behavioral sciences. Let's say you read an article that you find to be very relevant to your research proposal and want to know what else the author has done. You might want to search by subject through abstracts as we have talked about, but you might also want to find other articles by the same author or on the same general topic. Tools like *SSCI* allow you to focus on your specific topic and access as much of the available information as possible. For example, do you want to find out who has mentioned the classic article "Mental and Physical Traits of a Thousand Gifted Children" (written by Louis Terman and published in 1925)? Look up Terman, L., in *SSCI* year by year, and you will find more references than you may know what to do with.

Finally, you can consult the *Bibliographic Index,* a compilation of bibliographies that results from a search of about 2,600 periodicals. Just think of the time you can save if you locate a relatively recent bibliography on whatever you are interested in.

Using Computers in Your Research Search

Imagine this if you will: You are in your apartment and it is late at night. You find that you need one more reference on the development of adolescent self-esteem to complete your literature review. You are tired. It is snowing. The library is about to close, and they might not have what you need anyway.

Both the computer as a tool and the library as a storehouse of information (and another tool) play different, but equally important, roles in the research process.

Zoom, you're on the Internet and you're on the way. Log onto some proprietary (which means you pay) database or just browse and search for the reference. In 20 seconds you have got the reference to read or to print. Is this for real? You bet, and there is a very good chance your professor already uses services that provide this capability. You can also bet that by the time you are finished with your undergraduate or graduate training, you will be zooming around databases and information providers using your personal computer and some simple, inexpensive hardware and software.

At home, in your office, or in the confines of the library, the use of computers for completing literature searches and reviews is booming and blooming, with new databases to search becoming available each day.

In a moment we'll start our explanation of some of this, but first a few words of "this can't be true, but it is." Many of you who are using this book may have never taken advantage of what your library services have to offer. Now, if you don't have access to the Internet at home because you can't afford a computer, (although the price of the equipment you need is coming down dramatically), that's entirely understandable. What is not understandable is why you are not accessing these resources from on campus. Almost every college or university provides *free* access to all these resources for its students. The personal computers you can use may be located in the computer center, in the library, in academic buildings or even in all three and more—but they are surely there for the using. And, probably a hefty chunk of the fees that you pay each semester goes toward purchasing new equipment and paying for these services. So, use them!

Also, the publishing industry is changing so rapidly that today, many important sets of references are no longer available as hard or printed copy. For example, what used to be *Psych Abstracts* is now *PsychInfo* and most institutions only have it available via CD or online. Why? Basically, it's not any more expensive than the paper copy, it's easier to use, and best of all, it takes up virtually no space (well, maybe a bunch of CDs—but that's lots better than a football field worth of shelves).

So while in the previous edition of *Exploring Research,* we would talk about both paper and electronic forms of a reference, today we're talking *only* about electronic forms if available in both forms. It's the way of the future and you better get used to it.

Using CD-ROMs

At the University of Kansas, you can walk into Watson Library (the main research library), sit down at a computer terminal, insert one of the CD-ROM (compact disk-read only memory) disks containing ERIC documents, and search through them in seconds for the reference you want. Not bad. You can also access centrally stored CD-ROMs that contain millions of abstracts, full length articles, and more.

For example, here is what happened during a search for references on teacher burnout in elementary schools. First, the characters teacher-burnout were entered. The hyphen represents the ERIC instruction to seek records that are related to both words. In three seconds, 366 records were found.

Second, the characters elementary-school-teachers were entered, and 559 records were reported as available.

Finally, to see how many records contain both types of information, the characters 1! and 2! were entered, telling ERIC to look for records containing both teacher-burnout and elementary-school-teacher references, 15 were listed on the screen. You can then print this information, read it off the screen, or save it to disk. Easy? Definitely. Expensive? In this case, it is free (read: taxes pay for it!). As additional disks and computers need to be purchased, there is sure to be a real dollar cost associated with search. Figure 3.6 shows an abstract taken right off line.

Another incredibly useful source of reference information that you can access through your personal computer on a CD-ROM is any one of the many different encyclopedias that are available on CD-ROM. You can see in Figure 3.7 how we found information on behavior modification using the *Compton Interactive Encyclopedia.* While this is not enough to write your term paper, it is certainly enough to give you a clue as to the general area.

Searching Online

Your library offers you some incredible resources for accessing information through the use of personal computers.

Researchers in universities, businesses, and the government are turning to online information providers more and more to find the key information they need, whether a specific reference or fact, such as the number of bicycles produced by Japan or the number of young adults who live in urban areas.

Your local city library as well as the university probably has tons of CDs that include valuable reference information.

Record 1 of 1 - ERIC 1992-1998/09

AN: ED417357

AU: Sugland,-Barbara-W.; Wilder,-Kathleen-J.; Chandra,-Anita

TI: Understanding Adolescents' Motivation To Prevent Pregnancy: A
Literature Review.

CS: Child Trends, Inc., Washington, DC. PY: 1996

NT: 107 p.

PR: EDRS Price - MF01/PC05 Plus Postage.

AB: Recent efforts targeting teenage pregnancy in the United States have marked a renewed conviction to reduce the level of childbearing among adolescents. Some of the behavioral, psychosocial, and ethnographic studies that explore the underlying motivation to delay sex and to effectively use contraception are the focus of this literature review. Eschewing the more traditional, demographic or descriptive approach to teenage pregnancy, the goal of this study is to understand adolescents' motivation to prevent pregnancy; subsequently, it focuses on research that addresses the transition to first sex, sexual activity, and the use of contraception. A select number of studies on pregnancy resolution are also included as they are helpful for understanding the broader context of factors that may encourage/discourage adolescent sex and contraceptive behavior. The studies under review address individual-level factors, the influence of partners, peers, siblings and family processes, community and policy influences. Key findings are summarized, areas in need of further exploration are discussed, and a preliminary framework for a model integrating current knowledge is presented. Two sections, "Literature Cited" and "Literature Reviewed," contain approximately 267 references. An appendix describes and compares 19 models for understanding adolescent pregnancy. (EMK)

Figure 3.6 A typical ERIC abstract.

The Value of Online Searches

Why conduct an online search if you can just as well let your fingers do the walking through the stacks, books, journals, abstracts, and indexes (tired yet?) discussed earlier in this chapter?

I am sure you guessed by now . . . basically, it's time and convenience. You can do a search using one of the online services in one quarter of the time it takes to do it manually. Just schlepping to the library can take 30 minutes. If you drive, you spend 15 minutes more looking for a parking space, and the list goes on.

Another important advantage of online searches, if your search skills are anywhere near competent, is that you are not likely to miss very much. The information providers (such as America Online) provide access to tens of thousands of documents,

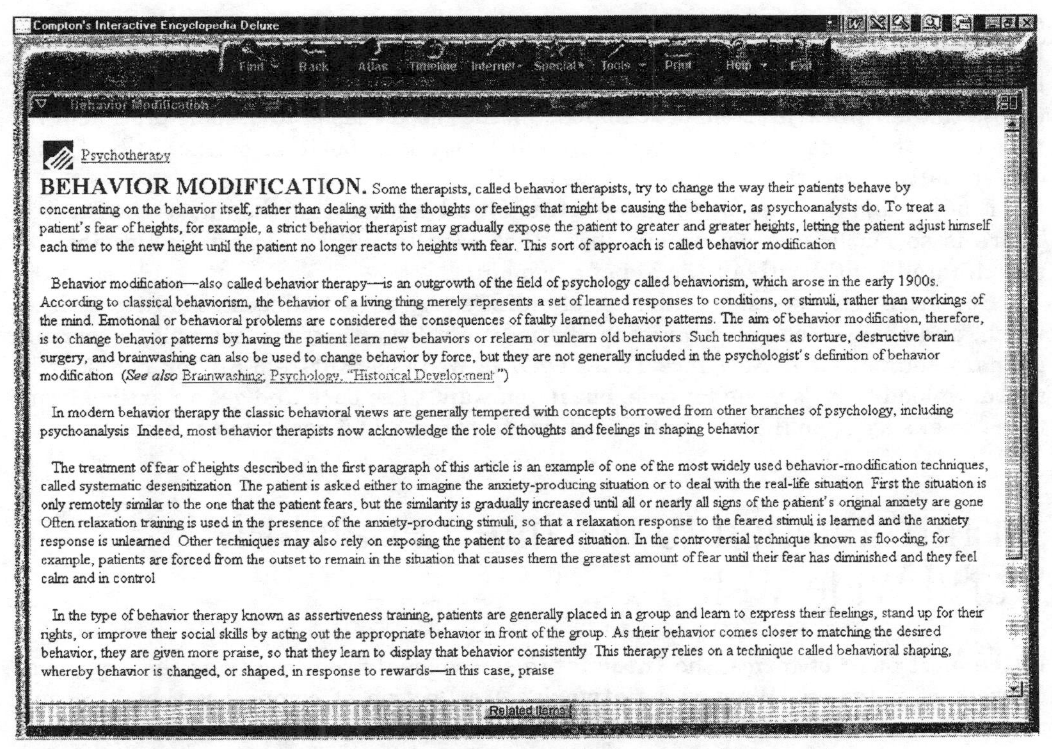
Compton's Interactive Encyclopedia Deluxe

Find Back Atlas Timeline Internet Special Tools Print Help Exit

Behavior Modification

Psychotherapy

BEHAVIOR MODIFICATION. Some therapists, called behavior therapists, try to change the way their patients behave by concentrating on the behavior itself, rather than dealing with the thoughts or feelings that might be causing the behavior, as psychoanalysts do. To treat a patient's fear of heights, for example, a strict behavior therapist may gradually expose the patient to greater and greater heights, letting the patient adjust himself each time to the new height until the patient no longer reacts to heights with fear. This sort of approach is called behavior modification

Behavior modification—also called behavior therapy—is an outgrowth of the field of psychology called behaviorism, which arose in the early 1900s. According to classical behaviorism, the behavior of a living thing merely represents a set of learned responses to conditions, or stimuli, rather than workings of the mind. Emotional or behavioral problems are considered the consequences of faulty learned behavior patterns. The aim of behavior modification, therefore, is to change behavior patterns by having the patient learn new behaviors or relearn or unlearn old behaviors Such techniques as torture, destructive brain surgery, and brainwashing can also be used to change behavior by force, but they are not generally included in the psychologist's definition of behavior modification (*See also* Brainwashing; Psychology, "Historical Development")

In modern behavior therapy the classic behavioral views are generally tempered with concepts borrowed from other branches of psychology, including psychoanalysis Indeed, most behavior therapists now acknowledge the role of thoughts and feelings in shaping behavior

The treatment of fear of heights described in the first paragraph of this article is an example of one of the most widely used behavior-modification techniques, called systematic desensitization The patient is asked either to imagine the anxiety-producing situation or to deal with the real-life situation First the situation is only remotely similar to the one that the patient fears, but the similarity is gradually increased until all or nearly all signs of the patient's original anxiety are gone Often relaxation training is used in the presence of the anxiety-producing stimuli, so that a relaxation response to the feared stimuli is learned and the anxiety response is unlearned Other techniques may also rely on exposing the patient to a feared situation. In the controversial technique known as flooding, for example, patients are forced from the outset to remain in the situation that causes them the greatest amount of fear until their fear has diminished and they feel calm and in control

In the type of behavior therapy known as assertiveness training, patients are generally placed in a group and learn to express their feelings, stand up for their rights, or improve their social skills by acting out the appropriate behavior in front of the group. As their behavior comes closer to matching the desired behavior, they are given more praise, so that they learn to display that behavior consistently This therapy relies on a technique called behavioral shaping, whereby behavior is changed, or shaped, in response to rewards—in this case, praise

Related Items

Figure 3.7 Using *Compton's Interactive Encyclopedia* for general information.

The New York Times on the Web - Netscape

File Edit View Go Communicator Help

Back Forward Reload Home Search Netscape Print Security Stop

Bookmarks Netsite: http://www.nytimes.com/ What's Related

The New York Times ON THE WEB

NYC Weather 40° F

EXPECT THE WORLD

TUESDAY, DECEMBER 29, 1998 | Site Updated 5:21 PM

QUICK NEWS
PAGE ONE PLUS
International
National/N.Y.
Politics
Business
Technology
Science
Sports
Weather
Opinion
Arts/Living
Automobiles
Books
Diversions
Job Market
Learning
Real Estate
Travel
SITE INDEX

FOR LISTINGS, VISIT NEWYORKtoday
- Movies
- Restaurants
- Theater
- Music
- Shopping
- Yellow Pages

Text Version

Khmer Rouge Leaders Call On Cambodians to Forget the Past

Two top Khmer Rouge leaders apologized Tuesday for the deaths of as many as 2 million people during their regime in the 1970's and asked their countrymen to "let bygones be bygones." Go to Article

Initial Data Indicate Surge for Online Retailers' Holiday Sales

Holiday sales for Internet retailers were even stronger than predictions that earlier this month seemed overblown, initial reports suggested. Go to Article

Challenging U.S., Iraq Claims To Be Flying in No-Fly Zone

Iraq is challenging "no-fly" zones over its northern and southern territory by flying its warplanes through skies patrolled by the United States and Britain, Iraq's vice president said on

The Supreme Court is being asked to reverse an order permitting Hugo P. and his sister, Gloria, to be adopted by different families. Go to Article

INTERNATIONAL
Three Tourists Killed in Yemen

ARTS
A Racial Divide Widens on Network TV

NATIONAL
Denver Stands Out in Trend Toward Downtown Living

http://www.nytimes.com/classified/

Figure 3.8 The *New York Times* on the Web.

either in their own databases, or others they can tap into. And dedicated databases, have millions of pieces (such as *PsychInfo* from the American psychological Association) of information. Keep in mind also that most colleges and universities now allow access to their libraries from off campus, another good reason to become proficient in this area. At the least, you can work through a catalog of holdings online. At best, you can actually access the holdings.

Finally, and this may be the most attractive advantage, it is the way of the future. There is so much information out there that soon it will be close to impossible to search intelligently without the aid of a computer.

But there is a down side to the use of online services as well: cost. There is no free lunch, and there is no free searching of the literature either. For example, a terrific primary source is *The New York Times On The Web* (see Figure 3.8). You can search and download today's issue for free, but if you want to go back and get an article from three weeks ago, you'll have to pay—not much (about $2.95 each), but it's not free.

An Introduction to the Internet and the World Wide Web

In the most basic of terms, the **Internet** (also commonly referred to as the **net**), is a network of networks. What is a **network?** A collection of computers that are connected to one another and that can communicate with each other. Imagine if all these networks were connected to one another and imagine hundreds of networks and thousands of computers of all different types attached to one another and millions of people using those computers. Now you have some idea how large the Internet is. In fact, it is growing geometrically (2, 4, 8, 16, etc.) and now millions of people connect each day for work (and a bit of fun as well).

Research Activities on the Net

If you are talking about information in all shapes and sizes, there is not much that you cannot do on the Internet. Here is a brief overview of how the Internet can be used for research purposes, whether it is contacting an expert in your field via e-mail, or finding the home page of the university (more on home pages later) where you would like to apply for graduate school, or getting a bibliography on a particular topic.

- The Internet is used most often for **electronic mail** or **e-mail.** Just as you exchange postal mail with a colleague across the United States or the world, so you can do the same without ever putting pen to paper. You create a message and send it to your correspondent's electronic address. It is fast, easy, and fun. For example, if you would like a reprint of an article that you find interesting, you could e-mail the author and ask for a copy. Almost all faculty and staff members at large and small educational institutions have e-mail.
- There are thousands of **electronic newsgroups** available to you on the Internet. These are places where information can be posted and shared among Internet users, with topics that range from space exploration to the authenticity of a Civil War era land deed. You can drop in and contribute to any of these newsgroups. For example, if you are interested in K-12 math curriculum, try the k12.ed.math newsgroups. How about pathological behavior? Try the sci.psychology.psychotherapy newsgroup. We mentioned these earlier and will return to them again later for a short demo.

- Finally, there is the **World Wide Web** or **WWW.** Here you can use a **browser** (such as Netscape or Internet Explorer) to make a connection to these graphical stops on the information highway. You can access the National Institutes of Health home page and see what types of funding programs are available or go to the latest timetable at the University of Kansas to find out when Statistics 1 is being offered and who is teaching it.

This chapter will limit its comments to e-mail, newsgroups, and an exploration of the World Wide Web using Netscape's browser, called Communicator—the most popular browser.

We'll provide examples of how these various Internet features can be used. In most cases, to connect to the Internet at school and use e-mail, newsgroups and "surf the Web," all it takes is sitting down and double-clicking on the browser icon.

Electronic Mail for Everyone

Imagine it is 1925, and you are sitting at your desk at college, writing a letter to a friend in England. You stamp the letter, mail it, and three weeks later an answer comes back. You are amazed at how fast the mail is and sit down to answer your friend's new questions about how much you like college and what you will do after you graduate.

Now imagine it is 1999, and you are writing to a friend in England. Only this time, you use electronic mail or e-mail. From your home, you compose the message, press the send key, and your friend has it in less than 30 minutes. The message back to you arrives within 20 minutes more and "attached" to the message is a special thank you note.

E-mail works much like conventional mail. You write a message and send it to an address. The big difference is that there is no paper involved. Rather, the messages you send travel from one computer to another in a matter of minutes or hours, rather than in days or weeks, as fast as your voice travels in a telephone conversation.

E-mail is the fastest and least expensive way to communicate and obtain specific information from others in your field.

Netscape and E-Mail

Here is a sample Netscape session where I write to a colleague and request a reprint. In Figure 3.9, I have composed a message to a colleague requesting a copy of an article. The Netscape screen is like many other mail program screens where you compose a letter.

- It has a location for the Internet address to whom the message is being sent (Dr. Lewis Margolis at the University of North Carolina).
- It shows the topic or subject of the message (Copy of article).
- The content of the message is shown in the main message area starting with "Dear Dr. Margolis."

Once the message is complete, I click the Send button at the top of the screen, and the message is sent to Lew Margolis.

If it was a message that I wanted to copy to other people, I can just enter those addresses as well. And, if I want I can "attach" a file (such as a paper or a graphic) that I want to send as well.

Usually, when any kind of mail is sent, be it e-mail or snail mail (another term for postal mail), the recipient answers. Netscape automatically checks my mailbox every set number of minutes (I decide how often) and lets me know if I have mail to read. If I do have mail, a chime sounds, and I double-click on the message and it opens.

You can see in any of the Netscape screens shown that there are many different buttons that can be clicked and many menus with lots of options from which you can

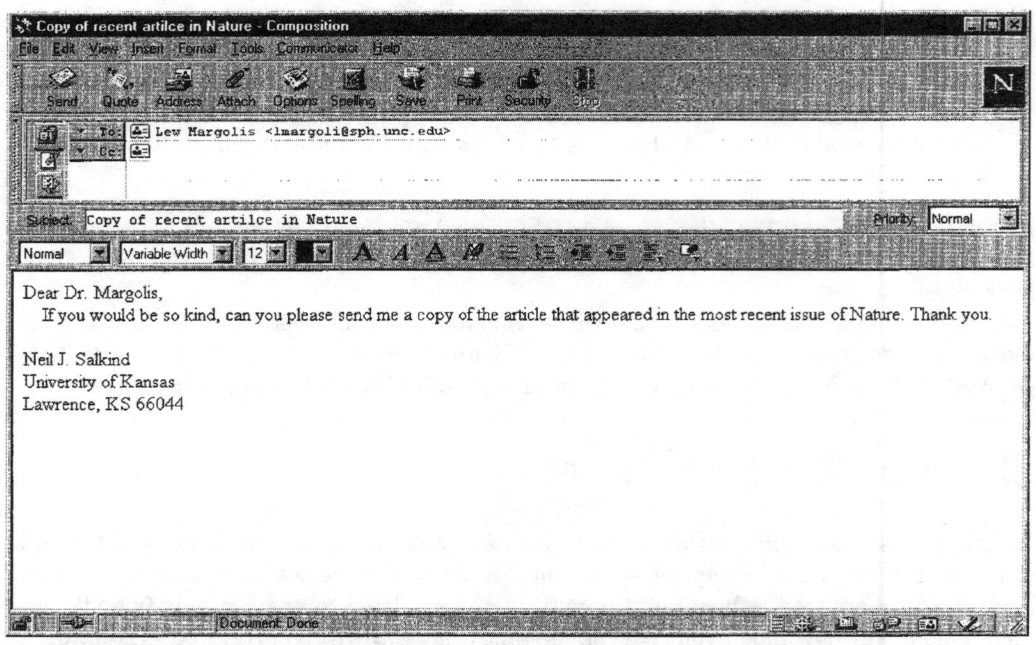

Figure 3.9 Composing a message in Netscape.

select. We are not going into any of those since our purpose is not to teach you how to use Netscape but only to show you easy e-mail is to use. However, it would be useful for you to have some idea what any good e-mail program can do, and Netscape is one of the best.

Its features allow you to

- Print mail messages.
- Have mail messages automatically placed in certain folders using filters.
- Forward mail messages to one or 100 other people.
- Include your "signature" with every mail message you send. This can be a quote or your e-mail address or whatever you feel works best. For example, here is the signature of a student of mine. It automatically appears at the end of every e-mail message he sends:

  Jim Williams | phone: (817) 555-4532
  Summit High School | voice mail: (817) 255-4399 ext. 52
  2318 Blue Pkwy | fax: (817) 555-3419
  Webster, MO 64063
  www:http://www.place.k12.mo.us/

- Have as many mailboxes as you want.
- Check spelling.
- Use nicknames (instead of "jtkuhub.cc.ukans.edu" I can use "Judy Turner").
- Store mail for later reading.

And how should you use e-mail? Well, first, if you're not already an e-mail user, get an account from your computer people and start. It's fun for social and family reasons, but indispensable as part of the research process. Imagine having a question about a particular test you want to use in a research study. E-mail the test's author. Imagine not being able to find a critical reference. E-mail the author. Imagine not being able to understand a point your professor made in class about a particular statistical technique. With permission, e-mail your professor. This stuff really works.

An Introduction to Newsgroups

Now, imagine being able to find information about 30,000 topics ranging from stereo systems to jokes (censored and otherwise) to the ethics of law to college football to astronomy. Where would you be able to find a collection of such diverse information that can be easily accessed? You guessed it. The Internet and the various newsgroup sites that ship news each day around the world. The news that fits in one category, such as college football or the ethics of law, forms a **newsgroup** (also called a group). A newsgroup is simply a collection of information about one topic.

To help manage the flow of articles, news sites are managed, moderated, administered, and censored by system administrators who work for institutions such as universities and corporations. Not all newsgroups reach each potential site or everyone who has access to an Internet site. The newsgroups from which you can select news are those that the system administrator makes available.

Newsgroups can be a small or huge discussion groups about a particular topic.

What's in the News?

Newsgroups are named and organized following a set of rules. The most general of these rules has to do with the name of the group itself. There is a hierarchical structure to a newsgroup name, with the highest level of the hierarchy appearing in the left-most position. For example, the newsgroup name k12.ed.tech means that within k12 (the general name for the kindergarten through twelfth-grade newsgroup), there is a subset named ed (for education) and within that another subset named tech (for technology).

Table 3.4 is a sample of some newsgroup names, what these groups are named, the general area they cover, and examples of what is in each of these groups.

To see how a newsgroup works, let's follow an example of someone interested in educational technology. Once again, we'll use Netscape. It wasn't too long ago when you would have to use a separate newsreader to read news. Now almost every browser, such as Netscape, comes with its own, built in and ready to go. The tools allow you to read existing news and post new messages.

The first thing you need to do when you are ready to access a newsgroup is to subscribe to it. In the Netscape Read Newsgroup option, you can usually see all the newsgroups that your site administrator allows access to (as shown in Figure 3.10). From those, you can select the ones you want to subscribe to. Each time you start your news reader, you will get the updated version of those newsgroups including all the news that has been added to that group since the last time you opened it.

The next step would be to open the k12.ed.tech newsgroup and examine the contents, as you see in Figure 3.11. Within newsgroups, you will see a listing of topics (in this case 3), each one started by an individual as a source for more information, a place to meet electronically, discuss issues, and so forth.

If someone wants to participate in a certain newsgroup, they can add a new topic at this level, or go into an existing newsgroup and make their own contribution.

In Figure 3.11, you can have a discussion about teaching keyboarding. At this level as well, someone can respond to this contribution by posting a message or even by writing directly to the author of this message (in which case the response would not be posted).

Using Mailing Lists

There is another really neat way to use newsgroups, and it is a great source of information. You can sign up for a **listserv discussion group.** A listserv discussion

Newsgroup	General Area	Examples
Alt	Everything that doesn't fit anywhere else and certainly lots of stuff out of the ordinary.	• Alt.actors.dustin-hoffman (welcome back to the Graduate) • Alt.amazon.women (Xena, the Princess Warrior and more) • Alt.anything (guess)
Comp	Information about computers, computer science, software and general interest computer topics.	• Comp.ai (Danger! Will Robinson!—all about artificial intelligence) • Comp.compression (a discussion of ways to compress or reduce files) • Comp.software engineering (so you want to design a new chip?)
News	Information about news, newsgroups, and the newsgroup network.	• News.admin.censorships (all about what should and shouldn't be on the net) • News.admin.net-abuse.email (don't like all that junk e-mail? Come here for advice) • News.accounce.conferences (where to go to be seen)
Biz	Information about business.	• Biz.healthcare (healthcare and $$$) • Biz.books.technical (new publications about business) • Biz.comp.accounting (the exciting world of accounting)
K12	Information about education from kindergarten through grade 12.	• K12.ed.science (teaching science from kindergarten through the 12th grade • K12.library (especially for librarians) • K12.lang.francais (mais oui!)
Bionet	Information about biology.	• Bionet.biophysics (light reading) • Bionet.jobs (where to turn after you get your Ph.D.) • Bionet.journals (where to publish the results of your Ph.D. dissertation)
Rec	Information about recreation, hobbies, the performing arts, and fun stuff.	• Rec.sport.swimming (make a splash) • Rec.bicycles.racing (what cool stuff to buy for your bike to go faster) • Rec.skydiving (take an extra chute)
Sci	Information about science, scientific research and discoveries, engineering, and some social science stuff.	• Sci.astro (astronomy) • Sci.cognitive (so that's what you're thinking) • Sci.skeptic (UFO's do exist!)
Soc	Information about the social sciences.	• Soc.couples (people getting along) • Soc.penpals (why people write to one another) • Soc.misc (stuff that doesn't fit anywhere else)

Table 3.4 Some major newsgroups and examples of their content.

Communicator: Subscribe to Newsgroups

All | Search | New

Server: news.sunflower.com

Newsgroup:

Newsgroup name	ubscrib	Messag
a.* (3 groups)		
aaa.inu-chan	•	0
ab.* (4 groups)		
abg.* (23 groups)		
acadia.* (2 groups)		
acs.* (3 groups)		
adass.* (2 groups)		
ahn.* (5 groups)		
airmail.* (6 groups)		
airnews.* (11 groups)		
ak.* (4 groups)		
akr.* (4 groups)		
alabama.* (20 groups)		
alc.* (11 groups)		
alt	•	0

Add Server... | Subscribe | Unsubscribe | Refresh List | Expand | Collapse All | Stop

OK | Cancel | Help

Document: Done

Figure 3.10 The partial list of newsgroups from which you can select.

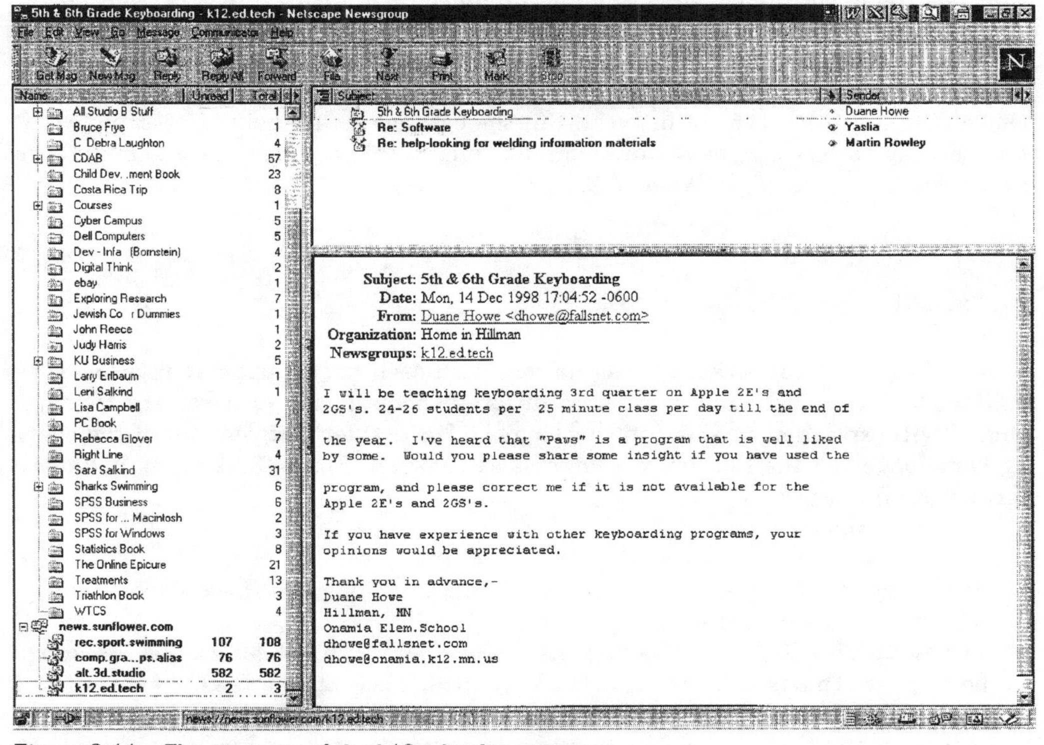

Figure 3.11 The contents of the k12.edtech newsgroup.

group is an automatic depository for information. If you subscribe to it, you receive everything that the list receives. A mail list is also known as a **listserv mailing list.**

For example, if you belong to the kindergarten through twelfth-grade educational technology mailing list, then each time someone sends mail to that list, you will receive it as well. There are more mail servers than you can imagine, and it will take some exploration to find out which ones fit your needs.

To subscribe to a mailing list, you need to send a message to the list's administrator. As soon as you do that, a constant stream of messages will come your way. But be careful; if a list is very active you can receive hundreds of messages in one day. If you go even a day without checking your mail, your electronic mailbox is likely to get so full of messages that you won't be able to read anything! Imagine your real mailbox outside your apartment or home. When it gets stuffed full, it is very difficult to pull out any one piece because the mail is packed so tightly. You need a bigger box, or you needed to empty the box before it gets so full. Such is the case with an Internet mailing list. Either get a larger e-mail box (ask for more storage space from the system administrator), or check your mail more than once a day.

Exploring the WWW

Now we are ready to actually explore the Internet and use what many people find to be the most attractive aspect of the Internet—the World Wide Web.

You already know that the Internet is a network of networks. The World Wide Web (or the Web) is a collection of graphical documents representing different locations that are linked to one another, such that clicking on a particular word or picture or sound in one can quickly take you to another. On the Web, you will find what are called distributed hypertext documents. These documents, also called home pages, contain hot links. These links connect one home page to another. To see and use these home pages and hot links, you need a viewer, and that is where Netscape comes in.

Netscape is one of many browsers that can be used for exploring the Web. There are other viewers and they all work pretty well. I selected Netscape for this book because it is available online and free. It is widely available and it is being used by more people than any other type of browser. But the best reason for using Netscape is that it is so easy to use and more fun than you might think possible. So get ready to browse and meet the World Wide Web.

All About Home Pages

A **home page** is a collection of information, with each home page having some very similar characteristics. You can get to different home pages in a variety of ways, which I will explain more about in this chapter. For now let's explore one of the opening home pages for the Library of Congress as shown in Figure 3.12, not a bad place to start for any search.

Let's see what we see.

- At the top of the page, you see the title Library of Congress Home Page. The title tells you what the current home page is.
- The Location text box shows you the address (http://lcweb.loc.gov/)of the active home page. This is an address on the Web and is also called a **URL** for **universal resource locator.** Once you know the URL for a particular home page, you can just enter the URL in the Location text box, press Enter, and Netscape will take

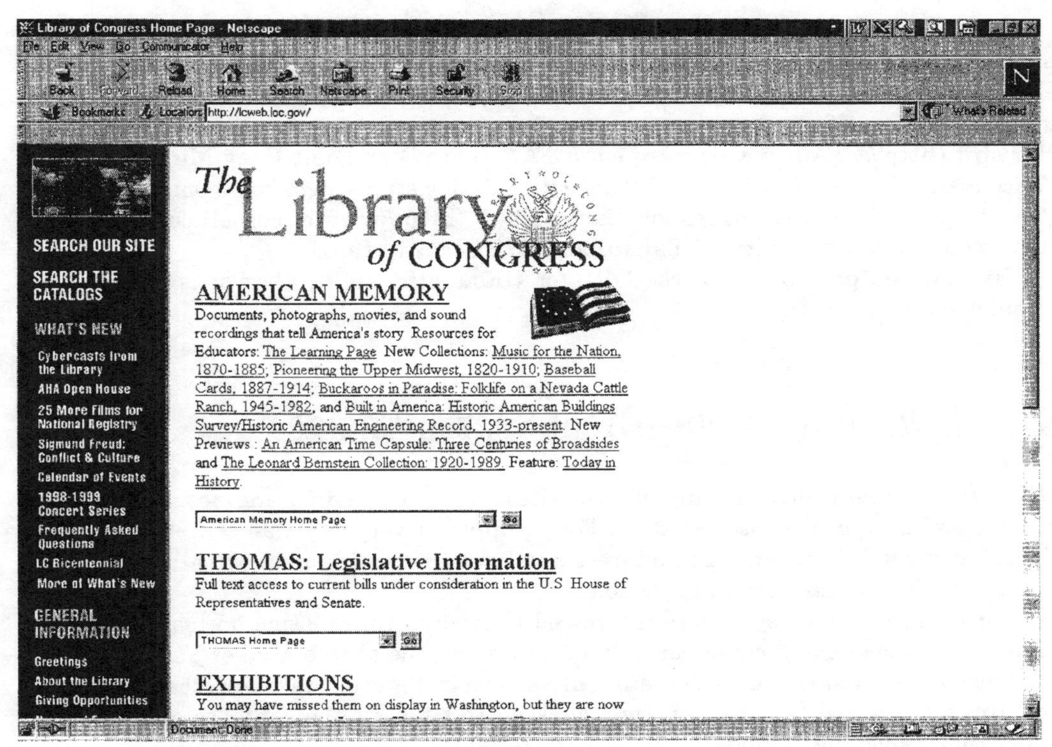

Figure 3.12 The home page for the Library of Congress.

you there. By their nature, URLs are cryptic, and it is tough to tell where one is physically located or what institution is sponsoring the home page. That means it is handy to keep a running list of URLs you like and want to visit once again. That is exactly what the Bookmark pull-down menu does.

➤ Then there's the main portion of the screen showing the contents of the home page, which starts with a nice graphic showing the Library of Congress main building and a listing of various options that you can click, such as the SEARCH OUR SITE button that will allow you to search the entire Library of Congress, all millions of documents.

In all honesty, the utility of home pages is a function of how industrious the designer and the people behind the effort are. This home page (Figure 3.12) can let you access endless documents.

So where do you find great home pages? Not only ones that are fun (like the Motley Fool at *www.fool.com*), but ones that you would find useful for your own work? This is the $64,000 question. There is no central listing of home pages, so you cannot go to a directory or some other source and find something like "All the Home Pages on the World Wide Web." You cannot do this because the Web and the number of pages on it are changing rapidly. Many books offer different listings, but some of those books are out of date before they are published. Nonetheless, such a book may be a good place to start.

The best way to find home pages, however, is to explore the Web using a **search engine.** These are sophisticated tools that use algorithms or logical systems to search for what it is that you might want to find.

We'll get to search engines in the next section of this chapter, but never forget to talk with your colleagues to find out what they are discovering. When you find a terrific home page, save its location as a bookmark, and share that information with a friend.

Got some time right now and want to have some fun? Try UrouLette. This home page, created at the University of Kansas, allows you to click on a roulette wheel (what else?) and go to a home page. Which one? It selects home pages at random, so you might find yourself at a home page on x-rays in Uganda, or solar and stellar physics at Harvard (http://CFAûwww.harvard.edu/CFA/ssp.html) or Point Grey Mini School in Vancouver, British Columbia (http://trinculo.educ.sfu.ca/pgm/pgmhome.html), or "Gleanings from the Writings of Baha'u'llah" (http//:www.cs.cornell.edu/Information/People/kalantar/Writings/Bahaullah/GWB/secû24.html).

By now you probably want the URL for URouLette, right? Here it is http://www.uroulette.com. Have fun.

Searching on the Web—Great Search Engines

While there is no central listing of Web sites, there are search engines, which help you find what you are interested in. For example, a very popular search engine is Yahoo! at www.yahoo.com. That address gets you an opening page with hundreds of links to topics in every area imaginable.

For example, let's say we are interested in finding information on hyperactivity. Figure 3.13 shows the term hyperactivity entered in the search area of Yahoo!

Once the search is done, the results are shown in Figure 3.14 where there are several links suggested that we can then click on to find out the contents of the home pages that Yahoo! has found.

Yahoo is one of many different search engines which helps you find information that may be contained in a home page on the Web. And wouldn't you know it, some ambitious webmeister placed hundreds of search engines on one page. You can locate

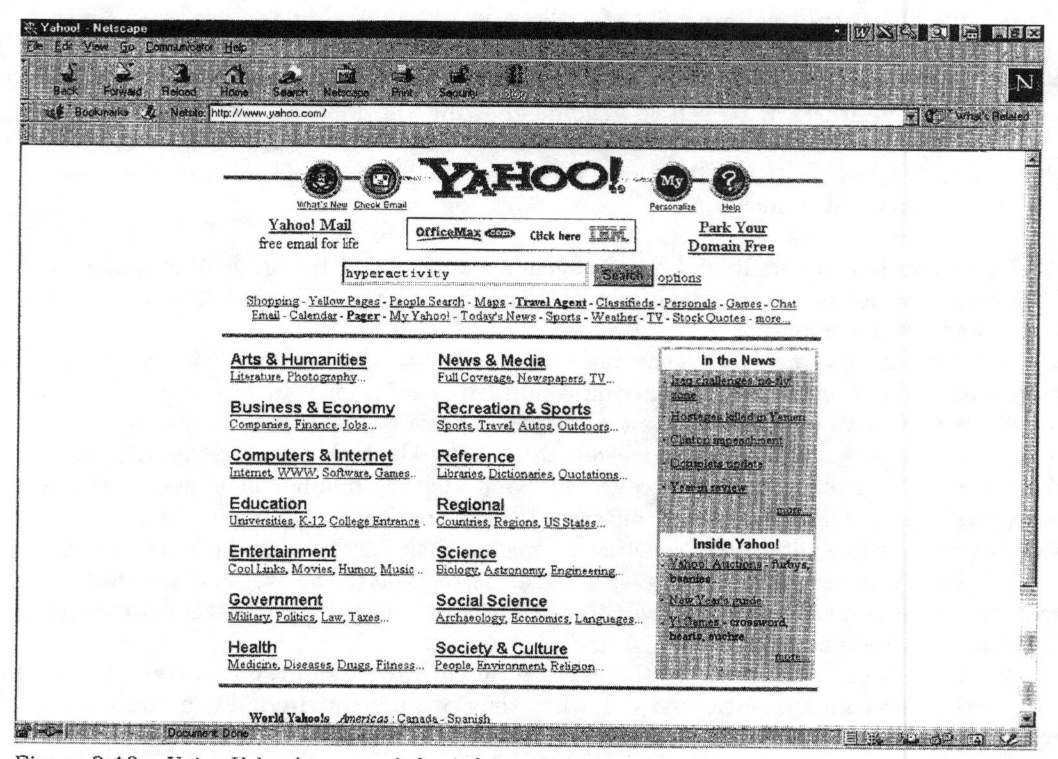

Figure 3.13 Using Yahoo! to search for information.

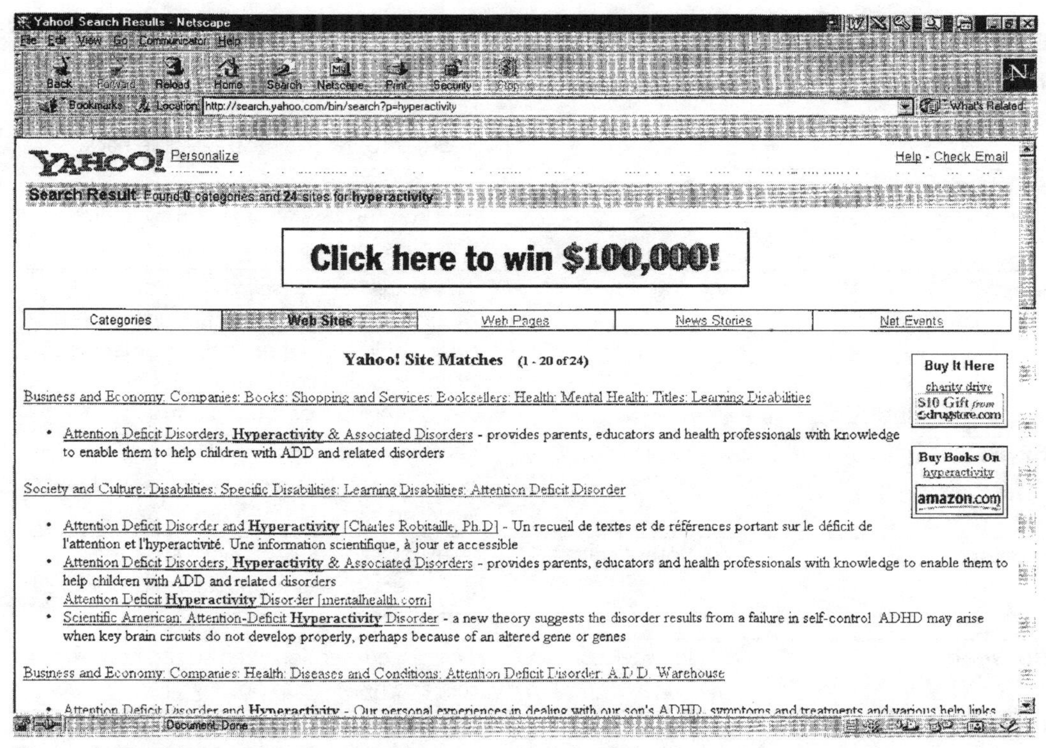

Figure 3.14 The results of a yahoo! search.

the All-In-One search page by pointing your World Wide Web browser at http://www.albany.net/allinone and then search by people, subjects, and even the news and weather.

Are all search engines created equally? No. Some give you very precise results while others give you general categories from which you can begin your search. It's best to experiment with several different search engines until you find the one that best suits the way you like to work or the one that finds what you want.

Table 3.5 shows you the whole kit and kaboodle—a brief description of many of the most popular search engines available today including their name, home page, and description.

And how to best use a search engine? Here are some tips:

- Enter the most narrow search terms you can and then get more broad from there. Entering intelligence will find lots of stuff, most of it irrelevant. But, intelligence and children and school, will make the results much more manageable and closer to what you want. Remember that the fewer the words you enter, the more general the results.
- If you use more than one word, either join them with the conjunction and, or use quotes, such as bilingual and education or "bilingual education."
- Look at our table on search engines and try to pick the one that best fits your purpose for searching.
- If there is a help file or function that comes along with the search engine, open it and read it. It will have invaluable information that will save you time and effort.
- When you get more used to using a search engine, look for the more advanced searching techniques and use them.
- Didn't get what you wanted? The most simple solution? Check your typing. Simple typos spell disaster.
- Try a synonym for the term or terms you're looking for. There's more than one way to eviscerate a feline (get it?).

Search Engine Name	URL	Description
Alta Vista	www.altavista.net	An exhaustive tool that requires you to learn something about its search language in order to get the most possible back.
Ask Jeeves	www.askjeeves.com	Especially good for beginners, Jeeves will lead you through your search by asking you questions.
Dogpile	www.dogpile.com	This search engine searches through 13 other Web search engines, more than two dozen online news services or other types of sources, and sorts the results by the search engine that found them.
Excite	www.excite.com	Gives you a broad general search and adds other information to the returns like headlines and such.
Hotbot	www.hotbot.com	Ever read *Wired* magazine? This is their search engine and is an excellent tool for finding specific information.
Infoseek	www.infoseek.com	The place to go for Web pages, news stories, and newsgroup postings.
Internet Sleuth	www.isleuth.com	Combs through a collection of 3,000 specialized online databases and up to six other search sites for Web pages and news.
Lycos	www.lycos.com	Specializes in advanced search capabilities, like the ability to search for specific file types.
Metacrawler	www.metacrawler.com	Another metasearch site that goes through Yahoo, Excite, and five other search engines.
Northern Light	www.nlsearch.com	Searches the regular Web page base, but also searches through pay-per-view articles from periodicals and books.
Yahoo!	www.yahoo.com	Unique to the Web and more of a Web directory. Yahoo! is a directory put together by humans (really!) and places findings in categories.

Table 3.5 A guide to some of the most popular search engines.

Writing the Literature Review

It is now time to take all the information you have collected and organize it somehow so it begins to make sense. This is your review of literature, and now you need to actually write it (horrors!). Here are some writing hints.

First, read other literature reviews. There is no arguing with success. Ask a student who has already been through this course or your adviser for a successful proposal. Look carefully at the format as well as the content of the literature review. Also, look at some of the sources mentioned earlier in this chapter, especially sources that are reviews of literature, journal articles, and other review papers.

Second, create a unified theme, or a line of thought, throughout the review. Your review of literature is not supposed to be a novel, but most good literature reviews build from a very general argument to a more specific one and set the stage for the purpose of the research. You should bring the reader "into the fold" and create some interest in where you will be going with this research that other people have not gone.

Third, use a system to organize your materials. Most reviews of the literature will be organized chronologically within topics. For example, if you are studying gender differences among adults in anxiety and verbal ability, you would organize all the references by topic area (anxiety and verbal ability) and then within each of these topics begin your review with the earliest dated reference. This way you move from the earliest to the latest and provide some historical perspective.

Fourth, work from an outline. If you are an accomplished and skilled writer, you can ignore this suggestion. But if you are just starting out, it is a good idea to use this tool to help organize the main thought in your proposal before you begin the actual writing process.

Fifth, build bridges between the different areas that you review. For example, if you are conducting a cross-cultural study comparing the way that East Indian and American parents discipline their children, you might not find a great deal of literature on that specific topic. But there is certainly voluminous literature on child rearing in America and in India and tons of references on discipline. Part of the creative effort in writing a proposal is being able to show where these two come together in an interesting and potentially fruitful way.

Sixth, practice may not always make perfect but it certainly doesn't hurt. For some reason, most people believe a person is born with or without a talent for writing. Any successful writer would admit that to be a class A basketball player or an accomplished violinist you have to practice. Should it be any different for a writer? Should you have any doubts about this question, find a serious writer and ask him (or her) how many hours a day or week he or she practices that craft. More often than not, you will see it is the equivalent of the ball player or the musician. In fact, a writing friend of mine gives this advice to people who want to write but don't have a good idea about the level of involvement it requires. She says, "Just sit down at your typewriter or word processor, and open a vein." That is how easy it is.

So the last (but really the first) hint is to practice your writing. As you work at it and find out where you need to improve (get feedback from other students and professors), you will indeed see a change for the better.

Summary

Everyone who does research starts somewhere, and most of the time a review of the literature puts ideas and goals into perspective. The literature, and all the tools available to work with the literature, is your first and best ally in putting together a well-researched and comprehensive discussion of what has occurred in the past. Once important variables are identified, you need to turn your attention to how these variables can be measured, the focus of the next chapter.

Exercises

1. Make a list of 10 topics you would find interesting to pursue research in. These can be any topics dealing with education or psychology that you might glean from

newspapers, radio and television news, magazines, research journals, and even overheard conversations. Rank these various ideas by level of interest, and for each of the top five write one sentence explaining why it appeals to you.

2. Take the idea that you ranked #1 above and do the following:
   (a) Write a one-paragraph description of a study that incorporates that idea.
   (b) List the steps you could take in reviewing the specific literature relevant to this topic.
   (c) From this idea, generate three more questions derived from the original question or idea.

3. Use the idea that you ranked #2 above and do the following:
   (a) Locate a reference from a journal, and write out the complete citation.
   (b) Locate an abstract from a study that focuses on the topic.

4. Find 10 other sources of information about any of the topics you listed in #1 above, and write out the complete citation for each. Try to complete a set of other sources that is as diverse as possible.

5. Go to your library and find five journals in your field of study. After you have located the journals, examine them to determine:
   (a) What type of articles are published (reviews of literature, empirical studies, etc.).
   (b) Whether the journal is published by a professional organization (such as the American Psychological Association) or by a private group (such as Sage Press).
   (c) The number of articles in each journal and if there is any similarity in the topic areas covered within each issue of the journal.
   (d) How often the journal is published and other information about its editorial policies (e.g., guidelines, features).

6. Select any topic that you are interested in and use three different search engines to obtain online information. How do the results differ? Which one gave you the most interesting and useful information? How might you revise your search terms to get the same degree of usefulness from other search engines?

7. Find three abstracts from recent research journals. For each abstract identify the following:
   (a) The purpose
   (b) The hypothesis
   (c) The type of study (correlational, experimental, etc.)
   (d) The conclusion

8. Discuss some of the advantages of online searching.

9. You have been assigned the topic of gender differences in adolescent development of independence for a research study. Formulate five research questions that address this topic.

10. Use the Internet to find five references on any of the topics in which you have an interest (as you defined in earlier questions).

Want to Know More?

Further Readings

Collins, M.E. (1988). Search strategies: Teaching research in children's literature to graduate education students using ERIC. *Research Strategies, 6,* 127–132.

Shows how to use ERIC databases to research children's literature materials using both thesaurus and subject indexes. Also lists advantages of using online searching to retrieve citations.

Kahn, R. (1988). Making a difference: A review of the user interface features in six CD-ROM databases products. *Optical Information Systems, 8,* 169–183.

Reviews BRS MEDLINE, Wilson Disk Cumulative Book Index, MLA International Bibliography, Dialog OnDisc, ERIC, SilverPlatter Sociofile, CCOHS, and Knowledge Finder MEDLINE. Describes each as to how to browse, use menus, search, access online versions, print, and save.

Stewart, L., & Olsen, J. (1988). Compact disk databases: Are they good for users? *Online, 12,* 48–52.

Looks at four groups of undergraduate students researching assigned topics with use of printed and CD-ROM versions of ERIC. One group was given formal instruction with the CD-ROM, one group used CD-ROM without instruction, a third group used the printed version with instruction, and the last group used the printed version without instruction. Results illustrate the advantages of using CD-ROM for searches.

Maclay, V. (1989). Selected sources of United States agency decisions. *Government Publications Review, 16*(3), 271–301.

Discusses frequently used sources of U.S. agency decisions, including computer, assisted legal research systems, and the availability of online research systems.

Strunk, W., & White, E.B. (1959). The elements of style. New York: Macmillan.

The book containing simple and straightforward rules and tips on how to improve your writing. A must for anyone who writes anything!

Readings of Other Interest

Edelman, G.M. (1989). *The remembered present.* New York: Basic Books.

After stating the problem, presents author's theory of the brain (neural Darwinism) with supportive logic, past information, and opinion. You see how a problem can be connected to a theory and the logic used.

Goldberg, F.S. (1988). Telecommunications and the classroom: Where we've been and where we should be going. *Computing Teacher, 15*(8), 26–30.

Discusses the use of telecommunications, and highlights projects designed by the New York City Board of Education to investigate telecommunications alternatives for the classroom. Some of the models described are online research, user-supported libraries, and computer mediated dialogues.

Huntington, R.B. (1993). Networks for success: Using the BITNET and Internet in institutional research. *Journal of Maryland Association for Institutional Research, 2,* 78–87.

Discusses the advantages of using online database searches' availability to investigate research issues in greater depth prior to conducting research. Overall, covers various issues of using online searches and this technology's impact on institutional research.

Chapter 2

International Business

Chapter 2a

the global perspective

Beacons

A Look at This Chapter

This chapter presents a global view of business activities. We begin by describing the forces behind globalization, explaining why companies "go international," and showing what types of companies are involved. We then discuss the main elements of the global perspective on business. We close by briefly discussing the importance of ethics and social responsibility.

A Look Ahead

PART II, covering Chapters 2 to 4, introduces us to different national business environments. Chapter 2 describes important cultural differences among nations. Chapter 3 examines different political and legal systems. Chapter 4 shows how nations differ in economic systems and stages of development and explains how companies adapt to these differences.

Learning Objectives

After studying this chapter, you should be able to

1. Describe *international business* and the process of *globalization.*
2. Explain why companies pursue *international business activity*.
3. Identify the *types of companies* that participate in international business.
4. Explain the *global perspective* on business and identify its three main elements.

Hari Darmawan is an entrepreneur who is concerned about the future of the company he founded, PT Matahari Putra Prima. "Wal-Mart," he laments, "must play fair. That is the Indonesian Way. Indonesians do not try to put one another out of business. It's just not done." With annual sales of $600 million, Matahari Putra Prima is Indonesia's largest retailer. But today the company is preparing to do battle with the world's largest companies.

Competitors from France and the United States are storming into Indonesia's market to challenge Matahari. French retail giant Carrefour expects to have six stores in Indonesia by the early 2000s. Price Venture and JCPenney, both of the United States, will soon open Indonesian outlets. Wal-Mart, with the global muscle of 3,000 stores and annual sales of $300 billion, poses the greatest threat. Wal-Mart will soon have nine stores in the capital of Jakarta and sees Matahari as a strong competitor. Accordingly, it has proceeded cautiously, recently delaying one store opening for fear that staff members weren't quite ready.

"Conventional wisdom," reports one local retail analyst, "has it that Matahari will be crushed by the stampede. But that stance ignores Matahari's intimate knowledge of local conditions." Although large international companies

have the marketing muscle and low prices to make inroads in Indonesia, Matahari's managers understand how to operate in the local market. Matahari will need its firsthand knowledge of Indonesian consumers and business practices to survive this competitive onslaught. Indeed, even for companies that consider their business purely domestic, international competition is the rule rather than the exception today.[1]

Although PT Matahari Putra Prima operates only in Indonesia, it is discovering the global nature of the retailing industry. Even though the company does not currently compete in other markets, international business is coming to Matahari.

International business affects the activities of every consumer, worker, company, and government. Falling trade barriers, increasing competition, and converging consumer tastes are creating global markets for many products. *Consumers* enjoy greater product selection at better prices than ever before. *Workers* often find themselves competing for jobs against workers in another country thousands of miles away. *Companies* directly involved in international production or marketing confront cultures, political systems, and economic systems that can differ greatly from their own. Local, regional, and national *governments* work to attract jobs by offering incentives for companies to locate in specific places. As PT Matahari Putra Prima has learned, domestic companies are not isolated from international business. More and more international companies are invading home markets everywhere.

In this chapter, we develop a global perspective on business activity. We investigate important issues currently facing consumers, workers, and international companies. The world atlas at the end of the chapter provides a reference for our discussion of international business as we proceed through the book.

WHY STUDY INTERNATIONAL BUSINESS?

Each of us experiences the result of dozens of international business transactions every day. Your radio-alarm clock was probably made in China. The news broadcast buzzing in your ears comes from Britain's BBC radio. You slip into a Gap T-shirt made in Egypt, Levi's made in Bangladesh, and Nikes assembled in Vietnam from components made in several other countries. You get into your Japanese Toyota (which was made in Kentucky) and pop in a Dutch-made CD of music performed by a Swedish band. At the local espresso bar, you charge up with coffee brewed from beans harvested in Colombia or Kenya.

imports
All goods and services brought into a country that were purchased from organizations located in other countries.

You don't even have to set foot out of a small town to be affected by international business. No matter where you live, you'll be surrounded by **imports**—all the goods and services brought into a country that were purchased from organizations located in other countries. Your counterparts around the world will undoubtedly spend the day using your nation's **exports**—all the goods and services sent from one country to other nations.

exports
All goods and services sent from one country to other nations.

But international business is not just about companies selling their products to customers in other countries. It is also about crossing borders to get products made in the first place. This is particularly true in the information age. Say you're an IBM computer programmer based in Seattle. You may never leave the state of Washington, but you'll be working with colleagues in places such as central Europe and India. Consider the following actual example:

- A team of computer programmers at Beijing's Tsignhua University writes software using Java technology for IBM. At the end of each day, they send their work over the Internet to an IBM facility in Seattle. There, programmers build on it before zapping it 5,000 miles to the Institute of Computer Science in Belarus and the Software House Group in Latvia. From there, the work goes to India's Tata Group, which passes the software back to Tsignhua by the next morning. The process repeats itself until the project is done.[2]

IBM's vice president for Internet technology calls this global relay race "Java around the Clock," and it is fast becoming the way things are done. Even a traditional manufacturer such as General Motors is considering reorganizing around a single global auto-development team. It stands to reason, then, that skills in international business—from cross-cultural understanding and communication to a knowledge of international monetary systems and distribution practices—is crucial if you want to become a more valuable player on your global team.

Already, firms like Solid State Measurements Inc., a Pittsburgh-based company with over 65 percent of its sales going abroad, are finding it hard to locate executives with adequate international experience.[3] As more and more companies locate operations beyond their borders, they will hire people who are best equipped to manage their international operations, regardless of citizenship. In Tokyo, for example, Sony Corporation is on the verge of becoming an "un-Japanese" company. Already, Sony's worldwide workforce is split roughly 50/50 between Japanese and non-Japanese. As Sony continues to relocate many of its factories to Mexico, a substantial majority of its workforce will be outside Japan.[4]

INTERNATIONAL BUSINESS AND GLOBALIZATION

As we've seen, international business affects many aspects of our lives. Let's begin, therefore, by explaining just what *international business* is and then describing in greater detail the impact of *globalization*.

WHAT IS INTERNATIONAL BUSINESS?

International business is the total of all business transactions that cross the borders of two or more nations. Consumers, companies, financial institutions, and governments are all important to international business activity. Consumers demand quality products from the international companies that sell and service them. Financial institutions help companies engaging in international business to finance investments, exchange currencies, and transfer money around the globe. Governments regulate flows of goods, services, people, and capital across national borders. Here are just a handful of typical international business transactions:

international business
Total of all business transactions that cross the borders of two or more nations.

- Italian media firm AGB conducts market research in Hungary to identify the television shows that people watch there.
- To provide financing for companies entering the Polish market, Daiwa Securities of Japan opens an office in Warsaw, Poland.
- American Honda Motor Corporation sends cars from the United States to Honda Motor Corporation in Japan.
- Three young entrepreneurs import premium coffee into China to serve urban customers in Beijing and Tianjin.

Map 1.1 shows the total value of goods and services, including both imports and exports, now crossing each nation's borders. The annual total value is a staggering

MAP 1.1
INTERNATIONAL TRADE VOLUME (MILLIONS OF U.S. DOLLARS)

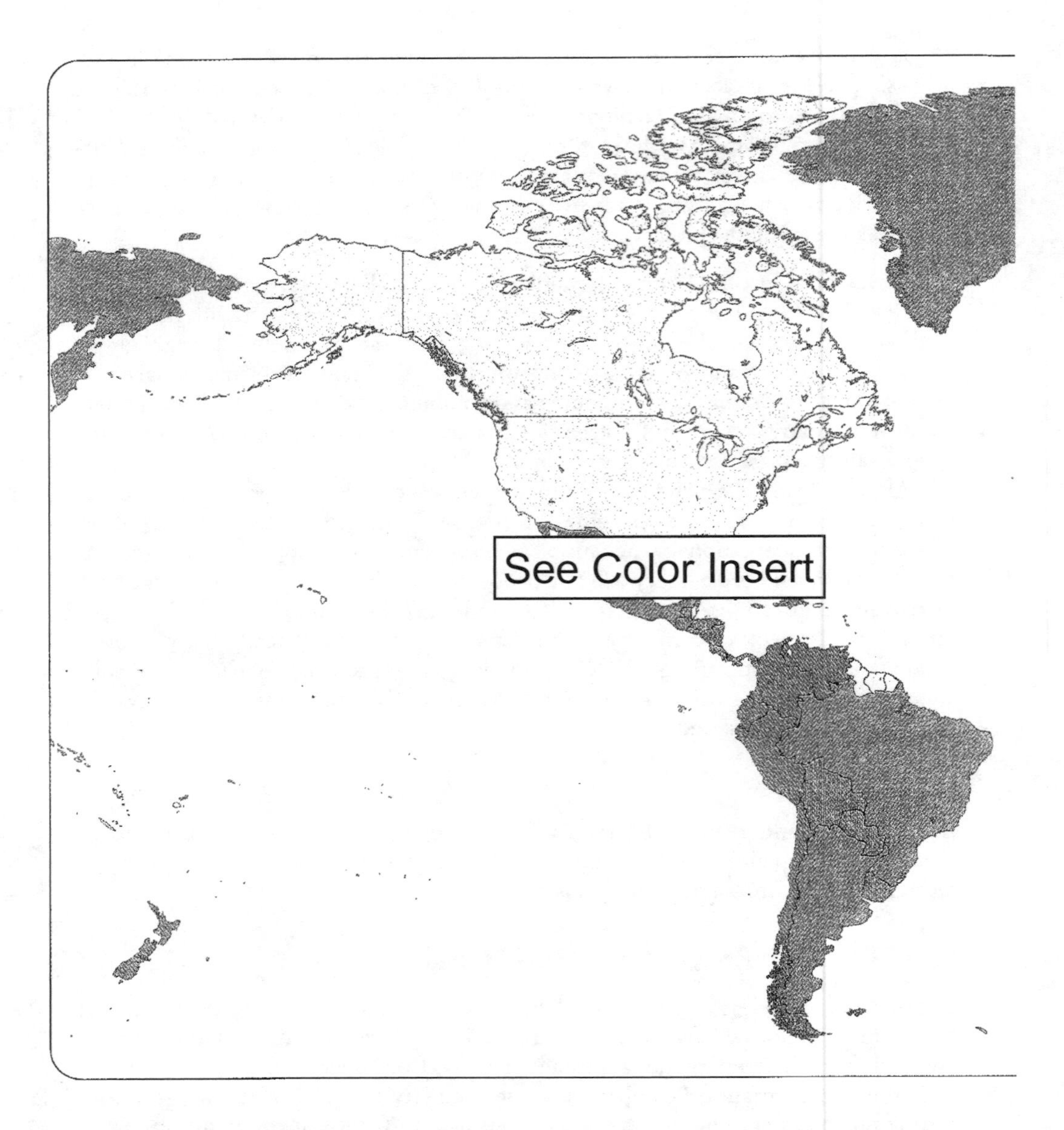

$13,649,858,000,000 (more than $13.6 trillion)—$2 trillion more than the combined annual revenues of the *Fortune Global 500* (the 500 largest companies in the world). This value of trade is more than 76 times the annual revenue of the world's largest company, General Motors.

WHAT IS GLOBALIZATION?

globalization
Process involving the integration of national economies.

Although national governments retain ultimate control over the products, people, and capital passing through their markets, the global economy is becoming increasingly intertwined. The process involving the integration of national economies is called **globalization**. Let's now examine globalization in detail.

Globalized Markets Globalization of *markets* (places where buyers and sellers meet to exchange goods and services) is very important to our study of international business. For instance, consumer preferences for some products are converging around the world. Sony, L.L. Bean, Nike, The Gap, Calvin Klein, Coca-Cola, and McDonald's

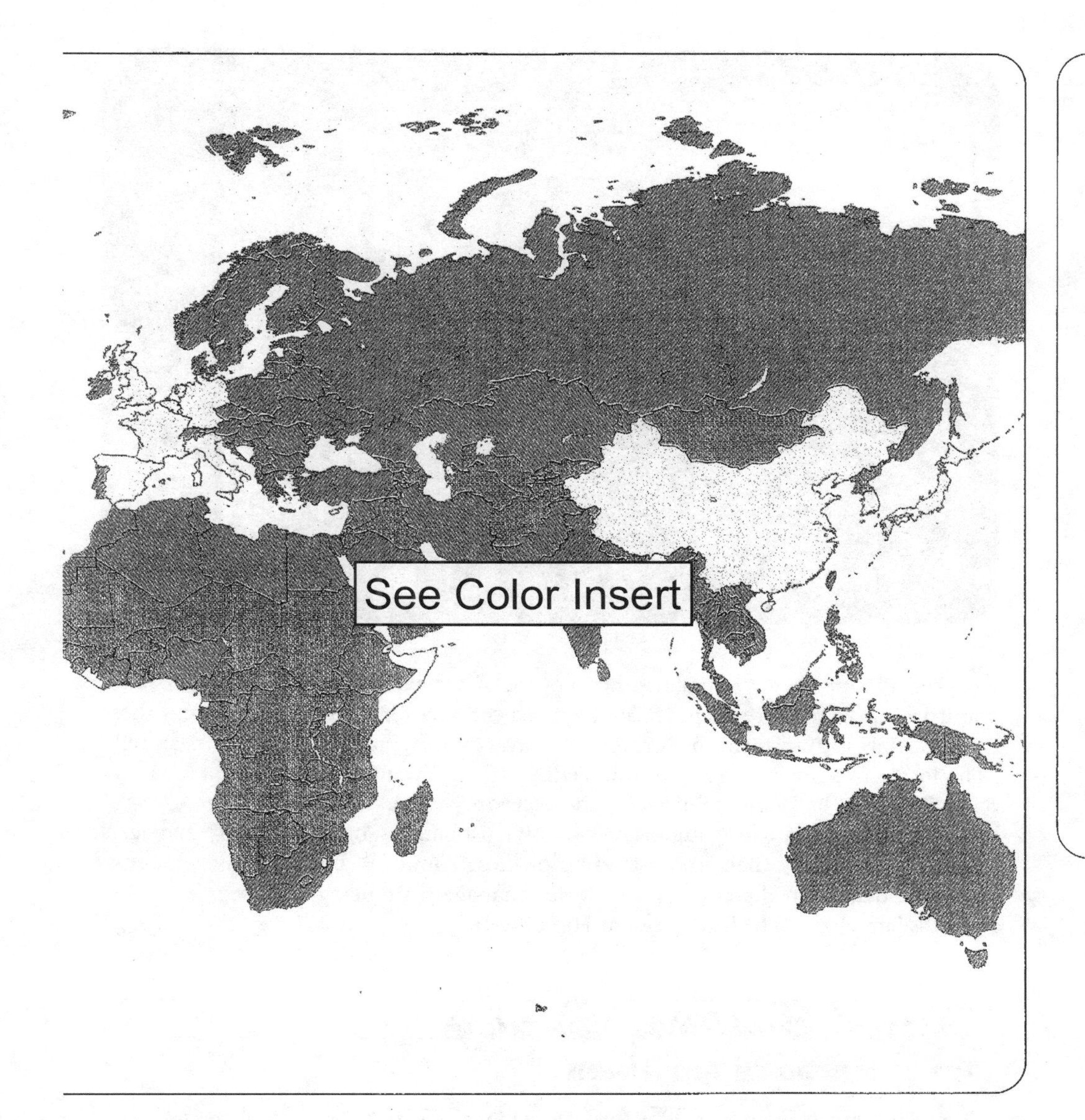

TRADE VOLUME
(millions of U.S. dollars)

- $220,000 and up
- 40,000–219,999
- 10,000–39,999
- 0–9,999
- No data

Top Fourteen

United States	1,777,826
Germany	1,167,470
Japan	955,663
France	718,384
United Kingdom	690,263
Italy	590,981
Canada	433,620
Netherlands	432,849
Belgium	396,006
Hong Kong, China	379,287
China	333,066
South Korea	330,088
Singapore	304,647
Spain	292,975

are just a few companies that sell so-called *global products*—products marketed in all countries essentially without any changes. Sometimes they make small modifications to suit local tastes. In southern Japan, for example, Coca-Cola sweetened its traditional formula to compete with sweeter-tasting Pepsi.[5] In India, where cows are sacred and the consumption of beef taboo, McDonald's markets the "Maharaja Mac"—two all-mutton patties on a sesame-seed bun with all the usual toppings.[6]

Globalized Production Activities Today, many production activities are also becoming global. Technology allows any product to be made practically anywhere it is cheapest to do so.[7] Local, regional, and national governments offer firms various incentives to construct factories in their regions or countries. This strategy brings jobs to the country that wins the factory, but can bring unemployment to another if, as a consequence, a factory in that location is closed.

For example, competing business hubs in Asia—such as Kuala Lumpur (Malaysia), Singapore, Shanghai (China), and the Philippines' Subic Bay—routinely entice global companies with favorable tax deals and subsidized rents and worker train-

Despite recent economic turmoil, the Philippines slowly strengthened its economy over the past decade, making it an attractive trade hub to international companies such as Intel and Seagate. Subic Bay, which lies at the southern tip of the Philippine island of Luzon, has become attractive to international investors because it is a free port with few trade restrictions, and because the local people have an affinity for speaking English. Acer, Taiwan's biggest computer maker, plans to make Subic Bay the home of its Central Asian operations facility.

ing. The Philippine government, once notorious for tying up investors from other countries in reams of red tape, recently paved the way for Federal Express and three other carriers to transform the former U.S. naval base at Subic Bay into an Asian hub. "The local government," explains one FedEx official, "wanted to make us a tenant at Subic Bay. That had a big influence on the decision."[8]

Because of the growing importance of low-cost nations, more and more managers will need to increase their understanding of these countries' business environments. For more details on the countries to which managers are being sent, see the World Business Survey on "The International Top Fifteen."

World Business Survey

The International Top Fifteen

A recent survey uncovered the top international destinations of U.S. managers. Asian countries ranked lower in the most recent poll because financial crises there since 1997 have reduced relocations to the region. However, as economies in Asia recover, they will once again move higher in the rankings. Here are the top 15 destinations:

Top 15 Destinations		
1. United Kingdom	6. Mexico	11. Singapore
2. Germany	7. Brazil	12. Thailand
3. Australia	8. Saudi Arabia	13. Switzerland
4. Japan	9. Puerto Rico	14. China
5. France	10. Netherlands	15. Peru

Forces Spurring Globalization Two main forces are spurring the globalization of markets and production: *lower trade and investment barriers* and *increased innovation*. Let's take a look at each of these factors in greater detail.

Lower Trade and Investment Barriers: GATT In 1947, 23 nations made history when they created the *General Agreement on Tariffs and Trade (GATT)*. The GATT is an international treaty setting specific rules for international trade designed to pry open national markets by reducing *tariffs* (taxes on traded goods) and *nontariff barriers* such as quotas (restrictions on the volume of goods allowed into a country). Today, GATT has 133 members.

Because merchandise accounted for the majority of total world trade at the time, the 1947 GATT agreement focused on *merchandise* trade. The treaty was quite successful: In 1988, world merchandise trade was 20 times larger than in 1947, and average tariffs dropped from 40 percent to 5 percent. But by the late 1980s, trade conflicts had caused nontariff barriers to increase 45 percent. In addition, service industries grew increasingly important, accounting for 25 percent to 30 percent of total world trade. A 1994 revision of GATT modified the original treaty in several important ways:[9]

- Average tariffs on merchandise trade were to be reduced further.
- Subsidies (price supports) for agricultural products were to be reduced significantly.
- *Intellectual property rights* were clearly defined, giving protection to copyrights (including computer programs, databases, sound records, films), trademarks and service marks, and patents (including trade secrets and know-how).
- The *World Trade Organization (WTO)* was established with power to enforce the new GATT—an agency that the 1947 GATT lacked.

Role of Trade Blocs Nations are integrating their economies as never before. For example, the *North American Free Trade Agreement (NAFTA)* groups three nations (Canada, Mexico, and the United States) into a free-trade bloc. The even more ambitious *European Union (EU)* combines 15 countries. The *Asia Pacific Economic Cooperation (APEC)* forum consists of 18 nations committed to creating a free-trade zone around the Pacific. All these agreements aim to lower trade barriers. As a result of such initiatives, growth in international trade now outpaces growth in worldwide production. Map 1.2 identifies the countries belonging to these and other free-trade blocs.

Innovation in Information Technology As lower barriers to trade and investment encourage globalization, increased innovation is accelerating the process. Advancements in information technology and transportation are making it easier, faster, and less costly to move data, goods, equipment, and people around the world.

Business activities, such as managing employees and scheduling production in several locations, are more difficult and costly when conducted across borders and time zones. But new computer technologies are speeding up the flow of information, making coordination and control easier and cheaper. With electronic mail (e-mail), for instance, managers can stay in contact with international operations and respond quickly to important matters. Videoconferencing allows lawyers to meet while still in different branch offices, and engineers to collaborate on designs from remote locations. Consistent with this, worldwide sales of videoconferencing equipment were about $7 billion in 1998—up from $1.6 billion in 1996.[10]

e·biz

Internets, Intranets, and Extranets Companies also use the Internet and World Wide Web to stay in touch with international production and distribution activities. A recent study revealed that 61 percent of executives feel that knowledge of the Internet will make them more marketable managers; 76 percent believe that being Net-savvy will advance their careers within five years.[11]

e·biz

MAP 1.2

FREE TRADE BLOCS OF THE WORLD

Note: Chile and Bolivia are associate members of MERCOSUR.

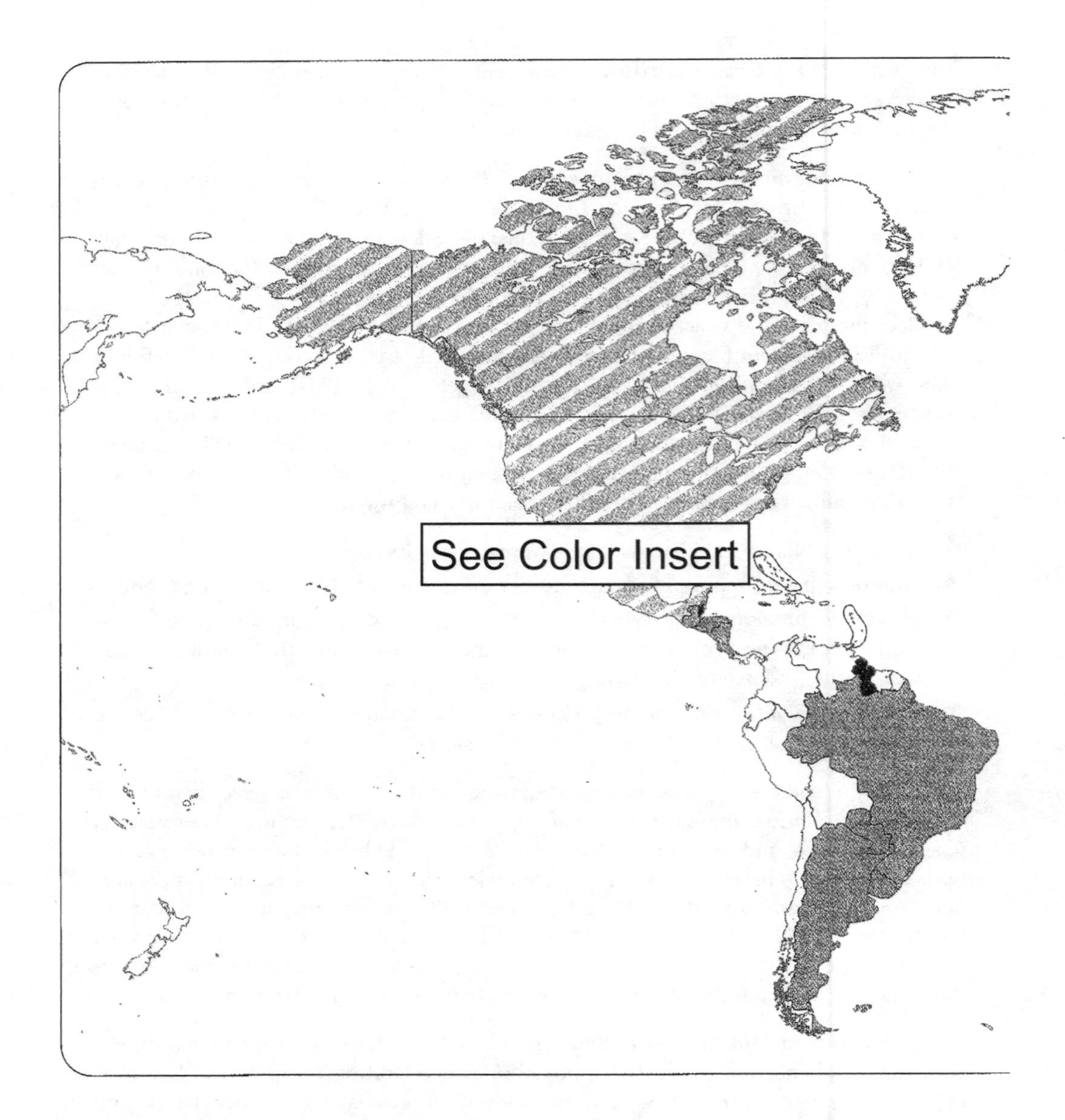

Private networks of internal company Web sites and other information sources (called *intranets*) allow employees to access their company's information from distant locations with desktop computers and modems. Microsoft reports that sales-analysis data have been accessed five times more often since becoming available on the company intranet.[12] Today, so-called *extranets* are being developed to give distributors and suppliers access to a company's database so that they can place orders or restock inventories electronically and automatically. All these new technologies permit managers to respond to both internal and external conditions more quickly than ever before.[13]

Technology and Small Business Computer technologies can also increase the competitiveness of small companies by reducing the costs of reaching an international customer base. In fact, small companies were among the first to use the Web as a global marketing tool, and many are still able to respond faster than large companies to shifting market conditions.

These "webpreneurs" are increasingly gaining a leg up on larger competitors who are neither as nimble nor as Net-savvy. "I think we're fairly typical," says Jim Macintyre

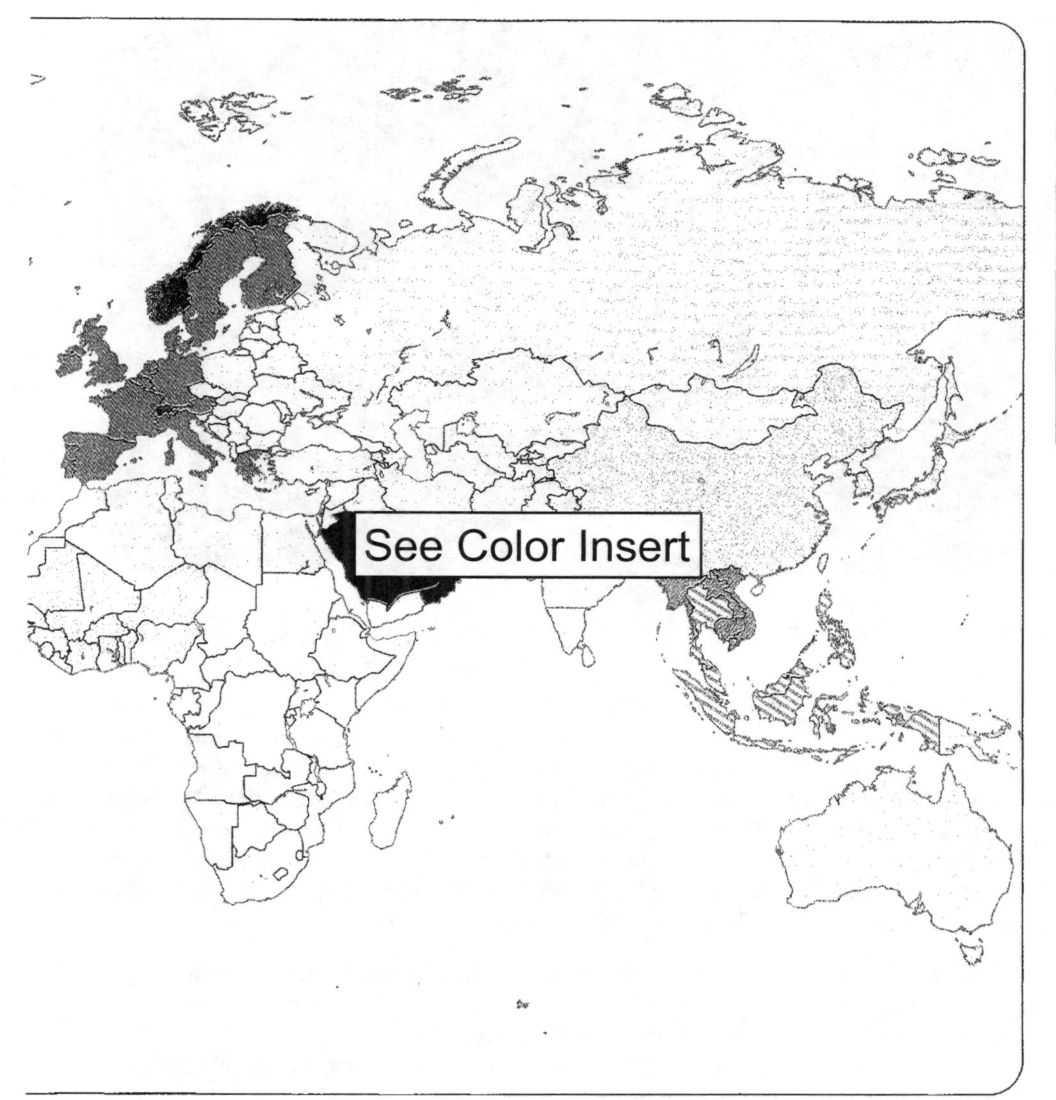

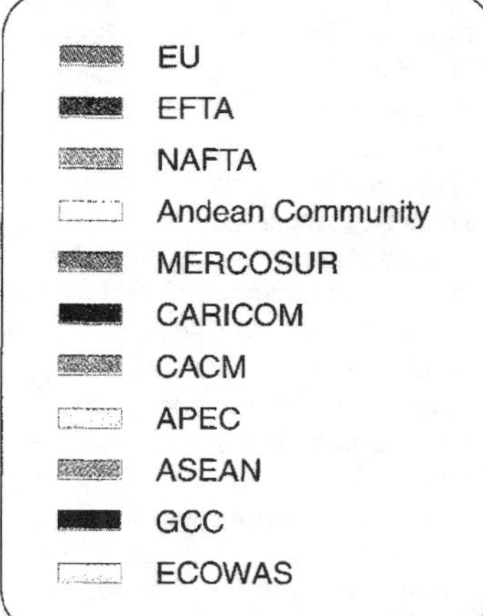

of Tropical Jim's Remake Shop, a Web designer located in Caracas, Venezuela. "Our firm was in the red until we started selling to the American market. Now 90 percent of our customers are Americans." For Jonathan Strum, a Tropical Jim's customer based in Los Angeles, the Web makes Caracas seem like next-door. "Not long ago," he admits, "I would have thought depending on a firm in Caracas for the services we need for our business was outlandish. Now I am importing all my graphic design and most of my programming from overseas."[14]

Some Pros and Cons of Technology Some businesses are finding it hard to survive on the Internet. Most Internet sites suffer losses for at least three years before they turn profits—much too long for the majority of small companies. Those who do survive tend to sell the sort of low-priced goods that have broad appeal. But even the hottest-selling items can be hard to peddle on the Internet, especially when buyers are still hesitant about sending credit card information through cyberspace. One recent survey found that only 15 percent of Internet users had actually bought anything on-line.[15] Apparently "window shopping" and information gathering are more common activities.

Videoconferencing, which allows for "face-to-face" communication in real time, is helping to ease communications in the global community. The World Economic Forum, a global nonprofit organization with 2,000 members from government, academia, business, and the media, recently embraced videoconferencing as a means to communicate quickly and easily with members across the globe. Likewise, doctors at two children's hospitals, Sri Ramachandra Medical College in India and Toronto's Hospital for Sick Children, use videoconferencing to share visual data instantly—a need that e-mail and telephones can't meet.

With the number of Internet sites growing daily, a company without a partner in cyberspace might be disappointed with traffic in its cyberstore. On-line intermediaries (called portals), such as America Online (AOL), Yahoo, and Excite, offer to funnel Web surfers to your site for a fee. However, the cost of such a partnership can be enormous. Recently, three securities firms—DLJ-direct, E*Trade Securities, and Waterhouse Securities—each paid AOL $25 million for its services over a two-year period. Thus generating traffic in an online store is more difficult than originally imagined. As one expert noted, "Launching an e-commerce site without a portal partner is like opening a retail store in the desert. Sure, it's cheap, but does anybody stop there?"[16]

Technology and the Business of Distribution Some Internet-based companies pose a threat to competitors who rely solely on traditional distribution methods. On average, for example, 62 percent of a product's cost results from *activities occurring after the production process.*[17] Using sites on the World Wide Web to bypass intermediaries like wholesalers and retailers, companies can enter global markets, cut postproduction costs, and pass on savings to customers.

This strategy is best suited to firms offering products such as music, books, computer software, and travel services. In fact, travel services are expected to receive the biggest jump in on-line revenue by the year 2003 (see Figure 1.1). Amazon.com is a bookseller whose "store" exists only on the Internet. Now slugging it out with long-established booksellers Borders Books and Barnes & Noble, Amazon.com calls itself "Earth's Biggest Bookstore" (playing off B&N's billing as "The World's Biggest Bookstore") and offers more than 2.5 million titles. Brisk sales at Amazon.com prompted Barnes & Noble to create its own Web-based bookstore, barnesandnoble.com.

Innovation in Transportation Technology Like advances in computer technology, advances in transportation methods are helping to globalize both markets and production activities. Advances in air travel allow managers to travel more quickly and cheaply to locations in other countries. As incomes rise and travel grows more affordable, more and more consumers take international vacations. As a result, consumer tastes become more global as travelers encounter products in other countries and create demand for them at home.

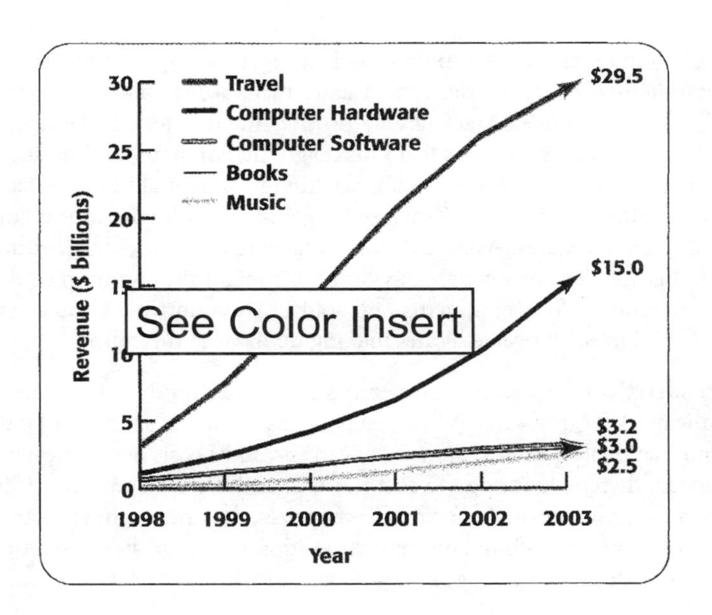

FIGURE 1.1
MAJOR ON-LINE RETAIL SECTORS BY 2003

Advances in shipping methods have also spurred globalization. The development of huge freighters that carry an enormous amount of goods on a single trip has greatly lowered the cost of overseas shipping. Container-shipment methods are becoming popular as well. Because the same containers can now be placed on trucks, trains, and ships, shipping is faster and costs associated with using two or more means to transport a shipment are lower.

WHY DO COMPANIES GO INTERNATIONAL?

Why do companies choose to engage in international business? Basically, they do so for the same reasons that they decide to expand in the domestic market: to *increase sales* and to *access resources.*

INCREASE SALES

The goal of increasing sales is attractive when a firm must deal with either of two conditions: *international sales growth opportunities* or *excess production capacity.*

International Sales Growth Opportunities As PT Matahari Putra Prima discovered in this chapter's opening example, companies often go international to increase sales. Saturated home markets or an economic slowdown there often forces companies to explore international sales opportunities.

Another impetus for companies to seek international sales is uneven income. Companies might be able to level off their income stream by supplementing domestic sales with international sales. This also helps avoid wild production swings characterized by cycles of overwork and slack capacity. In particular, firms take the leap into international markets when they're confident that buyers in other cultures are receptive to a product and can afford it. Consider the current strategy of McDonald's. Although there is one McDonald's outlet for every 29,000 people in the United States, there is only one for every 40 million people in China. Not surprisingly, McDonald's is aggressively expanding in China (indeed, all across Asia), where long-term growth potential is enormous.[18]

Consider another example. Though nearly as large in area as the United States, Australia has only 17.7 million people, compared to 260 million in the United States.

Thus the Australian Trade Commission is helping small to medium-size companies reach their potential by providing export assistance. Some small exporters have met remarkable success. Duncan MacGillivray of Adelaide developed Two Dogs alcoholic lemonade by using surplus lemons from his neighbor's orchard, adding sugar, and fermenting the mix with yeast. After quickly reaching its potential in Australia, Two Dogs expanded into Hong Kong, New Zealand, Singapore, South Africa, the United Kingdom, and the United States. Asian consumers have received the drink enthusiastically because lemons are a popular source of vitamin C to fight the common cold there. Two Dogs is now made on four continents and sold in 44 countries. Annual revenue now exceeds $39 million, with overseas sales making up most of this figure.[19]

Excess Production Capacity Sometimes companies produce more goods and services than the market can absorb. When that happens, resources sit idle. But if the firm can find new international sources of demand, it can spread its costs over a greater number of units produced, thereby lowering the cost per unit and increasing profits. If it passes on these benefits to consumers in the form of lower prices, the firm might also capture market share from competitors. A dominant market position means greater market power, providing the firm with greater leverage in negotiating with both suppliers and buyers.

ACCESS RESOURCES

natural resources
Products from nature that are economically or technologically useful.

Companies also go international to access resources that are unavailable or more costly at home. What commonly draws companies into international markets is the quest for **natural resources**—products from nature that are economically or technologically useful. Japan, for example, is a small, densely populated island nation with very few natural resources of its own, especially forests. Thus Japan's largest paper company, Nippon Seishi, must do more than simply import wood pulp. It owns huge forests and corresponding processing facilities in Australia, Canada, and the United States. By controlling earlier stages in the papermaking process, the company guarantees a steady flow of an important input (wood pulp) that is less subject to the uncertainties associated with buying pulp on the open market. Likewise, to access cheaper energy resources used in other manufacturing industries, a variety of Japanese firms are locating in China, Mexico, Taiwan, and Vietnam where energy costs are lower.

Labor markets also draw companies into international business. One way firms try to keep their prices internationally competitive is by locating production in countries with low-cost labor. But if low-cost labor were the only reason a nation attracted international companies, businesses would stampede into places like Afghanistan and Somalia. In order to be attractive, a location must offer low-cost, adequately skilled workers in an environment with acceptable levels of social, political, and economic stability. When these conditions exist, the long-term investment necessary for economic development will flow into a country. We discuss the factors that attract international business to different countries more fully in Part II of this book.

WHO PARTICIPATES IN INTERNATIONAL BUSINESS?

Companies of all types and sizes, and in all sorts of industries, enter into international business activities. Manufacturing companies, service companies, and retail companies all search for customers beyond their borders. An **international company** is a business that engages directly in any form of international business activity such as exporting, importing, or international production. Thus companies vary in the extent to which they get involved in international business. For instance, although an importer only purchases from its supplier(s) abroad, it is considered an international company. Likewise, a large company with factories scattered around the world is an international company but is also called a **multinational corporation (MNC)**—a business that has direct investments (in the form of marketing or manufacturing subsidiaries) abroad in several or more countries. Thus although *all* companies involved in some aspect of international trade or investment are considered international companies, only those with direct investments abroad are called multinationals. These multinationals are also sometimes called *global* companies when they operate in practically all countries around the world. However, the *strategies* companies employ in their international business activities is another matter—we discuss *multinational* versus *global strategies* in Chapter 12. Let's now take a closer look at the different types of international companies.

international company
Business that engages directly in any form of international business activity.

multinational corporation (MNC)
Business that has direct investments abroad in several or more countries.

ENTREPRENEURS AND SMALL BUSINESSES

Small companies are becoming increasingly active in international trade and investment. One recent study reports that companies are exporting earlier and growing faster as a result.[20] As noted earlier, technology has toppled some real barriers to exporting for small businesses.

e-biz

Whereas traditional distribution channels often gave only large companies access to distant markets, electronic distribution is a cheap and effective alternative for many small businesses.[21] Some small companies reside exclusively in cyberspace, reaching out to customers around the world solely through the World Wide Web. For instance, Alessandro Naldi's *Weekend a Firenze* (*Weekend in Florence*) Web site at **www.waf.it/mall** offers global villagers more authentic Florentine products than they'll find in the scores of overpriced tourist shops crowded into downtown Florence. A Florentine himself, Naldi established his site to sell high-quality, authentic Italian merchandise made only in the many small factories of Tuscany. Currently, Weekend a Firenze averages 20,000 visitors each month, with 40 percent of its "guests" coming from Japan, 30 percent from the United States, and the remainder from Greece, Australia, Canada, Mexico, Saudi Arabia, and Italy.[22]

Unfortunately, many small businesses that are capable of exporting have not yet begun to do so. For example, in one recent year only 10 percent of companies in the United States with fewer than 100 employees were exporting compared to 18 percent of companies of all sizes. Although there are certain real obstacles to exporting for small businesses—lack of investment capital, for example—some common myths create artificial obstacles. To explore some of these myths and the facts that dispute them, see the Entrepreneurial Focus "Untapped Potential: Four Myths That Keep Small Businesses from Export Success."

MULTINATIONAL CORPORATIONS

Multinational corporations vary widely in size, being as small as the security firm Pinkerton, with about $900 million in annual revenue, and as large as Mitsubishi Corporation, with revenue of more than $128 billion. Other well-known multinationals are Boeing (U.S.), Sony (Japan), Volvo (Sweden), Coca-Cola (U.S.), and Samsung Electronics (South Korea).

The units of large international companies can function either rather independently or as parts of a tightly integrated global network. Independent operations tend to have a good understanding of local culture and are often able to adapt quickly to changing local market conditions. On the other hand, firms that operate as global networks often find it easier to respond to changing conditions by shifting production, marketing, and other activities among national units. Depending on the type of business, either structure can be appropriate. As stated earlier, we discuss these alternative strategies and structures more fully in Chapter 12.

Entrepreneurial Focus

Untapped Potential: Four Myths That Keep Small Businesses from Export Success

MYTH 1: ONLY LARGE COMPANIES CAN EXPORT SUCCESSFULLY.

Fact: Exporting increases sales and profitability for small firms and can make both manufacturers and distributors less dependent on the health of the domestic economy. It can also help businesses avoid seasonal fluctuations in sales. In addition, selling abroad gives small businesses the advantage of competing with companies from other countries *before* they enter the domestic market.

MYTH 2: SMALL BUSINESSES HAVE NO PLACE TO TURN FOR EXPORT ADVICE.

Fact: Whether a company is just starting out or is already exporting profitably, the federal government has an assistance program to meet its needs. The Trade Information Center (TIC) of the U.S. Department of Commerce is a comprehensive resource for information on all federal export-assistance programs. Firms can get advice from international trade specialists on how to locate and use federal, state, local, and private-sector programs. They also receive free information on sources of market research, trade leads, financing, and trade events.

MYTH 3: THE LICENSING REQUIREMENTS NEEDED FOR EXPORTING ARE NOT WORTH THE EFFORT.

Fact: "Most products," according to international trade specialist Linda Jones, "don't need export licenses. Exporters simply write 'NLR' for 'no license required' on their Shipper's Export Declaration. There is no onerous paperwork involved." A license is needed only when exporting certain restricted commodities (such as high technology or defense-related goods) or when shipping to a country currently under U.S. trade embargo or other restriction. To find out about license requirements, companies can call the Commerce Department's Bureau of Export Administration (BXA).

MYTH 4: THERE IS NO EXPORT FINANCING AVAILABLE FOR SMALL BUSINESS.

Fact: In 1995, the Small Business Administration (SBA) and the Export-Import Bank joined forces to lend money to small businesses. Whereas the SBA is responsible for loan requests below $750,000, Ex-Im Bank handles transactions above $750,000. The Overseas Private Investment Corporation and the Trade and Development Agency also help small and medium-size firms obtain financing for international projects.

Economic Importance of Multinationals If, as we have seen, small and medium-size firms are so important to a country's economy, why do business headlines focus so sharply on large international companies? There are two main reasons:

1. *Their economic and political muscle makes them highly visible.* Large companies generate a large number of jobs, greater investment, and significant tax revenue for the areas in which they operate. Likewise, announced factory closings of large international companies make headlines because of the hundreds, perhaps thousands, of lost jobs.
2. *Their dealings involve large sums of money.* It is common for the income and dealings of large companies, such as mergers and acquisitions, to be valued in the hundreds of millions, sometimes billions, of dollars. In 1998, Germany's Daimler-Benz announced a merger with Chrysler Corporation valued at $40 billion; in December that year two global petroleum companies, Exxon and Mobil, agreed to create a merged company worth $86 billion.

Multinationals and GDP We can see the enormous economic clout of multinational corporations when we compare the revenues of companies in the *Fortune*

Global 500 to the value of goods and services generated by various countries. In Table 1.1, we inserted the nine multinationals with the highest annual revenues into a list of nations ranked from twenty-fourth to thirty-fourth in terms of national output. Our measure of national output is **gross domestic product** (GDP)—the total market value of all goods and services produced during a one-year period with resources located within a country. This means that if General Motors were a country, it would weigh in as a rich nation and rank ahead of both Denmark and Norway. Even the five hundredth largest firm in the world, Sun of the United States, has revenues larger than the GDPs of many countries. The government-owned U.S. Postal Service has 898,384 employees—the most of any company in the *Global 500.* Wal-Mart Stores is second, with 825,000 employees, General Motors third, with 608,000. All types of industries are represented in the *Global 500,* ranging from food and beverages to mining and crude oil production.[23]

gross domestic product (GDP) *Total market value of all goods and services produced during a one-year period with resources located within a country.*

Table 1.2 augments the listing of the MNCs with the highest annual revenues (from tenth to twenty-ninth), and Table 1.3 shows the international distribution of the Global 500.[24]

Merger Mania Not only do the largest multinationals dwarf the total economic output of some nations, but the biggest companies are getting bigger. In 1998 alone, the world's largest firms were involved in $1.6 *trillion* worth of mergers; this figure was up from $1 trillion in 1997.[25] But as the chairman of the Federal Trade Commission points out, "More and more deals . . . should be judged on a global-market scale. . . .

TABLE 1.1 ***Comparing the Global 500 with Selected Countries***

Country/Company	GDP/Revenue (millions of U.S. Dollars)
24. Turkey	181,464
General Motors	178,174
25. Denmark	174,247
26. Norway	157,802
27. Hong Kong, China	154,767
Ford Motor	153,627
Mitsui	142,688
28. Poland	134,477
Mitsubishi	128,922
Royal Dutch/Shell Group	128,142
Itochu	126,632
29. South Africa	126,301
30. Saudi Arabia	126,266
31. Finland	123,966
32. Greece	122,946
Wal-Mart Stores	122,379
Marubeni	111,121
33. Portugal	104,000
Sumitomo	102,395
34. Malaysia	99,213

TABLE 1.2 ***More of the* Global 500**

Company	Revenue (millions of U.S. Dollars)
10. Toyota Motor	95,137
11. General Electric	90,840
12. Nissho Iwai	81,894
13. International Business Machines (IBM)	78,508
14. Nippon Telegraph & Telephone	76,984
15. AXA	76,874
16. Daimler-Benz	71,561
17. Daewoo	71,526
18. Nippon Life Insurance	71,388
19. British Petroleum	71,194
20. Hitachi	68,567
21. Volkswagen	65,328
22. Matsushita Electric Industrial	64,281
23. Siemens	63,755
24. Chrysler	61,147
25. Mobil	59,978
26. U.S. Postal Service	58,216
27. Allianz	56,785
28. Philip Morris	56,114
29. Sony	55,033

TABLE 1.3 ***Distribution of the* Global 500**

Country	Number of Companies
United States	172
Japan	112
Germany	42
France	38
Britain	35
Italy	13
South Korea	12
Switzerland	12
Netherlands	9
Canada	8
All others	47

Mergers go through now that would have been challenged just 10 years ago because competition now comes from all corners of the world."[26]

Figure 1.2 highlights the rapid growth in mergers and acquisitions since 1980. It shows that international acquisitions by U.S. firms and acquisition of U.S. firms by non-U.S. buyers played a big role in the recent wave of mergers, especially between 1991 and 1997.

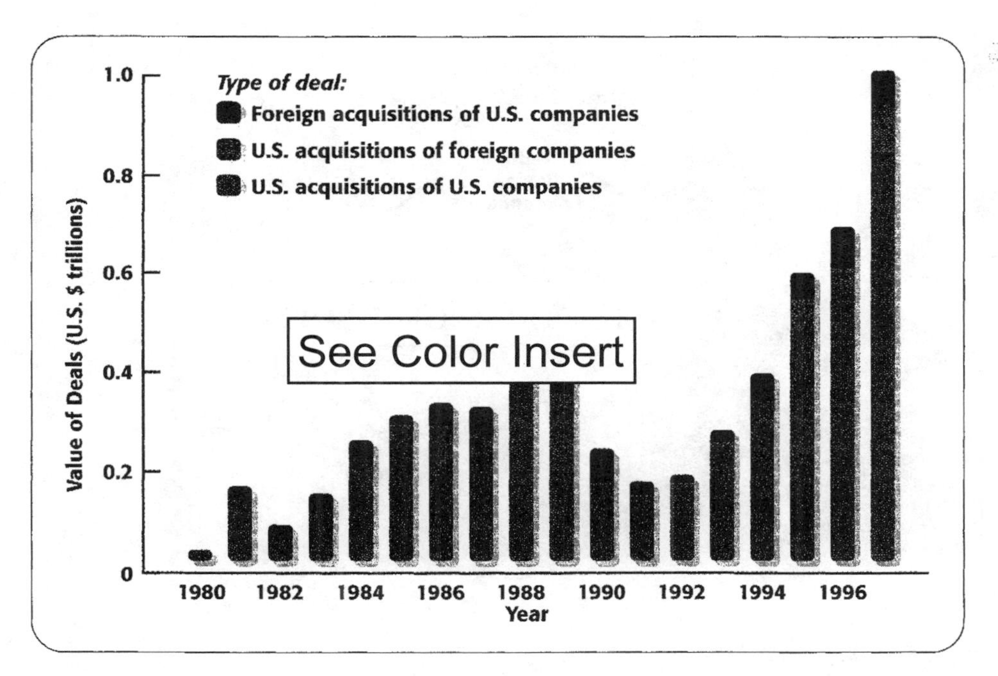

FIGURE 1.2
THE GROWING VALUE OF MERGERS AND ACQUISITIONS

BUSINESS: THE GLOBAL PERSPECTIVE

Some people regard international business as an us-against-them proposition. This defensive mentality causes nations to barricade their markets, cutting off one another from both potential markets and investment opportunities. Following the First World War, countries tried to reduce the outflow of their wealth in the form of gold by discouraging imports and protecting domestic industries. By the early 1930s, this mode of thinking was one factor contributing to the worldwide Great Depression. Thinking globally helps reduce the potential danger associated with this way of thinking.

Businesspeople must try to break out of the boundaries placed upon them by years of living and working within their respective cultures. They must strive to view the global marketplace through the eyes of others with different cultural backgrounds. Today, more and more companies want their managers to think from a global perspective, unhindered by the blinders of nationalism. As we saw earlier in this chapter, for instance, Sony Corporation is in the process of creating a dual-headquarters organization. Global activities in the financial, legal, and business strategy areas that were previously performed only in Tokyo will now be shared with Sony's New York office. "If our headquarters remains in regulation-bound Japan," explains one high-ranking executive, "our managers' thinking will be skewed in a way which limits the development of strategies with a global perspective." At the same time, however, all top executives remain Japanese. Observers argue that for Sony to develop a "truly global" company and culture, top management must include executives with different cultural backgrounds.[27]

Figure 1.3 displays the three elements of the global perspective:

1. Many *national business environments*
2. The *international business environment*
3. The *international business management* of companies

Figure 1.3 also implies that both the national and international business environments influence international business management. Let's examine these three components.

FIGURE 1.3
A GLOBAL PERSPECTIVE ON BUSINESS

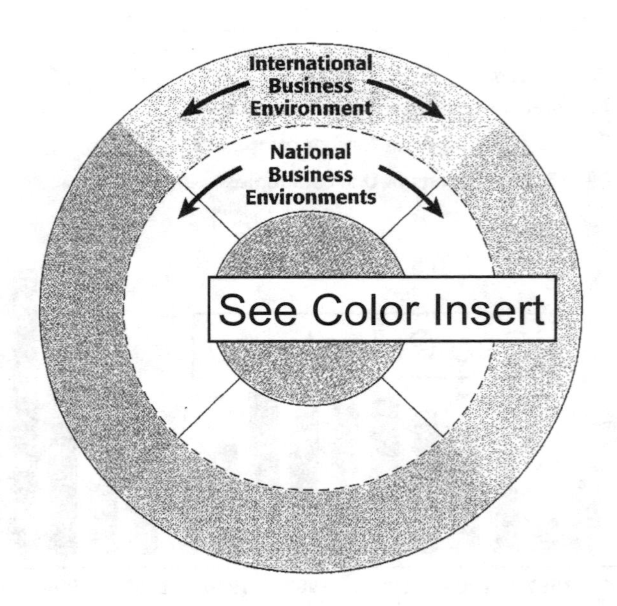

NATIONAL BUSINESS ENVIRONMENTS

Although globalization is drawing the world's economies closer together, many differences among countries remain. Each *national business environment* includes all the elements that are external to a company but that can potentially affect its performance. Each of these elements belongs to one of four external environmental forces: *cultural, political and legal, economic,* and *competitive.*

Four Environmental Forces Following are the key features of these four forces:

- *Cultural forces* reflect a people's aesthetics, values and attitudes, manners and customs, social structure, religion, personal communication, education, and physical and material environments. Understanding national culture helps managers to be more effective at managing their sales and production activities.
- *Political and legal forces* are matters of governmental and regulatory importance that concern the management of businesses. Political forces include the stability of government, the level of corruption in the political system, and the political processes that influence economic policies. Legal forces include laws governing the payment of minimum wages, the safety of workers, the protection of the environment and consumers, and what is ruled legal or illegal competitive behavior.
- *Economic forces* include financial and economic variables, such as interest and tax rates, consumption patterns, productivity levels, and output levels. They also include infrastructure variables, such as telecommunications, physical distribution networks (roads, highways, airports, and so forth), and the availability and cost of energy.
- *Competitive forces* include factors such as the numbers of a company's competitors and their strategies, cost structures, and product quality. It also includes how competition affects the cost and availability of resources such as labor, financial capital, and raw materials. Finally, it involves customers' characteristics, behaviors, and preferences toward the products of a company and its competitors.

These four groups of external forces influence the way all companies operate in any nation's business environment. Entrepreneurs and small to medium-size businesses not involved in international activities can be particularly affected. They must typically employ labor and acquire financial resources in their national or regional market where a limited supply can increase costs.

INTERNATIONAL BUSINESS ENVIRONMENT

Managers of domestic companies are concerned mainly with how external forces *in that one national environment* affect performance. In contrast, managers of international companies must be concerned with external forces in *all of the national business environments in which the company is involved.*

International institutions and processes help shape international business activity. In the *international business environment,* the activities of consumers, workers, companies, financial institutions and governments from different countries converge. The international environment, therefore, links the world's national business environments and is the conduit by which external forces in one country affect companies in others.

Five Influential Groups Information, capital, people, and products all move about in the international business environment. Five groups account for such movements:

- *Consumers* around the world are beginning to develop similar wants and needs, especially in such product categories as personal computers, stereos, music, and movies. In addition, they are increasingly knowledgeable about the value of products available in the global marketplace. Today, such merchandise may be purchased directly from manufacturers or retailers over the World Wide Web (and delivered electronically or by conventional means) no matter where either party is physically located.

e-biz

- *Workers* relocate when employment opportunities dwindle in home countries. The formation of free trade areas (such as the European Union) can greatly enhance the mobility of workers among member nations.
- *Companies* sell goods and services around the world and acquire investment capital through international financial markets. Multinational corporations transfer employees, information, and capital between their national subsidiaries and compete head-to-head in one another's markets.
- *Governments* procure products from international suppliers to accomplish social, economic, and military goals. They also regulate international flows of products, labor, information, and capital. Whereas the global economy benefits from laws that protect consumers and the environment, it can be harmed by laws that are simply barriers to trade and investment.
- *Financial institutions* play several important roles in the international business environment. First, they supply companies with the currencies of other countries in order to pay for needed imports. They also buy the currencies of other nations on behalf of companies when managers want to reduce the risk of an international deal. Finally, financial institutions help companies raise capital and invest excess cash in world financial markets.

INTERNATIONAL BUSINESS MANAGEMENT

When a business decides to go international, it faces many challenges. At that point, a firm's internal forces encounter new cultural, political and legal, economic, and competitive external forces. Companies' *internal forces* are those elements within a company over which it has a large degree of control and include:

- Human resource staffing policies and employee training and development programs
- Organizational culture and the strength with which shared values are emphasized

- The acquisition and allocation of financial resources
- Production methods and scheduling
- Marketing decisions regarding products, pricing, promotion, and distribution
- Policies regarding the evaluation of managers and company performance

Standardization versus Adaptation International business management is usually subject to the two opposing forces of standardization and adaptation. These forces usually entail a basic decision about doing business abroad. On the one hand, companies can obtain cost savings by *standardizing* various elements of their activities, including production methods, marketing strategy, and corporate policy. On the other hand, they may achieve greater success by *adapting* activities to satisfy the needs of buyers in each local culture—a practice that normally raises costs. Companies must balance the need to cut costs against the special needs of local consumers.

To meet these and other challenges, many companies are working to dissolve the divisions between *business functions* (marketing, production, finance, research and development, and so forth). They are organizing themselves around the processes that create value for their customers, contribute to quality or competitive advantage, or help win new sales contracts. Others are turning to *cross-functional teams* to solve common problems. Teams that cut across functional and cultural boundaries often work to create innovative solutions to problems facing the company in different national markets. We discuss these topics fully in part V of this book.

Ethics and Social Responsibility When companies venture into international business activities, managers are exposed to different cultures and, therefore, to different ideas about how employees should be treated, different conceptions of ethical behavior, and different guidelines for socially responsible behavior. Firms are often forced to alter their products, advertising, human resource practices, company-wide strategies, and even their organizational structures. Confronting and adapting to such unfamiliar elements presents companies with both tremendous opportunities and potential pitfalls.

Issues such as plant closings, the use of child labor, human rights abuses, and protecting the environment increasingly invade debates on international trade. Whereas ethics pertain to the behavior of individuals, social responsibility relates to the actions of organizations. Let's take a brief look at each of these.

ethical behavior
Personal behavior that is in accordance with rules or standards for right conduct or morality.

Ethical Behavior Personal behavior that is in accordance with rules or standards for right conduct or morality is called **ethical behavior**. Ethical dilemmas are not legal questions. When a law exists to guide a manager toward a legally correct action, the legally correct path must necessarily be followed. But in ethical dilemmas there are no right or wrong decisions but alternative choices, each of which may be equally valid, depending on one's perspective.

Ethical questions often arise when managers attempt to either abide by local management practices or import their own practices from the home country. One viewpoint agrees with the old saying "When in Rome, do as the Romans do." This philosophy, however, often runs into trouble when large international companies from developed nations do business in developing nations. Consider one case publicized by human rights and labor groups investigating charges of worker abuse at the factory of one of Nike's Vietnamese suppliers. Twelve of 56 female employees reportedly fainted when a supervisor forced them to run around the factory as punishment for not wearing regulation shoes. Nike confirmed the report and, in suspending the supervisor, took steps to implement practices more in keeping with the company's home-country ethics.[28]

Another viewpoint believes that home-country policies should be implemented wherever a company operates. However, this policy can also create ethical questions. Home-country practice initially won out in 1996 at a Mitsubishi Motors plant in Normal, Illinois. But 30 women later filed a civil suit charging that plant managers fostered an atmosphere conducive to sexual harassment because they let offensive behavior go unpunished. The Equal Employment Opportunity Commission also filed a lawsuit, and Mitsubishi eventually instituted company-wide changes in its human resource policies. Some experts observed that cultural differences and the practices of Mitsubishi that were implemented in the United States from Japan may have contributed to a tolerance of sexual harassment at the Normal plant.

Social Responsibility In addition to individual managers behaving ethically, corporations are expected to exercise **social responsibility**—the practice of going beyond legal obligations to actively balance commitments to investors, customers, other companies, and communities. In recent years governments, labor unions, consumer groups, and human rights activists have combined to drive apparel companies from developed nations to implement codes of conduct and monitoring principles in their international production activities. Pertinent issues include trade initiatives with developing nations (a government issue), the relocation of home-country factories to locations abroad (a labor issue), and the treatment of workers by local contractors abroad (a human rights issue).

social responsibility
Practice of companies going beyond legal obligations to actively balance commitments to investors, customers, other companies, and communities.

Today, companies often don't wait for governments to pressure them before undertaking policy changes. Most business leaders realize that the future of their companies rests on healthy workforces and environments worldwide. Thus some companies have introduced codes of conduct that set standards for working conditions in manufacturing facilities abroad. Starbucks, for instance, introduced a Framework for a Code of Conduct for coffee-exporting countries from which it obtains its coffee beans. This code reflects a larger effort to initiate an industry-wide dialogue among coffee retailers, exporters, and growers to encourage social responsibility.

Levi-Strauss pioneered the use of guidelines in 1992, and company-wide policies have evolved into a set of practical codes. Levi-Strauss relies on these codes both to control working conditions at contractors' facilities and to assess countries as potential locations for doing business. A global staff of about 50 people monitors working conditions in the factories of Levi's contractors abroad.[29] Figure 1.4 summarizes Levi's "Guidelines for Country Selection."

As globalization continues, companies acting in socially irresponsible ways anywhere in the world will come under increasing pressure. The reason is simple: Labor unions, consumer groups, and human rights organizations are also transforming themselves into global organizations. Labor activists in the United States have been instrumental in helping Mexican unions free themselves from decades-long control by a government-backed union that has been accused of not truly supporting workers' rights. For instance, although union leaders in the United States oppose policies that encourage home-based companies to relocate to countries like Mexico, they are now forging closer ties with their Mexican counterparts. Why are they assisting Mexican labor unions in this way? Improved wages and working conditions in Mexico help workers in the United States by reducing the incentive for U.S. firms to move to Mexico.[30]

For some insight into traits (in addition to behaving ethically and acting in a socially responsible manner) that can help managers and their companies succeed in the international marketplace, see the Global Manager "The Keys to Success."

FIGURE 1.4
LEVI STRAUSS & CO. GUIDELINES FOR COUNTRY SELECTION

1. **Brand Image**
   We will not initiate or renew contractual relationships in countries where sourcing would have an adverse effect on our global brand image.
2. **Health & Safety**
   We will not initiate or renew contractual relationships in locations where there is evidence that Company employees or representatives would be exposed to unreasonable risk.
3. **Human Rights**
   We should not initiate or renew contractual relationships in countries where there are pervasive violations of basic human rights.
4. **Legal Requirements**
   We will not initiate or renew contractual relationships in countries where the legal environment creates unreasonable risk to our trademarks or to other important commercial interests or seriously impedes our ability to implement these guidelines.
5. **Political or Social Stability**
   We will not initiate or renew contractual relationships in countries where political or social turmoil unreasonably threatens our commercial interests.

Global Manager

The Keys to Success

Despite the difficulties of managing internationally, many companies prosper when competing beyond their domestic market. Although they assemble everything from 99-cent hamburgers (McDonald's) to $150 million jumbo jets (Boeing), their executives acknowledge certain common threads in their management styles. The most successful global managers offer the following advice:

- **Know the Customer** The successful manager has detailed knowledge of what different international customers want and ensures that the company is flexible enough to customize products to meet those needs.
- **Emphasize Global Awareness** Good global managers ensure that the company designs and builds products and services for export from the beginning, not as an afterthought following the conquest of domestic markets.
- **Market a World-Class Product** Successful managers insist on high-quality products; they know that customers everywhere demand reliability.
- **Give Workers a Stake in the Company** The best global companies provide special incentives for employees who perform well.
- **Know How to Analyze Problems** Successful managers rarely start out with solutions. Instead, they tackle problems one piece at a time by experimenting and taking risks as necessary.
- **Understand Technology** The best managers find ways to match technology with the customer's environment. They do not, for example, make changes out of love for technology but will build new product lines using new, cheaper material when it becomes available.
- **Keep an Eye on Exchange Rates** The increasing popularity of using exchange rates to control trade means that global managers must constantly deal with shifts in currency values. In short, they must understand how exchange rates function.

PLAN OF THIS BOOK

The main theme of this chapter is that the world's national economies are becoming increasingly intertwined. Cultural, political, legal, and economic events in one nation are increasingly affecting business activities in others. As globalization strengthens the bonds among national economies, this trend will continue. By the same token, as globalization penetrates further into national business environments, managers everywhere should take a global perspective on their business activities.

Figure 1.5 shows the path this book takes through the study of international business. Notice that each of the three rings in Figure 1.5 corresponds to the three main elements of Figure 1.3—*the international business environment, national business environments,* and *international business management.* In addition, each component of Figure 1.5 corresponds to a chapter in this book.

In Part II, we explore *national business environments,* showing how people's attitudes, values, beliefs, and institutions differ from one culture to another. We also explain how companies modify business practices and strategies when operating under different political, legal, and economic systems.

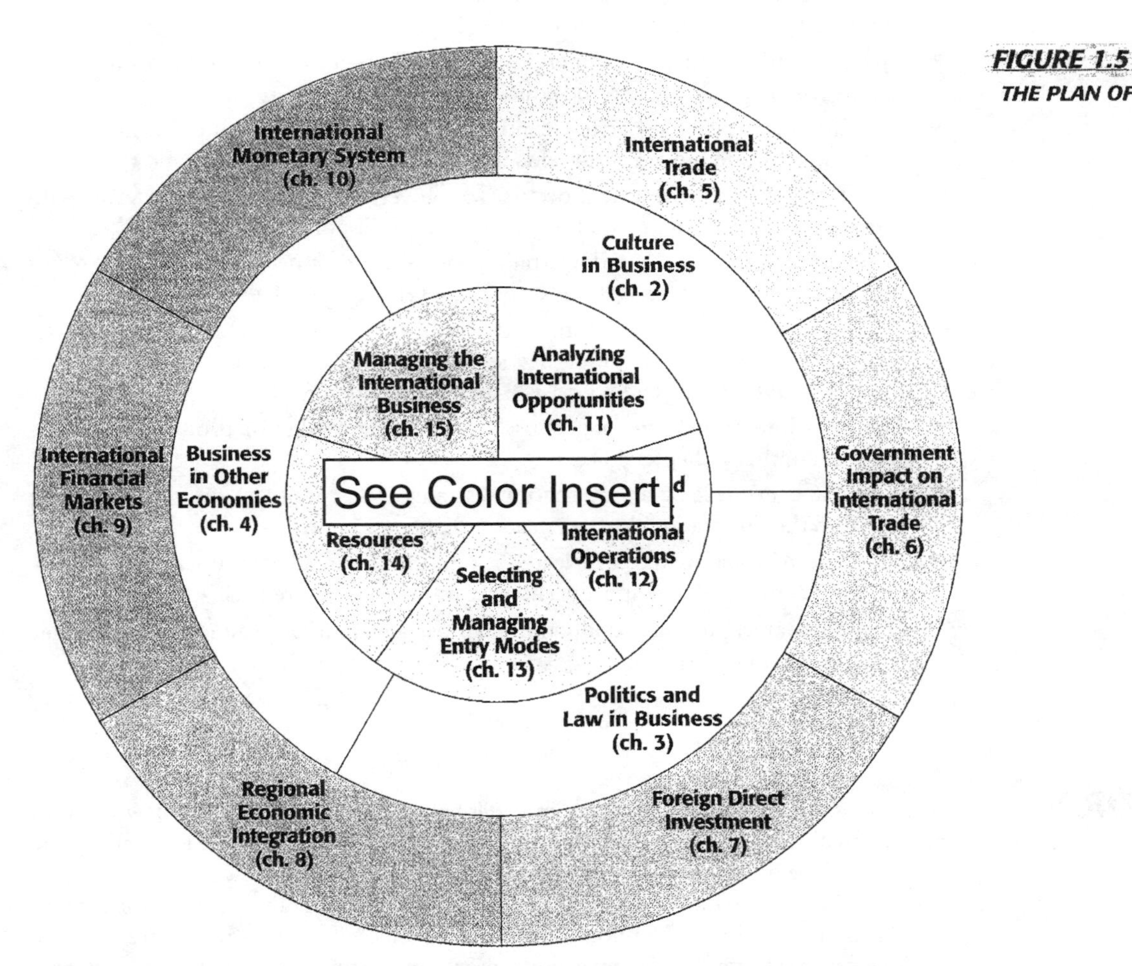

FIGURE 1.5
THE PLAN OF THIS BOOK

We discuss the major components of the *international business environment* in Parts III and IV. We learn why trade and investment flow across borders and why governments try to encourage or discourage their movement. We also explore the process of regional economic integration sweeping the global economy and outline its implications for international companies. Finally, we explain how global financial markets and the global monetary system function and show how they influence companies' international business activities.

In Part V, we describe the ways in which *international business management* is different from managing a purely domestic firm. We discuss how a company analyzes and decides on the markets in which it will sell or manufacture its products. We explain how a company plans and organizes itself for international operations. We explore why different companies choose to enter markets in different ways, and how they acquire and manage their business resources. Among the coming attractions in later chapters, we will explore:

- How companies can make marketing and production blunders when they fail to fully understand a people's culture (Chapter 2).
- The political and legal obstacles international businesses must overcome, including industrial espionage and terrorism (Chapter 3).
- The continuing struggle of emerging countries in recovering from communism and its costly socialist economic policies (Chapter 4).
- Why international trade occurs, its positive and negative economic and social benefits, and why and how governments intervene in trade (Chapters 5 and 6).
- Why foreign direct investment occurs, why governments insist on interfering with international investment, and how managers can respond (Chapter 7).
- Whether continually expanding trading blocs are destined to become fortresses that exclude nonmember nations or become vehicles for freer trade (Chapter 8).
- The globalization of financial markets and how currency speculators become extremely wealthy while wreaking havoc with national economies—such as during the 1997–1998 Asian currency crisis (Chapters 9 and 10).
- The tools international managers use to select one market or production site instead of another (Chapter 11).
- How managers develop an international strategy and choose an entry mode for the leap into the international marketplace (Chapters 12 and 13).
- How international managers selected for an international assignment can fall victim to "culture shock" if appropriate precautions are ignored (Chapter 14).
- How companies manage production facilities and market products in unfamiliar cultures (Chapter 15).

A FINAL WORD

No business today can escape the grip of globalization—it will breathe new life into some companies and force others into bankruptcy. By thoroughly understanding the dynamics of the international marketplace, you will increase your own chances for success. Whether you work for a global firm in a large cosmopolitan city or for a small business in a rural town, the information in this book will make you a more valuable employee, a more effective manager, or a more successful entrepreneur. This chapter has simply introduced you to the study of international business. We hope you enjoy the rest of your journey as you continue to discover the truly rich and dynamic nature of international business!

There is a variety of additional material available on the companion Web site that accompanies this text. You can access this information by visiting the Web site at ⟨**www.prenhall.com/wild**⟩.

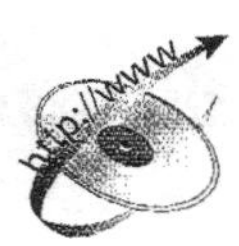

summary

1. **Describe *international business* and the process of *globalization*.** *International business* is the total of all business transactions crossing the borders of two or more nations. By means of international business, more and more nations are integrating their national economies into the global economy. This process of integration is called *globalization*. Two main forces behind the increasing globalization of business are (1) *lower trade and investment barriers* and (2) *increased innovation*, particularly in the areas of information and transportation technology.

2. **Explain why companies pursue *international business activity*.** Companies engage in international business for two main reasons: (1) to *increase sales* and (2) to *access resources*. Increasing sales is an attractive option when a firm is presented with either of two conditions: (1) an international sales growth opportunity or (2) excess production capacity. Firms try to access both *natural resources* (products supplied by nature) and *labor markets* in countries where low-cost labor helps them to be more competitive.

3. **Identify the *types of companies* that participate in international business.** Almost any company can participate in international business. Thanks to the Internet and other technologies that permit them to surmount such obstacles as prohibitively high advertising and distribution costs, many small businesses have become increasingly active in international trade and investment. However, large *multinational corporations (MNCs)* conduct most international business transactions. Multinationals dominate the international business news for two reasons: (1) They are highly visible because they have so much economic muscle; (2) their mergers and acquisitions are often valued in the billions of dollars.

4. **Explain the *global perspective* on business and identify its three main elements.** Adopting a *global perspective* means breaking out of the boundaries placed on us by years of living within our respective cultures. The consideration of three elements goes into the global perspective on business: (a) Separate *national business environments*, which include all the elements that are external to a company but that can affect its performance. These elements belong to one of four external environmental forces: *cultural, political/legal, economic*, and *competitive*. (b) The *international business environment*, which refers to the institutions and processes that shape international business activity. It links national environments by conducting the flow of information, capital, people, and products. In turn, five groups account for these flows: consumers, workers, companies, governments, and financial institutions. (c) *International business management* involves (among other things) balancing a firm's internal forces (human resource policies, organizational culture, production methods, and so forth) with external environmental forces (cultural, political/legal, economic, and competitive).

questions for review

1. What is *international business*? Give several examples of international business transactions (other than those included in the chapter).
2. What two major factors have led to greater *globalization* in markets and production? Explain each briefly.
3. For what two main reasons do companies "go international"?
4. What types of companies get involved in international business activities? Explain why large companies capture so much of the international business headlines.
5. What do we mean by "the *global perspective* on business?" Explain how its three main elements interact.
6. What is the *national business environment*? Identify the four external forces that comprise it.
7. What is the *international business environment*? Identify the five groups that account for the international flow of information, capital, people, and products.
8. How does managing an international business differ from managing a domestic company?
9. Why do the issues of *ethical behavior* and *social responsibility* arise in the international marketplace? Explain how these two concepts differ from one another.

questions for discussion

1. International businesspeople must think globally about production and sales opportunities. The World Business Survey "The International Top Fifteen" on page 8 reveals the nations that are expected to attract managers in the future. What can companies do now to prepare themselves for these new markets? What can entrepreneurs and small businesses with limited resources do?
2. In the past, national governments greatly affected the pace of globalization through agreements to lower barriers to international trade and investment. Is the pace of change now outpacing the ability of governments to manage the global economy? Will national governments become more or less important to international business in the future? Explain your answer.
3. Information and communication technologies are developing at a faster rate than ever before. How have these technologies affected globalization? Give specific examples. Do you think globalization will continue until we all live in one "global village"? Why or why not?
4. Consider the following statement: "Globalization and the resulting increase in competition harm people as international companies play one government against another to get the best deal possible. Meanwhile, governments continually ask for greater concessions from their citizens, demanding that they work harder and longer for less pay." Do you agree? Why or why not?

in practice

This chapter discussed the reasons why companies expand into international markets. Read the brief article below and answer the questions that follow.

BMW, VW Expand in Russsia

Two German carmakers—BMW and Volkswagen—have announced plans to build assembly plants in Russia. BMW said it has closely studied the projected long-term growth of the Russian auto market and decided to construct the facility in the Baltic city of Kaliningrad. BMW sales in Russia have declined by about 10 percent over the past several years. The German company has 19 dealerships in Russia, five of which are also licensed to sell Land Rovers produced by its British off-road division. Volkswagen AG's future plans call for the construction of a plant this year at an as-yet undisclosed location in Russia.

1. Given that sales of BMWs in Russia are in decline, why do you think the company is building an assembly plant there? Identify as many possible reasons as you can.
2. Go to the Web site of BMW ⟨**www.bmw.com**⟩ and access its most recent annual report. In what other locations does BMW produce auto parts or assemble cars? Based on the information at the Web site, report on one aspect of the company that interests you.
3. Why does the article refer to Kaliningrad as a "Baltic city?" *Hint:* You might want to take a look at the world atlas that follows this chapter.

projects

1. Imagine that you own a company that manufactures cheap sunglasses. To lower production costs, you want to move your factory from your developed country to a low-wage country. Choose a prospective country to which you will move. What elements of the national business environment will affect your move? Are there any obstacles to overcome in the international business environment? How will managing your company be different when you undertake international activities? What challenges will you face in managing your new employees?
2. With a group of classmates, select a country that interests you. What does its flag look like? What do the various colors and symbols, if any, represent? Identify any neighbors with which it shares borders. Give some important facts about the country, including its population, population density, land area, topography, climate, natural resources, and the locations of main industries. What products are produced there? Do any aspects of the natural environment help explain why it produces what it does? Present your findings to the class.

business case 1

MTV: GOING GLOBAL WITH A LOCAL BEAT

Perhaps no company exemplifies the maxim "Think globally, act locally" better than MTV. The company beams its irreverent and brash mix of music, news, and entertainment to 281 million homes in over 64 countries, including Brazil, Singapore, India, and 36 countries in Europe. Although style and format are largely driven by the U.S. youth culture, content is tailored to local markets.

In 1987, MTV commanded an audience of 61 million in the United States. But because demand was leveling off, the company took the music revolution global by starting MTV Europe and MTV Australia. Through its experiences in Europe, MTV refined its mix of programming to become a global national brand with local variations. At first, it took a pan-European approach, marketing the same product to all European countries. MTV broadcast primarily British and U.S. music (both of which were topping the charts throughout Europe) and used European "veejays" who spoke English. The European network was a huge overnight success.

Seven years later, however, MTV had become the victim of its own success. Now it had to compete with a new crop of upstart rivals that tailored content to language, culture, and current events in specific countries. One successful competitor is Germany's VIVA, launched in 1993 and featuring German veejays and more German artists (like Fantascishen 4 and Scooter) than MTV Europe. Managers at MTV Networks were not overly concerned because MTV was still extremely popular. But they did realize they were losing their edge (and some customers) to the new national networks. What should the company do? Split up MTV Europe into MTV Germany and MTV Spain?

Because they had spent almost two decades building a global brand identity, MTV executives initially rejected that idea. Little by little, however, they changed their collective mind. They decided to move forward because a certain technological innovation made it possible for MTV to think globally and act locally at very little cost. The breakthrough was digital compression technology, which allows suppliers to multiply the number of services offered on a single satellite feed. "Where there were three or four services," explained one MTV official, "now we can broadcast six or eight."

Today, not only teens in Europe but teens all over the world have their MTV cake and eat it, too. German teens, for instance, see shows created and produced in Germany—in German—along with the usual generous helpings of U.S., British, and international music and the ever-popular duo Beavis and Butthead. And there's an added side benefit for MTV: National advertisers who had shunned the channel during its pan-European days are now coming onboard to beam ads targeted specifically to their consumers.

thinking globally

1. The last decade has witnessed a growing similarity in the attitudes and spending habits of youthful consumers around the world. As one journalist puts it, "It may still be conventional wisdom to 'think globally and act locally,' but in the youth market, it is increasingly a case of one size fits all." Do you agree or disagree? Why or why not?
2. Some people are concerned that teens exposed to large doses of U.S. youth culture via 24-hour MTV networks will begin to identify less and less with their own cultures and societies. Others worry that teenage consumers in developing countries want more and more Western goods that they can't afford. MTV's response to such criticism: "It's just fun," says one network executive. "It's only TV."

   What do you think? Are there dangers in broadcasting U.S. programs and ads to both developed and developing countries?
3. Digital compression technology made it possible for MTV to program over a global network. Can you think of any other technological innovations that have helped companies to think globally and act locally?

a question of ethics

1. We often characterize ethical dilemmas as "right-versus-wrong" situations. But consider the opinion of Rushworth Kidder, president of the Institute for Global Ethics: "The very toughest choices people face are not questions of right versus wrong, but questions of right versus right," such as a choice between the values of truth and loyalty. For instance, should you tell the truth about a superior's wrongdoing, or should you remain loyal to your boss? Describe an ethical dilemma in which an international executive might face a tough choice between "right" and "right." Have you ever faced such a choice? How do *you* define ethical behavior? Do you think that people can be made to act ethically?[31]
2. Nike called upon civil rights leader Andrew Young to look into its labor practices at Asian plants in order to determine if the company was adhering to its own code of ethical conduct.

After a monthlong investigation, Young reported no evidence of widespread or systematic mistreatment of Nike workers abroad. Critics charged that the report was shallow because Young admitted to spending only three hours in any factory, always accompanied by Nike officials. They were also skeptical because Young presented his findings to Nike's board and senior management a week before making them public. If you were the CEO of Nike, how would you respond to these criticisms? Do you think that there are more effective or objective means of monitoring a company's overseas activities? If so, what are they?[32]

3. The North American Free Trade Agreement (NAFTA) requires the United States to spend over $1 billion for environmental cleanup. By the end of 1996, however, the United States had spent nothing in this area. According to Guillermo Perez Diaz, general manager of the water department of San Luis Rio Colorado, a Mexican border city, "The mutual promises made by our two governments have not yet been kept. Our city . . . has serious environmental problems. Our drainage system serves only 38 percent of the population, and our sewage, for which we have no treatment plant, is seriously contaminating the dry bed of the Colorado River. After more than a year of presenting projects to the Border Environment Cooperation Commission and the North American Development Bank, we have yet to receive any help." Do the businesses who have set up in San Luis Rio Colorado bear any responsibility for the environmental problems there? What can business leaders do when governments ignore environmental promises?[33]

integrative **video case**

PART ONE: OVERVIEW OF INTERNATIONAL BUSINESS

lands' end and yahoo!

background

This video case shows how two very different companies, Lands' End and Yahoo!, approached the same goal: expansion into international markets. Lands' End is a retail business that sells its products through its print and on-line catalogs. Yahoo! is an Internet search engine that supplies its service to Web surfers worldwide.

A firm may decide to go international for any number of reasons, including the drive to increase sales volume and to access resources in other national markets. Lands' End wanted to increase its sales volume in markets such as Japan, Germany, and the United Kingdom. Yahoo! wanted to dominate the global Internet industry by penetrating markets such as China, Japan, Sweden, Norway, France, and others. This video illustrates how the two companies entered a particular country and localized their products and services to meet the needs and preferences of consumers in new markets.

lands' end

In 1963, Gary C. Comer, a former advertising copywriter and an avid sailor, founded Lands' End, Inc., in Chicago, Illinois. The company began by selling sailboat hardware equipment by catalog. In 1978, Lands' End warehouse and phone operations moved to Dodgeville, Wisconsin, a rural community located 40 miles southwest of Madison, Wisconsin. In 1980, the company established a toll-free phone operation that ran 24 hours a day, and in 1985, the Lands' End catalog started coming out monthly. The company went public in 1986. In 1990, three new specialty catalogs were launched: Coming Home (bed and bath supplies), Lands' End Kids, and Beyond Buttonwoods (men's tailored clothing). In 1991, Lands' End sent its catalog to customers in the United Kingdom for the first time, and in 1993 the company opened a warehouse and phone center there. In 1994, Lands' End opened operations in Japan. That same year Lands' End purchased the trademark of Willis & Geiger, an U.S.-based adventure outfitters company. In 1995, Lands' End launched its Web site on the Internet. Still building its overseas presence, Lands' End opened a phone center in Germany in 1996. By 1997 Lands' End sales had reached $1.2 billion, making the company one of the largest apparel brands in the United States.

yahoo! inc.

Yahoo! is an Internet search engine headquartered in Santa Clara, California, that helps people navigate the World Wide Web. The company's principal product is an ad-supported Internet directory that links users to millions of Web pages. The site leads the field in traffic (95 million pages viewed each day) and is second only to Netscape in on-line advertising revenues. Yahoo! has targeted guides for geographic audiences (Yahoo! Finance and Yahoo! News), demographic audiences (see Yahooligans!, a Web guide for children), special-interest audiences (for example, Yahoo! Finance and Yahoo! News), and community services (Yahoo! Chat). The company is moving into the Internet access market through an alliance with AT&T and has agreed to acquire fellow Internet player GeoCities. Japan's SOFTBANK, which owns 28 percent of Yahoo!, has 15 international Web properties outside the United States. Yahoo! now has offices in Europe, the Asian Pacific, and Canada. Net income for 1998 was $25.6 million. In 1997, the company employed 386 people, and in 1998 its staff climbed to 803.

discussion questions

While you watch the video, keep the following discussion questions in mind. You might want to take notes.

1. Why did the two companies go international?
2. What is the difference between international and global? Answer this question from the perspectives of Lands' End and Yahoo!.
3. How did Lands' End succeed in establishing itself in Germany, the United Kingdom, and Japan?
4. How did Yahoo! succeed in Japan, France, Sweden, China, and Latin America?
5. What international issues have challenged the two companies?
6. How did Yahoo! localize its global products and services?

student exercises

1. Break into groups of two or three people. Discuss the national and international environments for Lands' End and Yahoo!. Present your analysis to the rest of the class with a 10- to 15-minute talk.
2. Choose any company from any country in the world and write up the reasons why this company should or should not go international.
3. Compare and contrast the differences between a global and an international business.

APPENDIX
world atlas

This atlas presents the global landscape in a series of maps designed to assist your understanding of global business. By knowing the locations of countries and the distances between them, managers in the global marketplace are able to make more informed decisions. Knowing the geography of a place also gives managers insight into the culture of the people living there. Because international managers must know where borders meet, this atlas captures the most recent changes in national political boundaries.

As the global marketplace continues to absorb previously isolated business environments, each one of us needs a thorough grasp of the global landscape. Familiarize yourself with each of the maps in this appendix and then try to answer the following 20 questions. We urge you to return to this atlas frequently in order to refresh your memory of the global landscape and especially when you encounter the name of an unfamiliar city or country.

MAP EXERCISES

1. Which of the following countries border the Atlantic Ocean?
   a. Bolivia
   b. Australia
   c. South Africa
   d. Japan
   e. United States
2. Which of the following countries are found in Africa?
   a. Guyana
   b. Morocco
   c. Egypt
   d. Pakistan
   e. Niger
3. Which one of the following countries does *not* border the Pacific Ocean?
   a. Australia
   b. Venezuela
   c. Japan
   d. Mexico
   e. Peru
4. Prague is the capital city of:
   a. Uruguay
   b. Czech Republic
   c. Portugal
   d. Tunisia
   e. Hungary
5. If transportation costs for getting your product from your market to Japan are high, which of the following countries might be good places to locate a manufacturing facility?
   a. Thailand
   b. Philippines
   c. South Africa
   d. Indonesia
   e. Portugal
6. Seoul is the capital city of:
   a. Vietnam
   b. Cambodia
   c. Malaysia
   d. China
   e. South Korea
7. Turkey, Romania, Ukraine, and Russia border the body of water called the ______________ Sea.
8. Thailand shares borders with:
   a. Cambodia
   b. Pakistan
   c. Singapore
   d. Malaysia
   e. Indonesia
9. Which of the following countries border no major ocean or sea?
   a. Austria
   b. Paraguay
   c. Switzerland
   d. Niger
   e. all of the above

10. Oslo is the capital city of:
    a. Germany
    b. Canada
    c. Brazil
    d. Australia
    e. Norway
11. Chile is located in:
    a. Africa
    b. Asia
    c. the Northern Hemisphere
    d. South America
    e. Central Europe
12. Saudi Arabia shares borders with:
    a. Jordan
    b. Kuwait
    c. Iraq
    d. United Arab Emirates
    e. all of the above
13. The body of water located between Sweden and Estonia is the ______________ Sea.
14. Which of the following countries are located on the Mediterranean Sea?
    a. Italy
    b. Croatia
    c. Turkey
    d. France
    e. Portugal
15. The distance between Sydney (Australia) and Tokyo (Japan) is shorter than that between:
    a. Tokyo and Cape Town (South Africa)
    b. Sydney and Hong Kong (China)
    c. Tokyo and London (England)
    d. Sydney and Jakarta (Indonesia)
    e. all of the above
16. Madrid is the capital city of (capitals are designated with red dots.):
    a. Madagascar
    b. Italy
    c. Mexico
    d. Spain
    e. United States
17. Which of the following countries is *not* located in central Asia?
    a. Afghanistan
    b. Uzbekistan
    c. Turkmenistan
    d. Kazakhstan
    e. Suriname
18. If you were shipping your products from your production facility in Pakistan to market in Australia, they would likely cross the ______________ Ocean.
19. Papua New Guinea, Guinea-Bissau, and Guinea are alternative names for the same country.
    a. true
    b. false
20. Which of the following countries are island nations?
    a. New Zealand
    b. Madagascar
    c. Japan
    d. Australia
    e. all of the above

Answers

1. c. South Africa, e. United States; 2. b. Morocco, c. Egypt, e. Niger; 3. b. Venezuela; 4. b. Czech Republic; 5. a. Thailand, b. Philippines, d. Indonesia; 6. e. South Korea; 7. Black; 8. a. Cambodia, d. Malaysia; 9. e. all of the above; 10. e. Norway; 11. d. South America; 12. e. all of the above; 13. Baltic; 14. a. Italy, c. Turkey, d. France; 15. a. Tokyo and Cape Town (South Africa), c. Tokyo and London (England); 16. d. Spain; 17. e. Suriname; 18. Indian; 19. b. false; 20. e. all of the above.

Self-Assessment

If you scored 15 correct answers or more, well done: You are well prepared for your international business journey. If you scored fewer than 8 correct answers, you may wish to review this atlas before moving on to Chapter 2.

Chapter 2b

culture in business

Beacons

A Look Back

CHAPTER 1 presented a global perspective on business. We learned why companies "go international" and about the many external and internal forces with which companies must deal when managing an international business.

A Look at This Chapter

This chapter introduces the important role of culture in international business. We explore the main elements of culture and show how they affect business policies and practices. We learn different methods of classifying cultures and how these methods can be applied to business.

A Look Ahead

CHAPTER 3 describes the political and legal systems of nations. We learn how these systems differ from one country to another and how they influence international business operations. We also show how managers reduce the effects of political risk.

Learning Objectives

After studying this chapter, you should be able to

1. Describe *culture* and explain the influence of both national culture and subcultures.
2. Identify the *components of culture* and describe their impact on business activities around the world.
3. Describe *cultural change* and explain how companies and culture affect one another.
4. Explain how the *physical environment* and *technology* influence culture.
5. Describe the *frameworks* and *dimensions* used to classify cultures and explain how they are applied.

Consumers around the world purchase personal computers, clothing, perfume, and soft drinks. Broad popular appeal, however, doesn't mean that a product can be made and marketed the same way in every country.

Lands' End, for example, modifies shirts, trousers, coats, sweaters, and almost every other article of clothing to accommodate differences in human physique, climate, and shopping habits worldwide. Commodore once used a photo of a naked young man to sell computers in Germany, but the same approach in Saudi Arabia would be highly offensive to Islamic values, not to mention illegal.

Even products that seem "universal" may need to be adapted for international markets. Arab-Malaysian Bank developed a credit card for Malaysians that doesn't allow purchases at "unholy" businesses such as gambling casinos, massage parlors, and nightclubs. But it does offer discounts on pilgrimages to Islam's holy city of Mecca, Saudi Arabia. Even the Walt Disney Company modified long-standing staffing policies at Disneyland Paris when French employees, complaining that Disney was disregarding local values, objected to bans on mustaches, beards, and short skirts.

Thus companies often adapt their marketing and management processes to suit local conditions. Careful evaluation of the local culture helps managers decide whether they will follow the maxim "When in Rome, do as the Romans do."[1]

This chapter is the first of three that discuss aspects of a nation's business environment (culture, politics, laws, and economics) that affect international business activities. One might ask, Why study topics that seem to be only indirectly related to international business? The short answer is they have *everything* to do with international business. Many failures by international businesses are directly related to their neglect of these crucial environmental factors.

The first step in the process of analyzing a nation's potential as a host for international business activity is to assess its overall business climate. This process means addressing some important questions. Are the local people open to new ideas and new ways of doing business? Is the political situation stable enough so that assets and employees are not placed at unacceptable levels of risk? Do government officials and the people want our business? By what ground rules do local businesses play? Answers to these kinds of questions—plus statistical data on such items as income level and labor costs—allow businesses to evaluate the attractiveness of a particular location as a place for doing business.

Understanding culture is crucial when a company does business in *its own* country. It is even more crucial when operating *across* cultures. From individual consumers to entrepreneurs to huge global firms, people inhabit the core of all business activity. When buyers and sellers from around the world come together to conduct business, they bring with them different backgrounds, expectations, and methods of communication. It is very important for businesspeople to understand how to communicate with their counterparts in other cultures.

This chapter defines *culture* in the context of international business. We explore the ways in which social institutions, religion, language, and other elements of culture affect international business activities. We learn how each nation's culture affects such things as its business practices and international competitiveness.

WHAT IS CULTURE?

culture
Set of values, beliefs, rules, and institutions held by a specific group of people.

When traveling in other countries, we often perceive differences in the way people live and work. In the United States dinner is commonly eaten around six; in Spain it's not served until eight or nine. In the United States people shop in large supermarkets once a week; Italians shop in small local grocery stores every day. These are differences in **culture**—the set of values, beliefs, rules, and institutions held by a specific group of people.[2] Culture is a highly complex portrait of a people. It includes everything from high tea in England, to the tropical climate of Barbados, to Mardi Gras in Brazil, to segregation of the sexes in Saudi Arabian schools. As we shall see later in this chapter, the main components of any culture include its *aesthetics, values* and *attitudes, manners* and *customs, social structure, religion, personal communication, education,* and *physical* and *material environments.*

ethnocentricity
Belief that one's own ethnic group or culture is superior to that of others.

Accommodating Culture: Overcoming Ethnocentricity Ethnocentricity is the belief that one's own ethnic group or culture is superior to that of others. It causes people to *view other cultures in terms of their own*—causing them to overlook important human and environmental differences among cultures.

International business projects are often undermined by ethnocentricity, primarily because firms' employees fail to be sensitive to cultural nuances. The annals of business are full of projects that failed because of resistance put up by government, labor, or the general public when companies tried to change something culturally fundamental at a factory or office in someone else's homeland.

Today globalization demands that businesspeople approach other cultures far differently than they did in the past. In particular, new technologies and their applications allow suppliers and buyers to treat the world as a single interconnected global

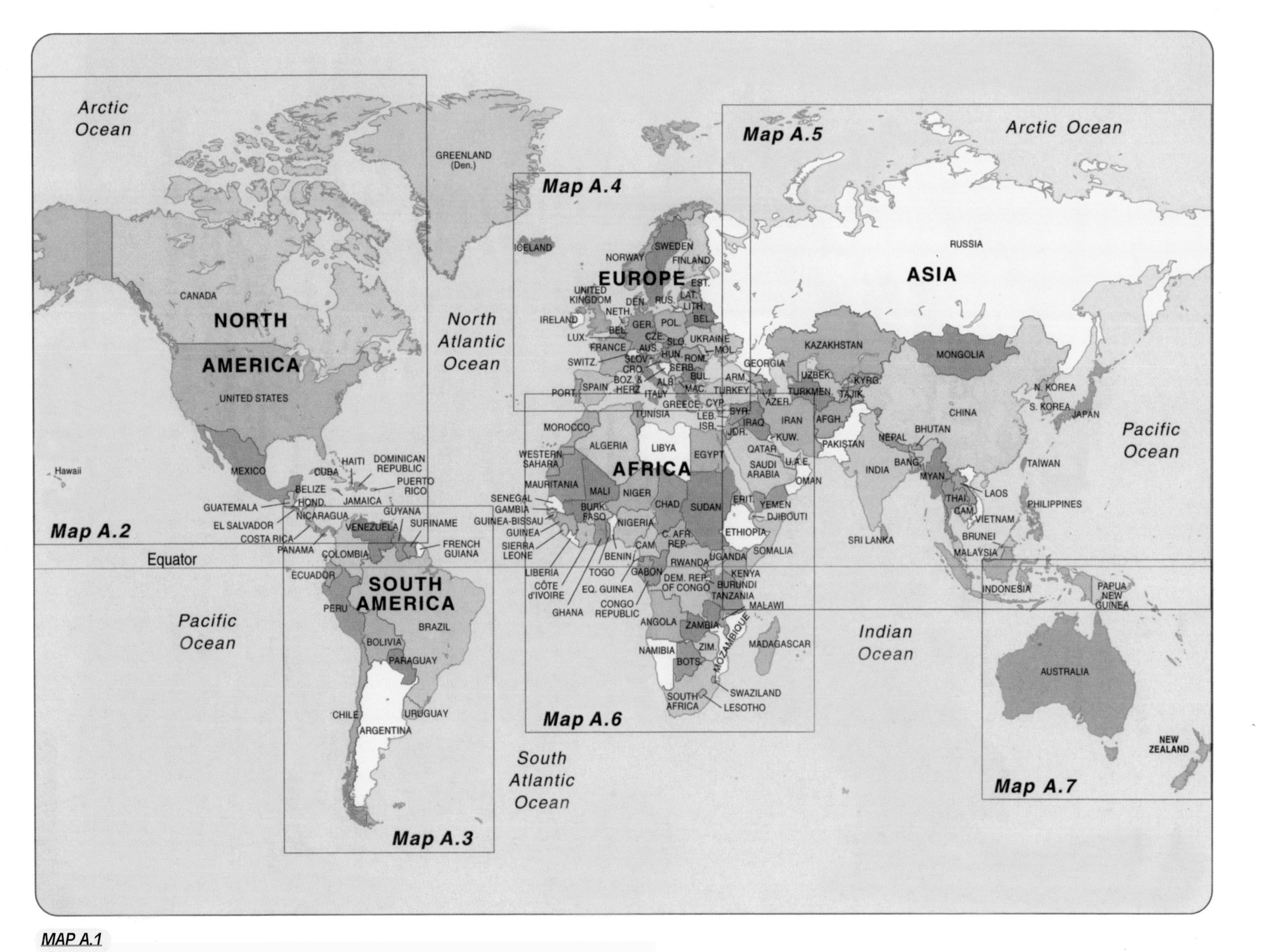

MAP A.1

THE WORLD IN 1999 This global view identifies each continent and acts as a reference for the six maps that follow.

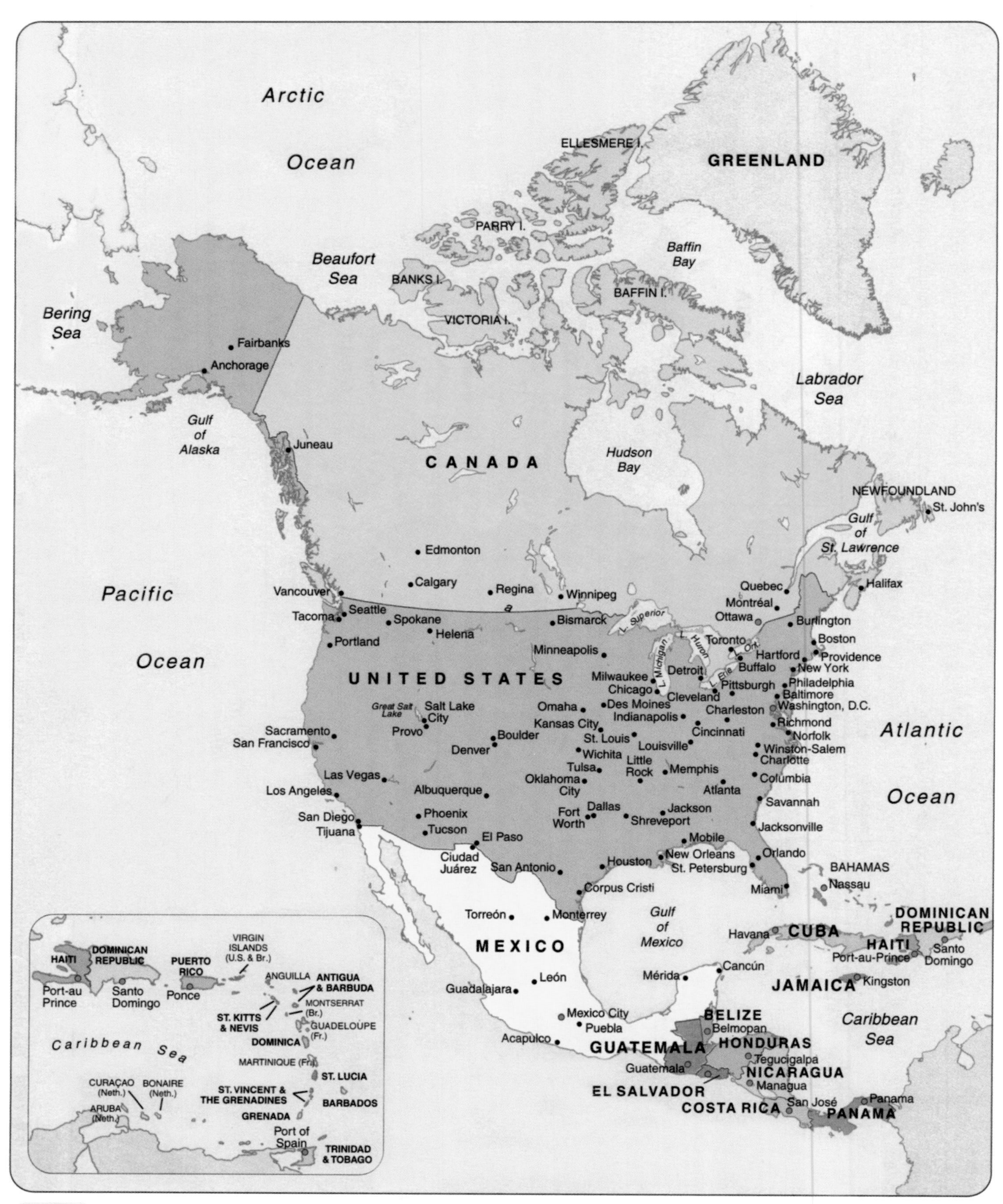

MAP A.2

NORTH AMERICA

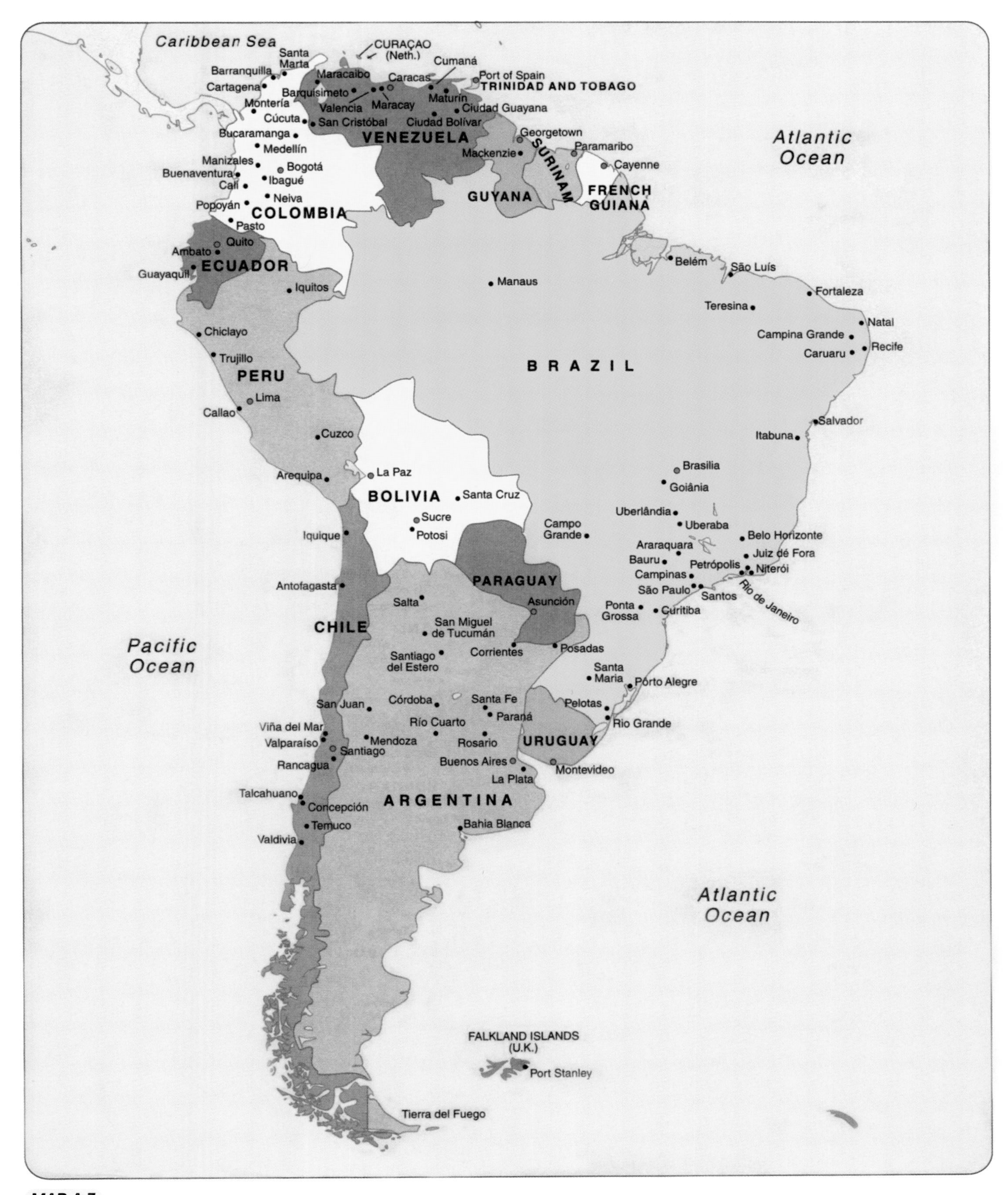

MAP A.3

SOUTH AMERICA

MAP A.4

EUROPE

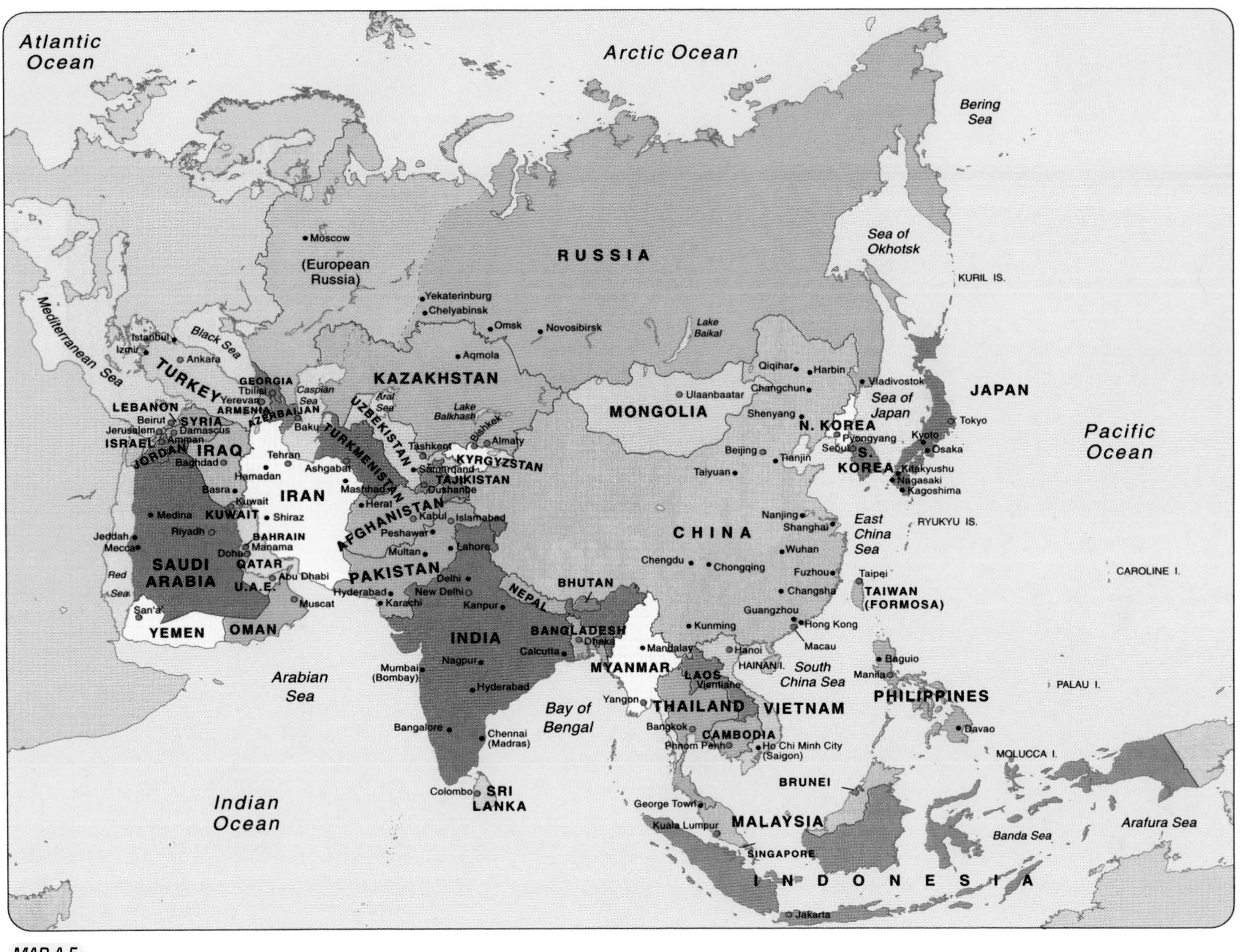
Atlantic Ocean
Arctic Ocean
Bering Sea
Sea of Okhotsk
KURIL IS.
RUSSIA
Moscow
(European Russia)
Yekaterinburg
Chelyabinsk
Omsk
Novosibirsk
Lake Baikal
Mediterranean Sea
Black Sea
Istanbul
Izmir
Ankara
TURKEY
GEORGIA
Tbilisi
Yerevan
ARMENIA
AZERBAIJAN
Baku
Caspian Sea
Aqmola
KAZAKHSTAN
Aral Sea
Lake Balkhash
UZBEKISTAN
TURKMENISTAN
Tashkent
Bishkek
Almaty
KYRGYZSTAN
Samarqand
Dushanbe
TAJIKISTAN
LEBANON
Beirut
SYRIA
Jerusalem
Damascus
ISRAEL
Amman
JORDAN
IRAQ
Baghdad
Tehran
Hamadan
Ashgabat
IRAN
Mashhad
Herat
Basra
Kuwait
KUWAIT
Shiraz
Medina
Riyadh
Jeddah
Mecca
BAHRAIN
Manama
Doha
QATAR
SAUDI ARABIA
Red Sea
Abu Dhabi
U.A.E.
Muscat
San'a'
YEMEN
OMAN
AFGHANISTAN
Kabul
Islamabad
Peshawar
Multan
Lahore
PAKISTAN
Hyderabad
Karachi
Delhi
New Delhi
Kanpur
NEPAL
BHUTAN
INDIA
BANGLADESH
Dhaka
Calcutta
Nagpur
Mumbai (Bombay)
Hyderabad
Arabian Sea
Bay of Bengal
Bangalore
Chennai (Madras)
Colombo
SRI LANKA
Indian Ocean
MONGOLIA
Ulaanbaatar
Qiqihar
Harbin
Changchun
Shenyang
Vladivostok
Sea of Japan
JAPAN
Tokyo
N. KOREA
Pyongyang
Seoul
S. KOREA
Kyoto
Osaka
Kitakyushu
Nagasaki
Kagoshima
Beijing
Tianjin
Taiyuan
Pacific Ocean
RYUKYU IS.
Nanjing
Shanghai
East China Sea
CHINA
Wuhan
Chengdu
Chongqing
Fuzhou
Taipei
TAIWAN (FORMOSA)
CAROLINE I.
Changsha
Guangzhou
Hong Kong
Macau
Kunming
Mandalay
MYANMAR
Hanoi
HAINAN I.
South China Sea
LAOS
Vientiane
Baguio
Manila
PHILIPPINES
PALAU I.
Yangon
THAILAND
VIETNAM
Bangkok
CAMBODIA
Phnom Penh
Ho Chi Minh City (Saigon)
Davao
MOLUCCA I.
BRUNEI
George Town
MALAYSIA
Kuala Lumpur
SINGAPORE
Banda Sea
Arafura Sea
INDONESIA
Jakarta

MAP A.5

ASIA

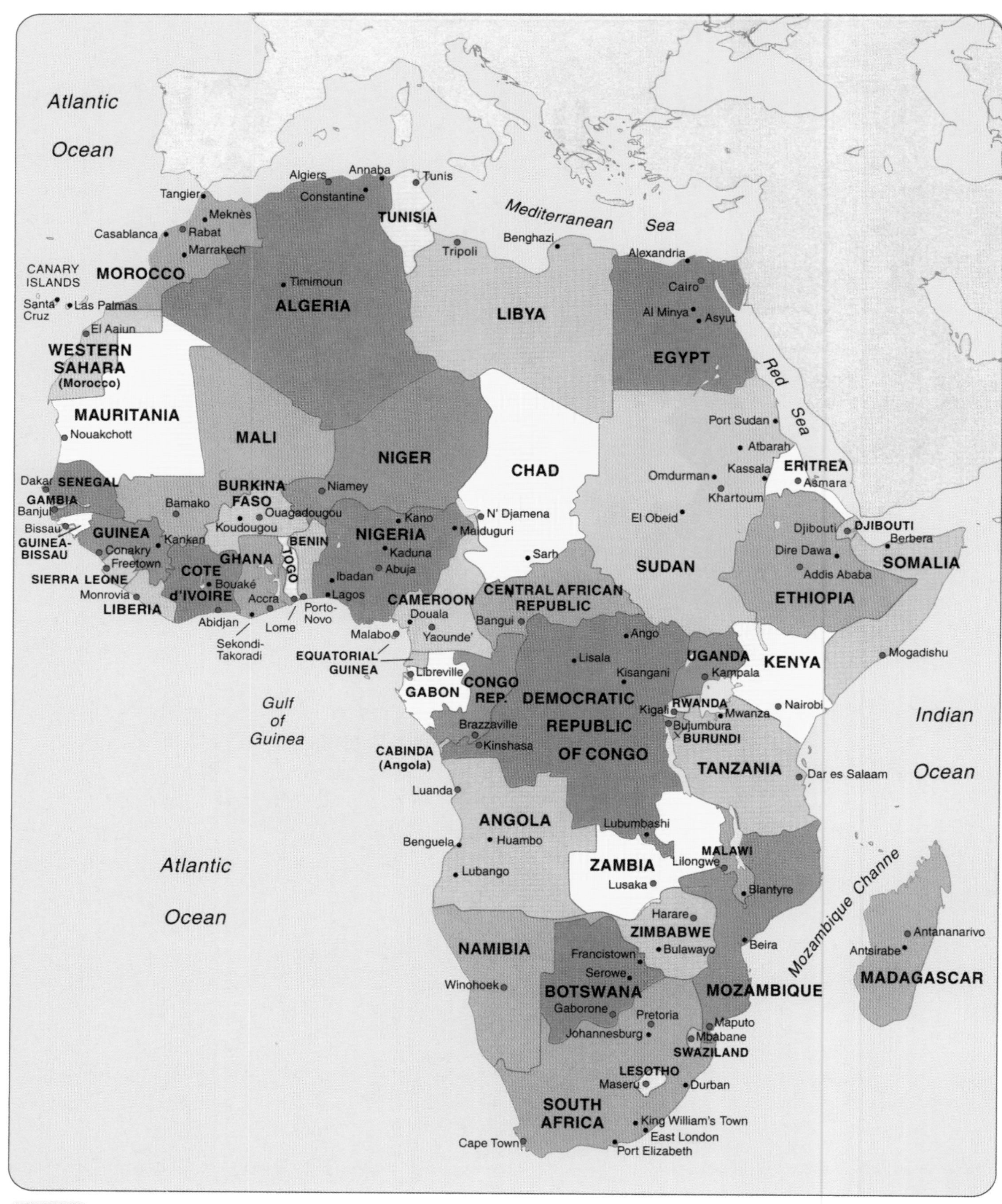

MAP A.6

AFRICA

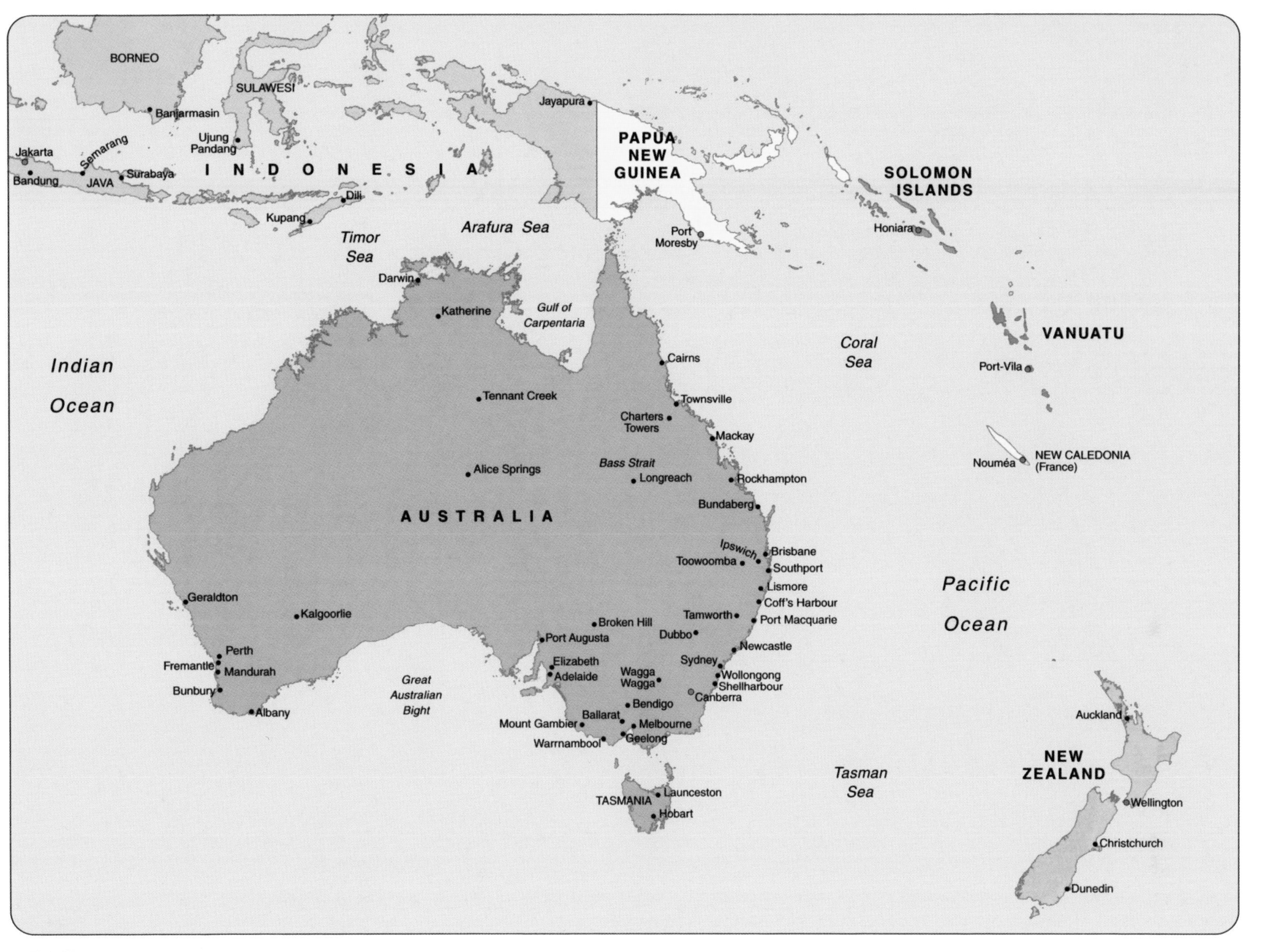

MAP A.7

OCEANIA

MAP 1.1

INTERNATIONAL TRADE VOLUME (MILLIONS OF U.S. DOLLARS)

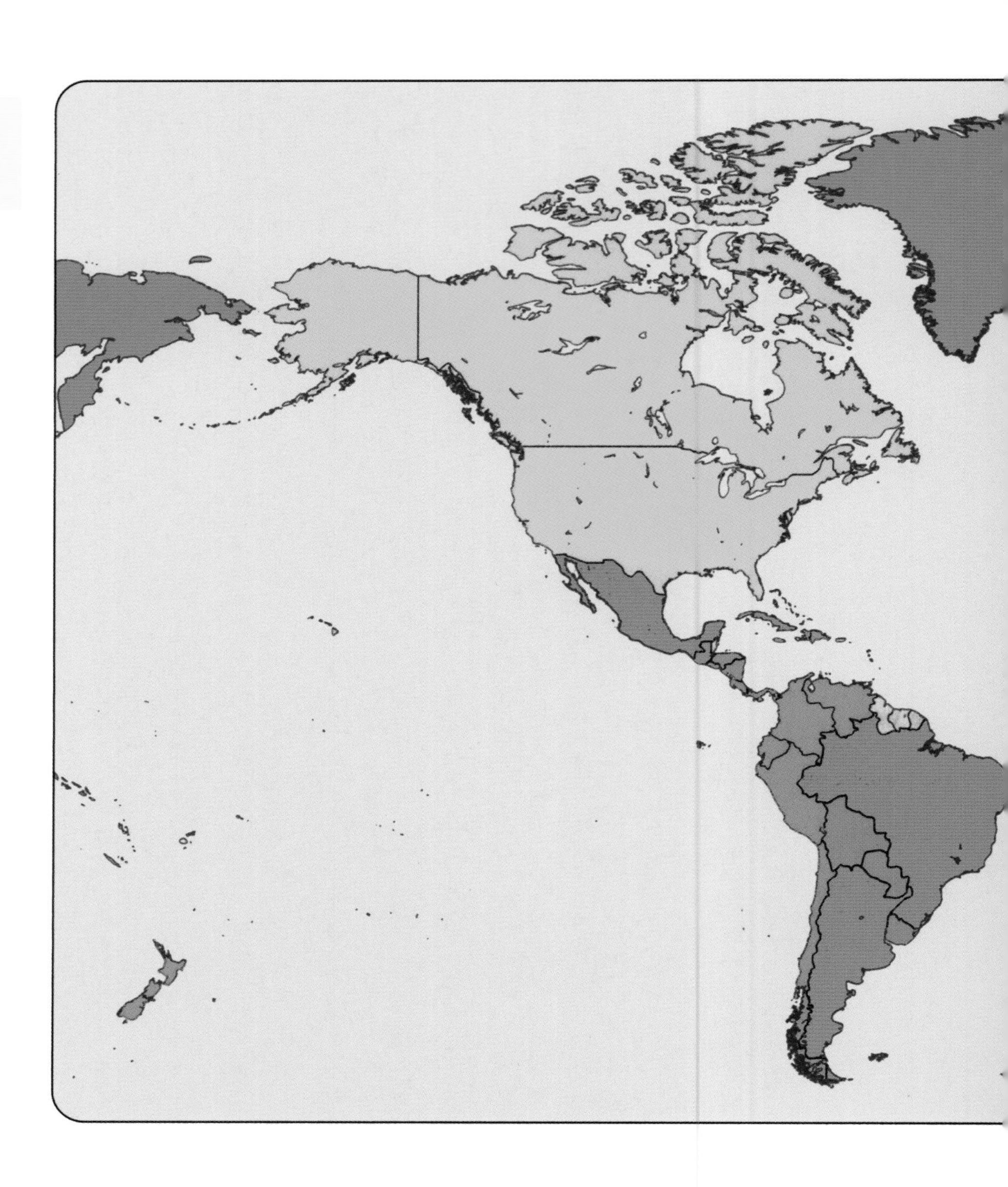

FIGURE 1.1

MAJOR ON-LINE RETAIL SECTORS BY 2003

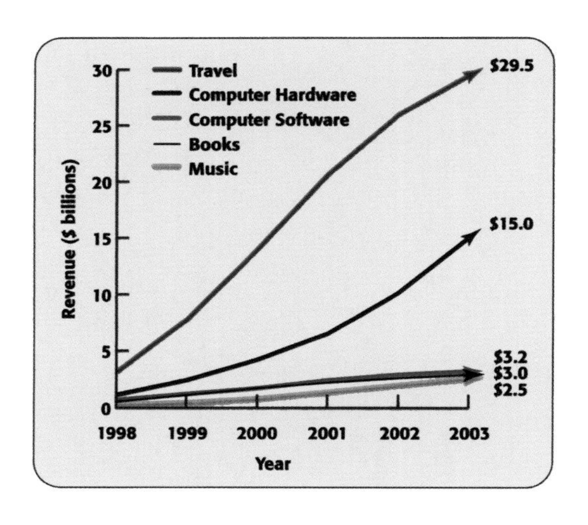

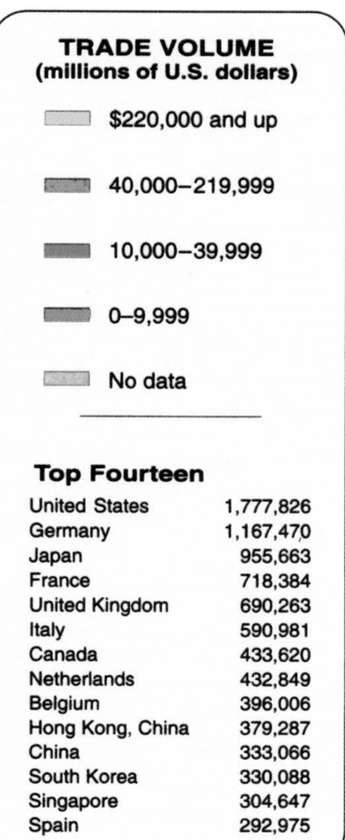

Top Fourteen

United States	1,777,826
Germany	1,167,470
Japan	955,663
France	718,384
United Kingdom	690,263
Italy	590,981
Canada	433,620
Netherlands	432,849
Belgium	396,006
Hong Kong, China	379,287
China	333,066
South Korea	330,088
Singapore	304,647
Spain	292,975

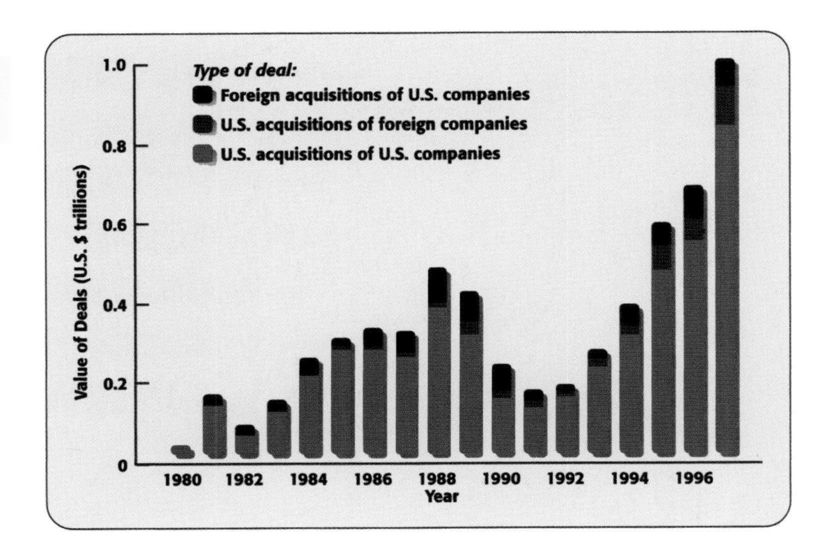

FIGURE 1.2

THE GROWING VALUE OF MERGERS AND ACQUISITIONS

MAP 1.2

FREE TRADE BLOCS OF THE WORLD

Note: Chile and Bolivia are associate members of MERCOSUR.

FIGURE 2.1

PERCENTAGE OF WOMEN-OWNED BUSINESSES

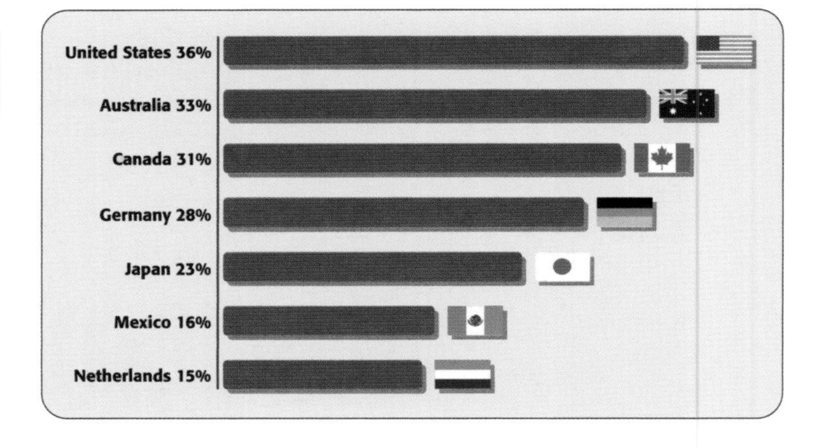

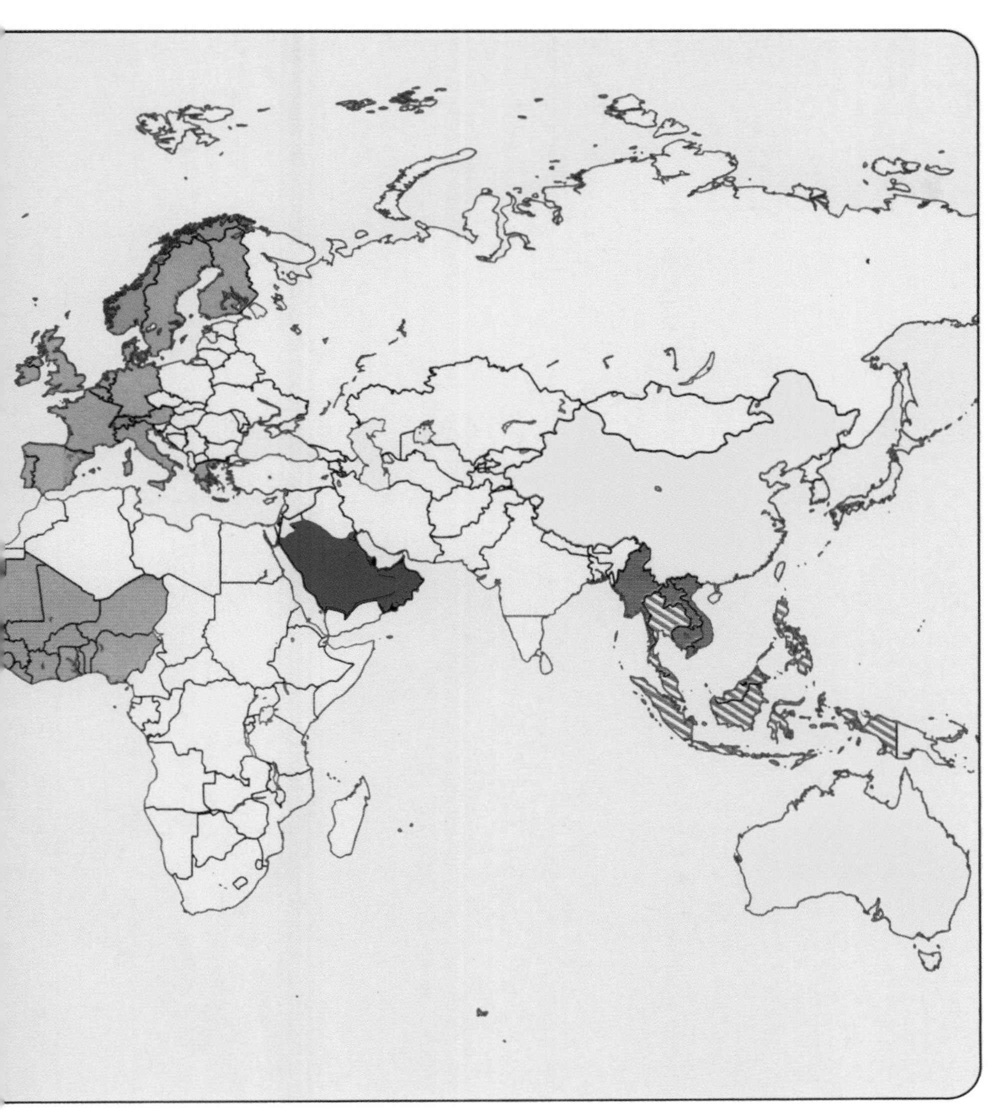

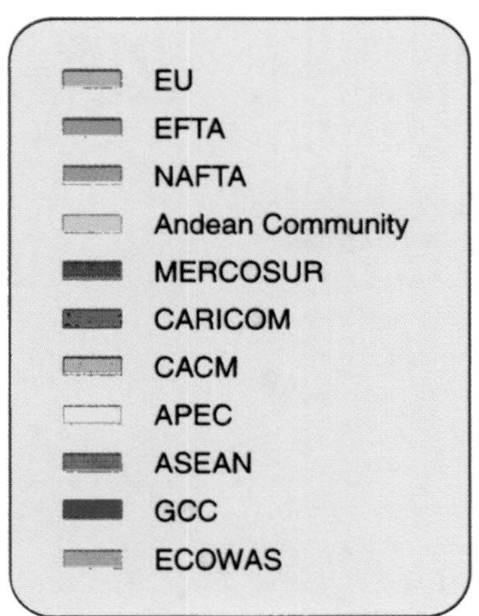

FIGURE 2.4
HOFSTEDE'S DIMENSIONS

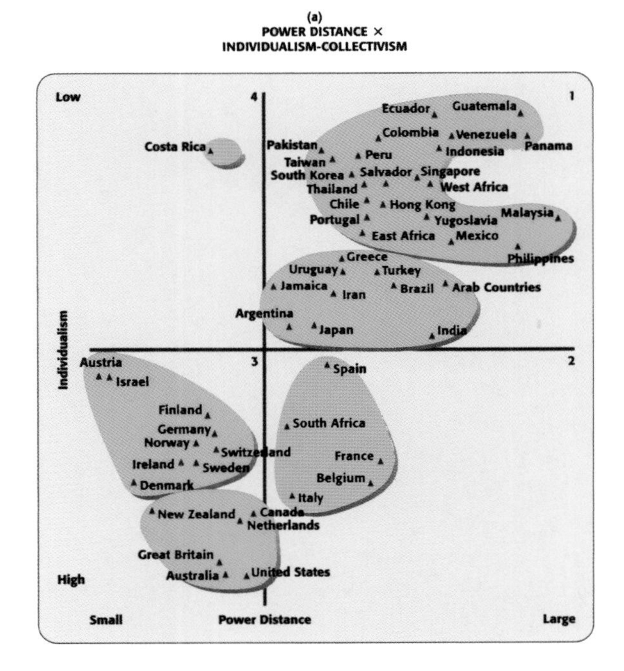

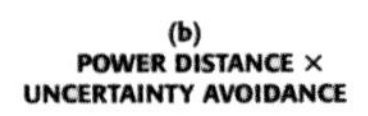

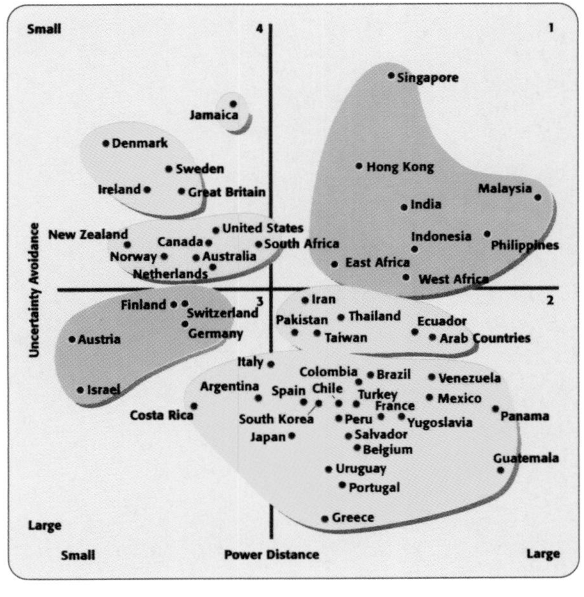

MAP 2.1

MAJOR RELIGIONS OF THE WORLD

Religion is not confined to national political boundaries but can exist in different regions of the world simultaneously. Different religions can also dominate different regions in a single nation. This map shows where the world's major religions are prominent. The map shows several religions in addition to those discussed in this chapter including: **Taoism**, which began in the 100s B.C. in China. Taoists pray to a mixture of deceased humans who displayed extraordinary powers during their lives, and nonhuman spirits embodying various elements of Tao; **Sikhism**, dating back to 1469, teaches breaking the continuous cycle of reincarnation by waking early, cleansing, meditating, and devoting all activites to God; **Animism**, describes all religions involving honoring the souls of deceased humans and worshiping spirits in nature; **Lamaist Buddism** is a Buddhist sect that emphasizes meditation and has as its spiritual leader, the Dalai Lama; and **Southern Buddhism**, the Buddhist sect that is older than Lamaism and stresses following the teachings of the Buddha.

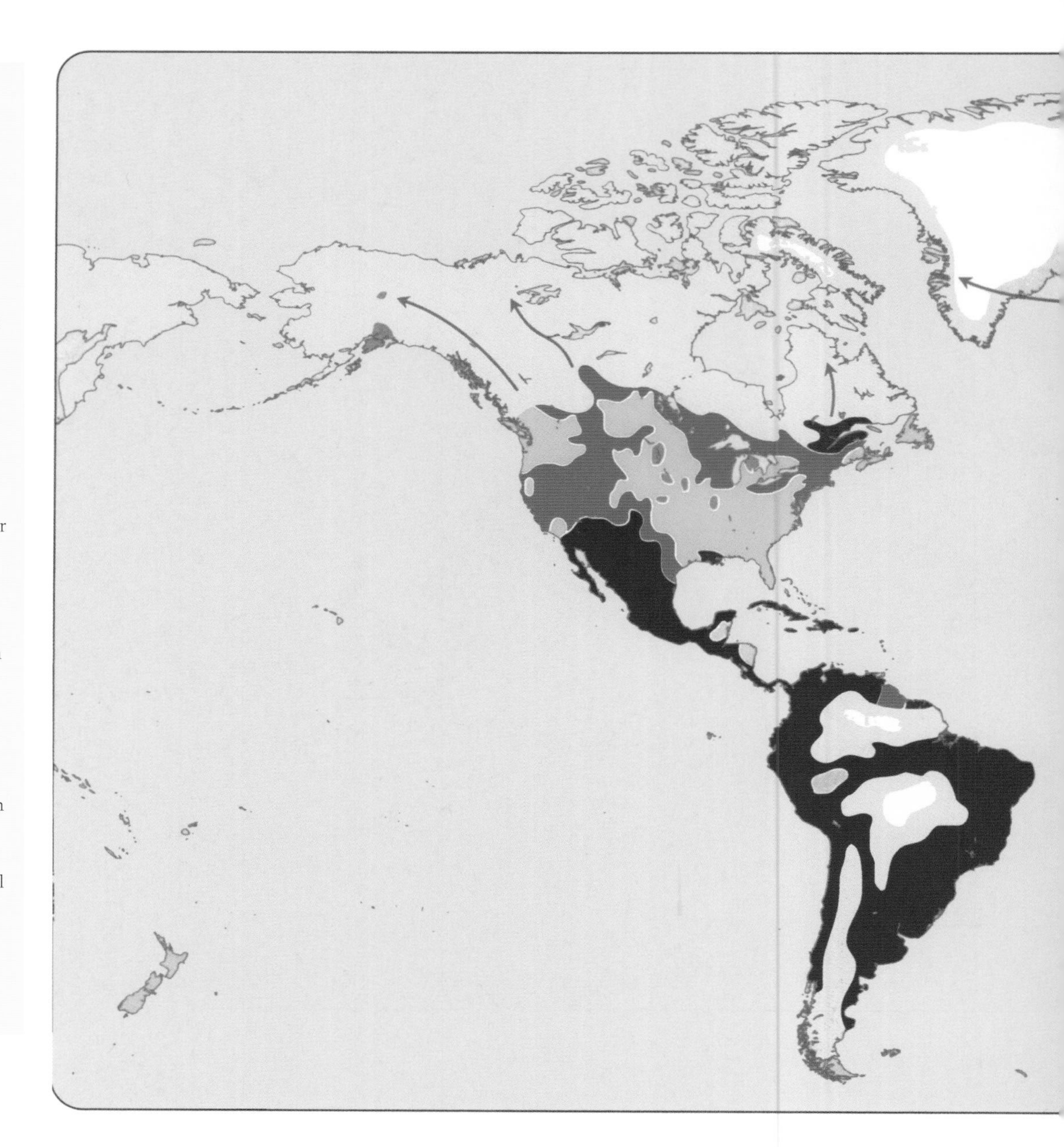

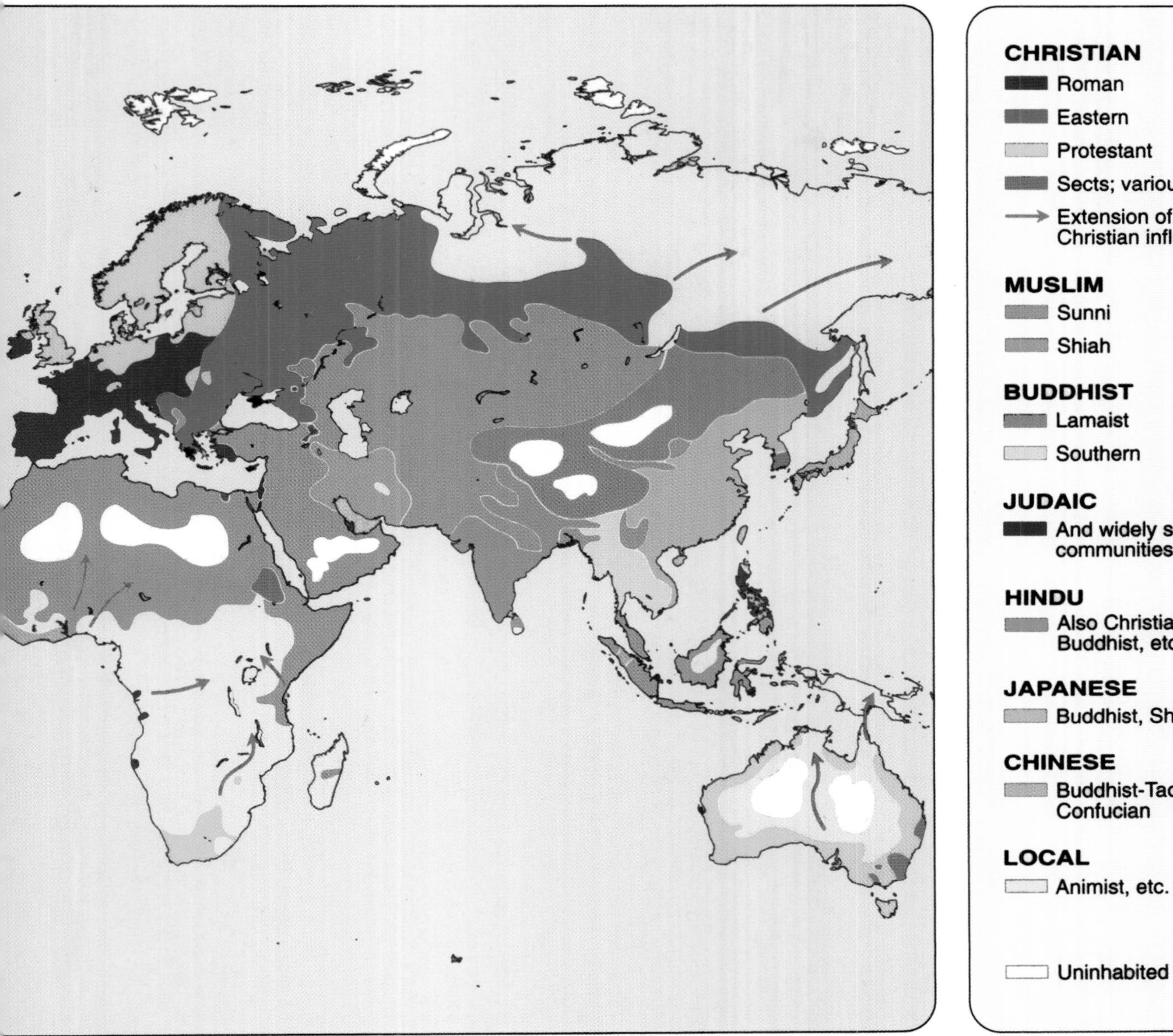

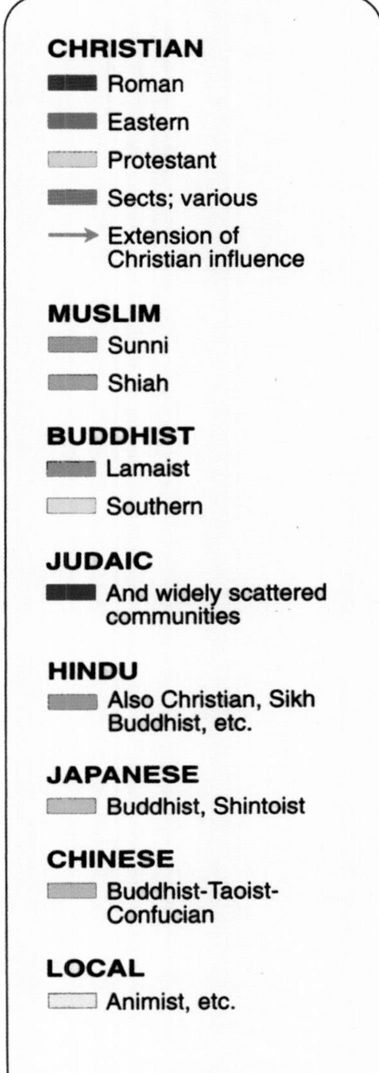

CHRISTIAN
Roman
Eastern
Protestant
Sects; various
Extension of Christian influence
MUSLIM
Sunni
Shiah
BUDDHIST
Lamaist
Southern
JUDAIC
And widely scattered communities
HINDU
Also Christian, Sikh Buddhist, etc.
JAPANESE
Buddhist, Shintoist
CHINESE
Buddhist-Taoist-Confucian
LOCAL
Animist, etc.
Uninhabited

MAP 2.2

A SYNTHESIS OF COUNTRY CLUSTERS

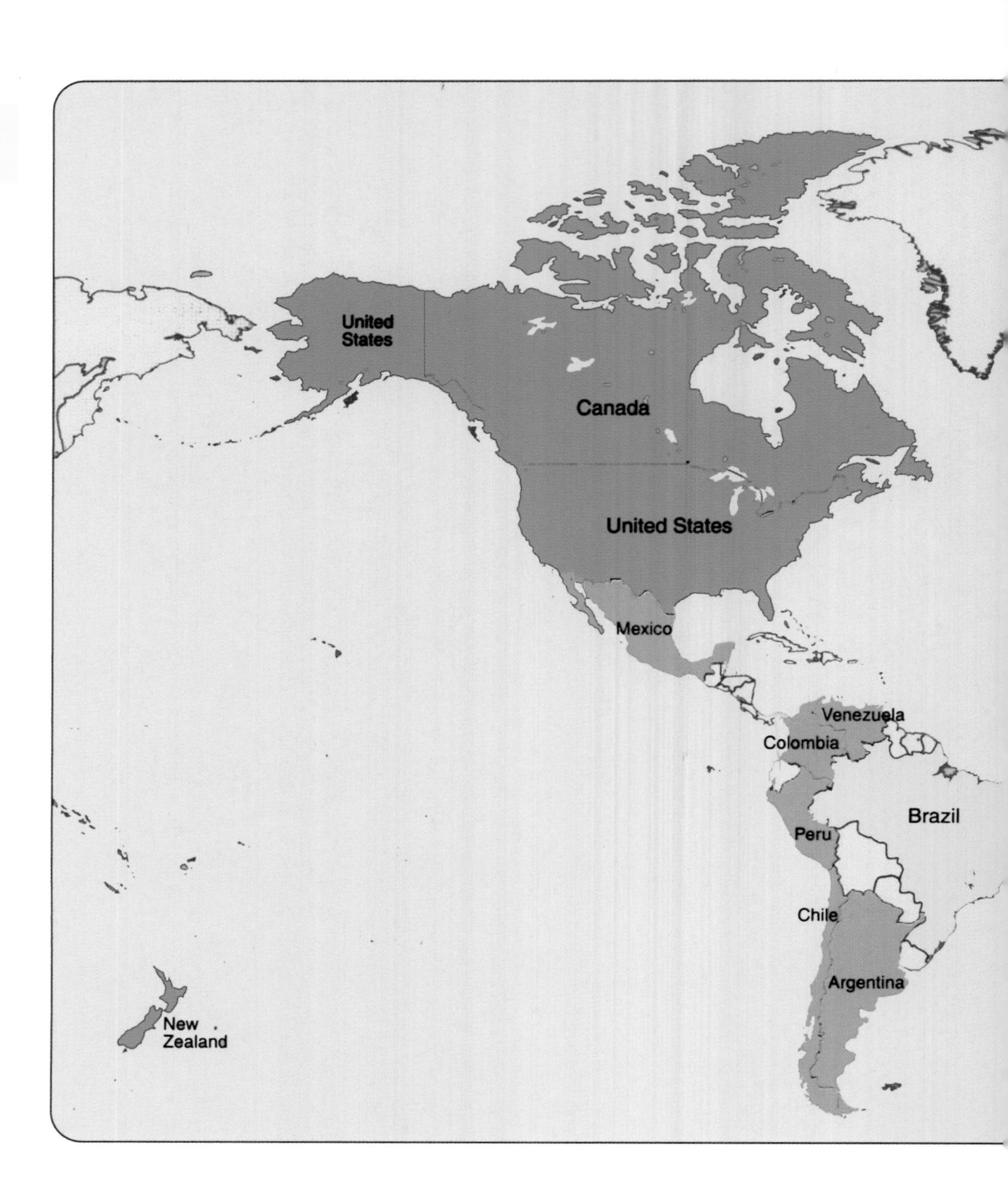

Finland
Sweden
Norway
U.K.
Denmark
Germany
Belgium
France
Austria
Switzerland
Spain
Italy
Greece
Turkey
Israel
Iran
Kuwait
Bahrain
Saudi Arabia
Abu-Dhabi
U.A.E
Oman
India
Hong Kong
Taiwan
Japan
Thailand
Vietnam
Philippines
Malaysia
Singapore
Indonesia
Australia
South Africa

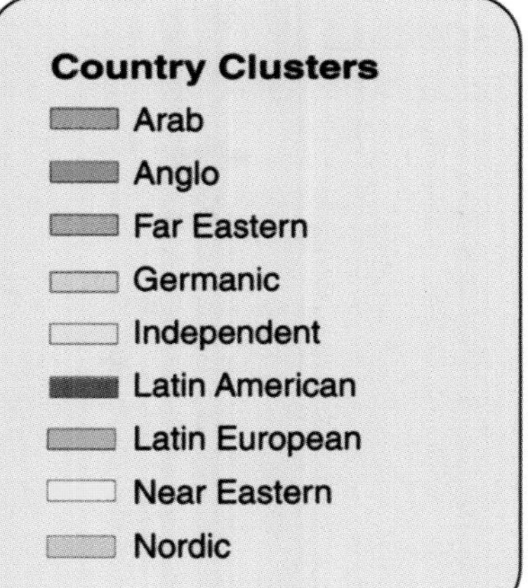
Country Clusters
Arab
Anglo
Far Eastern
Germanic
Independent
Latin American
Latin European
Near Eastern
Nordic

FIGURE 1.3

A GLOBAL PERSPECTIVE ON BUSINESS

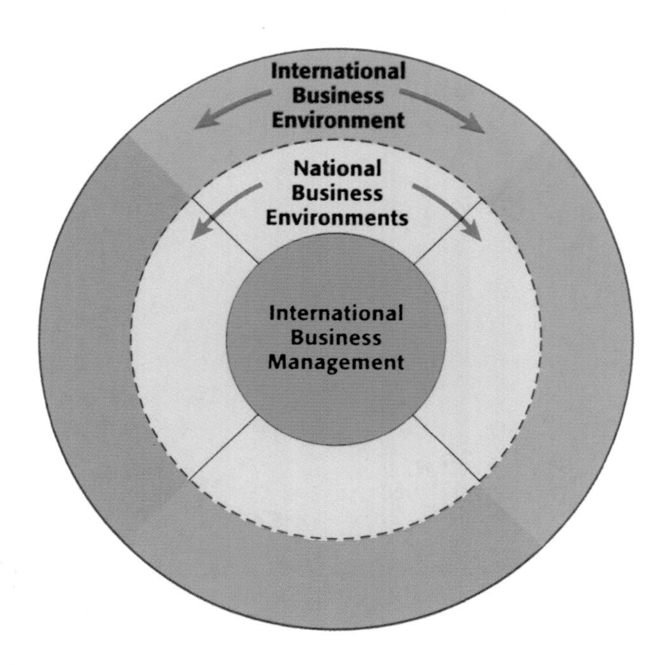

FIGURE 1.5

THE PLAN OF THIS BOOK

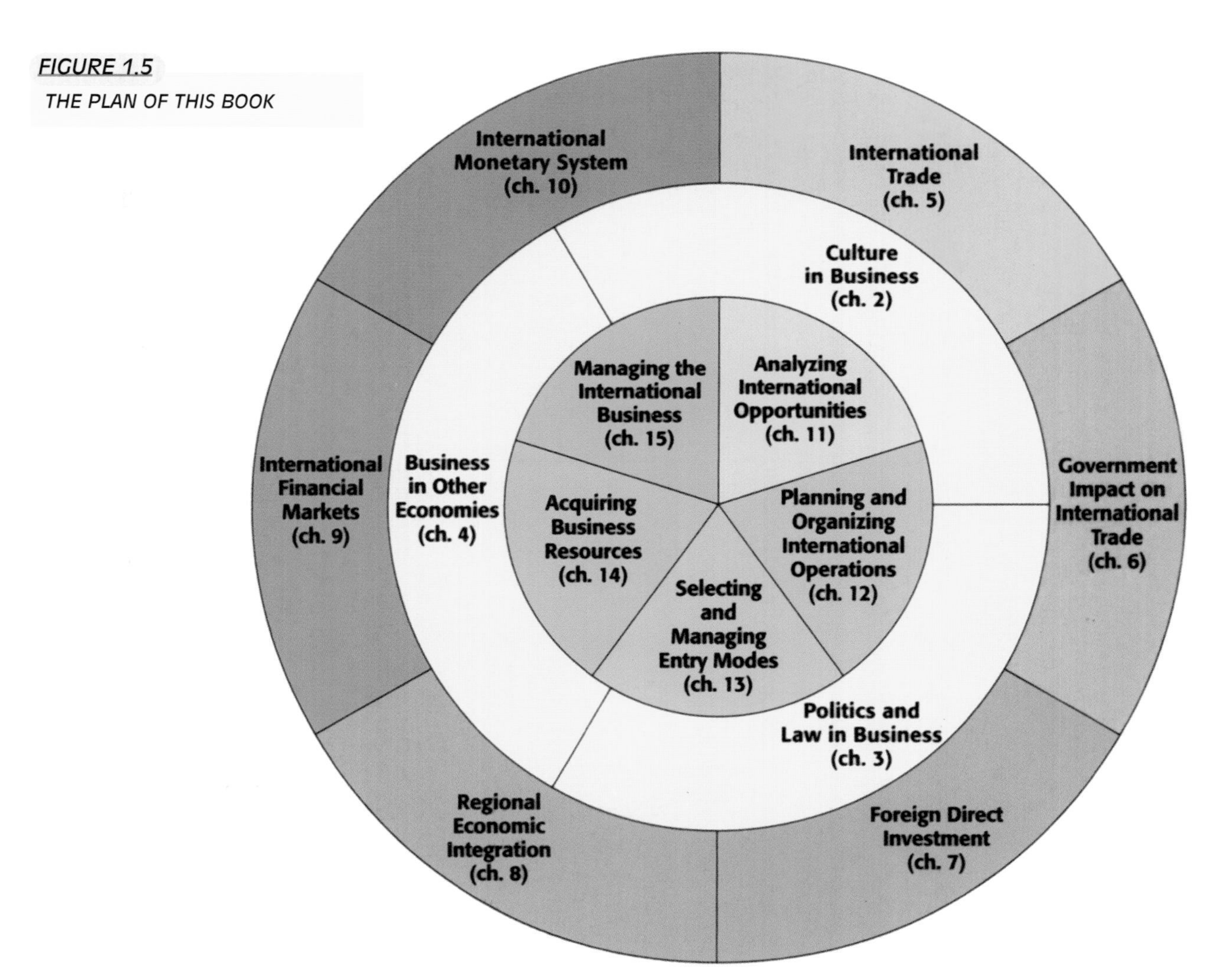

• **Outer Ring:** International Business Environment • **Middle Ring:** National Business Environments
• **Core:** International Business Management

marketplace. Because globalization is bringing companies face-to-face with each other and their global customers, companies need employees who are not blinded by ethnocentricity.

Understanding Culture: Developing Cultural Literacy Globalization demands that everyone involved in business exhibit a certain degree of **cultural literacy**—detailed knowledge about a culture that enables people to live and work within it. Cultural literacy improves the ability to manage employees, market products, and conduct negotiations in other countries. Global brand names like MTV and Gucci provide a competitive advantage, but cultural differences continue to force modifications to suit local markets. Because culture still dictates that many products incorporate local tastes and preferences, cultural literacy brings us closer to customer needs and desires and improves our competitiveness. We discuss different types of cultural training used for developing cultural literacy in Chapter 14.

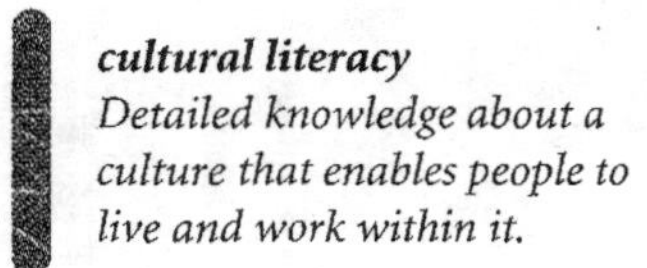
cultural literacy
Detailed knowledge about a culture that enables people to live and work within it.

NATIONAL CULTURE AND SUBCULTURES

Whether rightly or wrongly, we tend to invoke the concept of the *nation-state* when speaking of culture. In other words, we usually refer to British and Indonesian cultures as if all Britons and all Indonesians were culturally identical. Why? Because we have been conditioned to think in terms of *national culture*. But this is at best a generalization. For example, campaigns for Scottish and Welsh independence in Great Britain continue to gain momentum. In remote parts of Indonesia, people build homes in the treetops even as other parts of the nation pursue ambitious economic development programs.

Let's take a closer look at national cultures and the diversity that lies within them.

National Culture Nation-states support and promote the concept of a national culture by building museums and monuments to preserve the legacies of important events and people. In so doing, they affirm the importance of national culture to their citizens and organizations.

Many companies take advantage of the public relations value of supporting national culture. In Russia, for example, where the national budget cannot afford adequate support for the arts, financially sound Russian firms are leading the way in buying Russian art and returning it to Russian museums. Consumers respond to such goodwill activities by purchasing these companies' products.

Nation-states also intervene in business to help preserve their national cultures. Most nations, for example, regulate culturally sensitive sectors of the economy such as filmmaking and broadcasting. In particular, France continues to voice fears that its language is being tainted with English and its media with U.S. programming.[3] To stem the English invasion, new French laws limit the use of English in product packaging and storefront signs. At peak listening times, at least 40 percent of all radio station programming must be reserved for French artists. Similar laws apply to television broadcasting. Recently, the French government even fined the local branch of a U.S. university for failing to provide a French translation on its English-language site on the World Wide Web.

e·biz

Subcultures A group of people who share a unique way of life within a larger, dominant culture is called a **subculture**. Unfortunately, our impressions of the cultures of many nations often do not incorporate the influence of important subcultures. Subcultures can differ from the dominant culture in language, race, lifestyle, values, attitudes, or other characteristics. They often play important roles in forming the national image and in the determination of the business strategies that companies employ.

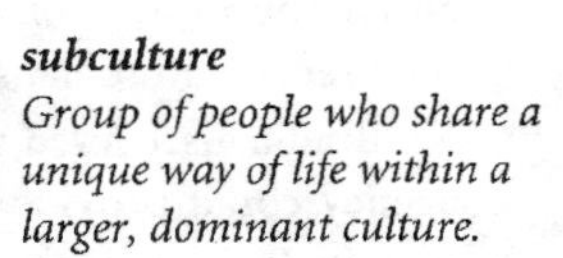
subculture
Group of people who share a unique way of life within a larger, dominant culture.

Subcultures exist in all nations. For example, the official portrait of Chinese culture often ignores the fact that the total population of China is comprised of more than 50 distinct ethnic groups. Decisions regarding product design, packaging, and advertising must consider each group's distinct culture. Marketing directed at Tibetans must respect their unique history and ethnic pride. Tibetans would resent any campaign referring to them as Chinese. Marketing campaigns in China must also acknowledge that Chinese dialects in the Shanghai and Canton regions differ from those of smaller areas in the country's interior. Not everyone is fluent in the official Mandarin dialect.

Firms must take special care when marketing medicines, dangerous chemicals, and other products requiring detailed instructions. If a product's labels and warnings cannot be read and understood by all subcultures, it might be more likely to inflict physical harm than to satisfy a need.

Although nation-states play a role in the development of national culture, political boundaries do not always correspond to cultural boundaries. This means that subcultures sometimes cross national borders. People who live in different nations but share the same subculture can have more in common with one another than with fellow nationals. Arab culture, for instance, extends from northwest Africa to the Middle East. Arabs—who include any of the Semitic peoples who were once native to Saudi Arabia but who now inhabit every surrounding land—also live in Turkey, in many European countries, and in the United States. Because Arabs tend to share attitudes and purchasing behaviors related to Islamic religious beliefs, marketing to Arab subcultures can sometimes be accomplished with a single marketing campaign. A common language (Arabic) also eliminates translation costs and increases the likelihood of correct message interpretation. To see how small businesses can exploit the knowledge of subcultures and cultural literacy, see the Entrepreneurial Focus "Entrepreneurs Respect Culture."

Entrepreneurial Focus

Entrepreneurs Respect Culture

What do Clifford Lichaytoo in the Philippines, Jiri Bradle in the Czech Republic, and Sterry Chong in China possibly have in common? They are small-business owners who have taken risks because they live in cultures that value and reward risk taking. A close look at the businesses founded by these three entrepreneurs shows how cultural forces affect small businesses.

- Clifford Lichaytoo learned the cruel reality of the global economy when he lost textile contracts to competitors in countries like Nicaragua, which have 75 percent lower labor costs. So he started a company in a higher-value-added business—importing premium wines. As Filipinos have prospered, their consumer behavior has begun to resemble that of consumers in other industrialized countries—for example, drinking fine wines, as the French and Italians do.
- Jiri Bradle discovered the value that his new advertising agency could provide Western companies doing business in Prague, capital of the Czech Republic. Having learned some lessons in cultural literacy, Colgate Palmolive hired Bradle to integrate Czech culture into its marketing campaign for Colgate toothpaste.
- Sterry Chong and his brother hope to strike it rich in a U.S.-China joint venture with TCBY (The Country's Best Yogurt). As their spending power has grown, Chinese consumers, like Filipinos, have begun to behave like consumers in any industrialized nation. Because they are in the market for healthier diets, the selection of available goods has widened. The Chongs are exploiting this trend and their thorough understanding of Chinese culture. "Each city," explains Sterry Chong, "is very different; each province has its own culture. You can't just make one single television commercial and broadcast it across the country. You have to find out what the interest is in each city or province." Accordingly, the Chongs are designing yogurt products and flavors to suit the needs of each individual market in the country.

COMPONENTS OF CULTURE

Both the actions of nation-states and the presence of subcultures help define the culture of a group of people. But a people's culture also includes what they consider beautiful and tasteful, their underlying beliefs, their traditional habits, and the ways in which they relate to one another and their surroundings. This section covers the main components of culture: *aesthetics, values* and *attitudes, manners* and *customs, social structure, religion, personal communication, education,* and *physical* and *material environments.*

AESTHETICS

What a culture considers to be in "good taste" in the arts (including music, painting, dance, drama, and architecture), the imagery evoked by certain expressions, and even the symbolism of certain colors is called **aesthetics**.

aesthetics
What a culture considers to be in "good taste" in the arts, the imagery evoked by certain expressions, and the symbolism of certain colors.

Aesthetics are important when a firm considers doing business in another culture. Major blunders can result from selecting inappropriate colors for advertising, product packaging, and even work uniforms. For instance, green is a favorable color in Islam and adorns the national flags of most Islamic nations, including Jordan, Pakistan, and Saudi Arabia. This results in product packaging that is often green to take advantage of this emotional attachment. Across much of Asia, on the other hand, green is associated with sickness. In Europe, Mexico, and the United States, black is the color of death and mourning; in Japan and most of Asia, it's white.

Consider this actual example of the importance of both color imagery and symbolism in marketing. In 1997, Britain transferred administrative control of Hong Kong to the Chinese after its 99-year lease expired. Understandably, the residents of Hong Kong were fearful about what Communist Chinese control would mean for their civil liberties. American Craft Brewing International wished to mark the occasion by brewing a special red-colored lager at its Hong Kong brewery. Because red is a favorite color in China and dawn is the symbol for change, the brewer called its product Red Dawn. For Hong Kong's residents, however, *red* is also seen as the official color of the Chinese Communist Party. Moreover, *dawn* stirs memories of the popular communist song "Dong Fang Hong." These are hardly the images with which Hong Kong residents wanted to relax while pondering the transfer of control to China. As a rule, companies must carefully research product colors and names to be sure they do not evoke any unintended response.[4]

Likewise, music is deeply embedded in culture and should be considered when developing promotions. It can be used in clever and creative ways or in ways that are offensive to the local population. The architecture of buildings and other structures should also be researched to avoid making cultural blunders due to the symbolism of certain shapes and forms.

VALUES AND ATTITUDES

Ideas, beliefs, and customs to which people are emotionally attached are **values**. Values include things like honesty, marital faithfulness, freedom, and responsibility.

values
Ideas, beliefs, and customs to which people are emotionally attached.

Values are important to business because they affect a people's work ethic and desire for material possessions. Whereas certain cultures (say, Singapore) value hard work and material success, others (Greece, for instance) value leisure and a modest lifestyle. The United Kingdom and United States value individual freedom, whereas Japan and South Korea value group consensus. Because values are so important to both individuals and groups, the influx of values from other cultures can be fiercely resisted. Muslims believe drugs, alcohol, and certain kinds of music and literature will undermine important values. Nations under Islamic law (such as Iran and Saudi Arabia) exact severe penalties for the possession of such items as drugs and alcohol.

attitudes
Positive or negative evaluations, feelings, and tendencies that individuals harbor toward objects or concepts.

Attitudes are positive or negative evaluations, feelings, and tendencies that individuals harbor toward objects or concepts. For instance, a Westerner expresses an attitude if he or she were to say, "I do not like the Japanese purification ritual because it involves being naked in a communal bath." Attitudes reflect underlying values. The Westerner quoted above, for instance, might hold conservative beliefs regarding exposure of the body.

Like values, attitudes are learned from role models, including parents, teachers, and religious leaders. Like values, they also differ from one country to another because they are formed within a cultural context. Generally, although values concern only important matters, people hold attitudes toward both important and unimportant aspects of life. And whereas values are quite rigid over time, attitudes are more flexible.

Cultural knowledge can tell a businessperson when products or promotions must be adapted to local preferences that reflect values and attitudes. In most countries, for instance, Virginia Slims fosters an image of its cigarette as a cigarette especially for women. Hence, a recent U.S. ad campaign bearing the slogan "It's a Woman Thing." But because South Korean men find its mild taste appealing and similar to the country's traditional brand, Virginia Slims adapted its advertising plans to exploit this attitude toward its cigarette, using such advertisement tag lines in South Korea as "The Cigarette for the Successful Man."[5] Among the important aspects of life that directly affect business activities, people tend to have different cultural attitudes toward time, work and achievement, and cultural change.

Attitudes toward Time People in many Latin American and Mediterranean cultures are casual about time. They maintain flexible schedules and would rather enjoy their time than sacrifice it to unbending efficiency. Businesspeople, for example, often arrive after scheduled meeting times and prefer to spend time building personal trust before discussing business. Not surprisingly, it usually takes longer to conduct business in these parts of the world than in the United States or northern Europe.

In contrast, people in Japan and the United States typically arrive promptly for meetings, keep tight schedules, and work long hours.[6] The emphasis on using time efficiently reflects the underlying value of hard work in both these countries. However, Japanese and Americans sometimes differ in how they use their work time. Americans, for example, strive toward workplace efficiency and sometimes leave early if the day's tasks are done. This attitude reflects the value that Americans place on producing individual results. In Japan, it is important to look busy in the eyes of others even when business is slow. Japanese workers want to demonstrate their dedication to superiors and co-workers—an attitude grounded in values such as the concern for group cohesion, loyalty, and harmony.

Attitudes toward Work Whereas some cultures display a strong work ethic, others stress a more balanced pace in juggling work and leisure. People in southern France like to say "We work to live, while people in the United States live to work." Work, they say, is for them a means to an end. In the United States, they charge, it is an end in itself. Not surprisingly, the lifestyle in southern France is slower paced. People tend to concentrate on earning enough money to enjoy food, wine, and good times. Businesses practically close down during August, when many workers take month-long paid holidays (usually outside the country). This attitude is unheard of in many Asian countries, including Japan.

The perceived opportunity for success and reward is a strong element in a culture's attitude toward work. People tend to work hard when risk taking is rewarded with low

In the new China, the state-owned sector has been radically downsized. China is in the midst of converting about 300,000 state-owned businesses into shareholder-owned corporations managed to compete on a global scale. Beijing Enterprises, a conglomerate that franchises tourist concessions, is one of thousands of companies trying to survive in a market economy. Such firms support a rapidly growing middle class of independent businesspeople, professionals, and corporate employees whose attitudes toward work and success has changed significantly. You can find out more about Beijing Enterprises, which handles Chinese McDonald's franchises, at ⟨**www.irasia.com/listco/hk/behl/index.htm**⟩.

taxes on profits and when capital is available for new business start-ups. In both the United Kingdom and France, start-ups are considered quite risky, and capital for entrepreneurial ventures is scarce. If at some point an entrepreneur's venture in those countries goes bust, he or she can find it very hard to obtain financing for future projects. The opposite attitude tends to prevail in the United States. Reference to prior bankruptcy in a business plan is sometimes considered valuable learning experience (assuming, of course, that some lessons were learned). As long as U.S. bankers see promising business plans, they are generally willing to loan money.

Today, many European nations are trying to foster an entrepreneurial spirit like that in the United States. If we look at the record on job creation, the reason is simple. For every 100 jobs in the United States 25 years ago, there are now 160; for every 100 jobs in the European Union 25 years ago, there are now 96.[7]

e·biz

The need to compete globally is another strong cultural influence on attitudes toward work. Europeans, for example, have not adopted computer technology in the way companies have in the United States, nor is there any equivalent to the support from the public sector that fostered the Internet in the United States. Over a recent 10-year period, for example, 35 percent of all U.S. investment dollars went into technology; in Britain, the total was 16 percent. U.S. venture capitalists—companies that invest in firms with high growth potential—pumped $2.3 billion into new technology in 1996 alone; in Britain, the total was $1.1 billion. But British and other European firms are beginning to realize that global markets require them to connect to the Internet and forge alliances in Asia and the United States. Venture capitalist firms are sprouting up across Europe with large amounts of capital at their disposal.[8]

Finally, people's attitudes toward work are being affected in countries undergoing transition to free market economies. Employees in many of these nations are no longer satisfied with the old dictatorial ways of doing things and want fulfillment from their jobs. A recent poll of soon-to-be business and engineering graduates in eastern Europe found that 65 percent want their ideal manager to be receptive to their ideas. The students also desire their managers to be highly skilled at their jobs. Thirty-seven percent want managers with solid industry experience and 34 percent want managers

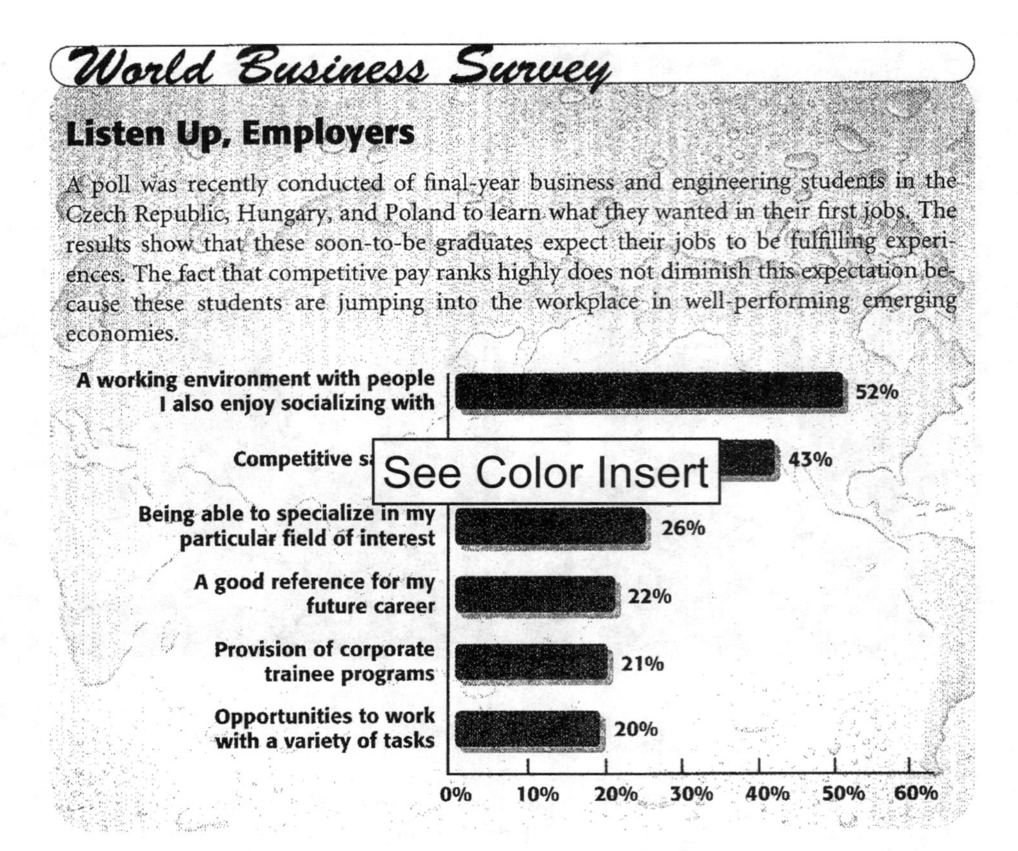

that display rational decision making. For more on what these students desire in their first jobs, see the World Business Survey "Listen Up, Employers."

cultural trait
Anything that represents a culture's way of life, including gestures, material objects, traditions, and concepts.

Attitudes toward Cultural Change A **cultural trait** is anything that represents a culture's way of life, including gestures, material objects, traditions, and concepts. Such traits include bowing to show respect in Japan *(gesture)*, a Buddhist temple in Thailand *(material object)*, relaxing in a *dwaniyah* (tearoom) in Kuwait *(tradition)*, and practicing democracy in the United States *(concept)*. Let's look more closely at how cultures change over time and the roles that international companies play in cultural change.

cultural diffusion
Process whereby cultural traits spread from one culture to another.

Cultural Diffusion The process whereby cultural traits spread from one culture to another is called **cultural diffusion**. *Cultural change* occurs as new traits are accepted and absorbed into a culture. It occurs naturally and, as a rule, gradually. Globalization and technological advances are increasing the pace of both cultural change and diffusion. Satellite television, videoconferencing, and the Internet are increasing the frequency of international contact and exposing people of different nations to new ideas and practices.

e-biz

cultural imperialism
Replacement of one culture's traditions, folk heroes, and artifacts with substitutes from another.

When Companies Change Culture: Cultural Imperialism International companies are often agents of cultural change. As trade and investment barriers fall, for example, consumer-goods and entertainment companies—Coca-Cola, Walt Disney, and MTV among them—are moving into untapped markets. Critics in some target markets charge that in exporting the products of such firms, the United States is practicing **cultural imperialism**—that is, the replacement of one culture's traditions, folk heroes, and artifacts with substitutes from another. Thus products from the Walt Disney

Company and its Disneyland Paris theme park met opposition from the French, who saw them as harmful to local culture. Some central and eastern Europeans resent Ronald McDonald and Mickey Mouse because they so quickly dominate domestic markets. Politicians in Russia have decried the so-called Snickerization of their culture—a snide term that refers to the popularity of Snickers candy bars.

Conservative groups in India criticized the Miss World Pageant when it was recently held in the southern city of Bangalore. Farmers criticized Western corporate sponsors for spreading messages of consumerism. More than 500 women protested the portrayal of women as sex objects and threatened to set themselves on fire if the contest took place. One man reportedly burned himself to death in protest.

Companies must be sensitive to the needs and desires of people in every culture in which they do business. They must not only focus on meeting people's product needs, but on how their activities and products affect people's traditional ways and habits. When resistance to cultural change peaks, it often leads to laws designed to preserve culture. In such cases, rather than view their effects on culture as the inevitable consequence of doing business, companies can take several steps to soften those effects.

Policies and practices that are at odds with deeply held beliefs must be introduced gradually. Managers should consult highly respected individuals in the local culture about such activities (in many developing countries elders play a leading role). There are, of course, volatile times in every society, and trying to inject new values or attitudes into an already unstable environment could be disastrous. Launching new investment projects or implementing unfamiliar management methods are best reserved for times when a culture is experiencing relative stability. In any case, managers should always make clear to workers the benefits of any proposed changes.

When Cultures Change Companies Firms often need to adapt policies and practices to local cultures. Managers from the United States, for instance, often encounter cultural differences that force changes in how they motivate Mexican employees. Although it's a time-consuming practice, they might try *situational management*, a system in which a supervisor walks an employee through every step of an

Among the "have" countries of Eastern Europe, Poland enjoys a booming consumer economy (fueled largely by an annual 24 percent growth in exports). Poles once considered interest payments a capitalist evil, but retail credit has grown by 50 percent in each of the past two years. The credit binge hardly rivals that of the United States in the 1960s, but the changes in lifestyles and values are similar: "I see a lot of people around me going into debt," says one young professional, "so it's less embarrassing now to buy on credit."

assignment or task and monitors the results at each stage. This technique helps employees fully understand the scope of their jobs and clarifies the boundaries of their responsibilities.

Exposure to new cultural practices can have subtle effects on a company's local operations. Many U.S. and European companies are rushing to build factories and encourage an emerging consumer culture in Vietnam. But because Vietnam has a traditionally agriculture-based economy, people's concept of time revolves around the seasons. The local "timepiece" is the monsoon, not the clock. Managers must consequently modify their approach and take a more patient, long-term view of business.

Companies also must often modify employee evaluation and reward systems. In Vietnam, individual criticism must be delivered privately to save employees from losing "face" among co-workers. Individual praise for good performance can be delivered either in private or publicly. But because the Vietnamese place great value on group harmony, an individual can be embarrassed if singled out publicly as superior to the rest of the work unit.[9]

Is a Global Culture Emerging? What does the world's high level of cultural change mean for international business? Are we witnessing the emergence of a new, truly global culture in which people around the world share similar lifestyles, values, and attitudes? The rapid pace of cultural diffusion and high degree of human interaction across national borders are causing cultures to converge to some extent. Perhaps it is even true that people in different cultures are developing similar perspectives on the world and beginning to think along similar lines.[10]

But it seems that just as often as we see signs of an emerging global culture, we discover some new habit unique to one culture. When that happens, we are reminded of the roles of history and tradition in defining culture. Whereas cultural convergence is certainly taking place in some market segments for some products (say the teenage market for pop music), it seems likely that a broader global culture will take a very long time to develop, if ever. Values and attitudes are under continually greater pressure as globalization continues. But because they are so deeply ingrained in culture, their transformation will continue to be gradual rather than abrupt.

MANNERS AND CUSTOMS

When doing business in another culture, it is important to understand a people's manners and customs. At a minimum, understanding manners and customs helps managers to avoid making embarrassing mistakes or offending people. In-depth knowledge, meanwhile, improves the ability to negotiate in other cultures, market products to them effectively, and manage international operations. Let's explore some of the important differences in manners and customs around the world.

manners
Appropriate ways of behaving, speaking, and dressing in a culture.

Manners Appropriate ways of behaving, speaking, and dressing in a culture are called **manners**. In Arab cultures from the Middle East to northwest Africa, one does not extend a hand to greet an older person unless the elder first offers the greeting. In going first, a younger person would be displaying bad manners. Moreover, because Arab culture considers the left hand the "toilet hand," using it to pour tea or serve a meal is considered very bad manners.

Conducting business during meals is common practice in the United States. In Mexico, however, it is poor manners to bring up business at mealtime unless the host does so first. Business discussions typically resume when coffee and brandy arrive. Likewise, toasts in the United States tend to be casual and sprinkled with lighthearted humor. A similar toast in Mexico, where it should be philosophical and full of passion, would be offensive.[11]

Customs When habits or ways of behaving in specific circumstances are passed down through generations, they become **customs**. They differ from manners in that they define appropriate habits or behaviors in *specific* situations. Sharing food gifts during the Islamic holy month of Ramadan is a custom, as is the Japanese tradition of throwing special parties for young women and men who turn age 20. We now define two types of customs and see how instances of each vary around the world.

customs
Habits or ways of behaving in specific circumstances that are passed down through generations in a culture.

Folk and Popular Customs A **folk custom** is behavior, often dating back several generations, that is practiced within a homogeneous group of people. The wearing of turbans by Muslims in southern Asia and the art of belly dancing in Turkey are folk customs.

folk custom
Behavior, often dating back several generations, that is practiced within a homogeneous group of people.

A **popular custom** is behavior shared by a heterogeneous group or by several groups. Popular customs can exist either in just one culture or in two or more cultures at the same time. Wearing blue jeans and playing golf are both popular customs. Many folk customs that have spread by cultural diffusion to other regions have developed into popular customs.

popular custom
Behavior shared by a heterogeneous group or by several groups.

We can distinguish between folk and popular food. Popular Western-style fast food, for instance, is rapidly replacing folk food around the world. In many Asian countries, widespread acceptance of "burgers 'n' fries" (born in the United States), and "fish 'n' chips" (born in Britain) is actually altering deep-seated dietary traditions, especially among young people. They are even becoming part of home-cooked meals in Japan and South Korea.

One custom that is similar across cultures is children's play patterns. Companies like Mattel take advantage of children's interest in similar types of toys. Although it relies on managers in each country to adapt promotions to local culture and languages, Mattel often markets standardized products globally.

The Business of Gift Giving Although giving token gifts to business and government associates is customary in many countries, the proper type of gift varies. A knife, for example, should not be offered to associates in Russia, France, or Germany, where it signals the severing of a relationship. In Japan, gifts must be wrapped in such a delicate way that it is wise to ask someone trained in the practice to do the honors. It is also Japanese custom not to open a gift in front of the gift giver. Tradition dictates that the giver protest that the gift is something small and unworthy of the recipient. In turn, the recipient waits until later to open the gift so that the giver is not embarrassed by the gift's insignificance. Remember, however, that this tradition does not endorse trivial gifts; it is simply a custom.

On the other hand, large gifts to business associates sometimes raise suspicion. Cultures differ in their legal and ethical rules against giving or accepting bribes. The U.S. Foreign Corrupt Practices Act, which prohibits companies from giving large gifts to win business favors, applies to U.S. firms operating at home *and* abroad. In many cultures, however, bribery is woven into a social fabric that has worn well for centuries. In Germany, bribe payments may even qualify for tax deductions.[12] However, the issue remains controversial. Although governments around the world are adopting stricter measures to control bribery, in some cultures large gifts continue to be an effective means of obtaining contracts, entering markets, and securing protection from global competition.

SOCIAL STRUCTURE

social structure
A culture's fundamental organization, including its groups and institutions, its system of social positions and their relationships, and the process by which its resoursces are distributed.

Social structure embodies a culture's fundamental organization, including its groups and institutions, its system of social positions and their relationships, and the process by which its resources are distributed. Naturally, social structure affects business decisions ranging from production-site selection to advertising methods and the costs of doing business in a country. Three important elements of social structure differ across cultures: *social group associations*, *social status*, and *social mobility*.

social group
Collection of two or more people who identify and interact with one another.

Social Group Associations People in all cultures associate themselves with a variety of **social groups**—collections of two or more people who identify and interact with one another. Social groups contribute to each individual's identity and self-image. Two groups that play especially important roles in affecting business activity everywhere are *family* and *gender*.*

Family There are two different types of family groups:

- The *nuclear family* consists of a person's immediate relatives, including parents, brothers, and sisters. This concept of family prevails in Australia, Canada, the United States, and much of Europe.
- The concept of the *extended family* broadens the nuclear family to include grandparents, aunts and uncles, cousins, and relatives through marriage. It is more important as a social group in much of Asia, the Middle East, North Africa, and Latin America.

Extended families can present some interesting situations for businesspeople unfamiliar with the concept. In some cultures, owners and managers in extended families obtain supplies and materials from another company in which someone in the family works before looking elsewhere. Gaining entry into such family arrangements can be difficult because quality and price are not sufficient motives to ignore family ties.

In extended-family cultures, managers and other employees often try to find jobs for relatives inside their own companies. This practice can present a challenge to the human resource operations of a Western company, which typically must establish explicit policies on nepotism (the practice of hiring relatives).

Gender Let's first define *gender*. Gender refers to socially learned traits associated with, and expected of, men or women. Gender refers to such socially learned behaviors and attitudes as styles of dress and activity preferences. It is not the same thing as sex, which refers to the biological fact that a person is either male or female.

Although many countries have made great strides toward gender equality in the workplace, others have not. For instance, countries operating under Islamic law sometimes segregate women and men in schools, universities, and social activities, and restrict women to certain professions. Sometimes they are allowed teaching careers but only in all-female classrooms. At other times they can be physicians but for female patients only.

In Japan, women have traditionally been denied equal opportunity in the workplace. While men held nearly all positions of responsibility, women generally served as office clerks and administrative assistants until their mid to late twenties when they were expected to marry and stay at home tending to family needs. Although this is still largely true today, progress is being made in expanding the role of women in Japan's business community. Figure 2.1 shows that women own 23 percent of all businesses in Japan. But many of these businesses are very small and do not carry a great deal of economic clout. The figure shows that greater gender equality prevails in Australia, Canada, Germany, and the United States. However, women in these countries still tend to earn less money than men in similar positions and are sometimes subjected to sexual harassment.

*We put these two "groups" together for the sake of convenience. Strictly speaking, a gender is not a group. Sociologists regard it as a category—people who share some status. A key to group membership is mutual *interaction*. Individuals in categories know that they are not alone in holding a particular status, but the vast majority remain strangers to one another.

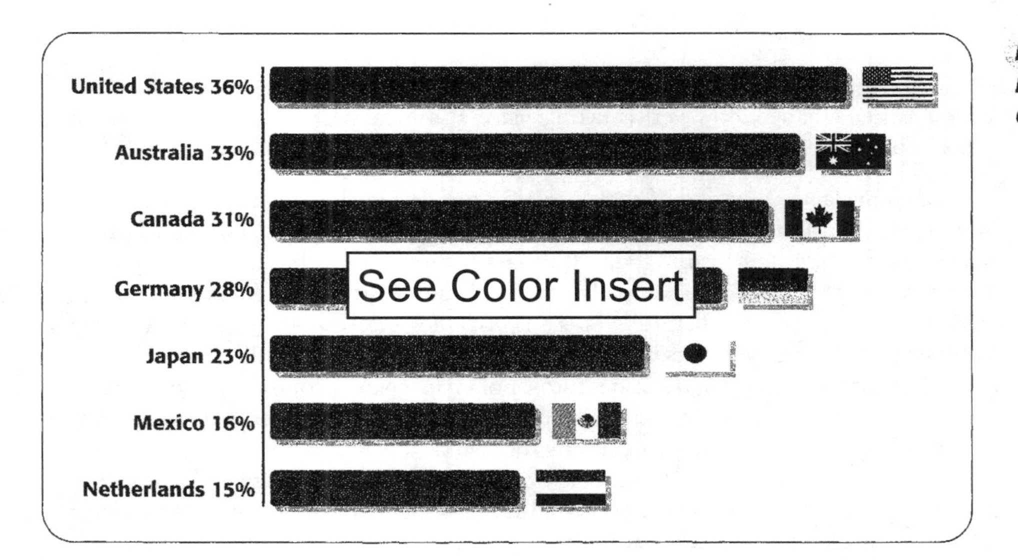

FIGURE 2.1
PERCENTAGE OF WOMEN-OWNED BUSINESSES

Social Status Another important aspect of social structure is the way a culture divides its population according to *status*—that is, according to positions within the structure. Although some cultures have only a few categories, others have many. The process of ranking people into social layers or classes is called **social stratification**. Class membership places individuals on a sort of "social ladder" that tends to persist across cultures.

social stratification
Process of ranking people into social layers or classes.

Social status is normally determined by one or more of the following three factors: family heritage, income, and occupation. In most societies, the highest social layers are occupied by royalty, government officials, and top business leaders. Scientists, medical doctors, and others with a university education occupy the middle rung. Below are those with vocational training or a secondary-school education that dominate the manual and clerical occupations. Although rankings are fairly stable, they can and do change over time. For example, because Confucianism (a major Chinese religion) stresses a life of learning, Chinese culture frowned on businesspeople for centuries. In modern China, however, those who have obtained wealth and power through business are now counted among those who are important role models for young people.

Social Mobility Moving to a higher social class is easy in some cultures and difficult or impossible in others. **Social mobility** is the ease with which individuals can move up or down a culture's social ladder. For much of the world's population today, one of two systems regulates social mobility: a *caste system* or a *class system*.

social mobility
Ease with which individuals can move up or down a culture's social ladder.

Caste Systems A **caste system** is a system of social stratification in which people are born into a social ranking, or *caste*, with no opportunity for social mobility. India is the classic example of a caste culture. Little social interaction occurs between castes, and marrying out of caste is taboo. Opportunities for work and advancement are defined within the system and certain occupations are reserved for members of each caste. Because personal clashes would be inevitable, a member of one caste cannot supervise someone of a higher caste. The caste system forces Western companies to make some hard ethical decisions when entering the Indian marketplace. For example, should they adjust to local human resource policies or import their own because they think of them as so-called "more developed?"

caste system
System of social stratification in which people are born into a social ranking, or caste, *with no opportunity for social mobility.*

Although the Indian constitution *officially* bans discrimination by caste, its influence persists. Change, however, is taking place at a breakneck pace in India, and as globalization introduces new values, the social system will undoubtedly adapt.

class system
System of social stratification in which personal ability and actions decide social status and mobility.

Class Systems A system of social stratification in which personal ability and actions decide social status and mobility is a **class system**. It is the most common form of social stratification in the world today. But class systems vary in the amount of mobility they allow. Highly class-conscious cultures offer less mobility and, not surprisingly, experience greater class conflict. In Western Europe, for instance, wealthy families have retained power for generations by restricting social mobility. As a result, they must deal with class conflict that often translates into labor-management conflict and so increases the cost of doing business. Strikes and property damage are common today when European companies announce plant closings or layoffs.

Conversely, lower levels of class consciousness encourage mobility and lessen conflict. Most U.S. citizens, for instance, share the belief that hard work can improve living standards and social status. They attribute higher status to greater income or wealth, but

MAP 2.1
MAJOR RELIGIONS OF THE WORLD
Religion is not confined to national political boundaries but can exist in different regions of the world simultaneously. Different religions can also dominate different regions in a single nation. This map shows where the world's major religions are prominent. The map shows several religions in addition to those discussed in this chapter including: **Taoism**, which began in the 100s B.C. in China. Taoists pray to a mixture of deceased humans who displayed extraordinary powers during their lives, and nonhuman spirits embodying various elements of Tao; **Sikhism**, dating back to 1469, teaches breaking the continuous cycle of reincarnation by waking early, cleansing, meditating, and devoting all activities to God; **Animism**, describes all religions involving honoring the souls of deceased humans and worshiping spirits in nature; **Lamaist Buddhism** is a Buddhist sect that emphasizes meditation and has as its spiritual leader, the Dalai Lama; and **Southern Buddhism**, the Buddhist sect that is older than Lamaism and stresses following the teachings of the Buddha.

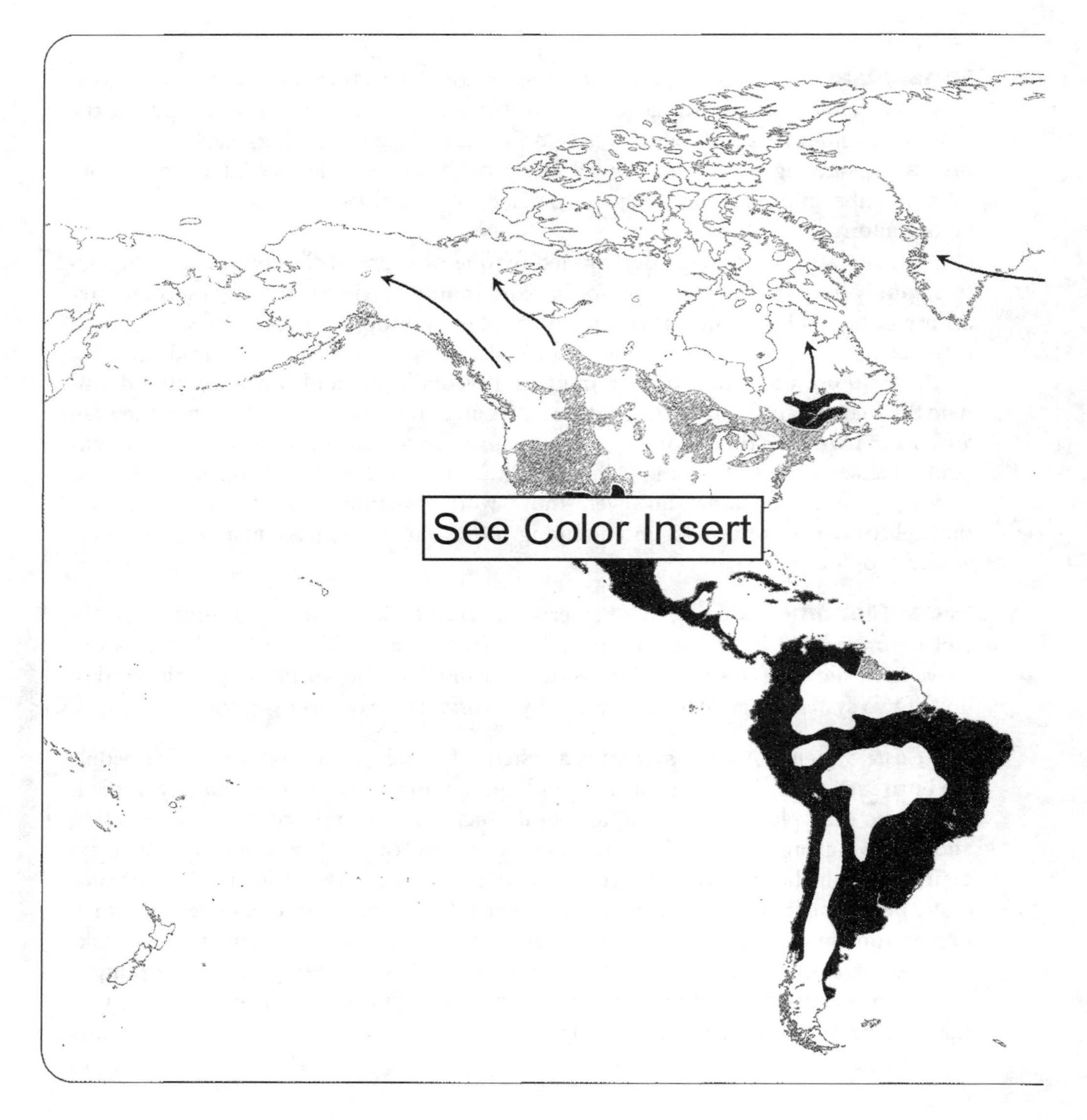

often with little regard for family background. Material well-being is important primarily because it affirms or improves status. A more cooperative atmosphere in the workplace tends to prevail when people feel that a higher social standing is within their reach.

RELIGION

Human values often derive from religious beliefs. Different religions take different views of work, savings, and material goods. Understanding why they do so helps us to understand why companies from certain cultures are more competitive than companies from other cultures. It also helps us understand why some countries develop more slowly than others do. Knowing how religion affects business practices is especially important in countries with religious governments.

Map 2.1 shows where the world's major religions are practiced. In the following sections, we explore several of these religions—Christianity, Islam, Hinduism, Buddhism, Confucianism, Judaism, and Shinto—to examine their effects, both positive and negative, on international business activity.

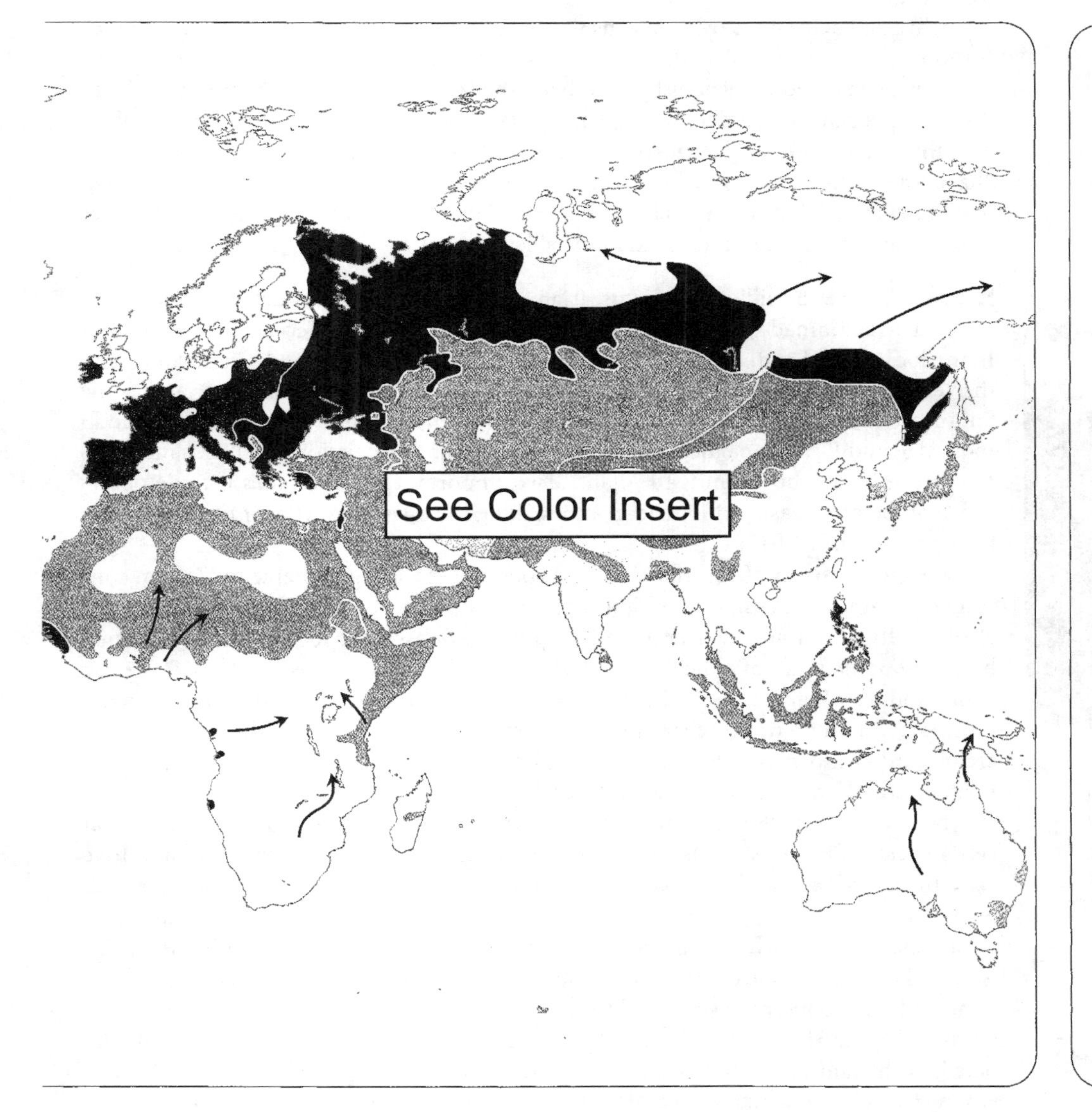

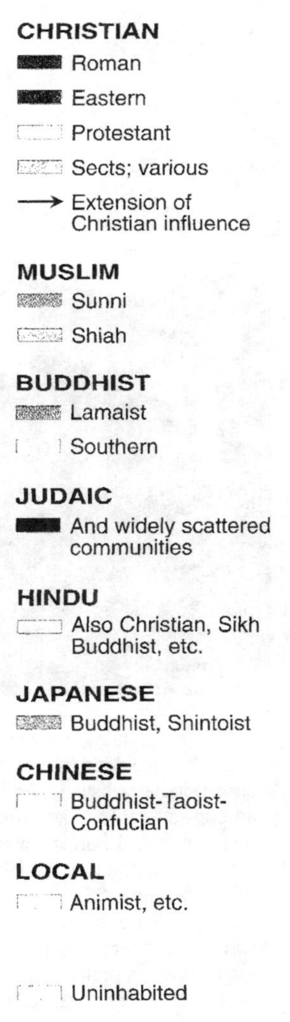

Christianity Christianity was born in Palestine nearly 2,000 years ago among Jews who believed that God sent Jesus of Nazareth to be their savior. Christianity now boasts more than 300 denominations, but most Christians belong to the Roman Catholic, Protestant, or Eastern Orthodox churches. With over 1.7 billion followers, Christianity is the world's single largest religion.

The Roman Catholic faith asks its followers to refrain from placing material possessions above God and others. Protestants believe that salvation comes from faith in God and that hard work gives glory to God—a tenet known widely as the Protestant work ethic. Many historians believe this conviction to be a main factor in the development of capitalism and free enterprise in nineteenth-century Europe.

Christian organizations sometimes get involved in social causes that affect business policy. For example, the political wings of some Christian groups have recently called for boycotts against the Walt Disney Company. Among other things, some conservative Christians have charged that in portraying young people as rejecting parental guidance, Disney films impede the moral development of young viewers worldwide.

Christian activism is by no means limited to the United States. In 1998, the French Bishops' Conference sued Volkswagen-France over a billboard ad that, according to the conference, insulted Christians by parodying the famous image of Leonardo Da Vinci's *The Last Supper*. The conference explained that it was reacting to increasing use of sacred things in advertising throughout Europe. "Advertising experts," said a spokesman, "have told us that ads aim for the sacred in order to shock because using sex does not work anymore." Volkswagen halted the $16 million campaign in response to the power of the church to mold opinion and marshal legal resources.[13]

In Islamic countries, where alcohol is forbidden, soft drinks are a popular substitute. And among soft drinks Coke is the preferred brand, hands down. Coke now sells a billion drinks per day—2 percent of the whole world's daily beverage consumption. Eighty percent of the company's profits come from outside the United States. The Arabic sign in this photo is read from right to left.

Islam With 925 million adherents, Islam is the world's second-largest religion. The prophet Muhammad founded Islam around the year 600 in Mecca, the holy city of Islam located in Saudi Arabia. Islam developed from Judaism and Christianity and thrives in northwestern Africa, the Middle East, Central Asia, Pakistan, and some Southeast Asian nations, including Indonesia. Muslim concentrations are also found in most U.S. and European cities. The word *Islam* means "submission to Allah," and *Muslim* means "one who submits to Allah." Two important religious rites include observance of the holy season of Ramadan and making the pilgrimage (the *Hajj*) to Mecca at least once in one's lifetime.

Religion strongly affects the kinds of goods and services acceptable to Muslim consumers. Islam, for example, prohibits the consumption of alcohol and pork. Popular alcohol substitutes are soda pop, coffee, and tea. Substitutes for pork include lamb, beef, and poultry (all of which must be slaughtered in a prescribed way). Because hot coffee and tea often play ceremonial roles in Muslim nations, the markets for them are quite large. Because usury (charging interest for money lent) violates the laws of Islam, credit card companies collect management fees rather than interest, and each cardholder's credit line is limited to an amount held on deposit.[14]

Nations governed by Islamic law (see Chapter 3) sometimes segregate the sexes at certain activities and locations such as in schools. In Saudi Arabia, women cannot drive cars. In orthodox Islamic nations, men cannot conduct market research surveys with women at home unless they are family members. Women visiting Islamic cultures need to be especially sensitive to Islamic beliefs and customs. In Iran, for instance, the Ministry of Islamic Guidance and Culture posts a reminder to visiting female journalists: "The body is a tool for the spirit and the spirit is a divine song. The holy tool should not be used for sexual intentions." Although the issue of *hejab* (Islamic dress) is hotly debated, both Iranian and non-Iranian women are officially expected to wear body-concealing garments and scarves over their hair (which is considered sexually alluring).[15]

Hinduism Formed around 4,000 years ago in present-day India, where over 90 percent of its nearly 690 million adherents live, Hinduism is the world's oldest religion. It is also the majority religion of Nepal and a secondary religion in Bangladesh, Bhutan, and Sri Lanka. Considered by some to be a way of life rather than a religion, Hinduism recalls no founder and recognizes no central authority or spiritual leader. Integral to the Hindu faith is the caste system described earlier.

Hindus believe in reincarnation—the rebirth of the human soul at the time of death. For many Hindus the highest goal of life is *moksha*—escaping from the cycle of reincarnation and entering a state of eternal happiness called *nirvana.* Hindus do not eat or willfully harm any living creature because it may be a reincarnated human soul. Because Hindus consider cows sacred animals they do not eat beef. However, consuming milk is considered a means of religious purification. Firms like McDonald's must work closely with government and religious officials to respect Hindu beliefs. In many Hindu regions, McDonald's has removed all beef products from its menu and prepares vegetable and fish products in separate kitchen areas.

In India, there have been attacks on Western consumer-goods companies in the name of preserving Indian culture and Hindu beliefs. Pepsi bottles have been smashed and posters burned, and local officials shut down a KFC restaurant for a time. Although it currently operates in India, Coca-Cola once left the market completely rather than succumb to demands that it must reveal its secret formula to authorities. India's investment environment has improved greatly in recent years. Yet labor-management relations have deteriorated to such a degree that regular strikes cut deeply into productivity. India, for example, makes just five cars per worker per year, compared to a global standard of forty.[16]

Buddhism Buddhism was founded about 2,600 years ago in India by a Hindu prince named Siddhartha Gautama. Today, Buddhism has approximately 311 million followers, mostly in such Asian nations as China, Tibet, Korea, Japan, Vietnam, and Thailand. There also are small numbers of Buddhists in Europe and North and South America. Although founded in India, Buddhism has relatively few adherents there, and unlike Hinduism, it rejects the sort of caste system that dominates Indian society. But like Hinduism, Buddhism promotes a life centered on spiritual rather than worldly matters. Buddhists seek *nirvana* (escape from reincarnation) through charity, modesty, compassion for others, restraint from violence, and general self-control.

Although monks at many rural temples are devoted to lives of meditation and discipline, many Buddhist priests are dedicated to lessening the burden of human suffering. They have financed schools and hospitals across Asia and have been active in worldwide peace movements. In Tibet, where most people still acknowledge the exiled Dalai Lama as the spiritual and political head of the Buddhist culture, the Chinese Communist government suppresses allegiance to any outside authority. Similarly, the official Catholic Church of China must reject the principle of the pope as supreme leader. In the United States, a coalition of religious groups, human rights advocates, and supporters of the Dalai Lama have pressed the U.S. Congress to apply economic sanctions against countries that, like China, are judged to practice religious persecution.[17]

Confucianism An exiled politician and philosopher named Kung-fu-dz (pronounced *Confucius* in English) began teaching his ideas in China nearly 2,500 years ago. Today, China is home to most of Confucianism's 150 million followers. Confucian thought is also ingrained in the cultures of Japan, South Korea, and nations with large numbers of ethnic Chinese, including Singapore.

South Korean business practice reflects Confucian thought in its rigid organizational structure and unswerving reverence for authority. Whereas Korean employees do not question strict chains of command, non-Korean managers and workers often feel differently. Efforts to apply Korean-style management in overseas subsidiaries have caused some high-profile disputes with U.S. executives and even physical confrontations with factory workers in Vietnam.[18]

Some observers contend that the Confucian work ethic and educational commitment helped spur east Asia's phenomenal economic growth. But others respond that the link between culture and economic growth is weak. They argue that economic, historical, and international factors are at least as important as culture.[19]

Chinese leaders distrusted Confucianism for centuries because they believed that it stunted economic growth. Likewise, many Chinese despised merchants and traders because their main objective (earning money) violated Confucian beliefs. As a result, many Chinese businesspeople moved to Indonesia, Malaysia, Singapore, and Thailand, where they launched successful businesses. Today, these countries (along with Taiwan) are continuing to develop and are financing much of China's economic growth.[20]

Judaism More than 3,000 years old, Judaism was the first religion to preach belief in a single God. Nowadays, Judaism has roughly 18 million followers worldwide. In Israel, Orthodox (or "fully observant") Jews make up 12 percent of the population and constitute an increasingly important economic segment. In Jerusalem, there is even a modeling agency that specializes in casting Orthodox Jews in ads aimed both inside and outside the Orthodox community. Models include scholars and even one rabbi. In keeping with Orthodox principles, women model only modest clothing and never appear in ads alongside men.[21]

Employers and human resource managers must be aware of important days in the Jewish faith. Because the Sabbath lasts from sundown on Friday to sundown on Saturday, work schedules might need adjustment. Devout Jews want to be home before sundown on Fridays. On the Sabbath itself, they do not work, travel, or carry money. Several other important observances are Rosh Ha-Shanah (the two-day Jewish New Year, in September or October), Yom Kippur (the Day of Atonement, ten days after New Year), Passover (which celebrates the Exodus from Egypt, in March or April each year), and Hanukkah (which celebrates an ancient victory over the Syrians, usually in December).

Marketers must take into account foods that are banned among strict Jews. Pork and shellfish (such as lobster and crab) are prohibited. Meat and milk are stored and served separately. Other meats must be slaughtered according to a practice called *shehitah.* Meals prepared according to Jewish dietary traditions are called *kosher.* Most airlines, for example, offer kosher meals.

Shinto Shinto (meaning "way of the gods") arose as the native religion of the Japanese. But today Shinto can claim only about 3.5 million strict adherents in Japan. Because modern Shinto preaches patriotism, it is sometimes said that Japan's real religion is nationalism. Shinto teaches sincere and ethical behavior, loyalty and respect toward others, and enjoyment of life.

Shinto beliefs are reflected in the workplace through the traditional practice of lifetime employment and through the traditional trust extended between firms and customers. Japanese competitiveness in world markets has benefited from loyal work forces, lower employee turnover, and greater labor-management cooperation. The success of Japanese companies since World War II gave rise to the concept of a Shinto work ethic, certain aspects of which have been emulated by Western managers.

communication
System of conveying thoughts, feelings, knowledge, and information to others through speech, actions, and writing.

PERSONAL COMMUNICATION

People in every culture have a **communication** system to convey thoughts, feelings, knowledge, and information through speech, actions, and writing. Understanding a culture's *spoken* language gives us great insight into why people think and act the way that they do. Understanding a culture's *unspoken* language helps us avoid sending unintended or embarrassing messages. Let's take a closer look at each of these.

Spoken Language Spoken language is the part of a culture's communication system that is embodied in its spoken and written vocabulary. It is the most obvious difference we notice when traveling in another country. We overhear and engage in a multitude of conversations, and must read many signs and documents to find our way. Because we can never truly understand a culture until we learn its language, language is critical to all international business activities.

Linguistically different segments of a population are often culturally, socially, and politically distinct. For instance, Malaysia's population is comprised of Malay (60 percent), Chinese (30 percent), and Indian (10 percent). Malay is the official national language, but each ethnic group speaks its own language and continues its traditions. The result has sometimes been physical confrontation. The United Kingdom includes England, Northern Ireland, Scotland, and Wales—each of which has its own language and traditions. Recently Scotland has vigorously renewed its drive for independence, and Ireland's native language, Gaelic, is staging a comeback on Irish television and in Gaelic-language schools.[22]

lingua franca
Third or "link" language that is understood by two parties who speak different languages.

Lingua Franca A ***lingua franca*** is a third or "link" language that is understood by two parties who speak different native languages. Although only 5 percent of the world population speaks English as a first language, it is the most common *lingua franca* in international business, followed by French and Spanish.[23] Even the Cantonese dialect of Chinese spoken in Hong Kong and the Mandarin dialect spoken in Taiwan and on the Chinese mainland are so different that a *lingua franca* is often preferred. Although India's official language is Hindi, its *lingua franca* is English because it was once a British colony. MTV is considering Indian programs in Hindi or Tamil, another widely spoken Indian language. "But for now," reports the president of MTV Networks in Asia, "Hinglish works. It's what young people are speaking." *Hinglish* is a combination of Hindi, Tamil, and English words alternated within a single sentence.[24]

Because they operate in many nations, each with its own language, multinationals sometimes choose a *lingua franca* for official internal communications. Philips NV (a Netherlands-based electronics firm) and Asea Brown Boveri AG (a Swiss-based industrial giant) use English for all internal correspondence. Japan-based Sony and Matsushita also use English abroad, even in some non-English-speaking countries.

Properly translating all communications is critical in international business. For instance, Microsoft Corporation recently purchased a thesaurus (a categorized index of terms) for the Spanish-language version of its word processing program. Unfortunately, the index offered some extremely offensive synonyms, equating *man-eater, cannibal,* and *barbarian* with a black person and *man-eating savage* with American Indian; *bastard* meant someone of mixed race, and *vicious* and *perverse* were associated with lesbian. Meanwhile, *Occidental* (referring to the Western Hemisphere) was equated with white, civilized, and cultured. Microsoft issued an apology but still suffered negative publicity in Spain, Mexico, and the United States.[25] (For some more linguistic mistakes made by well-known international companies, see Figure 2.2.)

Language proficiency is critical in production facilities where nonnative managers are supervising local employees. In the wake of the North American Free Trade Agreement, for example, U.S. corporations continue to expand operations in Mexico. Because Mexican factory workers generally appear relaxed and untroubled at work, one U.S. manager was confused when his workers went on strike at his seemingly happy plant. The problem lay in different cultural perspectives. Mexican workers do not take the initiative in matters of problem solving and workplace complaints. In this case, they concluded that the plant manager knew but did not care about their complaints because he did not trouble to question employees about work conditions.[26]

FIGURE 2.2
WHAT DID YOU SAY?

Advertising slogans and company documents must be translated carefully so that messages are received precisely as intended. Some humorous (but sometimes expensive) translation blunders include the following:

- Braniff Airlines' English-language slogan "Fly in Leather" was translated into "Fly Naked" in Spanish.
- A sign for non-Japanese-speaking guests in a Tokyo hotel read, "You are respectfully requested to take advantage of the chambermaids."
- An English sign in Moscow hotel read, "If this is your first visit to the USSR, you are welcome to it."
- A Japanese knife manufacturer labeled its exports to the United States with "Caution: Blade extremely sharp! Keep out of children."
- Japan-based Kinki Nippon Tourist Company changed its name in English-speaking markets after people called looking for "kinky" sex tours.

unspoken language *Language communicated through unspoken cues, including hand gestures, facial expressions, physical greetings, eye contact, and the manipulation of personal space.*

Unspoken Language **Unspoken language** communicates through unspoken cues, including hand gestures, facial expressions, physical greetings, eye contact, and the manipulation of personal space. Like spoken language, unspoken language communicates both information and feelings and differs greatly from one culture to another. Italians, French, Arabs, and Venezuelans, for example, animate conversations with lively hand gestures and other body motions. Japanese and Koreans, although more reserved, communicate just as much information through their own unspoken languages; a look of the eye can carry as much or more meaning as two flailing arms.

Bows of respect in many Asian cultures may carry different meanings, usually depending upon the recipient. Associates of equal standing bow about 15 degrees toward one another. But proper respect for an elder requires a bow of about 30 degrees. Bows of remorse or apology should be about 45 degrees.

Most unspoken language is subtle and takes time to recognize and interpret. Physical gestures, for example, often convey different meanings in different cultures: the thumbs-up sign is vulgar in Italy and Greece but means "all right" or even "great" in the United States. Former U.S. President George Bush once gave a backward peace sign with his fore- and middle fingers (meaning "peace" or "victory" in the United States) to a crowd in Australia. He was unaware that he was sending a message similar to that given in the United States with the middle finger. Figure 2.3 demonstrates how the meaning of certain gestures varies in different countries.

EDUCATION

Education is crucial for passing on traditions, customs, and values. Each culture educates its young people through schooling, parenting, religious teachings, and group memberships. Families and other groups provide informal instruction about customs and how to socialize with others. In most cultures, intellectual skills, including reading and mathematics, are taught in formal educational settings.

FIGURE 2.3
SOME REGIONAL DIFFERENCES IN THE MEANING OF GESTURES

Although Western Europe may be moving toward economic unity, its tapestry of cultures remains diverse. Gestures, for example, continue to reflect centuries of cultural differences. As in the United States, the thumb-and-index circle means "okay" in most of Europe; in Germany, it's an indelicate reference to the receiver's anatomy. In most of Great Britain—England and Scotland—the finger tapping the nose means, "You and I are in on the secret"; in nearby Wales, however, it means, "You're very nosy." If you tap your temple just about anywhere in Western Europe, you're suggesting that someone is "crazy"; in Holland, however, you'll be congratulating someone for being clever.

Education Level Data provided by governments on the education level of their people must be taken with a grain of salt. Because many nations rely on literacy tests of their own design, they often provide little basis for comparison across countries. Some administer standardized tests; others require only a signature as proof of literacy. Unfortunately, because few other options exist, searching for an untapped market and searching for a new factory site forces managers to rely on such undependable benchmarks. Moreover, as you can see from Table 2.1, some countries have further to go in increasing national literacy rates.

TABLE 2.1 ***Illiteracy Rates of Selected Countries***

Country	Adult Illiteracy Rate (Percent of People 15 and Above)	Country	Adult Illiteracy Rate (Percent of People 15 and Above)
Niger	86	South Africa	18
Pakistan	62	Turkey	18
Morocco	56	Brazil	17
Haiti	55	Indonesia	16
Egypt	49	Zimbabwe	15
India	48	Jordan	13
Guatemala	44	Mexico	10
Nigeria	43	Singapore	9
Rwanda	40	Venezuela	9
Saudi Arabia	37	Thailand	6
Cambodia	35	Vietnam	6
Nicaragua	34	Chile	5
Kenya	22	Philippines	5
China	19	Argentina	4

High-wage industries are often attracted to nations with excellent programs for basic education. Nations that invest in worker training are usually repaid in productivity increases and rising incomes. It is an undisputed fact that whereas nations with skilled, well-educated workforces attract all sorts of high-paying jobs, poorly educated countries attract the lowest-paying manufacturing jobs. By investing in education, a country can attract (and even create) the kind of high-wage industries that are often called "brainpower" industries.[27]

Newly industrialized economies in Asia owe much of their rapid economic development to solid education systems. Hong Kong, South Korea, Singapore, and Taiwan focus on rigorous mathematical training in primary and secondary schooling. University education concentrates on the hard sciences and aims to train engineers, scientists, and managers.

The "Brain Drain" Phenomenon Just as a country's quality of education affects its economic development, the level and pace of economic development affects its education system. **Brain drain** is the departure of highly educated people from one profession, geographic region, or nation to another. It transfers know-how from one profession to another because people can apply education and skills to alternate occupations. China is traditionally strong in teaching and research in the basic sciences and mathematics. But economic reform is stranding many university professors with much less income than they could earn by working for private companies or even starting their own businesses. A recent report states that more than 50 percent of those leaving teaching positions at Beijing Normal University have advanced degrees. It's easy to understand brain drain from education when we learn that while university professors in China earn as little as 400 renminbi ($50) per month, multinationals in the private sector are paying secretarial assistants 3,000 renminbi ($375) and bilingual administrative assistants 16,000 ($2,000).[28]

brain drain
Departure of highly educated people from one profession, geographic region, or nation to another.

e-biz

Although the United States controls two thirds of the $300 billion global market for software products and services, there are still nearly 200,000 unfilled high-tech jobs in the United States, mostly for computer programmers. Moreover, because the number of

In high-tech industries, the United States is suffering a severe shortage of brain power. Because they still have about 200,000 jobs to fill, companies like Microsoft have begun draining the brain power of such places as Europe, where 18 million workers are unemployed. These recruits in Ireland are among 3,000 Europeans who have received free training from Microsoft. Ninety-eight percent have found jobs. For the view of the National Science foundation on the mobility of highly skilled personnel, visit its Web site at **⟨www.nsf.gov⟩**, and search for the phrase "brain drain."

computer-science graduates at U.S. universities plummeted from 48,000 in 1984 to 26,000 in 1997, demand for brainpower in this field will continue to outstrip supply for another decade. More and more U.S. software firms are thus recruiting in markets like Europe, where 18 million people are unemployed. In one year alone, Microsoft put 3,000 Europeans through a free training program and proceeded to place 98 percent in U.S.-paid jobs.[29]

Meanwhile, many developing countries—India, Pakistan, Russia, South Africa, and Taiwan among them—are experiencing high levels of brain drain among scientists, engineers, and researchers in all fields, many of them to the United States. But as the economies of these and other nations continue to develop, they are luring professionals back to their homelands—a process known as *reverse brain drain.*

PHYSICAL AND MATERIAL ENVIRONMENTS

The physical environment and material surroundings of a culture heavily influence its development and pace of change. In this section, we learn how physical environment and culture are related. We then explore the important effect on business of material culture.

Physical Environment Although culture is *affected* by the physical environment, it is not directly *determined* by it. Two aspects of the physical environment—topography and climate—heavily influence a people's culture.

Topography All the physical features that characterize the surface of a geographic region constitute its **topography**. Some surface features such as navigable rivers and flat plains facilitate travel and contact with others. In contrast, treacherous mountain ranges and large bodies of water can discourage contact and cultural change. Cultures isolated by impassable mountains or large bodies of water will be less exposed to the cultural traits of other peoples. Cultural change tends to occur more slowly in isolated cultures than in cultures not isolated in such a manner.

topography
All the physical features that characterize the surface of a geographic region.

Topography can have an impact on consumers' product needs. There is little market for Honda scooters in most mountainous regions because their engines are too small. These are better markets for rugged, maneuverable, fuel-efficient motorcycles with larger engines. Thinner air at higher elevations might also entail modifications in carburetor design for gasoline-powered vehicles.

Topography and Communication Topography can have a profound impact on personal communication in a culture. For instance, two thirds of China is consumed by mountain ranges (including the Himalayas in southern Tibet) and the formidable Gobi Desert. Groups living in mountain valleys have in fact held to their own ways of life and developed their own languages. Although the Mandarin dialect was decreed the national language many years ago, the mountains, desert, and great land area of China still impair personal communication and the proliferation of Mandarin.

Climate The weather conditions of a geographic region are called its **climate**. Climate affects where people settle and helps direct systems of distribution. In Australia, for example, intensely hot and dry conditions in two large deserts, combined with jungle conditions in the northeast, have pushed settlement to coastal areas. As a result—and because water transport is less costly than land transport—coastal waters are still used to distribute products between distant cities.

climate
Weather conditions of a geographic region.

Climate, Lifestyle, and Work Climate plays a large role in lifestyle and work habits. In the countries of southern Europe, northern Africa, and the Middle East, because the heat of the summer sun grows intense in the early afternoon hours, people often take afternoon work breaks of one or two hours during July and August. During

This cartoon suggests that climate is a strong determinant of a culture's food preferences. Here, people in a cold-climate culture are shown enjoying a fire-cicle to warm up as opposed to having a pop-cicle to cool down in warm weather.

this time, people perform errands, such as shopping, or even take short naps before returning to work until about 7 or 8 P.M. Companies doing business in these regions must adapt. Production schedules, for instance, must be adjusted for periods during which machines stand idle. Shipping and receiving schedules must reflect afternoon downtime while accommodating shipments made during later working hours.

Climate and Customs Climate also impacts customs such as clothing and food. For instance, people in many tropical areas wear little clothing and wear it loosely because of the warm, humid climate. In the desert areas of the Middle East and North Africa, people also wear loose clothing, but they wear long robes to protect themselves from intense sunshine and blowing sand.

A culture's food customs are perhaps more influenced by the physical environment than by any other aspect of culture. But here, too, beliefs can have a major impact on diet. Pigs, for example, are a good source of protein in China, Europe, and the Pacific Islands. In the Middle East, however, they are regarded as unclean and prohibited by both Judaism and Islam. The taboo probably originated in environmental factors: They were expensive to feed and produced no materials for clothing. However, because some people were still tempted to squander resources by raising pigs, the prohibition became cultural and was incorporated into both Judaic and Islamic religious texts.[30]

material culture
All the technology employed in a culture to manufacture goods and provide services.

Material Culture All the technology employed in a culture to manufacture goods and provide services is called its **material culture**. Material culture is often used to measure the technological advancement of a nation's markets or industries. Generally, firms enter new markets under one of two conditions: (1) Demand for their products has developed, or (2) the market is capable of supporting its production operations. For example, companies are not flocking to the Southeast Asian nation of Myanmar

(Burma) because economic development under a repressive military government has been stalled by a wide range of political and social problems.

Changes in material culture often cause change in other aspects of a people's culture. Nigeria is the most populous African nation with more than 105 million people. However, the country has only four phone lines per 1,000 people and the typical wait for a phone is 3.5 years. DSC Communications Corporation of the United States recently announced its plans to provide fixed wireless phone service throughout most of Nigeria including the cities of Lagos, Abuja, Kano, Wam, and Port Harcourt.[31] As the African continent continues to upgrade its material culture through economic development programs, a consumer culture will begin to take root.

Uneven Material Culture Material culture often displays uneven development across a nation's geography, markets, and industries. For example, much of China's recent economic progress is occurring in coastal cities such as Shanghai. Shanghai has long played an important role in China's international trade because of its strategic location and superb harbor on the East China Sea. Although it is home to only 1 percent of the total population, Shanghai accounts for 4.3 percent of China's total output—including 12 percent of its industrial production and 11 percent of its financial-services output.[32]

Likewise, Bangkok, the capital city of Thailand, houses only 10 percent of the nation's population but accounts for about 40 percent of its economic output. Meanwhile, the northern parts of the country remain rural, containing farms, forests, and mountains.[33]

CLASSIFYING CULTURES

There are two widely accepted ways to study cultural differences: the *Kluckhohn-Strodtbeck* and *Hofstede frameworks.* Let's look at each of these tools in more detail.

KLUCKHOHN-STRODTBECK FRAMEWORK

The **Kluckhohn-Strodtbeck framework** compares cultures along six cultural dimensions. It studies a given culture by asking the following questions:[34]

Kluckhohn-Strodtbeck framework
Framework for studying cultural differences along six dimensions, such as focus on past or future events and belief in individual or group responsibility for personal well-being.

1. Do people believe that their environment controls them, that they control the environment, or that they are part of nature?
2. Do people focus on past events, on the present, or on the future implications of their actions?
3. Are people easily controlled and not to be trusted, or can they be trusted to act freely and responsibly?
4. Do people desire accomplishments in life, carefree lives, or spiritual and contemplative lives?
5. Do people believe that individuals or groups are responsible for each person's welfare?
6. Do people prefer to conduct most activities in private or in public?

Case: Dimensions of Japanese Culture By providing answers to each of these six questions, we can briefly apply the Kluckhohn-Strodtbeck framework to Japanese culture:

1. *Japanese believe in a delicate balance between people and environment that must be maintained.* Suppose an undetected flaw in a company's product harms customers

using it. In many countries, a high-stakes class-action lawsuit would be filed against the manufacturer on behalf of the victims' families. This scenario is rarely played out in Japan. Japanese culture does not feel that individuals can possibly control every situation—accidents happen. Japanese victims would receive heartfelt apologies, a promise it won't happen again, and a relatively small damage award.

2. *Japanese culture emphasizes the future.* Negotiators from the United States often divulge information about their position to their Japanese counterparts without even realizing it. They also tend to sweeten the deal when negotiations aren't progressing rapidly enough. Japanese negotiators, on the other hand, take a long-term orientation, taking advantage of their U.S. counterparts' desire to wrap things up.
3. *Japanese culture treats people as quite trustworthy.* Crime rates are quite low, and the streets of big cities are safe at night.
4. *Japanese are accomplishment oriented—not necessarily for themselves, but for their employers and work units.*
5. *Japanese culture emphasizes individual responsibility to the group and group responsibility to the individual.*
6. *The culture of Japan tends to be public.* You will often find top managers located in the center of a large, open office surrounded by the desks of many employees. By comparison, many Western executives are often ensconced in offices along outside walls in their home countries.

HOFSTEDE FRAMEWORK

Hofstede framework
Framework for studying cultural differences along four dimensions, such as individualism versus collectivism and power distance.

The **Hofstede framework** grew from a study of one company's worldwide personnel.[35] More than 110,000 people working in IBM subsidiaries in 40 countries responded to a 32-item questionnaire. Based on these responses, Danish psychologist Geert Hofstede developed four dimensions for examining cultures:[36]

1. *Individualism versus collectivism.* Identifies whether a culture holds individuals or the group responsible for each member's welfare. Businesses in individualist cultures place responsibility for poor decisions on the individual in charge; in collectivist cultures, blame for making bad decisions is shared among group members.
2. *Power distance.* Describes the degree of inequality between people in different occupations. In cultures with large power distance, leaders and supervisors enjoy special recognition and privileges. In cultures with small power distance, prestige and rewards are more equally shared between superiors and the company's rank-and-file employees.
3. *Uncertainty avoidance.* Identifies a culture's willingness to accept uncertainty about the future. Cultures that avoid uncertainty normally have lower employee turnover, more formal rules for regulating employee behavior, and more difficulty in implementing change. Organizations in risk-accepting cultures welcome practices from other cultures but suffer from greater employee turnover.
4. *Quantity versus quality of life.* Cultures focused on *quantity of life* emphasize accomplishments like power, wealth, and status. Cultures that stress *quality of life* generally have more relaxed lifestyles; people are more concerned with cultivating relationships and the general welfare of others.

Figure 2.4(a) shows how the Hofstede study ranked selected countries according to the power distance and individualism dimensions. Countries in Quadrant 1 feature little individualism and fairly inequitable reward systems. In contrast, countries in Quadrant 3 display individualistic tendencies and have more equitable cultures.

FIGURE 2.4

HOFSTEDE'S DIMENSIONS

(a)
POWER DISTANCE ×
INDIVIDUALISM-COLLECTIVISM

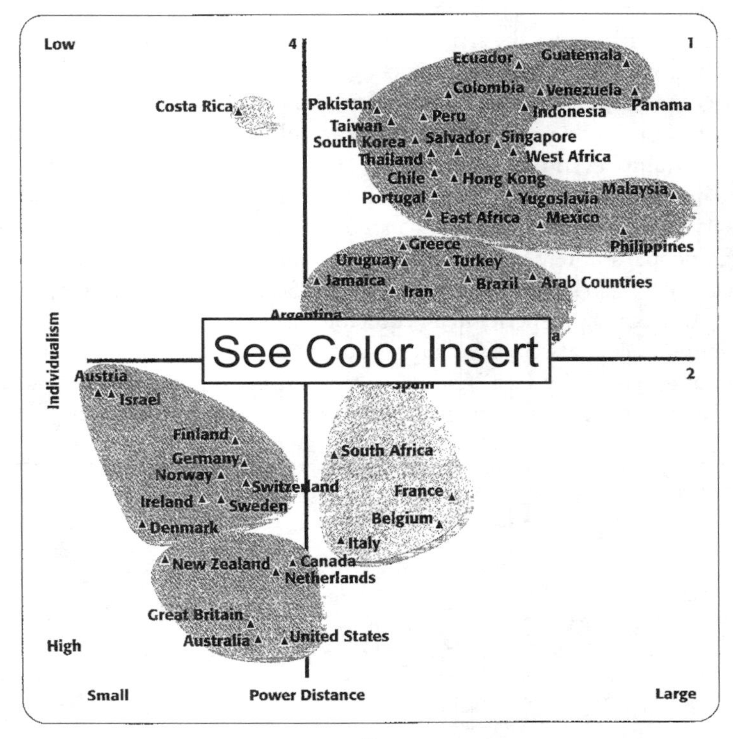

(b)
POWER DISTANCE ×
UNCERTAINTY AVOIDANCE

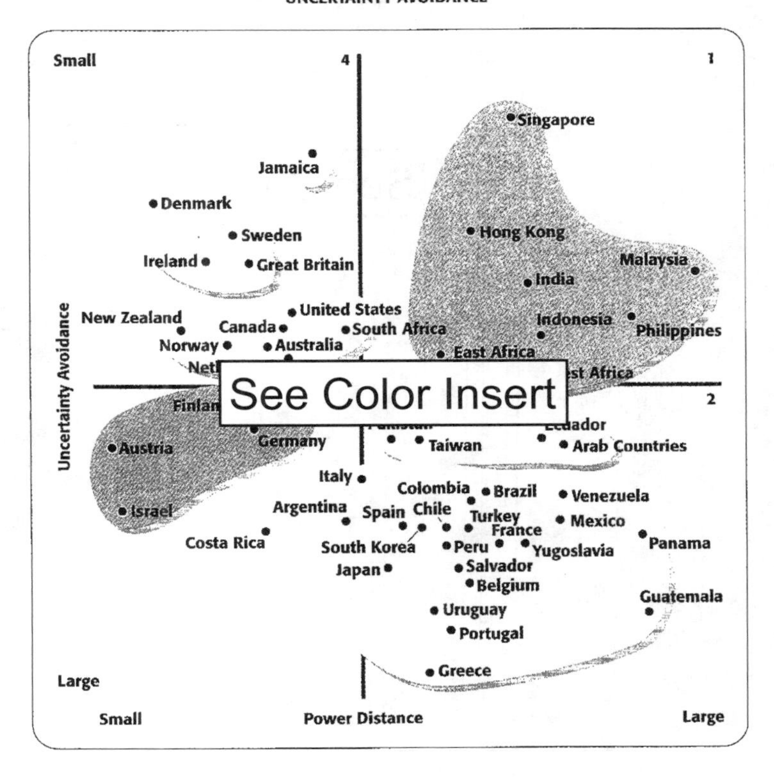

Quadrant 3 also features economies relying mostly on a free-market economic system. In other words, in terms of welfare and other government social programs, people in Quadrant 3 nations have substantial "safety nets."

Figure 2.4(b) ranks the same countries according to power distance and uncertainty avoidance. Quadrant 1 contains mostly Southeast Asian cultures that extend special privileges to those in power and whose people tend to avoid uncertainty. In Quadrant 2 lie Japan, Korea, and many South American cultures in which people accept greater risk and uncertainty even though the perks of power still exist. Companies are hierarchical and maintain formal, even rigid lines of communication. Quadrant 3 contains Israel and some Western European cultures in which benefits are fairly evenly rewarded even though people still rely largely on formal organizational rules. Quadrant 4 contains the United States, Canada, Great Britain, and the Scandinavian countries. People here share varying degrees of prosperity in an equitable fashion.

Some researchers classify cultures according to similarities in values, religion, language, and geography (see Map 2.2). *Most cross-cultural mistakes made by businesses occur between these clusters*, rather than between countries within any single cluster.

MAP 2.2

A SYNTHESIS OF COUNTRY CLUSTERS

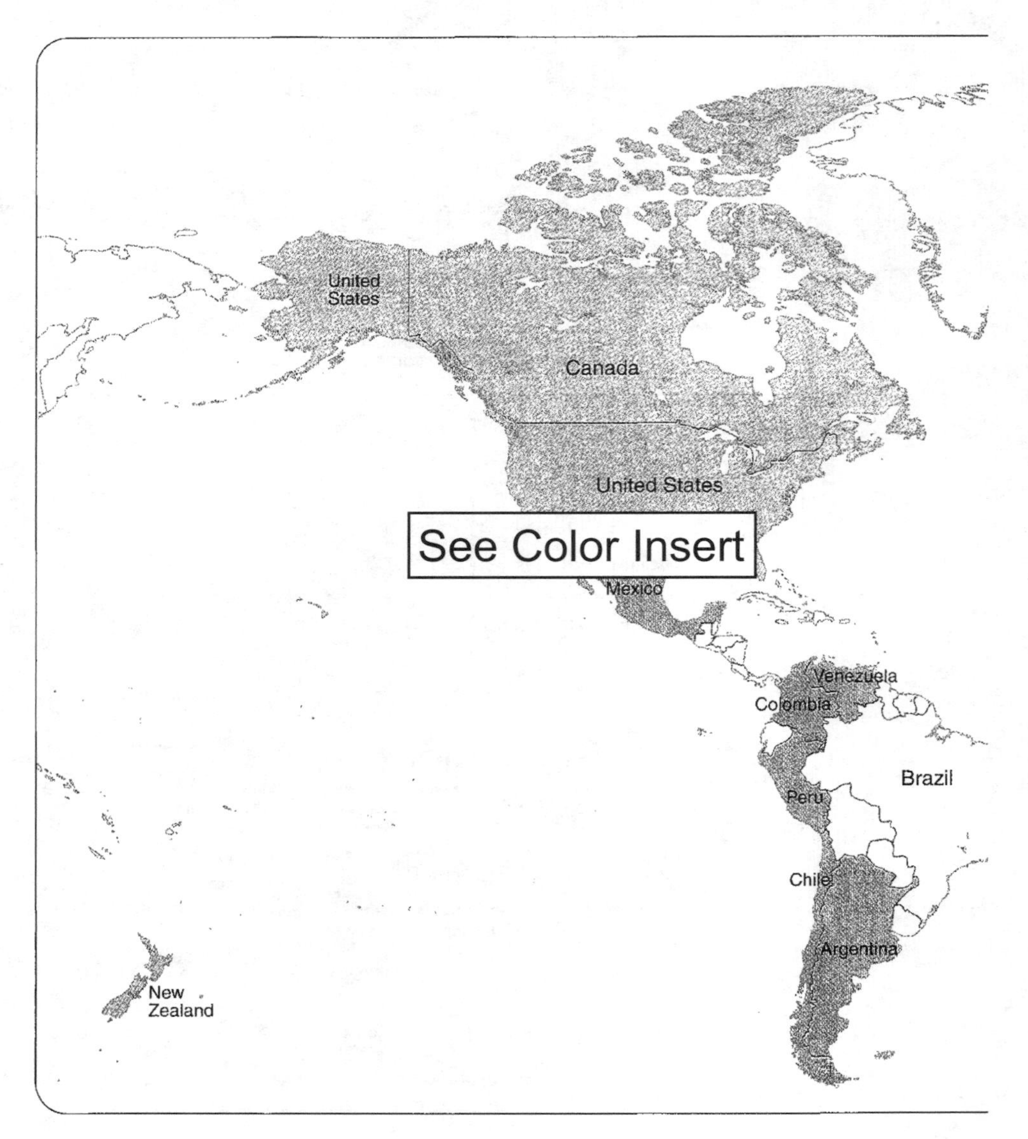

APPLYING THE TWO FRAMEWORKS

If we combine the Kluckhohn-Strodtbeck and Hofstede frameworks, we can recognize ten cultural dimensions that influence managerial decisions, including the design of employee-training programs and reward systems, and approaches to corporate change.[37] These ten dimensions also tell us a great deal about the ways in which people relate to one another and in which cultures organize their business-related institutions. Let's now apply these frameworks to see how cultures *differ* along one very important dimension—the emphasis placed on individual versus group responsibility.

individual-oriented culture *Culture in which each individual tends to be responsible for his or her own well-being.*

Individual-Oriented Cultures A culture in which each individual tends to be responsible for his or her own well-being is called an **individual-oriented culture**. This type of culture is found in Europe and North America, including Australia, Canada, Spain, Britain, and the United States. People are given freedom to focus on personal goals but are held responsible for their actions. Children are taught to

Country Clusters

- Arab
- Anglo
- Far Eastern
- Germanic
- Independent
- Latin American
- Latin European
- Near Eastern
- Nordic

be self-reliant and self-confident at a young age. Such cultures value hard work and entrepreneurial efforts, and the emphasis on individualism promotes risk taking, which in turn fosters invention and innovation. At the same time, the individualist emphasis is also blamed for high turnover among managers and other employees. It's an important consideration: If a key manager who possesses valuable information goes to work for a competitor, the former employer can lose its competitive edge virtually overnight.

It is sometimes hard to develop a cooperative work environment or "team spirit" among employees in individual-oriented cultures. People who are accustomed to receiving personal recognition tend to be more concerned with personal responsibilities than with company-wide performance. Because companies in individual-oriented cultures might find it more difficult to trust one another, cooperative ventures can run into trouble. Partners are more likely to pull out of the venture once their objectives are met.

group-oriented culture
Culture in which the group shares responsibility for the well-being of each member.

Group-Oriented Cultures A culture in which the group shares responsibility for the well-being of each member is called a **group-oriented culture**. People work toward collective rather than personal goals and are responsible to the group for their actions. All social, political, economic, and legal institutions reflect the group's critical role. The goal of maintaining group harmony is most evident in the family structure.

Japan is a classic group-oriented culture. Japanese children learn the importance of groups early by contributing to the upkeep of their schools. They share such duties as mopping floors, washing windows, cleaning chalkboards, and arranging desks and chairs. They carry habits learned in school into the adult workplace, where management and labor work together toward company goals. Japanese managers make decisions only after considering input from subordinates. Materials buyers, engineers, designers, factory floor supervisors, and marketers cooperate at every stage in product development.

Employee-manager trust has long been a hallmark of Japanese organizations. Traditionally, while subordinates promise hard work and loyalty, top managers promise job security. Today's slow-growth Japanese economy makes job security a more difficult promise to keep. From World War II until 1973, for instance, annual economic growth was 9 percent; from 1973 to 1990, it declined to 4 percent and remained at only 2 percent from 1990 to 1996. To remain internationally competitive, Japanese firms have been cutting payroll expenses by eliminating jobs and moving production to low-wage nations like China and Vietnam.[38] As such traditions as job security and the belief that non-Japanese employers provide less job stability fall by the wayside, more and more Japanese workers now consider employment with non-Japanese companies. They are finding that many non-Japanese firms offer better pay and quicker advancement.[39]

A FINAL WORD

This chapter discussed many of the cultural differences that impact international business. We saw how problems can erupt from cultural misunderstandings and learned how companies can improve their performance with cultural literacy. Being culturally literate can mean the difference between returning home with a contract in hand or returning empty-handed. As globalization propels more and more companies into the international business arena, "Thinking global, and acting local" can help managers succeed. Knowing a people's values, beliefs, rules, and institutions makes managers more effective marketers, negotiators, and production managers. In the next two chapters we explore differences between nations' political, legal, and economic systems.

There is a variety of additional material available on the companion Web site that accompanies this text. You can access this information by visiting the Web site at ⟨**www.prenhall.com/wild**⟩.

summary

1. **Describe *culture* and explain the influence of both national culture and subcultures.** *Culture* is the set of values, beliefs, rules, and institutions supported by a specific group of people. Successfully dealing with members of other cultures means overcoming *ethnocentricity* (the tendency to view one's own culture as superior to others) and developing *cultural literacy* (gaining the detailed knowledge necessary to work and live in another culture).

   We are conditioned to think in terms of *national culture*—that is, to equate a nation-state and its people with a single culture. In reality, most nation-states are home to numerous *subcultures*—groups of people who share a unique way of life within a larger, dominant culture. But nations affirm the importance of "national culture" by building museums and monuments to preserve national legacies that cut across subcultures. Nation-states often intervene in business to help protect the national culture from the unwanted influence of other cultures. Even so, subcultures contribute greatly to national culture and must be considered in marketing and production decisions.

2. **Identify the *components of culture* and describe their impact on business activities around the world.** Culture includes a people's beliefs and traditional habits and the ways in which they relate to one another. These factors fall into one or more of the eight major components of culture: (1) *aesthetics*; (2) *values* and *attitudes*; (3) *manners* and *customs*; (4) *social structure*; (5) *religion*; (6) *personal communication*; (7) *education*; and (8) *physical* and *material environments*.

   All of these components affect business activity. Aesthetics, for instance, determines which colors and symbols will be effective (or offensive) in advertising. Values influence a people's attitudes toward time, work and achievement, and cultural change. Knowledge of manners and customs is necessary for negotiating with people of other cultures, marketing products to them, and managing operations in their country. Social structure affects business decisions ranging from production-site selection to advertising methods to the costs of doing business in a country. Different religions take different views of work, savings, and material goods. Understanding a people's system of personal communication provides insight into their values and behavior. A culture's education level affects the quality of the workforce and standard of living. The physical and material environments influence work habits and preferences regarding such products as clothing and food.

3. **Describe *cultural change* and explain how companies and culture affect one another.** *Cultural change* occurs when a people integrate into their culture the gestures, material objects, traditions, or concepts of another culture. Globalization and technology are increasing the pace of cultural change around the world. Companies can influence culture when they import business practices or products into the host country. In order to avoid charges of *cultural imperialism*, they should import new products, policies, and practices during times of stability. Cultures also affect management styles, work scheduling, and reward systems. Adapting to local cultures around the world means heeding the maxim "Think global, act local."

4. **Explain how the *physical environment* and *technology* influence culture.** A people's *physical environment* includes topography and climate and the ways (good and bad) in which they relate to their surroundings. Cultures isolated by topographical barriers, such as mountains or seas, normally change very slowly, and their languages are often distinct. *Climate* affects the hours of the day that people work. For example, people in hot climates normally take siestas when afternoon temperatures soar. Climate also influences customs, such as the type of clothing a people wear and the types of foods they eat.

Material culture refers to all the technology that people employ to manufacture goods and provide services. It is often used to measure the technological advancement of a nation and often used by businesspeople to determine whether a market has developed adequate demand for a company's products and whether it can support production activities. Material culture tends to be uneven across most nations.

5 **Describe the *frameworks* and *dimensions* used to classify cultures and explain how they are applied.** There are two widely accepted frameworks for studying cultural differences: (1) The *Kluckhohn-Strodtbeck framework* compares cultures along six dimensions by seeking answers to certain questions including: Do people believe that their environment controls them or vice versa? Do people focus on past events or the future? Do they prefer to conduct activities in public or private? (2) The *Hofstede framework* develops four dimensions, such as individualism versus collectivism and quantity versus quality of life. In using one or both of these frameworks, we can analyze cultural differences to find out whether a culture is individual- or group-oriented. This orientation affects attitudes toward such business-related cultural values as risk taking, innovation, job mobility, team cooperation, pay levels, and hiring practices.

questions for review

1. What is *culture*? Explain how *ethnocentricity* distorts one's view of other cultures.
2. What is *cultural literacy*? What factors are forcing businesspeople to understand more about other *cultures*?
3. How do *nation-states* and *subcultures* affect a nation's cultural image?
4. What is meant by a culture's *aesthetics*? Give several examples from several different cultures.
5. How do *values* and *attitudes* differ? Explain how cultures differ in their attitudes toward time, work, and cultural change.
6. How do one culture's practices spread to other cultures? Why are practices from one culture not always welcome in another? Explain why international businesses should be sensitive to accusations of *cultural imperialism*.
7. How do *manners* and *customs* differ? Give some examples of each from several different cultures.
8. What are *folk* and *popular customs*? Describe how a folk custom can become a popular custom.
9. To what does *social structure* refer? How do social rank and mobility affect business activities?
10. Identify the dominant religion in each of the following countries.
    a. India
    b. Ireland
    c. Mexico
    d. Russia
    e. China
    f. Brazil
    g. Thailand
11. What specific advantages do companies gain when they learn how to communicate in another culture?
12. Why is the *education* of a country's people important to both native and nonnative companies operating there? What is meant by *brain drain* and *reverse brain drain*?
13. How are a people's culture and *physical environment* related? How does technology affect culture?
14. Describe the dimensions of the *Kluckhohn-Strodtbeck* and *Hofstede frameworks*. Contrast two cultures by applying each of these frameworks to them.
15. What are the primary characteristics of *individual-oriented cultures*? Of *group-oriented cultures*? How might business practices and competitiveness differ between these two types of cultures?

questions for discussion

1. Two students are discussing the various reasons why they are *not* studying international business. "International business doesn't affect me," declares the first. "I'm going to stay here, not work in some *foreign* country." "Yeah," agrees the second. "Besides, some cultures are real *strange*. The sooner other countries start doing business our way, the better."

   What counterarguments can you present to these students' perceptions?
2. A recent survey of European business executives obtained some interesting results. They were asked which nation's executives had the strongest work ethic and demonstrated the best leadership abilities. Germany ranked high on both di-

mensions. What parts of German culture do you think explain its high ratings? On the other hand, Greece received low ratings. What is it about Greek culture that, in your opinion, may explain its low rankings on each dimension? Give specific examples if you can.

3. In this exercise, two groups of four students each will debate the benefits and drawbacks of individual- versus group-oriented cultures. After the first student from each side has spoken, the second student questions the opponent's arguments, looking for holes and inconsistencies. A third student attempts to reply to these counterarguments. Then a fourth student summarizes each side's arguments. Finally, the class votes on which team has presented the more compelling case.

in practice

Read the short newspaper article below and answer the questions that follow.

Nike Building Playground at Virginia Mosque

FALLS CHURCH, Va. (AP) - Shoe manufacturer Nike Corp. has begun building a playground at a northern Virginia mosque, one of several projects to make amends for a marketing gaffe.

About two years ago, Nike emblazoned a new shoe model with the word "Air" written in what looked like flames. However, the squiggly lines made the word look like Arabic script for the word Allah.

Under threat of a worldwide boycott by hundreds of millions of Muslims, who considered it a sacrilege, Nike recalled more than 38,000 pairs of the shoes and agreed to build several playgrounds for Muslim communities.

Groundbreaking for the Falls Church playground took place Saturday at the Dar Al-Hijrah Islamic Center, and some 80 children told Nike representatives what the playground should include.

1. What components of culture did Nike disregard in its development of this new shoe? Briefly explain how they disregarded each one.
2. List the countries around the world in which a large percentage of their people would be offended by this marketing mistake.
3. Do you think Nike could have prevented such a gaffe from occurring? If so, what preventative steps could it have taken?
4. Write a short paragraph describing another company that offended a group of people by ignoring relevant cultural components.

projects

1. Select a recent business periodical in print or online—say, *Fortune* ⟨**www.fortune.com**⟩, the *Far Eastern Economic Review* ⟨**www.feer.com**⟩, or *CNN Interactive* ⟨**www.cnn.com**⟩—and find an article discussing the role of culture in international business. Then write a short summary detailing the cultural elements identified by the author, being sure to explain how they pertain to actual business activities in the country under discussion.
2. Select a company in your city or town that interests you and make an appointment to interview the owner or a manager. Your goal is to learn how international opportunities and competition affect the decisions of this owner/manager and his or her company. Be sure to ask for specific examples. Write a short report of your interview and present a brief talk on your findings to the class.
3. Go to your library or link to a business information service on the Internet. Locate annual reports or similar information issued by companies like Nike, Guess, Lands' End, or Coca-Cola—most libraries have annual reports in both paper and computer-readable form. Review this information and report on the (1) main products or services the company offers, (2) extent to which the company pursues international business operations (often expressed as percentage of sales or assets), and (3) ways that the company has adapted to local cultures around the world.

Many cultures in Asia are in the midst of an identity crisis. In effect, they are being torn between two worlds. Pulling in one direction is a traditional value system derived from agriculture-based communities and extended families—that is, elements of a culture in which relatives take care of one another and state-run welfare systems are unnecessary. Pulling from the opposite direction is a new set of values emerging from manufacturing- and finance-based economies—elements of a culture in which workers must often move to faraway cities to find work, sometimes leaving family members to fend for themselves.

For years, spectacular rates of economic growth elevated living standards in many Asian countries far beyond what was thought possible in a few short decades. Young people in countries like Malaysia and Thailand felt the lure of Western brands. Gucci handbags, Harley-Davidson motorcycles, and other global brand names became common symbols of success. Some parents even encouraged brand-consciousness among their teenage children because it signaled familywide success. Meanwhile, polls of young people showed them holding steadfast to traditional values such as respect for family and group harmony. Youth in Hong Kong, for example, overwhelmingly continued to believe that parents should have much to say about how hard they study, about how they treat family members and elders, and about their choice of friends.

But events took an unpleasant turn in the middle of 1997. The currencies of Thailand, Indonesia, Malaysia, South Korea, and other nations crumbled. Within weeks, currencies were worth about half as much as before and spending power was sharply reduced. Financial investments throughout Southeast Asia fled to safe havens in highly industrialized countries, and future investment plans were either scaled back or put on hold. Some Asians blame the West for the crippling economic crisis. Even more blame economic development and "westernization" for a decaying value system and declining morality. Many Asians, it seems, want modernization but also want to hold on to traditional beliefs and values. They do not want Western companies and governments imposing their ways of doing business on cultures that they might not fully comprehend. Nevertheless, following the crisis, Western companies are scooping up failing enterprises from Thailand to Japan and implementing Western business practices.

Prior to the financial crisis, Asians thought they had discovered an "Asian" way of doing business that was uniquely their own. Many respected analysts in Asia, Europe, and the United States discussed the virtues of the so-called "Asian model." But the crisis put an abrupt end to that discussion. Some observers say that talk of an "Asian" way of doing business was overstated and misplaced. They argue that belief in the importance of family became the practice of nepotism, belief in the importance of relationships became cronyism, belief in the building of consensus became corrupt politics, and belief in conservatism and respect for authority became rigidity and an inability to innovate. If Asian culture esteems family loyalty so highly, why was it necessary for Singapore to enact legislation *requiring* that children take care of elderly parents?

thinking globally

1. If your international firm were doing business in Asia, would you feel partly responsible for these social trends? Is there anything that your company could do to ease the tensions being experienced by these cultures? Be specific.
2. In your opinion, is globalization among the causes of the increasing incidence of divorce, crime, and drug abuse in Asia? Why or why not?
3. Broadly defined, Asia comprises over 60 percent of the world's population—a population that practices Buddhism, Confucianism, Islam, and numerous other religions. Given the fact that there are considerable cultural differences between countries such as China, India, Indonesia, Japan, and Malaysia, is it possible to carry on a valid discussion of "Asian" values? Why or why not?
4. Consider the following statement: "Economic development and capitalism require a certain style of doing business for the twenty-first century. The sooner Asian cultures adapt, the better." Do you agree or disagree? Explain.

a question **of ethics**

1. Some businesspeople and other experts argue that bribery helps cut through mounds of red tape. Do you agree? By calling for reforms in nations that condone bribery, are international agencies (strongly backed by U.S. interests) promoting a certain set of values and morals? Are they practicing cultural imperialism?
2. When international firms enter the Indian market, they soon learn about the various ways in which a rigid caste system can

affect business activities. Should these companies adjust to local management styles and human resource practices? Or should they import their own styles and practices because they are so-called "more developed" and equitable?

3. Companies often relocate factories from industrialized nations with high labor costs to such low-wage countries as China, India, Mexico, and the nations of Central America. Is there any reasonable response to charges that, in so doing, they frequently exploit child labor, force women to work 75-hour weeks, and destroy family units?

Module B

Teams and Diversity

Chapter 3

Team Building

Team Decision Making: Conformity, Pitfalls, and Solutions

"I . . . grabbed the photographic evidence showing the hot gas blow-by comparisons from previous flights and placed it on the table in view of the managers and somewhat angered, admonished them to look at the photos and not ignore what they were telling us; namely, that low temperature indeed caused significantly more hot gas blow-by to occur in the joints. I received cold stares . . . with looks as if to say, 'Go away and don't bother us with the facts.' No one in management wanted to discuss the facts; they just would not respond verbally to . . . me. I felt totally helpless at that moment and that further argument was fruitless, so I, too, stopped pressing my case" (Boisjoly, 1987, p. 7).

We all know that decisions made by committees can be of the worst caliber. It might seem, because the downside potential is so great, that team decisions are not worth the risk. However, good team decisions can be outstanding—far better than those attainable by any individual. The key, of course, is doing it right, and doing it right is the topic of this chapter.

The space shuttle *Challenger* disaster may have resulted, in part, from a poor team decision process. The opening quote from Roger Boisjoly, an engineer who tried to halt the flight in 1986, led the Presidential Commission to conclude that the disaster was, indeed, the result of a "flawed decision-making process."[1] Another example from the business world is the American Medical Association's decision to allow Sunbeam to use the AMA name as a product endorsement. Because bad team decisions can have disastrous consequences, it is important to understand the particular kinds of faults that lead to faulty decision making, specifically in teams.

DECISION MAKING IN TEAMS

Decision making is an integrated sequence of activities that includes gathering, interpreting, and exchanging information; creating and identifying alternative courses of action; choosing among alternatives by integrating the often differing perspectives and opinions of team members; and implementing a choice and monitoring its consequences (Guzzo, Salas, & Associates, 1995). Decision making is a key activity that teams must do, no matter what their governance structure—self-managing, manager-led, or self-directing. This is true for tactical, problem-solving, and creative teams. In teams, information is often distributed unequally among members and must be integrated, and

[1]Committee on Science and Technology, House of Representatives, House Report 99-1016, "Investigation of the Challenger Accident," October 29, 1986.

the integration process may be complicated by uncertainty, status differences among members, failure of members to appreciate the significance of the information they hold or of the information not held by others, and so on.

This chapter focuses on four decision-making pitfalls that teams often encounter. For each, we describe the problem and then provide preventative measures. The first problem that we focus on is groupthink, the tendency to conform to the consensus viewpoint in group decision making. We then discuss escalation of commitment and the Abilene paradox. Finally, we discuss group polarization.

The quality of group decision making is impacted by conformity, and conformity can lead to any of the four main pitfalls of group decision making. We begin the chapter with an analysis of conformity and then discuss the four main group decision-making pitfalls.

CONFORMITY: WHY IT OCCURS AND HOW IT WORKS IN TEAMS

Suppose that you are meeting with your team. The question facing your team is a simple one: Which of the three lines in panel 2 is equal in length to the line in panel 1? (See Figure 6-1.)

The team leader seeks a group consensus. She begins by asking the colleague sitting to your left for his opinion. To your shock, your colleague chooses line 1; then, each of the other four team members selects line 1—even though line 2 is clearly correct. You begin to wonder whether you are losing your mind. Finally, it's your turn to decide. What do you do?

Most people who read this example find it nearly impossible to imagine that they would choose line 1, even if everyone else had. Yet 76 percent make an erroneous, conforming judgment (e.g., choose line 1) on at least one question; on average, people conform one-third of the time when others give the obviously incorrect answer (Asch, 1956).

The line experiment is a dramatic illustration of the power of conformity pressure. **Conformity** occurs when people bring their behavior into alignment with a group's expectations and beliefs. In this example, the people who give the wrong answer know that the answer is wrong; nevertheless, they feel compelled to provide an answer that will be acceptable to the group.

Although many people think their beliefs and behavior are based on their own free will, social behavior is strongly influenced by others. Why do people conform? There are two main reasons: They want to do the "right" thing and they want to be liked.

The Need to Be Right

Groups are presumed to have access to a broader range of decision-making resources and, hence, to be better equipped to make high-quality decisions than any person can alone. By pooling their different backgrounds, training, and experience, group members have at least the potential for working in a more informed fashion than would be the case were the decision left to any single individual. The implication of these two assertions is that individuals are **information dependent**—that is, they often lack information that another member has. Consequently, individuals look to the team to provide infor-

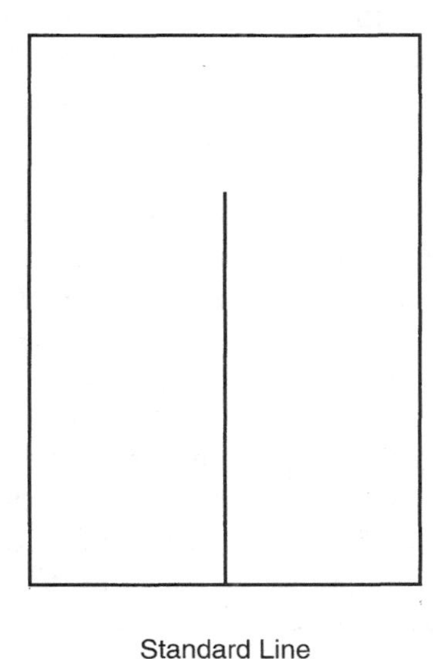

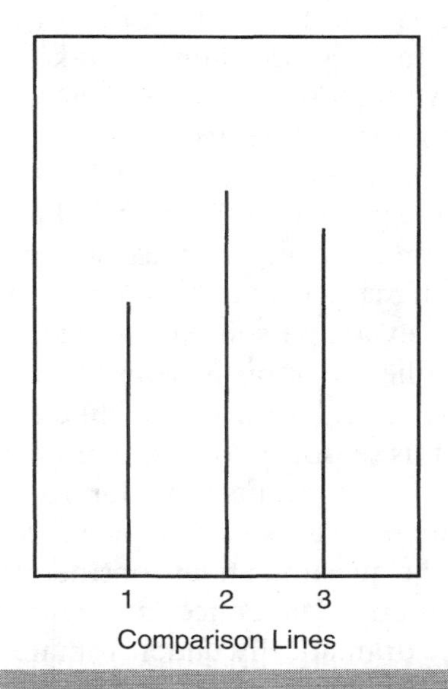

FIGURE 6-1 Conformity Pressure

Source: Adapted from Asch, S. E. 1956. "Studies of Independence and Conformity: A Minority of One against a Unanimous Majority." *Psychological Monographs, 70* (9, Whole No. 416).

mation that they do not know. On the one hand, this is an adaptive response. However, it can lead to problems when people treat others' opinions as facts and fail to question their validity. The need to be right, therefore, is the tendency to look to the group to define what reality is—and the more people who hold a particular opinion, the more right an answer appears to be. Whereas this information-seeking tendency would seem to be contradictory to the common information effect that we discussed in the previous chapter, the two processes are not inconsistent. The common information effect (and all of its undesirable consequences) are driven by a biased search for information. Conformity, or the adoption of group-level beliefs, is strongest when individuals feel unsure about their own position.

The Need to Be Liked

Most people have a fundamental need to be accepted and approved of by others. Conformity is often a ticket to group acceptance. There is good reason for this: Teams provide valuable resources. One of the most straightforward ways to gain immediate acceptance in a group is to express attitudes consistent with those of the group members. Stated another way, most people like others who conform to their own beliefs. This means that people in groups will become more extreme in the direction of the group's general opinion, because attitudes that are sympathetic toward the group are most likely to be positively rewarded. The need to be liked refers to the tendency for people to agree with a group so that they can feel more like a part of that group.

Conformity is greater when the judgment or opinion issue is difficult and when people are uncertain. People are especially likely to conform if they face an otherwise unanimous group consensus (Asch, 1956; Wilder & Allen, 1977). Conformity is greater when people value and admire their team—rejection from a desirable group is very threatening (Back, 1951). However, we do not want to paint the picture that managers lack integrity. People are more willing to take a stand when they feel confident about their expertise, have high social status (Harvey & Consalvi, 1960), are strongly committed to their initial view (Deutsch & Gerard, 1955), and do not like or respect the people trying to influence them (Hogg & Turner, 1987).

Coupled with the need to be liked is the desire not to be ostracized from one's team. There is good reason for concern, because individuals who deviate from their team's opinion are more harshly evaluated than are those who conform (Levine, 1989). A group may reject a deviant person even when they are not under pressure to reach complete consensus (Miller, Jackson, Mueller, & Schersching, 1987). Apparently, holding a different opinion is enough to trigger dislike even when it does not directly block the group's goals. For this reason, people are more likely to conform to the majority when they respond publicly (e.g., Deutsch & Gerard, 1955), anticipate future interaction with other group members (e.g., Lewis, Langan, & Hollander, 1972), are less confident (Allen, 1965), find the question under consideration to be ambiguous or difficult (Tajfel, 1978), and are interdependent concerning rewards (e.g., Deutsch & Gerard, 1955).

Most managers dramatically underestimate the conformity pressures that operate in groups. Perhaps this is because people like to think of themselves as individualists who are not afraid to speak their own minds. However, conformity pressures in groups are real and they affect the quality of team decision making. The key message for the manager is to anticipate conformity pressures in groups, to understand what drives it (i.e., the need to be liked and the desire to be right), and then to put into place group structures that will not allow conformity pressures to endanger the quality of group decision making. This leads us to the first of the decision-making problems that teams may encounter.

DECISION-MAKING PITFALL 1: GROUPTHINK

Groupthink occurs when team members place consensus above all other priorities—including using good judgment when the consensus reflects poor judgment, improper or immoral actions, and so on. Groupthink, at its core, involves a deterioration of mental efficiency, reality testing, and moral judgments as a result of group pressures toward conformity of opinion. For a list of groupthink decisions in the political and corporate world, see Box 6-1. The desire to agree can become so dominant that it can override the realistic appraisal of alternative courses of action (Janis, 1972, 1982). The reasons for groupthink may range from group pressures to conform to a sincere desire to incorporate and reflect the views of all team members. Such pressure may also come from management if the directive is to reach a decision that all can agree to, such as in cross-functional teams.

Conformity pressures can lead decision makers to censor their misgivings, ignore outside information, feel too confident, and adopt an attitude of invulnerability. The pressure for unanimity is thought to be a recipe for ineffective group decision making and explains how a group of otherwise intelligent and thoughtful people can make serious miscalculations that result in disastrous outcomes.

Symptoms of groupthink cannot be easily assessed by outside observers. Rather, most groupthink symptoms represent private feelings or beliefs held by group members or behaviors performed in private. There are three key symptoms of groupthink that take root and blossom in groups that succumb to pressures of reaching unanimity:

BOX 6-1

Instances of Groupthink in Politics and the Corporate World

EXAMPLES FROM POLITICS

- Neville Chamberlain's inner circle, whose members supported the policy of appeasement of Hitler during 1937 and 1938, despite repeated warnings and events that indicated it would have adverse consequences (Janis & Mann, 1977).
- President Truman's advisory group, whose members supported the decision to escalate the war in North Korea, despite firm warnings by the Chinese Communist government that U.S. entry into North Korea would be met with armed resistance from the Chinese (Janis & Mann, 1977).
- President Kennedy's inner circle, whose members supported the decision to launch the Bay of Pigs invasion of Cuba, despite the availability of information indicating that it would be an unsuccessful venture and would damage U.S. relations with other countries (Janis & Mann, 1977).
- President Johnson's close advisors, who supported the decision to escalate the war in Vietnam, despite intelligence reports and information indicating that this course of action would not defeat the Viet Cong or the North Vietnamese, and would generate unfavorable political consequences within the United States (Janis & Mann, 1977).
- The decision of the Reagan administration to exchange arms for hostages with Iran and to continue commitment to the Nicaraguan Contras in the face of several congressional amendments limiting or banning aid.

EXAMPLES FROM THE CORPORATE WORLD

- Gruenenthal Chemie's decision to market the drug thalidomide (Raven & Rubin, 1976).
- The price-fixing conspiracy involving the electrical manufacturing industry during the 1950s.
- The decision by Ford Motor Company to produce the Edsel (Huseman & Driver, 1979).
- The selling of millions of jars of "phony" apple juice by Beech-Nut, the second largest baby food producer in the United States.
- The involvement of E. F. Hutton in "check kiting," wherein a money manager at a Hutton branch office would write a check on an account in Bank A for more money than Hutton had in the account. Because of the time lag in the check-collection system, these overdrafts sometimes went undetected, and Hutton could deposit funds to cover the overdraft in the following day. The deposited money would start earning interest immediately. The scheme allowed Hutton to earn a day's interest on Bank A's account without having to pay anything for it—resulting in $250 million in free loans every day (*ABA Banking Journal,* 1985; Goleman, 1988).
- The illegal purchases by Salomon Brothers at U.S. Treasury auctions in the early 1990s (Sims, 1992).

- **Overestimation of the group:** Members of the group regard themselves as invulnerable and, at the same time, morally correct. This lethal combination can lead decision makers to believe they are above, and exempt from, standards.
- **Close-mindedness:** Members of the group engage in collective rationalization, often accompanied by stereotyping out-group members, a topic we discuss further in part III.
- **Pressures toward uniformity:** There is a strong intolerance in a groupthink situation for diversity of opinion. Dissenters are subject to enormous social pressure. This often leads group members to suppress their reservations. Thus, the group perceives itself to be unanimous.

Deficits arising from groupthink can lead to many shortcomings in the decision-making process. Consider, for example, the following lapses that often accompany groupthink:

- Incomplete survey of alternatives
- Incomplete survey of objectives
- Failure to reexamine alternatives
- Failure to examine preferred choices
- Selection bias
- Poor information search
- Failure to create contingency plans

Each of these behaviors thwarts the rational decision-making process we outlined at the beginning of this chapter.

Learning from History

Consider two decisions made by the same United States presidential cabinet—the Kennedy administration. The Kennedy cabinet was responsible for the Bay of Pigs operation and the Cuban Missile Crisis. The Bay of Pigs was a military operation concocted by the United States in an attempt to overthrow Fidel Castro, the leader of Cuba. The Bay of Pigs is often seen as one of the worst foreign policy mistakes in U.S. history. The operation was regarded as a disaster of epic proportions, resulting in the loss of lives and the disruption of foreign policy. It is also a kind of puzzle because the invasion, in retrospect, seems to have been so poorly planned and so poorly implemented—yet it was led by people whose individual talents seemed to make them eminently qualified to carry out an operation of this sort. What led capable people who should have known better to proceed with such a disastrous plan? In contrast, Kennedy's response to the Cuban Missile Crisis was regarded as a great foreign policy success. These examples, from the same organizational context and team, make an important point: Even smart and highly motivated people can make disastrous decisions under certain conditions. Kennedy's cabinet fell prey to groupthink in the Bay of Pigs decision, but not in the Cuban Missile Crisis. Why was the same cabinet so successful in one instance, but such a miserable failure in another?

A number of detailed historical analyses have been performed (Kramer, 1999; Peterson, Owens, Tetlock, Fan, & Martorana, 1998) comparing these two historical examples, as well as several others. Some sharp differences distinguish between groupthink and effective groups.

TABLE 6-1 Precipitating and Preventative Conditions for the Development of Groupthink		
Conditions	*Leader Behavior and Cognition*	*Team Behavior and Cognition*
Precipitous conditions *(likely to lead to group-think)*	• Narrow, defective appraisal of options • Analysis of options in terms of political repercussions • Concern about image and reputation • Loss-avoidance strategy	• Rigidity • Conformity • View roles in political terms (protecting political capital and status) • Large team size • High sense of collective efficacy • Perceived threat to social identity
Preventative conditions *(likely to engender effective decision making)*	• Being explicit and direct about policy preferences allows the team to know immediately where the leader stands	• Task orientation • Intellectual flexibility • Less consciousness of crisis • Less pessimism • Less corruption (i.e., more concerned with observing correct rules and procedures) • Less centralization • Openness and candidness • Adjustment to failing policies in timely fashion • Genuine commitment to solving problems • Encouraging dissent • Acting decisively in emergencies • Attuned to changes in environment • Focus on shared goals • Realization that trade-offs are necessary • Ability to improvise solutions to unexpected events
Inconclusive conditions *(unlikely to make much of a difference)*	• Strong, opinionated leadership	• Risk taking • Cohesion • Internal debate

Table 6-1 summarizes three kinds of critical evidence: (1) factors that may lead to groupthink; (2) factors that may promote sound decision making; and (3) factors that do not seem to induce groupthink. We focus on two types of behavior: That of the leader and that of the rest of the group.

A number of factors may lead to groupthink. Leader behavior that is associated with too much concern for political ramifications, or the analysis of alternatives in terms of their political repercussions, is a key determinant of groupthink. The same is also true for group behavior; when groups are overly concerned with their political image, they may not make sound decisions.

In terms of preventative conditions, the behavior of the team has a greater impact on the development of groupthink than does leader behavior. Sound group decision making can be achieved through task orientation, flexibility, less centralization, norms of openness, encouraging dissent, focus on shared goals, and realizing that trade-offs are necessary.

How to Avoid Groupthink

In this section, we identify some specific steps managers can take to prevent groupthink. Prevention is predicated on two broad goals: The stimulation of constructive, intellectual conflict and the reduction of concerns about how the group is viewed by others—a kind of conformity pressure. We focus primarily on team design factors because those are the ones managers have the greatest control over. None of these can guarantee success, but they can be effective in encouraging vigilant decision making.

Monitor Team Size

Team size is positively correlated with groupthink, with larger teams more likely to fall prey to groupthink (McCauley, 1998). People grow more intimidated and hesitant as team size increases. This is related to the principle of performance anxiety, which we discussed in chapter 2. There is no magic number for team size, but with teams larger than 10, individual members may feel less personal responsibility for team outcomes and their behaviors may be too risky.

Get Buy-In from Organizational Authorities

Teams whose members are preoccupied with their political image are less effective than are teams whose members do not get caught up in their self-image. This should not be construed to mean that teams should be completely oblivious to organizational issues. It is obvious that teams, like individuals, are sensitive to how they are viewed by the organization and relevant organizational authorities. When teams believe that their decisions are important to organizational authorities, they are more likely to make sound decisions than if they believe that their decisions are unimportant (Thompson, Kray, & Lind, 1998).

Provide a Face-Saving Mechanism for Teams

A small team who has the respect and support of their organization would seem to be in an ideal position to make effective decisions. Yet often, they fail to do so. One reason is that they are concerned with how their decision, and its fallout, will be viewed by others. Many teams are afraid of being blamed for poor decisions—even decisions for which it would have been impossible to predict the outcome. Often, face-saving concerns keep people from changing course, even when the current course is clearly doubtful. For this reason, it can be useful to provide teams with a face-saving mechanism or a reason for why outcomes might appear to be poor. This basically amounts to giving teams an external attribution for poor performance. Indeed, teams that are given an excuse for poor performance before knowing the outcome of their decision are less likely to succumb to groupthink than teams that do not have an excuse (Turner, Probasco, Pratkanis, & Leve, 1992).

The Risk Technique

The risk technique is a structured discussion situation designed to reduce group members' fears about making decisions (Maier, 1952). The discussion is structured so that team members talk about the dangers or risks involved in a decision and delay discussion of any potential gains. Following this is a discussion of controls or mechanisms for dealing with the risks or dangers. This strategy may sound touchy-feely, but it basically amounts to creating an atmosphere in which team members can express doubts and raise criticisms without fear of rejection or hostility from the team. There are many ways to create such an atmosphere. One way is to have a facilitator play the role of devil's advocate for a particular decision. The mere expression of doubt about an idea or plan by one person may liberate others to raise doubts and concerns. A second method may be to have members privately convey their concerns or doubts and then post this information in an unidentifiable manner. Again, this liberates members to talk about their doubts.

Adopt Different Perspectives

In this technique, team members assume the perspective of other constituencies with a stake in the decision (Turner & Pratkanis, 1998). For example, in the *Challenger* incident, group members might have been asked to assume the roles of the federal government, local citizens, space crew families, astronomers, and so on. Although the *Challenger* disaster happened in large part because of a disastrously poor understanding of how to interpret statistical data, the key point of adopting different perspectives is to create a mechanism that will instigate thinking more carefully about problems, which could prompt these groups to reconsider evidence.

Debias Training Techniques

The goal of debiasing training techniques is to expose how human decision making can be faulty and based on limited information. For this reason, it is often helpful to have a decision expert work with a team and elaborate upon key decision biases, ideally through simulations and exercises. It is usually unhelpful to simply inform teams about biases, because they appear to be absurdly obvious after the fact. Rather, it is best to actively challenge teams with a realistic decision scenario and then use the team context to discuss the process of decision making and methods for improving its quality.

Structure Discussion Principles

The goal of structured discussion principles is to delay solution selection and to increase the problem-solving phase. This prevents premature closure on a solution and extends problem analysis and evaluation. For example, teams may be given guidelines that emphasize continued solicitations of solutions, protection of individuals from criticism, keeping the discussion problem-centered, and listing all solutions before evaluating them (Maier, 1952).

Establish Procedures for Protecting Alternative Viewpoints

Although teams can generate high-quality decision alternatives, they frequently fail to adopt them as preferred solutions (Janis, 1982; Turner et al., 1992). This means that most problems that teams face are not simple, "eureka" types of decisions, in which the correct answer is obvious once it is put on the table. Rather, team members must convince others about the correctness of their views. This is a difficult task when things like conformity pressure are operating and especially after individual team members have publicly committed to a particular course of action. For these reasons, it can be useful to instruct members to keep a log of all alternatives suggested during each meeting.

Second Solution

This technique requires teams to identify a second solution or decision recommendation as an alternative to their first choice. This enhances the problem-solving and idea generation phases as well as performance quality (Hoffman & Maier, 1966).

Beware of Time Pressure

Decisions involve idealistic considerations, such as moral principles and ideals, as well as practical considerations, such as difficulty, cost, or situational pressures. Therefore, it is undeniable that decision makers often make trade-offs. Moral principles are more likely to guide decisions for the distant future than for the immediate future, whereas difficulty, cost, and situational pressures are more likely to be important in near future decisions. In other words, managers are more likely to compromise their principles in decisions regarding near future actions compared with distant future actions (Liberman & Trope, 1998).

DECISION-MAKING PITFALL 2: ESCALATION OF COMMITMENT

It would seem that one remedy for groupthink would be clear feedback as to the effectiveness of the decision-making process. For example, the Coca-Cola Company's decision to introduce New Coke was eventually recognized as a mistake and reversed. Do such clear failures prompt teams to revisit their decision-making process and improve upon it? Not necessarily. In fact, under some conditions, teams will persist with a losing course of action, even in the face of clear evidence to the contrary. This type of situation is known as the **escalation of commitment** phenomenon.

Consider the decision-making problem in Box 6-2.

BOX 6-2

New-Product Investment Decision

As the president of an airline company, you have invested $10 million of the company's money into a research project. The purpose was to build a plane that would not be detected by conventional radar, in other words, a radar-blank plane. When the project is 90 percent completed, another firm begins marketing a plane that cannot be detected by radar. Also, it is apparent that their plane is much faster and far more economical than the plan your company is building. The question is: Should you invest the last 10 percent of the research funds to finish your radar-blank plane?

☐ Yes, invest the money.

☐ No, drop the project.

Next, consider the following decision situations.

- A senior marketing manager at a major pet food corporation continues to promote a specific brand, despite clear evidence that the brand is losing market share to its competitors.
- A company continues to invest in a manager who is known to have handled many situations poorly and receives consistently subpar 360-degree evaluations.
- Quaker Oats continued to push Snapple, even though its market share dropped staggeringly.
- When the stock market tide is running, wildly enthusiastic investors will bid up companies' stock prices to levels known to be too high, in the certainty that they can "only go up." Two years later, they dump these companies at any price, believing with equal certainty that they are becoming worthless (Train, 1995).
- A company continues to drill for oil, despite being unable to turn a profit on drilling efforts in the past 3 years.
- John R. Silber, previous president of Boston University, decided to invest in Seragen, a biotechnology company with a promising cancer drug. After investing $1.7 million over 6 years, the value is now $43,000 (Barboza, 1998).

In all of these situations, individuals and teams committed further resources to what eventually proved to be a failing course of action. The decision bias known as the escalation of commitment. In most cases, the situation does not turn into a problem for a while. The situation becomes an escalation dilemma when the persons involved in the decision would make a different decision if they had not been involved up until that point, or when other objective persons would not choose that course of action. Often, in escalation situations, a decision is made to commit further resources to "turn the situation around." This process may repeat and escalate several times as additional resources are invested. The bigger the investment and the more severe the possible loss, the more prone people are to try to turn things around. Consider the situation faced by Lyndon Johnson during the early stage of the Vietnam War. Johnson received the following memo from George Ball, then undersecretary of state:

> The decision you face now is crucial. Once large numbers of U.S. troops are committed to direct combat, they will begin to take heavy casualties in a war they are ill-equipped to fight in a noncooperative if not downright hostile countryside. Once we suffer large casualties, we will have started a well-nigh irreversible process. Our involvement will be so great that we cannot—without national humiliation—stop short of achieving our complete objectives. Of the two possibilities I think humiliation will be more likely than the achievement of our objectives—even after we have paid terrible costs. (Sheehan et al., 1971, p. 450).

The escalation of commitment process is illustrated in Figure 6-2. In the first stage of the escalation of commitment, a decision-making team is confronted with questionable or negative outcomes (e.g., a price drop, decreasing market share, poor performance evaluations, or a malfunction). This external event prompts a reexamination of the team's current course of action, in which the utility of continuing is weighed against the utility of withdrawing or changing course. This decision determines the team's commitment to its current course of action. If this commitment is low, the team may withdraw from the project and assume its losses. If this commitment is high, however, the

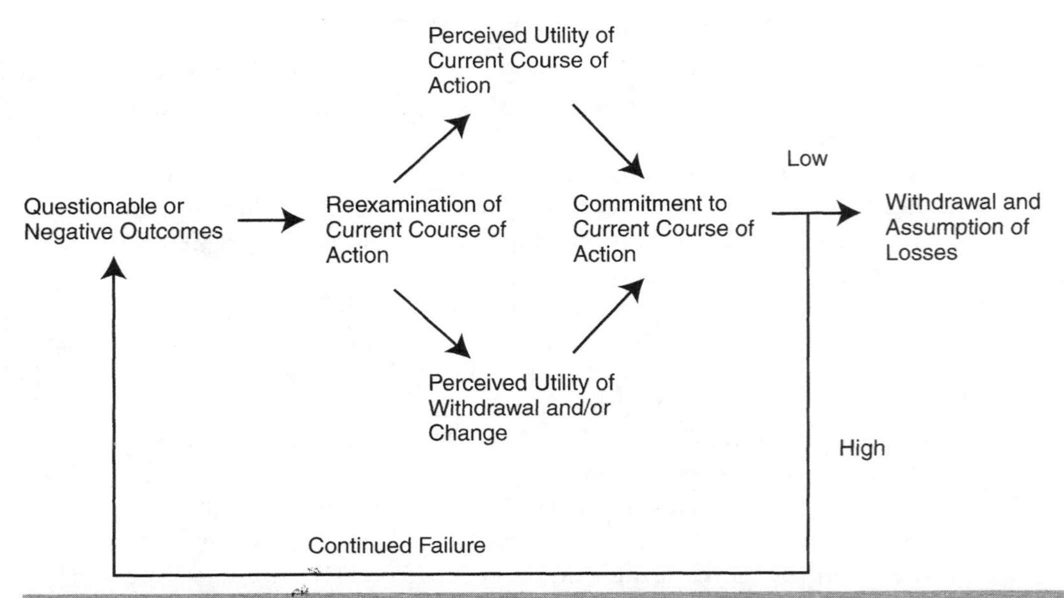

FIGURE 6-2 Escalation of Commitment

Source: Adapted from Ross, J., & Staw, B. M. 1993, August. "Organizational Escalation and Exit: Lessons from the Shoreham Nuclear Power Plant." *Academy of Management Journal,* 701–732.

team will continue commitment and continue to cycle through the decision stages. There are four key processes involved in the escalation of commitment cycle: Project-related determinants, psychological determinants, social determinants, and structural determinants (Ross & Staw, 1993).

Project Determinants

Project determinants are the objective features of the situation. Upon receiving negative feedback, team members ask whether the perceived setback is permanent or temporary (e.g., is reduced market share a meaningful trend or a simple perturbation in a noisy system?). If it is perceived to be temporary, there may appear to be little reason to reverse course. Then, when addressing questions like whether to increase investment in the project or to commit more time and energy to it, the team is essentially asking whether it wishes to escalate its commitment. Of course, this may often be the right choice, but it should be clear that such decisions also make it harder for the team to terminate that course of action if results continue to be poor.

Psychological Determinants

Psychological determinants refer to the cognitive and motivational factors that propel people to continue with a chosen course of action. When managers or teams receive indication that the outcomes of a project may be negative, they should ask themselves the following questions regarding their own involvement in the process:

What Are the Personal Rewards for Me in This Project?

In many cases, the *process* of the project itself, rather than the *outcome* of the project, becomes the reason for continuing the project. This leads to a self-perpetuating reinforcement trap, wherein the rewards for continuing are not aligned with the actual objectives of the project. Ironically, people who have high, rather than low, self-esteem are more likely to become victimized by psychological forces—people with high self-esteem have much more invested in their ego and its maintenance than do those with low self-esteem.

This advice may seem rather odd because it appears to be inconsistent with self-interest. That is, it would seem to be in a project manager's best interest to invest in the product, rather than to benefit the company as a whole. However, managers or teams who fall prey to escalation of commitment will ultimately end up losing because their product won't be successful, and they will have suffered more than if they simply cut off the project earlier on.

Is My Ego and the Team's Reputation on the Line?

"If I pull out of this project, would I feel stupid? Do I worry that other people would judge me to be stupid?" Ego protection often becomes a higher priority than the success of the project. When managers feel personally responsible for a decision, monetary allocations to the project increase at a much higher rate than when managers do not feel responsible for the initial decision (Staw, 1976).

In some sense, it does not seem too surprising that when managers personally oversee a project, they attempt to ensure that the project has every chance of success (e.g., by allocating more resources to it). After all, that is their job. A manager who works on a project through from beginning to end is going to know more about it and may be in a better position to judge it. Furthermore, personal commitment is essential for the success of many projects. Whereas it is certainly good to nurture projects so that they have their best chance of survival, it is nearly impossible for most managers to be completely objective about it. This is where it is important to have clear, unbiased criteria by which to evaluate the success of a project.

Are We Evaluating All of the Facts in an Unbiased Fashion?

The confirmation bias is the tendency for people to only see what they already believe to be true. When people are ego-invested in a project, the confirmation bias will even be stronger. It is striking how even upon the receipt of what appears to be unsupportive data, people who have fallen prey to the confirmation bias will maintain, and in some cases increase, their resolve. For example, the confirmation bias is related to the costly protraction of strike activity—a form of escalation of commitment. As a quick demonstration of the confirmation bias, take the test in Box 6-3.

Is the Glass Half-Empty or Half-Full?

If decision makers see themselves as trying to recover from a losing position, chances are they will engage in greater risk than if they see themselves as starting with a clean slate. Like the gambler in Las Vegas, decision makers who wait for their luck to turn around have fallen into the trap. For these reasons, decision makers who were initially responsible for the decision are likely to feel more compelled to continue to pursue the same course of action as compared to the successors of such managers. Escalation of commitment is partially responsible for some of the worst financial losses experienced by organizations. For example, from 1966 to 1989, the Long Island Lighting Company's investment in the

BOX 6-3

Card Test

Imagine that the following four cards are placed in front of you and are printed with the following symbols on one side:

Card 1	*Card 2*	*Card 3*	*Card 4*
E	K	4	7

Now, imagine you are told that a letter appears on one side of each card and a number on the other. Your task is to judge the validity of the following rule, which refers only to these four cards: "If a card has a vowel on one side, then it has an even number on the other side." Your task is to turn over only those cards that have to be turned over for the correctness of the rule to be judged. Which cards do you want to turn over? *(Stop here and decide which cards to turn over before reading on.)*

Averaging over a large number of investigations (Oaksford & Chater, 1994), 89 percent of people select E, which is a logically correct choice because an odd number on the other side would disconfirm the rule. However, 62 percent also choose to turn over the 4, which is not logically informative because neither a vowel nor a consonant on the other side would falsify the rule. Only 25 percent of people elect to turn over the 7, which is a logically informative choice because a vowel behind the 7 would falsify the rule. Only 16 percent elect to turn over K, which would not be an informative choice.

Thus, people display two types of logical errors in the task. First, they often turn over the 4, an example of the confirmation bias. However, even more striking is the failure to take the step of attempting to disconfirm what they believe is true—in other words, turning over the 7 (Wason & Johnson-Laird, 1972).

Shoreham Nuclear Power Plant escalated from $65 million to $5 billion, despite a steady flow of negative feedback. The plant was never opened (Ross & Staw, 1993).

Social Determinants

Most people want others to approve of them, accept them, and respect them. Consequently, they engage in actions and behaviors that they think will please most of the people most of the time, perhaps at the expense of doing the right thing, which may not be popular.

The need for approval and liking may be especially heightened among groups composed of friends. Indeed, groups of longtime friends are more likely to continue to invest in a losing course of action (41 percent) than groups composed of unacquainted persons (16 percent) when groups do not have buy-in from relevant organizational authorities. In contrast, when they are respected by their organization, groups of friends are extremely deft at extracting themselves from failing courses of action (Lind, Kray, & Thompson, 1998).

Structural Determinants

The same determinants that create groupthink on a team level also exist at the level of the institution. For instance, a project can itself become institutionalized, thereby removing it from critical evaluation. Instead, old-timers and newcomers learn to perceive the project as an integral part of the culture. It becomes impossible for these teams to consider removal or extinction of the project.

Often in organizations, political pressure can kill an otherwise viable project. Similarly, political support can keep a project alive that should be terminated. The escalation of commitment phenomenon implies that more often than not, teams will persevere with a losing course of action because of the psychological, social, and structural reinforcements in the situation. Teams become entrenched and committed to their positions and reluctant to move away from them.

Avoiding the Escalation of Commitment Problem

Most teams do not realize that they are in an escalation dilemma until it is too late. Complicating matters is the fact that, in most escalation dilemmas, the team might have some early "wins" or good signs that reinforce the initial decision. How can a team best get out of an escalation dilemma?

Unfortunately, there is no magical, overnight cure. The best advice is to adopt a policy of risk management: Be aware of the risks involved in the decision; learn how to best manage these risks; and set limits, effectively capping losses at a tolerable level. It is also important to find ways to get information and feedback on the project from a different perspective. More specifically:

Set Limits

Ideally, a team should determine at the outset what criteria and performance standards will be necessary to continue to invest in the project or program in question. These should be spelled out and distributed to all relevant personnel.

Avoid the Bystander Effect

In many situations, especially ambiguous ones, people quite frankly are not sure how to behave and, therefore, do nothing out of fear of acting foolishly. This dynamic explains the bystander effect, or the tendency to not help others who obviously need help in emergency situations (Latané & Darley, 1970). If team members have well-defined, predetermined limits, they need not try to interpret others' behavior; they can refer to their own judgment and act upon it.

Avoid Tunnel Vision

Get several perspectives on the problem. Ask people who are not personally involved in the situation for their appraisal. Be careful not to bias their evaluation with your own views, hopes, expectations, or other details, such as the cost of extricating the team from the situation, because that will only predispose them toward the team's point of view. This is not what you want—you want an honest, critical assessment.

Recognize Sunk Costs

Probably the most powerful way to escape escalation of commitment is to simply recognize and accept sunk costs. Sunk costs are basically water under the bridge: Money (or other commitments) previously spent that cannot be recovered. It is often helpful for teams to have built into their agenda a period in which they consider removal of the project, product, or program. In this way, the situation is redefined as one in which a decision will be made immediately about whether to invest or not; that is, if you were making the initial decision today, would you make the investment currently under consideration (as a continuing investment), or would you choose another course of action? If the decision is not one that you would choose anew, you might want to start thinking about how to terminate the project and move on to the next one.

External Review

In some cases, it is necessary to remove or replace the original decision makers from deliberations precisely because they are biased. One way to do this is with an external review of departments.

DECISION-MAKING PITFALL 3: THE ABILENE PARADOX

In the case of groupthink and escalation of commitment, teams pursue a course of action largely because they are personally involved; a decision to discontinue might involve admission of a poor earlier choice. There is another kind of behavior that can lead teams to make undesirable choices—choices, in fact, that none of the individuals would have made on their own. Known as the **Abilene paradox** (Harvey, 1974), it is a kind of consensus seeking that has its roots in the avoidance of conflict. The Abilene paradox is basically a form of **pluralistic ignorance:** Group members adopt a position because they feel other members desire it; team members don't challenge one another because they want to avoid conflict or achieve consensus. Although this is a kind of "expectational bubble"—a set of expectations about other people's expectations that could be burst if even one person expressed a contrary view—it can have a dramatic impact on the actual decision-making behavior of the team. The story in Box 6-4 illustrates the dilemma.

To the extent that team members are more interested in consensus than debate, they may end up in Abilene. Indeed, the mismanagement of agreement can be more problematic than the management of disagreement (Harvey, 1974). This may seem counterintuitive, but the consequences are very real.

It may seem strange to think that intelligent people who are in private agreement may somehow fail to realize the commonality of their beliefs and end up in Abilene. However, it is easy to see how this can happen if members fail to communicate their beliefs to each other.

Quandaries like the Abilene paradox may seem absurd, but they are easy to fall into. Strategies to avoid the situation include playing devil's advocate, careful questioning, and a commitment on the part of all team members to both fully air their opinions as well as respectfully listen to others. Note that none of these requires team members to abandon consensus seeking as a goal—if that is indeed their goal. However, it does require that consensus actually reflect the true beliefs of the team.

What factors lead to problems like the Abilene paradox? In general, if individual team members are intimidated or feel that their efforts will not be worthwhile, then they are less likely to air or defend their viewpoints. This is called *self-limiting behavior.*

BOX 6-4

The Abilene Paradox

The July afternoon in Coleman, Texas (population 5,607), was particularly hot—104 degrees as measured by the Walgreen's Rexall Ex-Lax temperature gauge. In addition, the wind was blowing fine-grained West Texas topsoil through the house. But the afternoon was still tolerable—even potentially enjoyable. There was a fan going on the back porch; there was cold lemonade; and finally, there was entertainment. Dominoes. Perfect for the conditions. The game required little more physical exertion than an occasional mumbled comment, "Shuffle 'em," and an unhurried movement of the arm to place the spots in the appropriate perspective on the table. All in all, it had the markings of an agreeable Sunday afternoon in Coleman—that is, it was until my father-in-law suddenly said, "Let's get in the car and go to Abilene and have dinner at the cafeteria."

I thought, "What, go to Abilene? Fifty-three miles? In this dust storm and heat? And in an un-air-conditioned 1958 Buick?"

But my wife chimed in with "Sounds like a great idea. I'd like to go. How about you, Jerry?" Since my own preferences were obviously out of step with the rest I replied, "Sounds good to me," and added, "I just hope your mother wants to go."

"Of course I want to go," said my mother-in-law. "I haven't been to Abilene in a long time."

So into the car and off to Abilene we went. My predictions were fulfilled. The heat was brutal. We were coated with a fine layer of dust that was cemented with perspiration by the time we arrived. The food at the cafeteria provided first-rate testimonial material for antacid commercials.

Some four hours and 106 miles later we returned to Coleman, hot and exhausted. We sat in front of the fan for a long time in silence. Then, both to be sociable and to break the silence, I said, "It was a great trip, wasn't it?"

No one spoke. Finally my mother-in-law said, with some irritation, "Well, to tell the truth, I really didn't enjoy it much and would rather have stayed here. I just went along because the three of you were so enthusiastic about going. I wouldn't have gone if you all hadn't pressured me into it."

I couldn't believe it. "What do you mean 'you all'?" I said. "Don't put me in the 'you all' group. I was delighted to be doing what we were doing. I didn't want to go. I only went to satisfy the rest of you. You're the culprits."

My wife looked shocked. "Don't call me a culprit. You and Daddy and Mama were the ones who wanted to go. I just went along to be sociable and to keep you happy. I would have had to be crazy to want to go out in heat like that."

Her father entered the conversation abruptly. "Hell!" he said.

He proceeded to expand on what was already absolutely clear. "Listen, I never wanted to go to Abilene. I just thought you might be bored. You visit so seldom I wanted to be sure you enjoyed it. I would have preferred to play another game of dominoes and eat the leftovers in the icebox."

After the outburst of recrimination we all sat back in silence. Here we were, four reasonably sensible people who, of our own volition, had just taken a 106-mile trip across a godforsaken desert in a furnace-like temperature through a cloud-like dust storm to eat unpalatable food at a hole-in-the-wall cafeteria in Abilene, when none of us had really wanted to go. In fact, to be more accurate, we'd done just the opposite of what we wanted to do. The whole situation simply didn't make sense (Harvey, 1974).

According to a survey of 569 managers by Mulvey, Veiga, & Elsass (1996), there are six key causes of self-limiting behavior in teams:

- **The presence of someone with expertise:** When team members perceive that another member of the team has expertise or is highly qualified to make a decision, they will self-limit. Members' perceptions of other teammates' competence play a key role, and these evaluations are formed quickly—often before a team meets for the first time.
- **The presentation of a compelling argument:** Frequently, the timing of a coherent argument influences decision making—such as when the decision is made after a lot of fruitless discussion.
- **A lack of confidence in one's ability to contribute:** If team members feel unsure about their ability to meaningfully contribute to the decision, they will be inclined to self-limit.
- **An unimportant or meaningless decision:** Unless the decision is seen as vital or important to the individual's well-being, there is a powerful tendency to adopt a "who cares" attitude.
- **Pressure from others to conform to the team's decision:** Roger Boisjoly reported that he felt incredible pressures to conform exerted by the management team.
- **A dysfunctional decision-making climate:** When team members believe that others are frustrated, indifferent, disorganized, or generally unwilling to commit themselves to making an effective decision, they are likely to self-limit. Such a climate can be created in the early stages of a decision by inadvertent remarks such as, "this is a ridiculous task," "nothing's going to change, so why bother," and so on.

How to Avoid the Abilene Paradox

The following suggestions are taken from Harvey (1974) and Mulvey et al. (1996).

Confront the Issue in a Team Setting

The most straightforward approach involves meeting with the organization members who are key figures in the problem and its solution. The first step is for the individual who proposes a solution to state it and then be open to any and all feedback. For example:

> I want to talk with you about the research project. Although I have previously said things to the contrary, I frankly don't think it will work and I am very anxious about it. I suspect that others may feel the same, but I don't know. Anyway, I am concerned that we may end up misleading one another, and if we aren't careful, we may continue to work on a problem that none of us wants and that might even bankrupt us. That's why I need to know where the rest of you stand. I would appreciate any of your thoughts about the project. Do you think it can succeed? (Harvey, 1974, p. 32).

Conduct a Private Vote

People often go along with what they think the team wants to do. Dissenting opinions are easier to express privately—pass out blank cards and ask team members to privately write their opinions. Guarantee them anonymity and then share the overall outcomes with the team.

Minimize Status Differences

High-status members are often at the center of communication, and lower status members are likely to feel pressures to conform more quickly. Although this can be difficult to avoid, reassurances by senior members about the importance of frank and honest discussion reinforced by the elimination of status symbols, like dress, meeting place, title, and so on, may be helpful.

Minimize the Size of the Team

As we have seen, teams that are too large often experience social loafing, free riding, and a diffusion of responsibility—all of which can contribute to making a trip to Abilene.

Frame the Task As a Decision to Be Made

Framing the task as a decision to be made, rather than a judgment (which suggests personal opinion), helps cast a tone of somber decision making, absent of the trappings of power or personal prestige. When team members are given a decision-making responsibility, they fundamentally approach the problem differently when the decision that needs to be made is framed as a *problem to be solved.* The typical approach is to view decisions as judgments, not problems. People typically view a problem as needing more analysis, such as pros and cons, and less opinion. Telling your team that you believe in "fact-based decision making" is a potentially helpful way of framing the decision.

Provide a Formal Forum for Controversial Views

This may be achieved by segmenting the discussion into pros and cons. Debate must be legitimized. Members should not have to worry about whether it is appropriate to bring up contrary views; it should be expected and encouraged.

Take Responsibility for Failure

It is important to create a climate where teams can make mistakes, own up to them, and then move on without fear of recrimination. Consider what happened to a three-man forge team, called the "Grumpy Old Men," at Eaton Corporation in the Forge Division plant. Through an assumption at the start of their shift, they made an error that resulted in about 1,200 pieces of scrap. It was not an inexpensive mistake, but it was not one that would close the plant. The team had jeopardized the plant's output to customers. The team came forward to the plant leadership, admitted their error, described its potential impact, and demanded to be allowed to take corrective action so that the problem could never occur again. They even took it a step further and demanded to be allowed to go before the entire workforce at the start of each of the three shifts and admit their error and describe what they were doing to make sure it would not happen again (Bergstrom, 1997).

DECISION-MAKING PITFALL 4: GROUP POLARIZATION

Consider the case in Box 6-5. Most people independently evaluating the problem state that the new company would need to have nearly a two-thirds probability of success before they would advise Mr. A. to leave his current job and accept a new position (Stoner, 1961). What do you think happens when the same people discuss Mr. A.'s situation and are instructed to reach consensus?

You might expect the outcome of the team to be the same as the average of the individuals considered separately. However, this is not what happens. The group advises Mr. A. to take the new job, even if it only has slightly better than a 50-50 chance of success! In other words, groups show a **risky shift.**

Now consider a situation in which a company is deciding the highest odds of an engine malfunction that could be tolerated on the release of a new vehicle. In this case, individual advisors are cautious, but when the same people are in a group, they collectively insist on even lower odds. Thus, they exhibit a **cautious shift.**

Why are teams both more risky and more cautious than are individuals, considering the identical situation? The reason for this apparent disparity has to do with some of the peculiarities of group dynamics. Teams are not inherently more risky or cautious than individuals; rather they are more *extreme* than individuals. **Group polarization** is the tendency for group discussion to intensify group opinion, producing more extreme judgment than might be obtained by pooling the individuals' views separately (see Figure 6-3).

Group polarization is not simply a case of social compliance or a bandwagon effect. The same individuals display the polarization effect when queried privately af-

BOX 6-5

Advice Question

Mr. A., an electrical engineer who is married and has one child, has been working for a large electronics corporation since graduating from college 5 years ago. He is assured of a lifetime job with a modest, though adequate, salary and liberal pension benefits upon retirement. On the other hand, it is very unlikely that his salary will increase much before he retires. While attending a convention, Mr. A. is offered a job with a small, newly founded company that has a highly uncertain future. The new job would pay more to start and would offer the possibility of a share in the ownership if the company survived the competition with larger firms.

Imagine that you are advising Mr. A. What is the *lowest* probability or odds of the new company proving financially sound that you would consider acceptable to make it worthwhile for Mr. A. to take the new job? Before reading on, indicate your response on a probability scale from zero to 100 percent.

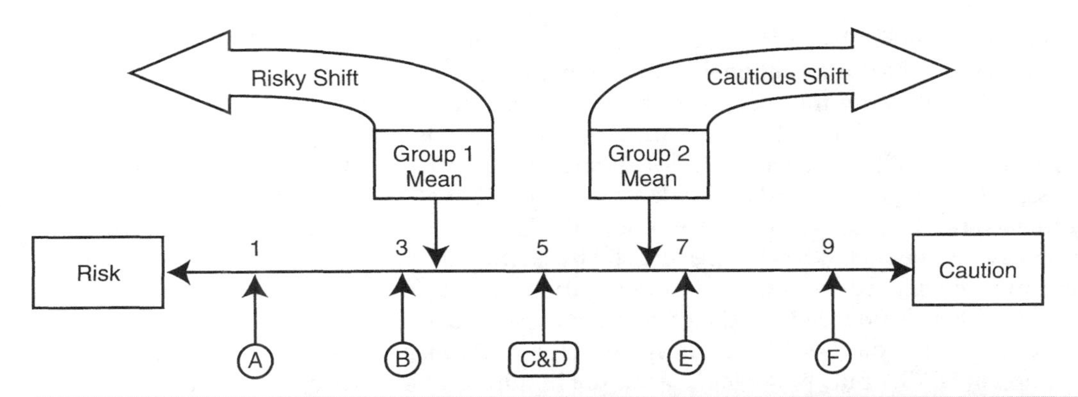

FIGURE 6-3 Group Polarization Processes. Imagine that Group 1 includes Person A (who chose 1), Person B (who chose 3), and Persons C and D (who both chose 5); the average of pregroup choices would be (1 + 3 + 5 + 5)/4, or 3.5. Because this mean is less than 5, a risky shift would probably occur in Group 1. If, in contrast, Group 2 contained persons C, D, E, and F, their pregroup average would be (5 + 5 + 7 + 9)/4 or 6.5. Because this mean is closer to the caution pole, a conservative shift would probably occur in the group.

Source: Adapted from Janis, I. L. 1982. *Victims of Groupthink* (2nd ed.). Boston: Houghton Mifflin.

ter group discussion. This means that people really believe the group's decision—they have conformed inwardly! The polarization effect does not happen in nominal groups. The polarization effect grows stronger with time, meaning that the same person who was in a group discussion 2 weeks earlier will be even more extreme in his or her judgment.

Two explanations for group polarization hearken back to our discussion of conformity at the beginning of the chapter: The need to be right and the need to be liked. Simply stated, people want to make the right decision and they want to be approved of by their team. Take the case concerning Mr. A., the electrical engineer. Most people are positively inclined when they agree to recommend to Mr. A. that he seriously consider a job change. However, they vary greatly in their reasons for why Mr. A. should change jobs. Someone in the group may feel that Mr. A. should leave the secure job because it does not represent a sufficient challenge; others may think that Mr. A. should leave the company because he should increase his standard of living. Thus, people feel that Mr. A. should consider a move, but they have different (yet complementary) reasons supporting their belief. This is the rational type of conformity we discussed earlier. At the same time, members of the team want to be accepted—part of the socialization process we outlined in chapter 4.

CONCLUSIONS

Teams make important decisions and some of them will not be good ones, despite the very best of intentions. It is unrealistic to suggest that poor decision making, or for that matter even disastrous decision making, is avoidable. The key message hearkens back to a point we made early in chapter 1, which has to do with creating an organization that can optimally learn from failure. Learning from failure is difficult when people suffer—especially innocent ones. As a case in point, consider the steps that were taken by NASA following the space shuttle *Challenger* accident, including the redesign of the joints and solid rocket booster, which went through hundreds of modifications; the institution of full hazard analysis for thousands of parts; certification of flight readiness, which includes verbal and video-recorded affirmation from a variety of NASA officials; the institution of a veto policy, in which anyone at any level can stop the process—a policy that has been exercised by NASA members; and creation of launch criteria, which occurs in the cool of the morning, rather than in the heat of the afternoon. Is there a downside to the creation and use of decision-making procedures and criteria that err on the side of safety? As Don McMonagle, manager of launch integration at NASA puts it: If every one of the hundreds of thousands of components on space vehicles were required to work perfectly, no one could ever launch and this would effectively paralyze the U.S. space program (personal communication, July 1998). The key for NASA and other decision-making teams within organizations is to develop and use decision-making procedures, such as veto policies and preestablished criteria to guide decision making. All of these decisions involve a certain level of risk, but that risk can be minimized.

3

A Guide for Creating Effective Study Groups

Most students enrolled in M.B.A. programs must work in groups to complete important projects and requirements en route to obtaining their degree. Some students work with the same group throughout their program; other students work with several different groups each semester. This is a guide for helping these groups to be as maximally effective as possible.

VERY EARLY ON

In the beginning, when the group is first forming, it is helpful to do some kind of structured exercise that moves beyond usual chit-chat. We suggest the "Team Management Skills Inventory" (exercise by Thompson, 1998)[1].

SOMETIME DURING THE FIRST WEEK OR TWO

There are a host of tensions and dilemmas that can threaten the effectiveness of any study group. We suggest the team meet and complete a "Team Contract" (exercise by Thompson, 1998).

We also suggest that groups that will work together for long periods of time discuss the following issues in the first week or two:

Team Goals

- **Learning:** "Are we here to learn and to help others learn or are we here to get a good grade?" There is not a right answer to this question, but differing goals in the group can hurt later performance.
- **Standards:** "Is perfectionism more important than being on time, or vice versa?"
- **Performance:** "Are we a high-pass (dean's list) group or a pass (survival) group?"

Thought Questions

- What happens if the project leader has lower standards than some other members about writing a paper or report?
- What happens if one group member is not very skilled at some topic area (i.e., how do you utilize that member's input on group projects and incorporate ideas that do not appear to be adding value)?

Person-Task Mapping

- Is it best to capitalize on the existing strengths of team members or to play to people's weaknesses?
- Suppose your team has a quantitative guru in it. Do you want to assign the "quant jock" to do all the math and econometrics problems, or use this as an opportunity to let other team members learn?

---

[1]The exercises cited in this appendix are written for the Kellogg Teams and Groups Center (KTAG) and are available through the Dispute Resolution Research Center (DRRC), Kellogg Graduate School of Management, Northwestern University, 2001 Sheridan Road, Evanston, Illinois 60208-2011. Phone: (847) 491-8068; e-mail: drrc@kellogg.nwu.edu.

Additional Questions

- **Member skills:** Do you want to use your study group meeting time to bring all group members up to speed or should those who need help get it on their own time?
- **Person-task focus:** Are people the group's first priority or is working the first priority?
- **Structure:** Should the team meeting be structured (e.g., agenda, timekeeper, assigned roles) or should it be free-form?
- **Interloper:** Are other people (outside the group) allowed to attend group meetings and have access to group notes, outlines, homework, and so on, or is group work considered confidential?
- **Communication standards:** Are group members expected to adapt to the most advanced methods of communication, or does group work happen at the lowest common denominator?
- **Project leader pacing:** There would seem to be an advantage for group members who volunteer early on for group projects because commitments and pressures build up later in the semester; how will the group meeting process adapt to increasing workloads?

AFTER THE GROUP IS WELL UNDER WAY

After the group is well under way, it is a good idea to take stock of how the group is working together. We suggest the "Group Assessment Inventory," ideally administered by a professor or another person acquainted with the study group (exercise by Thompson, Gruenfeld, Rothbard, & Naquin, 1999).

Another useful idea is to do some version of a peer-feedback performance review, wherein individuals receive confidential feedback and ratings about how they are viewed by other team members. This can often be completely computerized (see appendix 4).

ON A REGULAR BASIS

It is important that study groups revisit the team contract. Are the expectations being met? What issues and topics should be talked about that are not currently in the contract? What issues are in the contract that do not seem relevant?

SPECIAL TIPS FOR LONG-TERM STUDY GROUPS

Consider the actual advice from M.B.A. students who were enrolled in an intensive 2-year program. Their study groups were assigned to them and maintained throughout the 2-year program. During the time they worked together, members were asked for their input on what did and did not work in their study groups in regard to maximizing learning and using time effectively. Box A3-1 summarizes the students' responses.

BOX A3-1

Advice for Long-Term Study Groups

- An agenda should be distributed before each group meeting date so everyone can prepare properly. Decide upon the agenda for the next meeting before adjourning the current meeting.
- Define who is expected to do what for each project.
- A written outline or "straw man" is needed to focus the group discussion on any particular project. Several alternatives should be evaluated during the outline stage before selecting which alternative will be taken for any project.
- Each major group project has a project leader responsible for doing most of the writing (in some cases, all of the writing). Other group members provide input early in the project and after a draft has been written. Assignments can be done in parallel by using this method, which helps to meet deadlines.
- Some groups summarize class readings for the project leader during the weeks that they are busy completing the project.
- The workload is not divided equally on every project. Over a 2-year period everyone will get the chance to contribute.
- Rotate responsibilities with each module or semester. For example, one person in the group may be the agenda captain for an entire module. The agenda captain organizes the meeting agendas and runs the meetings for that entire module. Rotating responsibilities every week wastes time deciding who does what.
- Try to meet on the same day and time each week. This makes it easier to plan travel schedules in advance.
- At the end of each major assignment, review the effectiveness of the process used to fulfill requirements. Adjust the process to improve effectiveness.
- Improve communication within the group by using e-mail and standardized software.
- Focus on the goals of the meeting first, then socialize.
- Maintain a sense of humor!

Source: Taken from compiled lists from the Executive Masters Program, Kellogg School of Management, Northwestern University, Evanston, Illinois. Lists compiled by K. Murnighan (1998) and R. Weeks (1996).

Chapter 4

Building a Balanced Team

Building a Balanced Team

GOALS

- Grasp the importance of balance among member types for a productive team.
- Learn the main components that work together to create team balance.
- Become acquainted with techniques for building and restoring team balance.

Do you remember the process most of us used in elementary school to select team members for playground sports? Two captains (often self-selected!) would take turns choosing players for their teams. If you were one of the last chosen, that process was often painful indeed. Just as often, the teams ended up with various forms of imbalance: the boys against the girls, one set of friends against another set of friends, and so forth.

Teams in companies and other organizations cannot afford imbalance based on bias, whim, or accident. Just as a major league sports team endeavors to fill each position with talent, so a company tries to build teams whose members have complementary skills and backgrounds.

THE IMPORTANCE OF BALANCE

You can imagine the difficulties a company would encounter if it turned an important marketing project over to a team made up exclusively of accountants. It is likely that every aspect of the project would be judged solely and narrowly by its cost. Just as disastrous would be the assignment of financial reform in the company to a team made up of advertising specialists. In these examples, the presence of an accountant or an advertising person on the team is not in question; both would probably play a valuable role. Only when the team is composed of one employee type do difficulties often arise.

Consider the many ways in which teams can achieve balance:

- by mixing team member personality types
- by mixing team members according to their expertise and experience
- by mixing team members according to their place in the organization's hierarchy
- by mixing employee ethnicities
- by mixing employee genders

In all cases, the purpose for such balancing is not political correctness but improved bottom-line results for the team. The balance sought for any specific team depends on the purpose or project at hand, the audience to whom the team will report, and the company culture itself. Therefore, no single formula can be given as an ideal recipe for the balanced team. Instead, this chapter points out options and advantages you may want to consider when building a team in your organization. We focus especially on the advantages of gender balance.

INSIGHT 17

Balance in the membership of a team gives the company the differing perspectives of several stakeholders. Variety of opinion makes for more complete discussion of issues and, eventually, better decision making.

Your Turn

If you believe you have served or now serve on a balanced team, jot down any advantages and disadvantages that came as a result of the team's diverse membership. If you have never served on a balanced team, think about a recent team experience. Describe the kinds of members that, if added, would have made your team more balanced.

CAUSES OF TEAM IMBALANCE

Although imbalanced teams arise for many reasons, four causes in particular appear to account for most imbalanced teams.

The team as the boss's clones. In many companies, bosses have such high opinions of themselves that they appoint team members strictly in their image. For many years, IBM struggled with this cloning phenomenon on its sales teams: All IBM sales representatives seemed to look, act, dress, and think in remarkably similar ways. Certainly, in the last decade, IBM has acted aggressively to achieve the advantages of diversity in its workforce and on its key teams.

The team as the usual players. The old business adage asserts that "20 percent of the employees do 80 percent of the work." Unfortunately, some companies take this folk wisdom so literally that they keep appointing only that 20 percent to company teams.

The same people seem to appear on major company teams year after year and, with no surprise, probably tend to make the same kinds of decisions (or mistakes) year after year.

The team as those most suited for the task. At first glance, this form of imbalance makes a certain amount of sense. For example, it would seem logical to give a research project to a company team made up of researchers, but an imbalance of any one employee type yields less than satisfactory results. The team could no doubt profit from the addition of a member from the finance group or marketing department. These members could help researchers see the "big picture" and avoid intellectually interesting but impractical decisions.

The team as one personality type. Some companies make the right move in balancing teams with employees of differing backgrounds, only to make the greater mistake of choosing members all of whom share the same personality profile. For example, imagine a team composed entirely of obsessive planners, each with their Palm Pilot crammed with dates, deadlines, and schedules. Their team project will almost certainly be delivered on time, but may be sorely lacking in creativity and fresh thinking. The same general point could be made for teams composed entirely of any of the other personality types discussed later in this chapter.

INSIGHT 18

Uniformity in membership usually has little advantage to a team. Diverse personality types, expertise, experience, and other differences among members tend to enrich discussion and improve decision making.

Your Turn

As a speculative exercise, think of some work- or school-related project that might well be accomplished by a team. Describe the characteristics of at least five members—your "dream team"—that you would assemble to serve on that team. Explain why you aimed at the balance you describe.

HOW AND WHEN TO PLAN FOR BALANCE

Like balancing a car tire, the balancing of a team is better undertaken before the journey begins, so to speak, than when you're already on the road. Once you have formed a team, there is great stigma attached to removing a team member for any reason. Therefore, make it your priority to choose team members wisely from the outset of a project. Many managers follow these approximate steps in shaping the membership of a team:

- Write down the specific goals you want to achieve through your team.
- List any constraints (such as personnel availability, budget factors, and company policies or procedures) that will limit your choice of team members.
- Describe skill or expertise categories (not specific people) that should be represented on the team.
- Describe personality types that will help the team function optimally.
- Nominate in writing several people, if possible, for each of the skill or expertise categories you have described. For each person on this list, write down an educated guess about his or her basic personality type.
- Select team members who fulfill the desired skill or expertise categories and provide a useful distribution of personality types in relation to your project goals.
- Inform these individuals in a motivating, morale-building way of their membership on the team. (You will want to make yourself available for individual conferences to deal with questions and concerns.)
- Plan carefully for an inspiriting first meeting of the team, at which basic information regarding goals, team leadership, available resources, milestones, deliverables, and evaluation measures are thoroughly discussed.

INSIGHT 19

Productive teams rarely happen by chance. The effort a manager puts into the selection of team members is repaid many times over by the team's cooperative proceedings and significant achievements.

Your Turn

Think about a time when you found yourself as a member of a team that was apparently assembled without forethought or planning. If the efforts of the team were not successful, explain reasons for this failure. If the efforts of the team were successful, explain any adjustments team members had to make to deal with the lack of planning in the forming of the team.

THE LIMITS OF PERSONALITY TESTS

Team members typically exhibit personality tendencies that can be placed at some point on four continua:

Member —— Self
Thinker —— Empathizer
Planner —— Juggler
Closer —— Researcher

Experts in personality testing caution against an overly simplistic interpretation of personality types or test results. Human beings are complex bundles of intellectual and emotional potential that resist any single label. As you may have guessed, stress levels and other life circumstances can dramatically influence one's dominant personality type. For example, a Juggler (someone who likes to have many balls in the air at once and live in the excitement of the moment) may, during times of stress, revert to a rigid Planner mentality, complete with a daily "to-do" list of things to accomplish. A Thinker, who usually values proof, rationality, and logic can, under the impact of stress, exhibit qualities of the Empathizer.

The key to evaluating the personalities of team members (or potential team members) lies in knowing your people as thoroughly as possible. If you have not worked with them personally, talk at length with their previous supervisors and coworkers to learn about their work habits, attitudes, needs, and career goals.

INSIGHT 20

Personality tests are only a starting point for the accurate description of your own personality or someone else's. Use the results of such tests carefully and in combination with other evidence to develop an appropriate balance of personality types on a team.

Your Turn

Do you believe that your personality changes in significant ways during times of stress? If so, what are those changes?

MAKING THE MOST OF GENDER BALANCE

In the 1990s, several influential books (including Deborah Tannen's *You Just Don't Understand* and *Talking from 9 to 5*,[1] and Kathleen Reardon's *They Don't Get It, Do They?*[2]) have argued that many aspects of women's verbal and nonverbal communication in business are distinctly different from those of men. Moreover, these authors assert, women's communication habits sometimes put them at a disadvantage for leadership roles, team participation, promotion, recognition, and full participation in decision making in corporate life.

For our purposes, the goal of every team leader and member should be to understand possible communication differences between genders so that the contributions of both genders can be maximized. In some descriptions of team processes, the topic of women's modes of communication has been reduced to a latter-day version of Henry Higgins' complaint of Eliza Doolittle in *My Fair Lady*: "If only a woman could be more like a man!" Teams and team leaders who have a similar attitude toward women members are missing the unique contributions women bring to the team table. As Tannen, Reardon, and others point out, women's communication habits in business exist for reasons. To understand those reasons is to put ourselves as team members and leaders in a better position to make the most of the communication patterns of both men and women. In short, women and men who serve together on teams must learn to listen to themselves and to one another, then to make adjustments in communication styles to achieve fairness, make the best use of team resources, and successfully execute the organization's mission.

Let it be said at the outset that the following observations are by no means applicable to all women in business environments. No researcher of women's communication behaviors has claimed universality for the results of quite limited studies. In the words of Deborah Tannen,

> I do not imply that there is anything inherently male or female about particular ways of talking, nor to claim that every individual man or woman adheres to the pattern, but rather to observe that a larger percentage of

---

[1] Tannen, Deborah. *You Just Don't Understand.* 2d ed. New York: Quill, 2001; *Talking from 9 to 5.* 2d ed. New York: Quill, 2001.

[2] Reardon, Kathleen. *They Don't Get It, Do They?* New York: Little, Brown, 1995.

women or men as a group talk in a particular way, or individual women and men are more likely to talk one way or the other.[3]

Tannen's research, joined by dozens of supportive studies, makes the point that women do appear to communicate differently than men in work environments, including teams. Most often women have been judged negatively for this difference, and they have been instructed (often by women) to "talk the talk" (i.e., the male talk) if they want to rise to positions of power in companies and be taken seriously in teams. This effort to recreate women's communication patterns in men's images ignores the very real contributions women bring to the team through their ways of communicating. As a counterbalance, then, to the pervasive argument that women should learn to speak more like men, we offer brief interpretations of 20 gender communication patterns. These interpretations are intended to point out the value of women's communication patterns *as they are* without repair or alteration for modern teams.

INSIGHT 21

Gender-based patterns of communication, whether those of men or women, can be useful in a variety of business circumstances and are equally of value.

Your Turn

Give your own impressions of ways in which communication may differ somewhat depending on the gender of the communicator.

CHARACTERISTICS OF MEN'S AND WOMEN'S COMMUNICATION HABITS

1. Men are less likely to ask for information or directions in a public situation that would reveal their lack of knowledge.

Man: I don't need to stop at the gas station for directions. I can find the right street.

Woman: Why not stop and ask? It will save us time.

---

[3] Tannen, Deborah. *Talking from 9 to 5*, p. xxi.

The willingness of women to seek help in such situations can prove useful to what Peter Senge has called "the learning organization,"[4] including its learning teams. The reluctance, out of pride or embarrassment, of independent men on a team to seek assistance is counterproductive. The language habits of women in this case can be extended throughout the team as a way of encouraging openness to new information, reliance on team members as resources, and a constant readiness to ask questions and learn.

2. Women perceive the question, "What would you like to do?" as an invitation for discussion and negotiation. Men perceive the same question as the stimulus to a direct answer.

Woman: We have to arrange a holiday party. What would you like to do? [She is expecting conversation about past holiday parties, anecdotes, personal memories, and possibility thinking.]

Man: We have to arrange a holiday party. What would you like to do? [He is expecting places and times to be named.]

Women's willingness to delay decision making pending a multidimensional review of background information and influences is sometimes portrayed as a deficit, especially for would-be leaders of teams. However, that same communication tendency can be valued as an antidote to a team's tendency to rush to judgment or to ignore relevant input. On modern teams, leaders are cast less and less in the role of quick-draw decision maker and more in the role of seer, with wisdom and patience implied. The gender communication approach of women in this case fits well with the requirements of team leadership, where instant answers and quick decisions are often impossible or foolhardy.

3. Women misunderstand men's ultimatums as serious threats rather than one more negotiation strategy.

Man: This is nonnegotiable. [A bluff.]

Woman: Fine, then. Have it your way. [She accepts the bluff as reality.]

This may be a way of saying that women tend to attach meanings to words and assume that male speakers do as well. In this example, the woman speaker believes that the man knows what "nonnegotiable" means and chooses that word sincerely to describe his position. If the man knows that his position is negotiable but chooses to dissemble, are we to praise his strategy and recommend it to both genders? In George Orwell's fine phrase, "The great enemy of language is insincerity." Women have much to teach about integrity in saying what you mean and meaning what you say.

---

[4] Senge, Peter. *The Fifth Discipline: The Art and Practice of the Learning Organization.* New York: Doubleday, 1994..

INSIGHT 22

What men and women say is not always what they mean. Listen to subtle expressions of attitude and emotion and pay attention to nonverbal signs to determine the complete meaning of a statement.

Your Turn

Describe a time when a person's words to you revealed only a small portion of the complete meaning they were trying to communicate. How did you go about discovering the full intent of their communication?

4. In decision making, women are more likely to downplay their certainty; men are more likely to downplay their doubts.

> Woman: In making this recommendation, I think I've covered every base—at least the ones I'm aware of.
>
> Man: I make this recommendation with complete confidence.

This language tendency on the part of women is sometimes portrayed as an inability to stand strong as a confident decision maker. It can just as easily be regarded and valued as a reluctance to bluff the audience or to assume a posture of confidence that is neither felt by the speaker nor supported by the facts. Women, by their language of qualification as exemplified here, may be providing a necessary caution against the male tendency toward exaggeration and bravado. In effect, women are telling it like it is: "I'm not entirely sure about my conclusions and I'm not going to pretend otherwise. To do so would be lying to you and, ultimately, empowering myself at your expense."

5. Women tend to lead by making suggestions and explaining those suggestions in terms of the good of the team. Men are more likely to lead by giving orders, with explanations (if any) based on rationales related to project goals.

> Woman: Let's proceed by dividing into teams. I think we can make the most of our individual talents by working with one another in smaller groups.
>
> Man: We're going to break into teams to divide up the workload and meet our deadlines.

Modern teams obviously require both approaches to planning and decision making as a way of dealing with rapidly changing business conditions. For every occasion when the team must be nourished and encouraged there is also a circumstance when someone has to make decisions without consensus (or relying on a trust bond that already exists within the group). The important point is that neither style is dysfunctional; both can be useful on teams to serve different but complementary goals.

6. Women tend to apologize even when they have done nothing wrong. Men tend to avoid apologies as signs of weakness or concession.

Woman: I'm sorry, but I have to read you this e-mail that just arrived from the boss.

Man: Listen up. The boss just sent this e-mail.

In this case, only the most rigid literalist would interpret the phrase, "I'm sorry" as an apology for a mistake of some kind. These words instead reveal a recognition that the listener's feelings may be bruised by the ensuing message, and that the speaker is not unaware of or unresponsive to those feelings. In this way, the communication patterns of women tend to insert emotional buffers into sometimes turbulent business life. What on the surface may appear to be unjustified apologizing is, at a deeper level, an effort to humanize the team and soften harsh effects.

INSIGHT 23

Apologies and equivocations do not necessarily indicate guilt or a perception of wrongdoing on the part of the speaker. These phrases may be a way of attempting to deal gently with an uncomfortable moment or situation.

Your Turn

Consider your own use of apology phrases such as "I'm sorry, but . . ." or "Excuse me" beyond their literal meanings. Try to paraphrase exactly what you are attempting to communicate by the use of these phrases.

7. Women tend to accept blame as a way of smoothing awkward situations. Men tend to ignore blame or place it elsewhere.

Woman: I probably didn't welcome our Japanese visitors exactly as I should have, but I tried to be gracious and sincere.

Man: I met the Japanese visitors at the airport. Next time someone should tell me when and how to bow.

Teams require accountability, but it is hardly present in the male language pattern illustrated here. The woman is clearly accepting responsibility both for what went right and what went wrong in her efforts to greet the Japanese visitors. The man, by contrast, seeks to avoid personal accountability and instead to pass it on to a vague "someone" in the organization. When less-than-ideal situations in business occur, the language habits of women may be more likely to depict accurately the accountability involved.

8. Women tend to temper criticism with positive buffers. Men tend to give criticism directly.

Woman: You're doing a great job on this report, but you may want to look at page eight one more time. At least see what you think.

Man: Fix page eight, then let me reread your report one final time before we send it upstairs.

An awareness of the listener's feelings is not a bad thing for team relationships. In this woman's example, the speaker tries to preserve the relationship while changing the behavior. The man seems more willing to sacrifice or at least risk the relationship for the sake of behavior. That choice leads directly, on many teams, to low morale and excessive turnover of membership.

9. Women tend to insert unnecessary and unwarranted "thank you's" in conversations. Men tend to avoid thanks as a sign of weakness.

Woman: Thanks anyway, but I don't think I want to trade my parking place with Jack.

Man: No, I don't want to trade for Jack's spot.

The facade of thanks is only part of a complex architecture of courtesy and civility that women may tend to prefer in the team environment. By contrast, the apparent tone of the male response portrays the team environment as an arena for confrontation, victory, defeat, and perhaps bullying.

INSIGHT 24

Every manager must deliver constructive criticism, often hourly or daily. Your own way of delivering such criticism may be influenced by your gender.

Your Turn

Write down how you prefer to receive criticism of your work behavior when such criticism is necessary. Then describe how one or two recent supervisors have chosen to deliver performance evaluations or other forms of constructive criticism. Did their approach to delivering criticism meet with your approval? If so, how did you feel in receiving the criticism and what was the result? If not, how did you feel in receiving the criticism and what was the result?

10. Women tend to ask, "What do you think?" to build consensus. Men often perceive the question to be a sign of incompetence and lack of confidence.

> Woman: What do you think about dividing my office into a work area and a waiting area?
>
> Man [thinks]: It's her office. Can't she decide what she wants to do?

Let's assume that the woman in this case knows full well what she wants to do with her office. Her question is not a solicitation of permission (although the man takes it as such) nor a sign that she can't make her own decisions. Instead, it is another demonstration of the tendency we have already observed in women's language patterns to gather input and weigh opinions before acting.

11. Women tend to mix business talk with talk about their personal lives and expect other women to do so as well. Men mix business talk with banter about sports, politics, or jokes (many of them sexually oriented).

> Woman: I don't mind traveling to Cincinnati, but it will mean finding overnight care for our baby.
>
> Man: If I do go to Cincinnati, I'm taking an afternoon off to see a ball game. That's the least they can do.

This question is worth asking: Which gender is expressing most truthfully and accurately the impact team and business responsibilities have on personal life? Let's assume that the man in this case is a father and that he, no less than the working woman, has family matters to consider in arranging his business trip. He too must make provision for children, pets, and so forth. The point is that the woman tends to discuss with others how business duties influence her personal life. The man is reluctant to do so. Businesses probably operate best knowing what problems, obstacles, and burdens their employees face. By knowing an employee's circumstances, the business can adapt for win-win solutions.

12. Women feel that men aren't direct enough in telling them what they (women) are doing right. Men feel that women aren't direct enough in telling them what they (men) are doing wrong.

> Woman: I don't know how you feel about my work. [This is a request for more feedback.]
>
> Man: Just tell me right out if you don't like what I'm doing. [This is a request to avoid mixed signals.]

Feedback is a business buzzword that refuses to fade, perhaps because of its importance to employee motivation and quality management, including that of teams. Both genders in this example are asking for feedback, but the woman's way of asking is more in line with the 360-degree-feedback systems currently used for performance evaluations at all levels of teamwork. The woman's communication pattern allows for the possibility that feedback may include both positive and negative aspects, that is, the full range of evaluation. The man's communication pattern closes the door to praise almost entirely and solicits only negative feedback.

INSIGHT 25

Soliciting the opinions of others ("What do you think?") often is not an invitation to provide specific answers so much as an invitation to join in discussion and to offer an emotional response of some kind.

Your Turn

Recall a recent conversation with a member of the opposite sex in which you seemed to have different goals for the conversation or in some way "talked past" one another. As you reflect on that conversation, what do you believe the conversational expectations of the other person were? What were your conversational expectations?

13. Women bring up complaints and troubles with one another as a means of arousing sympathy and building rapport. Men bring up problems only when they want to hear solutions.

Woman: Our problem at home is just not having enough time with each other. I get home just as Bob is leaving for his job.

Man: We haven't been out to a show for months. Where do you find babysitters?

Sharing problems is not just an effort to build rapport and arouse sympathy. In addition, and perhaps more crucially, it is an effort to understand pain and thereby alleviate it. The woman's communication pattern assumes that the group may have insights and experiences that will enlighten the nature of the pain or frustration at hand. The man's communication pattern is cynical about the ability of the surrounding group to provide indepth perspectives or resonant ideas. The woman wants help in understanding the problem; the man wants help in postponing the problem.

14. Women's humor tends to be self-mocking. Men's humor tends to be razzing, teasing, and mock-hostile attacking.

Woman: So I said in my charming way, "You forgot to plug it in."

Man: So I said, "Did you notice anything strange about the cord lying on the floor?"

Freud wrote at length about "tendency humor"—our effort to disguise in humor what we really want to communicate, but dare not directly. The tendency of the male communication pattern illustrated here is to emphasize the person's stupidity or foolishness. By contrast, the person making the comment is to be seen as superior and smarter. The woman defuses this potential power play in her softened version of the verbal transaction. She recognizes that the person may feel insecure and awkward about the incident, and so consciously lowers her own status by self-mocking humor to avoid a threat to the relationship.

15. Women tend to give directions in indirect ways, a technique that may be perceived by men as confusing, less confident, or manipulative.

Woman: You can handle this account any way you want, but taking him out to lunch might be a possibility. Or meet in his office. Whatever you think. Lunch, though, might be the way to go.

Man [thinks]: Is she telling me to take him out to lunch or not? Is she setting me up for an I-told-you-so if I don't do it her way? And what is her way?

Teams make much of empowerment, which can only take place when the decision maker has options. In this example, the woman's communication pattern is conducive to empowerment because it leaves the decision maker free to choose, learn, and grow within a range of options. The man's apparent preference for a command style of management may allow short-term efficiencies, but does not encourage empowerment with its allied benefits of creativity, motivation, and loyalty.

INSIGHT 26

Humor often disguises messages that others are trying to share with us. Seeing through the humor to the underlying message can be a good way of determining the true nature of your relationship with the other person.

Your Turn

Think of someone in your work or social life who uses humor, perhaps in a mocking way, to say something to you and other people. Write down an approximate translation of what that person is usually trying to communicate by such humor. Why do you believe the person uses humor to disguise those messages?

16. When women and men gather in a team setting, women tend to change their communication styles to adapt to the presence of the men. Women also practice "silent applause" by smiling often, agreeing with others often, and giving more nonverbal signals of attentiveness than do men.

Audience adaptation is highly recommended in virtually all communication guides and textbooks. The apparent fact that women change their communication behaviors based on their audience is not a sign of uncertainty, deceit, or weakness. Instead, it is an effort to relate successfully.

17. Women in positions of team leadership tend to be less accustomed to dealing with conflict and attack than are men.

Woman: Why is everyone mad at me?

Man: This is an unpopular decision, but I've got to make it.

As consensus builders, women respond quickly and vocally to signs that consensus is failing and that relationships are threatened. For generations this behavior has been interpreted negatively: "If you can't stand the heat, stay out of the kitchen." It can just as well be interpreted positively for the purposes of modern teams. Women are no less tough for recognizing and responding to conflict and attack. It can be argued that they are all the more tough for their willingness to confront and deal with those forces rather than stoically or stubbornly ignoring them.

18. Women tend to be referred to more often by their first name than are men, sometimes as a sign of respect for women and sometimes as a sign of presumed familiarity or intimacy.

Man: Get Smith, Underwood, Connors, and Jill to go along with you on the sales call.

The use of the woman's first name in this example may or may not be a subtle way for the man to minimize the woman's professionalism. He may feel more gallant in calling women by their first names. As a team leader, however, he should choose one form of address or the other and apply it consistently to both genders.

19. Men tend to be uncomfortable with female peers, particularly those who may threaten their power.

Working for a woman is uncomfortable for many men, primarily because they misunderstand the communication patterns explained throughout this chapter. The male employee may complain about the woman boss's seeming lack of direct supervision and mixed messages, whereas the woman boss may simultaneously complain about the male employee's unwillingness to discuss problems openly, to work well with others on the team, and to share ideas.

20. Men tend to perceive a group of women in conversation as wasting time or hatching a plot of some kind. Women tend to perceive a group of men in conversation as doing business or working out power relations through bonding and joking.

These impressions from a distance of gender-exclusive groups tell volumes about the core misunderstandings between male and female members of a team. Interestingly, women credit men with more positive activities (doing business, etc.) than is the reverse (wasting time, hatching plots). Are women more sanguine about their fellow team members than are men? Do women tend to see the corporate glass as half full and men to see it as half empty?

INSIGHT 27

One's comfort level in working for or with members of the opposite gender can help or hinder career success. It is important to understand one's feelings about the role of gender in interpersonal relations.

Your Turn

Briefly describe in writing your own experiences and feelings about working for a member of the opposite gender. If you prefer, describe the attitudes of someone who has strong feelings (pro or con) about working for a member of the opposite sex. Explain their attitudes to the best of your ability.

Summing Up

Balancing the personal qualities, expertise, experience, and other factors of team members is important in achieving a harmonious team that discusses issues fully and reaches decisions only after gathering a wide range of data. An evaluation of personality types can be useful in establishing this balance, but such personality information should not be applied too narrowly or literally. In attempting to balance the influence and interaction of men and women on a productive team, a team leader or manager must bear in mind many communication differences associated with gender. Communication on the team can be improved if all members are aware of and respect the value of these communication differences.

Chapter 5

Developing Intercultural Teams

Developing Intercultural Teams

GOALS

- Recognize the increasing importance of intercultural and international teams in corporations and other organizations.
- Understand and adjust to the assumptions and practices of intercultural participants in teams.
- Make the most of the potential of intercultural teams to solve problems and seize opportunities.

Almost every major company you can name—Sears, Boeing, General Electric, IBM, and yes, McDonald's—has international branches that employ native workers. When these companies want to address a multinational problem or opportunity, they commonly assemble a team made up of members from their various branches throughout the world. Team members from India, Japan, France, Brazil, China, and the United States suddenly find themselves in a room—or in a teleconference—as members of an important team charged by the company to deal with a global issue of some kind. In a nutshell, that's the intercultural challenge facing more and more work teams in this new century—a challenge that may face you now or in your career future.

SHARED INFORMATION WITHOUT A SHARED CULTURE

Your team members on an intercultural team probably have access to the same company data that you do. As you sit around the meeting table, however, you soon realize that sharing data is not the same thing as sharing culture. Each person at the meeting brings quite different expectations about how and when to speak at the meeting, how to relate to the team leader and other members, when to socialize and when to talk business at meals, how to dress, and even when to arrive at team meetings.

These are all aspects of culture that we each carry with us, often unconsciously. Some things feel right and some things wrong, as judged by our cultural background. The goal of this chapter is not to ask you to set aside your own culture or become a devotee of another person's culture. Rather, the goal here is to become aware of the influence of various cultures on team processes. Once team members recognize the role of cultural difference operating within their team, they can deal constructively with those differences and often gain a competitive advantage because of them.

INSIGHT 65

Intercultural teams are a fact of business life. Their progress can be impeded if members are not skilled in making cultural adjustments.

Your Turn

If you have worked abroad, briefly describe the cultural adjustments you had to make to function effectively in that region of the world. If you have not worked abroad, describe the cultural differences you have observed in a visitor or work associate new to this country. What did they do differently from American businesspeople? What behaviors would you advise them to change if they plan to work for a prolonged period in the United States?

WHAT'S AT STAKE IN UNDERSTANDING CULTURAL DIFFERENCES

In earlier chapters we have seen how much the work of a team depends upon relationships forged among team members and with the team leader. In an intercultural team, the formation of these relationships depends, to a remarkable degree, on the willingness of all team members to

- be flexible and accepting of differences in values, beliefs, standards, and mores—even if they do not understand or personally believe in these differences
- be sensitive to verbal nuances and nonverbal behavior, as intercultural team members attempt to express their feelings as well as their thoughts
- be knowledgable about the religious, cultural, business, social, and dietary practices of other cultures
- be open in sharing aspects of your own culture at the same time you are learning about the cultures of your teammates

American team members sometimes have problems seeing beyond their own cultural assumptions in attempting to relate well with intercultural team members. By putting the spotlight on the following 10 assumptions, we can recognize them for what they are: American values and beliefs that may differ substantially from the perspectives of other, intercultural members of our team.

Assumption 1: Change Is Good

In the United States, change is often associated with progress, development, growth, and advancement. Many older world cultures do not share this basic belief. Instead, they view change as essentially disruptive and destructive. They value stability, preservation, tradition, and heritage.

Assumption 2: Time Controls Us

American businesspeople race against the clock and take time constraints seriously. Not to observe time commitments in the United States is a grave sign of disrespect or unprofessionalism. This is not so in much of the world. In many other cultures, business and other activities are not so rigidly controlled by time. "All in good time" is a common, relaxed attitude toward business projects in many cultures.

Assumption 3: We Are All Created Equal

Americans view equality as an important civic and social goal, but in most of the world, rank and status—often a part of one's birthright—are viewed as a natural part of everyday life and the source of one's authority. To many individuals in other cultures, personal progress out of their "class" is not a worthwhile goal. They have grown up knowing who they are and where they fit in the various strata of their society. Some, in fact, draw a sense of security from such knowledge.

Assumption 4: I Am an Individual with Special Interests and Needs, Including a Right to Privacy

Even though we are now a nation of more than 300 million people, each of us clings to some degree to the assumption of individualism, with attendant rights to be respected. In other cultures, where space is at a premium in homes, offices, and workplaces, and where large numbers of people are treated similarly, the American assumptions about individual rights and individual privacy are seen as merely quaint.

Assumption 5: We Are Self-Made People

In the United States we take cultural pride in making it on our own. We accept inherited wealth, but give the individual little personal credit for wealth secured from a parent. In other cultures, the self-made man or woman may not garner the respect accorded in the United States. "Old money" and old family or social connections may count much more for business influence than a person's track record of personal achievement.

Assumption 6: Competition Makes Us Feel Alive

Americans value competition and stress it as a desirable quality from the classroom to the sports field to the boardroom, but in societies that value cooperation, the intense competitiveness of the United States is not easy to comprehend. These societies place much more emphasis on the building of harmonious relationships among people, partnering with others to achieve common goals, and resisting the temptation to get ahead at the expense of others in the community or culture.

Assumption 7: The Future Looks Bright

People in the United States constantly work, plan, and strive for a better future. We set short- and long-term goals for our professional and financial lives. Much of the rest of the world, however, views an attempt to alter or improve the future as futile (and, in some cultures, even sinful). "What will be, will be" is a common attitude beyond our shores.

Assumption 8: Work Is the Only Game in Town

Americans work more hours per week than any other trading nation. Our work days and activities are scheduled weeks or even months in advance. We value work and the rewards of work so highly that many of us become workaholics. Many cultures do not share this obsessive attention to accomplishing productive labor; instead, they value a modicum of work balanced by a day strolling or meditating, frequent holidays with family and friends, and summer vacations much longer than their U.S. equivalents.

Assumption 9: We Tell It Like It Is

Americans are often viewed as being blunt to the point of rudeness. Our direct approach to people and situations may be difficult to understand for an individual who comes from a society where saving face is important or one in which an indirect method is used for conveying bad news or an uncomplimentary evaluation. Americans typically have little patience with people who hint at what they want to say rather than coming right out with it. From their vantage point, members of other cultures may have trouble trusting and respecting Americans who appear to have so little regard for the feelings of others.

Assumption 10: What Counts Is the Bottom Line

Americans are perceived around the world as being deeply materialistic. We talk about and care about our upscale appliances, cars, TVs, computers, and homes as our just rewards for hard work. Other cultures may view such materialism as spiritually shallow—the sad obsession of people who have not found deeper, less materialistic things to concern themselves with in life.

In this brief overview of some (but certainly not all) American assumptions and values, we have not attached labels of right or wrong to anyone's beliefs. Pointing out that much of the world does not share the American value system does not suggest that one group is correct and the other incorrect. Instead, we can use this knowledge of cultural difference to prepare ourselves for understanding and accepting intercultural team members on their own terms rather than assuming they are just like us.

INSIGHT 66

Americans preparing for membership on an intercultural team can begin by examining their own assumptions and behaviors.

Your Turn

Choose one aspect of American culture that you feel would not export well to another area of the world (of your choice). Explain why people in that area would have difficulty accepting the American cultural aspect you have chosen.

Team Manners for Intercultural Meetings

Most cultures are more formal than the United States in meeting behaviors, written documents, and oral presentations. Team members in the United States should be careful to use titles when addressing their team partners in Europe and Asia. It is almost always wise to use a surname and/or title when addressing a colleague in the work setting. A German professional may even be addressed as "Herr Dr. Professor" (three titles!).

In written communications with intercultural team members, opening sentences are usually introductory in nature rather than getting right to the point, in typical American fashion. Brief comments about a previous trip, the beauty of the locale, or other noncontroversial topic are quite appropriate as icebreakers for both written and spoken communications. Sensitive topics such as payments, behavior of company representatives, and errors or delays in shipping should be handled with deft timing, sensitivity, and tact.

In intercultural team conversations and meetings, American members should be careful to avoid terms that reflect superiority, power, or a lack of personal interest. This applies particularly to the giving and receiving of business cards from your intercultural associates. Throughout most of Asia, for example, it is expected that you will receive someone's business card with both hands, take a respectful moment to read it carefully and perhaps comment in a complimentary way on the person's title or company, then place the card in a special holder (rather than cramming it into an already over-stuffed wallet or purse). When giving your business card, you should extend it (again, with both hands) so that the print is readable from the perspective of the person receiving the card. This ritual almost always takes place upon first meeting your intercultural associate, not (as is often the case in American business practice) after a working relationship has been established.

Above all, take time to read about the cultural preferences, rituals, and habits of your intercultural associates before you meet them for the first time. You may even have the time and ability to master a few words in their native languages—a compliment to them, no matter how poorly you speak the words. Several good books on intercultural manners and mores are included in the Recommended Reading section at the end of this book.

INSIGHT 67

We tend to react in spite of ourselves to unusual verbal or nonverbal behaviors exhibited in meetings and other business occasions. Even though we understand that cultural differences explain these unusual behaviors, we often allow our attitudes and relationships to be shaped by our initial, judgmental reactions.

Your Turn

Tell about a time you were irritated or surprised by a verbal or nonverbal behavior on the part of a person new to U.S. culture. Did the person mean to offend you by the behavior? How can you avoid similar problems when you visit a culture that is new to you?

GRASPING THE DEEPER ASPECTS OF CULTURAL DIFFERENCE

If you intend to understand your intercultural team members in more than a surface way, you will inevitably have to come to terms with several profound cultural differences:

The perception of space. Animals, both wild and domestic, guard their territory. This concern for territoriality also exists in nations and cultures. To protect and define our territory we put up flags, fences, rows of bushes, signs, and so forth. The norms that govern our defense of territory are dictated by culture. Americans typically define an area of about 3 feet of open space around their personal territory (i.e., their bodies) as a comfort zone.

If you are a member of an intercultural team with participants from countries such as Mexico and Italy, you should expect them to intrude upon this culturally defined envelope of personal space. Your Italian member, for example, may be speaking with great excitement about a company development. As he does so, he moves to within a few inches of your face. You instinctively back up. Both of you experience an awkward and confusing intercultural moment. "Why is he moving so close to me?" you wonder. "Is he attacking me or is this a come-on of some kind?" Your Italian associate is just as confused. "Why is this person moving away from me? Am I saying something objectionable?"

Consider larger distributions of space from a cultural perspective. Look, for example, at the arrangement and division of space in a U.S. corporation. The president, in splendid isolation, occupies a large office on the top floor with corner windows. By contrast, French or Middle Eastern managing directors more commonly sit among their subordinates so they can observe all activities. Consider your Japanese associate who values a small, gem-like home characterized by elegant proportions and appointed with only the items needed for daily use. Contrast that attitude—and catch his looks of confusion—when he visits his first suburban American home measuring in the thousands of square feet and filled to the bursting point with possessions of all kinds.

INSIGHT 68

"Getting in my face" is considered a sign of hostility in the United States. It requires patience and practice to overcome these feelings when working on an intercultural team where social space is treated differently than in the United States.

Your Turn

Recall the last time that someone violated your personal space. Why did he or she do so? How did you react? What was the outcome of the situation?

The perception of time. Your intercultural team members may think of time quite differently than you do. In the United States, we save time, make time, spend time, waste time, and invest time. We distinguish between ordinary time and quality time. We become easily irritated when others do not observe time as obsessively as we do. Be prepared, therefore, for members of other cultures where punctuality is not a highly valued aspect of professional life; where "ripeness" of projects is more important than meeting deadlines; and where flexibility in scheduling and a casual attitude toward meeting times is the sign of a seasoned executive.

Friendships. As you get to know your intercultural team members over time, recognize that friendships are viewed differently from culture to culture. In the mobile U.S. society where people change jobs and locales frequently, we have all become accustomed to making new friends easily and quickly. New neighbors, church members, and work associates almost immediately become part of our social circle. When we attempt the same approach to friendship in other cultures—Germany, Japan, or Finland, for example—we may encounter a cultural surprise. Our acquaintances do not expect to become our friends. Friendships develop slowly and carefully in many cultures. In Welsh villages, for example, the "new couple" in town may have lived there 20 years or more—and still awaits full acceptance into the social life of the community. Be patient with intercultural team members, therefore, if they do not appear to warm up to you as quickly as you may have supposed they would. Instant friendship is often a new cultural experience for them.

Agreements. Perhaps most perplexing of all in working with intercultural team members is the question of "Do we have a deal or don't we?" To a U.S. businessperson, an agreement completed with a signed contract is almost sacred, but to many businesspeople in the Middle East, China, and elsewhere, a signed contract is just a piece of paper. More important by far in these cultures is the underlying relationship of trust established between parties over a series of meals. The signed contact, as many U.S. contractors have discovered to their dismay, is considered in many cultures to mark the beginning rather than the culmination of negotiation.

Ethical practices. These matters are among the most thorny for intercultural team members adjusting to one another's assumptions and business practices. What your intercultural team associate considers business as usual (including the giving of bribes or "commissions," as your team associate phrases it) may strike you as highly unethical. Certain comments or overt actions in a U.S. office between a man and woman may be termed sexual harrassment—actions that your intercultural team member views as harmless sport. It takes great skill to apprise your intercultural team members of the customary ethical codes and practices of your business environment without making them feel they are villains or worse. Difficult as it may be, this ethical education is crucial: You cannot afford to have a team representative acting on the basis of moral assumptions that are untenable and legally hazardous for your company.

INSIGHT 69

"When in Rome, do as the Romans do" is hardly an adequate guideline when basic matters of ethics and social justice are involved. When you confront assumptions or behaviors that offend your personal ethics or code of conduct, carefully review your options so that, if possible, you can achieve your business purpose without sacrificing your own integrity.

Your Turn

It is easy to think of the rest of the world as morally corrupt in contrast to a supposed law-and-order society here in the United States. Choose some part of the world, then put yourself in the shoes of a business visitor to the United States for the first time from that region. What aspects of American social or business life might that visitor find ethically or morally objectionable?

Male-female relationships. In interviews with intercultural teams, the topic that receives the most comment from team members is the matter of how men and women should relate in the workplace. Male-female relationships are a sensitive aspect of most cultures. If you visit a work associate in the Middle East, local custom dictates that you do not inquire about the health of his wife or daughters. Similarly off-limits are your inquiries into the whereabouts of wives as you are hosted by your male associates in Tokyo.

Americans have the most difficulty when they confront the spoken or unspoken assumption in intercultural team members that women are naturally subordinate to men in the order of things. The social, political, and moral dimensions of this issue come to a head when a U.S. businesswoman joins an intercultural team composed largely of members from cultures that suppress women. What is the woman to do? On the one hand, she could simply avoid contact with cultures who do not share her own culture's attitudes toward women. That option, however, may be professionally and economically hazardous for a woman's career. Although her specific choices will differ according to the culture and situation at hand, three trends have emerged in recent years:

1. Businesswomen are visiting sexually hostile cultures in increasing numbers. The American businesswoman in a Middle Eastern business meeting is no longer seen as an oddity.
2. When businesswomen anticipate problems due to sexual assumptions, they prepare in advance by establishing their professional status with their foreign clients through correspondence, telephone conversation, and mutual acquaintances. When they arrive in the foreign culture, these early contacts help these women arrive as "people" rather than as women.
3. Women sometimes make initial business contacts in the company of male associates, who then withdraw as the business relationship develops.

Attitudes toward women in business are quickly changing around the world as women assert themselves as professionals no less qualified than men to do business. It remains sad, however, when American-born Japanese businesswomen who speak fluent Japanese purposely speak only English when they visit Japan on business so that they will not be treated like a Japanese woman (i.e., given little professional respect).

INSIGHT 70

Women face an ongoing struggle throughout much of the world to be accepted on a par with men for business purposes. When women confront suppression and prejudice, they can strategize to overcome these factors.

Your Turn

If you are a woman, describe a time when you were devalued as a professional because of your gender. What did you do about the situation? If you are a man, describe a time when you observed a woman placed or kept in a subordinate role primarily because of her gender. What did you do about the situation?

COMMUNICATION IN THE INTERCULTURAL TEAM MEETING

People take for granted that verbal language differs from culture to culture, but your team members may be less aware that nonverbal language also varies dramatically across cultures. Mixed signals due to a misreading of nonverbal cues has proven a barrier in many intercultural team meetings.

Nonverbal signs and cues can range from touching and sniffing to gestures and body movement. The attitude in the United States toward the nonverbal area of touching another work associate is vastly different from that of many other cultures. It is not unusual throughout Europe and the Middle East to see two men walking arm in arm or with an arm encircling a shoulder. At a meeting, a work associate in these countries may place a hand on the forearm of the person sitting nearby and keep that hand there while talking.

Expected business posture also differs substantially from culture to culture. Discussion in a team meeting in the United States might find members in very relaxed postures. A man may even have a foot propped on a nearby chair or planted on a tabletop. Not so in Korea, the Middle East, China, Japan, and much of Europe. There, sitting "at attention" is a sign of respect to your team leader and fellow members. Showing the soles of your feet to your Saudi associates would be an insult indeed. Keeping your hands in your pockets while addressing your German or Austrian boss would be a sign of disrespect.

Perhaps most difficult to adjust to are cultural differences having to do with eye contact. In the United States we show concern when the other person does not look us in the eye or seems otherwise evasive. Is there a lack of honesty or integrity here, we wonder? But in Japan, a business leader may infer a lack of respect if a subordinate does give direct eye contact. When serving on an intercultural team, do not impute U.S. conclusions to eye contact behaviors exhibited by members of other cultures. This particular nonverbal difference is the first to be noticed and remains the hardest to change for intercultural team members attempting to adjust to U.S. ways.

INSIGHT 71

Among the most difficult intercultural differences to adjust to are touching, posture, and eye contact behaviors. We tend to have knee-jerk reactions to what we perceive as abnormal behaviors in these categories. We may experience difficulty in preventing these reactions from interfering with our relationships with intercultural team members.

Your Turn

Tell about a time when you noticed an unusual nonverbal behavior on the part of a visitor new to this country. How did you react? Why?

Summing Up

Intercultural teams are an increasing reality for U.S. businesspeople. The success of the team will depend in large part upon the willingness of team members to adjust to the many cultural differences they observe in one another. Learning to see a colleague as different but not "less than" is the key to productive team relationships. Members come to understand that they can respect and live with cultural differences in others even when they do not accept those values, practices, or worldviews for themselves.

Chapter 6

Diversity in the Workplace

Chapter 6a

DIVERSITY: AN OVERVIEW

chapter objectives

Upon completion of this chapter, you will be able to:

- Define **diversity**.
- Explain what is meant by our *changing cultural landscape.*
- Describe and give examples of demographic, social, and cultural changes that are responsible for the growing importance of diversity.
- Contrast **assimilation** and **pluralism** and give an example of each.
- List at least four characteristics of diversity.
- List and explain five diversity myths.
- Define **diversity consciousness**.
- Define **diversity education**.

Many cultures contribute to the richness of our world community. Just as every culture has time honored traditions that make its heritage unique, each of us has individual qualities and characteristics that make us special. Let us learn more of one another...in knowledge there is understanding; in understanding there is respect; and where there is respect, growth is possible.[1]

Diversity is defined in the dictionary as "a state of unlikeness" or "the condition of being different." Diversity can be viewed and defined in many different ways. In this book, **diversity** refers to *all* of the ways in which people are different. This includes individual, group, and cultural differences.

Today, diversity is getting a great deal of attention. We don't have to look far to see why. Imagine a group of employees at work or a class of students at college. Then imagine how that same group might have looked, thought, and acted differently two or three decades ago. Now picture how this same group might change by the year 2050.

OUR CHANGING CULTURAL LANDSCAPE

Traditionally, the concept of diversity is most often used in relation to culture. **Culture** refers to our way of life, including everything that is learned, shared, and transmitted from one generation to the next. Language, values, rules, beliefs, and even the material things we create are all part of one's culture. *Landscape* means a scene or a setting. When we talk about **cultural landscape**, we are referring to the different lifestyles, traditions, and perspectives that can be found in the United States and throughout the world. Our cultural landscape is changing constantly.

Demographic Changes in the United States

Diversity is not a new phenomenon. If we look back at the first U.S. Census in 1790, we see some interesting differences and similarities with today's society (see Fig. 1.1). The first U.S. Census revealed our rural character. Only 3 percent of the population lived in settlements of 8000 or more.[2] In 1790, almost one out of five residents (about 19 percent) was African-American. It is interesting to

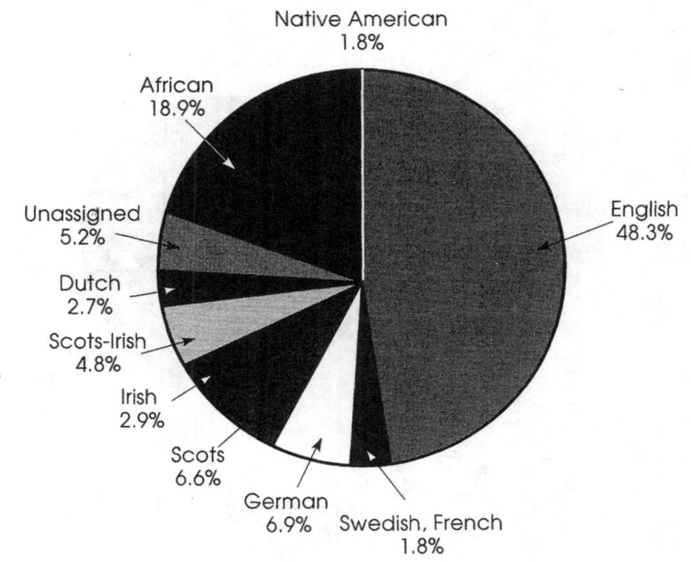

Figure 1.1: *Total U.S. population distribution in 1970. (From the U.S. Bureau of the Census,* Historical Statistics of the United States, *Part II, Series Z 20-132, U.S. Government Printing Office, 1976.) Washington, D.C.*

note the cultural diversity among Whites at that time. About 75 percent of the white population were White Anglo-Saxon Protestant (English, Scots, Scots-Irish); 25 percent were mainly Dutch, French, German, Irish, and Swedish.[3] These statistics show that early inhabitants of this country were not monocultural. In other words, they were not all culturally alike.

Since 1790, the cultural landscape of the United States has continued to change. We are no longer a rural society. Approximately 75 percent of our population lives in urban areas.[4] Our racial and ethnic mix has a different look as well. The percentage of African-Americans has declined from approximately 19 percent in 1790 to slightly more than 12 percent today. Asians and Pacific Islanders have steadily increased in numbers since they were first counted in the 1860 Census. This population is one of the fastest-growing ethnic groups in the United States. Census Bureau projections indicate that Hispanics, another rapidly growing population, will outnumber African-Americans in the near future. Currently, there are more Hispanic than African-American children in the United States. The percentage of Whites peaked in 1940 at approximately 90 percent, and the figure is now closer to 74 percent. The U.S. Census Bureau estimates that by the year 2050, racial and ethnic minorities will account for 47 percent of the nation's population (see Fig. 1.2). From now until that time, the percentage of Whites who are not Hispanic (Hispanics can be of any race) will shrink noticeably to 52.8 percent).

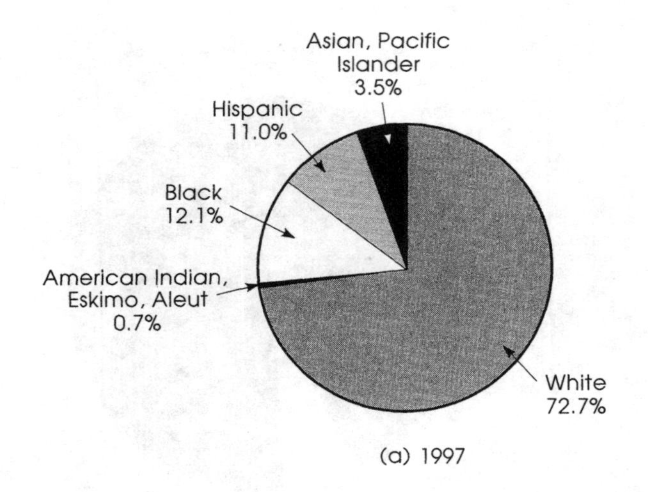

(a) 1997

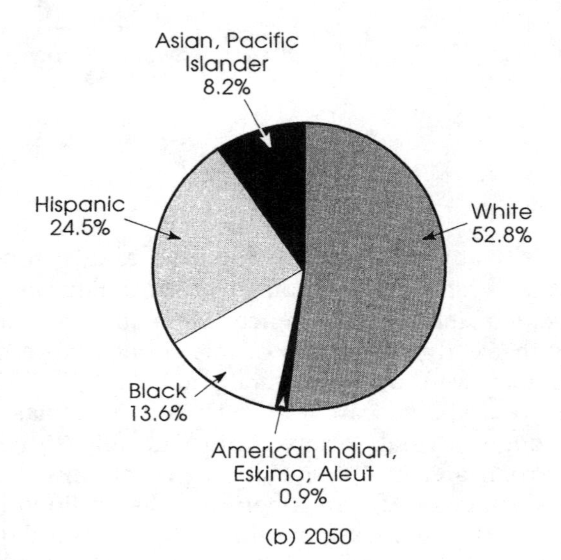

(b) 2050

Figure 1.2: *U.S. population distribution: (a) 1997 (total population = 267.6 million); (b) 2050 (projected; total population = 393.9 million). Data from the U.S. Census Bureau makes it possible to compare today's population by racial and ethnic distribution with projected figures for the year 2050. Projections are based on estimates of future birthrate and immigration trends. ((a) From U.S. Bureau of the Census,* Statistical Abstract of the United States, 1998, *118th ed., Washington, D.C., 1998; (b) from U.S. Bureau of the Census,* Current Population Reports, Series P25-1092 *(U.S. Government Printing Office, Washington, D.C., 1992), and* Statistical Abstract of the United States, 1994, *(U.S. Government Printing Office, Washington, D.C., 1994.))*

Census data must be interpreted cautiously. Different groupings have been used since the first Census. In 1870, for instance, the terms *quadroon* (one-fourth Black, or having one black grandparent) and *octoroon* (one-eighth black, or having one black great-grandparent) were used to indicate the exact amount of a person's black heritage.

In recent years, racial categories have been added and an increasing number of people have chosen to identify themselves as "other." Many people do not feel that they belong in a single category, and others do not want to be categorized at all. One student, who refuses to select any category, explains, "I'm not White, I'm not Black, and I sure don't want to be an *other*."

DON'T BOX ME IN

An increasing number of people are resisting the pressure to be boxed in by color. Tiger Woods, for example, has made it known that he objects to being called African-American. Rather, he prefers "Cablinasian," a term he made up that combines his Caucasian, Black, Indian, and Asian ancestry. Other well-known people who have affirmed their mixed ancestry are Keanu Reeves (Hawaiian, Chinese, Caucasian), Mariah Carey (Black, Venezuelan, Caucasian), and Johnny Depp (Cherokee, Caucasian). Groups such as Wesleyan University's Interracial Students Organization are becoming more common on college campuses. This trend will probably continue as interracial marriages become more common and society becomes more comfortable with different and new ways of defining one's heritage.

The racial options of the 2000 census have been modified to accommodate those who want to express their multiracial heritage. For the first time, Americans may choose more than one racial category when describing themselves. Consequently, "other" is no longer included as a choice. Other changes in the 2000 census include:

- Black reads "Black or African-American."
- Respondents are now given the choice Hispanic or Latino rather than just Hispanic. This change is based on research showing that Latino is a more popular term in the western United States.
- The old category "Asian or Pacific Islander" is now divided. Asian is one category and Native Hawaiian or other Pacific Islander is another.

I was born in 1959 and I was "black." I did not challenge forms when I was younger, because I did not realize then how important the information those forms requested would become to me. If the form asked me to check "negro," I did. I don't remember there being racial categories other than black/negro or white.

As I grew older and learned through family conversation that there was another culture that was part of me, I began a hesitant journey of uncovering who I am as a complete *person. This began with acknowledgment that my Native American heritage is as important to me as being Black. My first acknowledgment of my racial completeness was to check "other." Checking "other" was one of the most difficult things I have ever done. With that act came extreme guilt at the thought of abandoning my given culture and race.*

I soon discovered that the guilt came from a sense of having banished myself to neutrality. "Other" meant recognizing no race at all. I went back to checking "Black," which once again made me comfortable but incomplete. I have now settled on checking both "Native American" and "Black."

—A student's perspective

THINKING THROUGH DIVERSITY:
Would you describe yourself as multiracial, or do you see yourself as belonging to a single race?

It is clear that our nation's schools and workforce will feel the effects of growing diversity for some time. Demographic data indicates that

- Women, minorities, and people with disabilities will continue to account for the vast majority of new entries in the workforce.
- The nation's population of college students will grow increasingly diverse. Data from the U.S. Department of Education reveals that college students have become increasingly heterogeneous during the last two decades. This trend will continue as elementary and secondary students become even more racially and ethnically diverse in the future.
- The international student population in the United States is growing. The Institute of International Education estimates that there are 450,000 international students in the United States.[5] Most of these students come from Asian and Latin American countries.

AMERICA'S SCHOOLCHILDREN: A LOOK AT THE FUTURE

What if the entire population of elementary and secondary schools in the United States were shrunk into one class of 30 students? What would it look like? According to the National Center for Research on Cultural Diversity and Second Language Learning, 10 of the 30 students would come from racial or ethnic minority groups. Of these 10, six would come from homes in which languages other than English are spoken, and two would be from immigrant families. Of the six students who spoke another language, four would speak Spanish, one would speak an Asian language, and the other student would speak any one of more than 100 languages. Ten students, one-third of the class, would be poor.[6]

Technological and Social Changes

A number of social and technological changes have also altered the cultural landscape in recent years.

Globalization and Technology

Peoples and cultures throughout the world meet each day. Several forces make this possible, one being the growing interdependence of economies in various countries. Another is the speed and ease of modern transportation. Technological advances have transformed our social world into what Marshall McLuhan termed a *global village*.[7] In other words, increasingly we need to think of the entire world when we talk about our social environment. Computers, satellites, and communication technology have brought the world closer together and made cross-cultural encounters an everyday occurrence.

I am a citizen, not of Athens or Greece, but of the world.

—Socrates

Heightened Awareness of Diversity

Stories about diversity appear in the news each day. These stories deal with such issues as affirmative action, discrimination, social conflict, global education, and religious as well as language differences. Scholarship on the subject of diversity has mushroomed in recent years. Diversity itself has become a thriving industry. Books, Web sites, diversity consultants, courses, workshops, and conferences have proliferated as more and more money is spent in this area.

EXPERIENCING THE WORLD ON A DAILY BASIS

In the United States, globalization is part of our daily lives. It is evident from the time we get up to the time we go to sleep. Take an ordinary person such as Millie Jones. She attends school part-time and works full-time. A typical day in her life connects her with many different parts of the world.

Ms. Jones wakes up and brews coffee shipped from Brazil. After a quick breakfast, she has a few minutes to read the morning newspaper. Her eye catches articles about political unrest in the Middle East, the spread of AIDS in parts of Africa, and preparations for the Olympic Games in Athens, Greece.

Millie then drives her sports car to work. The car was assembled in Germany, with parts from all over the world. She arrives at work. Her employer is a large, multinational company that manufactures and markets computer software throughout the world. After checking her e-mail, she gets on the Internet. Millie checks the financial markets in Hong Kong, Paris, Sydney, and other parts of the world.

She leaves work early to attend two evening classes at a nearby community college. On the way to school, she picks up a late lunch at her favorite Mexican restaurant.

At school, Millie listens to a lecture by an Iranian professor in an advanced statistics class. On the way to the next class, she chats with two Nigerian students. In biology, she uses the Internet to get the latest research on *Loa loa*, a worm that infects the human eye and is found in African rain forests.

After school, she drives home, eats some leftovers, and turns on the computer. She spends some time on her online service's "International Chat Room." Before going to bed, Millie turns on a CD player made in Japan and listens to music performed by a rock group from Ireland.

Pride in our cultural roots is championed by popular music, movies, ethnic festivals, and cultural exhibits. As diversity has become more visible in everyday life, it is more apt to become an issue that is addressed, discussed, and debated publicly and privately.

Continued Cultural Separation in the Midst of Diversity

Although some parts of our cultural landscape are becoming more diverse, other parts show little of this change. Sociologists refer to this as **cultural lag**, a condition in which one part of culture is not keeping pace with another part. This lag or gap is becoming increasingly evident when we look at where we live, worship, go to school, and work. Consider the following examples.

1. Many residents of the United States continue to live in neighborhoods that are separated along racial, ethnic, and economic lines. The upper, middle, and lower social classes gravitate to separate communities. Hispanic barrios, Little Japans, Little Italys, and Chinatowns are commonplace. So too are "chocolate cities and vanilla suburbs," a phrase used by musical artist George Clinton. William Frey, in his analysis of recent population estimates from the Census Bureau, concludes that most communities in the United States lack significant racial and ethnic diversity. According to Frey, Asians, Hispanics, and to a lesser extent African-Americans continue to be concentrated in specific regions of the country and a handful of metropolitan areas.[8]

2. According to the U.S. Labor Department's Federal Glass Ceiling Commission, the upper levels of big business remain mostly white and mostly male.[9] The Commission found that the **glass ceiling**—attitudes and actions that block the promotion of minorities and women into top management positions—is still very much in place. These barriers may exist because of individual prejudices and discrimination, or they may be rooted in the policies, procedures, and culture of a business. Other barriers, referred to as *glass walls*, make it difficult to move from one position to another at the same level. For example, minority employees sometimes find it difficult to transfer into those departments that eventually provide more chances to move into upper-level management.

THINKING THROUGH DIVERSITY:
Have you or any member of your family ever encountered a glass ceiling or a glass wall?

3. Martin Luther King once called our time of worship the most segregated hour of the week. Despite the significant social changes during the past few decades, racial segregation remains in place at many religious services.

4. While the percentage of students of color is increasing significantly, racial diversification among teachers has not kept pace.

5. In recent years, there has been a resurgence of intergroup hostility and intolerance. This is not simply the work of a select few. When we think of intolerance, how many of us visualize a member of the Ku Klux Klan (KKK) or a skinhead? Unfortunately, intolerance can also come dressed in a three-piece suit, a military uniform, or more casual wear. College campuses throughout the country have recently witnessed an upsurge in hate crimes. Hate literature, graffiti on dormitory room doors, threatening e-mail and telephone calls, property damage, and physical violence can make it difficult for students to feel comfortable and concentrate on their studies.

CYBERHATE

A former student at the University of California–Irvine was the first person in the United States to be charged and convicted of committing a hate crime over the Internet. In 1996, he sent out an e-mail threat to 59 students, most of whom were Asian. The message read, in part: "I personally will make it my life's work to find and kill every one of you personally. OK? That's how determined I am. Do you hear me?"[10]

Hate speech on the Internet has grown rapidly in recent years. Web sites, e-mail, bulletin boards, and chat rooms may target, among other things, a person or group's race, creed, sexual orientation, religion, disability, or national origin. A number of universities have enacted policies to punish students who post hate messages on the World Wide Web. Other universities see this type of regulation as a violation of the First Amendment right to free speech. They maintain that suppressing hate speech is far more dangerous than permitting it.

People react differently to the social changes that result from the growing importance of diversity. Some adapt, others resist. In a way, it is a lot like the growing importance of computer technology. We may work to adapt and learn more because we know that if we do not become computer literate, our chances for success will be severely limited. The same holds true for diversity. Whether we realize it or not, diversity touches each of us on a daily basis. If we are not in a position to capitalize on diversity, we will be at a disadvantage socially and economically. In Chapter 2 we focus on the relationship between diversity and success.

VIEWS OF DIVERSITY: ASSIMILATION AND PLURALISM

Throughout our nation's history, our diversity has been described as a *melting pot, tossed salad, rainbow, quilt,* and *kaleidoscope.* These images illustrate the fact that we are different. Our differences, and the way we view them, change constantly.

In the early twentieth century, a Jewish immigrant named Israel Zangwill offered this description of the United States in his book *The Melting Pot:* "There she lies, the great melting pot—listen! Can't you hear the roaring and the bubbling? There gapes her mouth—the harbour where a thousand mammoth feeders come from the ends of the world to pour in their human freight. Ah, what a stirring and a seething—Celt and Latin, Slav and Teuton, Greek and Syrian, Black and Yellow... Jew and Gentile."[11]

According to Zangwill, European immigrants would gradually lose their traditional ways of life and blend together. A new mixed culture would emerge from this process. This is commonly referred to as **assimilation**, the process in which people lose their cultural differences and blend into the wider society. International students as well as those born and raised in the United States sometimes sense their culture slipping away. They have many ways to deal with the pressure to assimilate. Some see it as inevitable and desirable. Others see it as something to avoid at all costs. Still others find themselves assimilating up to a point. As one of my students put it, "I do it up to a point, as long as it does not rob me of my identity."

It took 22 years for me to develop my own personality and goals despite the struggles I have and the struggles my race still has. By assimilating—that is like saying Dr. Martin Luther King died for nothing. That Malcolm X and all of the other people who gave their lives so that I would have a chance died for nothing. To me, assimilation is another word for slavery.

Work is a perfect example of how I assimilate my identity so that I feel comfortable. If changing the way I dress and act makes me feel more accepted on the job, then that's what I want to do.

My personal background provides me with a very strong belief that I am to be who I am. I think my Jewish background as well as my mother's influence help me deal with assimilation. I know who I am, as far as race, culture, and personality. And I know that I'm not changing for anyone. Therefore, when the idea of assimilation is presented in any way to me, I instinctively decline.

In America, everyone at some point and time will be forced to assimilate themselves with another culture or group. Being a young black male, assimilation is probably the most frequently used pattern of interaction in my life. In my neighborhood, especially with my circle of friends, it is a cardinal sin to assimilate with the white culture. We see ourselves as the shunned group. At every possible opportunity, we thumb our collective noses at white society. By learning the "rules of the game" a long time ago, I know that assimilating with the majority society is a must. When forced to assimilate, I just separate my two worlds. I'm always going to be black with black sentiments and I'll never compromise that for anything. However, I will play by the rules dictated, at least to an extent, to further myself and my people.

—Students' perspectives

Many now question whether the model of the melting pot fits our society. They argue that people want to be accepted for who they are. A growing number of people are unwilling to give up what makes them distinctive, even if it is only for a certain period of time each day. When they go to work or school, they do not want to leave their culture at home. They feel that like the ingredients in a salad or the colors of a rainbow, differences can coexist and complement each other (see Fig. 1.3).

Figure 1.3: *"People call us a melting pot, but we never have been. What we really represent is a quilt of different colors, different textures, all held together by a common thread."—Kweisi Mfume, President of the NAACP. (Photo by Regina Bryan.)*

What Is an American?

How would you define the term *American*? For some, the term applies solely to those living in the United States. Others maintain that those who inhabit any of the countries in North, Central, or South America are Americans. Still others feel that the term has a racial connotation. Toni Morrison, in her book *Playing in the Dark*, has observed "deep within the word 'American' is its association with race...American means white."[12] A student of color sums up her feelings this way: "Being an American is a phrase way down on my list of descriptive words. America has caused me to describe myself in a lot of ways—Black, woman, minority. The word *American* is not part of that list. I wish I could feel a part of this country. But everyday I am quickly reminded that I am not an American, but a nuisance."

Do you feel that you are an American? What does *American* mean to you? What does an American look like? In his book *A Different Mirror: A History of Multicultural America*, Ronald Takaki describes an experience he had while riding in a taxi. The driver, who looked to be in his 40s, asked him how long he had been in the United States. Takaki replied that he had been born in the United States. He further explained that his family came here from Japan more than 100 years ago. The driver's assumption was that he didn't really look "American."[13]

Why do we make this kind of assumption? According to Takaki, schools have to accept at least part of the blame. He argues that from kindergarten to college, teachers and textbooks have cultivated a narrow view of U.S. history. Typically, the experiences of African-Americans, Hispanics, Native Americans, and Asian-Americans have been ignored. In addition to schools, our upbringing can influence our thinking. A college student elaborates: "The way I was brought up was to think that everybody who was the same as me were 'Americans,' and the other people were of 'such and such descent'."[14]

Pluralism is a process through which cultural differences are acknowledged and preserved. By way of illustration, advocates of multicultural education argue that the study of U.S. history should be more pluralistic. History should reflect the distinctive cultural experiences of all people. According to this perspective, courses in history often ignore the experiences, perspectives, and contributions of women or people of color. Those who share this opinion argue that if history courses were truly inclusive, there would be no need for a Black History Month or a Women's History Month.

DIMENSIONS OF DIVERSITY

Dimensions of diversity refer to specific traits viewed as distinguishing one person or group from another. Race, gender, and ethnicity are three examples. **Race** refers to a category of people who are *perceived* as physically distinctive on the basis of certain traits, such as skin color, hair texture, and facial features. Notice that what makes this group distinctive is our perception of their differences. The concept of race is discussed later in more detail.

Whereas race relates to physical differences, ethnicity focuses on cultural distinctiveness. **Ethnicity** is defined as the consciousness of a cultural heritage shared with other people. **Gender** has to do with the cultural differences that distinguish males from females. For instance, in any given culture, people raise males and females to act certain ways. Do not confuse the term *gender* with *sex*. Sex refers to biological differences, such as hormones and anatomy.

SOCIAL CLASS DIFFERENCES IN THE UNITED STATES

Social class refers to one's status in society. In the United States, status is usually determined by a variety of social and economic criteria, including wealth, power, and prestige. Even though social class influences where we work, live, and go to school, its importance is addressed infrequently. Perhaps class distinctions are downplayed or ignored because we are uncomfortable, psychologically speaking, acknowledging the tremendous inequality that exists in this society. Moreover, the concept of social class is "fuzzy" and inconsistent. For example, how would we classify other students in our class? *Lower, middle,* and *upper class* mean different things to different people.

When we talk about the dimensions of diversity, social class, sexual orientation, age, religion, learning style, and family background are invariably ignored. Some people may perceive these and other dimensions to be more important than race or gender. When students are asked what makes them unique, their answers reflect a very inclusive view of diversity (see Diversity Box: Who Am I?)

WHO AM I?

Students in a college success class were asked to write down five things that describe each of them. Then they wrote all of their descriptors on the board, as follows:

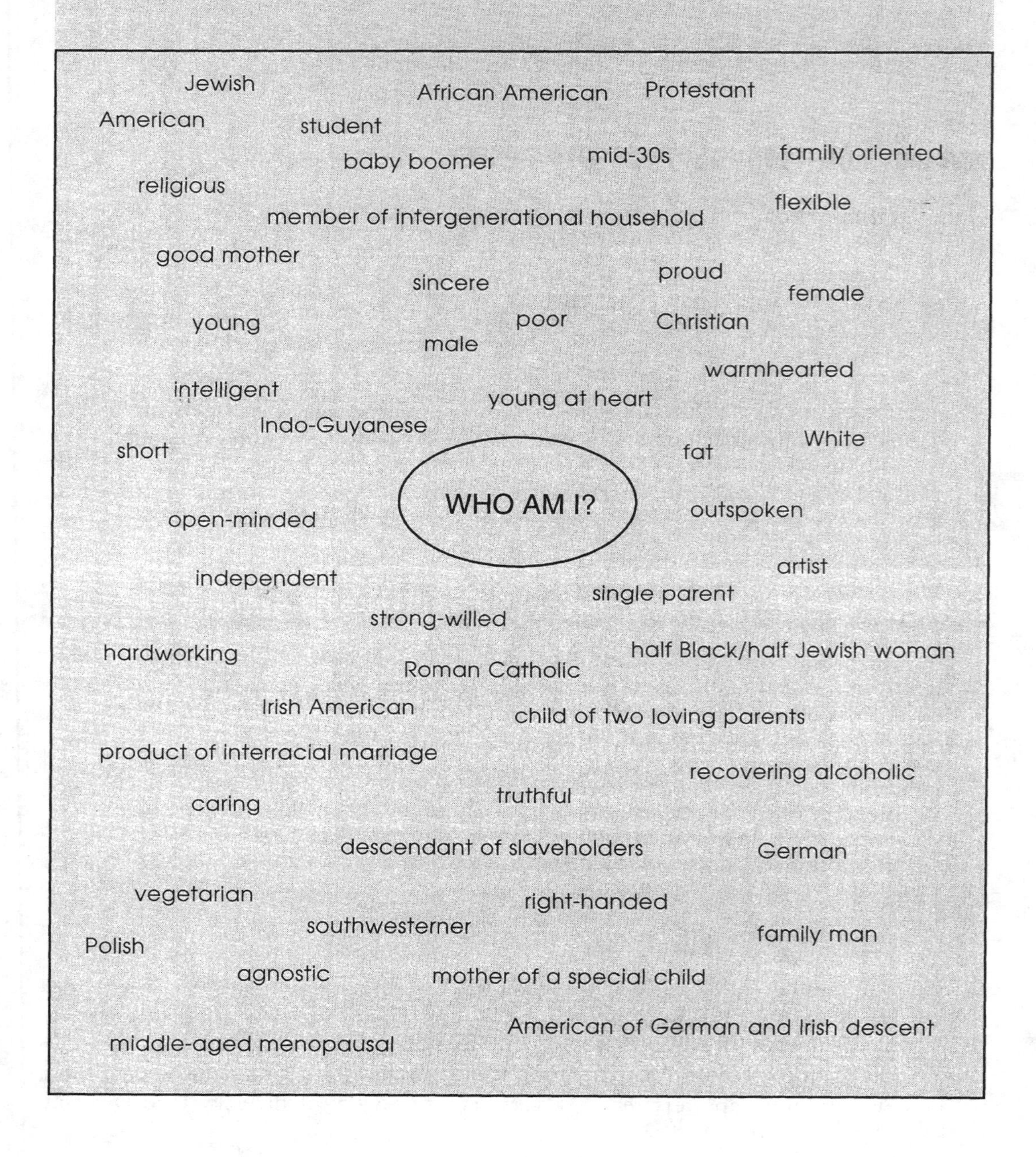

The meaning of the term *diversity* is expanding continually. Roosevelt Thomas, a leading expert on managing diversity in the workplace, makes this point in his book *Beyond Race and Gender.* He defines diversity in a way that includes everyone. According to Thomas, workforce diversity is not something that is simply defined by race or gender. Rather, it encompasses a variety of other dimensions, such as age, personal and corporate background, education, job function and position, geographic origin, lifestyle, sexual orientation, and personality.[15] To this list we can add ancestry, national origin, creed, religion, economic class, learning style, personality, family background, marital status, military background, and disability. The list goes on and on. In short, it includes whatever we think distinguishes us.

As you read about diversity and, in particular, various dimensions of diversity, keep these points in mind.

1. *Dimensions of diversity may be hidden or visible.* Diversity is not only skin deep. According to one theory, diversity is like a cultural iceberg. Only about 10 percent of it is visible. Most dimensions mentioned by students (see Diversity Box: Who Am I?) would be invisible in the classroom. For example, we would not know that a classmate was a descendant of slaveholders, a vegetarian, or a born-again Christian unless the person chose to share this with us.

2. *Dimensions of diversity are found within groups as well as within individuals.* People possess varied personalities and talents as well as different learning and communication styles. Similarly, everyone within a group is not the same. Differences within a group are often ignored when we distinguish between groups. Diversity within groups is addressed later in the chapter.

Master Status

People are often identified and distinguished by their **master statuses**, positions that stand out in the eyes of society and hide one's individuality. Ask yourself what is the first thing that people see when they look at you? Is it your race, gender, disability, or some other master status?

In his autobiography, Malcolm X discusses his experiences as a student in Mason, Michigan, a town just outside Lansing. He was one of the top students in his class and excelled in English. He vividly remembers talking with Mr. Ostrowski, his English teacher, about his plans for a career.

"'Malcolm, you ought to be thinking about a career,' said Mr. Ostrowski. 'Have you been giving it thought?' The truth is, I hadn't. I never have figured out why I told him, 'Well, yes, sir, I've been thinking I'd like to be a lawyer.' Lansing certainly had no Negro lawyers—or doctors either—in those days, to hold up an image I might have aspired to. All I really knew for certain was that a lawyer didn't wash dishes, as I was doing.

continued

MASTER STATUS (CONT'D)

Mr. Ostrowski looked surprised, I remember, and leaned back in his chair and clasped his hands behind his head. He kind of half-smiled and said, 'Malcolm, one of life's first needs is for us to be realistic. Don't misunderstand me, now. We all here like you, you know that. But you've got to be realistic about being a nigger. A lawyer—that's no realistic goal for a nigger. You need to think about something you *can* be. You're good with your hands—making things. Everybody admires your carpentry work. Why don't you plan on carpentry? People like you as a person—you'll get all kinds of work.'

The more I thought afterwards about what he said, the more uneasy it made me. It just kept treading around in my mind."[16]

It is clear from this excerpt that race was a master status during this period of Malcolm X's life. Although Mr. Ostrowski knew that Malcolm X was intelligent, he also understood the social norms that were in place at this time. From Mr. Ostrowski's point of view, it did not matter that Malcolm X was smart. He had to learn that aspiring to be a lawyer was at odds with the "place" reserved for him in the wider society.

3. *Dimensions of diversity are in a constant state of flux.* In different situations, we see ourselves and are seen by others differently. In some situations a student might want to be seen as a Muslim female. In another situation, she might simply want to be viewed as a student.

4. *Dimensions of diversity are not always clear-cut or easily defined.* Diversity means different things to different people. A good example is the term *race.* Even though we talk about race as if it can be biologically defined, there is no easy way to distinguish people based solely on their skin color, hair texture, shape or color of their eyes, or any other physical trait. Racial mixing has blurred the boundaries between races. Skin color, for example, is a common but unreliable indicator of race. There are Whites who are more dark-skinned than some Blacks. Many Hispanics have dark skin but do not consider themselves Black. Anthropologist Ashley Montagu addressed this issue in his book *Man's Most Dangerous Myth: The Fallacy of Race.* According to Montagu, the term *race* has no scientific basis and cannot be applied to real life.[17] There is almost total agreement among scientists today that race is arbitrarily and socially defined. Yet it is important because we make it important, and we model its importance for children (see Fig. 1.4).

In summary, diversity is multidimensional. Various dimensions may be hidden or visible. Moreover, they may or may not have anything to do with race or gender.

Figure 1.4: *(By permission from Copley News Service.)*

DIVERSITY BETWEEN AND WITHIN GROUPS

The United States is home to one of the most culturally diverse populations in the world. Nevertheless, we often ignore or gloss over these differences. When we focus our attention on race, we think in terms of Blacks and Whites or sometimes Latinos and Whites. Our society, and even our communities, are described as biracial rather than multiracial. This can be particularly uncomfortable and offensive to those who are constantly stereotyped or left out of the picture. An Iranian student describes how she has struggled with this dilemma: "I am an Iranian woman, one who can't pass as white because I'm too dark, but certainly can't pass as black because I have Middle-Eastern features...When I date black men, I receive animosity from those who feel that black men belong with black women. When I date white men, I've been accused of selling out and trying to be white. Iranian men who expect me to fit within a certain mold find me strange. I also seem to have this peculiar power to make people at airports and train stations visibly uncomfortable." She describes her feelings when she was informed she would not be allowed to join the BLSA—the Black Law Students Association—at her college. "My first impulse had been to argue with the man sitting behind the table with the introductory flyers. He looked me in the eye and said, 'Look, if you're not black, then as far as I'm concerned, you're white.' She goes on to say: "What was I to do, start an 'ILSA' of which I would be the sole member?"[18]

We may paint diversity with such a broad brush that we fail to capture the differences that exist within groups as well as between them. Indeed, the differences within groups are often greater. For instance, we tend to get caught up with how men and women differ from each other. We forget or ignore the significant differences that can be found when we simply look at a group of men or a group of women. Women can be assertive or passive, dependent or independent, and supporters or opponents of feminism. Similar differences exist among men.

Differences exist among the largest ethnic groups in this country. These groups include African-Americans, Latinos, Asian-Americans, and Native Americans. For this reason, we cannot talk about the Latino family any more than we can talk about the white family. Discussing *the* Asian-American or *the* Latino experience in this country ignores the diversity that exists within groups and individuals from these populations. Asian-Americans include Chinese, Japanese, Filipinos, Vietnamese, Laotians, Cambodians, Hmong, Koreans, Native Hawaiians, Samoans, and others. Latinos are also distinguished by a wide range of skin colors, ethnic or cultural lifestyles, religions, and languages. Many object to the term *Latino* or *Hispanic* because it masks the uniqueness of the particular culture. *Mexican, Puerto Rican, Cuban,* or some other term identifying one's nationality may be preferred.

DIVERSITY MYTHS

Diversity is a concept that means many things to many people. It can trigger a wide range of positive and negative feelings. Unfortunately, what we learn about this subject is often incomplete and inaccurate. Some of the more common misconceptions that surround diversity follow.

Myth 1: Diversity = women + minorities. Diversity includes everyone. All of us, for example, bring differences to school. This includes white males.

Myth 2: Diversity is a new phenomenon. There has always been diversity, but now it is receiving more attention. Some changes are not as new as we might believe. As an example, statistics indicate that more women are entering the job market than ever before. This masks the fact that a large percentage of women of color have always worked.

Myth 3: Diversity = deficiency. This myth is based on the premise that diversity results in standards being lowered. Today, professionals increasingly view diversity as a resource rather than a deficit. Big businesses such as IBM, Xerox, and Digital Equipment approach diversity as good business. According to the international diversity manager at Digital Equipment Corporation, "It's in the best interest of each and every one of us to do the personal growth work that valuing differences is about. We will be more synergistic, we will share power, we will be more collaborative, and we will be more creative, and at that point, we'll make more money."[19]

An advertisement by Atlantic Richfield Company (ARCO) makes the same point. The top of the ad reads, "The value of diversity is priceless."

Underneath the ad is a picture of foreign currency and these words: "As a multinational corporation, ARCO is committed to filling the needs of our customers at home and around the world. Diversity in our staff and in our business relationships help enhance our effectiveness in the global marketplace. It's a win–win situation, because diversity increases opportunity for others and strengthens our own organization. Diversity makes sense. And pounds, francs, yen..."

Myth 4: Diversity = divisiveness. Many assume that our society is divided because of our differences. Does the problem lie with our differences or our inability to respect and learn from these differences? Being exposed to diversity can bring people together.

In *What Matters in College?* Alexander Astin discusses findings from his research on 217 colleges and universities.[20] He found that a student's diversity experiences in college can be a potent way of bridging the gap between various groups and easing tensions. These experiences might take the form of a workshop or a course on diversity. Equally important was the frequency with which students interacted socially with persons from different racial and ethnic groups.

Myth 5: Diversity is to be feared. By focusing exclusively on our differences and ignoring our similarities, we create fear. Fear is cultivated by our ignorance of differences and similarities. Fear is compounded by our inability to communicate with people who disagree with us about difficult issues. People often shy away from talking about diversity because it is so emotionally charged. As one student put it, "All it takes is one slip of the tongue." In a video entitled *The Color of Fear*, a group of men of varying racial and ethnic backgrounds attend a retreat and "open up" to each other about the issue of race. After a few days, it appears the racial divisions among the men are almost insurmountable. Their fear and mistrust almost make it impossible for them to communicate effectively. Toward the end of the retreat, they begin to connect with each other by confronting their fears, sharing intimate feelings, and really listening. They become more aware of some of the feelings they have in common.

The kind of dialogue that unfolds in this video is rare because it is genuinely open and honest. Consequently, it can be very painful at times. Toward the end of the video, one of the participants comments on the anger and hurt that surfaces during the group's discussions. "Sometimes," he says, "the cure for the pain is in the pain."[21]

Differences aren't necessarily a burden but a blessing.

—A student's perspective

WHAT IS DIVERSITY CONSCIOUSNESS?

The definition of consciousness in the dictionary is being fully aware or sensitive to something. Another way of defining it is the full activity of the mind or senses. This state of mind is necessary to develop **diversity consciousness**; understanding, awareness, and skills in the area of diversity.

THINKING THROUGH DIVERSITY:

Should we always treat everybody the same and ignore differences? Are there any situations in which you should treat people differently?

Diversity consciousness is not simple and straightforward. It cannot be manufactured during a one-hour TV talk show or a day-long training session. Try to keep the following points in mind as you read about diversity consciousness.

Diversity consciousness is not

- *Simply common sense.* Common sense is not sufficient. We need to educate ourselves and each other. At the Boston Campus of the University of Massachusetts, the training of faculty includes dealing with diversity issues and instructing students from diverse backgrounds. Each year, employees at American Telephone and Telegraph (AT&T) are required to take 40 hours of continuing education courses in diversity and tolerance.
- *The result of good intentions.* I have heard people say, "If my heart is in the right place, that is enough." Trying extra hard to be fair and respectful of others or having the best of intentions are a good start, but only a start. It is possible to show insensitivity and ignorance even though you have the best of intentions. People who talk to adults with disabilities in a childlike manner may think that they are being kind. People who tell you to forget our differences and just "be human" may think they are offering helpful advice. Leonard Pitts, a columnist for the *Miami Herald*, writes, "I've lost count of the times well-meaning white people have advised me to quit being black and 'just be a person.'"[22]
- *The result of some simple formula or strategy.* This is a reflection of the "McDonaldization" of our society. Sociologists use this phrase to describe our preoccupation with doing things quickly and efficiently, much like McDonald's restaurants. However, diversity consciousness requires life-long soul searching, self-reflection, and learning.
- *Important for just some of us.* At your college, are events held during African-American History Month more apt to attract students and faculty of color than white students and faculty? Similarly, are Women's History Month events usually attended by more women than men? All

of us need to be culturally literate and responsive to survive and succeed in the twenty-first century. According to Dr. Benjamin Carson, one of the world's most renowned surgeons, it is a mistake to think that it's not my problem or it doesn't affect me. "All of our ancestors came to this country in different boats. But we're all in the same boat now. And if part of the boat sinks, eventually the rest of it goes down too."[23]

- *Simply ignoring differences and treating everybody the same.* It is necessary to distinguish between sameness and equal opportunity. Should an instructor, for example, always treat everybody the same? On one hand, she should have high expectations for all of her students regardless of who they are. That same instructor, however, will have to distinguish among students in determining how she can teach the material most effectively and how she can help individual students succeed.
- *Some "feel good" activity.* Diversity consciousness is not a matter of merely feeling good about ourselves and others. It goes deeper. Superficial acceptance is replaced by a deeper and more critical understanding.
- *A passing fad.* Diversity has always been with us, and responding to it effectively will become more and more important. A good example is our increasing life span. Census predictions point to a much grayer population by the year 2050 because we are living longer. America's "baby boomers" will begin to reach age 65 in the year 2010. By 2020, nearly one-fifth of the U.S. population will be 65 years of age or older.[24] People are not only living longer, but they are also healthier and retiring at a later age. Therefore, the older population will be a growing part of the diversity that surrounds us daily.

DIVERSITY EDUCATION

Diversity has always been a powerful, even a necessary, catalyst for intellectual progress.

—David H. Porter, President Emeritus, Skidmore College

Diversity education refers to all the strategies that enable us to develop diversity consciousness. Through diversity education, we develop awareness, understanding, and a variety of skills in the area of diversity. Throughout the book, these skills are referred to as **diversity skills**. Among these are flexible thinking, communication, teamwork, and leadership skills, as well as the ability to overcome personal and social barriers.

Diversity education takes many forms. It is something we can initiate and control, such as reading a book, attending a workshop, and exchanging ideas about diversity issues with thousands of people over the Internet. One form of diversity education, which has proliferated throughout the country in recent years, is study circles. Anyone can form a study circle.

STUDY CIRCLES ON DIVERSITY

The idea behind this kind of study circle is to involve communities in ongoing dialogues on diversity. Anyone or any group can initiate a study circle. In many communities, organizations such as churches, businesses, schools, and clubs sponsor study circles. Support from the Study Circles Resource Center (SCRC) is also available at no charge. SCRC provides free discussion materials and assistance.[25]

People who join study circles agree to meet regularly over an extended period of time. This long-term proactive approach to dialogue allows study circle participants to get to know one another and begin to share their innermost feelings. Everyone is given a "home" in the conversation. By participating in study circles, everyday people gain ownership of issues that relate to diversity. Typically, the discussion focuses initially on personal experiences and perspectives. Participants then examine how personal and community issues interrelate and what action needs to be taken. Unlike many other forms of diversity education which do not go beyond dialogue, study circles combine talk with action.

The experiences of study circles throughout the country show promise. In some cases, hundreds and thousands of people participate in community-wide dialogues. Roughly 500 people and 30 organizations in Minneapolis/St. Paul are involved in study circles on the challenge of racial segregation in housing and education. A statewide program in Oklahoma helped initiate sweeping changes in the corrections system. In Miami, Florida, the "Many Voices, One Community" project is addressing a number of diversity issues, including immigration and education, race relations, language differences, and job opportunities.

Typically, long-term relationships form out of circles. I have a best friend that I met in a study circle. Often, there is a need for a second level of the same circle that further narrows the focus. If the first circle was good, the participants are reluctant to leave. There is a bonding that takes place that transcends culture and race. This makes us simply human beings who have gained a wiser understanding of one another and the need to know more.

—A student's perspective

Unlike many other forms of learning, true diversity education requires continual, fundamental change. Change of this nature, what best-selling author Stephen Covey terms *real change*, takes place "from the inside out." In *The Seven Habits of Highly Successful People*, Covey elaborates. Real change "doesn't come from hacking at the leaves of attitude and behavior with quick fix personality ethic techniques. It comes from striking at the root—the fabric of our thought, the fundamental essential paradigms which give definition to our character and create the lens through which we see the world."[26] In other words, fundamental changes involve growing as a person, both intellectually and emotionally. Although change of this nature is not easy, the rewards are worth it.

Much of the dialogue regarding diversity in recent years equates diversity with diversity education. They are not the same. Diversity simply refers to our individual and collective differences. Without education, diversity is simply untapped potential.

In summary, the cultural landscape in the United States is changing due to the influence of demographic, technological, and social changes. The term *diversity* has gained new meaning; it does not simply refer to racial, ethnic, and gender differences. Despite the attention diversity receives, our views and understanding of diversity are often influenced by myths about diversity and the role it plays in our lives. Diversity education enables us to move beyond these myths and develop our diversity consciousness.

In the next chapter, we focus on skills that enable us to capitalize on diversity. We examine how diversity skills make us more successful at school and on the job. Additionally, we explore the numerous ways in which organizations benefit from the diversity skills of their employees.

Exercises

In-Class

Exercise 1: The Diversity within You

Each student will need the following materials for this exercise: 1 square foot of aluminum foil, 4 toothpicks, 2 paper clips, a foam cup, and a marker.

Directions for Instructor

1. Ask each student to create something from these materials that represents his or her diversity as an individual.
2. Once everybody has finished, ask each student to share his or her creation with other members of the class and explain what it represents.

Exercise 2: What Is an American?

Directions for Instructor

1. Ask students, "What does it mean to be an American?" Each student should write down a response that is no more than two sentences.
2. Ask students to form groups of two. Compare answers. How are their definitions of an American similar? How are they different?
3. Ask the entire class to share and analyze their responses. Who is included and excluded in their descriptions of an American?

OUT-OF-CLASS

Exercise 1: What Is Diversity?

1. Ask 10 students not in this class to complete this sentence:
   Diversity is ____.
   Record their responses.
2. Write a paragraph summarizing the responses of the 10 students. Do any of their responses reflect diversity myths? Explain.

Exercise 2: Thinking through My Cultural Diversity

Describe, in a reasonable amount of detail, your background in terms of the following dimensions of cultural diversity.

- Your early environment: the kind(s) of community(ies) in which you grew up (large city, suburb, small town, rural area)
- Your social class as you grew up, the jobs and levels of education of those who raised you, and the social class levels of your neighbors
- Your social heritage—specifically, your racial, ethnic (cultural), and religious background (you may not necessarily identify with all three)—and its importance to you
- The culture other than your own that has had the greatest impact on you, and why

Exercise 3: What's in a Name?

1. What is your full name? How do you feel about your name? Why?
2. Find out as much as you can about your name. For example, what is the history and significance of your name? What is the meaning of your name?

INTERNET ASSIGNMENT

1. Go to a search engine site such as www.Yahoo.com or www.hotbot.com. Do a search on "diversity education" (put the two words inside quotes so that the search is for that exact term).
2. Read the selection of links you receive and choose one that interests you. Go to that site and print either the home page or an article of interest.

3. Write a two-paragraph summary of what you learned from visiting this Web site and any links that you visited.

NOTES

[1]"Inclusion," *Book and Video Catalog* (Manhattan, KS: The MASTER Teacher, 1999), 5A.

[2]Vincent N. Parillo, *Diversity in America* (Thousand Oaks, CA: Pine Forge Press, 1996), 65.

[3]U.S. Bureau of the Census, *Historical Statistics of the United States, Part II*, Series Z 20-132 (Washington, DC: U.S. Government Printing Office, 1976).

[4]U.S. Bureau of the Census, *Statistical Abstract of the United States 1997*, 117th ed. (Washington, DC, U.S. Government Printing Office, 1997), 44.

[5]Barbara Fraser, "U.S. Colleges Step Up Recruiting in Latin America," *Chronicle of Higher Education*, XLIV(10), Oct. 31, 1997, A58–A59.

[6]Barry McLaughlin and Beverly McLeod, "Educating All Our Students: Improving Education for Children from Culturally and Linguistically Diverse Backgrounds." Online. World Wide Web. June 1966. Available: http://www.ncbe.gwu.edu/miscpubs/ncrcdsll/edall.htm.

[7]Marshall McLuhan, *The Mechanical Bride: Folklore of Industrial Man* (Boston: Beacon Press, 1967).

[8]William Frey, "The Diversity Myth," *American Demographics*, June 1998, 38–43.

[9]Federal Glass Ceiling Commission, *A Solid Investment: Making Full Use of the Nation's Human Capital* (Washington, DC: U.S. Department of Labor, 1995), 6.

[10]Southern Poverty Law Center, "E-mail on Trial," *Intelligence Report*, Winter 1988, 5.

[11]Israel Zangwill, *The Melting Pot* (New York: The Jewish Publication Society of America, 1909), 198–199.

[12]Toni Morrison, *Playing in the Dark* (Cambridge, Mass.: Harvard University Press, 1992), 47.

[13]Ronald Takaki. *A Different Mirror. A History of Multicultural America.* (Boston: Little, Brown, 1993).

[14]Ruth Frankenberg, *White Women, Race Matters: The Social Construction of Whiteness* (Minneapolis, MN: University of Minnesota Press, 1993), 198.

[15]Roosevelt Thomas. *Beyond Race and Gender: Unleashing the Power of Your Total Work Force by Managing Diversity* (New York: American Management Association, 1991).

[16]Malcolm X, *The Autobiography of Malcolm X* (New York: Ballantine Books, 1965), 36.

[17]Ashley Montagu. *Man's Most Dangerous Myth: The Fallacy of Race* (Cleveland, OH: World Publishing, 1964).

[18]Amanda Enayati, "Not Black, Not White," *The Washington Post*, July 13, 1997, C1.

[19]L. A. Kauffman, "The Diversity Game," *Voice*, Aug. 31, 1993, 31.

[20]Alexander Astin. *What Matters in College? Four Critical Years Revisited* (San Francisco: Jossey-Bass, 1993).

[21] *The Color of Fear* (video) (Oakland, CA: Stir Fry Productions, 1994).

[22]Leonard Pitts, Jr., "Watching Whites Struggle to Understand Their Whiteness," *The Sun*, Apr. 21, 1997, 9A.

[23]Benjamin Carson, "Carson Philosophy Is 'Think Big,'" *The Sun*, Aug. 24, 1997, 6H.

[24]Richard W. Judy and Carol D'Amico, *Workforce 2020: Executive Summary* (Indianapolis, IN: Hudson Institute, 1997), 3.

[25]For more information, contact Study Circles Resource Center, P.O. Box 203, 697 Pomfret Street, Pomfret, CT 06258; tel: 203-928-2616; fax: 203-928-3713.

[26]Stephen Covey, *The Seven Habits of Highly Effective People* (New York: Simon & Schuster, 1989).

Chapter 6b

DEVELOPING DIVERSITY CONSCIOUSNESS

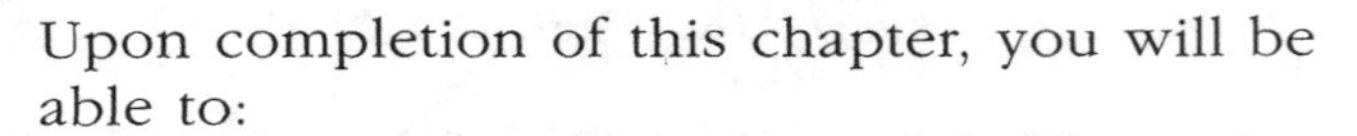

Upon completion of this chapter, you will be able to:

- Explain the importance of **diversity consciousness**.
- List and explain the six areas of development.
- Discuss at least three strategies for personal growth.
- Explain why the development of diversity consciousness is a continuing process.

> *Not to know is bad.*
> *Not to want to know is worse.*
> *Not to hope unthinkable.*
> *Not to care unforgivable.*
>
> *—Nigerian proverb*

DIVERSITY CONSCIOUSNESS

In this chapter we look at how each of us can develop our diversity consciousness. We examine the roots and impact of our cultural isolation, as well as how we can become more aware of ourselves and others. This ongoing process is not sequential; it does not occur in steps that follow one another neatly. Rather, many things feed into this process as we continually open ourselves up to other perspectives.

Regardless of your educational or career goals, diversity consciousness is important for a number of reasons:

1. *It enhances your diversity skills.* These skills, discussed throughout the book, include:

- Teamwork
- Ability to balance "fitting in" and "being yourself"
- Flexible thinking and adaptability
- Ability to network and learn from everyone and anyone
- Ability to recognize and respect diverse intellectual strengths and learning styles
- Ability to appreciate and maintain pride in your background and culture
- Ability to deal effectively with barriers to success
- Interpersonal relations and communication
- Self-evaluation
- Pluralistic leadership
- Conflict management
- Critical thinking

These skills will open up your mind to opportunities in all realms of life.

2. *It expands your horizons and empowers you.* Knowledge is power. Learning about yourself and others helps you to cope with all kinds of situations. Knowledge can give you confidence and instill pride in yourself and your culture. Unlike material possessions, it cannot be taken away from you. Vu Duc Vuong, a Vietnamese immigrant, makes this point when he talks about the economic hardships endured by refugees. They "often lose everything they have; everything can be taken away from a refugee: money, house, car, gold, souvenirs, job, status, friends, relatives, spouses, and even their own lives. You have heard these stories, and some of you may have even witnessed them firsthand. But among all the losses, there is one thing that will always be yours, that is your learning. No person, no circumstance, no law, and no catastrophe can take away what is inside your head. So, you owe it to yourself to learn as much as you can the rest of your life. That is one possession that is completely within your control, that is completely yours."[1]

Knowledge is better than riches.

—Cameroonian proverb

3. *It allows you to expand and enhance your social network.* By making contacts and developing relationships with people from a wide variety of backgrounds, you expand your social network. Thus you open up social, educational, and business opportunities. As you grow to value diversity, you will meet new and different kinds of people and expand your circle of friends. At school, diversity consciousness allows you to relate more effectively to a wide variety of instructors with diverse teaching styles. It enables you to learn more from other students. Additionally, the skills you develop as you become more conscious of diversity increase your value at work. Your assets will include your flexibility, creativity, and ability to communicate and work with all kinds of people. These are the same qualities that will make you a more effective leader or manager.

Opportunity isn't necessarily going to come along looking, talking, dressing, and acting like you. The more different kinds of people you can get along with, the more opportunities you will have.

—An instructor's perspective

ISOLATION

Are you the typical college student? In comparison to most other students, what makes you similar or different? The following quiz tests your assumptions about college students in the United States today.

True or false?

1. Most college students are between 18 and 21 years of age.
2. Of all college students, fewer than 25 percent are part-time.
3. Roughly half of those who begin college drop out.
4. Most college students are paying, on average, around $10,000 a year for tuition and other fees.
5. People classified as "minority" or "foreign" make up approximately 15 percent of all college students.
6. The proportion of women completing college is greater than that of men.

Note: Answers to each of these questions are provided on the next page.

When we think of what is typical, we tend to start with ourselves and our own little worlds: our families, neighborhoods, schools, and communities. This kind of thinking often gives rise to ethnocentrism, a concept we discussed in the last chapter. Ethnocentrism leads us to judge others or the larger world by our own limited experiences.

Sometimes, our narrow perspective expands a bit through exposure to the media. Indeed, for most people in the United States, various media are their primary source of information about the larger world. This can be dangerous since many people do not critically evaluate what they see or hear on television, in the newspapers, or elsewhere. According to research, the media often provide information that is stereotypical, superficial, and incomplete.

For example, the research group Women, Men, and Media periodically reviews the gender of newsmakers found on the front page of large and small newspapers. In a recent survey of news coverage, this group found that women rarely make the front page of newspapers. When they do, it is often because of a tragedy such as death or due to their relationship to a male newsmaker.[2] Another survey by the National Council of La Raza found that television and film often depict Hispanics as low status and criminals.[3] Many stories on poverty that appear in the media reveal a bias as well. According to a recent Yale University study by Martin Gilens,[4] stories about the poor in national news magazines picture African-Americans 62 percent of the time. This is likely to create the impression that most poor people are African-Americans. However, U.S. Census data paint a different picture of poverty. While roughly 25 percent of Americans who fall below the poverty line are African-American, 75 percent are not.[5]

If we cannot rely on the media, what about our personal lives? Why can't we simply fall back on what we know as a result of our past and present experiences? Your perception of college students might provide some answers to this question. Think back to the quiz on college students that appears above. How do your answers compare with data provided by the U.S. Department of Education and the College Board?

Figure 4.1: *Lifelong learning is becoming a reality for all Americans, regardless of age. (Courtesy of Senior Net.)*

1. Most college students are between 18 and 21 years of age—*false.* More than half of all college students are 22 years of age or older, and more than one-fourth are 30 or older.[6] Many older students are returning to college to learn new skills (see Fig. 4.1). Others have raised their families and are finally able to think about their own education. Although most of your classmates may be 18 to 22 year olds, this is not the norm, especially for community colleges.

2. Of all college students, fewer than 25 percent are part-time—*false.* Approximately 40 percent of college students attend part-time.[7] Many of these students are employed and some are parents. They do not have the time or the resources to attend full-time. Many older students are getting a feeling for college before they become full-time. Many of these students tend to be less visible on campus because they attend school at night or on weekends.

3. Roughly half of those who begin college drop out—*true.*[8] This figure may seem high to some of you. However, retention is a serious problem in higher education. Students drop out for any number of reasons and often times, it has nothing to do with their ability to do the work.

4. Most college students are paying, on average, around $10,000 a year for tuition and other fees—*false.* We often read articles or watch news stories about tuition and fees rising above $20,000. However, this is true of relatively few schools. Most students attend public two- and four-year colleges where the average cost of tuition and fees ranges from about $1500 to $3100 a year.[9]

5. People classified as "minority" or "foreign" make up approximately 15 percent of all college students—*false.* Minority and foreign students account for almost twice this percentage.[10] In recent years, most of the growth in college enrollment has been among students classified as African-American, Asian-American, Native American, and Hispanic American.

6. The proportion of women completing college is greater than that of men—*true.* This statement is supported by the Census Bureau's analysis of education statistics. Before 1985, men topped women consistently. Between 1985 and 1995, the completion rate for men and women was so close that the difference was considered statistically insignificant. In 1996, the proportion of women completing college topped that of men and the lead is widening.[11] This trend indicates that more and more women want careers and recognize the economic value of a college education.

Our perceptions of college students are a reflection of our experiences. Sometimes those experiences are what we might term "typical," but often they are not. When we show ethnocentrism and assume that our way of living or doing things is not only typical but also the only way, we can easily offend others and limit our own personal growth.

Isolation: Before College

Social isolation starts at a young age. It is apparent throughout **socialization**, the lifelong process of social interaction that enables us to learn about ourselves and others. We are inclined to make friends with other people who are like us. In many cases, we attend schools and live in neighborhoods that are racially and ethnically segregated. Social isolation prior to college is one of the major reasons why college life can be such an adjustment. After living in relatively segregated communities, students tend to become much more aware of their cultural identity when they enter college. One student commented: "Like now, I feel white. I feel different. I feel really different compared to other people."[12]

Students may find it difficult to adjust to college life when the cultural backgrounds of their fellow students are unlike those of people in their home communities. Faced with this situation, students typically become more focused on their own culture or minority status. As one student remarked, "I'm used to being the minority, but I wasn't used to living it day by day by day, morning, noon, and night."[13]

Prior to college, exposure to other groups and ways of life takes place largely through the media and popular culture. Students tend to experience exposure to some groups more than others. Larger groups, such as Latinos and African-Americans, tend to be more visible than smaller groups, such as Asian-Americans and Native Americans. Even when images in the media are accurate, they may lack balance. By way of illustration, a movie such as *The Joy Luck Club* provides us with certain negative images of Asian-American males. These images might accurately reflect *some* Asian-American men. However, these images are not adequately balanced by other, more positive portrayals.

Many students bring to school negative preconceptions about differences. Often, students form these views as a result of isolated experiences with members of another group. Some of these experiences are associated with considerable emotion and even pain. For instance, one student confided in me she had been raped by a Jamaican male. As a result, she makes a habit of staying away from any man who appears to be Jamaican.

Isolation: At College

College typically exposes students to a wider variety of human differences. However, this exposure does not necessarily lead to greater acceptance and interaction across group boundaries, due to a number of factors.

1. *Research shows that throwing diverse students together in the same setting is no guarantee that they will interact or get to know each other.* Whites, African-Americans, Latinos, and other minority students often are unlikely to develop personal relationships outside their group. Students in general may find it easier to socialize with others who they perceive as being more like them. Also, negative prior experiences or personal biases may make some students hesitant to develop any kind of meaningful relationship with someone who does not share their background or even their physical appearance.

This kind of self-segregation, in which people "keep with their own kind," is relatively common on college campuses. It occurs in residence halls, athletic teams, social clubs, and support groups. Contrary to popular belief, research findings indicate that self-segregation is more common among white students than among students of color. This is one of the major conclusions found in *The Impact of Diversity on Students*, a research report published by the Association of American Colleges and Universities.[14]

THINKING THROUGH DIVERSITY:

Take a look at your close circle of friends. How diverse is this group?

2. *The campus climate is "chilly" for some students.* **Campus climate** refers to the level of comfort that students experience in the classroom and on campus. Students may feel uncomfortable for any number of reasons, including gender. In *The Classroom Climate: A Chilly One for Women?*, a female student recalls: "I was discussing my work in a public setting when a professor cut me off and asked me if I had freckles all over my body."[15] A chilly climate can make it more difficult for students to focus on their schoolwork, communicate with others, and develop relationships with faculty and students. Unfortunately, research findings show that students feel there are very few opportunities to express their concerns about campus climate.[16]

3. *Opportunities to learn about diversity, and students' inclination to take advantage of these opportunities, vary greatly.* When it comes to providing students with opportunities to become more knowledgeable about diversity, some colleges do a lot and others do relatively little. At certain colleges, all students are required to take at least one course dealing with cultural diversity. An increasing number of college instructors are infusing diversity in their courses. Student and faculty programs, workshops, and activities dealing with diversity issues are commonplace.

Nevertheless, learning about diversity is not always a college-wide priority. Sometimes, it is only an issue if a particular student or faculty member makes it an issue. At some schools, diversity is seen as relevant only for a small group of students majoring in the social sciences or related areas. Consequently, many students discover that during their years in college, learning about diversity is up to them. If you take responsibility for learning more about others regardless of the college you attend, your diversity consciousness will grow. If you don't, it won't.

THINKING THROUGH DIVERSITY:
Look at what is being taught in your college classes. Do the readings, lectures, and discussions reflect the contributions of many cultures?

Cultural Immersion Program

The University of Indiana and the University of Nebraska have recently begun what they term a *cultural immersion program* for education majors. As part of their educational program, students are required to teach and live in a predominantly bilingual/bicultural setting. The program addresses the growing need for elementary and secondary school teachers with multicultural skills and training.

SIX AREAS OF DEVELOPMENT

Diversity consciousness is not an ideal level of awareness and understanding that we reach, after which we remain static. Rather, it is dynamic. Developing our diversity consciousness means committing ourselves to constant learning

Figure 4.2: Diversity consciousness: six areas of development.

and change. In this sense, it is a lot like developing computer know-how. There is always something new to learn and practice.

The development of diversity consciousness can be broken down into six areas (see Fig. 4.2): (1) examining yourself and your world, (2) expanding your knowledge of others and their worlds, (3) stepping outside of yourself, (4) gauging the level of the playing field, (5) checking up on yourself, and (6) following through. In the following sections we describe each of these areas.

Examining Yourself and Your World

It is a huge mistake to assume that we already have full knowledge of our own history and culture. Zora Neale Hurston, a well-known writer and anthropologist, stated: "I couldn't see it [culture] for wearing it. It was only when I was off in college, away from my native surroundings, that I could see myself like somebody else and stand off and look at my garment. I had to have the spyglass of Anthropology to look through at that."[17] Like many of us, Hurston was unaware of her culture because she was so immersed in it. When she went to college, she found herself in a different cultural and academic setting. By experiencing and learning about cultural diversity in this new environment, she was able to "stand back" and take a more critical look at her culture.

Before we begin to make sense of other cultures and cultural differences, we need to become aware of who we are. We do this by focusing on ourselves and the enormous diversity that exists within each of us. Each person is different and each is unique.

Our uniqueness is a reflection of both nature and nurture, which work together. **Nature** refers to our biological makeup. This includes our inborn or genetic traits. "Who we are," therefore, has something to do with nature. However, we cannot examine nature apart from nurture. **Nurture** includes those aspects of the environment that mold and shape us. Essentially, nurture simply describes how schools, families, peer groups, and other parts of our culture influence us. Each of us is reared in a distinctive environment. Even children from the same family are treated differently by their parents, watch different television shows, read different books, and have different friends.

You can reveal your own diversity by asking a number of questions about your background. What makes you unique? Is it your work ethic; talents, personality, sense of humor, or maybe all these things? Your upbringing, schooling, family background, and cultural roots further distinguish you from other people. Your answers to the following questions will provide greater insight into your diversity.

1. What is your name? What is the meaning or significance of your name?
2. Where were you born?
3. What is your family background? Who raised you? As you grew up, who did you consider "family?" Where did you live? Who were your closest friends?
4. What schools did you attend? In general, did you feel like you belonged, or did you feel like an outsider at school? Were the values you learned at school similar to the ones you learned at home? Did you feel the need to "leave your culture at home" in order to be accepted at school?
5. How has your identity been influenced by your race, gender, religion, ethnic background, sexual orientation, and/or social class?
6. What about your personality makes you unique? How are you different from other members of your family?
7. What motivates you? What are your interests and hobbies? What are your goals in life? How do you want to be remembered?
8. What kinds of learning experiences are meaningful for you? What kinds are not?

Every person has a name, and also his own story about his name. My name is Yuan Cai. I don't know what you think about that, but to me it just feels upside-down because I used to be called "Cai Yuan" or "Yuan

Yuan." That's why when I speak English I just tell you my name is "Yuan." "Yuan" is the end character of my name, so I feel I have told you all. You know, giving best names to children is so important in China. They look up in dictionary and search for the most beautiful sounds, perfect meanings, special and elegantly simple characters, and require the characters to have some relationships between family members. So you can imagine how hard a job it was for my parents to give me my name.

—A student's perspective

Examining our own diversity entails learning about our culture. This is a bigger job for some than others. How much do you know about your ancestors? Although most of us have an immigrant past, few of us know much about it. Whereas some students are very conscious of their cultural backgrounds, others are hardly aware of it at all. Still others wrestle with the history of their culture and how it reflects on them.

Sometimes, learning about your history can be difficult. In the book *Tearing the Silence*, Ursula Hegi talks about "what it means to be linked to two cultures."[18] Hegi, a German-American, devotes much of her book to the personal histories of Germans who were born during or after World War II and later migrated to the United States. When they arrived, they expected to find an open and tolerant society. Instead, they encountered many who scorned and mocked them because they were assumed to be Nazis.

Many of the German-Americans interviewed by Hegi wanted to leave their past behind. As one person put it: "I have a very difficult time dealing with the Holocaust. I think there is a collective burden in our generation because it is just so tremendous, so horrible. On the other side, I must say that we have this 'Gnade der spaten Geburt'—the grace of late birth. It's an easy way out....But it came to my mind that there is a shadow of a collective guilt. At the same time, I feel it is not my personal guilt, and there's nothing I can do."[19]

Your own cultural identity may be more or less visible to you for a number of reasons. For example, some students are more apt to be reminded of their cultural background on a daily basis. Language, music, food, holidays, and customs all serve to reinforce our sense of cultural belonging. Being treated as an outsider serves as a reminder as well. Because of their background, some students continually find themselves in situations in which they must decide whether to try to "fit in." Frequently, they may have to weigh the pros and cons of being "true" to their cultural roots, assimilating, or some combination of the two. On the other hand, other students do not have to make these choices. Their culture is the norm at school, home, and work.

There are also times when some students feel their culture is slipping away. "I was so anxious to assimilate, to blend in, that I started to forget who I was.... I just felt it wasn't cool to be a poor Latina girl from Harlem. It was better to mosh than merengue and to be able to go to a country home on the weekends. I almost forgot who I was and where I came from, and it's important not to do that. Remember, you come from beautifully vibrant cultures filled with rich music and traditions. Share that. Enlighten others with your history.... Try new things but don't forget the old.... Remember who you are."[20]

In the course of becoming aware of our cultural roots, it is important to remember that our environment has a lot to do with who we are. An African proverb states: "A person is a person through other people." We cannot escape the influence of culture; we are not the totally independent thinkers and learners we may think we are.

Up to this point we have focused on who we are and how we are interconnected with others. Frequently, it is difficult to make that connection for a number of reasons, including the following:

1. *The emphasis on individualism in U.S. society makes it difficult to see social influences.* In most cases, people in the United States are raised to believe that they think and act on their own. Consider the sayings, "Be all that you can be" and "You are your own worst enemy." Now contrast those with the African proverb, "It takes an entire village to raise a child." Asian cultures also tend to be more oriented toward "we" than "me." As an example, Japanese have a saying, "the nail that stands up gets pounded down." This notion that personal goals are not as important as the goals of the group is at odds with the saying in this country that "the squeaky wheel gets the grease."

Baseball in Japan and in the United States

Think for a moment about how we view baseball in the United States. How might people in other countries, such as Japan, view it differently? Some differences are captured in an article that appeared in *Sports Illustrated.*[21] While U.S. professional ballplayers are encouraged to "do their own thing," *kojinshugi* (the Japanese term for individualism) is frowned upon in Japan. In the United States, it is commonplace for a player to hold out for more money and sell his services to the highest bidder. This is highly unacceptable in Japan because it shows that a player is more concerned about himself than about his team. In the United States, each player gets himself into shape, whereas in Japan, everyone follows the same training regimen, even the superstars.

2. *Our cultural environment is so close to us that sometimes we do not see it.* Often, we do not even think about certain beliefs that are deeply embedded in each of us. Consequently, it is hard to step back and take a long hard look at our environment or imagine that anyone could think any other way. In *Patterns of Problem Solving,* Moshe Rubinstein provides us with insight into how people from different cultures might view the following hypothetical situation.[22] Imagine that you are in a boat with your mom, spouse, and child. If you could save yourself and only *one* of these three people, who would you save, and why? Most students in my classes answer child. They argue their children have their whole future ahead of them. Some students mention that their children are "part of them." Very few choose mom or spouse. Rubenstein relates how a man from an Arab culture chose "mother." Given this man's cultural background, he could not imagine choosing anyone else. His reasoning was that you can always have another child or spouse. However, you can only have one mother.

3. *Some people rarely experience what it is like to be viewed as an outsider.* Because of this, they have a difficult time seeing beyond their own world. On the other hand, if you are constantly being judged because of your race, class, or religion, you are apt to be more aware of its social significance. For example, consider an American history instructor who constantly calls on the only Mormon student in class to get "her people's" point of view. This experience may make this student feel like an outsider because she is constantly being singled out. In addition, the student may realize that other students in class are not called upon to represent their religions.

THINKING THROUGH DIVERSITY:
How can learning about others help us learn more about ourselves?

Expanding Your Knowledge of Others and Their Worlds

Learning about others is instrumental in laying the foundation for diversity consciousness. Furthermore, it enables us to learn more about ourselves. Anthropologists, for example, do not just study cultures that differ from their own. They also work to understand and interpret their own culture, often using what they learn about other cultures to do so. Visiting another country, similarly, can make you more aware of your cultural biases and provide you with a basis for comparison. After visiting another country, you may have a whole new outlook on parts of your culture that you take for granted, such as housing, recreation, education, or friendship.

I come from Zaire and one thing that I miss here most is the friendship of my neighbors and friends. In my country, and in Africa in general, people are hospitable. Friendship is the most important thing in life. In my country, you can't perish from hunger or illness, because members of your family must assist you and help you to improve your life. It's an obligation. Even the neighbors give you their assistance. For instance, when you are sick and you can't go to a hospital because you don't have enough money or you don't have a car, the one in your neighborhood who has a car must transport you to the hospital without hesitation. He has to do it with all his heart. You can even stop a car passing your way, to get help.

In America, however, I think this is not the same. People live in mistrust of each other. You can't count on your neighbors because either they don't know you or don't want to be involved. You are condemned to live without any moral support from anyone in the neighborhood. You can be ill and can die alone in your apartment and no one is likely to notice it. Here I think friendship takes place only when there is an interest. Last week I finished my milk and went to ask a neighbor for a half cup of milk. She gave it to me, but a few days later, she asked for some sugar from me and gave it back to me in the evening. I was very surprised because this is not done among neighbors.

Maybe I am wrong in my opinion, but the facts show that friendships in America are very different from friendships in my country.

—A student's perspective

Malcolm X, in his autobiography, talks about his visit to Saudi Arabia as well as a number of countries in Africa as being one of the turning points in his life.[23] His experiences in that part of the world gave him an entirely different view of race relations in the United States. Moving to another country can provide students with new insight into their ethnic background. A college student from Colombia talks about her interaction with other Latin Americans in the United States. "I have met a lot of Latin Americans. Although we have the same cultural background, we are different. We have different accents in our language and use different words to mean the same things. I have learned about exotic foods from other Latin American countries that I have never seen before. It's incredible that I have learned about Latin American culture in a non–Latin American country. When you are in a foreign country, you have the opportunity to recognize your own roots because you see things from a different point of view."

Differences

Typically, students learn about cultural differences by sampling and studying a few noteworthy events and people. A good example of this is the "group of the month" approach adopted by many schools. With this approach, students are exposed to various elements of African-American culture during Black History Month. Similarly, there are months reserved for women, Latinos, Native Americans, people with disabilities, and other groups.

This kind of approach may be attractive because it is simple and easy to implement. Unfortunately, it promotes a superficial and distorted view of differences. The historical experiences of African-Americans or women, for example, cannot be separated and studied in any kind of meaningful way in a single month. At best, this approach gives us a "taste" of a few noteworthy people or events. At worst, it excludes some students who wonder why their groups are never a "group of the month." Such an approach can also lead to even more stereotypical assumptions.

Although sampling different ways of life may have some value, it is not without dangers. After riding in a wheelchair for 15 minutes or attending a one-hour lecture on disability awareness, some people may begin to feel that they now know what it is like to have a disability. They may generalize what they learn or experience to all people with disabilities. In addition, they may forget the lesson learned shortly thereafter, unless it is reaffirmed time and again.

What then is the best way to learn about differences? A number of specific strategies will be discussed later in the chapter. It is impossible to know every aspect of every culture. However, we need to approach cultural differences with a number of things in mind:

1. *Do not simply sample differences from a distance.* This promotes an "us" versus "them" attitude. In the mid-1970s, I remember a student in one of my classes correcting me on something I had said about Black Muslims. The student, Lola X, was a Black Muslim. She then invited me and my wife to her local temple. We accepted. When we arrived, we were frisked for our own safety. At that time there were concerns about the threat of violence. We were then taken into the temple. My wife was seated with the women on one side and I took my seat with the men. We discovered that we were the only two Whites in a congregation of more than 300 people of color. The sermon was powerful and positive. Everybody, it seemed, tried to make us feel welcome. After the service, a number of people came up to us, introduced themselves, and invited us back. As I look back at that experience, I realize how being there helped me learn and appreciate Lola and her religion. Based on what I had read and heard, I fully expected to be surrounded by people who were angry and hateful toward Whites. What I saw and felt were strong, loving people who went out of their way to make my wife and me feel at home.

2. *Seek to understand how the histories, perspectives, and contributions of different cultures are interconnected.* In 1927, the American historian Carter Woodson made this point with regard to "Negro history." Woodson argued that the focus should be on the Negro *in* history rather than on Negro history.[24]

3. *Try to decrease the social distance between you and those groups or individuals about whom you know little if anything.* **Social distance** is a concept that was coined by a scientist named Emory Bogardus.[25] It refers to the degree to which we are willing to interact and develop relationships with certain racial and ethnic groups. Bogardus created a scale to measure whether we would accept certain people as neighbors, classmates, co-workers, or even spouses. He found that we tend to separate ourselves from others who we think are not like us. This is particularly true of our inner social circles. Take a look at your close friends. How closely do they resemble the racial, ethnic, and social class mix of the students in your school? Would you be comfortable bringing someone of a different religion or sexual orientation home for a few days to spend some time with your family? Our tendency to gravitate toward people who are like us promotes **cultural encapsulation**, meaning a lack of contact with other cultures.

THINKING THROUGH DIVERSITY:
In your life, what groups or cultures are most socially distant?

4. *Focus on ordinary people and occurrences.* Learning about a few remarkable people and events from another culture is not sufficient. Often, stories like these tell us very little about a culture. You can learn a lot more from people who do not make the headlines or the history books, such as a friend, a fellow student, or the employee who works in the cafeteria. Think about the "student perspectives" that appear throughout this book. What have you learned from them?

Similarities

Too often, we preoccupy ourselves so much with individual and cultural differences that we ignore our similarities. Some similarities are harder to see because they lie beneath the surface. In a poem entitled, "Underneath We're All the Same," a student addresses the fact that we all share certain feelings.

He prayed—it wasn't my religion.
He ate—it wasn't what I ate.
He spoke—it wasn't my language.
He dressed—it wasn't what I wore.
He took my hand—it wasn't the color of mine.
But when he laughed—it was how I laughed,
and when he cried—it was how I cried.

—Amy Maddox, as quoted in *Teaching Tolerance* Magazine[26]

Picture yourself in one of your classes. With whom do you have the most in common? Perhaps it is someone who looks like you or shares your cultural background. It might be the Hispanic student who sits next to you: Even though your race is different, you both grew up in a middle-class, urban neighborhood and are very close to your families. Then again, it might be the white woman who sits in front of you. Unlike you, she is married and has five children. Yet she is the one person in class who shares your passion for computers. Both of you hope to find jobs as computer programmers. Our differences often hide our similarities. Until we really get to know a person, we often fail to realize just how much we share in common.

As students encountering each other for the first time, we tend to notice differences. During the course of a semester, similarities among races, cultures, and other groups can become more apparent. The following comments were written by students who were part of a semester-long study group on racial and ethnic diversity.

I look at things differently because with me being a single parent, I do struggle and I realize that it's not just a "black thing." Everybody struggles.

I learned that Whites hurt just like I do, they cry just like I do. I never knew that some Whites have the same fears about race that I have.

I remember the day we listed the qualities that make us who we are. I realize most of us are alike in a lot of ways, and different in fewer ways. It was very reassuring to see other students agree with me on the same qualities.

—Students' perspectives

Stepping Outside of Yourself

One way to step outside of yourself is to put yourself in somebody else's place. For instance, when you study for a test, you might try to put yourself in the place of your instructor. You might say to yourself: "What questions would I ask on the test if I were the instructor?" This can give you valuable insight into what your instructor is thinking and what to study.

The ability to "put yourself in somebody else's moccasins" increases your awareness, understanding, and diversity skills—your diversity consciousness. By stepping outside of yourself and your culture, you can gain a deeper appreciation of other people's experiences. As a result, your ability to think flexibly and to communicate effectively improve.

Stepping outside of yourself is important for other reasons as well. It increases your awareness of your own frame of reference and how this shapes what you see. By adopting another perspective, you become more aware of your own. You also begin to realize that your perspective is just one of many.

THINKING THROUGH DIVERSITY:

Imagine that you are being forced to change your gender (select male/female) or your race/ethnicity (select a "new" racial/ethnic group) or your sexual orientation (select homosexual/heterosexual). Which would you change, and why?

ONLY SKIN DEEP

Joshua Solomon, a white student at the University of Maryland, remembers the day he read the book *Black Like Me* by John Howard Griffin.[27] He spent the entire day reading it and thinking about little else. Back in 1959, Griffin, a journalist, took a drug to change his skin from white to brown. He then traveled throughout the South and recorded his experiences. (A white woman by the name of Grace Halsell did something similar in the 1970s. Over the course of three years, she wrote three books about life as a Hispanic, Native American, and African-American woman.)

Solomon decided that he too would change the color of his skin and venture into the South. He did some research and talked to a physician at Yale University. He found the drug that Griffin had taken. Once he started taking it daily and spending time at a tanning salon, the effects became very noticeable.

Solomon decided to visit Atlanta, Georgia first. Almost immediately, he found himself trying to be polite when people stared at him or looked away. Even though he had never had any difficulty making friends, this was no longer true. People acted differently toward him. A hostess at a half-filled restaurant made it clear to him that there would be a long wait. A police officer stopped him and gave him a warning even though he had done nothing wrong. And a lady who sat next to him while he was eating warned him not to venture into an all-white area north of Atlanta. She made it clear that "you people" ruin white neighborhoods.

Solomon cut short his "experiment" after a couple of days because he had grown increasingly angry and depressed. He had always thought that many black people used racism as a crutch or an excuse. Because of this experience, he developed new insight into how pervasive and debilitating racism can be.

For some, learning to step outside of your own world can be a matter of survival. W. E. B. Dubois addresses this issue in his book *The Souls of Black Folk*.[28] According to Dubois, **double consciousness** refers to a person's awareness of his or her own perspective and the perspective of others. It is like looking at the same thing in different ways. Double consciousness makes it possible to shift your perspective back and forth continuously.

Why is shifting one's perspective so important? Imagine driving through the Deep South years ago. For many, driving through Mississippi or Texas on a long trip was like driving anywhere else. They drove as far as they wanted and then stopped for gas, food, or rest. They stopped when it was convenient. Others may recall their trips through this part of the country differently. They had to be constantly aware of where they were at all times. Some remember filling their car with gas and then driving for miles without stopping for gas, food, or lodging. Given the racial climate in the area, they may have even feared for their lives. They found themselves in two worlds divided by race. As they drove, they had to understand the perspective of people who lived in the surrounding areas. If they did not, their safety might be at risk.

Gauging the Level of the Playing Field

For some of us, college is the first time we really wrestle with inequality. This is particularly true of students who have lived around people of similar means all of their life. George Pillsbury, heir to the Pillsbury Flour Company family fortune, recalls that he never saw people living in poverty during his youth. He grew up on a private estate, attended an elite boarding school, and spent his leisure time at a country club. When he started attending classes at Yale University in New Haven, Connecticut, he was exposed to a radically different social world. "It was the first time I'd ever lived in the city—a real city with housing projects with poor people. I began to see poverty where I never had before....I saw the inequities and felt them personally for the first time. I felt a lot of guilt at first, but then it became an emotional and intellectual process toward dedicating myself to positive social change."[29] As Pillsbury discovered, learning about diversity means coming to grips with social inequality.

THINKING THROUGH DIVERSITY:
Are you *solely* responsible for opening and closing the doors of opportunity in your life?

Social inequality refers to the unequal distribution of resources, such as wealth, power, and prestige. In *Where Do We Go From Here*, Martin Luther King addresses the fact that people have different amounts of power.[30] He says, "There is nothing essentially wrong with power. The problem is America's power is unequally distributed."

As a result of social inequality, we belong to different social classes. A **social class** is a category of people who share similar amounts of wealth, power, and prestige. As mentioned earlier, social class is one dimension of diversity. Social class in the United States is not simply a matter of economics. Education, lifestyle, interests, and values relate to one's class position as well.

Diversity and social inequality are closely related. A sense of worth is often attached to differences. For example, in the United States we attach a lot of significance to age. We distinguish between old and young people, and unlike many other countries, we value youth. Billions of dollars are spent each year by people trying to avoid being perceived as old. A relationship exists between social inequality and people's perceptions. One example of social inequality is **ageism**, discrimination on the basis of age. Other examples of social inequality revolve around other dimensions of diversity, including gender, race, ethnicity, class, religion, and sexual orientation. In each case of social inequality, we categorize certain people as different and treat them unequally.

Thinking through inequality is difficult. Living in this society constantly exposes us to advantages and disadvantages connected with social inequality. However, in our own lives, we somehow fail to see many of our *advantages.* Think back to the example of George Pillsbury. He was surrounded by economic advantages throughout his childhood, yet he was not really aware of them because of his social isolation.

Why do we remain oblivious to many of our advantages or privileges? Why are we more aware of our disadvantages than our privileges? Why do we assume that we deserve these privileges and that others do not? **Unearned privileges** are those benefits in life that we have through no effort of our own. Perhaps we were born into a wealthy family or maybe we have certain benefits in school because of our religious background, gender, or race.

Unlike my wife, I was challenged by my teachers to pursue science or math as a possible career. I did not think twice about this advantage until my wife shared with me that she was always led to believe that math was for males. As a result, she opted not to pursue her interest in math even though she exhibited a tremendous amount of potential in this field. After graduating from college and teaching music for a number of years, she went back to school to pursue her lifelong dream of being a mathematician. She is now teaching this subject to high school students.

Privileges are invisible for a number of reasons. When we have something, we tend to take it for granted. For example, we might not truly appreciate freedom until we lose it. Those with privileges naturally want to hold on to them as long as possible. One way of preserving privileges is to discount or ignore them. The education we receive in schools typically focuses on how certain groups are disadvantaged, not advantaged. Discussing individual privileges is seen as too personal and threatening. We also live in a society that values individual achievement, competition, and equality. Because of this, we do not like to acknowledge our privileges, especially those that we do not earn. If we are privileged in some way, we assume that we deserve it. If others are not, we assume that they are not as good or worthy or qualified.

Thinking through privileges and disadvantages requires more than just learning about these things in an abstract way. Rather, we need to recognize them in our own life and in the lives of others. In each of our lives, we have an assortment of privileges as well as disadvantages. The power, number, and consequences of these privileges or disadvantages vary from person to person. Ask yourself: How are you privileged? What privileges do you enjoy? Did you earn them? Writing them down might help you bring them into sharper focus. One of the exercises at the end of this chapter will ask you to do this.

In *White Privilege and Male Privilege*, Peggy McIntosh talks about some of the privileges of being White. She examines an "invisible, weightless knapsack of special provisions, assurances, tools, maps, guides...." McIntosh cites some of the privileges operating in her own life, such as "I am never asked to speak for all the people of my racial group." Another one of the 47 unearned privileges mentioned by McIntosh is: "I can be pretty sure that if I ask to talk to 'the person in charge,' I will be facing a person of my race." In addition, she states "I can easily buy posters, post-cards, picture books, greeting cards, dolls, toys, and children's magazines featuring people of my race."[31]

There is considerable disagreement when we attempt to explain why everybody in the United States does not have an equal "piece of the pie." Recent polls show that the vast majority of white Americans believe racial and ethnic inequality is a thing of the past. When inequality is acknowledged, Whites tend to view it as a personal problem. People of color are more apt to see inequality as a problem that is rooted in society and is still very much with us.

People who do not encounter discrimination on a daily basis are more apt to see it as an aberration; it happens but it is rare and relatively inconsequential. In an ABC news segment entitled "True Colors," the everyday activities of a white and a black male were videotaped for two and one-half weeks in a large metropolitan area in the Midwest. Both of these men were "testers," meaning that they were trained in presenting themselves in exactly the same way. One white student's reaction to the video is found in the following perspective:

When it comes to discrimination, I don't think I am as naive as some of my friends. I realize that it still exists in America. Before seeing this video, I assumed that maybe the cameras would catch a few things, like a salesman tailing the black man in a store, or perhaps a few not giving the black man the same friendly service. I was amazed when I saw not one but two car salesmen charging the black man a higher price than the white man for the exact same car. I saw a landlord giving the white man the keys and a welcomed tour of an apartment. The same landlord, however, told the black man this apartment was not available: a blatant lie. When the reporters entered the landlord's office with both the black and white man, they showed the landlord footage of the tape and asked him for an explanation. Although he had obviously just discriminated against the black man, he got upset and replied, "I am not a racist, I got Mexicans, and 'Jewies,' I got 'em all here." Not only was this man extremely racist when telling the black man that there was no apartment available, but he didn't even realize it. It seems to me that some people think that as long as you are not calling Blacks by derogatory names or telling them to their face they cannot do something because they are Black, that they are not discriminating.

—A student's perspective

The use of testers as shown in "True Colors" has yielded similar results in many other cities and suburbs throughout the United States. If you were constantly subjected to the kind of treatment that was documented in this video, what would be its cumulative effect on you? What would be the psychological *and* economic implications?

In gauging the level of the playing field, it is important to ask yourself the following questions:

1. *Are you blaming the individual or society?* When we blame individuals, we find fault with their characters, work ethics, attitudes, or some other individual difference. We assume that individuals are holding themselves back. Blaming society changes the focus from problem people to people with problems. These problems or barriers, which are found in the larger society, act as obstacles or detours. Social barriers might take the form of racism, a concept discussed earlier, sexism, and classism. **Sexism** refers to the thinking that one sex is superior to another and that unequal treatment is therefore justifiable. **Classism** can be defined in the same way, with the focus on social class. Both the individual and societal points of view are shortsighted and incomplete. One assumes total control over one's fate, the other assumes almost a total lack of control. The individual and society are both important and interconnected. Individuals do have the freedom to choose. People are not at the mercy of their environment. On the other hand, inequality does exist. We do not live in a **meritocracy**, a system in which people get ahead *solely* on the basis of merit. Factors that have nothing to do with ability can affect your move up the economic ladder, regardless of your motivation. These factors include who you know, your looks, and other people's preconceived notions about you.

2. *Are you assuming that if one person can succeed, anybody can?* How do you feel when people in the public eye are held up as evidence that anyone can make it to the top? What about when someone compares your school grades with someone else in your family or with a close friend? We are all different and unique, with our own strengths and limitations. A goal that is realistic or obtainable for one person may be out of someone else's reach or vision. Holding up one person as an example that anything is possible is an example of tunnel vision. People, for example, may point to a female CEO or Supreme Court Justice and cite her success as proof of equal opportunity for men and women. We cannot assume that what happens to one person necessarily applies to the entire group. If we focus exclusively on the one or two who "make it big," we may ignore the vast majority who do not. Circumstances vary from person to person and from one field of employment to another. To draw meaningful conclusions, we need considerably more data about the experiences of men and women in general. Moreover, we cannot gather and analyze evidence haphazardly.

3. *Do you see power and privilege as an all-or-nothing proposition?* Part of the problem with the terms *minority* and *majority* is that they create the impression that we are one or the other. When discussing social inequality, majority and minority refer to power, not numbers. **Majority** refers to the group with power and privilege. **Minority** is the group at a disadvantage in terms of power and privilege. In reality, the division between the more and less powerful is not that easy to see. As an example, a student's majority statuses might include being White, male, and upper class. This same student's minority statuses might be that he is gay and has a disability. Depending on the situation, people may consider him a majority- or a minority-group member. It is a mistake to ignore our multiple statuses and their impact on us.

4. *Do you immerse yourself in your own victimization to the point that you cannot see or comprehend the victimization of others?* Victimization can take many forms, including lost opportunities and the loss of self-esteem. People can feel like victims because of their minority and/or majority statuses. Awareness of our own victimization can make us more or less sensitive to the victimization of others. At times, we may use it as an excuse to stop trying. We *can* empower ourselves. Learning from our own experiences and observing how others have resisted victimization can help us think through social inequality. Experiencing what it is like to be a victim may sensitize us to the subtle and not so subtle ways in which our actions victimize others.

Checking Up on Yourself

Many of us shy away from self-examination. We would rather focus on other people and their shortcomings. In a way, it is much more difficult to confront our own prejudices, stereotypes, and ethnocentrism because it requires us to closely examine our assumptions. These assumptions can be difficult for us to see. They are often so embedded in us that we take them for granted.

A good example is the belief that "women, by nature, make better nurses than men." For some of us, this is an absolute truth. The media, school, and family cultivate and reinforce this assumption. It is difficult to step back and look at this commonplace assumption in an uncommon way. What are the sources of this assumption? Are these sources reliable? Historically, why did the nursing profession become predominantly female? How does this assumption affect our thinking and behavior toward male and female nurses? Wrestling with questions such as these is difficult. It also requires **critical thinking**, the ability to freely question and evaluate ideas and information.

Critical thinking is a diversity skill that enables us to recognize our biases and those of others. It can help us understand that our point of view is one of many. Critical thinking can also reveal gaps or inconsistencies in our assumptions. Research has shown that one key factor in reducing bias is the ability to think critically. In general, students who question what they hear from others and think things through show less prejudice than those who simply accept things at face value.

Checking up on yourself requires constant questioning, reevaluation, and self-reflection. Questions, such as those that follow, provide us with valuable insight into our thinking and behavior throughout the day.

1. *Are you more comfortable around certain types of people?* Why? For example, are you uncomfortable doing business with men who come across as aggressive? If so, are you equally uncomfortable around white and black men who act this way? What does this teach you about with whom you are comfortable and with whom you are not? James Box, a paraplegic and founder of a high-tech wheelchair company, suggests that we need to confront our discomfort and wrestle with it. If something "turns us off" or repulses us, we need to examine it for a while and ask questions of others and ourselves until we can figure out why we are uncomfortable.

2. *Do you make snap judgments about people?* When you are walking through a shopping mall, for example, what assumptions do you make based on clothing, hairstyle, and physical features?

3. *Who do you tend to include in your social circle?* Who do you tend to leave out? How might you expand your social circle?

4. *When you communicate, what messages are you sending?* What about your body language? Do you simply assume that people interpret your communication as you intended?

5. *Is your behavior consistent with your thinking?* In *To Be Equal,* Whitney Young addresses the need to do more than use language that is inoffensive. A change of vocabulary, according to Young, is something quite different from changes in behaviors and attitudes.[32]

Self-examination is ongoing. Since our environment is constantly changing, our awareness and understanding needs constantly to keep pace. We need to grow and adapt as our world and life experiences expand. Checking up on ourselves gives us direction. Companies, for example, regularly conduct assessments before they draw up a plan of action. Individuals need to do the same thing. Before we are able to improve and develop skills such as teamwork, leadership, and communication, it is necessary to think through where we are and in what direction we are going. This takes time, commitment, patience, and awareness of self.

Following Through

Diversity consciousness does not refer simply to our awareness of ourselves and others. It extends to how we behave and interact with others. In other words, we need to apply our knowledge and awareness constantly to real-life situations. We learn by doing. For example, hearing your instructor lecture about computers or reading your textbook is not sufficient to develop your computer skills. Think how much more you learn by sitting down at a computer and actually using it time and time again.

We can only develop and refine diversity skills through constant use and self-evaluation. For instance, many of us regard listening as passive. However, we can improve our listening skills through **active listening**, taking a more active role in hearing and digesting what is being said as well as encouraging the speaker. Specific techniques for developing this skill are found in Chapter 5.

It is very important for me to maintain control of my wandering mind. I try to avoid all of the listening traps, such as dwelling on one thought while the person continues speaking or thinking about tomorrow's list of errands. I focus on the one thing the speaker says that enlightens me for the moment. Also, I always carry a note pad and pen so that I will not cause my own frustration by forgetting my own opinion about whatever is being shared. Often, everyone is so intent on being able to speak that no one actually listens for content, but for cues that the end of the last sentence is about to arrive. A lot is missed in that kind of environment.

—A student's perspective

Practicing a diversity skill is not a feel-good activity. There is an element of risk taking. Try not to get too down on yourself or allow others to frustrate you. As time goes by, you will realize that it is worth the struggle.

STRATEGIES FOR DEVELOPING DIVERSITY CONSCIOUSNESS

Developing diversity consciousness is an uneven process, meaning that it is very unpredictable and sporadic. There is no magical moment when you develop diversity consciousness and say to yourself, "Ah ha, I got it." You may find the more you learn about diversity, the less knowledgeable you feel. As you grow, you may go from feeling, "I'm not prejudiced" to "maybe I am" to "I am prejudiced."

Ultimately, each of us must take responsibility for our development in this area. The following eight strategies, which revolve around education, self-examination, and networking, can help you move toward that goal.

1. *Expand your knowledge through reading.* Articles, novels, and personal narratives can provide you with realistic and dramatic portrayals of diversity. This is especially true of first-person accounts. These accounts or stories tend to be much more real, intimate, and varied. They remind us that Americans represent many cultures and come from many countries. When we read about history, different accounts emerge. To illustrate, the westward expansion by early European settlers is a different story when told by Native Americans. For them, the expansion meant encroachment, death, and disease.

A number of first-person accounts are included in the Bibliography and Suggested Readings at the end of the book.

2. *Put yourself in a learning mode in any multicultural setting.* Suspend judgment and adopt a childlike kind of inquisitiveness when trying to make sense out of a situation. One of my students compared this to starting over or "wiping the slate clean." She went on to say that her English instructor told her on the first day of class to forget everything that she had learned about English. The instructor was pushing her to relearn the subject matter and undo her bad habits. In a similar vein, each of us has to shed what we know in certain situations. Only then can we look at people and lifestyles as if we were encountering them for the first time.

3. *Remember that your own life experiences are one of many important sources of knowledge.* This applies to everyone. In the book *Women's Ways of Knowing*, women who live ordinary lives are interviewed about how they perceive themselves and the world around them.[33] Many of these women had little respect for their own minds, ideas, and experiences. At work, school, and home, they relied on others to feed them information and felt voiceless much of the time. Despite their own feelings of inadequacy, the interviews revealed that these women were extremely knowledgeable as well as talented.

4. *Move beyond your comfort zone.* Sometimes, learning can be difficult and uncomfortable. However, this is a necessary part of opening up intellectually and emotionally. The company Hoechst Celanese requires its top executives to join two organizations in which they are an "outsider," so to speak. The rationale for this policy was summarized by the CEO: "The only way to break out of comfort zones is to be exposed to other people. When we are, it becomes clear that all people are similar."[34]

5. *Be modest.* A few years ago, Bill Cosby told a graduating class at George Washington University: "Don't ever think you know more than the person mopping a floor." Everybody has something of value to share. Be aware that no matter how much you know or have seen, you can still learn from anyone. This perspective will make you more open to differences and more willing to learn from those around you.

6. *Don't be too hard on yourself if misunderstandings arise.* No matter how hard we try, there will be situations in which we show our lack of knowledge of other cultures. We may do this without even knowing it. The important thing is to acknowledge our mistakes and learn from them.

7. *Realize that you are not alone.* There are other people out there who care about you and will support you as you grow, learn, and wrestle with diversity issues. Surround yourself with these kinds of people.

journal entry

THINKING THROUGH DIVERSITY:

Do you think you can honor and respect diversity without understanding it?

8. *Take advantage of learning opportunities.* Opportunities to learn and grow can arise at any moment. Learning can be triggered by any number of experiences, such as overhearing an insensitive comment, attending a workshop on diversity, or doing something that might seem totally unrelated to diversity. In the next section we describe a range of opportunities available to students.

Some Specific Opportunities for Diversity Education

We are surrounded by opportunities to learn more about diversity. Whether we avail ourselves of these opportunities is up to us. For example, a wide range of diversity education programs and courses are available on most college campuses. If these opportunities are not available, you might suggest them to your instructor or someone in charge of student programming.

Individuals, groups, and entire communities can initiate and participate in diversity education. Eight possible activities follow:

1. *Computer technology.* New uses of technology, such as the Internet/World Wide Web (WWW), distance learning, and teleconferences make it possible to cross cultural boundaries very easily and quickly. Computer simulations are available that allow students to work through self-paced lessons on diversity issues.

2. *Taping.* If you have ever heard or seen yourself on tape, you know that this can be a real learning experience. It is not uncommon to uncover cultural biases that may surprise you.

3. *Courses.* More and more faculty are integrating diversity into their courses. This is true of a wide range of courses, including literature, art, business, math, allied health, student success, and social sciences. If diversity is not the focus of the entire course, it is likely to be discussed in one or more units of a course.

4. *Travel and opportunities for study abroad.* Students who study abroad learn the importance of a world view. This is particularly true of extensive trips abroad which provide opportunities for studying, working, and socializing (see Fig. 4.3).

5. *Racial/cultural awareness workshops.* Academic departments, offices dealing with student affairs, and community groups frequently offer workshops of this nature. Although one two-hour workshop is not going to change your thinking and behavior dramatically, it can deepen your understanding of diversity issues and put you in touch with people who may have similar interests and concerns. In his comprehensive study of undergraduates throughout the country, Astin found that participation in workshops increases students' awareness that (1) discrimination is still a problem and (2) individuals can bring about change in society.[35]

Figure 4.3: *Students visit a museum in Cairo, Egypt. The students, who are spending a semester on board a cruise ship, are enrolled in the University of Pittsburgh's "Semester at Sea" course. Each semester, more than 600 students take classes on board a cruise ship and then experience what they study by visiting countries throughout the world. (Courtesy of the Institute for Shipboard Education, University of Pittsburgh, Pittsburgh, PA.)*

6. *School programs.* Many programs aim at promoting the understanding and celebration of cultural differences. Many colleges offer these programs in connection with Black History Month, International Women's Day, AIDS Awareness Day, and other events. Lectures, dramatic presentations, art exhibits, and field trips are cocurricular activities that can enhance and broaden your education. Additionally, these programs are motivational as well as informative.

7. *Cultural activities in the community.* Plays, movies, art exhibits, museums, and community resources and events provide numerous opportunities to learn about diversity. Sometimes it makes sense to do this as a group so that you can share your thoughts and feelings afterward. With a minimal amount of expense or planning, student groups can rent and watch videos such as *Philadelphia, Beloved, Schindler's List, The Joy Luck Club, Rain Man, Smoke Signals,* and *Hoop Dreams.* This type of experience can break the ice and provide insight into history, culture, and different life experiences. It can also make it easier to talk about a variety of issues dealing with diversity.

Music and art have shown me the common ground between people and what we can do for each other.

—An instructor's perspective

8. *Study circles/groups.* As discussed earlier, study circles are small group discussions that focus on any number of issues, including diversity. The basic idea is that a group of perhaps 8 to 12 people commit to meeting regularly over a period of time. This type of discussion allows people to get to know each other, discover common ground, and take action. Schools, businesses, and communities throughout the country have adopted the study circle concept.

A CONTINUING PROCESS

> *The greater our knowledge increases, the greater our ignorance unfolds.*
>
> —John Fitzgerald Kennedy

Diversity consciousness is not something we can develop, store, and then consult periodically. It is not something that "kicks in" at school or work. Rather, it is an unending process. We need to reevaluate our knowledge of ourselves and others continuously as we gain new knowledge. As our thinking changes, so does our behavior. This kind of change requires both time and effort.

As we develop diversity consciousness, a number of positive changes will gradually occur:

- Our thinking will become less rigid and more flexible.
- Our awareness and appreciation of human differences will heighten our ability to see and value similarities.
- We will move from a perspective that centers on ourselves and our immediate environment to one that is more inclusive and global.

It should be clear from this chapter that it is extremely difficult to develop diversity consciousness. For many of us, just tolerating certain differences requires a radical change in our thinking and behavior. In many cases it means unlearning much that we have been taught. Diversity consciousness moves us beyond tolerance. Rather than putting up with differences, it makes it possible for us to understand, respect, and value differences. This kind of personal transformation requires not only time but also commitment.

> *Education is all a matter of building bridges.*
>
> —Ralph Ellison

In the next two chapters we examine two diversity skills: communication (Chapter 5) and teamwork (Chapter 6). As our society becomes more diverse and the larger world becomes more interconnected, it is increasingly important for us to understand the significance of these skills and their relationship to diversity consciousness.

Exercises

IN-CLASS

Exercise 1: The Name Game

Directions for Instructor.

Ask each student to respond to the following questions in writing:

1. Each of us learns about many famous people who have shaped history. Draw on this knowledge and name three well-known people (living or dead) who are:
   a. Upper class
   b. Lower class
   c. Gay and Lesbian
   d. Asian-American
   e. Native American
   f. Female
   g. Male
   h. Disabled
2. Have students pair up. Ask each pair of students to review the names each of them listed for the eight categories. Which categories of people were the easiest to name? Why? Which categories of people were the most difficult to name? Why?
3. As a class, discuss what this exercise reveals about you and your upbringing. Discuss what it reveals about your education.

Exercise 2: Family Stories

The African proverb "a person is a person through other persons" applies to each of us. In particular, it describes our relationship with family members. As we get older, we become more aware of these relationships.

Directions for Instructor

1. Ask each student to think of stories that have been passed down from generation to generation in her or his family. Students should select

one story that has influenced their lives in some way, such as making them stronger or altering how they view what is really important in life. They should try to remember as much of the story as possible.

2. Have students pair up. Each student shares his or her story. Also, the student should explain how the story affects her or him.
3. As a class, discuss the following questions: Is there anything that your stories have in common? In what ways are they different? Why do you think that some family stories are forgotten and others remain with us? What have you learned from these stories?

Exercise 3: Unearned Privileges

Each of us has privileges as well as disadvantages. Many of these relate to different dimensions of diversity, such as race, ethnicity, class, gender, sexual orientation, and religion. In the case of privileges, some are earned whereas others are unearned.

Directions for Instructor

1. Ask each student to list in writing three privileges he or she has that are *earned.* Then list three that are *unearned.* Be as specific as possible. Share these with the class.
2. As a class, discuss which of our privileges—earned or unearned—are easier for us to identify. Why?

Out-of-Class

Exercise 1: Shifting Perspectives in the Classroom

You are sitting in a college classroom. It is the first day of class. Your instructor, whom you have never met, walks in, introduces himself, and hands each student a course syllabus. Prior to going over the syllabus, the instructor reviews his expectations for classroom interaction.

- Students should act as if they understand everything and never ask any questions.
- Students should never raise questions about tests or grades at any time.
- Students should not look directly at the instructor when he speaks.

Answer the following questions.

1. In general, how did you feel about these expectations? Why do you feel this way? How is your cultural background related to your feelings?
2. Talk to other students who have attended schools outside the United States. How do they feel about the expectations outlined above? How have their educational experiences differed from yours?

Exercise 2: Cross-Cultural Interview and Analysis

Interview. Interview someone who was born and grew up in a country other than your own. This person should be a fellow student or a member of the faculty or staff. When interviewing someone, find a comfortable place to talk. Begin by getting acquainted with each other. Then focus your questions on the following topics related to the interviewee:

- Family background
- Cultural background
- Educational background
- Community in which he or she was raised
- Leisure activities as a child
- Religious background
- Other areas of interest

Analysis. Once the interview is completed, think through how you might have responded to these questions. Compare your responses with those of the interviewee.

1. List some of the major differences in your backgrounds. What are some of the major similarities?
2. Create a poster that represents these differences and/or similarities. Do not use any words; rather, express yourself through images. The images may be drawn by hand or created on the computer. You may include clippings from newspapers and magazines as well as photographs.

Exercise 3: The Challenge of Diversity Consciousness

What do you think will be your most difficult challenge as you work on increasing your own diversity consciousness?

Internet Assignment

1. Go to your college Web site. Search it thoroughly for courses, programs, and/or activities relative to diversity. Make a list of all you are able to find. (*Note:* If your college does not have a comprehensive Web site, do this using your college catalog.)
2. Go to another college Web site (www.collegeboard.org is a good starting point). Find one that has significantly more or fewer diversity programs, courses, and activities. List these as well.

NOTES

[1]Juan L. Gonzales, Jr., *The Lives of Ethnic Americans,* 2nd ed. (Dubuque, IA: Kendall/Hunt, 1994), 98.

[2]"Women, Men, and Media," in M. Junior Bridge, *Marginalizing Women* (Unabridged Communications, 1996).

[3]National Council of La Raza, *Don't Blink: Hispanics in Television Entertainment* (Washington, DC: Center for Media and Public Affairs, 1996).

[4]Martin Gilens, "Race and Poverty in America: Public Misperceptions and the American News Media," *Public Opinion Quarterly*, 60, 1996, 515–541.

[5]Associated Press, "Number Living in Poverty Drops for 3rd Year in a Row, U.S. Says," *The Sun*, Sept. 25, 1998, 3A.

[6]National Center for Education Statistics, *Digest of Education Statistics, 1997*, NCES 98-015 (Washington, DC: U.S. Department of Education, 1997), 186.

[7]Ibid.

[8]Ibid., 324.

[9]"Facts about Higher Education in the U.S.," *Chronicle of Higher Education Almanac Issue 1998/1999*, XLV(1), Aug. 28, 1998, 38.

[10]Ibid., 5.

[11]Associated Press, "More Women Finish College Than Men," *The Sun*, June 29, 1998, 3A.

[12]Charles Gallagher, "White Reconstruction in the University," *Socialist Review*, 24, 1994, 165.

[13]Cheryl Tan, "For College Students, Degrees of Ethnicity," *The Washington Post*, Sept. 3, 1996, B1.

[14]Morgan Appel, David Cartwright, Daryl Smith, and Lisa Wolf, *The Impact of Diversity on Students* (Washington, DC: Association of American Colleges and Universities, 1996), x.

[15]Roberta Hall and Bernice Sandler, *The Classroom Climate: A Chilly One for Women* (Washington, DC: Association of American Colleges, 1982), 3.

[16]Ansley A. Abraham, *Racial Issues on Campus: How Students View Them* (Atlanta, GA: Southern Regional Education Board, 1990), 2.

[17]Zora Neale Hurston, as found in Dorothy W. Riley (ed.), *My Soul Looks Back, 'Less I Forget*, (New York: Harper Collins, 1993), 81.

[18]Ursula Heigi, *Tearing the Silence*. (New York: Simon & Schuster, 1997).

[19]Jonathan Yardley, "Coping with History," *The Washington Post: Book World*, July 6, 1997, 3.

[20]John Lahr, "Speaking across the Divide," *The New Yorker*, Jan. 27, 1997, 41–42.

[21]Robert Whiting, "You've Gotta Have 'Wa'," *Sports Illustrated*, September 24, 1979, 60+.

[22]Moshe Rubinstein, *Patterns of Problem Solving* (Englewood Cliffs, NJ: Prentice Hall, 1975).

[23]Malcolm X, *The Autobiography of Malcolm X* (New York: Ballantine Books, 1965).

[24]Carter Woodson, as quoted in Dorothy W. Riley, ed., *My Soul Looks Back, 'Less I Forget: A Collection of Quotations by People of Color* (New York: Harper Collins, 1995), 189.

[25]Emory Bogardus, "Measuring Social Distance," *Journal of Applied Sociology*, 9, Mar./Apr. 1925, 299–308.

[26]Amy Maddox, "Underneath We're All the Same," *Teaching Tolerance*, Spring 1995, 65.

[27]John H. Griffin, *Black Like Me*. (New York: NAL/Dutton, 1999).

[28]W. E. B. Dubois, *The Souls of Black Folk* (New York: Fawcett, 1961).

[29]George Pillsbury, as quoted in John Sedgwick, *Rich Kids* (New York: William Morrow, 1985), 120.

[30]Martin Luther King, Jr., *Where Do We Go from Here: Chaos or Community?* (Boston: Beacon Press, 1968).

[31]Peggy McIntosh, *White Privilege and Male Privilege* (Wellesley, MA: Wellesley College Center for Research on Women, 1988), 7.

[32]Whitney Young, *To Be Equal* (New York: McGraw-Hill, 1966).

[33]Mary Belenky, Blythe Clinchy, Nancy Goldberger, and Jill Tarule, *Women's Ways of Knowing* (New York: Basic Books, 1986).

[34]Fay Rice, "How to Make Diversity Pay," *Fortune*, Aug. 8, 1994, 82.

[35]Alexander Astin, "Diversity and Multiculturalism on the Campus: How Are Students Affected?" *Change*, Mar./Apr. 1993, 47.

Chapter 7

Diversity in the Workplace

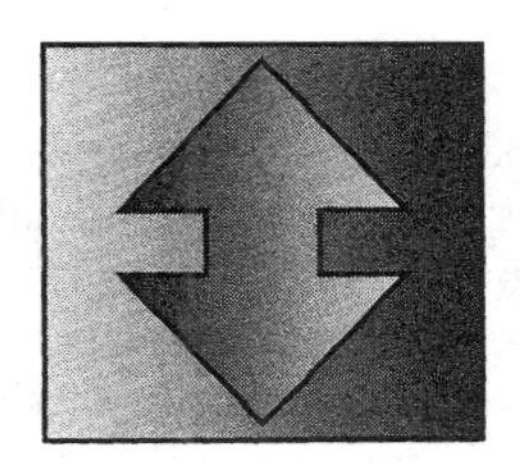

Have Affirmative Action Programs Outlived Their Usefulness?

The Civil Rights Act, with its sweeping antidiscrimination provisions, was signed into law in July of 1964. The hope was that this law would narrow the vast socioeconomic gap between the races.

That same year Daniel Patrick Moynihan, then assistant secretary of labor and future senator, wrote *The Negro Family: A Case for National Action.* Moynihan noted that progress had been made in giving black Americans full recognition of their civil rights, but he warned that this achievement was not cause for complacency because a new crisis was looming. Unless equal opportunity meant "roughly equal results," blacks would become frustrated and not feel a part of American society. The three centuries of slavery and its unimaginable treatment meant that blacks could not compete on equal terms. A new approach was needed.

Later that year, following on this theme, then President Lyndon Johnson noted, "You do not take a person who, for years, has been hobbled by chains and liberate him, bring him up to the starting line in a race and then say, 'you are free to compete.'" It was not enough just to open the gates of opportunity; all citizens also had to have the ability to walk through those gates, Johnson noted. "Equality as a fact and as a result" should be the goal.

Johnson's September 1965 Executive Order 11246 directed companies supplying goods and services to the federal government to "take affirmative action to ensure that minority applicants are employed." At the time, that meant aggressive recruitment—making extra efforts to locate black talent that had been overlooked and to give that talent the chance to develop.

Soon, concern that these policies were not working as quickly as was hoped led to the second meaning of affirmative action, one which emphasized equality of result for groups, and assumed that the best way to improve the situation of blacks was through quotas or special preferences.

Ironically, affirmative action quotas were first introduced in 1969 by the Nixon administration. George Shultz, Nixon's first secretary of labor, issued an administrative order that set hiring quotas for workers in the Philadelphia construction industry, an area in which employers and unions were cooperating to keep blacks out. The policy was soon extended to other cities. Other Nixon officeholders pressed similar programs with regard to faculty and students in higher education.

From these beginnings the various programs that exist today in many areas of American business and academia emerged.

Public opinion polls of whites have shown that they are opposed to preferential treatment and affirmative action. The opposition to affirmative action does not necessarily mean that whites think blacks have attained equality or that the government should not outlaw discrimination. Poll data reveals that on the central issues involving racial discrimination and Jim Crow practices, the American public is strongly against discrimination. The general agreement dissolves, however, when compulsory integration and quotas are involved. Many people oppose such efforts, not because they oppose racial equality but because they feel these measures violate their individual freedom. Most Americans do approve of concrete federal programs to help the disadvantaged and combat racial discrimination. Given a choice, however, between government intervention to solve social problems and "leaving people on their own" to work out their problems for themselves, the public tends to choose the latter (Lipset 1995).

Walter E. Williams, in "Affirmative Action Can't Be Mended," argues that affirmative action is a violation of justice and fair play, as well as racially polarizing. It is also, he says, a poor cover-up for the real work that needs to be done. Affirmative action focuses our attention on discrimination instead of trying to correct such factors as fraudulent education, family disintegration, and hostile economic climates in black neighborhoods.

Nathan Glazer, on the other hand, in his article "In Defense of Preference," argues that we have to continue racial preferences for blacks: first, because the United States has a special obligation to blacks that has not been fully discharged; second, because the strict application of the principle of qualifications would send a message of despair to many blacks, a message that the nation is indifferent to their difficulties and problems.

Affirmative Action Can't Be Mended

Walter E. Williams

For the last several decades, affirmative action has been the basic component of the civil rights agenda. But affirmative action, in the form of racial preferences, has worn out its political welcome. In Gallup Polls, between 1987 and 1990, people were asked if they agreed with the statement: "We should make every effort to improve the position of blacks and other minorities even if it means giving them preferential treatment." More than 70 percent of the respondents opposed preferential treatment while only 24 percent supported it. Among blacks, 66 percent opposed preferential treatment and 32 percent supported it (Lipset 1992: 66–69).

The rejection of racial preferences by the broad public and increasingly by the Supreme Court has been partially recognized by even supporters of affirmative action. While they have not forsaken their goals, they have begun to distance themselves from some of the language of affirmative action. Thus, many business, government, and university affirmative action offices have been renamed "equity offices." Racial preferences are increasingly referred to as "diversity multiculturalism." What is it about affirmative action that gives rise to its contentiousness?

...

Yesteryear civil rights organizations fought against the use of race in hiring, access to public schools, and university admissions. Today, civil rights organizations fight for the use of race in hiring, access to public schools, and university admissions. Yesteryear, civil rights organizations fought against restricted association in the forms of racially segregated schools, libraries, and private organizations. Today, they fight for restricted associations. They

From *Cato Journal* 17, no. 1 (spring/summer 1997). Copyright © 1997 by The Cato Institute. Reprinted with the permission of The Cato Institute, http://www.cato.org.

use state power, not unlike the racists they fought, to enforce racial associations they deem desirable. They protest that blacks should be a certain percentage of a company's workforce or clientele, a certain percentage of a student body, and even a certain percentage of an advertiser's models.

Civil rights organizations, in their successful struggle against state-sanctioned segregation, have lost sight of what it means to be truly committed to liberty, especially the freedom of association. The true test of that commitment does not come when we allow people to be free to associate in ways we deem appropriate. The true test is when we allow people to form those voluntary associations we deem offensive. It is the same principle we apply to our commitment to free speech. What tests our commitment to free speech is our willingness to permit people the freedom to say things we find offensive.

Zero-Sum Games

...

A zero-sum game is defined as any transaction where one person's gain necessarily results in another person's loss. The simplest example of a zero-sum game is poker. A winner's gain is matched precisely by the losses of one or more persons. In this respect, the only essential difference between affirmative action and poker is that in poker participation is voluntary. Another difference is the loser is readily identifiable, a point to which I will return later.

The University of California, Berkeley's affirmative action program for blacks captures the essence of a zero-sum game. Blacks are admitted with considerably lower average SAT scores (952) than the typical white (1232) and Asian student (1254) (Sowell 1993: 144). Between UCLA and UC Berkeley, more than 2,000 white and Asian straight A students are turned away in order to provide spaces for black and Hispanic students (Lynch 1989: 163). The admissions gains by blacks are exactly matched by admissions losses by white and Asian students. Thus, any preferential treatment program results in a zero-sum game almost by definition.

More generally, government allocation of resources is a zero-sum game primarily because government has no resources of its very own. When government gives some citizens food stamps, crop subsidies, or disaster relief payments, the recipients of the largesse gain. Losers are identified by asking: Where does government acquire the resources to confer the largesse? In order for government to give to some citizens, it must through intimidation, threats, and coercion take from other citizens. Those who lose the rights to their earnings, to finance government largesse, are the losers.

Government-mandated racial preferential treatment programs produce a similar result. When government creates a special advantage for one ethnic group, it necessarily comes at the expense of other ethnic groups for whom government simultaneously creates a special disadvantage in the form of reduced alternatives. If a college or employer has X amount of positions, and R of them have been set aside for blacks or some other group, that necessarily means there are (X-R) fewer positions for which other ethnic groups might compete. At a time when there were restrictions against blacks, that operated in favor of whites, those restrictions translated into a reduced opportunity set for blacks. It is a zero-sum game independent of the race or ethnicity of the winners and losers.

...

Tentative Victim Identification

In California, voters passed the California Civil Rights Initiative of 1996 (CCRI) that says: "The state shall not discriminate against, or grant preferential treatment to, any individual or group on the basis of race, sex, color, ethnicity, or national origin in the operation of public employment, public education, or public contracting." Therefore, California public universities can no longer have preferential admission policies that include race as a factor in deciding whom to admit.

For illustrative purposes, let us pretend that CCRI had not been adopted and the UCLA School of Law accepted 108 black students as it had in 1996 and UC Berkeley accepted 75. That being the case, 83 more blacks would be accepted to UCLA Law School for the 1997–98 academic year and 61 more blacks would be accepted to UC Berkeley's Law School. Clearly, the preferential admissions program, at least in terms of being accepted to these law schools, benefits blacks. However, that benefit is not without costs. With preferential admission programs in place, both UCLA and UC Berkeley law schools would have had to turn away 144 white and Asian students, with higher academic credentials, in order to have room for black students.

In the case of UC Berkeley's preferential admissions for blacks, those whites and Asians who have significantly higher SAT scores and grades than the admitted blacks are victims of reverse discrimination. However, in the eyes of the courts, others, and possibly themselves, they are invisible victims. In other words, no one can tell for sure who among those turned away would have gained entry to UC Berkeley were it not for the preferential treatment given to blacks.

...

Affirmative Action and Supply

An important focus of affirmative action is statistical underrepresentation of different racial and ethnic groups on college and university campuses. If the percentages of blacks and Mexican-Americans, for example, are not at a level deemed appropriate by a court, administrative agency, or university administrator, racial preference programs are instituted. The inference made from the underrepresentation argument is that, in the absence of racial discrimination, groups would be represented on college campuses in proportion to their numbers in the relevant population. In making that argument, little attention is paid to the supply issue—that is, to the pool of students available that meet the standards or qualifications of the university in question.

... If blacks scoring 600 or higher on the quantitative portion of the SAT (assuming their performance on the verbal portion of the examination gave them a composite SAT score of 1200 or higher) were recruited to elite colleges and universities, there would be less than 33 black students available per university. At none of those universities would blacks be represented according to their numbers in the population.

There is no evidence that suggests that university admissions offices practice racial discrimination by turning away blacks with SAT scores of 1200 or higher. In reality, there are not enough blacks to be admitted to leading colleges and universities on the same terms as other students, such that their numbers in the campus population bears any resemblance to their numbers in the general population.

Attempts by affirmative action programs to increase the percent of blacks admitted to top schools, regardless of whether blacks match the academic characteristics of the general student body, often produce disastrous results. In order to meet affirmative action guidelines, leading colleges and universities recruit and admit black students whose academic qualifications are well below the norm for other students. For example, of the 317 black students admitted to UC Berkeley in 1985, all were admitted under affirmative action criteria rather than academic qualifications. Those students had an average SAT score of 952 compared to the national average of 900 among all students. However, their SAT scores were well below UC Berkeley's average of nearly 1200. More than 70 percent of the black students failed to graduate from UC Berkeley (Sowell 1993: 144).

...

There is no question that preferential admissions is unjust to both white and Asian students who may be qualified but are turned away to make room for less-qualified students in the "right" ethnic group. However, viewed from a solely black self-interest point of view, the question should be asked whether such affirmative action programs serve the best interests of blacks. Is there such an abundance of black students who score above the national average on the SAT, such as those admitted to UC Berkeley, that blacks as a group can afford to have those students turned into artificial failures in the name of diversity, multiculturalism, or racial justice? The affirmative action debate needs to go beyond simply an issue of whether blacks are benefited at the expense of whites. Whites and Asians who are turned away to accommodate blacks are still better off than the blacks who were admitted. After all, graduating from the university of one's second choice is preferable to flunking out of the university of one's first choice.

To the extent racial preferences in admission produce an academic mismatch of students, the critics may be unnecessarily alarmed, assuming their concern is with black students actually graduating from college. If black students who score 952 on the SAT are not admitted to UC Berkeley, that does not mean that they cannot gain admittance to one of America's 3,000 other colleges. It means that they will gain admittance to some other college where their academic characteristics will be more similar to those of their peers. There will not be as much of an academic mismatch. To the extent this is true, we may see an increase in black graduation rates. Moreover, if black students find themselves more similar to their white peers in terms of college grades and graduation honors, they are less likely to feel academically isolated and harbor feelings of low self-esteem.

Affirmative Action and Justice

Aside from any other question, we might ask what case can be made for the morality or justice of turning away more highly credentialed white and Asian students so as to be able to admit more blacks. Clearly, blacks as a group have suffered past injustices, including discrimination in college and university admissions. However, that fact does not spontaneously yield sensible policy proposals for today. The fact is that a special privilege cannot be created for one person without creating a special disadvantage for another. In the case of preferential admissions, a special privilege for black students translates into a special disadvantage for white and Asian students. Thus, we must ask what have those individual white and Asian students done to deserve punishment? Were they at all responsible for the injustices, either in the past or present, suffered by blacks? If, as so often is the case, the justification for preferential treatment is to redress past grievances, how just is it to have a policy where a black of today is helped by punishing a white of today for what a white of yesterday did to a black of yesterday? Such an idea becomes even more questionable in light of the fact that so many whites and Asians cannot trace the American part of their ancestry back as much as two or three generations.

Affirmative Action and Racial Resentment

In addition to the injustices that are a result of preferential treatment, such treatment has given rise to racial resentment where it otherwise might not exist. While few people support racial resentment and its manifestations, if one sees some of affirmative action's flagrant attacks on fairness and equality before the law, one can readily understand why resentment is on the rise.

...

Affirmative action proponents cling to the notion that racial discrimination satisfactorily explains black/white socioeconomic differences. While every vestige of racial discrimination has not been eliminated in our society, current social discrimination cannot begin to explain all that affirmative action proponents' purport it explains. Rather than focusing our attention on discrimination, a higher payoff can be realized by focusing on real factors such as fraudulent education, family disintegration, and hostile economic climates in black neighborhoods. Even if affirmative action was not a violation of justice and fair play, was not a zero-sum game, was not racially polarizing, it is a poor cover-up for the real work that needs to be done.

References

Cunico v. Pueblo School District No. 60 (1990) 917 F. 2D 431 (10th Circuit).

Eastland, T. (1996). *Ending Affirmative Action: The Case for Colorblind Justice.* New York: Basic Books.

Lipset, S. M. (1992). "Equal Chances versus Equal Results." In H. Orlans and J. O'Neill, eds. *Affirmative Action Revisited; Annuals of the American Academy of Political and Social Science* (September): 63–74.

Lynch, F. R. (1989). *Invisible Victims: White Males and the Crisis of Affirmative Action.* New York: Greenwood Press.

Roberts, P. C., and Stratton, L. M. (1995). *The Color Line: How Quotas and Privilege Destroy Democracy.* Washington, D.C.: Regnery.

Sowell, T. (1990). *Preferential Policies: An International Perspective.* New York: William Morrow.

———. (1993). *Inside American Education: The Decline, the Deception, the Dogmas.* New York: The Free Press.

United States General Accounting Office. (1995). *Efforts by the Office for Civil Rights to Resolve Asian-American Complaints.* Washington, D.C.: Government Printing Office (December).

Weiss, K. R. (1997). "UC Law Schools' New Rules Cost Minorities Spots." *Los Angeles Times,* 15 May.

Wygant v. Jackson Board of Education (1982) 546 F. Supp. 1195.

Wygant v. Jackson Board of Education (1986) 476 U.S. 267.

In Defense of Preference

Nathan Glazer

The battle over affirmative action today is a contest between a clear principle on the one hand and a clear reality on the other. The principle is that ability, qualifications, and merit, independent of race, national origin, or sex should prevail when one applies for a job or promotion, or for entry into selective institutions for higher education, or when one bids for contracts. The reality is that strict adherence to this principle would result in few African Americans getting jobs, admissions, and contracts. What makes the debate so confused is that the facts that make a compelling case for affirmative action are often obscured by the defenders of affirmative action themselves. They have resisted acknowledging how serious the gaps are between African Americans and others, how deep the preferences reach, how systematic they have become. Considerably more than a mild bent in the direction of diversity now exists, but it exists because painful facts make it necessary if blacks are to participate in more than token numbers in some key institutions of our society. The opponents of affirmative action can also be faulted: They have not fully confronted the consequences that must follow from the implementation of the principle that measured ability, qualification, merit, applied without regard to color, should be our only guide.

...

The reality of this enormous gap is clearest where the tests in use are the most objective, the most reliable, and the best validated, as in the case of the various tests used for admission to selective institutions of higher education, for entry into elite occupations such as law and medicine, or for civil service jobs. These tests have been developed over many years specifically for the purpose of eliminating biases in admissions and appointments. As

From *The New Republic* 218, no. 14 (April 6, 1998). Copyright © 1998 by The New Republic, Inc. Reprinted with the permission of The New Republic.

defenders of affirmative action often point out, paper-and-pencil tests of information, reading comprehension, vocabulary, reasoning, and the like are not perfect indicators of individual ability. But they are the best measures we have for success in college and professional schools, which, after all, require just the skills the tests measure. And the tests can clearly differentiate the literate teacher from the illiterate one or the policeman who can make out a coherent arrest report from one who cannot.

...

There is no way of getting around this reality. Perhaps the tests are irrelevant to success in college? That cannot be sustained. They have been improved and revised over decades and predict achievement in college better than any alternative. Some of the revisions have been carried out in a near-desperate effort to exclude items which would discriminate against blacks. Some institutions have decided they will not use the tests, not because they are invalid per se, but because they pose a barrier to the increased admission of black students. Nor would emphasizing other admissions criteria, such as high school grades, make a radical difference. In any case, there is considerable value to a uniform national standard, given the enormous differences among high schools.

Do qualifications at the time of admission matter? Isn't the important thing what the institutions manage to do with those they admit? If they graduate, are they not qualified? Yes, but many do not graduate. Two or three times as many African American students as white students drop out before graduation. And the tests for admission to graduate schools show the same radical disparities between blacks and others. Are there not also preferences for athletes, children of alumni, students gifted in some particular respect? Yes, but except for athletes, the disparities in academic aptitude that result from such preferences are not nearly as substantial as those which must be elided in order to reach target figures for black students. Can we not substitute for the tests other factors—such as the poverty and other hardships students have overcome to reach the point of applying to college? This might keep up the number of African Americans, but not by much, if the studies are to be believed. A good number of white and Asian applicants would also benefit from such "class-based" affirmative action.

...

How, then, should we respond to this undeniable reality? The opponents of affirmative action say, "Let standards prevail whatever the result." So what if black students are reduced to two percent of our selective and elite student bodies? Those who gain entry will know that they are properly qualified for entry, that they have been selected without discrimination, and their classmates will know it too. The result will actually be improved race relations and a continuance of the improvements we have seen in black performance in recent decades. Fifteen years from now, perhaps three or four percent of students in the top schools will be black. Until then, blacks can go to less competitive institutions of higher education, perhaps gaining greater advantage from their education in so doing. And, meanwhile, let us improve elementary and high school education—as we have been trying to do for the last 15 years or more.

Yet we cannot be quite so cavalier about the impact on public opinion—black and white—of a radical reduction in the number of black students at the Harvards, the Berkeleys, and the Amhersts. These institutions have become, for better or worse, the gateways to prominence, privilege, wealth, and power in American society. To admit blacks under affirmative action no doubt undermines the American meritocracy, but to exclude blacks from them by abolishing affirmative action would undermine the legitimacy of American democracy.

My argument is rooted in history. African Americans—and the struggle for their full and fair inclusion in U.S. society—have been a part of American history from the beginning. Our Constitution took special—but grossly unfair—account of their status, our greatest war was fought over their status, and our most important constitutional amendments were adopted because of the need to right past wrongs done to them. And, amid the civil rights revolution of the 1960s, affirmative action was instituted to compensate for the damage done to black achievement and life chances by almost 400 years of slavery, followed by state-sanctioned discrimination and massive prejudice.

Yet, today, a vast gulf of difference persists between the educational and occupational status of blacks and whites, a gulf that encompasses statistical measures of wealth, residential segregation, and social relationships with other Americans. Thirty years ago, with the passage of the great civil rights laws, one could have reasonably expected—as I did—that all would be set right by now. But today, even after taking account of substantial progress and change, it is borne upon us how continuous, rooted, and substantial the differences between African Americans and other Americans remain.

The judgment of the elites who support affirmative action—the college presidents and trustees, the religious leaders, the corporate executives—and the judgment even of many of those who oppose it but hesitate to act against it—the Republican leaders in Congress, for example—is that the banning of preference would be bad for the country. I agree. Not that everyone's motives are entirely admirable; many conservative congressmen, for example, are simply afraid of being portrayed as racists even if their opposition to affirmative action is based on a sincere desire to support meritocratic principle. The college presidents who support affirmative action, under the fashionable mantra of diversity, also undoubtedly fear the student demonstrations that would occur if they were to speak out against preferences.

But there are also good-faith motives in this stand, and there is something behind the argument for diversity. What kind of institutions of higher education would we have if blacks suddenly dropped from six or seven percent of enrollment to one or two percent? The presence of blacks, in classes in social studies and the humanities, immediately introduces another tone, another range of questions (often to the discomfort of black students who do not want this representational burden placed upon them). The tone may be one of embarrassment and hesitation and self-censorship among whites (students and faculty). But must we not all learn how to face these questions together with our fellow citizens? We should not be able to escape from this embarrassment by the reduction of black students to minuscule numbers.

...

... But I believe the main reasons we have to continue racial preferences for blacks are, first, because this country has a special obligation to blacks that has not been fully discharged, and second, because strict application of the principle of qualification would send a message of despair to many blacks, a message that the nation is indifferent to their difficulties and problems.

...

Whatever the case one may make in general for affirmative action, many difficult issues remain: What kind, to what extent, how long, imposed by whom, by what decision-making process? It is important to bear in mind that affirmative action in higher education admissions is, for the most part, a policy that has been chosen (albeit sometimes under political pressure) by the institutions themselves....

...

We should retain the freedom of institutions of higher and professional education to make these determinations for themselves. As we know, they would almost all make room for a larger percentage of black students than would otherwise qualify. This is what these institutions do today. They defend what they do with the argument that diversity is a good thing. I think what they really mean is that a large segment of the American population, significant not only demographically but historically and politically and morally, cannot be so thoroughly excluded. I agree with them.

...

... Preference is no final answer (just as the elimination of preference is no final answer). It is rather what is necessary to respond to the reality that, for some years to come, yes, we are still two nations, and both nations must participate in the society to some reasonable degree.

Fortunately, those two nations, by and large, want to become more united. The United States is not Canada or Bosnia, Lebanon or Malaysia. But, for the foreseeable future, the strict use of certain generally reasonable tests as a benchmark criterion for admissions would mean the de facto exclusion of one of the two nations from a key institutional system of the society, higher education. Higher education's governing principle is qualification—merit. Should it make room for another and quite different principle, equal participation? The latter should never become dominant. Racial proportional representation would be a disaster. But basically the answer is yes—the principle of equal participation can and should be given some role. This decision has costs. But the alternative is too grim to contemplate.

KEY WEBSITES

AAD PROJECT

The Affirmative Action and Diversity Project is a web page designed to stimulate discussion and debate about affirmative action and diversity issues regarding culture, gender, race, and color. It provides links to pending court cases, state and federal legislation, and an annotated bibliography.
http://humanitas.ucsb.edu/aa.html

AAUP—DIVERSITY AND AFFIRMATIVE ACTION IN HIGHER EDUCATION

This website, compiled by the American Association of University Professors, contains essays, articles, and background information about affirmative action in higher education.
http://www.aaup.org/aacntnts.htm

AFFACT WEB: HOME PAGE OF THE AMERICAN ASSOCIATION FOR AFFIRMATIVE ACTION (AAAA)

AffAct Web contains information, news, and Web links related to Affirmative Action issues and Congress, federal agencies, the White House, the courts, and various states.
http://www.affirmativeaction.org/

AFFIRMATIVE ACTION: MYTHS VS. FACTS

This website, compiled by the Coalition against Bigotry and Bias, a Washington-state-based organization, contains statistics and information about affirmative action.
http://www.bbcc.ctc.edu/~webb/cabb.htm

AFFIRMATIVE ACTION WEB RESOURCES

This website provides links to dozens of websites, online newspaper and journal articles, and university policies and programs prepared by the Affirmative Action and Diversity Project at the University of California at Santa Barbara.
http://humanitas.ucsb.edu/projects/aa/pages/a-action.htmltop

AMERICANS AGAINST DISCRIMINATION AND PREFERENCES

This group works for the abolition of racial and gender discrimination and preferences at the local, state, and federal levels, along the lines established by California's Proposition 209. The website includes daily updates of links to news articles on affirmative action and race.
http://www.aadap.org/

AMERICANS UNITED FOR AFFIRMATIVE ACTION

Americans United for Affirmative Action is a national, nonprofit organization committed to educating the public on the importance of maintaining affirmative action programs and the principles of equal opportunity in employment and education.

http://www.auaa.org/index.html

U.S. SUPREME COURT SYLLABI: AFFIRMATIVE ACTION

This website, compiled by Cornell University's Legal Information Institute, provides a searchable index to identify affirmative action cases heard by the Supreme Court.

http://www4.law.cornell.edu/cgi-bin/fx?DB=SupctSyllabi&TOPDOC=0&P=affirmative+action

Module C

Critical Thinking and Business Ethics

Chapter 8

Critical Thinking

Chapter 8a

INTRODUCTION

The mind is its own place and in itself can make a hell of heaven or a heaven of hell.

John Milton, *Paradise Lost*

How Skilled Is Your Thinking Right Now?

There is nothing more practical than sound thinking. No matter what your circumstance or goals, no matter where you are or what problems you face, you are better off if your thinking is skilled. As a student, shopper, employee, citizen, lover, friend, parent—in every realm and situation of your life—good thinking pays off. Poor thinking, in contrast, inevitably causes problems, wastes time and energy, and engenders frustration and pain.

Critical thinking is the disciplined art of ensuring that you use the best thinking you are capable of in any set of circumstances. The general goal of thinking is to figure out the "lay of the land." We all have multiple choices to make. We need the best information to make the best choices.

What is really going on in this or that situation? Does so-and-so really care about me? Am I deceiving myself when I believe that . . . ? What are the likely consequences of failing to . . . ? If I want to do . . . , what is the best way to prepare? How can I be more successful in doing . . . ? Is this my biggest problem, or do I need to focus my attention on that? Responding to questions such as these successfully is the daily work of thinking. That's why we are *thinkers*.

Nothing you can do will guarantee that you will find the complete truth about anything, but there is a way to get better at it. Excellence of thought and skill in thinking are real possibilities. To maximize the quality of your thinking, however, you must learn how to become an effective critic of your thinking. And to become an effective critic of your thinking, you have to make *learning about thinking* a priority.

Consider for a minute all of what you have learned in your life: about sports, money, friendship, anger and fear, love and hate, your mother and father, nature, the city you live in, manners and taboos, human nature and human behavior. Learning is a natural, and inevitable, process. We learn in many directions. One direction in which learning is not natural is inward learning—self-knowledge, knowledge of the workings of our own mind, of how and why we think as we do.

Begin by answering these—rather unusual—questions: What have you learned about how you think? Did you ever *study* your thinking? What information do you have, for example, about the intellectual processes involved in how your mind thinks? More to the point, perhaps, what do you really know about how to analyze, evaluate, or reconstruct your thinking? Where does your thinking come from? How much of it is of "good" quality? How much of it is of "poor" quality? How much of your thinking is vague, muddled, inconsistent, inaccurate, illogical, or superficial? Are you, in any real sense, in control of your thinking? Do you know how to test it? Do you have any conscious standards for determining when you are thinking well and when you are thinking poorly? Have you ever discovered a significant problem in your thinking and then changed it by a conscious act of will? If anyone asked you to teach him or her what you have learned about thinking thus far in your life, would you have any idea what that was or how you learned it?

If you are like most people, the only honest answers to these questions run along the lines of: "Well, I suppose I don't know much about my thinking or about thinking in general. I suppose in my life I have more or less taken my thinking for granted. I don't really know how it works. I have never studied it. I don't know how I test it, or even if I *do* test it. It just happens in my mind automatically."

Serious study of thinking, serious thinking about thinking, is rare in human life. It is not a subject in most schools. It is not a subject taught at home. But if you focus your attention for a moment on the role that thinking is playing in your life, you may come to recognize that everything you do or want or feel is influenced by your thinking. And if you become persuaded of that, you will be surprised that humans show so little interest in thinking. We are like monkeys uninterested in what goes on when we "monkey" around. What is more, if you start to pay attention to thinking in a manner analogous to the way a botanist observes plants, you will be on your way to becoming a truly exceptional person. You will begin to notice what few others notice. You will be the rare monkey who knows what monkeying around is all about. You will be the rare monkey who knows how and why he or she is monkeying around, the rare monkey skilled in assessing and improving monkeying.

Some things you will eventually discover are: All of us, somewhere along the way, have picked up bad habits of thinking. All of us, for example, make generalizations when we don't have the evidence to back them up, allow stereotypes to influence our thinking, form some false beliefs, tend to look at the world from one fixed point of view, ignore or attack points of view that conflict with our own, fabricate illusions and myths that we subconsciously confuse with what is true and real, and think deceptively about many aspects of our experience. As you discover these problems in your thinking, we hope you will begin to ask yourself some key questions: Is it possible for me to learn to avoid bad habits of thought? Is it possible for me to develop good habits of thought? Is it possible for me to think at a high, or at least *higher,* level?

These are problems and questions that few discover or ask. Nevertheless, every major insight you gain into good or bad thinking can enhance your life significantly. You can begin to make better decisions. You can gain power, important power, that you presently lack. You can open up new doors for yourself, see new options, minimize significant mistakes, maximize potential understandings. If you're going to live your life as a monkey, why not get good at monkeying around?

I.1 *Think for Yourself*

BEGINNING TO THINK ABOUT YOUR THINKING

See if you can identify any discovery you made about your thinking before you started to read this book. If you can't think of any, write out your best explanation as to why not. If you do think of something, explain what you learned about your thinking.

GOOD THINKING REQUIRES HARD WORK

There is a catch—there always is. To make significant gains in the quality of your thinking, you will have to engage in a kind of work that most humans find unpleasant, if not painful: intellectual work. This is the price you have to pay if you want the gain. One doesn't become a skillful critic of thinking overnight any more than one becomes a skillful basketball player or dancer overnight. To become a student of thinking, you must be willing to put the work into thinking that skilled improvement requires. When thinking of what physical conditioning requires, we say, "No pain, no gain!" In this case, it would be more precise to say, "No *intellectual* pain, no *intellectual* gain!"

This means you must be willing to practice special "acts" of thinking that are, initially at least, uncomfortable, and sometimes challenging and difficult. You have to learn to do "moves" with your mind analogous to what accomplished athletes learn to do through practice and feedback with their body. Improvement in thinking, then, is similar to improvement in other domains of performance in which progress is a product of sound theory, commitment, hard work, and practice. Although this book will point the way to what you need to practice to become a skilled thinker, it cannot provide you with the internal motivation to do the required work. This must come from you. You must be willing, as it were, to be the monkey who comes down from the trees and starts to

FIGURE I.1 *Critical thinkers use theories to explain how the mind works. Then they apply those theories to the way they live every day.*

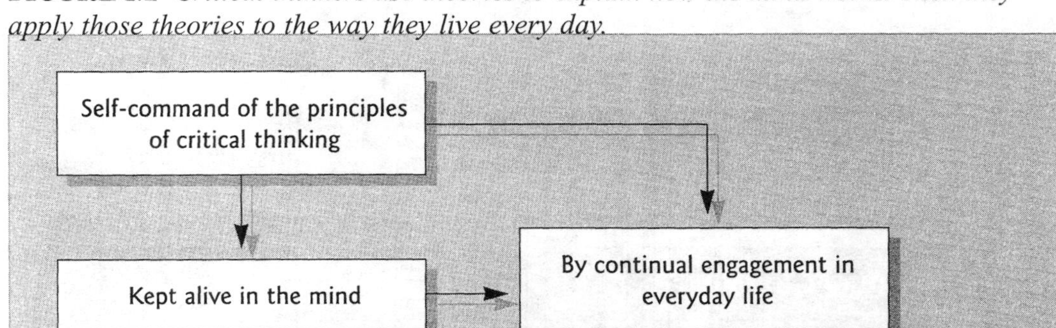

observe your fellow monkeys in action. You must be willing to examine mental films of your own monkeying around, as well.

Let's now develop further the analogy between physical and intellectual development. This analogy, we believe, goes a long way, and provides us with just the right prototype to keep before our minds. If you play tennis and you want to play better, there is nothing more advantageous than to look at some films of excellent players in action and then painstakingly compare how they, in comparison to you, address the ball. You study their performance. You note what you need to do more of, what you need to do less of, and you practice, practice, practice. You go through many cycles of practice/feedback/practice. Your practice heightens your awareness of the ins and outs of the art. You develop a vocabulary for talking about your performance. Perhaps you get a coach. And slowly, progressively, you improve. Similar points could be made for ballet, distance running, piano playing, chess, reading, writing, parenting, teaching, studying, and so on.

One major problem, however, is that all the activities of skill development with which we are typically familiar are visible. We could watch a film of the skill in action. But imagine a film of a person sitting in a chair *thinking*. It would look like the person was doing nothing. Yet, increasingly, workers are being paid precisely for the thinking they are able to do, not for their physical strength or physical activity. Therefore, though most of our thinking is invisible, it represents one of the most important things about us. Its quality in all likelihood will determine whether we will become rich or poor, powerful or weak. Yet we typically think without explicitly noticing how we are doing it. We take our thinking for granted.

For example, important concepts, such as love, friendship, integrity, freedom, democracy, and ethics, are often unconsciously twisted and distorted in common life and thought. Our subconscious interest is often in getting what we want, not in describing ourselves or the world truly and honestly, and well.

In any case, most of our concepts are invisible to us, though implicit in our talk and behavior. So is much of our thinking. We would be amazed, and sometimes shocked, if we were to see all of our thinking displayed for us on a large screen.

FIGURE I.2 *Critical thinking is the way we should approach everything we do.*

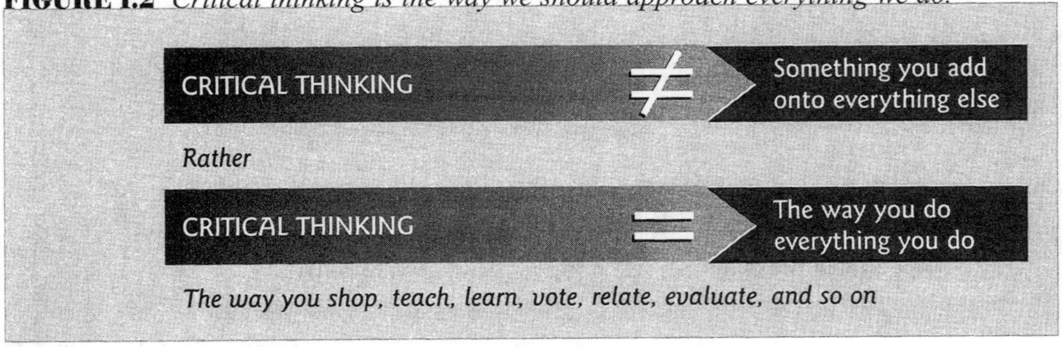

To develop as a thinker, you must begin to think of your thinking as involving an implicit set of structures—concepts being one important set—whose use can be improved only when you begin to take the tools of thinking seriously. You develop as a thinker when you explicitly notice what your thinking is doing and when you become committed to recognizing both strengths and weaknesses in that thinking. You develop as a thinker as you build your own "large screen" on which to view your thinking.

Critical thinking, then, provides the tools of mind you need to think through any and everything that requires thought—in college and in life. As your intellectual skills develop, you gain instruments that you can use deliberately and mindfully to better reason through the thinking tasks implicit in your short- and long-range goals. There are better and worse ways to pursue whatever you are after. Good thinking enables you to maximize the first and minimize the second.

I.2 *Think for Yourself*

UNDERSTANDING THE IMPORTANCE OF CONCEPTS

See if you can think of a time in which you "misused" an important concept. Hint: Think of an idea that you commonly use in your thinking, such as friendship, trust, truthfulness, or respect. Have you ever implied you were someone's friend but acted against that person (such as gossiping behind that person's back)? Write out your answer or explain orally.

Only by applying the fundamentals to a wide range of human problems can one begin to appreciate their power and usefulness. Think of it this way. If we were coaching you in tennis, we would remind you again and again to keep your eye on the ball. Could you imagine saying to your coach, "Why do I have to keep my eye on the ball? I already did that once." The same logic applies to the principles of skilled thinking. If you want to be proficient, you have to redirect your eyes to the fundamentals, again and again and again.

BECOME A CRITIC OF YOUR THINKING

One of the most important things you can do for yourself is to begin the process of becoming a critic of your thinking. You do this not to negate or dump on yourself but, instead, to improve yourself, to begin to practice the art of skilled thinking and lifelong learning. To do this, you must discover your thinking, see its structure, observe its implications, and recognize its basis and vantage point. You must come to recognize that, through commitment and daily practice, you can make foundational changes in your thinking. You need to learn about your bad habits of thought and about what you are striving for—good habits of thought. At whatever level you think, you need to recognize that you can learn to think better.

FIGURE I.3 *Critical thinking applies to everything about which we think.*

CRITICAL
THINKING
ABOUT
Teaching and learning
Emotions
Habits
Listening
Writing
Speaking
Religion
Reading
Problem-solving
Politics
Nursing
Medicine
Well-being
Intuition
Creativity

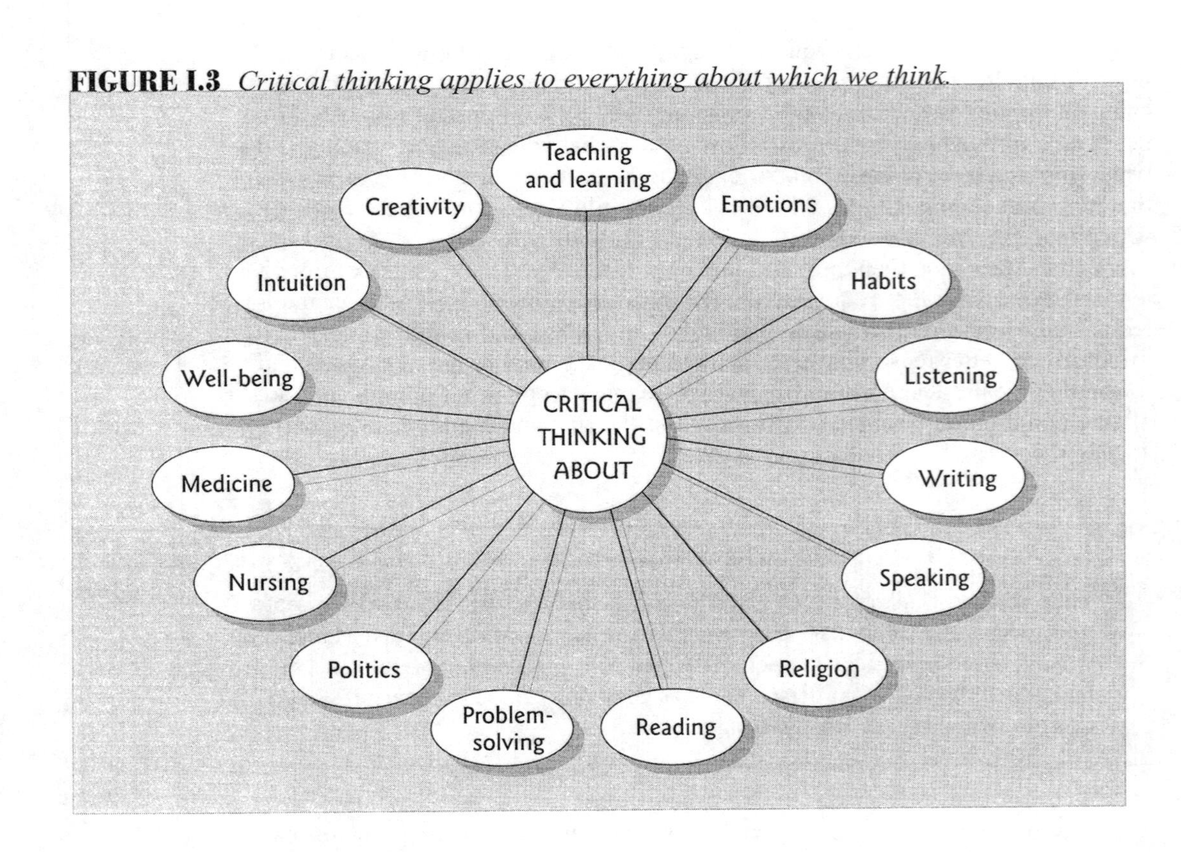

FIGURE I.4 *Critical thinking adds a second level of thinking to ordinary thinking. The second level analyzes and assesses our ordinary thinking.*

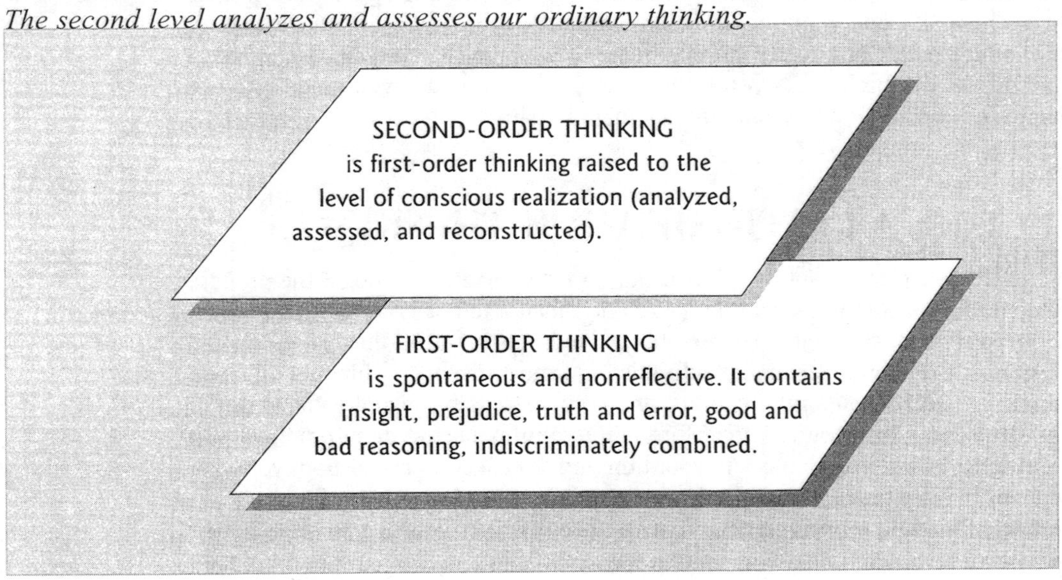

SECOND-ORDER THINKING
is first-order thinking raised to the level of conscious realization (analyzed, assessed, and reconstructed).
FIRST-ORDER THINKING
is spontaneous and nonreflective. It contains insight, prejudice, truth and error, good and bad reasoning, indiscriminately combined.

I.3 *Think for Yourself*

BEGINNING TO THINK ABOUT YOUR THINKING

Consider your thinking in personal relationships, in sports, in dealing with others of your gender, in relating to the opposite sex, as a reader, as a writer, as a listener to lectures, as an employee, in planning your life, in dealing with your emotions, in figuring out complex situations. Complete these statements:

1. Right now, I believe my thinking across all domains of my life is of ______________ quality. I base this judgment on ______________________________.

2. In the following areas, I think very well:
   a. ______________________________
   b. ______________________________
   c. ______________________________

3. In the following areas, my thinking is okay, not great, but not terrible either:
   a. ______________________________
   b. ______________________________
   c. ______________________________

4. In the following areas, my thinking is probably poor:
   a. ______________________________
   b. ______________________________
   c. ______________________________

ESTABLISH NEW HABITS OF THOUGHT

Most of us get through school by modifying our thinking the hard way—through trial and error. Most of us have little help in learning how to become a critic of our thinking. We develop few thinking tools. The result is that we use our native capacities to think in a largely unconscious fashion. We develop some good habits of thought, and we develop many bad habits of thought. The good and bad become intermixed and hard to disentangle. We learn without a clear sense of the *ideal* in thinking. We are not clear about our goals as thinkers. We treat each class like a new set of tasks to mechanically complete. We fail to learn important ideas that enable us to learn better and better.

To learn at a deeper level, you need to get powerful leverage on learning. You need a clearer perspective on what you should be striving to achieve and powerful tools for upgrading your thinking and learning.

Critical thinking works. It is practical. It will enable you to be more successful, to save time and energy, and to experience more positive and fulfilling emotions. It is in your interest to become a better critic of your own thinking: as a student, scholar, parent, consumer, citizen, and other roles, as well. If you are not progressively improving the quality of your life, you have not yet discovered the true power of critical thinking. We hope this book will serve as an impetus for this shift. Good thinking works—for everyone.

Think for Yourself I.4

CHANGING YOUR HABITS

Have you ever changed a habit as a result of your conscious effort and planning? What do you have to do to change a habit? Is it easy? If not, why not? What do you think you would have to do to change habits of thought? Write out your answer or explain orally.

FIGURE I.5 *Why critical thinking?*

THE PROBLEM

Everyone thinks. It is our nature to do so. But much of our thinking, left to itself, is biased, distorted, partial, uninformed, or downright prejudiced. Yet the quality of our life and that of what we produce, make, or build depends precisely on the quality of our thought. Shoddy thinking is costly, both in money and in quality of life. Excellence in thought, however, must be systematically cultivated.

A DEFINITION

Critical thinking is that mode of thinking—about any subject, content, or problem—in which the thinker improves the quality of his or her thinking by skillfully taking charge of the structures inherent in thinking and imposing intellectual standards upon them.

THE RESULT

A well-cultivated critical thinker:

- raises vital questions and problems, formulating them clearly and precisely;
- gathers and assesses relevant information, and can effectively interpret it;
- comes to well-reasoned conclusions and solutions, testing them against relevant criteria and standards;
- thinks openmindedly within alternative systems of thought, recognizing and assessing, as need be, their assumptions, implications, and practical consequences; and
- communicates effectively with others in figuring out solutions to complex problems.

Critical thinking is, in short, self-directed, self-disciplined, self-monitored, and self-corrective thinking. It presupposes assent to rigorous standards of excellence and mindful command of their use. It entails effective communication and problem-solving abilities.

Chapter 8b

THE STANDARDS FOR THINKING

One of the fundamentals of critical thinking is the ability to assess one's own reasoning. To be good at assessment requires that we consistently take apart our thinking and examine the parts with respect to standards of quality. We do this using *criteria* based on clarity, accuracy, precision, relevance, depth, breadth, logicalness, and significance. Critical thinkers recognize that, whenever they are reasoning, they reason to some *purpose* (element of reasoning). Implicit goals are built into their thought processes. But their reasoning is improved when they are *clear* (intellectual standard) about that purpose or goal. Similarly, to reason well, they need to know that, consciously or unconsciously, they are using *information* (element of reasoning) in thinking. But their reasoning improves if and when they make sure that the information they are using is *accurate* (intellectual standard).

Put another way, when we assess our reasoning, we want to know how well we are reasoning. We do not identify the elements of reasoning for the fun of it, or just to satisfy some authority. Rather, we assess our reasoning using intellectual standards because we realize the negative consequences of failing to do so. In assessing our reasoning, then, we recommend these intellectual standards as minimal:

- clarity
- accuracy
- precision
- relevance
- depth
- breadth
- logicalness
- significance
- fairness

These are not the *only* intellectual standards a person might use. They are simply among those that are most fundamental. In this respect, the elements of thought are more basic, because the eight elements we have identified are *universal*—present in all reasoning of all subjects in all cultures for all time. On the one hand, one cannot reason with no information about no question from no point of view with no assumptions. On the other hand, there is a wide variety of intellectual standards from which to choose—such as credibility, predictability, feasibility, and completeness—that we don't use routinely in assessing reasoning.

As critical thinkers, then, we think about our thinking with these kinds of questions in mind: Am I being clear? Accurate? Precise? Relevant? Am I thinking logically? Am I dealing with a matter of significance? Is my thinking justifiable in context? Typically, we apply these standards to one or more elements.

Think for Yourself 5.1

IDENTIFYING INAPPROPRIATE STANDARDS

Can you identify a class you took in the past, either in high school or in college, in which you think your work was graded, at least in part, by one or more inappropriate standards? What was the class? What was the standard? What was the result? Can you see the importance in education of basing all grades on appropriate intellectual standards? Write out or orally explain your answer.

TAKING A DEEPER LOOK AT UNIVERSAL INTELLECTUAL STANDARDS

Thinking critically requires command of fundamental intellectual standards. Critical thinkers routinely ask questions that apply intellectual standards to thinking. The ultimate goal is for these questions to become so spontaneous in thinking that they form a natural part of our inner voice, guiding us to better and better reasoning. In this section, we focus on the standards and questions that apply across the various facets of your life.

Clarity

Questions that focus on clarity include:

- Could you elaborate on that point?
- Could you express that point in another way?
- Could you give me an illustration?

- Could you give me an example?
- Let me state in my own words what I think you just said. Tell me if I am clear about your meaning.

Clarity is a gateway standard. If a statement is unclear, we cannot determine whether it is accurate or relevant. In fact, we cannot tell anything about it because we don't yet know what it is saying. For example, the question "What can be done about the education system in America?" is unclear. To adequately address the question, we would need a clearer understanding of what the person asking the question is considering the "problem" to be. A clearer question might be, "What can educators do to ensure that students learn the skills and abilities that help them function successfully on the job and in their daily decision-making?" This question, because of its increased clarity, provides a better guide to thinking. It lays out in a more definitive way the intellectual task at hand.

5.2 *Think for Yourself*

CONVERTING UNCLEAR THOUGHTS TO CLEAR THOUGHTS

Can you convert an unclear thought to one that is clear? Suppose you are engaged in a discussion about welfare and one person says, "Let's face it—welfare is corrupt!" What does this mean? What could it mean?

It could mean some very different things. It could mean, "The very idea of giving people goods and services they have not personally earned is equivalent to stealing money from those who have earned it" (a moral claim). Or it could mean, "The welfare laws have so many loopholes that people are receiving money and services that were not envisioned when the laws were initially formulated" (a legal claim). Or it could mean, "The people who receive welfare so often lie and cheat to falsify the documents they submit that they should be thrown in jail" (a claim about the ethical character of the recipients).

Now, for practice in making thoughts clear, take this statement: "She is a good person." This statement is unclear. Because we don't know the context within which this statement is being made, we aren't sure in what way "she" is "good." Formulate three possible meanings of this statement.

Now take the statement, "He is a jerk." Again, formulate three possible different meanings of this statement.

When you become skilled in differentiating what is clear and what is unclear, you will find that much of the time we are unclear both about what we are thinking and about what we are saying.

Accuracy

Questions focusing on making thinking more accurate include:

- Is that really true?
- How could we check to see if that is accurate?

- How could we find out if that is true?

A statement may be clear but not accurate, as in, "Most dogs weigh more than 300 pounds." To be accurate is to represent something in accordance with the way it actually is. People often present or describe things or events in a way that is not in accordance with the way things actually are. People frequently misrepresent or falsely describe things, especially when they have a vested interest in the description. Advertisers often do this to keep a buyer from seeing the weaknesses in a product. If an advertisement states, "Our water is 100% pure" when in fact the water contains small parts of chemicals such as chlorine and lead, it is inaccurate. If an advertisement says, "this bread contains 100% whole wheat" when the whole wheat has been bleached and enriched and the bread contains many additives, the advertisement is inaccurate.

Good thinkers listen carefully to statements and, when there is reason for skepticism, question whether what they hear is true and accurate. In the same way, they question the extent to which what they read is correct, when asserted as fact. Critical thinking, then, implies a healthy skepticism about public descriptions as to what is and is not fact.

At the same time, because we tend to think from a narrow, self-serving perspective, assessing ideas for accuracy can be difficult. We naturally tend to believe that our thoughts are automatically accurate just because they are ours, and therefore that the thoughts of those who disagree with us are inaccurate. We also fail to question statements that others make that conform to what we already believe, while we tend to question statements that conflict with our views. But as critical thinkers, we force ourselves to accurately assess our own views as well as those of others. We do this even if it means facing deficiencies in our thinking.

Think for Yourself 5.3, 5.4

RECOGNIZING INACCURATE STATEMENTS

Can you identify a statement that you heard recently that was clear but inaccurate? You will find an abundance of examples in everyday statements that people often make in praise or criticism. People in general have a tendency to make two kinds of inaccurate statements: false positives about the people they personally like (these would be untrue positive statements about people they like) and false negatives about the people they personally dislike (untrue negative things about people they don't like). Politically motivated statements tend to follow a similar pattern. See if you can think of an example of an inaccurate statement from your recent experience. Write out or orally explain your answer.

IN SEARCH OF THE FACTS

One of the most important critical thinking skills is the skill of assessing the accuracy of "factual" claims (someone's assertion that such-and-so is a fact).

In an ad in the *New York Times* (Nov. 29, 1999, p. A15), a coalition of 60 nonprofit organizations accused the World Trade Organization (a coalition of 134 nation states) of operating in secret, undermining democratic institutions and the environment. In the process of doing this, the nonprofit coalition argued that the working class and the poor have not significantly benefited as a result of the last 20 years of rapid expansion of global trade. They alleged, among other things, the following facts:

1. "American CEOs are now paid, on average, 419 times more than line workers, and the ratio is increasing."
2. "Median hourly wages for workers are down by 10% in the last 10 years."
3. "The top 20% of the U.S. population owns 84.6% of the country's wealth."
4. "The wealth of the world's 475 billionaires now equals the annual incomes of more than 50% of the world population *combined.*"

Using whatever sources you can find (including the Website of the Turning Point Project, the nonprofit coalition, www.turnpoint.org, discuss the probable accuracy of the factual claims. For example, find the Website (if there is one) of the World Trade Organization. They might challenge some of the facts alleged or advance facts of their own that put the charges of the nonprofit coalition into a different perspective.

Precision

Questions focusing on making thinking more precise include:

- Could you give me more details?
- Could you be more specific?

A statement can be both clear and accurate but not precise, as in "Jack is overweight." (We don't know how overweight Jack is—1 pound or 500 pounds.) To be precise is to give the details needed for someone to understand exactly what is meant. Some situations don't call for detail. If you ask, "Is there any milk in the refrigerator?" and I answer "Yes," both the question and the answer are probably precise enough for the circumstance (though it might be relevant to specify how much milk is there). Or imagine that you are ill and go to the doctor. He wouldn't say, "Take 1.4876946 antibiotic pills twice per day." This level of specificity, or precision, would be beyond that which is useful in the situation.

In many situations, however, specifics are essential to good thinking. Let's say that your friend is having financial problems and asks you, "What should I do about my situation?" In this case, you want to probe her thinking for specifics. Without the full specifics, you could not help her. You might ask questions such as, "What *precisely* is the problem? What *exactly* are the variables that bear on the problem? What are some possible solutions to the problem—in detail?

Think for Yourself 5.5

RECOGNIZING IMPRECISE STATEMENTS

Can you think of a recent situation in which you needed more details to figure something out, a circumstance in which, because you didn't have the details, you experienced some negative consequences? For example, have you ever been given directions to someone's house, directions that seemed precise enough at the time, but when you tried to find the person's house, you got lost because of lack of details in the directions?

First identify a situation in which the details and specifics were important (for example, in buying a computer, a car, or a stereo system). Then identify the negative consequences that resulted because you didn't get the details you needed to think well in the situation. Write out or orally explain your answer.

Relevance

Questions focusing on relevance include:

- How is this idea connected to the question?
- How does that bear on the issue?
- How does this idea relate to this other idea?
- How does your question relate to the issue we are dealing with?

A statement can be clear, accurate, and precise, but not relevant to the question at issue. For example, students often think the amount of effort they put into a course should contribute to raising their grade in the course. Often, however, effort does not measure the quality of student learning and therefore is irrelevant to the grade. Something is relevant when it is directly connected with and bears upon the issue at hand. Something is relevant when it is pertinent or applicable to a problem we are trying to solve. Irrelevant thinking encourages us to consider what we should set aside. Thinking that is relevant stays on track. People are often irrelevant in their thinking because they lack discipline in thinking. They don't know how to analyze an issue for what truly bears on it. Therefore, they aren't able to effectively think their way through the problems and issues they face.

Think for Yourself 5.6

RECOGNIZING IRRELEVANT STATEMENTS

Can you identify a statement you heard recently that was clear, accurate, and sufficiently precise, but irrelevant to the circumstance, problem, or issue? Though we all sometimes stray from a question or task, we need to be sensitive to when failure to stay on task may have a significant negative implication.

Identify, first, circumstances in which people tend to introduce irrelevant considerations into a discussion (for example, in meetings, in response to questions in class, in everyday dialogue when they have a hidden agenda—or simply want to get control of the conversation for some reason). Write out or orally explain your answer.

Depth

Questions focusing on depth of thought include:

- How does your answer address the complexities in the question?
- How are you taking into account the problems in the question?
- How are you dealing with the most significant factors in the problem?

We think deeply when we get beneath the surface of an issue or problem, identify the complexities inherent in it, and then deal with those complexities in an intellectually responsible way. Even when we think deeply, even when we deal well with the complexities in a question, we may find the question difficult to address. Still, our thinking will work better for us when we can recognize complicated questions and address each area of complexity in it.

A statement can be clear, accurate, precise, and relevant, but superficial—lacking in depth. Let's say you are asked what should be done about the problem of drug use in America and you answer by saying, "Just say no." This slogan, which was for several years used to discourage children and teens from using drugs, is clear, accurate, precise, and relevant. Nevertheless, it lacks depth because it treats an extremely complex issue—the pervasive problem of drug use among people in our culture—superficially. It does not address the history of the problem, the politics of the problem, the economics of the problem, the psychology of addiction, and so on.

5.7 *Think for Yourself*

RECOGNIZING SUPERFICIAL APPROACHES

Identify a newspaper article that contains a statement that is clear, accurate, precise, and relevant, but superficial with respect to a complex issue. For example, a number of laws take a Band-Aid approach to systemic problems such as drugs and crime.

1. State the problem at issue.
2. State how the article deals with the problem and why the approach taken is superficial.
3. Beginning to focus on the complexity of the issue, state how the problem might be dealt with.

Breadth

Questions focusing on making thinking broader include:

- Do we need to consider another point of view?
- Is there another way to look at this question?
- What would this look like from a conservative standpoint?
- What would this look like from the point of view of . . . ?

A line of reasoning may be clear, accurate, precise, relevant, and deep, but lack breadth. Examples are arguments from either the conservative or the liberal standpoint that get deeply into an issue but show insight into only one side of the question.

When we consider the issue at hand from every *relevant* viewpoint, we think in a broad way. When multiple points of view are pertinent to the issue, yet we fail to give due consideration to those perspectives, we think myopically, or narrow-mindedly. We do not try to enter alternative, or opposing, viewpoints.

Humans are frequently guilty of narrow-mindedness for many reasons: limited education, innate sociocentrism, natural selfishness, self-deception, and intellectual arrogance. Points of view that significantly disagree with our own often threaten us. It's much easier to ignore perspectives with which we disagree than to consider them, when we know at some level that to consider them would mean to be forced to reconsider our views.

Let's say, for example, that you are I are roommates and that I like to play loud music that annoys you. The question at issue, then, is: "Should I play loud music in the dorm room when you are present?" Both your viewpoint and mine are relevant to the question at issue. When I recognize your viewpoint as relevant, and then intellectually empathize with it—when I enter your way of thinking so as to actually understand it—I will be forced to see that imposing my loud music on you is unfair and inconsiderate. I will be able to imagine what it would be like to be forced to listen to loud music that I find annoying. But if I don't force myself to enter your viewpoint, I do not have to change my self-serving behavior. One of the primary mechanisms the mind uses to avoid giving up what it wants is unconsciously to refuse to enter viewpoints that differ from its own.

Think for Yourself 5.8

THINKING BROADLY ABOUT AN ISSUE

Take the question, "Is abortion morally justified?" Some argue that abortion is not morally justifiable, and others argue that it is. Try to state and elaborate on each of these points of view in detail. Articulate each point of view objectively, regardless of your personal views. Present each point of view in such a way that a person who actually takes that position would assess it as *accurate*. Each line of reasoning should be clear, accurate, precise, relevant, and deep. Do not take a position on it yourself.

Logicalness

Questions that focus on making thinking more logical include:

- Does all of this fit together logically?
- Does this really make sense?
- Does that follow from what you said?
- How does that follow from the evidence?
- Before, you implied this, and now you are saying that. I don't see how both can be true.

When we think, we bring together a variety of thoughts in some order. When the combined thoughts are mutually supporting and make sense in combination, the thinking is logical. When the combination is not mutually supporting, is contradictory in some sense, or does not make sense, the combination is not logical. Because humans often maintain conflicting beliefs without being aware that we are doing so, it is not unusual to find inconsistencies in human life and thought.

Let's say we know, by looking at standardized tests of students in schools and the actual work they are able to produce, that for the most part students are deficient in basic academic skills such as reading, writing, speaking, and the core disciplines such as math, science, and history. Despite this evidence, teachers often conclude that there is nothing they can do to change their instruction to improve student learning (and in fact that there is nothing fundamentally wrong with the way they teach). Given the evidence, this conclusion seems illogical. The conclusion doesn't seem to follow from the facts.

Let's take another example. Say that you know a person who has had a heart attack, and her doctors have told her she must be careful what she eats, to avoid problems in the future. Yet she concludes that what she eats really doesn't matter. Given the evidence, her conclusion is illogical. It doesn't make sense.

5.9 *Think for Yourself*

RECOGNIZING ILLOGICAL THINKING

Identify a newspaper article that contains an example of illogical thinking—thinking that doesn't make sense to you.

1. State the issue that the thinking revolves around.
2. State the thinking that you believe is illogical, and why you think it is illogical.
3. State some implications of the illogical thinking. What are some consequences likely to follow from the illogical thinking?

Significance

Questions that focus on making thinking more significant include:

- What is the most significant information we need to address this issue?

- How is that fact important in context?
- Which of these questions is the most significant?
- Which of these ideas or concepts is the most important?

When we reason through issues, we want to concentrate on the most important information (relevant to the issue) in our reasoning and take into account the most important ideas or concepts. Too often we fail in our thinking because we do not recognize that, though many ideas may be relevant to an issue, it does not follow that all are equally important. In a similar way, we often fail to ask the most important questions and are trapped by thinking only in terms of superficial questions, questions of little weight. In college, for example, few students focus on important questions such as, "What does it mean to be an educated person? What do I need to do to become educated?" Instead, students tend to ask questions such as, "What do I need to do to get an 'A' in this course? How many pages does this paper have to be? What do I have to do to satisfy this professor?"

Think for Yourself 5.10

FOCUSING ON SIGNIFICANCE IN THINKING

Think about your life, about the way you spend your time, in terms of the amount of time you spend on significant versus trivial things. As you do so, write the answers to these questions:

1. What is the most important goal or purpose you should focus on at this point in your life? Why is this purpose important? How much time do you spend focused on it?
2. What are the most trivial or superficial things you spend time focused on (things such as your appearance, impressing your friends, chatting about insignificant things at parties, and the like)?
3. What can you do to reduce the amount of time you spend on the trivial, and increase the amount of time you spend on the significant?

Fairness

Questions that focus on ensuring that thinking is fair include:

- Is my thinking justified given the evidence?
- Am I taking into account the weight of the evidence that others might advance in the situation?
- Are these assumptions justified?
- Is my purpose fair given the implications of my behavior?

- Is the manner in which I am addressing the problem fair-or is my vested interest keeping me from considering the problem from alternative viewpoints?
- Am I using concepts justifiably, or am I using them unfairly in other to manipulate someone (and selfishly get what I want)?

When we think through problems, we want to make sure that our thinking is justified. To be justified is to think fairly in context. In other words, it is to think in accord with reason. If you are vigilant in using the other intellectual standards covered thus far in the chapter you will (by implication) satisfy the standard of justifiability. We include fairness in its own section because of the powerful nature of self-deception in human thinking. For example, we often deceive ourselves into thinking that we are being fair and justified in our thinking when in fact we are refusing to consider significant relevant information that would cause us to change our view (and therefore not pursue our selfish interest). We often pursue unjustified purposes in order to get what we want even if we have to hurt others to get it. We often use concepts in an unjustified way in order to manipulate people. And we often make unjustified assumptions, unsupported by facts, that then lead to faulty inferences.

Let's focus on an example where the problem is unjustified thinking due to ignoring relevant facts. Let's say, for instance, that Kristi and Abbey are roommates. Kristi is cold-natured and Abbey is warm-natured. During the winter, Abbey likes to have the window in the dorm room open while Kristi likes to keep it closed. But Abbey insists that is "extremely uncomfortable" with the window closed. The information she is using in her reasoning all centers around her own point of view—that she is hot, that she can't study if she's hot, that if Kristi is cold she can wear a sweater. But the fact is that Abbey is not justified in her thinking. She refuses to enter Kristi's point of view, to consider information supporting Kristi's perspective, because to do so would mean that she would have to give something up. She would have to adopt a more reasonable, or fair, point of view.

People who are manipulative often use concepts in ways that are not justified. Take, for instance, John. Let's imagine that John is interested in borrowing Jay's portable stereo for a trip he is going to take. He therefore begins to regularly hang out with Jay. When they are with others, John introduces Jay as his "friend." As a result, Jay comes to define John as his friend. So when John asks to borrow Jay's stereo Jay readily agrees (since John is his friend). But when John fails to return the stereo and Jay asks for it back, John lies and says he lost it. The fact is that John never intended to return the stereo, and obviously never considered Jay a friend. He just used the term "friend" to get what he selfishly wanted. Therefore his use of the concept of friend was for the purpose of manipulation and was not fair in context.

When we reason to conclusions, we want to check to make sure that the assumptions we are using to come to those conclusions are justifiable given the facts of the situation. For example, all of our prejudices and stereotypes function as assumptions in thinking. And no prejudices and stereotypes are justifiable given their very nature. For example, we often make broad sweeping generalizations such as:

- Liberals are soft on crime
- Elderly people aren't interested in sex
- Young men are only interested in sex
- Jocks are cool
- Blondes are dumb
- Cheerleaders are airheads
- Intellectuals are nerds
- Learning is boring
- School doesn't have anything to do with life

The problem with assumptions like these is that they cause us to make basic—and often serious—mistakes in thinking. Because they aren't *justifiable,* they cause us to prejudge situations and people and draw faulty inferences—or conclusions—about them. For example, if we believe that all intellectuals are nerds, whenever we meet an intellectual we will infer that he or she is a nerd (and act unfairly toward the person).

In sum, justifiability, or fairness, is an important standard in thinking because it forces us to see how we are distorting our thinking in order to achieve our self-serving ends (or to see how others are distorting their thinking to achieve selfish ends).

Think for Yourself 5.11, 5.12

ANALYZING ASSUMPTIONS FOR JUSTIFIABILITY (FAIRNESS)

Look back at the assumptions you came up with for Think for Yourself 4.11. For each one, decide whether it is justifiable given the situation. For each assumption that is not justifiable, recreate an assumption that would be justified in context.

APPLYING INTELLECTUAL STANDARDS TO EVERYDAY LIFE DISCUSSIONS

Tape-record a discussion/debate between you and a group of your friends on an important controversial issue (for example, "What is the best solution to the drug problem in this country?"). Then play back the recording two or three remarks at a time. Comment on which of the standards are being met and which are violated each "step" along the way. Notice how seldom people tend to use intellectual standards in their thinking. Notice how unclear everyday thinking often is. Notice how people may feel just as confident in their positions even after you point out violations of intellectual standards. What does that tell you about them?

FIGURE 5.1 *Powerful questions are implied by the intellectual standards. Critical thinkers routinely ask them.*

CLARITY

Could you elaborate?
Could you illustrate what you mean?
Could you give me an example?

ACCURACY

How could we check on that?
How could we find out if that is true?
How could we verify or test that?

PRECISION

Could you be more specific?
Could you give me more details?
Could you be more exact?

DEPTH

What factors make this a difficult problem?
What are some of the complexities of this question?
What are some of the difficulties we need to deal with?

RELEVANCE

How does that relate to the problem?
How does that bear on the question?
How does that help us with the issue?

LOGICALNESS

Does all of this make sense together?
Does your first paragraph fit in with your last?
Does what you say follow from the evidence?

SIGNIFICANCE

Is this the most important problem to consider?
Is this the central idea to focus on?
Which of these facts are the most important?

BREADTH

Do we need to look at this from another perspective?
Do we need to consider another point of view?
Do we need to look at this in other ways?

FAIRNESS

Is my thinking justifiable in context?
Are my assumptions supported by evidence?
Is my purpose fair given the situation?
Am I using my concepts in keeping with educated usage or am I distorting them to get what I want?

BRINGING TOGETHER THE ELEMENTS OF REASONING AND THE INTELLECTUAL STANDARDS

We have considered the elements of reasoning and the importance of being able to take them apart, to analyze them so we can begin to recognize flaws in our thinking. We also have introduced the intellectual standards as tools for assessment. Now let us look at how the intellectual standards are used to assess the elements of reason.

FIGURE 5.2 *Critical thinkers routinely apply the intellectual standards to the elements of reasoning.*

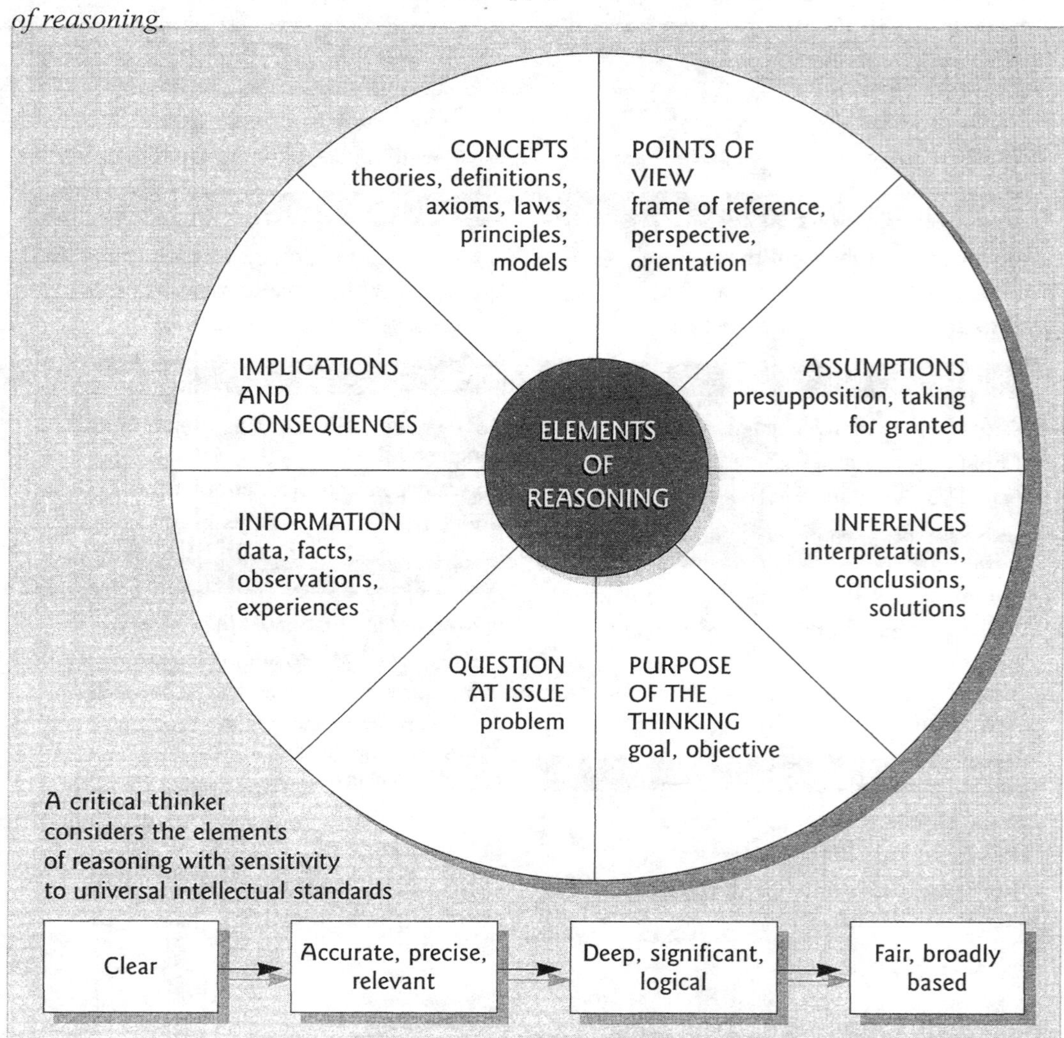

Purpose, Goal, or End in View

Whenever we reason, we reason to some end, to achieve some objective, to satisfy some desire or fulfill some need. One source of problems in human reasoning is traceable to defects at the level of goal, purpose, or end. If the goal is unrealistic, for example, or contradictory to other goals we have, if it is confused or muddled, the reasoning used to achieve it will suffer as a result.

As a developing critical thinker, then, you should get in the habit of explicitly stating the purposes you are trying to accomplish. You should strive to be clear about your purpose in every situation. If you fail to stick to your purpose, you are unlikely to achieve it. Let's say that your purpose in being in college is to obtain a degree so you can improve your chances of getting a good job and making a good income. If you keep that purpose clearly in mind and consistently work to achieve it, you are more likely to be successful. But it is easy to become so involved in the social life at college that you lose sight of your purpose and thus fail to achieve it.

As a student interested in developing your mind, you can begin to ask questions that improve your ability to focus on purpose in your classes. For example: Am I clear as to my purpose—in an essay, a research project, an oral report, a discussion? Can I specify my purpose precisely? Is my purpose a significant one? Realistic? Achievable? Justifiable? Do I have contradictory purposes?

5.13 *Think for Yourself*

BRINGING INTELLECTUAL STANDARDS TO BEAR UPON YOUR PURPOSE

Think of an important problem in your life. This can be a problem in a personal relationship, at your place of work, in college, or other situation. Now state your purpose in the situation *clearly* and *precisely*. What exactly are you trying to accomplish? Is your purpose *fair*, or *justifiable?* Is it *realistic?* Explain to a classmate.

Question at Issue or Problem to Be Solved

Whenever you attempt to reason something through, there is at least one question to answer—one question that emerges from the problem to be solved or issue to resolve. An area of concern in assessing reasoning, therefore, revolves around the very question at issue.

An important part of being able to think well is assessing your ability to formulate a problem in a clear and relevant way. It requires determining whether the question you are addressing is an important one, whether it is answerable, whether you understand the requirements for settling the question, for solving the problem.

As a student interested in developing your mind, you can begin to ask yourself questions that improve your ability to focus on the important questions in your classes. You begin to ask: What is the most fundamental question at issue (in this lecture, in this chapter, in this discussion)? What is the question, precisely? Is the question simple or complex? If it is complex, what makes it complex? Am I sticking to the question (in this discussion, in this paper I am working on)? Is there more than one important question to be considered here (in this lecture, etc.)?

Think for Yourself 5.14

BRINGING INTELLECTUAL STANDARDS TO BEAR UPON THE QUESTION AT ISSUE

Go back to the important problem in Think for Yourself 5.13. Now state the problem you are trying to address. Then state the question that emerges from that problem. State your question *clearly* and *precisely*. What complexities, if any, are inherent in the problem? Is there more than one question that you need to address to effectively reason through the problem? Explain to a classmate.

Point of View, or Frame of Reference

Whenever we reason, we must reason within some point of view or frame of reference. Any "defect" in that point of view or frame of reference is a possible source of problems in the reasoning.

A point of view may be too narrow, may be based on false or misleading information, may contain contradictions, and may be narrow or unfair. Critical thinkers strive to adopt a point of view that is fair to others, even to opposing points of view. They want their point of view to be broad, flexible, and justifiable, to be clearly stated and consistently adhered to. Good thinkers, then, consider alternative points of view as they reason through an issue.

As a student interested in developing your mind, you begin to ask yourself questions that improve your ability to focus on point of view in your classes. These questions might be: From what point of view am I looking at this issue? Am I so locked into my point of view that I am unable to see the issue from other points of view? Must I consider multiple points of view to reason well through the issue at hand? What is the point of view of this author? What is the frame of reference in this discipline? Are different world views implicit in these different perspectives?

Think for Yourself 5.15

BRINGING INTELLECTUAL STANDARDS TO BEAR UPON POINTS OF VIEW

Continue with the problem in Think for Yourself 5.14. Now state the point or points of view that are relevant to the issue at hand. State each point of view *clearly* and *precisely*. Make sure you are considering all relevant points of view (that you are thinking *broadly*), and that you are representing each point of view *accurately* (even if it means sympathetically expressing a view that you do not personally hold).

Information, Data, Experiences

Whenever we reason, there is some "stuff," some phenomena about which we are reasoning. Any "defect," then, in the experiences, data, evidence, or raw material upon which a person's reasoning is based is a possible source of problems.

Reasoners should be assessed on their ability to give evidence that is gathered and reported clearly, fairly, and accurately. Therefore, as a student, you should assess the information you use to come to conclusions, whether you are working on papers for class, reasoning through issues within the subjects you take, or reasoning through a problem in your personal life. You should assess whether the information you are using in reasoning is relevant to the issue at hand and adequate for achieving your purpose. You should assess whether you are taking the information into account consistently or distorting it to fit your own (often self-serving) point of view.

As a student interested in developing your mind, you begin to ask yourself questions that improve your ability to focus on information in your classes. These questions might be: What is the most important information I need to reason well through this issue? Are there alternate information sources I need to consider? How can I check to see if the information I am using is accurate? Am I sure that all of the information I am using is relevant to the issue at hand?

5.16 *Think for Yourself*

BRINGING INTELLECTUAL STANDARDS TO BEAR UPON THE INFORMATION YOU ARE USING IN REASONING

Continue with the problem you have been working on. Now state the information you are using in your thinking. This could be data, facts, or experiences that, in conjunction with your assumptions, lead you to conclusions. It could come from your experience, word of mouth, research, the media, or other sources. State the information clearly. How could you determine whether the information is *accurate* and *relevant* to the question at issue?

Concepts, Theories, Ideas

All reasoning uses some ideas or concepts and not others. These concepts include the theories, principles, axioms, and rules implicit in our reasoning. Any defect in the concepts or ideas of the reasoning is a possible source of problems in our reasoning.

As an aspiring critical thinker, you begin to focus more deeply on the concepts you use. You begin to assess the extent to which you are clear about those concepts, whether they are relevant to the issue at hand, whether your principles are inappropriately slanted by your point of view. You begin to direct your attention to how you use concepts, what concepts are most important, how concepts are intertwined in networks.

As a student interested in developing your mind, you begin to ask questions that improve your ability to focus on the importance of concepts in your classes. These questions may include: What is the most fundamental concept I need to learn in this class to help me in my life? How does this concept connect with other key concepts in the course? What are the most important theories in this class? Am I clear about the important concepts in the class? What questions do I need to ask to get clear about the concepts the teacher is explaining?

Think for Yourself 5.17

BRINGING INTELLECTUAL STANDARDS TO BEAR UPON THE CONCEPTS YOU USE

Continue with the problem you have been working on. Now state the most important concepts you are using to guide your reasoning. For example, if you are concerned with how you can keep in physical shape while also dedicating enough time to classes, work, and your boyfriend or girlfriend, your key concepts might be physical fitness, quality learning, and a good relationship. (You usually can find the key concepts you are using in your reasoning by looking at your question and purpose.) Elaborate on each of these concepts so you understand exactly how you are using them. State your concepts *clearly* and *precisely.*

Assumptions

All reasoning must begin somewhere. It must take some things for granted. Any defect in the assumptions or presuppositions with which reasoning begins is a possible source of problems in the reasoning.

Assessing skills of reasoning involves assessing our ability to recognize and articulate assumptions, again according to relevant standards. Our assumptions may be clear or unclear, justifiable or unjustifiable, consistent or contradictory.

As a student interested in developing your mind, you begin to ask questions that improve your ability to utilize important assumptions in your classes. These questions could include: What is taken for granted in this academic discipline (or in this lecture, or this discussion, or this article, or this experiment)? Are these assumptions justifiable, or should I question them? What does the author of this textbook assume in Chapter 2? Are these assumptions justified, or should they be questioned?

Think for Yourself 5.18

BRINGING INTELLECTUAL STANDARDS TO BEAR UPON YOUR ASSUMPTIONS

Continue with the problem you have been working on. Now state the most important assumptions you are making in your reasoning. What are you taking for granted that might be questioned? Using the previous example of how to keep in physical shape while also dedicating enough time to learning and your key relationship, your main assumptions might be:

1. Intellectual work is/is not more important than a relationship.
2. I know enough about fitness to do appropriate exercises.
3. I must spend some time working at a part-time job while in college (rather than getting a student loan).
4. I have enough time to do all of the above well.

State your assumptions *clearly* and *precisely*. Make sure they are *justifiable* in the context of the issue.

Implications and Consequences

Whenever we reason, implications follow from our reasoning. When we make decisions, consequences result from those decisions. As critical thinkers, we want to understand implications whenever and wherever they occur. We want to be able to trace logical consequences. We want to see what our actions are leading to. We want to anticipate possible problems before they arise.

No matter where we stop tracing implications, there always will be further implications. No matter what consequences we do see, there always will be other and further consequences. Any defect in our ability to follow the implications or consequences of our reasoning is a potential source of problems in our thinking. Our ability to reason well, then, is measured in part by our ability to understand and enunciate the implications and consequences of reasoning.

As a student interested in developing your mind, you begin to ask yourself questions that improve your ability to focus on the important implications in your thinking as a student. These questions could include, for example: What are the most significant implications of this biological theory, this phenomenon, this economic policy? What are the implications of this political practice? What are the implications of failing to act in this context? If we adopt this course of action, what are the likely consequences? What are the most significant implications of our tendency to solve this social problem in this way rather than that way? What were the implications (social, political, economic, cultural) of the United States' involvement in World War I?

5.19 *Think for Yourself*

THINKING THROUGH THE IMPLICATIONS OF YOUR REASONING

Continue with the problem you have been working on. Now state the most important implication of potential decisions you might make. Fill in these blanks: If I decide to do ____________, then ____________ is likely to follow. If I decide to act differently by doing ____________, then ____________ is likely to follow.

In this activity, you are emphasizing the *logical* implications and potential consequences of each potential decision. Make sure you emphasize important implications of each decision. For further practice, what would be the most likely implications of (1) getting married, (2) not going to college, (3) staying in your hometown for the whole of your life, (4) doing drugs for the fun of it?

Inferences

All reasoning proceeds by steps in which we reason as follows: "Because this is so, that also is so (or is probably so)" or, "Because this, therefore that." The mind perceives a situation or a set of facts and comes to a conclusion based on those facts. When this step of the mind occurs, an inference is made. Any defect in our ability to make logical inferences is a possible problem in our reasoning. For example, if you see a person sitting on the street corner wearing tattered clothing, a worn bed roll beside him and a bottle wrapped in a brown paper bag in his hand, you might infer that he is a bum. This inference is based on the facts you perceive in the situation and of what you assume about them. The inference, however, may or may not be logical in this situation.

Critical thinkers want to become adept at making sound inferences. First, you want to learn to identify when you or someone else has made an inference. What are the key inferences made in this article? Upon what are the inferences based? Are they justified? What is the key inference (or conclusion) I made in this paper? Was it justified? What is the key inference in this theory, in this way of proceeding, in solving this problem in this way? Is this inference logical? Is this conclusion significant? Is this interpretation justified? These are the kinds of questions you begin to ask.

As a student interested in developing your mind, you should ask questions that improve your ability to spot important inferences wherever they occur. Given the facts of this case, is there more than one logical inference (conclusion, interpretation) one could come to? What are some other logical conclusions that should be considered? From this point on, develop an inference detector, the skill of recognizing the inferences you are making in order to analyze them.

Think for Yourself 5.20

BRINGING INTELLECTUAL STANDARDS TO BEAR UPON YOUR INFERENCES

Continue with the problem you have been working on. Now state the inferences, or conclusions, you might come to (about the information you have) in solving your problem. You may have already stated these in Think for Yourself 5.19. Once you have thought through the potential conclusions you might come to in reasoning through the question at issue, state a possible final conclusion. Be clear and precise in stating each potential conclusion. Make sure your inferences make good sense, based on the information and concepts you are using.

USING INTELLECTUAL STANDARDS TO ASSESS YOUR THINKING: BRIEF GUIDELINES

As we have emphasized, all reasoning involves eight elements, each of which has a range of possible mistakes. Here we summarize some of the main "checkpoints" you should use in reasoning.

1. All reasoning has a *purpose.*
   - Take time to state your purpose *clearly.*
   - Choose *significant* and *realistic* purposes.
   - Distinguish your purpose from related purposes.
   - Make sure your purpose is *fair* in context (that it doesn't involve violating the rights of others).
   - Check periodically to be sure you are still focused on your purpose and haven't wandered from your target.
2. All reasoning is an attempt to figure out something, to settle some *question,* solve some problem.
   - Take time to *clearly* and *precisely* state the question at issue.
   - Express the question in several ways to *clarify* its meaning and scope.
   - Break the question into sub-questions (when you can).
   - Identify the type of question you are dealing with (historical, economic, biological, etc.) and whether the question has one right answer, is a matter of mere opinion, or requires reasoning from more than one point of view.
   - Think through the complexities of the question (think *deeply* through the question).
3. All reasoning is based on *assumptions.*
   - *Clearly* identify your assumptions and determine whether they are *justifiable.*
   - Consider how your assumptions are shaping your point of view.
4. All reasoning is done from some *point of view.*
   - *Clearly* identify your point of view.
   - Seek other *relevant* points of view and identify their strengths as well as weaknesses.
   - Strive to be fair-minded in evaluating all points of view.

5. All reasoning is based on data, *information,* and evidence.
   - Restrict your claims to those supported by the data you have.
   - Search for information that opposes your position as well as information that supports it.
   - Make sure that all information used is *clear, accurate,* and *relevant* to the question at issue.
   - Make sure you have gathered *sufficient* information.
   - Make sure, especially, that you have considered all *significant* information relevant to the issue.
6. All reasoning is expressed through, and shaped by, *concepts* and ideas.
   - *Clearly* identify key concepts.
   - Consider alternative concepts or alternative definitions for concepts.
   - Make sure you are using concepts with care and *precision.*
   - Use concepts *justifiably* (not distorting their established meanings).
7. All reasoning contains *inferences* or interpretations by which we draw conclusions and give meaning to data.
   - Infer only what the evidence implies.
   - Check inferences for their *consistency* with each other.
   - Identify assumptions that lead you to your inferences.
   - Make sure your inferences *logically* follow from the information.
8. All reasoning leads somewhere or has *implications* and consequences.
   - Trace the *logical* implications and consequences that follow from your reasoning.
   - Search for negative as well as positive implications.
   - Consider all possible significant consequences.

Think for Yourself 5.21

CHECKPOINTS IN THINKING

For all of the eight categories outlined, transform each checkpoint into a question or a set of questions; figure out one or more questions that the checkpoint implies. When you have completed your list and you are actively using the questions you formulated, you will have powerful tools for thinking.

Under the first category, *All reasoning has a purpose,* for example, the first checkpoint is, "Take time to state your purpose *clearly.*" Two questions implied by this checkpoint are: "What exactly is my purpose?" and "Am I clear about my purpose?"

FIGURE 5.3 *This chart focuses on* purpose in thinking. *It is useful in understanding the intellectual standards to be applied to purpose and in differentiating between the use of purpose in thinking by skilled and unskilled reasoners.*

PURPOSE

(All reasoning has a purpose.)

Primary standards: (1) clarity, (2) significance, (3) achievability, (4) consistency, (5) justifiability

Common problems: (1) unclear, (2) trivial, (3) unrealistic, (4) contradictory, (5) unfair

Principle: To reason well, you must clearly understand your purpose, and your purpose must be fair-minded.

SKILLED REASONERS	UNSKILLED REASONERS	CRITICAL REFLECTIONS
take the time to state their purpose clearly.	are often unclear about their central purpose.	Have I made the purpose of my reasoning clear? What exactly am I trying to achieve? Have I stated the purpose in several ways to clarify it?
distinguish it from related purposes.	oscillate between different, sometimes contradictory, purposes.	What different purposes do I have in mind? How do I see them as related? Am I going off in somewhat different directions? How can I reconcile these contradictory purposes?
periodically remind themselves of their purpose to determine whether they are straying from it.	lose track of their fundamental object or goal.	In writing this proposal, do I seem to be wandering from my purpose? How do my third and fourth paragraphs relate to my central goal?
adopt realistic purposes and goals.	adopt unrealistic purposes and set unrealistic goals.	Am I trying to accomplish too much in this project?
choose significant purposes and goals.	adopt trivial purposes and goals as if they were significant.	What is the significance of pursuing this particular purpose? Is there a more significant purpose I should be focused on?
choose goals and purposes that are consistent with other goals and purposes they have chosen.	inadvertently negate their own purposes. do not monitor their thinking for inconsistent goals.	Does one part of my proposal seem to undermine what I am trying to accomplish in another part?
adjust their thinking regularly to their purpose.	do not adjust their thinking regularly to their purpose.	Does my argument stick to the issue? Am I acting consistently within my purpose?
choose purposes that are fair-minded, considering the desires and rights of others equally with their own desires and rights.	choose purposes that are self-serving at the expense of others' needs and desires.	Is my purpose self-serving or concerned only with my own desires? Does it take into account the rights and needs of other people?

FIGURE 5.4 *This chart focuses on* question in thinking. *It is useful in understanding the intellectual standards to be applied to questions and in differentiating between the use of questions in thinking by skilled and unskilled reasoners.*

QUESTION AT ISSUE OR CENTRAL PROBLEM
(All reasoning is an attempt to figure something out, to settle some question, solve some problem.)

Primary standards: (1) clarity and precision, (2) significance, (3) answerability, (4) relevance

Common problems: (1) unclear and unprecise, (2) insignificant, (3) not answerable, (4) irrelevant

Principle: To settle a question, it must be answerable, and you must be clear about it and understand what is needed to adequately answer it.

SKILLED REASONERS	UNSKILLED REASONERS	CRITICAL REFLECTIONS
are clear about the question they are trying to settle.	are often unclear about the question they are asking.	Am I clear about the main question at issue? Am I able to state it precisely?
can re-express a question in a variety of ways.	express questions vaguely and find questions difficult to reformulate for clarity.	Am I able to reformulate my question in several ways to recognize the complexity of it?
can break a question into sub-questions.	are unable to break down the questions they are asking.	Have I broken down the main question into sub-questions? What are the sub-questions embedded in the main question?
routinely distinguish questions of different types.	confuse questions of different types and thus often respond inappropriately to the questions they ask.	Am I confused about the type of question I am asking? For example: Am I confusing a legal question with an ethical one? Am I confusing a question of preference with a question requiring judgment?
distinguish significant from trivial questions.	confuse trivial questions with significant ones.	Am I focusing on trivial questions while other significant questions have to be addressed?
distinguish relevant questions from irrelevant ones.	confuse irrelevant questions with relevant ones.	Are the questions I'm raising in this discussion relevant to the main question at issue?
are sensitive to the assumptions built into the questions they ask.	often ask loaded questions.	Is the way I'm putting the question loaded? Am I taking for granted from the outset the correctness of my own position?
distinguish questions they can answer from questions they can't.	try to answer questions they are not in a position to answer.	Am I in a position to answer this question? What information would I need to have before I could answer the question?

FIGURE 5.5 *This chart focuses on* point of view in thinking. *It is useful in understanding the intellectual standards to be applied to point of view and in differentiating between the use of point of view in thinking by skilled and unskilled reasoners.*

POINT OF VIEW
(All reasoning is done from some point of view.)

Primary standards: (1) flexibility, (2) fairness, (3) clarity, (4) breadth, (5) relevance

Common problems: (1) restricted, (2) biased, (3) unclear, (4) narrow, (5) irrelevant

Principle: To reason well, you must identify those points of view relevant to the issue and enter these viewpoints empathetically.

SKILLED REASONERS	UNSKILLED REASONERS	CRITICAL REFLECTIONS
keep in mind that people have different points of view, especially on controversial issues.	do not credit alternative reasonable viewpoints.	Have I articulated the point of view from which I am approaching this issue? Have I considered opposing points of view regarding this issue?
consistently articulate other points of view and reason from within those points of view to adequately understand other points of view.	cannot see issues from points of view that are significantly different from their own; cannot reason with empathy from alien points of view.	I may have characterized my own point of view, but have I considered the most significant aspects of the problem from the point of view of others?
seek other viewpoints, especially when the issue is one they believe in passionately.	can sometimes give other points of view when the issue is not emotionally charged but cannot do so for issues they feel strongly about.	Am I presenting X's point of view in an unfair manner? Am I having difficulty appreciating X's viewpoint because I am emotional about this issue?
confine their monological reasoning to problems that are clearly monological.*	confuse multilogical with monological issues; insist that there is only one frame of reference within which a given multilogical question must be decided.	Is the question here monological or multilogical? How can I tell? Am I reasoning as if only one point of view is relevant to this issue when in reality other viewpoints are relevant?
recognize when they are most likely to be prejudiced.	are unaware of their own prejudices.	Is this prejudiced or reasoned judgment? If prejudiced, where does it come from?
approach problems and issues with a richness of vision and an appropriately broad point of view.	reason from within inappropriately narrow or superficial points of view.	Is my approach to this question too narrow? Am I considering other viewpoints so I can adequately address the problem?

*Monological problems are ones for which there are definite correct and incorrect answers and definite procedures for getting those answers. In multilogical problems, there are competing schools of thought to be considered. (See the next chapter, on Questions.)

FIGURE 5.6 *This chart focuses on* information in thinking. *It is useful in understanding the intellectual standards to be applied to information and in differentiating between the use of information in thinking by skilled and unskilled reasoners.*

INFORMATION

(All reasoning is based on data, information, evidence, experience, research.)

Primary standards: (1) clear, (2) relevant, (3) fairly gathered and reported, (4) accurate, (5) adequate, (6) consistently applied

Common problems: (1) unclear, (2) irrelevant, (3) biased, (4) inaccurate, (5) insufficient, (6) inconsistently applied

Principle: Reasoning can be only as sound as the information it is based on.

SKILLED REASONERS	UNSKILLED REASONERS	CRITICAL REFLECTIONS
assert a claim only when they have sufficient evidence to back it up.	assert claims without considering all relevant information	Is my assertion supported by evidence?
can articulate and evaluate the information behind their claims.	don't articulate the information they are using in their reasoning and so do not subject it to rational scrutiny.	Do I have evidence to support my claim that I haven't clearly articulated? Have I evaluated for accuracy and relevance the information I am using?
actively search for information *against* (not just *for*) their own position.	gather information only when it supports their own point of view.	Where is a good place to look for evidence on the opposite side? Have I looked there? Have I honestly considered information that doesn't support my position?
focus on relevant information and disregard what is irrelevant to the question at issue.	do not carefully distinguish between relevant information and irrelevant information	Are my data relevant to the claim I'm making? Have I failed to consider relevant information?
draw conclusions only to the extent that they are supported by the data and sound reasoning.	make inferences that go beyond what the data support.	Does my claim go beyond the evidence I've cited?
state their evidence clearly and fairly.	distort the data or state it inaccurately.	Is my presentation of the pertinent information clear and coherent? Have I distorted information to support my position?

FIGURE 5.7 *This chart focuses on* concepts in thinking. *It is useful in understanding the intellectual standards to be applied to concepts and in differentiating between the use of concepts in thinking by skilled and unskilled reasoners.*

CONCEPTS AND IDEAS

(All reasoning is expressed through, and shaped by, concepts and ideas.)

Primary standards: (1) clarity, (2) relevance, (3) depth, (4) accuracy

Common problems: (1) unclear, (2) irrelevant, (3) superficial, (4) inaccurate

Principle: Reasoning can only be as clear, relevant, realistic, and deep as the concepts that shape it.

SKILLED REASONERS	UNSKILLED REASONERS	CRITICAL REFLECTIONS
are aware of the key concepts and ideas they and others use.	are unaware of the key concepts and ideas they and others use.	What is the main concept I am using in my thinking? What are the main concepts others are using?
are able to explain the basic implications of the key words and phrases they use.	cannot accurately explain basic implications of their key words and phrases.	Am I clear about the implications of key concepts? For example: Does the word *cunning* have negative implications that the word *clever* does not?
are able to distinguish special, nonstandard uses of words from standard uses.	are not able to recognize when their use of a word or phrase departs from educated usage.	Where did I get my definition of this central concept? For example: Where did I get my definition of the concept of . . . Have I put my unwarranted conclusions into the definition?
are aware of irrelevant concepts and ideas and use concepts and ideas in ways relevant to their functions.	use concepts in ways inappropriate to the subject or issue.	Am I using the concept of "love" appropriately? For example: Do I unknowingly act as if loving a person implies a right to treat them discourteously?
think deeply about the concepts they use.	fail to think deeply about the concepts they use.	Am I thinking deeply enough about this concept? For example: The concept of health care, as I describe it, does not take into account the patient's rights and privileges. Do I need to consider the idea of health care more deeply?

FIGURE 5.8 *This chart focuses on* assumptions in thinking. *It is useful in understanding the intellectual standards to be applied to assumptions and in differentiating between the use of assumptions in thinking by skilled and unskilled reasoners.*

ASSUMPTIONS

(All reasoning is based on assumptions—beliefs we take for granted.)

Primary standards: (1) clarity, (2) justifiability, (3) consistency

Common problems: (1) unclear, (2) unjustified, (3) contradictory

Principle: Reasoning can be only as sound as the assumptions it is based on.

SKILLED REASONERS	UNSKILLED REASONERS	CRITICAL REFLECTIONS
are clear about the assumptions they are making.	are often unclear about the assumptions they make.	Are my assumptions clear to me? Do I clearly understand what my assumptions are based upon?
make assumptions that are reasonable and justifiable given the situation and evidence.	often make unjustified or unreasonable assumptions.	Do I make assumptions about the future based on just one experience from the past? Can I fully justify what I am taking for granted? Are my assumptions justifiable given the evidence I am using to support them?
make assumptions that are consistent with each other.	often make assumptions that are contradictory.	Do the assumptions I made in the first part of my argument contradict the assumptions I am making now?
constantly seek to figure out what their assumptions are.	ignore their assumptions.	What assumptions am I making in this situation? Are they justifiable? Where did I get these assumptions?

FIGURE 5.9 *This chart focuses on* implications in thinking. *It is useful in understanding the intellectual standards to be applied to implications and in differentiating between how skilled and unskilled reasoners think about implications.*

IMPLICATIONS AND CONSEQUENCES

(All reasoning leads somewhere. It has implications and, when acted upon, has consequences.)

Primary standards: (1) significance, (2) logicalness, (3) clarity, (4) precision, (5) completeness

Common problems: (1) unimportant, (2) unrealistic, (3) unclear, (4) imprecise, (5) incomplete

Principle: To reason well through an issue, you must think through the implications that follow from your reasoning. You must think through the consequences likely to follow from the decisions you make.

SKILLED REASONERS	UNSKILLED REASONERS	CRITICAL REFLECTIONS
trace out a number of significant potential implications and consequences of their reasoning.	trace out few or none of the implications and consequences of holding a position or making a decision.	Did I spell out all the significant consequences of the action I am advocating? If I were to take this course of action, what other consequences might follow that I haven't considered?
clearly and precisely articulate the possible implications and consequences clearly and precisely.	are unclear and imprecise in the possible consequences they articulate.	Have I delineated clearly and precisely the consequences likely to follow from my chosen action?
search for potentially negative as well as potentially positive consequences.	trace out only the consequences they had in mind at the beginning, either positive or negative, but usually not both.	I may have done a good job of spelling out some positive implications of the decision I am about to make, but what are some of the possible negative implications or consequences?
anticipate the likelihood of unexpected negative and positive implications.	are surprised when their decisions have unexpected consequences.	If I make this decision, what are some possible unexpected implications? What are some variables out of my control that might lead to negative consequences?

FIGURE 5.10 *This chart focuses on* inferences in thinking. *It is useful in understanding the intellectual standards to be applied to inferences and indifferentiating between the kinds of inferences made by skilled and unskilled reasoners.*

INFERENCE AND INTERPRETATION

(All reasoning contains inferences from which we draw conclusions and give meaning to data and situations.)

Primary standards: (1) clarity, (2) logicalness, (3) justifiability, (4) profundity, (5) reasonability, (6) consistency

Common problems: (1) unclear, (2) illogical, (3) unjustified, (4) superficial, (5) unreasonable, (6) contradictory

Principle: Reasoning can be only as sound as the inferences it makes (or the conclusions it comes to).

SKILLED REASONERS	UNSKILLED REASONERS	CRITICAL REFLECTIONS
are clear about the inferences they are making clearly articulate their inferences.	are often unclear about the inferences they are making do not clearly articulate their inferences.	Am I clear about the inferences I am making? Have I clearly articulated my conclusions?
usually make inferences that follow from the evidence or reasons presented.	often make inferences that do not follow from the evidence or reasons presented.	Do my conclusions logically follow from the evidence and reasons presented?
often make inferences that are deep rather than superficial.	often make inferences that are superficial.	Are my conclusions superficial, given the problem?
often make inferences or come to conclusions that are reasonable.	often make inferences or come to conclusions that are unreasonable.	Are my conclusions reasonable?
make inferences or come to conclusions that are consistent with each other.	often make inferences or come to conclusions that are contradictory.	Do the conclusions I come to in the first part of my analysis seem to contradict the conclusions that I come to at the end?
understand the assumptions that lead to inferences.	do not seek to figure out the assumptions that lead to inferences.	Is my inference based on a faulty assumption? How would my inference be changed if I were to base it on a different, more justifiable assumption?

Chapter 8c

ASKING QUESTIONS THAT LEAD TO GOOD THINKING

It is not possible to become a good thinker and be a poor questioner. Thinking is not driven by answers but, rather, by questions. Had no questions been asked by those who laid the foundation for a field–for example, physics or biology–the field would not have been developed in the first place. Every intellectual field is born out of a cluster of questions to which answers are either needed or highly desirable. Furthermore, every field stays alive only to the extent that fresh questions are generated and taken seriously as the driving force in thinking. When a field of study is no longer pursuing answers to questions, it becomes extinct. To think through or rethink anything, one must ask questions that stimulate thought.

THE IMPORTANCE OF QUESTIONING

Questions define tasks, express problems, and delineate issues. Answers, on the other hand, often signal a full stop in thought. Only when an answer generates further questions does thought continue its life as such. This is why it is true that only when you have questions are you really thinking and learning. Moreover, the quality of the questions you ask determines the quality of your thinking. When you have no questions, you are not concerned with pursuing any answers.

For example, biologists and biochemists make progress when they ask questions such as, "What are we made of? How do our bodies work? What is life?" They make even more progress when they take their questioning to the subcellular and molecular level. They ask questions about isolated molecules and events on the molecular level: "What are proteins? What are enzymes? What are enzyme reactions? How do molecular events underlie macroscopic phenomena?" (Jevons, 1964). By focusing on these subcellular questions, they can then move to important questions such as, "How do vitamins interact with chemistry in the body to produce healthier functioning? And how do cancer cells differ from normal cells? And what kinds of foods interact with the body's chemistry to lessen the likelihood of the development of cancerous cells?"

The best teachers are usually those who understand the relationship between learning and asking questions. As Jevons (1964) says of his students, "Those who asked questions helped me most, but even those who merely looked puzzled helped a little, by stimulating me to find more effective ways of making myself understood."

Thinking is of no use, then, unless it goes somewhere productive. And the questions we ask determine where our thinking goes. Only when our thinking leads us somewhere important can we learn anything of value to us.

Think for Yourself 6.1

QUESTIONING YOUR QUESTIONS

Answer this question: What are the questions you would most like to answer for yourself? Once you have a short list of three or four, answer these questions: Where are these questions taking you? How is your focus on these questions affecting your behavior, your emotions, your experience, and the quality of your life? For example, too much emphasis on the question, "How can I make the most money?" may lead you to miss the significance of this question, "Am I developing a loving relationship with someone I respect?"

Consider the following ways that questions focusing on the elements of reasoning and intellectual standards force our thinking to a more disciplined level. *Deep* questions drive our thought underneath the surface of things, force us to deal with complexity.

- Questions of *purpose* force us to define our task.

- Questions of *information* force us to look at our sources of information as well as at the quality of our information.
- Questions of *interpretation* force us to examine how we are organizing or giving meaning to information and to consider alternative ways of giving meaning.
- Questions of *assumption* force us to examine what we are taking for granted.
- Questions of *implication* force us to follow where our thinking is leading us.
- Questions of *point of view* force us to examine our point of view and to consider other *relevant* points of view.
- Questions of *relevance* force us to discriminate what does and what does not bear on a question.
- Questions of *accuracy* force us to evaluate and test for truth and correctness.
- Questions of *precision* force us to give details and be specific.
- Questions of *consistency* force us to examine our thinking for contradictions.
- Questions of *logic* force us to consider how we are putting the whole of our thought together, to make sure that it all adds up and makes sense within a reasonable system of some kind.

6.2 *Think for Yourself*

QUESTIONING THE DEPTH OF YOUR QUESTIONS

Write out your answers to these questions: Are any of the questions you are focused on in your life *deep* questions? To what extent are you questioning your *purposes* and goals? Your *assumptions?* The *implications* of your thought and action? Do you ever question your *point of view?* Do you ever wonder whether your point of view is keeping you from seeing things from an opposing perspective? When?

Do you ever question the *consistency* of your thought and behavior? Do you question the *logicalness* of your thinking? What did answering the above questions, and your reflection on them, tell you about yourself and about your habits of questioning?

DEAD QUESTIONS REFLECT INERT MINDS

Most students ask virtually none of the above thought-stimulating types of questions. Most tend to stick to dead questions such as, "Is this going to be on the test?" Questions such as this usually imply the desire not to think.

We must continually remind ourselves that thinking begins within some content only when questions are generated. No questions (asked) equals no understanding (achieved). Superficial questions equal superficial understanding, unclear questions equal unclear understanding. If you sit in class in silence, your mind will probably be silent as well. When this is the case, either you will ask no questions or your questions will tend to be superficial, ill-formed, and self-serving. You should strive for a state of mind in which, even when you are outwardly quiet, you are inwardly asking questions. You should formulate questions that will lead you to productive learning.

If you want to learn deeply and independently, you should always strive to study so that what you do stimulates your thinking with questions that lead to further questions.

Think for Yourself 6.3, 6.4

QUESTIONING WHEN YOU READ

Read a chapter in one of your textbooks for the primary purpose of generating questions. Only when you are asking questions as you read are you reading critically. After reading each section, or every few paragraphs, make a list of all the questions you have about what you are reading. Then see if you can answer these questions—either by looking in the textbook or by raising them in class.

QUESTIONING YOUR QUESTIONING ABILITY

At this point in your intellectual development, to what extent would you call yourself a skilled or deep questioner? That is, how would you rate the overall quality of the questions you are asking (both those that you share with others and those you keep to yourself)? Do you know anyone who you would say is a deep questioner? If so, what makes you think this person questions deeply?

COMING TO TERMS WITH THREE CATEGORIES OF QUESTIONS

Before we go further in our discussion about how to question deeply, we want to introduce a way of categorizing questions that is useful. This way of classifying questions provides a sort of "jumpstart" in figuring out the kind of reasoning a question calls for.

The three categories of questions are:

1. QUESTIONS OF FACT. Questions with one right answer (factual questions fall into this category).

- What is the boiling point of lead?
- What is the size of this room?
- What is the differential of this equation?
- How does the hard drive on a computer operate?

FIGURE 6.1 *In approaching a question, it is useful to figure out what type it is. Is it a question with one definitive answer? Is it a question that calls for a subjective choice? Or does the question require you to consider competing answers?*

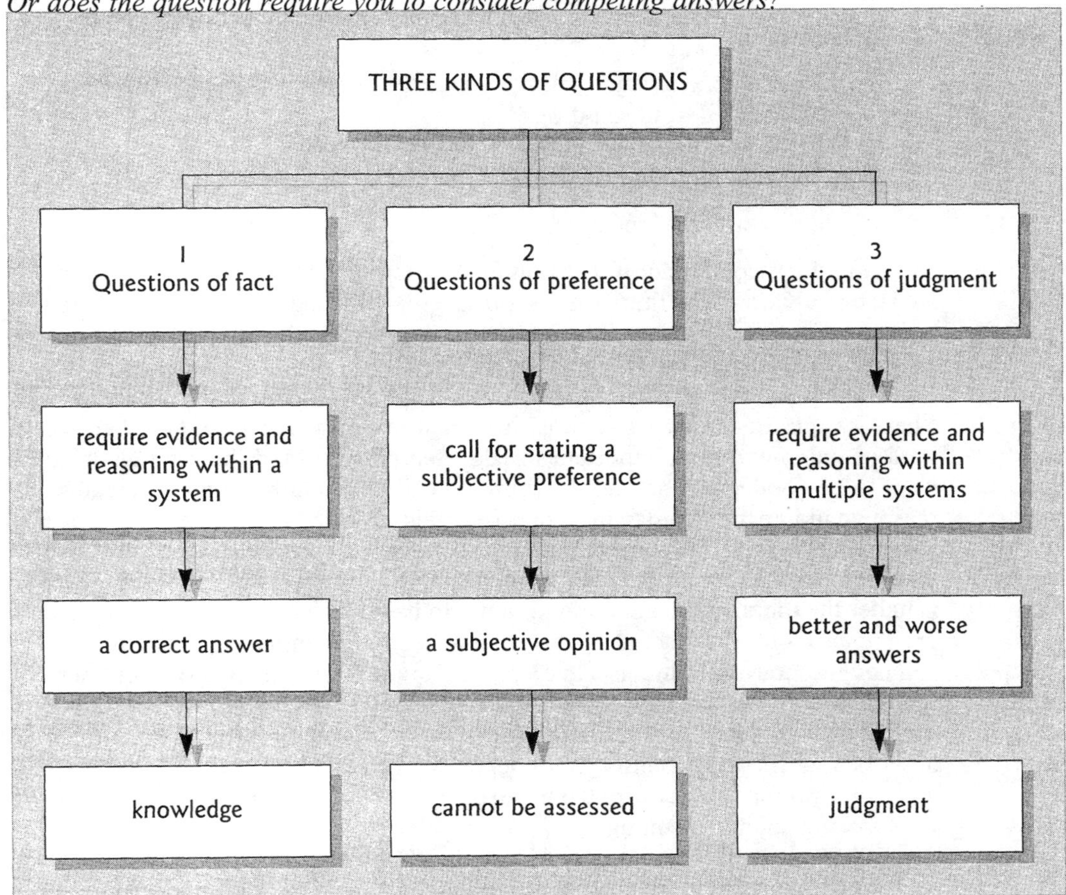

2. QUESTIONS OF PREFERENCE. Questions with as many answers as there are different human preferences (a category in which mere subjective opinion rules). These are questions that ask you to express a preference.

- Which would you prefer, a vacation in the mountains or one at the seashore?
- How do you like to wear your hair?
- Do you like to go to the opera?
- What is your favorite type of food?

3. QUESTIONS OF JUDGMENT. Questions requiring reasoning, but with more than one defensible answer. These are questions that make sense to debate, ques-

tions with better-or-worse answers (well-reasoned or poorly reasoned answers). Here we are seeking the best possible answer given the range of possibilities.

- How can we best address the most basic and significant economic problems of the nation today?
- What can be done to significantly reduce the number of people who become addicted to illegal drugs?
- What is the best thing we can do to save the earth?
- Is abortion morally justifiable?
- Should capital punishment be abolished?

Only the second kind of question (a question of preference) calls for sheer subjective opinion. The third kind is a matter of reasoned judgment. We should rationally evaluate answers to the question using universal intellectual standards such as clarity, depth, consistency, and so forth.

Some people think of all judgments as either fact or subjective preference. They ask questions that elicit either a factual response or an opinion. Yet, the kind of judgment most important to educated people—and the kind we most want to be good at—falls into the third, now almost totally ignored, category: reasoned judgment. A judge in a court of law is expected to engage in reasoned judgment. The judge is expected not only to render a judgment but also to base that judgment on sound, relevant evidence and valid legal reasoning. A judge is under the moral and legal obligation not to base her judgments on subjective preferences, on her personal opinions, as such. Judgment based on sound reasoning goes beyond, and is never to be equated with, fact alone or mere opinion alone. Facts are typically used in reasoning, but good reasoning does more than state facts. Furthermore, a position that is well-reasoned is not to be described as simply "opinion." Of course, we sometimes call the judge's verdict an "opinion," but we not only expect, we *demand* that it be based on relevant and sound reasoning.

When questions that require reasoned judgment are treated as matters of preference, counterfeit critical thinking occurs. Some people, then, come to uncritically assume that everyone's "subjective opinion" is of equal value. Their capacity to appreciate the importance of intellectual standards diminishes, and we can expect to hear questions such as these: "What if I don't like these standards? Why shouldn't I use my own standards? Don't I have a right to my own opinion? What if I'm just an emotional person? What if I like to follow my intuition? What if I think spirituality is more important than reason? What if I don't believe in being 'rational?'" When people reject questions that call for reasoned judgment and deep thought, they fail to see the difference between offering legitimate reasons and evidence in support of a view and simply asserting the view as true.

Intellectually responsible persons, in contrast, recognize questions of judgment for what they are: questions that require the consideration of alternative ways of reasoning. Put another way, intellectually responsible persons recognize when a question calls for good reasoning, and they behave in accordance with that responsibility. This means that they realize when there is more than one reasonable way to answer a question. Moreover, they appreciate the responsibility they have to consider alternative ways of looking at the problem, of entering *in good faith* viewpoints that oppose their own before coming to final judgments.

To summarize, we all need to recognize that questions call on us to do one of three things:

1. to express a subjective preference,
2. to establish an objective fact (within a well-defined system), or
3. to come up with the best of competing answers (generated by competing systems).

We do not fully understand the task we are faced with until we know which of these three is called for in our thinking. Is the question calling for a subjective or personal choice? If so, let's make that choice in terms of our personal preferences. If not, then is there a way to come up with one correct answer to this question (a definite system in which to find the answer)? Or, finally, are we dealing with a question that could reasonably be answered differently within different points of view? In other words, is it debatable? If the latter, what is the best answer to the question, all things considered?

6.5 *Think for Yourself*

DISTINGUISHING TYPES OF QUESTIONS I

Make a random list of clear and precise questions. Then decide which questions are a matter of fact (with definite right or wrong answers), which questions are matters of subjective preference, and which questions require reasoning and judgment (within multiple perspectives). To make these determinations, you might think through each question in the following way:

1. Ask, "Are there any facts that a reasonable person would have to consider to answer this question?" (If there are some facts you need to consider, the question is not purely a matter of subjective preference.)
2. If there are facts relevant to the question, would all reasonable persons interpret those facts in the same way? If so, it is a question of fact. If not, then presumably the facts can be rationally interpreted differently from different competing reasonable perspectives. It is therefore a question of judgment.

As you study a subject, distinguish among the three types of questions. Look for the questions that have definitive or correct answers. These will be matters settled by definition or fixed, established, and recognized procedures. Identify those questions that are ultimately a matter of personal choice. And, most important, identify those questions that can be legitimately, or at least arguably, approached from more than one point of view. These latter will arise most commonly when there are competing traditions or schools or theories within the discipline. For example, in psychology there are many competing schools: Freudian, Jungian, Adlerian, rational-emotive, gestalt, and so on. Many issues in psychology will be reasoned through differently depending on the academic allegiance of the reasoner. These issues will call for considering argumentation from a variety of perspectives and will result in different reasoned judgments.

Think for Yourself 6.6

DISTINGUISHING TYPES OF QUESTIONS 2

Identify at least one subject you have studied in school that involves competing traditions or schools of thought. Then identify some questions that would be answered differently depending on the school of thought used to think through the question. Which of the schools of thought do you best understand or identify most with? How might this school of thought be questioned from the perspective of another competing school of thought?

BECOMING A SOCRATIC QUESTIONER

Now that you are beginning to understand how to categorize questions, let us discuss how we can approach questions in general, so our questions will lead us to better thinking.

As critical thinkers, we want to go beyond questions that are undisciplined, questions that go in multiple directions with neither rhyme nor reason. Therefore, we turn from merely questioning to what might be termed "Socratic questioning." What the word "Socratic" adds to ordinary questioning is *systematicity,* depth, and a keen interest in assessing the truth or plausibility of things.

One of the primary goals of critical thinking is to establish a disciplined, "executive" component of thinking in our thinking, a powerful inner voice of reason, to monitor, assess, and repair—in a more rational direction—our thinking, feelings, and action. Socratic questioning provides that inner voice. Here are some of the fundamentals of Socratic questioning, followed by examples of questions you might ask in Socratic dialogue to begin to deeply probe the thinking of another person.

- Seek to understand—when possible—the ultimate foundations for what is said or believed, and follow the implications of those foundations through further questions. (You might ask, for example, "On what do you base your beliefs? Could you explain your reasoning to me in more detail so I can more fully understand your position?")
- Recognize that any thought can exist fully only in a network of connected thoughts. Therefore, treat all assertions as a connecting point to further

FIGURE 6.2 *Socratic thinking is an integrated, disciplined approach to thinking.*

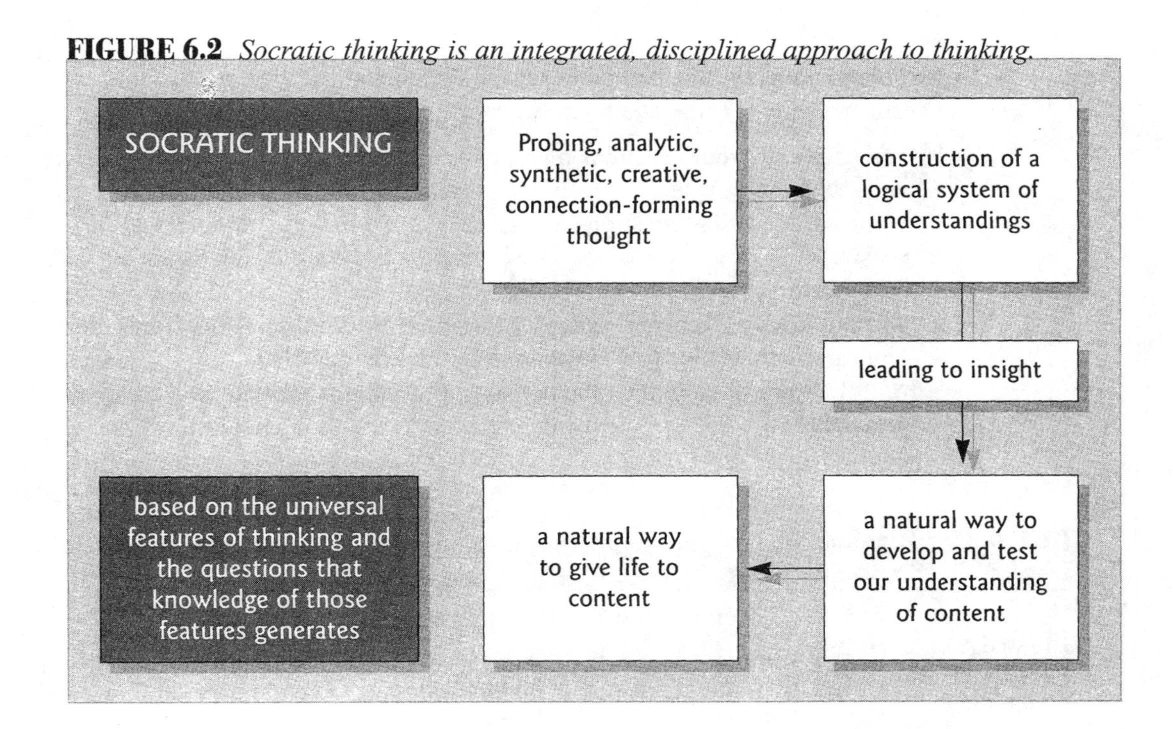

thoughts. Pursue those connections. (You might ask, for example, "If what you say is true, wouldn't x or y also be so?")

- Treat all thoughts as in need of development. (You might ask: "Could you elaborate on what you are saying so I can better understand you?")
- Recognize that all questions presuppose prior questions and all thinking presupposes prior thinking. When raising questions, be open to the questions they presuppose. (You might ask, for example, "To answer this complex question, what other questions do we need to answer?")

6.7 *Think for Yourself*

PRACTICING SOCRATIC QUESTIONING

When you become a Socratic questioner, a systematic questioner, you can question anyone about anything—effectively! Try out your questioning skills by questioning someone you know as systematically and as deeply as you can about something he or she deeply believes. Tape-record the discussion. Follow the suggestions given here. When finished, replay the tape and analyze your Socratic questioning abilities. Did you probe beneath the surface of the other person's thinking? Did you ask for elaboration when needed? Did you pursue connections? Overall, how you would rate yourself as a Socratic questioner?

To take your thinking to the level of disciplined questioning, to think or question Socratically, you can go in several directions:

1. You can focus your questions on types of questions (fact, preference, or judgment).
2. You can focus your questions on assessment, by targeting intellectual standards.
3. You can focus your questions on analysis, by targeting the elements of reasoning.
4. You can learn to "unpack" complex questions by developing questions one would have to answer prior to answering the lead question.
5. You can learn to determine the domains of questions inherent in a complex question.

FIGURE 6.3 *Here are four ways to generate questions that lead to disciplined thinking.*

Use your knowledge of structure of thought and logic of systems →	to focus on questions based on the elements of thought: Purpose, Question at issue, Concepts, Assumptions, Information, Interpretations, Implications, Point of view
Use your knowledge of systems →	to focus on three types of questions: ■ Questions with one right answer ■ Questions that are a matter of subjective preference ■ Questions requiring reasoned judgment
Use your knowledge of standards →	to focus on questions based on standards: Clarity, Accuracy, Precision, Relevance, Depth, Breadth, Logicalness, Fairness
Use your knowledge of disciplines and domains →	to focus on questions specific to a discipline or domain: Scientific questions, Mathematical questions, and so on, Historical questions, Literary questions

In the following discussion, we will elaborate these forms of Socratic questioning. Of course, the questions you would ask in a given situation will be determined by the context within which you are thinking. When you become skilled at using these questions, you will begin to see the powerful role they can play in your thinking. And, with practice, they eventually will become intuitive to you. You will begin to naturally ask questions of *clarification* when you are unclear. You will begin to naturally ask questions focused on *information* when the data seem to be inaccurate or otherwise questionable. You will intuitively recognize when people are mistakenly answering questions of judgment with their subjective preference, and so on. Again, intuitive ability comes only after a lot of practice.

Focus Your Thinking on the Type of Question Being Asked

As discussed earlier in this chapter, when you approach questions systematically, you are able to recognize that all thought has three possible functions: to express a subjective preference, to establish an objective fact (within a well-defined system), or to come up with the best of competing answers (generated by competing systems). Assume that you do not fully understand thinking until you know which type of thinking the question is focused on.

Questions you can ask that focus on getting at the type of question you are dealing with are:

- Is the question calling for a subjective or personal choice? If so, let's make that choice in terms of our personal preferences.
- If not, is this a question that has one correct answer, or a definite system in which to find the answer?
- Or are we dealing with a question that would be answered differently within different points of view?
- If the latter, what is the best answer to the question, all things considered?
- Is this person treating a question of judgment as a question of preference by saying he doesn't have to give reasoning for his answer when the question implies that he does?
- Is this person treating a question of judgment as a question for which there is one right answer?

Focus Your Questions on Universal Intellectual Standards for Thought

When you approach questions systematically, you recognize when people are failing to use the universal intellectual standards in their thinking. You also recognize when you are failing to use these standards in your thinking. And you ask questions, specifically targeting the intellectual standards, that upgrade thinking.

From discussions in previous chapters, the guidelines are:

1. Recognize that thinking is always more or less *clear.* Assume that you do not fully understand a thought except to the extent you can elaborate, illustrate, and exemplify it. Questions that focus on *clarity* in thinking are:
    - Could you elaborate on what you are saying?
    - Could you give me an example or illustration of your point?
    - I hear you saying "x." Am I hearing you correctly, or have I misunderstood you?
2. Recognize that thinking is always more or less *precise.* Assume that you do not fully understand it except to the extent that you can specify it in detail. Questions that focus on *precision* in thinking are:
    - Could you give me more details about that?
    - Could you be more specific?
    - Could you specify your allegations more fully?
3. Recognize that thinking is always more or less *accurate.* Assume that you have not fully assessed it except to the extent that you have checked to determine whether it represents things as they really are. Questions that focus on *accuracy* in thinking are:
    - How could we check that to see if it is true?
    - How could we verify these alleged facts?
    - Can we trust the accuracy of these data given the questionable source from which they come?
4. Recognize that thinking is always capable of straying from the task, question, problem, or issue under consideration. Assume that you have not fully assessed thinking except to the extent that you have ensured that all considerations used in addressing it are genuinely *relevant* to it. Questions that focus on *relevance* in thinking are:
    - I don't see how what you said bears on the question. Could you show me how it is relevant?
    - Could you explain what you think the connection is between your question and the question we have focused on?
5. Recognize that thinking can either function at the surface of things or probe beneath that surface to deeper matters and issues. Assume that you have not fully assessed a line of thinking except to the extent that you have determined the *depth* required for the task at hand (and compared that with the depth that actually has been achieved). (To figure out whether a question is deep, we need to determine whether it involves complexities that must be considered.) Questions that focus on *depth* in thinking are:
    - Is this question simple or complex? Is it easy or difficult to answer?
    - What makes this a complex question?
    - How are we dealing with the complexities inherent in the question?

6. Recognize that thinking can be more or less broad-minded (or narrow-minded) and that *breadth* of thinking requires the thinker to think insightfully within *more than one point of view or frame of reference.* Assume that you have not fully assessed a line of thinking except to the extent that you have determined how much *breadth* of thinking is required (and how much has in fact been exercised). Questions that focus on *breadth* in thinking are:
   - What points of view are relevant to this issue?
   - What relevant points of view have I ignored thus far?
   - Am I failing to consider this issue from an opposing viewpoint because I don't want to change my view?
   - Have I entered the opposing views in good faith, or only enough to find flaws in them?
   - I have looked at the question from an economic point of view. What is the moral point of view?
   - I have considered a liberal position on the issue. What would conservatives say?

6.8 *Think for Yourself*

FOCUSING YOUR QUESTIONS ON INTELLECTUAL STANDARDS

For each of the categories of questions focusing on intellectual standards (see the previous section), try to come up with one situation in which your failure to use intellectual standards had negative consequences. This might be a situation in which you should have asked a question of clarification and didn't, or should have asked a question focusing on precision and didn't, and so on. State what happened as a result of each failure. For example, you might recall a time when you asked for directions to someone's house but got lost because you failed to ask questions focused on important details.

Focus Your Questions on the Elements of Thought

Another powerful way to discipline your questions is to focus on the elements or parts of thinking. As you formulate your questions, recall the following guidelines:

1. All thought reflects an agenda or *purpose.* Assume that you do not fully understand someone's thought (including your own) until you understand the agenda behind it. Questions that focus on purpose in thinking include:
   - What are you trying to accomplish in saying this?
   - What is your central aim in this line of thought?
   - What is the purpose of this meeting?
   - What is the purpose of this chapter?

- What is the purpose of our relationship?
- What is my purpose for being in college?

2. All thoughts presuppose an *information* base. Assume that you do not fully understand the thought until you understand the background information (facts, data, experiences) that supports or informs it. Questions that focus on information in thinking include:
   - On what information are you basing that comment?
   - What experience convinced you of this? Could your experience be distorted?
   - How do we know this information is *accurate?*
   - Have we left out any important information that we need to consider?
3. All thought requires the making of *inferences,* the drawing of conclusions, the creation of meaning. Assume that you do not fully understand a thought until you understand the inferences that have shaped it. Questions that focus on inferences in thinking include:
   - How did you reach that conclusion?
   - Could you explain your reasoning?
   - Is there an alternative plausible conclusion?
   - Given all the facts what is the best possible conclusion?
4. All thought involves the application of *concepts.* Assume that you do not fully understand a thought until you understand the concepts that define and shape it. Questions that focus on concepts in thinking include:
   - What is the main idea you are using in your reasoning?
   - Could you explain that idea?
   - Are we using our concepts justifiably?
5. All thought rests upon other thoughts, which are taken for granted or *assumed.* Assume that you do not fully understand a thought until you understand what it takes for granted. Questions that focus on assumptions in thinking include:
   - What exactly are you taking for granted here?
   - Why are you assuming that?
   - Should I question the assumptions I am using about my roommate, my friends, my intimate other, my parents, my instructors, my country?
6. All thought is headed in a direction. It not only rests upon something (assumptions), but it is also going somewhere (*implications* and consequences). Assume that you do not fully understand a thought unless you know the implications and consequences that follow from it. Questions that focus on implications in thinking include:
   - What are you implying when you say that?
   - What is likely to happen if we do this versus that?
   - Are you implying that . . . ?

7. All thought takes place within a *point of view* or frame of reference. Assume that you do not fully understand a thought until you understand the point of view or frame of reference that places it on an intellectual map. Questions that focus on point of view in thinking include:
   - From what point of view are you looking at this?
   - Is there another point of view we should consider?
   - Which of these possible viewpoints makes the most sense given the situation?
8. All thought is responsive to a *question*. Assume that you do not fully understand the thought until you understand the question that gives rise to it. Questions that focus on question in thinking include:
   - I am not sure exactly what question you are raising. Could you explain it?
   - Is this question the best one to focus on at this point, or is there a more pressing question we need to address?
   - The question in my mind is this: How do you see the question?
   - How is your question related to the question we have been reasoning through?

6.9 *Think for Yourself*

FOCUSING YOUR QUESTIONS ON THE ELEMENTS OF REASONING

From each of the eight categories we just outlined, ask yourself at least one question about your view of marriage (or family). For example, you might begin with the question, "In my view, what is the basic purpose or goal of marriage?" (Answer each question after you ask it.)

Afterward, question a friend about his or her views, using the same questions (you should feel free to ask additional questions as they occur to you). Write out an analysis of your questioning process. Do you notice yourself beginning to think at a deeper level—given the questions you are now asking? Did you focus on all eight elements?

Focus Your Questions on Prior Questions

Whenever we are dealing with complex questions, another tool that is useful in disciplining our thinking is to construct prior questions—questions we need to answer before we can answer a more complex question.

Hence, to answer the question "What is multiculturalism?" we should be able to first settle the question, "What is culture?" And to settle that question, we should be able to settle the question, "What are the factors about a person that determine what culture he or she belongs to?" When you learn to formulate and pursue prior questions, you have another important "idea" that you can use to develop your ability to learn in any context.

To construct a list of prior questions, simply write down the main question upon which you are going to focus your discussion, and then formulate as many questions as you can think of that you would have to answer before you could answer the first. Then take this list and determine what question you would have to answer to answer these questions. Continue, following the same procedure for every new set of questions on your list.

As you proceed to construct your list, keep your attention focused on the first question on the list as well as on the last. If you do this well, you should end up with a list of questions that probe the logic of the first question.

As an example of how to construct logically prior questions, consider this list of questions we would need to answer to address the larger question, "What is history?"

- What do historians write about?
- What is "the past"?
- Is it possible to include all of the past in a history book?
- How many of the events during a given time period are left out in a history of that time period?
- Is more left out than is included?
- How does a historian know what to emphasize?
- Do historians make value judgments in deciding what to include and what to leave out?
- Is it possible to simply list facts in a history book, or does all history writing involve interpretations as well as facts?
- Is it possible to decide what to include and exclude and how to interpret facts without adopting a historical point of view?
- How can we begin to judge a historical interpretation?
- How can we begin to judge a historical point of view?

Think for Yourself 6.10

CONSTRUCTING A LIST OF PRIOR QUESTIONS

Formulate a complex question to which you would like to find an answer. Then use the procedure of constructing prior questions until you have a list of at least 10 questions. Afterward, see if you have gained insight into how the first question has to be thought-through in light of the prior questions you formulated.

When you have practiced formulating prior questions to complex questions, you will begin to develop a Socratic questioning tool that you can use whenever you need to answer a complicated question. You will notice your mind coming up with questions that are inherent in other questions. You are unpacking questions to better answer them. You should also then begin to recognize when others are failing to consider the complexities in a question.

Focus Your Questions on Domains of Thinking

When you are addressing a complex question that covers more than one domain of thought, you can target your prior questions by figuring out the domains of thinking inherent in the question. Does the complex question, for example, include an economic dimension? Does it include a biological, sociological, cultural, political, ethical, psychological, religious, historical, or some other dimensions? For each dimension of thinking inherent in the question, you can formulate questions that force you to consider complexities you otherwise may miss. Consider the following question, some of the domains imbedded in the question, and some of the questions imbedded in those domains.

FIGURE 6.4 *Complex questions have multiple domains. This figure shows just a few domains that might be imbedded in a complex question.*

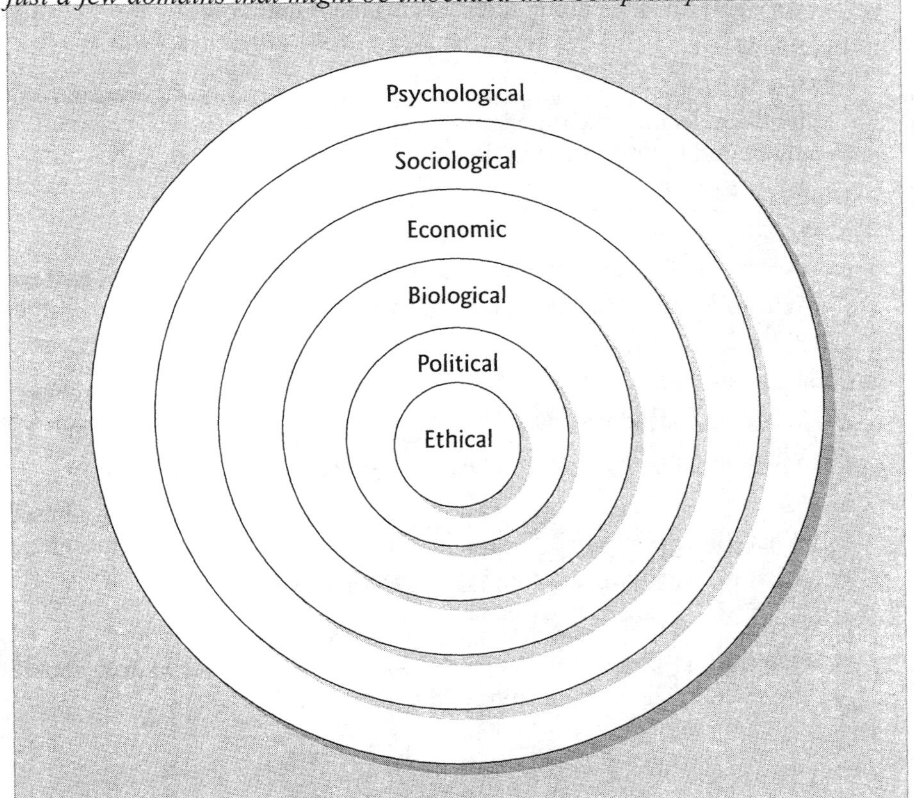

Complex question: What can be done about the number of people who abuse illegal drugs?

Domains inherent in the question, along with some questions we would have to address within each domain before we could answer our complex question are:

1. Economic
   - What economic forces support drug use?
   - What can be done to minimize the influence of money involved in drug sales?
2. Political
   - What possible solutions to drug abuse are politically unacceptable?
   - Are there any realistic solutions that the power structure would accept?
   - To what extent does the political structure exacerbate the problem?
3. Social/Sociological
   - What social structures and practices support drug abuse?
   - How does gang membership contribute to drug abuse?
   - How does membership within any group contribute to the problem or, conversely, insulate group members from abusing drugs?
4. Psychological
   - How do factors such as stress, individual personality differences, and childhood traumas support drug abuse?
   - What role, if any, does human irrationality play in drug abuse?
5. Biological
   - How do genetics play a role in drug abuse?
   - What biological changes in the body resulting from drug abuse contribute to the problem?
6. Educational
   - What can educational institutions do to reduce the incidence of drug abuse?
   - What role are they now playing to support or diminish the problem?
7. Religious
   - What can religious institutions do to reduce the incidence of drug abuse?
   - What role are they now playing in regard to the problem?
8. Cultural
   - What cultural beliefs support the drug-abuse problem?
   - What can we learn from cultures that have a low incidence of drug abuse?

6.11 *Think for Yourself*

FORMULATING QUESTIONS WITHIN DOMAINS OF THINKING

Focus on the question: What can be done to significantly improve the health of the ecosystems on Earth? Using the model above, figure out as many domains within the question that you would have to think within to address the complexities in the question. Then formulate as many questions as you can within each domain. (The question you are originally addressing determines the domains within which you need to think.)

When we can approach questions to target the domains inherent in them, we are able to ask questions such as:

- What are the domains of questions inherent in this complex question?
- Is this person dealing with all the relevant domains within the question?
- Am I leaving out some important domains when reasoning through this issue?

CONCLUSION

Questions play an important role in the mind of a critical thinker. The three types of questions are questions of fact, questions of preference, and questions of judgment. A critical thinker is able to distinguish these forms of questions so as to determine the kind of thinking the question calls for. The ability to ask questions in and of itself is not enough for high-quality thinking to follow, though. Socratic or systematic questioning is a means to disciplined thinking. One method of approaching Socratic questioning is by developing prior questions.

Because there is a sense in which "you think only as well as the questions you ask," you want to force yourself as a developing thinker to focus on the role that questions are playing in your thinking. To what extent are you asking significant questions? To what extent are you able to figure out whether a question is asking for a factual answer, preference, or reasoned judgment? To what extent are you asking questions that follow a disciplined path, leading to rationally defensible answers? To what extent are you able to take apart complex questions, to figure out questions you would have to answer prior to answering those questions? When you are practicing the fundamental questioning steps we have explored in this chapter, you will find yourself progressing as a questioner—and as a thinker.

Chapter 9

Critical Thinking

Chapter 9a

Introduction

Thinking Critically

The alarm clock goes off. Tanya, a first-year student at Cromwell College, is immediately confronted with the need to make a decision. Possibilities abound: Should she turn off the alarm and go back to sleep, missing her 8:00 A.M. class? Should she let the alarm buzz for awhile, thereby ensuring that she is fully awake but perhaps, in the meantime, awakening her roommate who was up late studying and who has no reason to rise for another hour? Should she vent her frustration at her continual lack of sleep by hurling the clock against the wall? Should she turn the alarm off immediately and, by sheer strength of will, bound out of bed?

This is just the first of many decision-making moments Tanya will face in her day. Indeed, at every minute she will encounter the need to make decisions: some trivial (whether to wear the black socks or the brown ones) and some significant (whether to cheat on her chemistry exam). What does she need to do to make conscious, well-reasoned decisions? What kind of questions should she ask as she assesses the situations facing her?

Tanya needs to be a critical thinker. She needs to evaluate the situations she encounters carefully and thoughtfully. She needs to become familiar with a set of techniques and approaches that will enable her to examine critically not only the texts she reads in her classes, but the everyday events of college life.

WHAT'S THE POINT?

One of the first questions Tanya should ask as she works through an assigned reading or as she launches into a debate with her best friend is, "What's the point?" In other words, what is the central **issue** under discussion? Once she figures this out, she can then investigate the thesis or **conclusion** being offered concerning the issue at hand. The conclusion is the message being conveyed; it is what an author or speaker is trying to prove.

Let's say Tanya's friend Kevin presents her with the following statement:

> My persnickety sociology professor takes attendance every day, and if you miss a certain number of class meetings, then he takes points off your grade. He's always whining about how ditching classes shows a careless attitude, and he claims that you can't do well if you don't show up. He seems to want to control student behavior like professors decades ago who required college students to attend chapel services. But we're living in a different age now, and the faculty can't exert that kind of control anymore. And anyway, I don't think he's taking a just approach to grading, because he isn't dealing with us fairly. In my opinion, as long as you do the work, showing up for class should be irrelevant.
>
> The point is, why should attendance have any impact on our grades? Students like us know we should be able to choose for ourselves whether or not to go to class. We're smart; we know what we're doing. We're in college now, and we're mature enough to be responsible. Sure, a few people may skip too many classes and end up not learning the material, but that's just a small minority. And if we don't get a chance to make mistakes, how will we ever learn to stand on our own two feet? Professors need to either leave the choice of attending classes to us or admit that they don't want to treat us like adults.
>
> You know, some people may not need to come to class every day—they may be familiar with the subject matter already, or they may be able to learn it just by doing the reading or talking to their classmates. If they can get the papers done, pass the tests, and so on, I don't see why attendance should have anything to do with their grades. After all, three students missed the review session our sociology professor held in the class meeting before our last exam, and these three students all got A's on the exam. It looks like missing class can actually help your course performance!
>
> I've done pretty well on all the written course work so far, too, even though I've been unable to attend at least seven classes. Maybe the professor resents that—I guess it makes him look bad if students can do okay without actually having to be in the same room with him all the time. I have a hunch that's why he's threatening to drastically lower my grade. He's just being malicious and trying to get back at me. It's no surprise that he has such low teaching evaluations. My friend Susan, who's a senior sociology major, says she heard he's really insecure. That makes sense to me, because if he was secure in himself, he wouldn't be so concerned about us showing up.
>
> Actually, lots of Cromwell faculty members agree with me about the attendance issue. Of the four courses I'm taking this semester, the professor takes attendance in only one of them; three out of four just don't see the point of doing it. My roommate Quentin, who's an education major, just did a study for a term paper that shows that most

> education professors don't take attendance either and that there isn't any difference in grade distributions between the professors who do take attendance and the ones who don't. My sociology professor is just out of step.
>
> Using attendance as a factor in grading is like judging people's artistic talent by how much time they spend in the studio. It's narrow and neurotic. Next thing you know, they'll start asking how long it takes us to do the assigned reading and give higher grades to people who take longer!

Tanya should be able to identify the issue at stake here: Should class attendance in itself have an impact on a student's course grade? Kevin, after all, makes it fairly easy for her to locate the main issue by highlighting it at the beginning of the second paragraph with the key phrase "The point is. . . . "

Tanya should also be able to identify Kevin's conclusion concerning the issue: Showing up for class—or not showing up for class—should have no bearing on the grading process ("as long as you do the work, showing up for class should be irrelevant"). Again, he gives her a tip-off phrase ("In my opinion . . . ") that serves as a handy signpost. Even without such indicators, however, Tanya—if she is to approach Kevin's presentation critically—must be able to locate his conclusion before she can proceed to evaluate the reasoning he uses to support it.

SO WHAT?

Before she invests too much time in discussing the issue with Kevin, however, Tanya needs to ask another set of questions: Is this a **significant** issue? Is the matter at hand really meaningful to her? Is it worth her time and energy? Is it just Kevin's pet peeve, or does it have larger importance? Could engaging in this discussion bring her to any new realizations? Could she learn something?

All right, Kevin's sociology professor takes attendance into account when assigning course grades—so what? Why should Tanya care? If she can't think of any reasons why she *should* care, then maybe she needs to change the subject. If, upon reflection, she decides that the issue does have some importance for her, then she can continue to examine Kevin's statement.

IS THAT A FACT?

Kevin's conclusion is supported by a set of **reasons** that explain *why* he believes in his conclusion. The conclusion and the reasons supporting it work together to constitute Kevin's **argument.** Throughout his argument, Kevin makes a number of **claims** or assertions about the way things are or the way they ought to be. Tanya needs to assess the truth of Kevin's claims; one way to begin doing this is to determine whether they are factually based.

For example, Kevin says that one reason why class attendance should be irrelevant in grading is because "we're mature enough to be responsible." Is that a fact? A **fact** is something that is known to be true, something that has been verified. A **tentative truth** is something that *may* be true, but that needs verification. An **opinion** is something that may be *believed* to be true, but that is questionable or debatable. Where, among these possibilities, does Kevin's claim fall?

Tanya needs to determine the extent to which Kevin is going beyond logical, factually-based reasoning and using strategies simply to affect her feelings. For instance, Tanya, like Kevin, is a student; he may be trying to use their shared position as students ("we're in college now") in order to engage her support for his cause. She needs to remain critically aware of such techniques in Kevin's argument.

PROVE IT!

Tanya can gain a clearer sense of the validity of Kevin's argument by assessing the **evidence** he provides in support of his claims. If Kevin wants one of his assertions to be convincing, he needs to prove it—to back it up with credible, or believable, evidence. What kind of evidence does he provide, and how credible is it?

In fact, Kevin offers various types of evidence, including personal experience and individual example, intuition, appeal to authority, and a research study. Tanya must evaluate *all* forms of evidence in Kevin's argument to determine its credibility.

To begin with, Kevin provides his own **personal experience** to support his case: he has "done pretty well" in his course work even though he has missed a number of classes. Tanya needs to consider whether Kevin's view of his own experience is really an objective one—*he* may think he has "done pretty well," but would his professor agree? She also must think about whether Kevin's experience is necessarily representative or typical of the experience of all students. Whenever someone offers a specific **example** or **case study** of a single individual's experience (whether it is their own experience or the experience of another), the question of whether or not the experience is representative must be addressed.

After Kevin asserts that he does not need to attend all his classes in order to complete the course work successfully, he goes on to claim, "Maybe the professor resents that—I guess it makes him look bad if students can do okay without actually having to be in the same room with him all the time." Expressions such as "maybe," "I guess," and "I have a hunch" in Kevin's remarks suggest that he does not know *for a fact* that the professor feels this way; he merely infers it based on his **intuition.**

Kevin appeals to external **authority** when he cites the information provided by his friend Susan, a senior sociology major: "she heard he's really insecure." Although her presence in the sociology department may give Susan some acquaintance with its faculty members, does it really endow her with enough **expertise** (special knowledge about the subject) to determine that Kevin's professor is insecure? In fact, Kevin himself notes that this is just something that Susan has "heard"—a point which may do even more to call her credibility into question.

Kevin appeals to another sort of authority when he brings up his roommate Quentin's term paper, a **research study** that he offers as evidence to corroborate his reasoning. Tanya should consider a number of factors in reference to this study. First of all, she may wonder about the qualifications and expertise of the researcher, as well as his neutrality. Is a college senior necessarily the most authoritative source on this subject? She may also wonder about the credibility of a single, rather limited research study. Is the **sample** (the selection of people studied) large, broad, and representative enough? Has this study been replicated by other researchers? Have other studies demonstrated the same findings?

Of course Tanya must not forget to assess the relevance of this study to the matter at hand. Kevin mentions that Quentin's study determined that "there doesn't seem to be any difference in grade distributions between the professors who do take attendance and the ones who don't." What bearing does this have on the issue of whether or not attendance *should* play a part in course grading? Tanya must be alert to any confusion between a **descriptive** issue (one that involves what *does* occur) and a **prescriptive** issue (one that involves what *should* occur).

CHECK THE NUMBERS!

Tanya also needs to take a closer look at the **statistics** Kevin offers in support of his argument; specifically, the statistical evidence ("three out of four professors") in the fifth paragraph. Is this figure a convincing component of Kevin's reasoning? Is Kevin's sample (the four professors he happens to have this semester) too limited to be persuasive?

Does it even matter how many professors do or do not take attendance? If what we are trying to evaluate is whether or not attendance *should* be a component in professors' grading criteria, is it really relevant to assess to what extent it *is* a component? Once again, we may have a confusion between the descriptive and the prescriptive.

WHO SAYS?

No matter how much evidence Kevin provides, Tanya needs to make sure that the sources of his evidence are reliable. We have already seen that there may be questions about the credibility of Susan and Quentin as authoritative, dependable sources. In fact, Kevin's own credibility could be called into question as well. He admits, in the fourth paragraph, that his sociology professor is threatening to lower Kevin's grade because of repeated absences. Is it possible that this threat has affected Kevin's perspective on the issue of attendance as a component of grading? Tanya should be alert to the possibility of **bias** in the sources of Kevin's evidence, and in his own approach to the subject.

WHERE ARE YOU COMING FROM?

Kevin's approach to the subject may be governed by the unspoken thoughts he brings to his argument. In order to determine where Kevin is coming from, Tanya needs to explore what Kevin does *not* explicitly express: the **assumptions** he takes for granted about how the world is or should be.

For example, Kevin asserts that "as long as you do the work, showing up for class should be irrelevant." There are a number of unspoken assumptions underlying this claim. One of the most significant is that "the work" of a course is what is done outside of regular class meetings—papers, exams, problem sets, lab reports, and other out-of-class assignments. Kevin's reasoning can proceed only by conceiving "course work" as something that is not undertaken in class. If we were to consider participation in class discussion or taking notes on a lecture as part of the work of a course, then it would be more difficult to reach the conclusion that "showing up for class should be irrelevant." Kevin's **descriptive assumption** concerning what course work *is* governs his entire argument.

Kevin also makes a number of **prescriptive** or **value assumptions** about how things *ought* to be, and these, too, govern his argument. For instance, Kevin asks this question: "And if we don't get a chance to make mistakes, how will we ever learn to stand on our own two feet?" Here he presupposes that learning "to stand on our own two feet" is a valuable component of a college education. If we do not agree that this is part of what we *should* be learning, then we will be unconvinced by Kevin's reasoning.

SAY WHAT?

Because of the assumptions he makes and the biases he brings to the issue at hand, Kevin's language may not always be as neutral or precise as it could be. Tanya would be well advised to look closely at Kevin's choice of specific words and phrases.

Some of the terms Kevin uses are obviously slanted. For instance, he refers at the beginning of his argument to his "persnickety" professor's "whining," and he uses the word "neurotic" at the very end. In other cases, the slanting of terminology is a bit more subtle. For example, Kevin says that his professor "claims that you can't do well if you don't show up." By using a word such as "claims" (rather than, say, "states"), Kevin conveys a sense of questionability, suggesting that what the professor says is opinion rather than fact.

In some cases, Kevin's use of loaded language can be characterized as **euphemism** or **dysphemism.** A euphemism is a gentle or positive-sounding word or phrase that may be used to soften a harsh or negative meaning; for example, when speaking of the sociology classes he has missed, Kevin refers to them as classes he has "been unable to attend." Dysphemism—the opposite of euphemism, and so the use of harsh or negative language—can be seen when Kevin reports on his professor's attitude towards students "ditching" classes.

In all cases, whether the loaded language is subtle or overt, Tanya must think critically about the effects of Kevin's specific terminology, looking beyond the mere **denotation** of a word (its explicit meaning or definition) and taking into account its potential **connotations** (the meanings associated with or suggested by it).

Tanya should also be aware that many of the words Kevin uses are **ambiguous**—they may have multiple meanings, or they may simply be vague and undefined. For example, in his second paragraph he says college students are "mature enough to be responsible." What exactly do words such as "mature" and "responsible" mean here? Could they have different meanings for different people? What about words like "just" and "fairly," which Kevin uses in the first paragraph? How might such ambiguity affect Kevin's overall argument?

RUN THAT BY ME AGAIN!

So far Tanya has come across a number of areas in which Kevin's argument could bear further examination. As she investigates possible weaknesses in his reasoning, she may want to run through a checklist of common logical **fallacies**—flaws in reasoning that can seriously undermine the credibility of an argument.

1. Emotive language: As we have already seen, Kevin has a tendency to depend on emotional appeals and emotion-laden language. Specific logical fallacies that fall under the category of emotive language include appeals to fear, appeals to pity, flattery, and peer pressure. For example, Kevin uses flattery when he says, "We're smart; we know what we're doing." He appeals to the vanity of his student audience in order to draw them into his argument.

2. False dilemma: Sometimes called the "either-or" fallacy, this describes the strategy of presenting only two extreme alternatives and excluding any middle ground. Kevin does this when he says, "Professors need to either leave the choice of attending classes to us or admit that they don't want to treat us like adults." Are those really the only available options?

3. Slippery slope: Often presented in the form of an "if-then" or "the next thing you know" statement, this fallacy suggests that if one thing happens, something else will necessarily follow. This may also be familiar as the "domino theory" or "ripple effect." We can see Kevin making use of this approach at the end of his argument: "Next thing you know, they'll start asking how long it takes us to do the assigned reading and give higher grades to people who take longer!" The problem is that we have no logical reason to believe that the first thing (using attendance to determine grades) will necessarily lead to the second (using length of reading time).

4. Circular reasoning: Sometimes described as a form of "begging the question" (that is, avoiding the issue), circular reasoning moves—as you might guess—in a circle. In other words, the justification of a claim is simply a restatement of the claim itself in a slightly altered form. When Kevin says, "I don't think he's taking a just approach to grading, because he isn't dealing with us fairly," his explanation simply proceeds by the use of near-synonyms: the approach isn't just because it isn't fair. Has he really explained anything?

5. Ad hominem: From the Latin phrase meaning "to the person," this fallacy uses a personal attack on an individual as a substitute for a reasoned critique of the individual's position. When Kevin refers to his sociology professor as "persnickety" and "insecure," and when he says, "He's just being malicious and trying to get back at me," he is engaging in ad hominem attacks.

6. Ad populum: From the Latin phrase meaning "to the people," this fallacy makes an appeal to the shared values or beliefs of the audience, playing on people's natural desire to be part of a group. Kevin uses this strategy in his second paragraph when he refers to what "students like us know."

7. Common practice: Here the appeal is not to popular beliefs, but to popular behavior—an "everyone is doing it" or "bandwagon" approach. When Kevin argues that three of his four professors do not take attendance and that, according to Quentin's study, most education professors do not take attendance either, he seems to suggest that the majority behavior is the norm, and that his sociology professor's policy is an aberration which should be rectified.

8. Red herring: This fallacy is a classic example of distraction—using an unrelated point to distract the audience's attention from the real issue at hand. Its name derives from the old practice of using a dead fish to distract dogs from the scent of their prey. One "dead fish" in Kevin's argument can be found when he refers in his fourth paragraph to his sociology professor's "low teaching evaluations." What does this point have to do with the issue of using attendance as a factor in grading?

9. Straw man: When the arguments of the opposition are exaggerated or distorted and then attacked, we end up with a "straw man" that is easily knocked down. In his opening paragraph, Kevin says that his sociology professor "seems to want to control student behavior like professors decades ago who required college students to attend chapel services." He then continues, "But we're living in a different age now, and the faculty can't exert that kind of control anymore." Is Kevin necessarily giving an accurate portrayal of his professor's position when he talks about what his professor "seems to want"? When he makes the point that "we're living in a different age now," is he rebutting his professor's actual position, or merely an imaginary position that Kevin himself has created?

10. Generalizations: Frequently signaled by such words as "all," "every," "always," "never," and "none," **broad generalizations** or **overstatements** are unqualified statements about all members of a category or group. Stereotyping is one form of overstatement. A conclusion based on a limited or unrepresentative sample is a **hasty generalization.** We see Kevin falling into this fallacy when he provides the "three out of four professors" statistic and draws the conclusion that "lots of Cromwell faculty members agree with me about the attendance issue." Based on his sample of only four professors, can he legitimately draw a conclusion about the views of "lots of Cromwell faculty members"?

11. False analogy: An **analogy** is a comparison that highlights the resemblance or similarity between two different things. When evaluating the soundness of an analogy, we need to examine how similar the two things being compared actually are and how significant the similarities may be. In his final paragraph Kevin says, "Using attendance as a factor in grading is like judging people's artistic talent by how much time they spend in the studio." Is grading a student in a particular course really comparable to judging artistic ability? Is attending class really comparable to spending time in an art studio?

12. Post hoc: Sometimes referred to as "false cause" reasoning, this fallacy takes its name from the Latin phrase *post hoc ergo propter hoc,* meaning "after this, therefore because of this." The suggestion is that there is a cause-effect relationship between two events simply because one came first. We can see this reasoning in Kevin's third paragraph: "After all, three students missed the review session our sociology professor held in the class meeting before our last exam, and these three students all got A's on the exam. It looks like missing class can actually help your course performance!" The implication is that the students got A's on the exam *because* they missed the prior review session—but of course the two events could be entirely unrelated.

13. Non sequitur: In Latin, this means "it does not follow." It can refer to any portion of an argument in which the reasoning simply does not make sense; for example, when Kevin says that if his sociology professor "was secure in himself, he wouldn't be so concerned about us showing up." What exactly is the link between the professor's possible insecurity and his grading policy? It may make sense to Kevin, but the connection may not be clear to anyone else.

WHAT'S MISSING?

Tanya needs to consider not only whether the argument Kevin presents is flawed or slanted, but whether he is leaving out any important factors. Altogether, Kevin may be presenting a rather limited view of the issue. Are there alternative ways to interpret the information he has offered? For example, Kevin notes that three of his professors this semester do not take attendance, and leads us to the claim that they do not do so because they do not think it is a legitimate component of grading. But could it instead be because their courses are so hugely enrolled that attendance-taking would be difficult? Could it be due to the nature of their courses, their goals and methods as teachers, or even their laziness?

Tanya also needs to consider whether there may be any negative consequences to Kevin's view that he neglects to mention. What might happen if attendance were never taken into consideration in the grading process? Is it possible that students would then be less likely to show up for classes? Might this create any problems?

There are many more examples of weaknesses in Kevin's argument than we have so far explored. Tanya would do well to undertake further examination of his presentation, attempting to uncover additional examples of problems with his reasoning.

Once Tanya has fully evaluated Kevin's argument, she will be ready to reply with an argument of her own. She will be able to use her analysis of Kevin's argument to build her case, for an awareness of the flaws in his reasoning will enable her to avoid such flaws herself.

PLAY IT AGAIN

Just to make sure that she has fully absorbed a critical-thinking approach, Tanya might want to examine another argument. She had an excellent opportunity to do so the day after her conversation with Kevin about class attendance and grading. As she settled into her favorite seat near the back of her English composition classroom a few minutes before her class was scheduled to begin, she overheard two of her classmates, Elise and Dalton, engage in the following discussion:

> "Don't you think that T-shirt you're wearing is tacky?" asked Elise.
>
> "Why should I think it's tacky? I'm showing my school pride! Don't you support the Cromwell Chiefs?" Dalton replied.
>
> "I have nothing against our athletes," Elise explained, "but I do have a problem with the school's mascot, especially the way he's portrayed on your T-shirt—feathers, war paint, and tomahawk in hand. I've taken a couple of courses here at Cromwell about Native American literature and culture, and I know that the image on your T-shirt doesn't reflect reality. It's just a representation of every possible mindless cliche. Just calling the athletic teams 'the Chiefs' is bad enough; the name alone gives a limited, stereotypical view of Native Americans. And when you associate that name with the cartoonish figure on your T-shirt, it's even worse."
>
> "Oh, come on, Elise. First of all, it's just a picture. Why make such a big deal over it? And what's wrong with calling our teams 'the Chiefs'? It's a positive image, after all—noble, courageous, in charge. It's a name that's been associated with our athletic program for generations, ever since Cromwell was founded. You can't change that kind of long-standing tradition—the alumni would never go for it. You can see that if you read the letters to the editor in Cromwell's alumni magazine; three-fourths of them point out all the ways the college is changing for the worse. What would you want to change the name to, anyway? Something nice and sweet like 'the Cromwell Chrysanthemums'? A team name is supposed to connote strength, victory, power. A word like 'Chiefs' does that perfectly."
>
> "But it's not the only powerful choice," Elise pointed out. "We could be 'the Cromwell Cougars,' for example, which at least wouldn't be offensive. I've never heard of anyone on any campus objecting to a name like that."
>
> "How do you know? Probably some animal rights fanatics out there would have a problem with it," Dalton said. "Wasn't there some big blow-up at Ralston College when they named their newspaper *The Ralston Roadkill*?"

"Now you're just being dumb. I don't know why I listen to anything a jerk like you has to say about serious issues."

At that point the professor entered the classroom. The conversation ceased, but Tanya continued to think about what she had overheard. She knew there were a number of points she needed to consider as she pondered Elise and Dalton's interchange.

- **What's the issue at hand?** What exactly is the point of the discussion: the alleged tackiness of Dalton's T-shirt or the larger issue of associating a college team with a specific cultural image or artifact?
- **Is it significant?** Does Tanya herself care enough about this issue to spend any more time thinking about it?
- **Is there a factual basis to the claims being made?** For example, when Dalton asserts that Cromwell alumni "would never go for" a change in the team name, is he stating a fact?
- **What kind of evidence is being provided in support of the claims?** When Elise notes that she has "never heard of anyone on any campus objecting" to animal names being used for athletic teams, is she providing adequate concrete support to back up her assertions?
- **Is the use of statistics or other numerical evidence credible?** What should Tanya make of Dalton's point about three-fourths of the letters to the editor in the alumni magazine pointing out "all the ways the college is changing for the worse"? Is this a legitimate use of statistical evidence?
- **How credible is the speaker as well as the sources cited?** Are Elise and Dalton presenting themselves, and the other sources they cite, as credible? For instance, when Elise points out that she's taken a couple of college courses dealing with Native American culture, does this establish her as an authoritative figure?
- **What assumptions are underlying any claims being made?** What do Elise and Dalton take for granted? What perceptions or attitudes govern the ways in which they view the issue at hand?
- **Is the language that is being used loaded or slanted in any way?** Do phrases such as "mindless cliche" and "long-standing tradition" affect the messages being conveyed by Elise and Dalton?
- **Are there any logical fallacies in the argument?** Are there examples throughout the discussion of such fallacies as emotive language ("Don't you support the Cromwell Chiefs?"), false dilemma ("What would you want to change the name to, anyway? Something nice and sweet like 'the Cromwell Chrysanthemums'?"), ad hominem attacks ("I don't know why I listen to anything a jerk like you has to say about serious issues"), or false analogy ("Wasn't there some big

blow-up at Ralston College when they named their newspaper *The Ralston Roadkill?*")?

- **Is anything important being left out of the presentation?** Are Elise and Dalton neglecting to consider negative consequences or alternative interpretations?

After exploring each of these questions in some depth, Tanya will have a much fuller understanding of the arguments that Elise and Dalton are presenting. As she did with Kevin's argument, she will be able to evaluate the positions being presented to her and at the same time construct a position of her own that is clear, coherent, and convincing. Tanya will be able to do this effectively because she has learned to think critically.

ONE MORE TIME

See if you, like Tanya, can think critically about college life by examining the following argument presented by Tanya's friend Hope.

> I know a lot of people complain about the children of alumni having an easier time getting into Cromwell than other applicants. I've heard from a friend of mine who does work-study in the admissions office that the average applicant to Cromwell has a one in ten chance of being admitted, but alumni children—they call them "legacies"—have a four in ten chance. It may seem like an unfair advantage, but I don't agree. I think legacies *do* deserve extra consideration from the admissions office. My dad is a Cromwell alumnus and I got admitted as a legacy, so I know what I'm talking about.
>
> Legacy applicants are more likely to do well when they get to Cromwell, because they have a clearer sense of what the college is all about. They already feel committed to the school because of their family connection to it, so they won't want to do anything to jeopardize their success here. They probably have higher retention rates, because legacies won't ever want to transfer to another school. Besides, if your parents graduated from Cromwell, that means they must have been smart—and since intelligence is genetic, that means you're smart, too, so you deserve a greater chance of admission to the college.
>
> And we shouldn't forget that legacies aren't the only ones who get favorable treatment in the admissions process. Cromwell gives special consideration to other groups, too: athletes, underrepresented minorities, students with special artistic or musical talents, and so on. Why not add alumni children to the list?
>
> The real clincher, though, is that alumni children, when they become alumni themselves, are going to be major donors to the college. The more of a family tradition you have of being connected to the school, the more likely you are to fork over major contributions. In

Cromwell's alumni magazine, I read about a study that showed that in their first two years after graduation, 78 percent of legacies donated a total of $100 or more to Cromwell. Only 36 percent of non-legacy graduates donated $100 or more in their first two years out. Like most colleges, Cromwell depends on alumni support to raise the necessary funds. If we cut down our number of legacy admissions, what would happen to the college budget? How would we be able to keep things running?

I think the people who complain about legacy admissions are just jealous. They need to calm down and take a longer view of things. After all, their children will be able to benefit from the legacy admission advantage as well!

How effective is Hope's presentation? How could she have presented her case more effectively? Can you think of any counterarguments to her stated positions? Can you locate any points where her reasoning is flawed or incomplete? In short, how would you approach her statement now that you, like Tanya, are learning to think critically?

Chapter 9b

On Your Honor

Academic Dishonesty and Its Consequences

PART ONE

As the semester wore on, the students of Cromwell College focused more and more on their studies, becoming almost obsessive in their academic concern as midterm examinations approached. Cromwell's first-year students were particularly anxious about midterms, since this would be their initial experience with college-level examinations. They could be seen at all hours with textbooks spread open on their laps, highlighters in their hands, and a glazed look in their eyes as they struggled to absorb information they had neglected in the press of more exciting events.

Lucy Donovan, one of the brightest students in this year's entering class, was perhaps even more apprehensive than the rest of her classmates. The past few weeks had not been easy for her. To begin with, she had had to fight a long battle with her parents about going away to school. Although Cromwell was only an hour's drive from her hometown, Lucy's mother and father—who were very strict and, in her opinion, old-fashioned in their approach to their only daughter—were worried about what might happen if Lucy was exposed to "the wrong element" while away at college. Lucy managed to talk them into letting her attend Cromwell and live in the residence halls, but her parents made it clear that she'd have to request a room in Reynolds Hall, the all-female residence, and that they'd bring her back home at the slightest hint of a problem, whether academic or personal.

Upon her arrival at Cromwell, Lucy found that residence life had its own set of troubles. She didn't get along with her roommate, her hallway was incredibly noisy, and her resident adviser did nothing to control the chaos. At first, Lucy began to wonder whether she wouldn't be happier back home—and then she met Frank McFarland.

Lucy had never known anyone like Frank. Aside from a rather remarkable mechanical ineptitude (it had taken him six hours to hook up his stereo system), he was a brilliant young man, witty and unconventional yet with a warm, sensitive, and loving side. After his first conversation with Lucy, he was determined to show her just how warm, sensitive, and loving he could be.

Frank's appearance didn't make a good first impression on Lucy: earring, ponytail, and ripped jeans were not the norm among her male friends back home. But ten minutes of whispered conversation during a particularly boring American history lecture won her over. Soon the two became "an item." And soon Lucy started doing something she had never expected to do: against residence hall visitation rules she found herself spending frequent nights in Frank's room in Blaine Hall, the all-male residence hall in the Lower Quad. Frank's roommate had dropped out of school after the second week of classes due to psychological problems, and since then Frank occupied a single room, an almost unheard-of luxury among first-year students and a setup that certainly didn't discourage Lucy's overnight visits. Meanwhile, Lucy was living in fear that her parents would phone her early in the morning and discover that she wasn't in her own room. So far she had been lucky, but she continued to be nervous about the situation. She was convinced that if her parents found out about her relationship with Frank, they would immediately pull her out of Cromwell.

Lucy's anxiety about her parents, together with her delight in spending time with Frank, had begun to get in the way of her studies. Intelligent as she was, Lucy was not quite as brilliant a student as Frank. Although he seemed to be able to pull A's in all his classes with no effort, she needed to work hard for her good grades. And lately she just hadn't been able, or willing, to work as hard as she should. She knew that it was crucial for her to do well on her midterm exams: every semester Cromwell College sent a brief report of midterm progress to the parents of each student, and if a poor midterm report were to reach Lucy's parents she was certain they would use it as an excuse to drag her back home. So Lucy now started putting in a lot of study time, desperately trying to make up for all the work she hadn't done in the first weeks of the semester.

Lucy wasn't too worried about her midterm grades in most of her classes, because all that went on the midterm report was an S (satisfactory) or a U (unsatisfactory). She had been doing well in English composition, and although she had fallen behind in her reading for

American history, she quickly caught up. Biology was basically a rehash of her high school Advanced Placement Biology class, and she was confident that a night or two of review would adequately prepare her for the midterm exam. Her once-a-week tutorial in violin technique wasn't a problem, either. There was no question that she'd pull S's in all these courses.

So far so good—but there was one more class to contend with. Lucy had been sure, when she'd signed up for Introduction to American Politics, that it would be one of her favorite courses. She had always been interested in politics, and spent the summer after her junior year in high school as an intern in the district office of her local congresswoman. But her expectations were dashed the first day she walked into Tom Sanders' class.

Professor Sanders spent most of the first class telling off-color jokes, recounting his collegiate exploits, and denouncing just about every politician currently in office. "These money-grubbing, power-hungry fools in Washington have just about ruined our country!" he proclaimed, but never offered any evidence to support his negative perspective.

Lucy tried to make the best of the situation. She kept telling herself that it was good for her to be exposed to all points of view, and tried to convince herself that she might learn something valuable from Prof. Sanders' approach to the issues. The problem, however, was that Prof. Sanders never really discussed any issues. Although their syllabus listed several required texts, students in the class didn't bother with the readings, since Prof. Sanders never referred to them. In class after class, he rarely got beyond jokes and anecdotes. His occasional treatment of concepts from the readings—federalism vs. state rights, for example—was so sketchy and disorganized, and so slanted toward his own idiosyncratic viewpoint, that Lucy found herself just as uninformed after his lectures as she was before they began.

None of this would have mattered to Lucy if not for the fact that Prof. Sanders' tests bore no relation whatsoever to his classes. It was as if he was using the exams of some other professor who was teaching a rigorous and challenging version of the political science curriculum. Indeed, the rumor was that Prof. Sanders copied his exams from those used last year by another Cromwell professor, Luther Jackson, who was known to be a much more thorough instructor. Lucy would have registered for Prof. Jackson's section of the American politics class to begin with, but he was on leave this year. By the time she realized she should drop the course and switch to something else, it was too late.

The two short tests already taken by Lucy's American politics class would have been challenging for students who were being well-taught; for those in Prof. Sanders' class, they were virtually impossible. Some students who had access to fraternity and sorority test files or knew people who had taken Prof. Jackson's class last year, managed to pass. Lucy, who had no such resources and who would have scorned them as unethical even if she did have access to them, performed miserably. She was going into the midterm with a D average. Prof. Sanders had indicated that everyone who earned a C or better on the midterm exam would receive an S on their midterm report, even if they'd done poorly on the previous tests. Lucy didn't have much hope, but figured she'd better do whatever she could to pull the crucial C.

And so she devoted most of her study time to reading and trying to understand all the material listed in the first half of the Introduction to American Politics syllabus. Frank, who wasn't taking the course, tried to help her, but there was so much to cover that Lucy was beginning to feel overwhelmed. "I'm never going to pass this exam," she moaned, "and then my parents will get my midterm grades, see the U, and it'll be good-bye Cromwell!"

By Tuesday morning, the day before the exam, Lucy was panic-stricken. She forgot to show up for her work-study job in the political science department office; when Frank dropped by her room to check on her, he found her still in her nightgown, staring blankly at the wall. He reminded her that she was supposed to be at work in ten minutes, and Lucy—who had never been late before, in spite of the fact that she was supposed to show up at the ungodly hour of 8:30 A.M.—miraculously made it on time. This feat was even more impressive because Poretski Hall, where the political science department was located, was on the opposite side of the campus from her room in Reynolds Hall.

When she made her breathless arrival at the office, she was greeted with a grunt from Adele Zeller, the office manager. This was one of the busiest times of the year for Ms. Zeller, and she was trying to delegate as much work as possible to her office assistant and her two work-study employees. Lucy was the first of the employees to arrive for the day. Ms. Zeller handed her a sheaf of job application letters that had been received in answer to a recent advertisement for a faculty opening at CC, and asked her to make two copies of each. "And you'd better collate and staple them properly this time—not backwards, like you did yesterday!" commanded Ms. Zeller, as Lucy sheepishly took the letters into the photocopying room.

As she lifted the cover of the photocopying machine, Lucy realized that the previous user had left a sheet of paper there. She picked it up to get it out of the way, and glanced at it to see whose it might be. Absent-minded faculty members often left papers on the machine, and if there was a name on it, office policy was to return the forgotten paper to the appropriate professor's mailbox. Much to her surprise, Lucy realized that she was staring at Tom Sanders' midterm exam for Introduction to American Politics.

Smack at the top of the page was the topic for an essay question that was worth 50 percent of the total exam grade. Before she was aware of what she was doing, Lucy read the question: "Briefly summarize the positions on federalism taken by Madison and Hamilton; analyze the divergences between their positions, and provide your own evaluation of which position is most convincing using specific evidence from the two authors' writings."

Once Lucy realized the nature of the document she was holding in her hand, she immediately put it facedown on the table next to her in order to keep from seeing the questions on the multiple-choice section of the exam. The essay topic, however, was already etched in her memory. She looked wildly around her, but realized she was alone in the photocopying room and no one else was aware of what she had seen. She stepped into the main office, and that, too, was deserted. Ms. Zeller must have left for a moment and the office assistant and the other work-study employee had not yet arrived.

Everything in the office—typewriters, computers, bookshelves, and filing cabinets—seemed to turn into a blur before Lucy's eyes. The only objects she saw clearly were the faculty mailboxes, arranged in a phalanx on the office's back wall. She darted over to Prof. Sanders' box, slipped the exam into it, quickly scrawled a note ("I'm feeling really sick and have gone home to bed—Lucy") and left it on Ms. Zeller's desk. She ran back to her room, locked the door behind her, got into bed, and pulled the covers up over her head.

Lucy's mind was racing. What should she do? Should she tell Prof. Sanders that she'd seen the exam? That would be the most honorable course. After all, wouldn't she be in violation of Cromwell's Honor Code, which prohibits "unauthorized assistance" on exams, if she were to go ahead and take the exam given the knowledge she had of its most significant question?

Well, actually Lucy wasn't so sure. It wasn't like she had intentionally set out to cheat, she reasoned. She wasn't *trying* to get a look at the exam, and as soon as she realized what it was, she prevented herself from seeing anything further. Besides, she'd heard what everyone said about Prof. Sanders' exams being copied from Prof. Jackson's materials from last year, and she knew that many students had access to those materials. Why shouldn't she have the same advantage they did? No one would ever know that she had seen the exam. All she'd need to do would be to spend the twenty-four hours before the test rereading *The Federalist Papers* and preparing a coherent response to the essay question. With any luck, she'd be able to get some of the multiple-choice questions right too. Surely she'd make a C, thereby earning the coveted midterm grade of S.

After a couple of hours of agonizing, Lucy's mind was made up. When Ms. Zeller phoned later in the morning to see how she was feeling and ask her about putting in some work time in the afternoon, Lucy told her she had a stomach virus and wouldn't be able to come back to the office that day. She pulled out her copy of *The Federalist Papers* and began taking notes.

When Frank stopped by later to walk with her to lunch, she begged off. "I'm really not hungry," she said, "and I'd rather spend my time studying for Sanders' exam. I think I'd just like to be alone all day so that I can focus on my reading." As Frank shrugged his shoulders and left, Lucy was stung by pangs of guilt, but she put them out of her mind in order to concentrate on writing an outline for her essay.

On Wednesday morning Lucy walked into her American politics classroom and sat down in her usual seat. As soon as Prof. Sanders handed out the exam, she glanced at the essay question, picked up her pen, opened her examination book, and began writing. Once she finished her essay, she turned to the multiple choice section. She was sure she knew the answers to at least half of the questions. Those, together with the essay, would certainly earn her the C that she so desperately needed! By the end of the exam period, she was exhausted yet satisfied, and slowly walked back toward her room for a short rest before lunch.

As Lucy meandered along, her dormant conscience stirred. "Oh, no!" she thought to herself, "What have I done? I always swore I'd never use old exam files or anything like that. I always thought of myself as somehow more ethical than my classmates. Now I've fallen far below them. No matter how you look at it, I've cheated on this exam. How will I ever be able to live with myself?"

After much consideration, Lucy came to a decision. She was determined to turn herself in to David Nadler, Cromwell's dean of academic affairs, and ask him to convene the honor council to hear her case. "I just don't see anything else to do," she thought. "Maybe if I turn myself in, they'll go a little easier on me—but in any case, my conscience just won't let me get away with cheating. It will probably mean that I'll have to go back home to my parents, but that can't be helped."

With those thoughts, she turned back in the direction of Vanburen Hall, where the academic dean's office was located. Dean Nadler's secretary told Lucy that he was available and immediately showed her into his office. There she told her tale, in all its depressing detail.

"I have no choice but to report this infraction to the honor council," the Dean sadly remarked after hearing her story, "though I must admit that I hope they'll show leniency in your case. We'll convene the council immediately. As you know, it consists of three faculty members selected yearly by me, as well as three students elected every spring."

The three faculty members were Selena Weil, a young, easy-going biology professor who also served on Cromwell's Judicial Advisory Committee; Hal Banner, a demanding but popular philosophy professor; and Carla Lombardo, a detail-minded sociology professor who was a stickler for rules. Dean Nadler told Lucy that the faculty and student members of the council would meet to consider the facts in her case on Thursday afternoon. She had no hope that the council would find her anything but guilty, but she was resigned to her fate and anxiously awaited the group's deliberations.

Some Questions to Consider

Is Lucy justified in her actions? Has she violated Cromwell's Honor Code? (See the appendix for a full statement of the code.) What should she have done when she discovered Prof. Sanders' exam on the photocopying machine? Has she done the right thing by turning herself in? Has the dean done the right thing by deciding to convene the honor council? What should Lucy do now?

SMALL-GROUP EXERCISE

Group 1 Lucy's Best Friends

Talking It Out

On the way back to her room after informing Dean Nadler of what she perceives to be her violation of the Honor Code, Lucy comes across the group of you sitting on the grass in front of Reynolds Hall. She immediately joins you and tells you the whole story.

"You folks are really my best friends here at CC," Lucy concludes. "You've stuck by me before; given me good advice on how to deal with my parents, my roommate, Frank—everything. Now it seems like it's all going up in smoke for me. I know I made a big mistake when I walked in and took that exam without telling Prof. Sanders I had seen the essay question. I feel that turning myself in was the only thing I could do and still live with my conscience. I know I deserve to face the consequences of my actions.

"But I also know that my life at Cromwell is over now. The honor council is sure to convict me; after all, I admitted myself that I cheated on the exam. When they reach a guilty verdict, they have no choice but to either suspend me for a year or expel me permanently—the Honor Code states that all violators must receive one of those two punishments. Even if I'm just suspended, my parents will never let me come back here. Knowing them, they probably won't even let me out of the house! I'll never be able to see Frank again, and I'll never be able to see any of you again."

You try to convince Lucy that things aren't as bleak as she perceives them, but she shakes her head. "I don't know," she says, "I don't see any way around it. I can't think of any way to present my case—to the honor council, to my friends, and most of all to my parents—that doesn't make it seem like I've totally disgraced my family and everything I've ever been taught to believe. You say things might not be as bad as I picture them. Well, can you give me any concrete suggestions for how to deal with my situation so that it's survivable? What should I say at the honor council hearing tomorrow? When should I tell my parents about all this? *How* should I tell them? *What* should I tell them? You've always given me good advice before. What advice can you give me now?"

Before you have a chance to say a word, Lucy sees Frank walking by and runs over to him. As she leaves, you begin to discuss her problems among yourselves, and try to reach a consensus about what advice you should give her.

Writing It Out

As you discuss Lucy's problems, you decide it might help her if you were to write her a note, as a group, giving her the concrete suggestions she wants. What will you write in response to her request?

SMALL-GROUP EXERCISE

Group 2 Members of a Group Opposed to the Honor Code

Talking It Out

Ever since the Honor Code was implemented at Cromwell several years ago, a vocal minority of students has expressed their opposition to it. They've cited a number of reasons; some are practically based (i.e., the code doesn't work to deter cheating), some are ethically based (i.e., the code is morally wrong), and some are logically based (i.e., the code is contradictory, hypocritical, or ambiguous).

After hearing a number of these arguments, you have begun to wonder about the Honor Code, and even attended a few meetings of the Committee to Reconsider the Honor Code (CRHC). When rumors about Lucy's case reach the CRHC, the group decides to hold a meeting to determine whether this incident raises any questions or problems that should be addressed.

At the meeting, one group member brings up the code's inflexibility that prevents the honor council from taking extenuating factors into consideration. For example, the code states that anyone found guilty of a violation *must* receive one of two punishments: a one-year suspension or total expulsion from the college. Shouldn't it make a difference that Lucy turned herself in? The code, however, allows for no consideration of such factors.

Another group member points out that at the same time the code is inflexible on the issue of punishment, it is ambiguous on the definition of a violation itself; "unauthorized assistance" is forbidden, but does that really apply to Lucy's case? Or does the inadvertent nature by which Lucy came upon the "assistance" exonerate her? How about Prof. Sanders' apparent disregard for his students' "study" methods? If he knowingly uses easily-accessible tests from last year, doesn't that in some sense tacitly "authorize" whatever assistance students find available?

After a few minutes of discussion, it becomes clear that Lucy's case raises enough questions to justify a reconsideration of Cromwell's Honor Code. How should these questions be posed in order to convince the Cromwell Student Government (CSG) to convene an open forum so that all members of the CC community who wish to could express their sentiments about the code?

Writing It Out

You've been delegated to serve on a subcommittee to prepare a memo to the CSG explaining why the issues raised by Lucy's case are significant enough to merit a total re-examination of the Honor Code and why an open forum would be the appropriate means to begin this re-examination. The CRHC has asked you to decide together how best to persuade the CSG that the time for action on the Honor Code is now, and to jointly draw up a draft of the memo. What will you write in response to this request?

SMALL-GROUP EXERCISE

Group 3 Lucy's American Politics Classmates

Talking It Out

The American politics exam is over and done. You have no idea how you performed on it, but at least it's behind you now. After a short nap on a sofa in the student union, you head off to the cafeteria for lunch, and there you hear the rumor that's all over campus: Lucy Donovan turned herself in for cheating on the American politics exam. It never ceases to amaze you how quickly news travels at Cromwell, and how detailed the news can be. One of your acquaintances who has a couple of friends on the faculty heard the whole story, and tells you the fine points of the scandal.

As you walk back to the serving area to get a second helping of Jello Jewels, you pass a table full of your American politics classmates and their friends. "Have you heard the news about Lucy?" one of them asks. You nod and sit down, filling your classmates in on everything you've picked up.

The roommate of one of your classmates, who isn't taking American politics but who is a close friend of Lucy's, pipes up: "As Lucy's classmates, how do you feel about this? Do you feel that she *has* cheated and betrayed the rest of the students in the class? Or do you feel what she did was justified, given Prof. Sanders' teaching incompetence and the fact that half the class makes use of 'assistance,' like test files, that isn't officially authorized by the professor?

"Have any of *you* ever used old tests to study from, without them being 'authorized'? What would *you* have done if you had been in Lucy's place? What do you think the honor council should do with her case? You know that if they find her guilty of receiving 'unauthorized assistance' they have to either suspend her from school for a year or else expel her totally—the Honor Code explicitly states that one of these two punishments *must* be implemented. What would you advise the members of the council to do?"

All thoughts of lunch are abandoned as you spend the rest of your mealtime discussing these questions with your classmates.

Writing It Out

After further discussing the case, you and your classmates agree that it would be a good idea for members of the class to draft a memo to the honor council. Lucy's friend suggests, "Why don't you try to reach some kind of consensus among yourselves, and then write a memo to the honor council stating your feelings as Lucy's fellow classmates in the American politics course, and making some recommendations for their interpretation of the case?" What will you write in response to this request?

SMALL-GROUP EXERCISE

Group 4 *The Cromwell Clarion* Editorial Staff

Talking It Out

When you first arrived at Cromwell, you thought you were the hottest thing on earth because you had been editor of your high school newspaper. When you decided to join the staff of *The Cromwell Clarion,* you were sure the editors would recognize your potential and award you a position of prominence. But it turned out that about half the CC student body had been the editors of their high school papers, and the only thing you've been allowed to do so far has been to proofread the letters to the editor.

Now, however, it looks like you're going to get a chance to make it into the journalistic major leagues. The editorial page editor has learned about Lucy's case, and has decided that it raises issues significant enough to warrant a *Clarion* editorial. Unfortunately, he's too swamped by midterms to write it himself, so he asks you and several other *Clarion* staffers to work together as a group to produce an editorial.

To give you some background, he sits down and explains some of the doubts and questions that have surrounded the Cromwell Honor Code; many of them raised by a group called the Committee to Reconsider the Honor Code (CRHC). CRHC members have noted that the code's inflexibility prevents the honor council from taking extenuating factors into consideration. For example, the code states that anyone found guilty of a violation *must* receive one of two punishments: a one-year suspension, or total expulsion from the college. Shouldn't it make a difference that Lucy turned herself in? The code, however, allows for no such considerations.

Moreover, CRHC members maintain that although the code is inflexible on the issue of punishment, it is ambiguous on the definition of a violation itself; "unauthorized assistance" is forbidden, but does that apply to Lucy's case? Or does the inadvertent nature of Lucy's discovery of "assistance" exonerate her? How about Prof. Sanders' apparent disregard for his students' "study" methods and his use of easily-accessible tests from last year?

Does Lucy's case raise enough questions to justify a reconsideration of Cromwell's Honor Code? Even if a total re-evaluation of the code is not justified, are there recommendations that could be made about this individual incident? How should the honor council deal with the case?

Writing It Out

After you've had a chance to discuss Lucy's case with your fellow newspaper staffers, the editor returns and says, "You can make the editorial as broad or as specific as you like. You can make large points about the code, or just speak about the particular case at hand. But whatever you do, I want you to take a stand, and to argue it clearly, concisely, and convincingly." What will you write in response to this request?

PART TWO

By Thursday afternoon, the student members of the honor council were visibly on edge. None of them wanted Lucy thrown out of the college. In their opinion, the circumstances surrounding her case pointed to a more merciful treatment. Even the most lenient punishment available, a full year's suspension, appeared harsh to them. Knowing the reputation of Lucy's parents, the members were certain they'd never let her come back to Cromwell even after the period of suspension was over. Nevertheless, the facts in the case seemed to be incontrovertible. Lucy had seen Prof. Sanders' exam beforehand—she admitted this—and this was clearly a case of receiving "unauthorized assistance."

Or was it? Selena Weil, one of the faculty members on the honor council, had a chat with the student members on Thursday morning and made her views known to them. Prof. Weil argued that Lucy's preview of the exam was *not* in fact "unauthorized." It was her contention that Prof. Sanders' behavior throughout the course of the term—his neglect of course material, his choice to use exams that were easily accessible to students, his negligence in leaving the exam on the photocopying machine—pointed to an "anything goes" attitude. The fact that he had never "de-authorized" the use of past exams as study aids, even though he knew that these past exams were readily available and were identical to the ones he was going to give to his current students, seemed to Prof. Weil to be further evidence that Prof. Sanders sanctioned the use of any means whatsoever to prepare for his exams. Moreover, though almost all of the professors at Cromwell included a statement regarding the penalties for academic fraud as a part of their course syllabi, Prof. Sanders' syllabus made no mention of the issue.

Prof. Weil hypothesized that if Prof. Sanders had known that Lucy had seen the actual exam the day before it was to be administered, he wouldn't have cared. She maintained that Lucy would have been justified in assuming that he would not object, given what she already knew about Prof. Sanders' attitudes. Therefore, Prof. Weil claimed, Prof. Sanders had tacitly "authorized" Lucy's use of her exam preview by sending an unspoken message that he didn't care what his students did; academic fraud appeared to be irrelevant to him. Given this interpretation of the situation, Prof. Weil was prepared to find Lucy not guilty of violating the Honor Code.

She was not the only one considering this position. As the members of the honor council filed into Dean Nadler's office at 2:00 P.M. Thursday, several of them were thinking about the possibility of a "not guilty" verdict, though others thought that the evidence plainly indicated an Honor Code violation. All were waiting to hear the dean's statement of the case, as well as any additional remarks Lucy chose to make.

Dean Nadler had invited Prof. Sanders to make a statement as well, but he declined, maintaining that he would not be able to contribute anything significant to the hearing. After all, he pointed out, it was Lucy herself, not her professor, who had brought the case to the dean's attention. Thus it was decided that Lucy's testimony would be sufficient to lead to a verdict.

Once the council members and Lucy were present, Dean Nadler closed his office door and began recounting the details of the case to "refresh everyone's memories," as he put it. He then presented the group with a memo from Lucy's American politics classmates and asked them to take the classmates' recommendations into consideration.

After giving the council members a few minutes to read the memo, the dean turned to Lucy and asked if she had anything to add. She looked confused, started to speak, then stopped. After a long pause, she said, "Some of my friends have urged me to speak out in my own defense, but I really don't know how that would help. There's nothing I could say that would alter the facts of the case, so I guess I'll just keep quiet." Dean Nadler waited a few moments to give her the opportunity to change her mind, but Lucy seemed determined to remain silent. He then turned to the council and informed them that it was time to reach a verdict in the case. He passed each one a slip of paper on which to record their secret vote.

Selena Weil was the first to turn in her ballot; as was expected, her verdict was "not guilty." Carla Lombardo handed her vote in almost as quickly—she had reached the conclusion that, by the letter of the law, Lucy was guilty, and she did not feel that the law should be bent in this or any other case. Hal Banner was the last of the three faculty members to submit his verdict. Although he had genuine sympathy for Lucy, he too was concerned about setting a precedent indicating that the code could be applied elastically. After much consideration, he handed in his "guilty" vote, planning to recommend suspension rather than expulsion.

It was now up to the student members of the council to decide the final verdict. Slowly and deliberately they marked their ballots and passed them to Dean Nadler.

Some Questions to Consider

Is Selena Weil's argument concerning Lucy's innocence convincing? Why or why not? Has there been any change in your perception of whether Lucy's action was an incidence of cheating, a violation of the Cromwell Honor Code preventing "unauthorized assistance" on exams? If you determine it to be a case of cheating, which of the two punishments authorized by CC's Honor Code would be most appropriate: a one-year suspension or total expulsion from the college? Why?

PART THREE

As he unfolded each of the secret ballots, Dean Nadler's face grew grimmer. When the votes were counted, he turned sadly to Lucy and said, "I'm sorry to inform you that the honor council has found you guilty of violating the code. We now ask you to leave the room while we discuss which penalty would be appropriate in your case."

Lucy left the office in a daze, and sank into the chair offered by the dean's secretary. Frank and some of her close friends had come to give her their support, and they waited with her for what seemed like an eternity. In reality, it was only a few moments before Dean Nadler opened the door and again invited Lucy into the office.

She entered the office, sat down, and looked blankly from one member of the council to another. The dean said gently, "Lucy, we've decided to give you the less severe punishment of one year's suspension from Cromwell. We believe that you've learned a good deal from this incident, and that you'll never succumb to a similar temptation again. At the end of a year, we'll be happy to welcome you back to our community. I will speak with your parents myself and explain the situation to them as fairly and as generously as I can."

At the mention of her parents, Lucy became deathly pale. She rose from her chair, turned toward the office door, and collapsed in a faint. Dean Nadler's office was plunged into chaos as honor council members huddled around Lucy, trying to revive her. The dean's secretary called the college infirmary and in a few minutes a nurse arrived. As Lucy regained consciousness, Dean Nadler telephoned her parents.

The Donovans wasted no time in coming to the "rescue" of their daughter. This may have been the only time in his life that Lucy's father broke the law—he averaged 75 m.p.h. on the highway, and drove only slightly slower once he got onto the city streets. By that night, all of Lucy's belongings had been packed into the family station wagon. Her parents couldn't wait to get Lucy away from the den of iniquity they perceived Cromwell College to be, and they told her in no uncertain terms that they would never permit her to return or to stay in touch with any of the "evil influences" she had met during her brief stay.

Lucy sat mutely in the backseat of the car, staring out the window at her closest friends who were waving good-bye from the front steps of Reynolds Hall. Frank was nowhere to be seen. He had been by Lucy's side throughout the afternoon, staying with her while the nurse revived her and refusing to leave her even after her parents, in the first desperate moments after their arrival, threatened to have him arrested. Lucy, who seemed to be in a state of shock, finally summoned the last dregs of energy she had remaining.

"I can't stand listening to my mom and dad rant and rave at you," she told Frank. "It's just tearing me up inside. Please leave for now, and maybe they'll calm down a bit. I'll find a way to get in touch with you soon." Lucy's parents harrumphed when they heard this, but Frank simply nodded and went on his way.

Frank spent the evening telling the rest of the campus about the outcome of the honor council's deliberations. He was determined to avenge Lucy in whatever way he could, and he chose to do this by attacking the Honor Code itself.

"What kind of justice is this, what kind of honor, when someone everyone knows did no real wrong is suspended from the college, getting the same punishment as others who commit much worse infractions?" he demanded. "We need to rethink the Honor Code and rework it so that it can respond to the circumstances of individual cases."

Many Cromwell students listened sympathetically to Frank's arguments. Members of the Cromwell Student Government (CSG), who had been considering holding an open forum to discuss the code, decided to hold the meeting immediately. They set the forum for Sunday evening and asked a number of student, faculty, and administrative representatives to make presentations. As Lucy drove home with her parents, CSG members—who had moved with impressive speed—were already posting flyers across the campus, announcing the forum and inviting the full participation of the entire CC community.

Some Questions to Consider

How do you feel about the honor council's decision to convict Lucy of academic fraud? What about their decision to penalize her with a one-year suspension? What do you think of the reaction of Lucy? Of her parents? Of Frank? What impact could the open forum have on Lucy's case or on future cases of possible academic fraud?

WRITING EXERCISE

Lucy managed to survive her first agonizing weekend at home, but it hadn't been easy. She was in disgrace; her parents were determined that she'd never return to Cromwell, and planned to keep her from seeing any of her CC friends, especially Frank McFarland.

Lucy tried to tell them her version of the story, but they didn't seem willing to listen. They were convinced that what Lucy did *was* cheating, and that she fell to this low point because of her unfortunate association with disreputable acquaintances. One look at Frank was enough to tell them that he was *not* the kind of young man they wanted their daughter dating. The "excessive" physical contact that they witnessed between Lucy and Frank signalled to them that Lucy was in danger of falling even deeper into the pit of sin—if, indeed, she had not already fallen! They decided they would allow her to enroll at Cascade Community College for the spring term, but that was the only concession they were willing to make.

Lucy had yet to fully recover from her state of shock. Aside from a few feeble attempts to explain the circumstances to her parents, she simply gave in to all their demands.

Meanwhile, word of Lucy's situation spread across campus, and the students were outraged. There was talk of a boycott of Prof.

Sanders' classes; others suggested focusing on the Honor Code itself. The Sunday evening forum to discuss changes in the code drew a large portion of the campus, from students to faculty to administrators, and there appeared to be widespread sentiment for a clearer and more flexible code. The CSG, after conferring with the Committee to Reconsider the Honor Code (CRHC), recommended particular revisions that would clarify the meaning of "unauthorized assistance" and that would provide a greater range of punishments depending on the circumstances surrounding a particular violation.

The CSG/CRHC recommendation was presented to a faculty/administrative committee that would be meeting on Tuesday afternoon to determine whether immediate action needed to be taken. Hal Banner, the honor council member who was serving as chair of the ad-hoc committee, invited any additional comments on the matter to be submitted to him as soon as possible.

What would it take for this tale of Lucy and the Honor Code to have a happy ending? Could Lucy be persuaded to abandon her state of lethargy and take some action on her own behalf? Could her parents be persuaded to let their "precious jewel" risk returning to the "sullying" environment of Cromwell College? Could Prof. Banner, as chair of the ad-hoc committee to rework the Honor Code, be persuaded that the code needs to be changed immediately to prevent future outcomes even more questionable than Lucy's case?

Decide which *one* of these three audiences (Lucy, her parents, or Prof. Banner) you would like to address; plan a letter to your target audience that makes a specific proposal and argues for it as clearly and concretely as possible, and write your letter coherently, concisely, and convincingly.

PART FOUR

After being back home for a few days and wandering around the house in a mental fog, Lucy shook off her lethargy and worked up the courage to face her parents. She had received a number of encouraging calls and letters from her Cromwell friends and their words of support motivated her to confront her parents at the breakfast table on Wednesday —exactly one week after she had taken Prof. Sanders' midterm exam. She looked them straight in the eyes, and said, "Mom and Dad, you know that I love you and that I appreciate all you're doing to keep me on the right path. But I've got to learn to stand on my own two feet.

"I'm not denying that I made a mistake regarding Prof. Sanders' exam, but you have to realize that to some extent you played a role in that mistake. If you hadn't gotten me so afraid that you would pull me out of school at the slightest provocation, I never would have felt the temptation to use questionable information on the test. You can't keep giving me the message that you don't trust me to take care of myself; otherwise, how will I ever grow or mature? After all, you're not always going to be around to look after me. The long and the short of it is that if I'm ever going to become a responsible adult, I need the opportunity to live my own life, to make my own decisions—and, maybe, my own mistakes.

"I guarantee you that I'll never again make the same mistake: getting so worried about my academic performance that I do something I know is ethically wrong. But I also have to be honest with you and let you know that I'll continue to keep in touch with my Cromwell friends. They had nothing to do with this mistake, and I'm sure all of my friends, especially Frank, would have counseled me to act honorably had I asked their advice beforehand. I can't cut myself off from my friends; they've come to mean so much to me in the past few weeks. You have no idea what happiness Frank has brought into my life—and isn't my happiness what you're ultimately after?

"Please don't judge Frank and the rest of my friends just by appearances. Give them a chance. After all, if everyone went on first impressions, what do you think my friends would think of *you?* The way you barged onto campus, insulted everyone, dragged me into the car—do you think this made a good impression on them? Well, I'd expect them to give you a second chance, and I'd like you to give my friends that same chance to prove to you that they're worthy of my friendship.

"I'm going to go back to Cromwell next year, when my suspension is over. I'd like to do it with your love and approval, but I'll do without it, if I have to. If you refuse to give me your financial support, I'll apply for financial aid—grants, loans, whatever I can get. I'll find a way."

Lucy's parents were stunned by this unaccustomed assertiveness from their daughter. But they, too, had been considering the situation and had to admit there was some truth in what she said. Lucy had not been the only one to receive thought-provoking calls and letters; Dean Nadler had already telephoned her parents three times, and some members of the Cromwell community had written directly to the Donovans, asking them to rethink their attitude toward their daughter's circumstances.

These words of concern from outside sources had a great impact on their views. They asked Lucy for a little time to think things over and later that day told her of their decision: they would allow her to stay in touch with her Cromwell friends and to take courses at nearby Cascade Community College in order to keep up with her studies. After her year of suspension, they would accept her return to Cromwell with their unconditional financial and emotional support. At the end of that second year, they would consider Lucy's situation and determine whether she could continue her education at CC.

Lucy was elated; this was a better outcome than she had expected! She rushed to the telephone to call Frank and tell him that she'd be able to see him as soon as he could make the long drive to her house. He was thrilled to hear the news, but had even more exciting news of his own.

"I was just about to call and tell you, but you beat me to it," he said. "You'll never believe it, Lucy, but the verdict in your case has just been overturned! You know, your case prompted an entire reconsideration of the Honor Code. A committee has just finished holding intensive meetings on the matter, and they apparently received some very convincing statements from various members of the CC community persuading them that the code is both too inflexible and too ambiguous. A subcommittee of the group has already drafted a new version of the code that more precisely defines 'unauthorized assistance' and offers a greater latitude of punishments.

"Because it was your case that prompted the revision, they thought it was only fair that the new code be applied retroactively to you. The honor council has decided that, under this new version of the code, they'll be able to grant you a much less severe punishment: a zero on the American politics exam. They're sending a letter to you by overnight mail indicating this change in the penalty. This means you're not suspended after all—you can return to campus right away."

"I can't believe it!" Lucy exclaimed. "I never dreamed I might be able to come back to Cromwell so soon, and I never expected such a positive result to come out of my case! I guess everything that happened had some kind of purpose. It makes me all the more eager to get back to school," said Lucy.

"I'll be waiting for you with open arms," Frank murmured.

The rest of their conversation may not be appropriate for outside ears. Suffice it to say that Lucy did receive a letter from the honor council the next day, inviting her to return to Cromwell immediately with the understanding that she would receive a zero on Prof. Sanders' exam. She convinced her parents to permit her to return, and Frank was indeed waiting for her with open arms. That night the two of them once again broke the residence hall visitation rules.

Some Questions to Consider

How do you feel about the conclusion of Lucy's case? Do you agree with the changes that have resulted in a more flexible Honor Code at Cromwell College? Do you think it's legitimate to retroactively apply these changes to Lucy's case? Do you think Lucy has gotten off too easily, given her own admission of guilt?

Thinking Critically

Lucy's case is rather complex and raises a number of issues surrounding academic fraud at Cromwell College, ranging from faculty responsibilities to penalties for cheating. Can you identify all the issues raised by this case? Can you identify the conclusions presented by the various participants in the case in response to these issues?

Connecting the Cases

In several Cromwell cases we have been faced with students who have violated college policies. In your opinion, are all of the CC regulations listed in the appendix equally valid? Are all stated as clearly as they could be? Are there any instances of ambiguous wording or potential loopholes? Are there differences in the ways in which policies can be or are applied—for example, differences between the application of the Honor Code in Lucy's case, the Sexual Misconduct policy in Angelica's case, and the Discriminatory Harassment policy in Frank's case?

Bringing It Home

What are the current student attitudes on your campus regarding academic fraud? What are your college's policies and procedures for dealing with cheating and plagiarism? Do you believe that your college's policies affect student behavior in this area? Do you support the idea of college honor codes or other academic honesty guidelines as a deterrent to cheating? Why or why not?

Suggestions for Writing

1. Write a letter to a close friend unfamiliar with the Cromwell scene, briefly explaining the facts of Lucy's case and exploring what you would have done had you been in Lucy's place and had inadvertently come across a crucial exam question. How would your actions have differed from—or resembled—hers?
2. The editor of your former high school newspaper decides to do a special issue on cheating. He approaches you to write a feature article on the issue from the college perspective, basing your discussion on interviews with current college students as well as on previously published material dealing with academic fraud on the university level.

Out Loud

You have decided to attend the CSG's open forum on the Honor Code. Make an oral presentation to the other forum participants that conveys your own position on the code, using Lucy's case as necessary to support, illuminate, or explain your position.

Chapter 9c

Cromwell College Regulations and Responsibilities

(excerpted from *CC: A Student's Guide to Cromwell College*)

DISCRIMINATORY HARASSMENT

It is the policy of Cromwell College that employees and students be able to work, study, and live in a campus community free of discriminatory harassment. Such harassment directed against an individual or group that is based on race, religious belief, color, sexual orientation, national origin, physical disability, age, or gender is prohibited. Any student or employee who violates this policy may be subject to disciplinary action up to and including dismissal from the college. Student organizations in violation of this policy may be subject to the loss of official recognition.

Discriminatory harassment includes conduct (oral, written, graphic, or physical) directed against any person or group of persons because of their race, religious belief, color, sexual orientation, national origin, physical disability, age, or gender and that has the purpose or reasonably foreseeable effect of creating an offensive, demeaning, intimidating, or hostile environment for that person or group of persons. Such conduct includes, but is not limited to, objectionable epithets, demeaning depictions or treatment, and threatened or actual abuse or harm.

Complaints relating to misconduct involving discriminatory harassment should be reported to the dean of students. Complaints will be carefully investigated, and cases that may require disciplinary action will be handled according to the established procedures of the college.

SEXUAL MISCONDUCT

Cromwell College prohibits any student from engaging in sexual conduct with another person without the consent of that person. Sexual conduct is defined as including vaginal intercourse; anal intercourse; fellatio; cunnilingus; touching of the genitals, buttocks, or inner thighs; or any other physical conduct or touching of a sexual nature.

Students are subject to this policy whether misconduct occurs on college premises, at college-sponsored activities, or at any off-campus location when such conduct is brought to the attention of college officials.

Complaints relating to sexual misconduct should be reported to the dean of students. Complaints will be carefully investigated, and cases that may require disciplinary action will be handled according to the established procedures of the college.

FACULTY-STUDENT RELATIONSHIPS

To guard against abuses of power, relationships of a sexual nature between faculty members and students are absolutely forbidden at Cromwell College, whether or not the student in question is currently enrolled in one of the faculty member's classes. The policy covers full-time, part-time, and temporary faculty, as well as full-time and part-time students.

This prohibition applies to vaginal intercourse; anal intercourse; fellatio; cunnilingus; touching of the genitals, buttocks, or inner thighs; or any other physical conduct or touching of a sexual nature. Consent of the parties involved is not a relevant factor; the prohibition applies regardless of consent.

Complaints relating to sexual relationships between faculty members and students should be reported to the provost. Complaints will be carefully investigated, and cases that may require disciplinary action will be handled according to the established procedures of the college.

HAZING

Cromwell College prohibits the hazing of students as a requirement for membership in any student organization, club, fraternity, or sorority.

Hazing is defined as: (1) any act involving physical mistreatment of a student, causing undue discomfort or bodily injury; (2) any act involving psychological mistreatment of a student, including acts of personal servitude or humiliation; (3) any act that endangers the life and health of the student; or (4) any act that interferes with regularly scheduled classes or academic pursuits of a student.

Complaints or information concerning an alleged violation of the hazing policy should be reported to the dean of students. Complaints will be carefully investigated, and cases that may require disciplinary action will be handled according to the established procedures of the college.

STUDENT PUBLICATIONS

Cromwell College supports the publication of a student newspaper, *The Cromwell Clarion;* a campus yearbook, *Kaleidoscope;* and a literary magazine, *Chiaroscuro*. Since these publications are funded by revenues collected by the college, the ultimate responsibility for the publications lies with the college.

Cromwell College values freedom of expression, and expects campus publications to function responsibly as autonomous student organizations. However, should a publication funded by the college present material detrimental to the college's educational mission, or should staff members of a publication violate existing Cromwell policies or use their positions irresponsibly, the college administration reserves the right to intervene.

THE HONOR CODE

To promote the value of intellectual honesty, all academic work at Cromwell College is done under the provisions of an honor code. Violations of the code are: (1) cheating—using unauthorized assistance (materials, resources, etc.) during or in preparation for an examination, and (2) plagiarism—representing someone else's words, ideas, data, or original research as one's own and failing to acknowledge the source of such work.

Both students and faculty have the responsibility of reporting suspected violations; failure to report a violation is in itself a violation of the Honor Code. Reports should be made to the dean of academic affairs, whose responsibility it is to determine whether there is sufficient evidence of a violation. If the evidence appears to be adequate, an honor council of three faculty members appointed by the dean of academic affairs and three students elected yearly by the student body will be convened to conduct a hearing, decide guilt or innocence, and in the event of guilt levy one of two penalties: a one-year suspension, or permanent expulsion from the university.

Upon deciding to matriculate at Cromwell College, all students will sign a statement indicating that they have read and understood the provisions of the Honor Code, and that they agree to abide by its stipulations. Ignorance of the code can thus be no excuse for its violation.

Chapter 10

Introduction to the Ethical Process

The Ethical Process helps us clarify and evaluate our responses to controversial issues. I consider "controversial issues" the type of issues where people have different views of the right thing to do. Whether to abuse children or not, for example, is not a controversial issue. I assume that everyone agrees child abuse is wrong. Whether child abusers should be given prison terms or extensive counseling might be a controversial issue. In other words, controversial issues are not only conflicts between right and wrong but also conflicts between different views of what is right.

The process presented here does not automatically resolve these kinds of conflicts. It helps us learn more about controversial issues by engaging in dialogue with people who disagree with us and by examining our positions in the light of different ethical theories. In some instances, we will change our minds, or at least consider changing them. In most instances, we will emerge from the process with a better idea of the merits and the limitations of different positions.

Our decisions are as good as the resources we use to make them. Most poor decisions are made, not because decision makers want to make poor decisions, but because they lack important resources. Often this could have been remedied by inviting alternative points of view. By entering into dialogue with others, we give others and ourselves the chance to increase our resources for making decisions.

The Ethical Process, then, is a way of working together to make better decisions and fewer mistakes. It is a learning activity. Its goal is to increase our knowledge, which will increase the likelihood that our decisions will be the right ones.

The Ethical Process is a guide, not a substitute, for thinking. Filling in the blanks on the worksheets is only the beginning of the process, not the end. If the worksheets open up new areas for reflection, increase your conceptual basis for analysis, and allow your conversations with others to move beyond exchanging opinions to exploring what's behind the opinions, then the process has served you well.

KEY CHARACTERISTICS OF THE ETHICAL PROCESS

The process is designed for people who are willing to discuss controversial issues with others. Individuals can use the process alone, however, by considering alternative views.

The process begins with people stating their views of what should be done. In this way the process differs from those decision-making models that begin with gathering information. The advantage of beginning with people taking positions on issues is that it helps everyone understand why people have selected some information which supports their position, and have ignored other information which does not support their position.

The process uses argumentative structures to uncover the observations and values on which people rely when taking positions on issues. Thus, the process uses argument as a method for inquiry rather than as a means of fighting.

The process balances advocacy and inquiry. People begin by advocating their positions on an issue and then turn to inquiring about the reasons that support these positions. This can be a mutual process of exploring the different personal, social, and cultural backgrounds of different positions. The inquiry aso includes looking at how different ethical approaches might interpret the issues. After this period of inquiry, the process returns to advocating positions that are based on what has been learned.

The process includes both descriptive and normative analysis. Descriptive analysis looks at what is and normative analysis looks at what should be. The process enables both types of analysis by first describing the observations, values, and assumptions that support each proposal and then applying different normative criteria to evaluate the strengths of each argument.

The process connects dialogue and argument in such a way that students can develop "argumentative dialogues" by working together to find the best decision possible.

THE PROGRESSION OF THE ETHICAL PROCESS

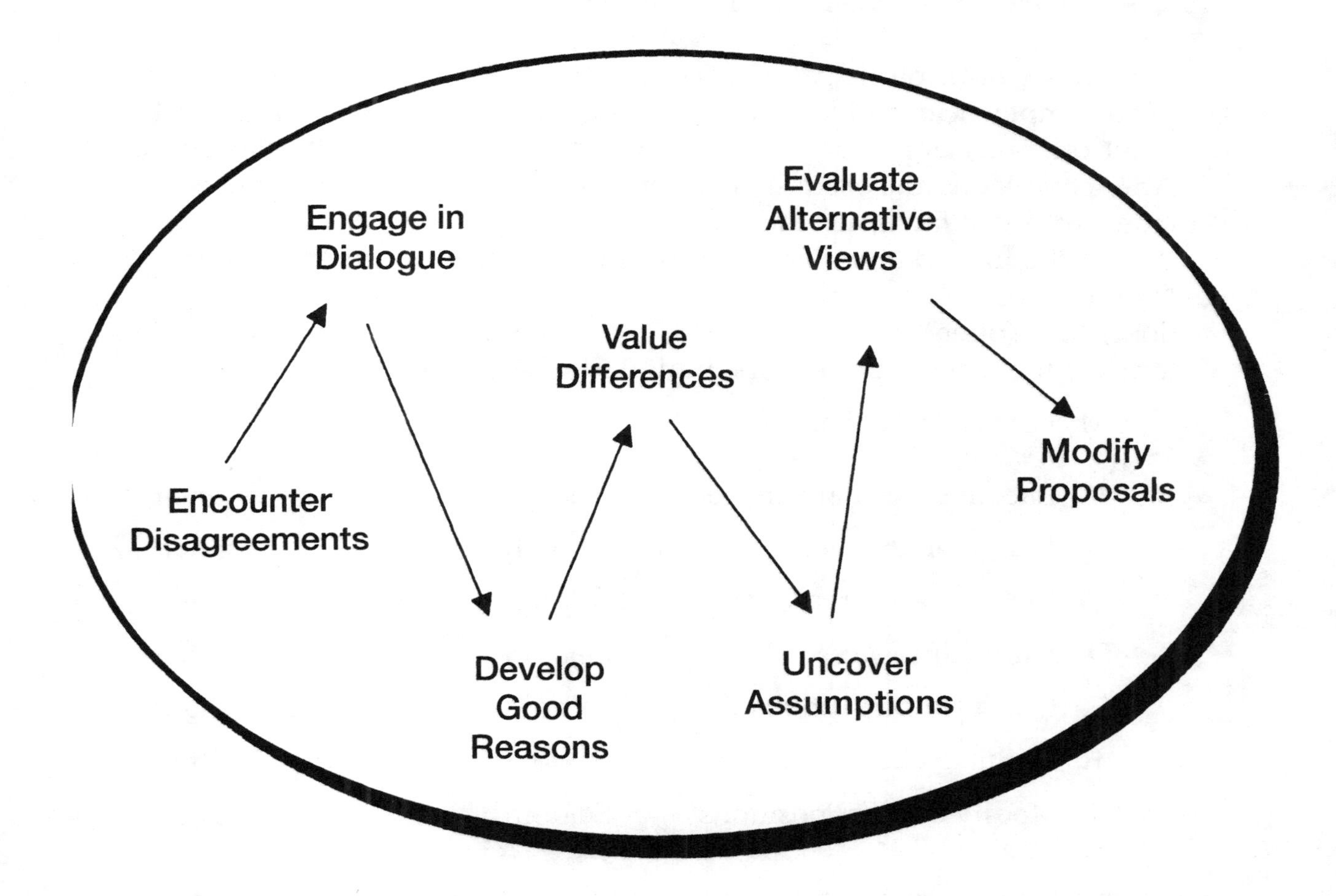

The Ethical Process involves a series of moves or moments that begin with disagreement about what should be done. By engaging in dialogue, members are able to both value differences and develop good reasons for their views. To understand each other's reasons, they uncover the assumptions behind them. With this new understanding, they can work together to evaluate the different views by applying different ethical standards of conduct. The process concludes with participants acknowledging what they have learned from each other by developing "modified proposals." The modified proposals show how the strengths of the different views alter their original positions. In this way, the final decision captures what the group has learned by engaging in the Ethical Process.

ACKNOWLEDGING OUR EVERYDAY COMPETENCE FOR ENGAGING IN ETHICAL REFLECTION

Most of us have participated in conversations in which we have developed competencies similar to those used in the Ethical Process. This worksheet offers an opportunity to highlight these conversational capacities. After completing the exercise, you can discuss with others the kind of relationships that facilitate ethical reflection.

In the first column, list seven people with whom you communicate. Include people from different settings. Then, using the scale from 1 (seldom) to 5 (often), evaluate each of the communicative relationships in terms of the seven aspects of the Ethical Process listed below.

My conversational partner and I:

A.	Encounter disagreements	Seldom	1 2 3 4 5	Often
B.	Engage in dialogue	Seldom	1 2 3 4 5	Often
C.	Develop good reasons	Seldom	1 2 3 4 5	Often
D.	Value differences	Seldom	1 2 3 4 5	Often
E.	Uncover assumptions	Seldom	1 2 3 4 5	Often
F.	Evaluate alternative views	Seldom	1 2 3 4 5	Often
G.	Modify original positions	Seldom	1 2 3 4 5	Often

Conversational Partners	A	B	C	D	E	F	G

EXPERIENCES WITH DISAGREEMENT

This workbook presents ethics as a way of responding to controversial issues. Such issues include the "big" issues of the day, as well as the everyday issues that we face in trying to make decisions with others. "Controversial issues" are any issues that arise from disagreement about the right thing to do. A group's pattern of responding to disagreement, therefore, may determine whether ethical reflection is even possible. So the next pages explore our experiences with, and attitudes toward, disagreement.

List three frequent responses to disagreement you have experienced at work, school, or at home.

1. ______________________________

____

____

____

____

2. ______________________________

____

____

____

____

3. ______________________________

____

____

____

____

Discuss with others in small groups the reasons for the different types of responses to disagreement that you have experienced. The reasons may be individual capacity, group patterns and expectations, organizational structures and cultures, and/or social norms. The following pages focus on our perceptions of group patterns and expectations.

FACING DISAGREEMENT

To explore attitudes toward disagreement, ask people whether they agree or disagree with the following statements.

- Most people do what they think is right, considering the world they think they live in.
- If people disagree with me, it's probably because they don't understand me.
- If you are right, then I am wrong.
- We can consider our disagreements only because of our agreements.
- We learn more from people who disagree with us than from people who agree with us.
- If people ignore their disagreements, they will usually become more productive.
- Many mistakes occur because people refuse to listen to other views.

ADVANTAGES AND DISADVANTAGES OF DISAGREEMENT

Although disagreements provide opportunities for learning and for making better decisions, they also entail some risks. Examine this list of the advantages and disadvantages of disagreement.

ADVANTAGES	DISADVANTAGES
Allows us to examine reasons.	May threaten cooperation.
Increases the pool of resources.	Can create a debating game of winners and losers.
Can reveal a proposal's limits.	May delay action.
May prevent mistakes.	May favor "argumentative" types over others.
Can promote a more inclusive and realistic proposal.	May stifle participation.
Creates opportunity for learning.	

If you look closely, you will notice that the advantages column refers more to reasons and decisions, and the disadvantages column more to feelings and relations. To benefit from the advantages and to minimize the disadvantages, people need to make sure that their conversations are supportive of different views and of different ways of expressing them. Sometimes, it will be necessary to examine and perhaps change an organization's culture and structure to enable such conversations. In any case, a group can usually increase its capacity to take advantage of disagreements if it chooses to engage in dialogue rather than debate.

THE DIALOGICAL CHOICE

The first, and perhaps the most important, step in the process of ethical reflection is choosing to engage in dialogue. This choice allows us to become co-learners in a mutual process of exploration. Dialogue involves listening to each other—inquiring, exploring, and reflecting. Choosing dialogue does not mean that we cannot disagree. Quite the contrary. It means that disagreement becomes a resource for discovering more than either of us knew before.

In contrast to a debate, which pits one person against another to see who wins and who loses, dialogue brings people together in a joint endeavor to increase their understanding.

Dialogue	**Debate**
Is driven by implicit meanings	Is driven by individual interests
Supports strengths	Exploits weaknesses
Strengthens community	Increases alienation
Allows participants to explore positions	Forces participants to protect positions
Allows participants to face each other as partners	Forces participants to face each other as combatants

WORKSHEET #1-1

Learning Through Dialogue

Select a partner and work together in answering the following questions.

1. "How do we differ?" (List three significant experiences that your partner has had that you have not.)

____

____

____

2. "What does your partner know from these experiences that you do not know?" (Ask questions of inquiry to understand more about your partner's knowledge.)

____

____

____

3. Share with the larger group what you have learned that your partner knows that you did not know.

____

____

____

STARTING POINTS

THE SETTING:	A group of people must decide what is the best response to a controversial issue. An issue is controversial when people disagree about the right course of action.
THE ACTORS:	People whose moral responses to issues are based on their beliefs, feelings, and relationships. As moral beings, their senses of right and wrong are rooted in their social, emotional, and cognitive development. Although they disagree with one another on an issue, they agree to investigate the reasons for their different views by engaging in the Ethical Process.
THE ACTIVITY:	A dialogical process that enables participants to work together to discover and then to evaluate the value judgments and assumptions implicit in their proposals.
THE PURPOSE:	To increase everyone's resources so that they can make the best decision possible.

Chapter 11

Ethics in the World of Business

CASE 1.1 Johnson & Johnson: The Tylenol Crisis

On September 30, 1982, James Burke, the CEO of Johnson & Johnson, received word that several deaths in the Chicago area might be linked to one of the company's products.[1] Reports were sketchy at first, but authorities eventually determined that seven people died from taking cyanide-laced capsules of Extra-Strength Tylenol. The news riveted the nation's attention, and Burke faced the challenge of his career.

Tylenol is one of Johnson & Johnson's most successful products. The nonaspirin pain reliever was developed in the mid-1950s by McNeil Laboratories and sold initially as a prescription drug, primarily for hospital use. After Johnson & Johnson acquired McNeil Laboratories in 1959, the company recognized the drug's potential and gained approval to sell it as an over-the-counter medication. Sales increased slowly but steadily, and by 1982 Tylenol had captured over 35 percent of the $1 billion analgesic market—over three times the market share of its nearest competitor. The product provided 7 percent of Johnson & Johnson sales and a whopping 17 percent of the company's profits.

Tylenol's success was achieved by heavy advertising and price reductions. Because the only active ingredient, acetaminophen, can easily be manufactured, the drug was open prey to competitors, and when Bristol-Myers introduced Datril in 1975, Johnson & Johnson had to move quickly. The company protected its market share by slashing prices by 30 percent and boosting advertising to $4 million in 1976 (from $142,000 the year before). The figure rose to $40 million in 1982, and during the seven-year period from 1976 to 1982, Johnson & Johnson spent over $155 million to promote the Tylenol brand. Developing a best-selling brand had been expensive, but by 1982 the company was reaping the rewards of its investment.

The cyanide that caused the deaths was placed in capsules of Extra-Strength Tylenol. Advertised as "the most potent pain reliever you can buy without a prescription," the extra-strength product—which contains 500 milligrams of acetaminophen as compared with 350 milligrams in regular Tylenol—was sold at the time in both capsule and tablet form. Extra-Strength Tylenol was instantly popular, and by 1979 it accounted for 70 percent of all Tylenol sales. The capsule form appealed to consumers because it was easier to swallow and also because of an association of capsules with strength. Capsules are susceptible to tampering, however, because they can be pulled apart and refilled, and the fact that all of the deaths occurred in one area—and that only a few capsules in each of the bottles contained cyanide—suggested that someone (who has never been apprehended) took advantage of the ease with which capsules can be used to kill.

James Burke and his staff quickly concluded that the tampering had not occurred at a McNeil production facility, and so the company was not responsible for the cyanide contamination itself. Still, the poisonings were associated with the Tylenol name, and sales of the brand were dropping rapidly. The public reaction was fueled by confusion, which was furthered by false reports of Tylenol-related deaths in several other states, and the company feared a rash of copycat incidents, especially as Halloween approached.

Johnson & Johnson faced two problems. One was how to respond to public concerns—and to the possibility that more cyanide-laced capsules might still be found. What information should the company release to the media and to worried customers? What changes, if any, should be made in the advertising for Tylenol, or should all advertising be suspended? Should Johnson & Johnson recall capsules of Extra-Strength Tylenol only in the Chicago area, or should the company pull all capsules from store shelves nationwide? A nationwide recall would involve an estimated 31 million bottles with a retail value of $100 million. Removal of the product would also cede valuable shelf space to Tylenol's competitors and risk a permanent loss of market share.

The problem, moreover, was tampering, which could occur with any medication in capsule form, and indeed with any over-the-counter drug. The pharmaceutical industry, and not merely Johnson & Johnson, was threatened by the Tylenol poisonings. The cost of a recall outside of the Chicago area was out of proportion to the risk, and consumers faced far greater risk from adverse reactions to many pharmaceutical products that were regarded as safe. On the other hand, capsules of Extra-Strength Tylenol on store shelves (which no longer belonged to Johnson & Johnson) was so much "dead stock" that might never be sold, and the loss would be borne by distributors and retailers.

The second problem was whether—and if so, how—to save the Tylenol brand name. Many marketing experts were convinced that the brand was doomed—that the public would forever associate Tylenol with death—and that a new identity should be sought for an acetaminophen product before the company's competitors could capture the market. James Burke was convinced that the brand name could be saved if Johnson & Johnson restored public confidence quickly, but doing so would require not only reassuring words but steps to make tampering less likely. An aggressive campaign could backfire, however, if another poisoning occurred, because the company could be accused of being more concerned with profits than consumer safety.

In addressing these problems, James Burke and others at Johnson & Johnson had the benefit of goodwill from a public that recognized that the company was also a victim of a senseless crime. The company also had an invaluable resource in the relation of trust that had been built through decades of adherence to the Johnson & Johnson credo. This declaration of the company's responsibility to customers, employees, and the community—as well as stockholders—had enabled Johnson & Johnson to prosper so far. Could it also be a guide in the current crisis?

INTRODUCTION

The Tylenol crisis created an unusual, and fortunately rare, test for the managers of Johnson & Johnson. The ethical dilemmas of management are generally less dramatic. Still, this case exhibits some typical features of ethical decision making in business. Johnson & Johnson managers faced ethical issues that were inextricably bound to practical business concerns. Their job was not merely to do the right thing but also to make a sound business decision. The future of the company was at stake. They had to act, moreover, in a highly competitive market environment under severe time pressure without adequate information. In the Tylenol crisis, the managers of Johnson & Johnson had to consider issues that were outside their expertise and not commonly a part of corporate decision making. They benefited, however, from the values expressed in the Johnson & Johnson credo.

This book is about the ethical issues that arise for managers—and, indeed, for all people, including employees, consumers, and members of the public. Corporate activities affect us all, and so the conduct of business is a matter of concern for everyone with a stake in ethical management. The ethical issues we will be examining are those considered by managers in the ordinary course of their work, but they are also issues that are discussed in the pages of the business press, debated in the halls of Congress, and scrutinized by the courts. This is because ethical issues in business are closely tied to important matters of public policy and to the legislative and judicial processes of government. They are often only part of a complex set of issues.

Case 1.2 Four Business Decisions

The Sales Rep

A sales representative for a struggling computer supply firm has a chance to close a multimillion-dollar deal for an office system to be installed over a two-year period. The machines for the first delivery are in the company's warehouse, but the remainder would have to be ordered from the manufacturer. Because the manufacturer is having difficulty meeting the heavy demand for the popular model, the sales representative is not sure that subsequent deliveries can be made on time. Any delay in converting to the new system would be costly to the customer; however, the blame could be placed on the manufacturer. Should the sales representative close the deal without advising the customer of the problem?

The Research Director

The director of research in a large aerospace firm recently promoted a woman to head an engineering team charged with designing a critical component for a new plane. She was tapped for the job because of her superior knowledge of the engineering aspects of the project, but the men under her direction have been expressing resentment at working for a woman by subtly sabotaging the work of the team. The director believes that it is unfair to deprive the woman of advancement merely because of the prejudice of her male colleagues, but quick completion of the designs and the building of a prototype are vital to the success of the company. Should he remove the woman as head of the engineering team?

The Marketing VP

The vice president of marketing for a major brewing company is aware that college students account for a large proportion of beer sales and that people in this age group form lifelong loyalties to particular brands of beer. The executive is personally uncomfortable with the tasteless gimmicks used by her competitors in the industry to encourage drinking on campuses, including beach parties and beer-drinking contests. She worries about the company's contribution to underage drinking and alcohol abuse among college students. Should she go along with the competition?

The CEO

The CEO of a midsize producer of a popular line of kitchen appliances is approached about merging with a larger company. The terms offered by the suitor are very advantageous to the CEO, who would receive a large severance package. The shareholders of the firm would also benefit, because the offer for their stock is substantially above the current market price. The CEO learns, however, that plans call for closing a plant that is the major employer in a small town. The firm has always taken its social responsibility seriously, but the CEO is now unsure of how to balance the welfare of the employees who would be thrown out of work and the community where the plant is located against the interests of the shareholders. He is also not sure how much to take his own interests into account. Should he bail out in order to enrich himself?

BUSINESS DECISION MAKING

These four hypothetical examples give some idea of the ethical issues that arise at all levels of business. The individuals in these cases are faced with questions about ethics in their relations with customers, employees, and members of the larger society. Frequently the ethically correct course of action is clear, and people in business act accordingly. Exceptions occur, however, when there is uncertainty about ethical obligations in particular situations or when considerations of ethics come into conflict with the practical demands of business. The sales representative might not be sure, for example, about the extent to which he is obligated to provide information about possible delays in delivery. And the director of research, although convinced that discrimination is wrong, might still feel that he has no choice but to remove the woman as head of the team in order to get the job done.

In deciding on an ethical course of action, we can rely to some extent on the rules of right conduct that we employ in everyday life. Deception is wrong, for example, whether we deceive a friend or a customer. And corporations no less than persons have an obligation not to discriminate or cause harm. Unfortunately, business activity also has some features that limit the applicability of our ordinary ethical views. What we ought to do depends to some extent on our situation and on the particular roles we occupy, and slightly different rules or codes of ethics are needed to guide us in the different departments of our lives. The CEO, by virtue of his position, has responsibilities to several different constituencies, and his problem in part is to find the proper balance.

One of the features that distinguishes business activity is its *economic* character. In the world of business, we interact with each other not as family members, friends, or neighbors but as buyers and sellers, employers and employees, and the like. Trading, for example, is often accompanied by hard bargaining, in which both sides conceal their full hand and perhaps engage in some bluffing. And a skilled salesperson is well versed in the art of arousing a customer's attention (sometimes by a bit of puffery) to clinch the sale. Still, there is an "ethics of trading" that prohibits the use of false or deceptive claims and tricks such as "bait-and-switch" advertising.

Employment is also recognized as a special relation with its own standards of right and wrong. Employers are generally entitled to hire and promote whomever they wish and to lay off or terminate workers without regard for the consequences. (This right is being increasingly challenged, however, by those who hold that employers ought to fire only for cause and to give employees an opportunity to defend themselves.) Employees also have some protections, such as a right not to be discriminated against or to be exposed to workplace hazards. There are many controversies in the workplace, such as the rights of employers and employees with regard to drug testing.

The ethics of business, then, is at least in part the ethics of economic relations—such as those involving buyers and sellers and employers and employees. So we need to ask, what are the rules that ought to govern these kinds of relations? And how do these rules differ from those that apply in other spheres of life?

A second distinguishing feature of business activity is that it typically takes place in large, impersonal *organizations*. An organization, according to organizational theory, is a hierarchical system of functionally defined positions designed to achieve some goal or set of goals. Consequently, the members of a business organization, in assuming a particular position—such as sales representative or vice president for marketing or CEO—take on new obligations to pursue the goals of the firm. Thus, the marketing executive is not free to act solely on her own standards of good taste and social responsibility at the expense of sales for the brewing company.

Nor can the CEO rightfully ignore the interests of shareholders and consider only the impact of the merger on one group of employees and their community any more than he can consider only his self-interest.

Levels of Decision Making

Decision making occurs on several distinct levels: the level of the *individual*, the level of the *organization*, and the level of the *business system*. Situations that confront individuals in the workplace and require them to make a decision about their own response are on the level of individual decision making. An employee with an unreasonably demanding boss, for example, or a boss who is discovered padding his expense account faces the question: What do I do? Whether to live with the difficult boss or to blow the whistle on the padding are questions to be answered by the individual and acted on accordingly.

Many ethical problems occur at the level of the organization in the sense that the individual decision maker is acting on behalf of the organization in bringing about some organizational change. Sexual harassment, for example, is an individual matter for the person suffering the abuse (and for the harasser), but a manager in an office where sexual harassment is happening must take steps not only to rectify the situation but also to ensure that it does not occur again. The decision in this case may be a disciplinary action, which involves a manager acting within his or her organizational role. The manager may also institute training to prevent sexual harassment and possibly develop a sexual harassment policy, which not only prohibits certain behavior but also creates procedures for handling complaints. Developing a policy with regard to sexual harassment, as opposed to dealing with harassment of one's self, involves decisions on the organizational level rather than the level of the individual.

Problems that result from accepted business practices or from features of the economic system cannot effectively be addressed by any single organization, much less a lone individual. Sales practices within an industry, for example, are difficult for one company to change singlehandedly, because the company is constrained by competition with possibly less ethical competitors. The most effective solution is likely to be an industrywide code of ethics, agreed to by all. Similarly, the lower pay of women's work, which is discussed in Chapter 9, results from structural features of the labor market, which no one company or even industry can alter. A single employer can adopt a policy of comparable worth as one possible solution because the problem is systemic, and consequently any substantial change must be on the level of the system. Systemic problems are best solved by some form of regulation or economic reform.

Identifying the appropriate level for a decision is important, because an ethical problem may have no solution on the level at which it is approached. The beer marketer described in Case 1.2 may have little choice but to follow the competition in using tasteless gimmicks, because the problem has no real solution on the individual or organizational level. An effective response requires that she place the problem on the systemic level and seek a solution appropriate to that level. Richard T. DeGeorge has described such a move as "ethical displacement," which consists of addressing a problem on a level other than the one on which the problem appears.[2] The fact that some problems can be solved only by displacing them to a higher level is a source of great distress for individuals in difficult situations, because they still must find some less-than-perfect response on a lower level.

Three Points of View

Decision making in business involves many factors, of which ethics is only one. In order to gain an understanding of the relevance of ethics for the conduct of business, it will be useful to begin with a description of three points of view from which decisions in business can be made: the economic, the legal, and the moral. Then we can see how these points of view may be integrated to form an approach to business decision making that can aid people facing difficult ethical situations.

Closing the deal for the sale of an office computer system is good from a strictly economic or business point of view, as long as there are no repercussions. The quick completion of the design for the airplane component and increasing beer sales among college students are good for the same reason. The individuals involved might also evaluate different courses of action from the point of view of their own careers and ask: What is best for me? What should I do from the point of view of self-interest? Or the individuals involved might consider the law and take a legal point of view. Would removing the woman from her job as head of the engineering team be considered illegal sexual discrimination? Would it be legal to oppose the merger merely to avoid closing the plant? Finally, the individuals involved might consider the moral point of view when making their decisions. Morally speaking, what is the best thing to do?

The Moral Point of View. In order to understand what it means to decide something from the moral point of view, let us consider the case of the sales representative. In deciding whether to disclose the possible delays in delivery, he might ask: What is accepted business practice? What would my boss expect me to do? What would other sales representatives in my company or the industry do? What kind of conduct is generally regarded as legally permissible? To proceed in these ways is to seek guidance from what is conventionally thought by one's peers or society at large to be right or wrong. Unable to find an answer, or perhaps wanting to make sure that he had found the correct one, the sales representative might push further and ask for the reasons that he ought to act in one way rather than another. Three reasons readily suggest themselves.

First, informing the customer about the possibility of a delay might result in losing the sale and a handsome commission. Judged purely by considerations of benefit to himself, he ought to close the deal, unless, of course, he would suffer greater harm if the company is unable to fulfill the contract. If benefit and harm to himself are reasons for acting in some way, why should he not consider the benefit and harm for the customer as well? The fact that the customer might suffer substantial losses would seem to be a morally relevant reason for revealing the possible delivery problems. But the sales representative might think, "I have no obligation to look out for this customer's welfare. If he suffers a loss, that's his problem, not mine; I am not going to pass up a sale to protect him."

On further reflection, however, he might realize that trust is essential in his line of work. If he and the company acquire a reputation for dishonesty, doing business will be more difficult in the future. In addition, if trust is lost in business as a whole so that buyers and sellers can no longer rely on each other's word in their dealings, then everyone suffers. Full disclosure in trade is of value because, on the whole, it helps everyone. In terms of benefit and harm for all concerned, therefore, it is a good policy to inform a customer of matters such as the possibility of delays.

Second, insofar as not revealing the information is misrepresentation, it is a form of lying, and we have been taught since childhood that lying is wrong. Misrepresentation does not require that something false actually be said. If the sales representative assures the customer that there will be no problem with the deliveries, then he is lying. But a person can lie by remaining silent or even saying something true. Consider a person selling a used car who says that the transmission was checked by a mechanic only last week but fails to add that the mechanic found serious problems. If the seller's words would lead a hearer to conclude that the transmission is in sound condition, misrepresentation has occurred.

If we wish to push the matter further, we can ask, what is morally wrong with lying or misrepresentation? If we appeal to the harm done, so that the rule "Do not lie" is itself based on benefit and harm, then this second reason is no different from the first. However, a different line of reasoning can be sketched as follows. To intentionally bring about a false belief so that another person cannot make a rational decision about some matter of importance is to manipulate that person. Manipulating or using another person is morally objectionable because it involves treating people as "things" for satisfying our desires and preventing them from acting to satisfy their own desires. In short, manipulation shows a lack of respect for the essential humanity of others. And the idea of respect for persons is an important moral consideration—different from benefit and harm—that supports the commonly accepted view that lying is wrong.

Third, the sales representative might ask: How would my action appear to the customer were he to know the full facts? Or how would I view it if I were in the customer's place? Would I want to be treated in the same way? These questions suggest a line of reasoning that is commonly expressed by the Golden Rule: Do unto others as you would have them do unto you. Part of the force of this rule is its insistence on equality, which is an important element of fairness or justice. To treat others in ways that we would not like to be treated is to make exceptions for ourselves and hence to depart from strict equality. The point is also expressed in the familiar slogan "What's fair for one is fair for all." Assuming that the sales representative would not want to have important information withheld from him, then it would be wrong for him to withhold the information from the customer.

Two Features. The moral point of view has two important features.[3] First is a willingness to seek out and act on *reasons.* The best action, according to one writer, is "the course of action which is supported by the best reasons."[4] This does not get us very far without some account of what are the best reasons, but it indicates a commitment to use reason in deliberating about what to do and to construct moral arguments that are persuasive to ourselves and others. Moral rules should not be accepted merely because they are a part of the prevailing morality. Rather, we should attempt to justify the rules we act on by means of the most general and comprehensive kind of reasons available.

Second, the moral point of view requires us to be *impartial.* We must regard the interests of everyone, including ourselves, as equally worthy of consideration and give all interests equal weight in deciding what to do. The moral point of view is the opposite of being purely self-interested. The idea of a personal morality—that is, a morality to be followed only by ourselves—is absurd. Morality by its very nature is public, in the sense that it involves a shared set of rules that can be observed by everyone.[5] A good test of the moral point of view is whether we would feel comfortable if our colleagues, friends, and family were to know about a decision we had made. Would we be willing to have an article on it appear on the front page of the local newspaper, for example? A decision made from the moral point of view can withstand and even invites this kind of openness and scrutiny.

An Integrated Approach

The approach advocated in this book is that decision making in business should involve an integration of all three points of view: the economic, the legal, and the moral. Business ethics is, in part, the attempt to think clearly and deeply about ethical issues in business and to arrive at conclusions that are supported by the strongest possible arguments. An integrated approach requires that we give proper weight to the economic and legal aspects of a problem, but to think that sound business decisions could be made solely from a perspective that excludes ethics is just as wrongheaded as it is to think that they could be made on the basis of ethical reasoning alone.

Integrating different points of view is nothing new; we do it all the time. Managers must juggle financial, production, marketing, personnel, and a host of other factors in taking just the economic point of view. Inevitably, there is tension between the three points of view, but the ideal resolution is not a trade-off between ethics and other considerations. The outcome, instead, should be a decision that is ethically defensible while at the same time satisfying the legitimate demands of economic performance and a company's legal obligations.

An example of an integrated approach is provided by Johnson & Johnson's response to the Tylenol crisis (see Case 1.1). Under the leadership of CEO James

Burke, the company quickly cleared all bottles of Extra-Strength Tylenol capsules off store shelves in the Chicago area and recalled all bottles from the two batches that had been identified in the poisonings. A decision was made to be completely candid with the medical community, the media, and the public. Accordingly, the company issued warnings to physicians and hospitals around the world, briefed the press fully, and provided a toll-free telephone number for answering consumer inquiries. In addition, all advertising for Tylenol was temporarily suspended. On October 6, 1982, one week after the first Tylenol-related deaths, Johnson & Johnson instituted a nationwide recall of the 31 million bottles of Regular- and Extra-Strength Tylenol capsules that remained unsold.

James Burke was convinced that the Tylenol brand name could be saved with a well-designed strategy. The key was to protect consumers by developing a tamper-resistant package that would both discourage tampering and make tampering more evident. The Tylenol crisis had alerted the pharmaceutical industry to the need for tamper-resistant packaging, and on November 4, 1982, the Food and Drug Administration (FDA) made such protection mandatory. By acting quickly to develop the technology, Johnson & Johnson could establish an industry leadership position. The company decided on a three-point protection system consisting of a tape seal on the box, a wrapper on the cap, and a seal over the mouth of the bottle. By late November, Extra-Strength Tylenol in capsule form was once again on store shelves. Advertising was resumed in December, and more than 80 million coupons were distributed for the product in its new tamper-resistant packaging. The direct cost for this recovery effort has been estimated at $150 million.

The response of Johnson & Johnson to the Tylenol crisis can be explained as sound business decision making. The effort to restore a valuable brand name was costly, but the high-stakes gamble paid off. The decision for a nationwide recall of all capsule products may appear obvious in retrospect because of the crucial role it played in assuring consumers of the company's commitment to safety. Strong arguments were made at the time against a recall, however, including the tremendous expense and the success of other companies in dismissing product tampering as isolated incidents.

An important factor in deciding on a recall was the Johnson & Johnson credo (see Exhibit 1.1). Developed in the 1940s as an expression of the company's way of doing business, the credo guided several generations of Johnson & Johnson employees. One of James Burke's first acts upon becoming CEO was to hold a series of credo "challenges," to determine whether the document was still relevant to management decision making, and the outcome was a gratifying reaffirmation of the credo's continuing force. Although economic and legal considerations played a role in Johnson & Johnson's response to the Tylenol crisis, the credo served too, and the clear statements of responsibility that it contained enabled the company to make some really tough, but ultimately right, decisions.

In retrospect, however, the company might be faulted for one decision: to continue marketing Extra-Strength Tylenol in capsule form. Consumer surveys found that a segment of the market strongly preferred medication in a capsule. But

Exhibit 1
Johnson & Johnson: Our Credo

We believe our first responsibility is to the doctors, nurses and patients, to mothers and fathers and all others who use our products and services. In meeting their needs everything we do must be of high quality. We must constantly strive to reduce our costs in order to maintain reasonable prices. Customers' orders must be serviced promptly and accurately. Our suppliers and distributors must have an opportunity to make a fair profit.

We are responsible to our employees, the men and women who work with us throughout the world. Everyone must be considered as an individual. We must respect their dignity and recognize their merit. They must have a sense of security in their jobs. Compensation must be fair and adequate, and working conditions clean, orderly and safe. We must be mindful of ways to help our employees fulfill their family responsibilities. Employees must feel free to make suggestions and complaints. There must be equal opportunity for employment, development, and advancement for those qualified. We must provide competent management, and their actions must be just and ethical.

We are responsible to the communities in which we live and work and to the world community as well. We must be good citizens—support good works and charities and bear our fair share of taxes. We must encourage civic improvements and better health and education. We must maintain in good order the property we are privileged to use, protecting the environment and natural resources.

Our final responsibility is to our stockholders. Business must make a sound profit. We must experiment with new ideas. Research must be carried on, innovative programs developed and mistakes paid for. New equipment must be purchased, new facilities provided and new products launched. Reserves must be created to provide for adverse times. When we operate according to these principles, the stockholders should realize a fair return.

Johnson & Johnson, the statement *Our Credo,* reprinted by permission.

a tampering incident about three years later, in February 1986, took the life of a 23-year-old New York State woman and finally convinced Burke that the safety of capsules could not be assured, even with tamper-resistant packaging. Production of Tylenol in capsule form was terminated, and a new product, Tylenol caplets—tablets shaped like capsules—was introduced. At the time, approximately one-third of all Tylenol sold was in capsule form, and the change was estimated to reduce Tylenol sales by about 6 percent annually. Perhaps Johnson & Johnson should have taken this step three years earlier.

Case 1.3 The Ethics of Hardball

Toys "R" Us: Fair or Foul?

Hardball tactics are often applauded in business, but when Child World was the victim, the toy retailer cried foul.[6] Its complaint was directed against a major competitor, Toys "R" Us, whose employees allegedly bought Child World inventory off the shelves during a promotion in which customers received $25 gift certificates for buying merchandise worth $100. The employees of Toys "R" Us were accused of selecting products that Child World sells close to cost, such as diapers, baby food, and infant formula. These items could be resold by Toys "R" Us at a profit, because the purchase price at Child World was barely above what a wholesaler would charge, and then Toys "R" Us could redeem the certificates for additional free merchandise, which could be resold at an even higher profit. Child World claims that its competitor bought up to $1.5 million worth of merchandise in this undercover manner and received as much as $375,000 worth of gift certificates. The practice is apparently legal, although Child World stated that the promotion excluded dealers, wholesalers, and retailers. Executives at Toys "R" Us do not deny the accusation and contend that the practice is common in the industry. Child World may have left itself open to such a hardball tactic by slashing prices and offering the certificates in an effort to increase market share against its larger rival.

Home Depot: Good Ethics or Shrewd Business?

When weather forecasters predicted that Hurricane Andrew would strike the Miami area with full force, customers rushed to stock up on plywood and other building materials.[7] That weekend the 19 Home Depot stores in southern Florida sold more 4-foot-by-8-foot sheets of exterior plywood than they usually sell in two weeks. On August 24, 1992, the hurricane struck, destroying or damaging more than 75,000 homes, and in the wake of the devastation, individual price gougers were able to sell basics like water and food as well as building materials at wildly inflated prices. But not Home Depot. The chain's stores initially kept prices on plywood at prehurricane levels, and when wholesale prices rose on average 28 percent, the company announced that it would sell plywood, roofing materials, and plastic sheeting at cost and take no profit on the sales. It did limit quantities, however, to prevent price gougers from reselling the goods at higher prices. In addition, Home Depot successfully negotiated with its suppliers of plywood, including Georgia-Pacific, the nation's largest plywood producer, to roll back prices to prehurricane levels. Georgia-Pacific, like Home Depot, has a large presence in Florida; the company runs 16 mills and distribution centers in the state and owns 500,000 acres of timberland. Although prices increased early in anticipation of Hurricane Andrew, Home Depot was still able, with the cooperation of suppliers, to sell half-inch plywood sheets for $10.15 after the hurricane, compared with a price of $8.65 before, thereby limiting the increase to less than 18 percent. Home Depot executives explained their decision as an act of good ethics by not profiting from human misery. Others contend, however, that the company made a shrewd business decision.

ETHICS, ECONOMICS, AND LAW

Businesses are economic organizations that operate within a framework of law. They are organized primarily to provide goods and services as well as jobs, and their success depends on efficient operation. In a capitalist system, firms must compete effectively in an open market and make a profit. American business has often been described as a game, in which the aim is to make as much profit as possible while staying within the rules of the game, which are set mainly by government.[8] On this view, it may be helpful and even essential to observe certain ethical standards, but doing so is merely a means to the end of profit making.

Both economics and law are critical to business decision making, but the view that they are the only relevant considerations and that ethics does not apply is plainly false. Even hard-fought games like football have a code of sportsmanship in addition to a rule book, and business, too, is governed by more than the legal rules. In addition, a competitive business system, in which everyone pursues his or her self-interest, depends for its existence on ethical behavior and is justified on ethical grounds. However, the relation of business ethics to economics and the law is very complicated and not easily summarized. The following discussion is intended to clarify these relations.

The Relation of Ethics and Economics

According to economic theory, firms in a free market utilize scarce resources or factors of production (labor, raw materials, and capital) in order to produce an output (goods and services). The demand for this output is determined by the preferences of individual consumers who select from among the available goods and services so as to maximize the satisfaction of their preferences, which is called utility. Firms also seek to maximize their preferences or utility by increasing their output up to the point where the amount received from the sale of goods and services equals the amount spent for labor, raw materials, and capital—that is, where marginal revenues equal marginal costs. Under fully competitive conditions, the result is economic efficiency, which means the production of the maximum output for the least amount of input.

Economics thus provides an explanatory account of the choices of economic actors, whether they be individuals or firms. On this account, the sole reason for any choice is to maximize utility. However, ethics considers many other kinds of reasons, including rights and justice and noneconomic values. To make a choice on the basis of ethics—that is, to use ethical reasons in making a decision—appears at first glance to be incompatible with economic choice. To make decisions on economic grounds and on ethical grounds is to employ two different kinds of reasoning. This apparent incompatibility dissolves on closer inspection. If the economists' account of economic reasoning is intended to be merely an explanation, then it tells us how we do reason in making economic choices but not how we *ought* to reason. Economics as a science need do no more than offer explanations, but economists generally hold that economic reasoning is also justified. That is, economic actors ought to make utility maximizing choices.

The Justification of the Market System. The argument for this position is the classical defense of the market system, which is discussed in Chapter 4. In *The Wealth of Nations,* Adam Smith, the "father" of modern economics, justified the pursuit of self-interest in exchange on the grounds that by making trades for our own advantage, we promote the interests of others. The justification for a free market capitalist system is, in part, that by pursuing profit, business firms promote the welfare of the whole society. Commentators on Adam Smith have observed that this argument assumes a well-ordered civil society with a high level of honesty and trust and an abundance of other moral virtues. Smith's argument would not apply well to a chaotic society marked by pervasive corruption and mistrust. Furthermore, in his defense of the free market in *The Wealth of Nations,* Smith was speaking about *exchange,* whereas economics also includes *production* and *distribution.*[9] The distribution of goods, for example, is heavily influenced by different initial endowments, access to natural resources, and the vagaries of fortune, among other factors. Whether the vast disparities in wealth in the world are justified is a question of distribution, not exchange, and is not addressed by Smith's argument.

Moreover, certain conditions must be satisfied in order for business activity to benefit society. These include the observance of minimal moral restraints to prevent theft, fraud, and the like. Markets must be fully competitive, with easy entry and exit, and everyone must possess all relevant information. In addition, all costs of production should be reflected in the prices that firms and consumers pay. For example, unintended consequences of business activity, such as job-related accidents, injuries from defective products, and pollution, are costs of production that are often not covered or internalized by the manufacturer but passed to others as spillover effects or *externalities.* Many business ethics problems arise when these conditions for the operation of a free market are not satisfied.

Some Conditions for Free Markets. A common view is that ensuring the conditions for free markets and correcting for their absence is a job for government. It is government's role, in other words, to create the rules of the game that allow managers to make decisions solely on economic grounds. However, the task of maintaining the marketplace cannot be handled by government alone, and the failure of government to do its job may create an obligation for business to help. Although government does enact and enforce laws against theft and fraud, including such specialized forms as the theft of trade secrets and fraud in securities transactions, there are many gray areas in which self-regulation and restraint should be exercised. Hardball tactics like those allegedly employed by Toys "R" Us (Case 1.3) are apparently legal, but many companies would consider such deliberate sabotage of a competitor to be an unacceptable business practice that is incompatible with the market system.

Recent work in economics has revealed the influence of ethics on people's economic behavior. Economists have shown how a reputation for honesty and trustworthiness, for example, attracts customers and potential business partners, thus creating economic opportunities that would not be available otherwise. Similarly, people and firms with an unsavory reputation are punished in the market. People are also motivated in their market behavior by consideration of fairness. This is illustrated by the "ultimatum bargaining game," in which two people are given a certain amount of money (say $10) on the condition that one person proposes how the money is to be divided (for example, $5 to each) and the second person accepts or rejects the proposed division. The first person can make only one proposal, and if the proposal is rejected by the second person, the money is taken away and each person receives nothing. Economic theory suggests that the second person would accept any proposal, no matter how small the share, if the alternative is no money at all. Hence, the first person could offer to share as little as $1 or less. But many people who play the game will refuse a proposal in which they receive a share that is considered too small and hence unfair.[10]

Economists explain the behavior of companies like Home Depot (Case 1.3) by the fact that considerations of fairness force firms to limit profit-seeking behavior. Consumers remember price gouging and other practices that they consider unfair and will punish the wrongdoers by ceasing to do business with them or even engaging in boycotts. One study found that people do not believe that scarcity is an acceptable reason for raising prices (despite what economists teach about supply and demand),[11] and so Home Depot and Georgia-Pacific, which are there for the long haul, have more to lose than gain by taking advantage of a natural disaster. Evidence also indicates that people in a natural disaster feel that everyone ought to make some sacrifice, so that profit seeking by a few is perceived as shirking a fair share of the burden.[12]

Finally, when economics is used in practice to support matters of public policy, it must be guided by noneconomic values. Economic analysis can be applied to the market for cocaine as easily as the soybean market, but it cannot tell us whether we should allow both markets. That is a decision for public policy makers on the basis of other considerations. A tax system, for example, depends on sound economic analysis, but the U.S. tax code attempts to achieve many aims simultaneously and to be accepted as fair. A demonstration that a particular system is the most efficient from a purely economic perspective would not necessarily be persuasive to a legislator in drafting a new tax code.

The Relation of Ethics and the Law

Business activity takes place within an extensive framework of law, and some people hold that law is the only set of rules that applies to business activity. Law, not ethics, is the only relevant guide. The reasons that lead people to hold this view are varied, but two predominate.[13]

Two Schools of Thought. One school of thought is that law and ethics govern two different realms. Law prevails in public life, whereas ethics is a private matter. The law is a clearly defined set of enforceable rules that applies to everyone, whereas ethics is a matter of personal opinion that reflects how we choose to lead our own lives. Consequently, it would be a mistake to apply ethical rules in business, just as it would be a mistake to apply the rules of poker to tennis. A variant of this position is that the law represents a minimal level of expected conduct that everyone should observe. Ethics, on the other hand, is a higher, optional level. It's "nice" to be ethical, but our conduct *has* to be legal.

The other school of thought is that the law embodies the ethics of business. There are ethical rules that apply to business, according to this position, and they have been enacted by legislators into laws, which are enforceable by judges in a court. As a form of social control, law has many advantages over ethics. Law provides more precise and detailed rules than ethics, and the courts not only enforce these rules with state power but also are available to interpret them when the wording is unclear. A common set of rules known to all also provides a level playing field. Imagine the chaos if competing teams each decided for themselves what the rules of a game ought to be. For these reasons, some people hold that it is morally sufficient in business merely to observe the law. Their motto is "If it's legal, then it's morally okay."[14]

Why the Law Is Not Enough. Despite their differences, these two schools of thought have the same practical implication: Managers need consider only the law in making decisions. This implication is not only false but also highly dangerous. Regardless of the view that a practicing manager takes on the relation of law and ethics, reliance on the law alone is prescription for disaster, as many individuals and firms have discovered. Approval from a company's legal department does not always assure a successful legal resolution, and companies have prevailed in court only to suffer adverse consequences in the marketplace. As a practical matter, then, managers need to consider both the ethical and legal aspects of a situation in making a decision for many reasons, including the following.

First, the law is inappropriate for regulating certain aspects of business activity. Not everything that is immoral is illegal. Some ethical issues in business concern interpersonal relations at work or relations between competitors, which would be difficult to regulate by law. Taking credit for someone else's work, making unreasonable demands on subordinates, and unjustly reprimanding an employee are all ethically objectionable practices, but they are best left outside the law. Some hardball tactics against competitors may also be legal but ethically objectionable. Whether the effort of Toys "R" Us to sabotage a promotion by its competitor is acceptable behavior (see Case 1.3) is open to dispute, but not every legal competitive maneuver is ethical. Generally, legislatures and the courts are reluctant to intervene in ordinary business decisions unless significant rights and interests are at stake. They rightly feel that outsiders should not second-guess the business judgment of people closer to a problem and impose broad rules for problems that require a more flexible approach. Companies also prefer to handle many problems without outside interference. Still, just because it is not illegal to do certain things does not mean that it is morally okay.

Second, the law is often slow to develop in new areas of concern. Christopher D. Stone points out that the law is primarily reactive, responding to problems that people in the business world can anticipate and deal with long before they come to public attention.[15] The legislative and judicial processes themselves take a long time, and meanwhile much damage can be done. This is true not only for newly emergent problems but also for long-recognized problems where the law has lagged behind public awareness. For example, racial and sexual discrimination was legal—and widely practiced in business—before the passage of the Civil Rights Act of 1964. It should not take a major piece of legislation to make corporate managers aware that discrimination is wrong. They should have recognized this and changed their discriminatory practices long before Congress finally got around to passing a law. At the present time, legal protection for employees who blow the whistle and those who are unjustly dismissed is just beginning to develop. Employers should not wait until they are forced by law to act on such matters of growing concern.

Third, the law itself often employs moral concepts that are not precisely defined, so it is impossible in some instances to understand the law without considering matters of morality. The requirement of *good faith*, for example, is ubiquitous in law. The National Labor Relations Act requires employers and the representatives of employees to bargain "in good faith." One defense against a charge of price discrimination is that a lower price was offered in a good-faith attempt to meet the price of a competitor. Yet the notion of good faith is not precisely defined in either instance. Abiding by the law, therefore, requires decision makers to have an understanding of this key moral concept.

The *fiduciary duty* of a person, such as a trustee, to act in the best interests of a beneficiary is another example. The classic statement of this duty was given by Justice Benjamin Cardozo in the case *Meinhard* v. *Salmon*:

> Many forms of conduct permissible in a workaday world for those acting at arm's length, are forbidden to those bound by fiduciary ties. A trustee is held to something stricter than the morals of the market place. Not honesty alone, but the punctilio of an honor the most sensitive, is then the standard of behavior.[16]

A person in a fiduciary relation, then, must act with reference to a very high standard that is properly a part of morality.

A fourth argument, closely related to the preceding one, is that the law itself is often unsettled, so that whether some course of action is legal must be decided by the courts. And in making a decision, the courts are often guided by moral considerations. Many people have thought that their actions, although perhaps immoral, were still legal, only to discover otherwise. The courts often refuse to interpret the law literally when doing so gives legal sanction to blatant immorality. Judges have some leeway or discretion in making decisions. In exercising this discretion, judges are not necessarily substituting morality for law but rather expressing a morality that is embodied in the law. Instead of the motto "If it's legal, it's morally okay," another motto is perhaps more accurate: "If it's morally wrong, it's probably also illegal." Where there is doubt about what the law is, morality is a good predictor of how the courts will decide.

Fifth, a pragmatic argument is that the law is a rather inefficient instrument, and an exclusive reliance on law alone invites legislation and litigation where it is not necessary. Many landmark enactments, such as the Civil Rights Act of 1964, the

National Environment Policy Act of 1969, the Occupational Safety and Health Act of 1970, and the Consumer Protection Act of 1972, were passed by Congress in response to public outrage over the well-documented failure of American businesses to act responsibly. Although business leaders lament the explosion of product liability suits by consumers injured by defective products, for example, consumers are left with little choice but to use the legal system when manufacturers themselves hide behind "If it's legal, it's morally okay." Adopting this motto, then, is often shortsighted, and businesses may often advance their self-interest more effectively by considering ethics in making decisions.

ETHICS AND MANAGEMENT

Most managers think of themselves as ethical persons, but some still question whether ethics is relevant to their role as a manager. It is important for people in business to be ethical, they might say, but being ethical in business is no different than being ethical in private life. The implication is that a manager need only be an ethical person. There is no need, in other words, to have specialized knowledge or skills in ethics.

Nothing could be further from the truth. Although there is no separate ethics of business, situations arise in business that are not easily addressed by ordinary ethical rules. We have already observed that the obligation to tell the truth is difficult to apply to the dilemma faced by the sales rep in Case 1.2. In addition, the manager of sales reps might face the task of determining the rules of acceptable sales practices for the whole organization and ensuring that the rules are followed. More broadly, high-level managers have a responsibility for creating and maintaining an ethical corporate climate that protects the organization against unethical and illegal conduct by its members. Furthermore, a well-defined value system serves to guide organizations in uncertain situations and to guard against the pursuit of unwise short-term gains.

Ethical Management and the Management of Ethics

A useful distinction can be made between *ethical management* and the *management of ethics.* Business ethics is often conceived as acting ethically as a manager by doing the right thing. This is *ethical management.* Acting ethically is important, both for individual success and organizational effectiveness. Ethical misconduct has ended more than a few promising careers, and some business firms have been severely harmed and even destroyed by the actions of a few individuals. Major scandals in the news attract our attention, but people in business face less momentous ethical dilemmas in the ordinary course of their work. These dilemmas sometimes result from misconduct by others, as when a subordinate is ordered to commit an unethical or illegal act, but they are also inherent in typical business situations.

The *management of ethics* is acting effectively in situations that have an ethical aspect. These situations occur in both the internal and the external environment of a business firm. Internally, organizations bind members together through myriad rules, procedures, policies, and values that must be carefully managed. Some of these, such as a policy on conflict of interest or the values expressed by the Johnson & Johnson credo, explicitly involve ethics. Effective organizational functioning also depends on gaining the acceptance of the rules, policies, and other guides, and this acceptance requires a perception of fairness and commitment. For example, an organization that does not "walk the talk" when it professes to value diversity is unlikely to gain the full cooperation of its employees. With respect to the external environment, corporations must successfully manage the demands for ethical conduct from groups concerned with racial justice, human rights, the environment, and other matters.

In order to practice both ethical management and the management of ethics, it is necessary for managers to possess some specialized *knowledge.* Many ethical issues have a factual background that must be understood. In dealing with a whistle-blower or developing a whistle-blowing policy, for example, the managers of a company should be aware of the motivation of whistle-blowers, the measures that other companies have found effective, and, not least, the relevant law. Some of this background is provided in Chapter 5 on whistle-blowing. In addition, many ethical issues involve competing theoretical perspectives that need to be understood by a manager. Whether it is ethical to use confidential information about a competitor or personal information about an employee depends on theories about intellectual property rights and the right to privacy that are debated by philosophers and legal theorists. Although a manager need not be equipped to participate in these debates, some familiarity with the theoretical considerations is helpful in dealing with practical situations.

To make sound ethical decisions and to implement them in a corporate environment are *skills* that come with experience and training. Some managers make mistakes because they fail to see the ethical dimensions of a situation. Other managers are unable to give proper weight to competing ethical factors or to see other people's perspectives. Thus, a manager may settle a controversial question to his or her satisfaction, only to discover that others still disagree. Moral imagination is often needed to arrive at creative solutions to problems. Finally, the resolution of a problem usually involves persuading others of the rightness of a position, and so the ability to explain one's reasoning is a valuable skill.

The need for specialized knowledge and skills is especially acute when business is conducted abroad.[17] In global business, there is a lack of consensus on acceptable standards of conduct, and practices that work well at home may fare badly elsewhere. This is especially true in less developed countries with lower standards and weak institutions. How should a manager proceed, for example, in a country with exploitive labor conditions, lax environmental regulation, and pervasive corruption? Even the most ethical manager must rethink his or her beliefs about how business ought to be conducted in other parts of the world.

Ethics and the Role of Managers

Every person in business occupies a role. A role is a structured set of relationships with accompanying rights and obligations. Thus, to be a purchasing agent or a personnel director or an internal auditor is to occupy a role. In occupying a role, a person assumes certain rights that are not held by everyone as well as certain role-specific obligations. Thus, a purchasing agent is empowered to make purchases on behalf of an organization and has a responsibility to make purchasing decisions that are best for the organization. To be a "good" purchasing agent is to do the job of a purchasing agent well.

The obligations of a particular role are sometimes added to those of ordinary morality. That is, a person who occupies a role generally assumes obligations over and above those of everyday life. Sometimes, however, role obligations come into conflict with our other obligations. In selecting people for promotion, a personnel director, for example, is obligated to set aside any considerations of friendship and to be wholly impartial. A person in this position may also be forced to terminate an employee for the good of the organization, without regard for the impact on the employee's life. A personnel director may even be required to implement a decision that he or she believes to be morally wrong, such as terminating an employee for inadequate cause. In such situations, the obligations of a role appear to be in conflict with the obligations of ordinary morality.

The idea of a role morality—that is, a morality that is specific to a particular role—is especially applicable to the situation of *professionals*, such as physicians, lawyers, engineers, and accountants. For example, accountants, including internal auditors and public accountants, have a stringent obligation to ensure the accuracy and completeness of financial information. This responsibility requires that they not only observe high standards of objectivity and integrity but also follow a prescribed course of action in reporting any financial irregularities. Internal auditors are required by their professional code of ethics to disclose their findings to top management and to resign if appropriate action is not taken. But they are prohibited from releasing any information to the public, even if doing so would protect some groups such as investors from great harm. The assumption is that the auditor's role is merely to inform top managers of any financial irregularities and that it is the role of those managers to take appropriate action.

Various justifications have been offered for role obligations. One justification is simply that people in certain positions have responsibilities to many different groups and hence must consider a wide range of interests. The decisions of a personnel director have an impact on everyone connected with a business organization, and so denying a friend a promotion or terminating an employee may be the right thing to do, all things considered. A more sophisticated justification is that roles are created in order to serve society better as a whole. A well-designed system of roles, with accompanying rights and obligations, enables a society to achieve more and thereby benefits everyone. A system of roles thus constitutes a kind of division of labor. As in Adam Smith's pin factory, in which workers who perform specific operations can be more productive than individuals working alone, so, too, a business organization with a multiplicity of roles can be more productive and better serve society. Of course, this justification requires that any system of roles be well designed, and there can be disagreement over the design of any given system. Some have argued, for example, that internal auditors ought to report financial irregularities to outside authorities if management does not take appropriate action.

What Is the Role of Managers?

We cannot understand the rights and obligations of managers without knowing their specific role. Managers serve at all levels of an organization and fulfill a variety of roles. Usually, these are defined by a job description, such as the role of a purchasing agent or a personnel director. Uncertainty arises mainly when we ask about the role of high-level corporate executives who make key decisions about policy and strategy. These questions often take the form: To whom are top managers responsible? Whose interests should they serve? What goals should they strive to achieve? To these questions, three main answers have been proposed.

Managers as Economic Actors. According to one widely accepted view, the manager's role is to make sound economic decisions that enable a firm to succeed in a competitive market. As economic actors, managers are expected to consider primarily economic factors in making decisions, and the main measure of success is profitability. The position is commonly expressed by saying that managers are agents of the shareholders, with an obligation to operate a corporation in the shareholders' interests. Legally, managers are not agents of the shareholders, but the law does impose an obligation on managers to seek a maximum return on all investments. This is the goal of managers who serve as economic actors even if they operate a sole proprietorship, a partnership, or any other kind of business enterprise.

Managers as Trustees. As leaders of business organizations, managers are entrusted with enormous assets and given a charge to manage these assets prudently. Employees, suppliers, customers, investors, and other so-called stakeholders have a stake in the success of a firm, and managers are expected to meet all of their legitimate expectations and to balance any conflicting interests. Generally, trustees have a fiduciary duty to act in all matters in the interests of the designated beneficiaries. A critical question, therefore, is whether managers are trustees or fiduciaries for shareholders alone or for all corporate constituencies.

Managers as Quasi-Public Servants. Managers exert enormous power both inside and outside their organizations. Although they are not elected in a democratic process, they nevertheless have many attributes of government officials, such as the power to make major investment decisions for society. Moreover, managers exercise their power by participating in the political process and cooperating with political bodies, including regulatory agencies. In any political system, power must be legitimized by showing how it serves some generally accepted societal goals, and managerial power is no exception. So managers are expected to demonstrate corporate leadership.

The debate over the role of managers at the highest level of business organizations cannot be settled here. Many of the issues of corporate ethics are discussed in Chapter 14. However, it is important to note that the relation of ethics and management cannot fully be explained without developing a full account of the manager's role, with its attendant rights and obligations.

MORALITY, ETHICS, AND ETHICAL THEORY

Before proceeding further, we need to clarify the meaning of the key terms *morality* and *ethics* and the cognates *moral* and *ethical* and *morally* and *ethically*. Generally, *morality* and *ethics*, *moral* and *ethical*, and so on are interchangeable. The presence of two words in the English language with the same meaning is due to the fact that they derive from different roots: *morality*, from the Latin word *moralitas*, and *ethics*, from the Greek *ethikos*. There is no difference, therefore, between describing discrimination as a moral issue and as an ethical issue, or between saying that discrimination is morally wrong and that it is ethically wrong. There are some subtle differences, however, between *morality* and *ethics*.

Morality is generally used to describe a sociological phenomenon, namely, the existence in a society of rules and standards of conduct. Every society has a morality, because this constitutes the basis for mutually beneficial interaction. Without such fundamental rules as "Do not kill" and "Do not steal," for example, stable communities would be impossible. Not all rules and standards are part of morality, of course. Eating peas with a knife, for example, is a breach of etiquette but not a moral wrong, and the rule "Look both ways before crossing the street" is a rule of prudence, not morality. Etiquette and prudence, therefore, constitute sets of nonmoral rules and standards. Morality also has many complex ties to the law, as we have already observed.

Moralities are also specific to societies and exist at certain times and places. Thus, we can speak of the morality of the Trobriand Islanders or the colonial settlers. The morality of Americans in the 1990s is different from that in the 1950s or the 1850s. We can even speak, as Karl Marx did, of the morality of different classes in society. In a highly developed society such as our own, morality also includes a complex vocabulary and patterns of reasoning that permit the members of the society to engage in moral discourse for the purpose of evaluating the actions of individuals and the practices and institutions of the society. *Ethics* is roughly a synonym for *morality*, but it is often restricted to the rules and norms of specific kinds of conduct or the codes of conduct for specialized groups. Thus, we talk about the ethics of stockbrokers or the code of ethics for the accounting profession but usually not about the morality of these groups.

The term *ethics* also has another, quite different, use which is to denote the field of *moral philosophy*. Ethics, along with logic, epistemology, and metaphysics, is a traditional area of philosophical inquiry that dates back to the time of the ancient Greeks. Ethics as a philosophical endeavor is the study of morality. Such a study is either *descriptive* or *normative*. Descriptive ethics may involve an empirical inquiry into the actual rules or standards of a particular group, or it could also consist of understanding the ethical reasoning process. A sociological study of the values of American business managers would be an example of the former, and the work of psychologists on moral development would illustrate the latter. Normative ethics is concerned largely with the possibility of justification. It takes morality as its subject matter and asks such questions as: Are there any means for showing that the rules and standards of our morality are the right ones? Are there any ultimate moral principles that can be used to resolve inconsistencies or conflicts? Normative ethics is concerned not with what people *believe* we ought to do but with what we *really* ought to do and is determined by reasoning or moral argument. Philosophical ethics is not a substitute for morality; rather, it seeks to organize our ordinary moral beliefs in a precise and consistent manner and to discover whatever justification they have.

Conclusion

In the next few chapters, three major theories of ethics are presented as the basis for our beliefs about moral obligations, rights, and justice, and they are applied in discussions of a number of issues concerning the rights and obligations of employees in a firm, employee relations, the protection of employees and consumers, and the responsibility of corporations to the public at large. We will discover a large measure of disagreement among these ethical theories in their content and in the results of applying them to specific cases. The differences between theories should not lead us to despair of resolving ethical issues or to conclude that one resolution is as good as another. Nor should we be discouraged by the fact that agreement on complex ethical issues is seldom achieved. The best we can do is to analyze the issues as fully as possible, which means getting the facts straight and achieving definitional clarity, and then develop the strongest and most complete arguments we can for what we consider to be the correct conclusions.

Case 1.4 A Sticky Situation

Kent Graham is still on the telephone, receiving the good news that he has just secured his largest order as an account manager for Dura-Stick Label Products.[18] His joy is tinged with uncertainty, however.

Dura-Stick is a leader in label converting for the durable-products marketplace. Label converting consists of converting log rolls of various substrates (paper, polyester, vinyl) into die-cut, printed labels. The company specializes in high-performance labels for the automotive, lawn and garden, and appliance industries. Dura-Stick has a well-deserved reputation for quality, technical knowledge, and service that enables the company to command a premium price for its products in a very competitive market.

Kent Graham has been with Dura-Stick for two years. Because he came to the company with ten years in the label industry, he was able to negotiate a very good salary and compensation plan, but his accomplishments since joining Dura-Stick have been mediocre at best. Kent fears that his time with Dura-Stick might be limited unless he starts closing some big accounts. Furthermore, with a wife and two children to support, losing his job would be disastrous. Kent was on a mission to land a big account.

Kent called on Jack Olson at Spray-On Inc., a manufacturer of industrial spraying systems for the automotive painting industry. Dura-Stick has been providing Spray-On with various warning and instructional labels for about twenty years. Jack has been very pleased with Dura-Stick's performance, especially the quality of its manufacturing department under the direction of Tim Davis. After giving Kent another excellent vendor evaluation report, Jack began to describe a new project at Spray-On, a paint sprayer for household consumer use that needs a seven-color label with very precise graphics. This label is different from the industrial two-color labels that Dura-Stick currently supplies to Spray-On.

Jack explained that this was the biggest project that Spray-On has undertaken in recent years and that it would generate a very large order for some label company. Jack then asked Kent, "Does Dura-Stick produce these multicolor, consumer-type labels?" Kent thought for a moment. He knew that a "yes" would give him a better shot at the business, and Dura-Stick might be able to handle the job, even though the company's experience to date was only with two-color labels. Almost without thinking, he replied, "Sure we can handle it, Jack, that's right up our alley!" "That's great news," Jack shot back. "Now take this sample and give me your proposal by Monday. Oh, and by the way, I hope your proposal looks good, because I would really feel confident if this important project were in the hands of your production people!"

Kent gave the sample to Marty Klein, who is responsible for coordinating the costs and price quotes for new opportunities. Marty took one look at the sample and said emphatically, "We'll have to farm this one out." Kent's heart sank down to his shoes. He knew that Jack would want to work with Dura-Stick only if the labels were produced at Dura-Stick's facility. Yet, he still allowed Marty to put the numbers together for the proposal. Kent presented the proposal to Jack at Spray-On. "Gee, Kent, these prices are pretty high, about 20 percent higher than your competition. That's pretty hard to swallow."

Kent knew that the price would be high because it included the cost of another company producing the labels plus Dura-Stick's usual profit margin, but he countered cheerily, "You know the quality that we provide and how important this project is to your company. Isn't it worth the extra 20 percent for the peace of mind that you will have?"

"Let me think about it," Jack replied.

The next day, Kent got a phone call from Jack. "Congratulations, Kent, Dura-Stick has been awarded the business. It was a tough sell to my people, but I convinced them that the extra money would be well spent because of the excellent production department that you have. If it wasn't for the fact that Tim Davis will personally oversee production, you guys probably would not have gotten this business."

Kent had to bite his tongue. He knew that Tim would not be involved because the labels would be produced in Kansas City by Labeltec, which would then send the finished labels to Dura-Stick for shipment to Spray-On's facility. Kent also knew that Jack would be completely satisfied with the quality of the labels. Besides, this order was crucial to his job security, not to mention the well-being of his company.

While Jack continued to explain Spray-On's decision, Kent pondered how he should close this conversation.

Case 1.5 Argus Incorporated: A Leasing Triangle

Susan Solomon walked slowly down the hall to Craig Dunston's office.[19] She was pondering a telephone call she had just received from an irate Mr. Hayes, who was demanding his missing monthly lease payments. Susan, a computer operations manager for Argus Incorporated, was disturbed because the lease in question was with TekUSA, not Mr. Hayes, and the lease had been terminated four months ago. In fact, the early termination was such an achievement that the Argus CEO had personally commended Susan and Craig. Now their triumph might be turning into a disaster.

As the computer operations manager for Argus Incorporated, a commercial real estate and property management company, Susan was responsible for the lease, purchase, maintenance, and disposition of all computer equipment and services for Argus. Craig hired her as a senior project manager four years ago because of her hands-on technical background and flair for explaining technology to employees and clients. During this time, Susan worked on a wide variety of projects under Craig's direction and showed her range of talents and skills. When the previous computer operations manager left, eight months ago, Craig immediately promoted Susan to this position.

As director of shared services, Craig was Susan's immediate superior, with responsibility for computer services in all of Argus's offices. Although Craig had strong managerial abilities and a thorough knowledge of the company's business, he lacked Susan's technical expertise. As a result, Argus had lagged behind the competition in offering sophisticated services. Craig had hoped that he and Susan could combine their strengths to make Argus the leader in their market.

Susan shared Craig's vision, and they became a powerful team. Their latest success had been to terminate the TekUSA lease eight months early. The agreement required Argus to make a lump-sum payment of $380,000 and return the old equipment to TekUSA. The savings in ongoing costs and the strategic opportunities provided by the new leased equipment more than compensated Argus for the cost of terminating the old lease. A critical factor in securing the early lease termination and negotiating a new lease was Susan's relationship with TekUSA. Although TekUSA had been one of Argus's most unreliable and expensive suppliers, Susan had confidence in its potential. The problem, she concluded, was that TekUSA did not understand Argus's business requirements. However, after a series of meetings that clarified each company's expectations, TekUSA was awarded the bulk of Argus's business for leased technology products.

The Master Lease Agreement allowed TekUSA to sell its interest in the leased equipment to a third party. Mr. Hayes claimed that he had bought the lease rights from TekUSA more than a year ago. If so, then Argus should have sent the final $380,000 payment and the old equipment to Mr. Hayes rather than TekUSA, not to mention the lease payments. TekUSA was required by the lease agreement to notify Argus if any portion of its rights were assigned to a third party. If a Notice of Assignment had been sent by TekUSA, then Argus had made a mistake that would be difficult, and costly, to rectify. If, on the other hand, a Notice of Assignment had not been sent, then the fault lay with TekUSA, which would be responsible for dealing with Mr. Hayes. Because all lease documents and invoices were sent to Craig, Susan made a beeline for his office.

"Well, Susan," Craig sighed as he pulled out the TekUSA lease contract file, "I can't imagine that we could've let something like this fall through the cracks, can you?" Shaking her head, Susan scanned the contract and quickly found the section that allowed TekUSA to assign its rights to a third party, provided notice was given to Argus. When Craig pulled out the invoice folder, they discovered that the invoices were generated by TekUSA with their logo on top, but Mr. Hayes's name and address were in the "remit to" box. Susan's heart sank. Now they had to determine whether Argus had ever received a Notice of Assignment.

Craig reached nervously into another folder and pulled out the Notice of Assignment from TekUSA. It was addressed to Craig and dated just over one year ago, four months before Susan's promotion. The Notice clearly stated that TekUSA was transferring the rights to the lease payments and the equipment to Mr. Hayes. Stunned, Susan realized that Argus had negotiated early termination with the wrong party. Argus was now liable for a second $380,000 and a year's lease payments to Mr. Hayes. Worse, Susan and Craig knew that TekUSA had destroyed as junk the equipment that rightly belonged to Mr. Hayes.

In spite of TekUSA's profitable relationship with Argus, the company was struggling with a serious slump in sales, and it had just been forced to lay off 300 people, a fifth of its work force. The odds of getting the payments back from TekUSA to send to Mr. Hayes were bleak. Worse, because the equipment had been junked, Mr. Hayes might ask for compensation based on its fair market value, which could run as high as $1 million. In its current state, TekUSA could not meet these demands without severe damage to its business. In addition, Argus could not permit such a blow to fall on TekUSA. As a critical supplier, TekUSA had to be kept afloat.

Craig spoke first. "Look, Susan, this Notice of Assignment has no Argus countersignature on it, nor was it sent certified mail with return receipt requested. No one knows we have this document, and no one can prove that we ever got it. Let me shred it and you just tell this Hayes guy that Argus never received a Notice of Assignment. Then his problem is with TekUSA, not with us."

Susan had never known Craig to suggest anything unethical, so they must be in serious trouble. TekUSA was seriously remiss in accepting the payments and negotiating the termination of a lease that it had assigned to someone else. Mr. Hayes had also contributed to the problem by not complaining months earlier. But Argus, and especially Craig, were at fault for overlooking the Notice of Assignment. Should Susan go along with Craig's suggestion in order to protect him and Argus?

Susan had a reputation for resolving tough situations. Her usual strategy was to encourage all parties to cooperate in developing a "win-win" solution. Perhaps she could persuade TekUSA to repay the misdirected funds by reducing Argus's monthly lease payments. Perhaps Mr. Hayes would be satisfied to receive similar equipment in place of the original which had already been destroyed. This would be a hard sell with no guarantee of success, and there were a lot of details to be worked out. Claiming that Argus had never received the notice would be a lot easier, and attempting to work out a solution would put Susan's reputation, and even her career, on the line. She wondered whether the effort was worth it.

NOTES

1. Material on this case is taken from "James Burke: A Career in American Business (A) & (B)," Harvard Business School, 1989; "The 1982 Tylenol Poisoning Episode," in Ronald M. Green, *The Ethical Manager: A New Method for Business Ethics* (New York: Macmillan, 1994), 208–19; and Robert F. Hartley, *Business Ethics: Violations of Public Trust* (New York: Wiley, 1993), 295–309.
2. Richard T. DeGeorge, *Competing with Integrity in International Business* (New York: Oxford University Press, 1993), 97–99.
3. The concept of the moral point of view is developed in Kurt Baier, *The Moral Point of View: A Rational Basis of Ethics* (Ithaca, NY: Cornell University Press, 1958). A similar account is offered in James Rachels, *The Elements of Moral Philosophy*, 3d ed. (New York: Random House, 1998), chap. 1.
4. Baier, *Moral Point of View*, 88.
5. Ibid., 195–96.
6. This case is adapted from Suzanne Alexander, "Child World Says Rival Cheats; Toys 'R' Us Answers: 'Grow Up,'" *Wall Street Journal*, 19 September 1991, B1, B10.
7. This case is adapted from Steve Lohr, "Lessons from a Hurricane: It Pays Not to Gouge," *New York Times*, 22 September 1992, D1, D2.
8. Albert Z. Carr, "Is Business Bluffing Ethical?" *Harvard Business Review*, 46 (January–February 1968), 148.
9. Amartya Sen, "Does Business Ethics Make Economic Sense?" *Business Ethics Quarterly*, 3 (1993), 45-54.
10. The results of experiments with the ultimatum bargaining game are presented in Robert H. Frank, *Passions within Reason: The Strategic Role of the Emotions* (New York: W. W. Norton, 1988), 170-74. For a discussion of the implications for business ethics, see Norman E. Bowie, "Challenging the Egoistic Paradigm," *Business Ethics Quarterly*, 1 (1991), 1-21.
11. Daniel Kahneman, Jack L. Knetch, and Richard Thaler, "Fairness as a Constraint of Profit-Seeking: Entitlements in the Market," *American Economic Review*, 76 (1986), 728–41.

12. Douglas C. Dacy and Howard Kunreuther, *The Economics of Natural Disasters* (New York: Free Press, 1969), 115–16.
13. Lynn Sharp Paine, "Law, Ethics, and Managerial Judgment," *Journal of Legal Studies Education*, 12 (1994), 153-69.
14. This phrase is taken from Norman E. Bowie, "Fair Markets," *Journal of Business Ethics*, 7 (1988), 89–98.
15. Christopher D. Stone, *Where the Law Ends: The Social Control of Corporate Behavior* (New York: Harper & Row, 1975), 94.
16. *Meinhard* v. *Salmon*, 164 N.E. 545 (1928).
17. See Thomas Donaldson, "Values in Tension: Ethics Away from Home," *Harvard Business Review*, 4 (September–October 1996), 48-62.
18. This case was prepared by Kerry Winans under the supervision of Professor John R. Boatright. Copyright 1995 by John R. Boatright.
19. This case was prepared by Kate Abele under the supervision of Professor John R. Boatright. Copyright 1998 by John R. Boatright.

Chapter 12

Ethics and Corporations

Case 14.1 The Nun and the CEO

In 1996, a nun from Philadelphia sparked a debate with a Silicon Valley CEO over corporate social responsibility.[1] Sister Doris Gormley of the Sisters of St. Francis, whose retirement fund held 7,000 shares of Cypress Semiconductor stock, wrote a letter to the company protesting the lack of women and minorities on the board of directors. Speaking for a religious congregation of approximately 1,000 women, Sister Gormely wrote, "We belive that a company is best represented by a Board of qualified Directors reflecting the equality of the sexes, races and ethnic groups.... Therefore our policy is to withhold authority to vote for nominees of a Board of Directors that does not include women and minorities."

T. J. Rodgers, the CEO of Cypress, an international distributor of semiconductors with about $600 million in annual sales, composed a six-page response in which he labeled the Sister's view "immoral" and urged her to get down from her "moral high horse."[2] His letter reads in part:

> Thank you for your letter criticizing the lack of racial and gender diversity of Cypress's Board of Directors.... The semiconductor business is a tough one with significant competition....For [this] reason, our Board of Directors is not a ceremonial watchdog, but a critical management function. The essential criteria for Cypress board membership are as follows:
>
> - Experience as a CEO of an important technology company.
> - Direct expertise in the semiconductor business based on education and management experience.
> - Direct experience in the management of a company that buys from the semiconductor industry.

A search based on these criteria usually yields a male who is 50-plus years old, has a Master's degree in an engineering science, and has moved up the managerial ladder to the top spot in one or more corporations. Unfortunately, there are currently few minorities and almost no women who chose to be engineering graduate students thirty years ago.... Bluntly stated, a "woman's view" on how to run our semiconductor company does not help us, unless that woman has an advance technical degree and experience as CEO.... Therefore, not only does Cypress not meet your requirements for boardroom diversification, but we are unlikely to, because it is very difficult to find qualified directors, let alone directors that also meet investors' racial and gender preferences....

I presume you believe your organization does good work and that the people who spend their careers in its service deserve to retire with the necessities of life assured. If your investment in Cypress is intended for that purpose, I can tell you that each of the retired Sisters of St. Francis would suffer if I were forced to run Cypress on anything but a profit-making basis. The retirement plans of thousands of other people also depend on Cypress stock.... Any choice I would make to jeopardize retirees and other investors from achieving their lifetime goals would be fundamentally wrong.... If all companies in the U.S. were forced to operate according to some arbitrary social agenda, rather than for profit, all American companies would operate at a disadvantage to their foreign competitors, all Americans would become less well off (some laid off), and charitable giving would decline precipitously. Making Americans poorer and reducing charitable giving in order to force companies to follow an arbitrary social agenda is fundamentally wrong....

You have voted against me and the other directors of the company, which is your right as a shareholder. But here is a synopsis of what you voted against:

- Employee ownership. Every employee of Cypress is a shareholder and every employee of Cypress—including the lowest-paid—receives new Cypress stock options every year....
- Excellent pay. Our employees in San Jose averaged $78,741 in salary and benefits in 1995....
- A significant boost to our economy. In 1995, our company paid out $150 million to its employees. That money did a lot of good: it bought a lot of houses, cars, movie tickets, eyeglasses, and college education.
- A flexible health-care program. A Cypress-paid health-care budget is granted to all employees to secure the health-care options they want....
- Profit sharing. Cypress shares it profits with its employees. In 1995, profit sharing added up to $5,000 per employee, given in equal shares, regardless of rank or salary....
- Charitable work. Cypress supports Silicon Valley. We support the Second Harvest Food Bank ... I was chairman of the 1993 food drive, and Cypress has won the good-giving title three years running.... We also give to the Valley Medical Center, our Santa Clara-based public hospital....

I believe you should support management teams that hold our values and have the courage to put them into practice. So, that's my reply. Choosing a Board of Directors based on race and gender is a lousy way to run a company. Cypress will never do it. Furthermore, we will never be pressured into it, because bowing to well-meaning, special-interest groups is an immoral way to run a company, given all the people it would hurt. We simply cannot allow arbitrary rules to be forced on us by organizations that lack business expertise. I would rather be labeled as a person who is unkind to religious groups than as a coward who harms his employees and investors by mindlessly following high-sounding, but false, standards of right and wrong.... With regard to shareholders who exercise their right to vote according to a social agenda, we suggest that they reconsider whether or not their strategy will do net good—after all of the real costs are considered.

T. J. Rodgers asserted that "Cypress is run under a set of carefully considered moral principles," although one of these principles is that making a profit is the primary objective of the company. He disagreed with Sister Doris on whether morality requires a company to have a diverse board of directors. Such diversity is, in his view, more a matter of "political correctness." Sister Doris claimed, however, that her letter had nothing to do with "political correctness" but simply expressed "concern for the social integrity of business." After the exchange of letters, Sister Doris discovered that the order's retirement fund had sold its 7,000 shares of Cypress stock for unrelated reasons, thus bringing to an end the debate between the nun and the CEO.

INTRODUCTION

Although corporations are primarily business organizations run for the benefit of shareholders, they have a wide-ranging set of responsibilities—to their own employees, to customers and suppliers, to the communities in which they are located, and to society at large. Most corporations recognize these responsibilities and make a serious effort to fulfill them. Often, these responsibilities are set out in formal statements of a company's principles or beliefs. Corporations do not always succeed in fulfilling the responsibilities they acknowledge, however, and disagreements inevitably arise over the responsibilities of corporations in particular situations.

For example, T. J. Rodgers believes that Cypress Semiconductor is socially responsible, as witness the good deeds he describes. He contends, however, that profit must come first, as the fuel for doing good, and he objects to pressure from outside sources, especially when they do not understand business. He admits, though, that Sister Doris has a right as a shareholder to vote according to her views, but do not other members of society not have a right to make demands on corporations through their economic and political choices? At issue, then, are two questions: What is the social responsibility of business, and who has the right to make this determination?

There are no easy answers to such questions, but some help can be obtained from the theories of corporate social responsibility examined in this chapter. These range from a very restricted position—that corporations have no social responsibility beyond making a profit—to the position that corporations ought to assume a more active role in addressing major social problems. The social responsibility of corporations cannot be understood without an examination of the nature of corporations and their objectives. The fundamental question of corporate governance is, whose interests ought corporations to serve? This question is examined in a section on corporate governance. Finally, this chapter considers the ethics programs that many corporations have adopted to ensure ethical conduct by their employees.

CORPORATE SOCIAL RESPONSIBILITY

The concept of corporate social responsibility originated in the 1950s when American corporations rapidly increased in size and power. The concept continued to figure prominently in public debate during the 1960s and 1970s as the nation confronted pressing social problems such as poverty, unemployment, race relations, urban blight, and pollution.[3] Corporate social responsibility became a rallying cry for diverse groups demanding change in American business. In the last two decades of the twentieth century, corporations generally recognized a responsibility to society, but that responsibility was weighed against the demands of being competitive in a rapidly changing global economy. Pressure for improved performance was exerted by institutional investors, especially mutual and pension fund managers, who have a fiduciary duty to their investors to push for maximum return. During this period, the wealth of many American households was closely tied to the stock market, and so increasing stock price became a strong imperative for corporate managers.

The Debate over Social Responsibility

Some contend that corporate social responsibility is altogether a pernicious idea. The well-known conservative economist Milton Friedman writes in *Capitalism and Freedom*, "Few trends could so thoroughly undermine the very foundations of our free society as the acceptance by corporate officials of a social responsibility other than making as much money for their stockholders as possible."[4] He continues:

> The view has been gaining widespread acceptance that corporate officials ... have a "social responsibility" that goes beyond serving the interest of their stockholders.... This view shows a fundamental misconception of the character and nature of a free economy. In such an economy, there is one and only one social responsibility of business—to use its resources and engage in activities designed to increase its profits so long as it stays within the rules of the game, which is to say, engages in open and free competition, without deception or fraud.... It is the responsibility of the rest of us to establish a framework of law such that an individual pursuing his own interest is, to quote Adam Smith ..., "led by an invisible hand to promote an end which was no part of his intention."[5]

At the other extreme are critics who would like corporations to be more socially responsible but are mistrustful. They consider talk about corporate social responsibility to be a public relations ploy designed to legitimize the role of corporations in present-day American society and to divert attention away from the destructive social consequences of corporate activity. Even those who are more favorably disposed to the idea have reservations about the ability of corporations, especially as they are currently structured, to respond effectively to social issues. Businesses are single-purpose institutions, conceived, organized, and managed solely in order to engage in economic activity. As such, they lack the resources and the expertise for solving major social problems, and some add that they lack the legitimacy as well. Corporate executives are not elected officials with a mandate from the American people to apply the resources under their control to just any ends that they deem worthwhile.

Furthermore, the idea that corporations should be more socially responsible fails to give adequate ethical guidance to the executives who must decide which causes to pursue and how much to commit to them. This problem is especially acute in view of the fact that all choices involve trade-offs. A program to increase minority employment, for example, might reduce efficiency, thereby reducing wages for employees or raising prices for consumers. Or such a program might be adopted at the expense of achieving a greater reduction in the amount of pollution. Corporations committed to exercising greater social responsibility need more specific moral rules or principles to give them reasons for acting in one way rather than another.

The Definition of the Concept

All accounts of corporate social responsibility recognize that business firms have not one but many different kinds of responsibility, including economic and legal responsibilities. Corporations have an *economic* responsibility to produce goods and services and to provide jobs and good wages to the work force while earning a profit. Economic responsibility also includes the obligation to seek out supplies of raw materials, to discover new resources and technological improvements, and to develop new products. In addition, business firms have certain *legal* responsibilities. One of these is to act as a fiduciary, managing the assets of a corporation in the interests of shareholders, but corporations also have numerous legal responsibilities to employees, customers, suppliers, and other parties. The vast body of business law is constantly increasing as legislatures, regulatory agencies, and the courts respond to greater societal expectations and impose new legal obligations on business.

The concept of corporate social responsibility is often expressed as the voluntary assumption of responsibilities that go beyond the purely economic and legal responsibilities of business firms.[6] More specifically, social responsibility, according to some accounts, is the selection of corporate goals and the evaluation of outcomes not solely by the criteria of profitability and organizational well-being but by ethical standards or judgments of social desirability. The exercise of social responsibility, in this view, must be consistent with the corporate objective of earning a satisfactory level of profit, but it implies a willingness to forgo a certain measure of profit in order to achieve noneconomic ends.

Archie B. Carroll views social responsibility as a four-stage continuum.[7] Beyond economic and legal responsibilities lie ethical responsibilities, which are "additional behaviors and activities that are not necessarily codified into law but nevertheless are expected of business by society's members."[8] At the far end of the continuum are discretionary responsibilities. These responsibilities are not legally required or even demanded by ethics; but corporations accept them in order to meet society's expectations. S. Prakash Sethi notes that social responsibility is a relative concept: What is only a vague ideal at one point in time or in one culture may be a definite legal requirement at another point in time or in another culture. In most of the advanced nations of the world, fulfilling traditional economic and legal responsibilities is no longer regarded as sufficient for legitimizing the activity of large corporations. Corporate social responsibility can thus be defined as "bringing corporate behavior up to a level where it is congruent with the prevailing social norms, values, and expectations of performance."[9]

In 1971, the Committee for Economic Development issued an influential report that characterized corporate social responsibility in a similar fashion but without an explicit mention of legal responsibilities. The responsibilities of corporations are described in this report as consisting of three concentric circles.

> The *inner circle* includes the clear-cut basic responsibilities for the efficient execution of the economic function—products, jobs, and economic growth.
>
> The *intermediate circle* encompasses responsibility to exercise this economic function with a sensitive awareness of changing social values and priorities: for example, with respect to environmental conservation; hiring and relations with employees; and more rigorous expectations of customers for information, fair treatment, and protection from injury.
>
> The *outer circle* outlines newly emerging and still amorphous responsibilities that business should assume to become more broadly involved in actively improving the social environment. Society is beginning to turn to corporations for help with major social problems such as poverty and urban blight. This is not so much because the public considers business singularly responsible for creating these problems, but because it feels large corporations possess considerable resources and skills that could make a critical difference in solving these problems.[10]

Examples of Social Responsibility. Although there are some disagreements about the meaning of corporate social responsibility, there is general agreement on the types of corporate activities that show social responsibility. Among these are

1. Choosing to operate on an ethical level that is higher than what the law requires.
2. Making contributions to civic and charitable organizations and nonprofit institutions.
3. Providing benefits for employees and improving the quality of life in the workplace beyond economic and legal requirements.
4. Taking advantage of an economic opportunity that is judged to be less profitable but more socially desirable than some alternatives.

5. Using corporate resources to operate a program that addresses some major social problem.

Although these activities are all beyond the economic and legal responsibilities of corporations and may involve some sacrifice of profit, they are not necessarily antithetical to corporate interests. For example, corporate philanthropy that makes the community in which a company is located a better place to live and work results in direct benefits. The "goodwill" that socially responsible activities create makes it easier for corporations to conduct their business. It should come as no surprise, then, that some of the most successful corporations are also among the most socially responsible. They are led by executives who see that even the narrow economic and legal responsibilities of corporations cannot be fulfilled without the articulation of noneconomic values to guide corporate decision making and the adoption of nontraditional business activities that satisfy the demands of diverse constituencies.

Going beyond Social Responsibility. An important aspect of corporate social responsibility is the responsiveness of corporations—that is, the ability of corporations to respond in a socially responsible manner to new challenges.[11] William C. Frederick explains that the concept of *corporate social responsiveness* "refers to the capacity of a corporation to respond to social pressures."[12] The emphasis of corporate social responsiveness, in other words, is on the *process* of responding or the readiness to respond, rather than on the *content* of an actual response. Thus, a socially responsive corporation uses its resources to anticipate social issues and develop policies, programs, and other means of dealing with them. The management of social issues in a socially responsive corporation is integrated into the strategic planning process, instead of being handled as an ad hoc reaction to specific crises.

The *content* of a response is also important because it represents the outcome of being socially responsible. Donna Wood has combined all three elements—the *principle* of being socially responsible, the *process* of social responsiveness, and the socially responsible *outcome*—in the concept of *corporate social performance.*[13] Using the example of environmental concerns about packaging, the *principles* of corporate social responsibility would be those that lead the company to recognize an obligation to change its packaging in order to protect the environment. The *processes* might consist of establishing an office of environmental affairs or working with environmentalists to develop new packaging. The *outcomes* could include the switch to environmentally responsible packaging and perhaps building facilities to recycle the packaging.

The Classical View

The dominant conception of the corporation, at least in the United States, is called the *classical view.* This view, which prevailed in the nineteenth century, is still very influential today, especially among economists. It is expressed by James W. McKie in three basic propositions.

1. Economic behavior is separate and distinct from other types of behavior, and business organizations are distinct from other organizations, even though the same individuals may be involved in business and nonbusiness affairs. Business organizations do not serve the same goals as other organizations in a pluralistic society.
2. The primary criteria of business performance are economic efficiency and growth in production of goods and services, including improvements in technology and innovations in goods and services.
3. The primary goal and motivating force for business organizations is profit. The firm attempts to make as large a profit as it can, thereby maintaining its efficiency and taking advantage of available opportunities to innovate and contribute to growth.[14]

In the classical view, corporations should engage in purely economic activity and be judged in purely economic terms. Social concerns are not unimportant, but they should be left to other institutions in society.

The classical view is part of a larger debate about the legitimate role of the corporation in a democracy. In his introduction to the influential volume *The Corporation in Modern Society*, Edward Mason described the problem of the modern corporation as follows: America is a "society of large corporations ... [whose] management is in the hands of a few thousand men. Who selected these men, if not to rule over us, at least to exercise vast authority, and to whom are they responsible?"[15] The classical view is a response to this problem that recognizes that corporate power must be harnessed to a larger social good if it is not to become tyrannical. Confining corporations to economic ends is intended, in part, to limit their role in society so as to preserve other kinds of institutions, both public and private.

Arguments for Social Responsibility

Business activity, in the classical view, is justified partly on the ground that it secures the well-being of society as a whole. The crux of this argument is the efficacy of Adam Smith's invisible hand in harmonizing self-interested behavior to secure an end that is not a part of anyone's intention. This justification also depends on the ability of the rest of society to create the conditions necessary for the invisible hand to operate and to address social problems without the aid of business. The debate over the workings of the invisible hand cannot be settled here (it is examined at some length in Chapter 4), but the invisible hand argument, upon which the classical view depends, is not incompatible with certain arguments for corporate social responsibility.

The Moral Minimum of the Market. First, a certain level of ethical conduct is necessary for the invisible hand to operate, or indeed for business activity to take place at all. Milton Friedman speaks of the "rules of the game," by which he means "open and free competition, without deception or fraud." Theodore Levitt, in his article "The Dangers of Social Responsibility," says that, aside from seeking material gain, business has only one responsibility, and that is "to obey the elementary canons of everyday face-to-face civility (honesty, good faith, and so on)."[16] The "rules of the game" and "face-to-face civility" impose not inconsequential constraints on business. Presumably, the prohibition against deception and fraud obligates corporations to deal fairly with employees, customers, and the public and to avoid sharp sales practices, misleading advertising, and the like.

The moral minimum of the market also includes an obligation to engage in business without inflicting injury on others. Critics of Levitt's position observe:

> ... Levitt presents the reader with a choice between, on the one hand, getting involved in the management of society ... and, on the other hand, fulfilling the profit-making function. But such a choice excludes another meaning of corporate responsibility: the making of profits in such a way as to minimize social injury. Levitt at no point considers the possibility that business activity may at times injure others and that it may be necessary to regulate the social consequences of one's business activities accordingly.[17]

Thus, corporations in a free market have an obligation not to pollute the environment and to clean up any pollution they cause.

It may also be in the best interests of a corporation to operate above the moral minimum of the market. Corporations that adhere only to the moral minimum leave themselves open to pressure from society and regulation by government. One of the major reasons advanced for corporations to exercise greater social responsibility is to avoid such external interference. By "internalizing" the expectations of society, corporations retain control over decision making and avoid the costs associated with government regulation.

Power and Responsibility. Second, corporations have become so large and powerful that they are not effectively restrained by market forces and government regulation, as the invisible hand argument assumes. Some self-imposed restraint in the form of a voluntary assumption of greater social responsibility is necessary, therefore, for corporate activity to secure the public welfare. Keith Davis expressed this point succinctly in the proposition "*social responsibility arises from social power.*"[18] He also cited what he calls the Iron Law of Responsibility: "In the long run, those who do not use power in a manner which society considers responsible will tend to lose it."[19] The need for greater social responsibility by corporations, then, is an inevitable result of their increasing size and influence in American society.

Holders of the classical theory argue in reply that precisely because of the immense power of corporations, it would be dangerous to unleash it from the discipline of the market in order to achieve vaguely defined social goals.[20] Kenneth E. Goodpaster and John B. Matthews, Jr., concede that this is a matter for serious concern but argue in response:

> What seems not to be appreciated is the fact that power affects when it is used as well as when it is not used. A decision by [a corporation] ... not to exercise its economic influence according to "non-economic" criteria is inevitably a moral decision and

just as inevitably affects the community. The issue in the end is not whether corporations (and other organizations) should be "unleashed" to exert moral force in our society but rather how critically and self-consciously they should choose to do so.[21]

Giving a Helping Hand to Government. Third, the classical view assumes that business is best-suited to provide for the economic well-being of the members of a society, whereas noneconomic goals are best left to government and the other noneconomic institutions of society. This sharp division of responsibility is true at best only as a generalization, and it does not follow that corporations have *no* responsibility to provide a helping hand. Corporations cannot attempt to solve every social problem, of course, and so some criteria are needed for distinguishing those situations in which corporations have an obligation to assist other institutions. John G. Simon, Charles W. Powers, and Jon P. Gunnemann propose the following four criteria:[22]

1. The urgency of the need;
2. The proximity of a corporation to the need;
3. The capability of a corporation to respond effectively;
4. The likelihood that the need will not be met unless a corporation acts.

Accordingly, a corporation has an obligation to address social problems that involve more substantial threats to the well-being of large numbers of people, that are close at hand and related in some way to the corporation's activity, that the corporation has the resources and expertise to solve, and that would likely persist without some action by the corporation.

Friedman's Argument against Social Responsibility

Perhaps the best-known critic of corporate social responsibility is Milton Friedman. Friedman's main argument against corporate social responsibility is that corporate executives, when they are acting in their official capacity and not as private persons, are agents of the stockholders of the corporation. As such, executives of a corporation have an obligation to make decisions in the interests of the stockholders, who are ultimately their employers. He has asked:

> What does it mean to say that the corporate executive has a "social responsibility" in his capacity as businessman? If this statement is not pure rhetoric, it must mean that he is to act in some way that is not in the interest of his employers. For example, that he is to refrain from increasing the price of the product in order to contribute to the social objective of preventing inflation, even though a price increase would be in the best interests of the corporation. Or that he is to make expenditures on reducing pollution beyond the amount that is in the best interests of the corporation or that is required by law in order to contribute to the social objective of improving the environment. Or that, at the expense of corporate profits, he is to hire "hardcore" unem-

> ployed instead of better-qualified available workmen to contribute to the social objective of reducing poverty.
>
> In each of these cases, the corporate executive would be spending someone else's money for a general social interest. Insofar as his actions in accord with his "social responsibility" reduce returns to stockholders, he is spending their money. Insofar as his actions raise the price to customers, he is spending the customers' money. Insofar as his actions lower the wages of some employees, he is spending their money.[23]

When corporate executives act in the way Friedman describes, they take on a role of imposing taxes and spending the proceeds that properly belongs only to elected officials. They become, in effect, civil servants with the power to tax, and as civil servants, they ought to be elected through the political process instead of being selected by the stockholders of private business firms.[24]

Criticism of Friedman's Argument. The classical view does not sanction an unrestrained pursuit of profit. Friedman himself acknowledges that business must observe certain essential limitations on permissible conduct, which he describes as the "rules of the game." Presumably, he would also grant the necessity of government with limited powers for setting and enforcing rules. Business activity requires, in other words, a minimal state in order to prevent anticompetitive practices and to enforce the basics of commercial law. Friedman recognizes, further, that many supposed socially responsible actions are really disguised forms of self-interest. Contributions to schools, hospitals, community organizations, cultural groups, and the like are compatible with the classical view insofar as corporations receive indirect benefits from the contributions. All Friedman asks is that corporations recognize these as effective means for making a profit and not as philanthropic activities.

In addition, holders of the classical view generally admit the legitimacy of three other functions of government that place limits on business activity.[25] First, business activity generates many *externalities,* that is, social harms, such as worker injury, which result indirectly from the operation of business firms. In order to prevent these harms or to correct them after they occur, it is proper for government to act—by requiring safer working conditions, for example, or by taxing employers to fund workers' compensation programs.[26] Second, the operation of a free market economy results in considerable *inequalities* in the distribution of income and wealth. Insofar as it is desirable as a matter of public policy to reduce these inequalities, it is appropriate for government to undertake the task by such means as progressive taxation and redistribution schemes. It is the job of government, in other words, and not business, to manage the equity/efficiency trade-off.[27] Third, free markets are prone to *instability* that manifests itself in inflation, recessions, unemployment, and other economic ills. Individual firms are too small to have much effect on the economy as a whole, and so government must step in and use its powers of taxation, public expenditure, control of the money supply, and the like to make the economy more stable.

The classical view is compatible, then, with some intervention in business activity by government in order to secure the public welfare. The important point to recognize is that the restraints are almost entirely *external.* The primary burden for ensuring that corporations act in a way that is generally beneficial rests on society as a whole, which is charged by Friedman with the task of creating a framework of law that allows business firms to operate solely in their self-interest. The classical theory, therefore, does not permit corporations to *act* in a socially irresponsible manner; it only relieves them of the need to *think* about matters of social responsibility. In a well-ordered society, corporations attend to business while government and other institutions fulfill their proper roles.

The "Taxation" Argument. The objections to Friedman's argument against corporate social responsibility discussed so far do not address his point that in exercising corporate social responsibility, managers are spending someone else's money. Investors, according to the "taxation" argument, entrust their money to the managers of corporations in order to make profits for the shareholders. Spending money to pursue social ends is thus a form of taxation.

Many things are wrong with the "taxation" argument. To say, as Friedman does, that corporate assets belong to the shareholders, that it's *their* money, is not wholly accurate. The role of shareholders in corporate governance is a rather complex issue, however, that is examined in the next section. Even if Friedman's assumption is accepted, it does not follow that corporations have no social responsibility.

First, managers of a corporation do not have an obligation to earn the greatest amount of profit for shareholders without regard for the means used. A taxi driver hired to take a passenger to the airport as fast as possible, for example, is not obligated to break traffic laws and endanger everyone else on the road. Similarly, money spent on product safety or pollution control may reduce the potential return to shareholders, but the alternative is to conduct business in a way that threatens the well-being of others in society. Friedman would insist, of course, that managers carry out their responsibility to shareholders within the rules of the game, but the moral obligation of managers to be sensitive to the social impact of their actions is more extensive than the minimal restraints listed by Friedman.

Second, the obligation of managers is not merely to secure the maximum return but also to preserve the equity invested in a corporation. Securing the maximum return for shareholders consistent with the preservation of invested capital requires managers to take a long-term view that considers the stability and growth of the corporation. For corporations to survive, they must satisfy the legitimate expectations of society and serve the purposes for which they have been created. Friedman admits the legitimacy of acts of social responsibility as long as they are ultimately in the self-interest of the corporation. The main area of disagreement between proponents and critics of social responsibility is, how much socially responsible behavior is in a corporation's long-term self-interest?

Third, the interests of shareholders are not narrowly economic; corporations are generally expected by their owners to pursue some socially desirable ends. Shareholders are also consumers, environmentalists, and citizens in communities. Consequently, they are affected when corporations fail to act responsibly. In fact, shareholders may be morally opposed to some activities of a corporation and in favor of some changes. One writer contends that "there are conventionally motivated investors who have an interest in the social characteristics of their portfolios *as well* as dividends and capital gains."[28] If so, managers who exercise social responsibility are not "taxing" shareholders and spending the money contrary to their interests but quite the opposite; managers who do not act in a socially responsible manner are using shareholders' money in ways that are against the interests of their shareholders. Friedman's response is, if shareholders want certain social goals, let them use their dividends for that purpose. However, it may be more efficient for corporations to expend funds on environmental protection, for example, than for shareholders to spend the same amount in dividends for the same purpose.

For these reasons, then, the "taxation" argument against corporate social responsibility is not very compelling. Although the rights of shareholders place some limits on what businesses can justifiably do to address major social concerns, they do not yield the very narrowly circumscribed view of Friedman and others. However, the issues raised by the debate over corporate social responsibility on the classical view is only part of a larger controversy over the governance of the modern corporation. Who should control a corporation? Whose interests should the corporation serve? To these questions of corporate governance we now turn.

CORPORATE GOVERNANCE

A corporation brings together many different groups—most notably managers, employees, suppliers, customers, and, of course, investors—for the purpose of conducting business. Because these various corporate constituencies have different and sometimes conflicting interests, the question arises: In whose interest should the corporation be run?

Debate has long raged over the nature of the corporation. Is the corporation the private property of the stockholders who choose to do business in the corporate form, or is the corporation a public institution sanctioned by the state for some social good?[29] In the former view, which may be called the *property rights theory*, the right to incorporate is an extension of the property rights and the right of contract that belong to all persons.[30] The latter view—let us call it the *social institution theory*—holds that the right to incorporate is a privilege granted by the state and that corporate property has an inherent public aspect.[31] A third view is the *contractual theory* of the firm. In the contractual theory, shareholders, along with other investors, employees, and the like, each own assets that they make available to the firm. Thus, the firm results from the property rights and the right of contract of every corporate constituency and not from those of shareholders alone.

Whether corporations ought to serve the interests of shareholders alone or the interests of a wider range of constituencies depends on the theory of the firm that we accept. Even though holders of all three theories generally conclude that the interests of shareholders are primary, the arguments that they provide are different, and it is important to understand the logic of each argument.

The Property Rights and Social Institution Theories

The original form of the modern corporation was the joint stock company in which a small group of wealthy individuals pooled their money for some undertaking that they could not finance alone. In the property rights theory, this corporate form of business organization is justified on the grounds that it represents an extension of the property rights and the right of contract enjoyed by everyone. Just as individuals are entitled to conduct business with their own assets, so, too, have they a right to contract with others for the same purpose. Although individual shareholders in a joint stock company or a corporation have exchanged their personal assets for shares of stock, they jointly own the common enterprise, and as owners they are entitled to receive the full proceeds.

The social institution theory emphasizes that a corporation is not merely a *private* association created for the purpose of personal enrichment but also a *public* enterprise that is intended to serve some larger social good. The earliest joint stock companies were special grants that kings bestowed on favored subjects for specific purposes. Today, corporations are chartered by states, so that the opportunity for individuals to do business in the corporate form is a state-granted privilege. The courts have also held in decisions such as *Munn* v. *Illinois* (1876) that corporate property is "affected with a public interest" so that states have a right to regulate its use.[32] Corporations are thus not wholly private; they have an inherent public aspect.

In a pure expression of the property rights theory, the Michigan State Supreme Court ruled in 1919 that the Ford Motor Company could be forced to pay more dividends to the shareholders in spite of Henry Ford's view that the company had made too much profit and ought to share some of it with the public by reducing prices. In *Dodge* v. *Ford Motor Co.,* the court declared, "A business corporation is organized and carried on primarily for the profit of the stockholders."[33] The profit-making end of a corporation is set forth in its charter of incorporation, which represents a contract among the shareholders who have invested their money, and Henry Ford had no right to substitute another end by using corporate resources for an essentially philanthropic purpose.

The decision in *Dodge* v. *Ford Motor Co.* assumed that shareholders are the owners of a corporation. This assumption was true as long as corporations had relatively few shareholders who actively controlled the business. However, in 1932, a book by Adolf A. Berle, Jr., and Gardiner C. Means, *The Modern Corporation and Private Property,* documented a dramatic shift that had occurred in American business.[34] Stock ownership in large corporations had become dispersed among numerous investors who had little involvement in corporate affairs, and the actual control of corporations had passed to a class of professional managers. The result was a separation of ownership and control, and with this separation came a change in the nature of corporate property.

The Nature of Corporate Property. Strictly speaking, property is not a tangible thing like land, but a bundle of rights that defines what an owner is entitled to do with a thing. A property right, in the full sense of the term, involves control over the thing owned and an assumption of responsibility. In the separation of ownership and control, shareholders had relinquished both control and responsibility. As a result, shareholders of large publicly held corporations had ceased to be owners in the full sense and had become merely one kind of provider of the resources needed by a corporation.

According to Berle and Means, "The property owner who invests in a modern corporation so far surrenders his wealth to those in control of the corporation that he has exchanged the position of independent owner for one in which he may become merely recipient of the wages of capital."[35] They continued:

> ... [T]he owners of passive property, by surrendering control and responsibility over the active property have surrendered the right that the corporation should be operated in their sole interest —they have released the community from the obligation to protect them to the full extent implied in the doctrine of strict property rights. At the same time, the controlling groups ... have in their own interest broken the bars of tradition which require that the corporation be operated solely for the benefit of the owners of passive property.[36]

Because of the separation of ownership and control, managers have assumed the position of trustee for the immense resources of a modern corporation, and in this new position, they face the question: For whom are corporate managers trustees?

The Berle-Dodd Debate. In a famous 1932 exchange with Berle in the *Harvard Law Review*, E. Merrick Dodd, Jr., argued that the corporation is "an economic institution which has a social service as well as a profit-making function."[37] According to Dodd, the modern corporation had become a public institution, as opposed to a private activity of the shareholders, and as such, it had a social responsibility that could include the making of charitable contributions.[38] Because a corporation is property only in a "qualified sense," it may be regulated by society so that the interests of employees, customers, and others are protected. Corporate managers have a right, even a duty, to consider the interests of all those who deal with the corporation.[39]

Berle cautioned against Dodd's position because of the dangers posed by unrestrained managerial power. In a response to Dodd in the *Harvard Law Review*, Berle wrote, "When the fiduciary obligation of the corporate management and 'control' to stockholders is weakened or eliminated, the management and 'control' become for all practical purposes absolute."[40] It would be unwise, in Berle's estimation, for the law to release managers from a strict accountability to shareholders, not out of respect for their property rights as owners of a corporation but as a matter of sound public policy. He wrote:

> Unchecked by present legal balances, a social-economic absolutism of corporate administrators, even if benevolent, might be unsafe; and in any case it hardly affords the soundest base on which to construct the economic commonwealth which industrialism seems to require.[41]

Corporate law has evolved effective means for restraining managerial power by directing managers to act in the interests of the shareholders, but we lack effective means for ensuring that managers serve the interests of society as a whole. There is no guarantee that managers will exercise their newly acquired control in any interests but their own. Berle described the rise of corporate managers as a "seizure of power without recognition of responsibility—ambition without courage."[42] But in the absence of effective restraints on managerial power, Berle concludes, "... [W]e had best be protecting the interests we know, being no less swift to provide for the new interests as they successively appear."[43]

Eventually, the law loosened the restraints that were imposed in *Dodge* v. *Ford Motor Co.* and allowed corporations to expend some corporate funds for the good of society. In *A. P. Smith Manufacturing Co.* v. *Barlow* (1953), the New Jersey State Supreme Court ruled that the managers of the company were permitted by law to give $1,500 to Princeton University despite shareholder objections on the grounds that to bar corporations from making such contributions would threaten our democracy and the free enterprise system. The court agreed with the testimony of a former chairman of the board of United States Steel Company that if American business does not aid important institutions such as private universities, then it is not "properly protecting the long-range interests of its stockholders, its employees and its customers." After the decision in *A. P. Smith Manufacturing Co.* v. *Barlow,* Berle conceded defeat in his debate with Dodd. Public opinion and the law had accepted Dodd's contention that corporate powers ought to be held in trust for the whole of society.[44]

Although the separation of ownership and control documented by Berle and Means undermined the property rights theory, a fully developed social institution theory did not replace it. Instead, a conception of the corporation as a quasi-public institution emerged, in which managers have limited discretion to use the resources at their command for the good of employees, customers, and the larger society. In a world of giant corporations, managers are called upon to balance the interests of competing corporate constituencies, and in order to fill this role they have developed a sense of management as a profession with public responsibilities. Managers ceased being the exclusive servants of the stockholders and assumed the mantle of public-spirited leaders, albeit of profit-making business organizations.

In the last several decades, another theory of the firm has emerged that now dominates thinking in financial economics and corporate law. This is the contractual theory, in which the firm is viewed as a nexus of contracts among all corporate constituencies.

The Contractual Theory

The origin of the contractual, or nexus-of-contracts, theory is the work of the economist Ronald Coase, who claimed that firms exist as less costly alternatives to market transactions.[45] In a world where market exchanges could occur without any costs (what economists call *transaction costs*), economic activity would be achieved entirely by means of contracting among individuals in a free market. In the actual world, the transaction costs involved in market activity can be quite high, and some coordination can be achieved more cheaply by organizing economic activity in firms. Thus, there are two forms of economic coordination—firms and markets—and the choice between them is determined by transaction costs.

In the Coasean view, the firm is a market writ small in which parties with economic assets contract with the firm to deploy these assets in productive activity. Generally, an individual's assets are more productive when they are combined with the assets of others in joint or team production. Individuals will choose to deploy their assets in a firm instead of the market when the lower transaction costs of a firm combined with the benefits of team production yield them a higher return.

Deploying assets in a firm involves some risks, however, when those assets are *firm-specific.* Consider the situation of an employee who acquires skills that are needed by a particular employer. A worker with such skills will generally earn more than one with only generic skills, but only a few employers will value those special skills and be willing to pay the higher wages. An employee with special skills is also tied more closely to the firm because the skills in question are not easily transferable, and the employee would likely suffer a loss if forced to move to another employer. The assets of an employee that can be more profitably employed with one or a few firms are thus firm-specific. Firm-specific assets enable a worker to create more wealth, which makes possible the higher pay, but this wealth can also be appropriated by the firm itself, leaving the employee without adequate compensation for acquiring special skills.

Not only employees but also investors, suppliers, customers, and other groups have firm-specific assets, and these groups will make their assets available to a firm only with adequate safeguards against misappropriation. That is, each group will seek guarantees to ensure that they are adequately compensated for any assets that cannot easily be removed from joint productive activity. Most groups protect themselves by means of contracts. These may be either explicit, legally enforceable contracts or implicit contracts that have no legal standing. Thus, employees are often protected by employment contracts, suppliers by purchase contracts, consumers by warranties, and so on. An implicit contract is created, for example, when an employer creates an expectation about the conditions of employment. In the nexus-of-contracts firm, managers coordinate these contracts with the various corporate constituencies. The contracts with most corporate constituencies are relatively unproblematical, but one group raises special problems, namely shareholders.

The Role of Shareholders. In the usual interpretation of the contractual theory, shareholders along with bondholders and other investors, provide capital, but, more significantly, they also assume the residual risk of conducting business, which is the risk that remains after a firm has fulfilled all of its legal obligations. Residual risk could be borne by every group that contracts with a firm, but risk bearing can also be a specialized role in which one group bears the preponderance of risk. In the large, publicly held corporation, shareholders fill the role of residual risk bearer, and it is this role, rather than the role of capital provider, that sets them apart from other groups in the nexus of contracts.

The position of residual risk bearer is difficult to protect by ordinary contractual provisions, such as those available to bondholders, employees, customers, and other constituencies. Some protection is provided by the opportunity to diversify and by the limited liability that shareholders enjoy. Shareholders are also rewarded for their investment with prospects of a higher return than that assured to secured creditors such as bondholders. However, the most important protection for shareholders is corporate control. Corporate control is a package of rights that includes the right to select the board of directors and approve important changes. In addition, shareholders have a claim on management's allegiance. This is commonly expressed by saying that management has a fiduciary duty to operate the corporation in the shareholders' interest and that the objective of the firm is to maximize shareholder wealth.

The contractual theory of the firm itself does not assign this right to shareholders—or to any other group for that matter. Rather, corporate control is a benefit to be bargained for in the nexus-of-contracts firm, and through bargaining any constituency group could conceivably assume the right of control. Indeed, other groups take control when a corporation becomes employee-owned or customer-owned (a co-op, for example). Employees have also successfully bargained for representation on boards of directors, and bond indentures sometimes give bondholders the right to vote on certain risky ventures. When corporations are in bankruptcy, creditors take control from shareholders and the creditors' interests become primary until the firm recovers.

Still, the current system of corporate governance assigns control, for the most part, to shareholders. Some further argument is needed, however, for this assignment of rights. Why should shareholders, as residual risk bearers, control a corporation?

The Argument for Shareholder Control. The starting point of the argument for shareholder control is that this right is of greater value to residual claimants than to other constituencies. First, control is better suited than other kinds of protection for the special situation of shareholders. That is, control is a fitting solution for the problem of protecting the firm-specific assets of residual risk bearers. Second and more importantly, the return to shareholders is wholly dependent on the profitability of a firm, and so they value control as a means to spur a firm to the highest possible level of performance. By contrast, nonshareholder constituencies have little to gain from control because their fixed claims will be satisfied as long as the firm remains solvent. The right of control, therefore, is more valuable to whichever group settles for residual rather than fixed claims.

The contractual theory envisions the corporation as a nexus of contracts that is formed by bargaining among all corporate constituencies. In an actual or hypothetical bargaining situation, shareholders as residual claimants would insist on corporate control and be more willing to pay for this right. Moreover, other constituencies would agree to this arrangement. The reason is that bondholders, employees, and other groups would prefer different contractual terms. Employees, for example, would opt for contracts that assure them a specific wage and other benefits. Bargaining for control rights, such as the right to a seat on the board of directors, would require employees to give up something else, and the reluctance of employees to bargain for such rights suggests that the gain is not worth the price.

The contractual theory also holds that society benefits when shareholders control a corporation. Assuming that maximum wealth creation is the goal of business activity, control should go to the group with the appropriate incentives for making wealth-maximizing decisions, and this group—according to the argument—is the shareholders. It has already been observed that bondholders, employees, and other corporate constituencies with fixed claims tend to favor decisions that secure their claims and no more. Therefore, some profitable investment opportunities might not be pursued if these groups had control. Managers, too, lack the incentives to pursue all profitable ventures, especially those that would reduce their power or place them at risk. Wealth-maximizing decisions are more likely to be made by the residual risk bearers, because they incur the marginal costs and gain the marginal benefits of all new ventures. Shareholder control, therefore, is the ideal arrangement for the whole of society.

The contractual theory argument for shareholder control, then, is that corporations will create more wealth if decisions are made with only the shareholders' interests in mind. What is important to note about this argument is that the *ultimate* objective of the firm is the maximization of wealth for the whole of society. The objective of shareholder wealth maximization is merely a means to this larger end. This argument does not neglect other constituencies, such as employees, customers, suppliers, and the larger community. It assumes, rather, that these groups are well protected by other kinds of contracts and that, on the whole, they are well served by shareholder control. In other words, this arrangement is optimal not merely for shareholders but for society as a whole.

Frank H. Easterbrook and Daniel R. Fischel make the point in the following way:

> A successful firm provides jobs for workers and goods and services for consumers. The more appealing the goods to consumers, the more profit (and jobs). Prosperity for stockholders, workers, and communities goes hand in glove with better products for consumers. Other objectives, too, come with profit. Wealthy firms provide better working conditions and clean up their outfalls; high profits produce social wealth that strengthens the demand for cleanliness.... [W]ealthy societies purchase much cleaner and healthier environments than do poorer nations—in part because well-to-do citizens want cleaner air and water, and in part because they can afford to pay for it.[46]

As a result, they claim, "maximizing profit for equity investors assists the other 'constituencies' automatically."[47]

Criticism of the Contractual Theory

The contractual theory argument for shareholder control is similar to Adam Smith's famous invisible hand argument according to which each self-interested individual is, to quote from the *Wealth of Nations*, "led by an invisible hand to promote an end which was no part of his intention." Just as the invisible hand argument is subject to some well-known objections, so, too, is the contractual theory argument.

Externalities. One problem is posed by externalities, such as pollution. The welfare of society is not promoted, for example, when corporations make a profit for shareholders by polluting a stream. The idea that managers ought to consider only the interests of shareholders appears to invite, indeed require, actions that impose harms on other constituencies. Easterbrook and Fischel recognize this possibility but deny that it has any bearing on the argument for shareholder control. They write:

> We do not make the Panglossian claim that profit and social welfare are perfectly aligned. When costs fall on third parties—pollution is a common example—firms do injury because harm does not come back to them as private cost.... Users of the stream impose costs on the firm (and its consumers) as fully as the firm imposes costs on the users of the stream. No rearrangement of corporate governance structures can change this. The task is to establish property rights so that the firm treats the social costs as private ones, and so that its reactions, as managers try to maximize profits given these new costs, duplicate what all of the parties (downstream users and customers alike) would have agreed to were bargaining among all possible without cost.[48]

Easterbrook and Fischel contend that clear assignments of property rights would force firms to internalize what would otherwise be external costs.[49] Pollution can also be handled by other means, such as government regulation. At issue, then, is whether externalities such as pollution are due to shareholder control and hence whether any change in control would provide a solution.

Implicit Contracts. The contractual theory argument assumes that nonshareholder constituencies are well served by their various contractual arrangements. Explicit contracts, such as an employee contract or a sales agreement, are legally enforceable. However, many contracts are implicit, so that they depend on the goodwill of management. Although an employer may create an expectation of secure employment, for example, this implicit contract can be violated without any legal consequences. When longtime employees are terminated in corporate restructurings or downsizings, the charge is often made that the shareholders gain by violating the implicit contracts with those who are forced to leave. Similarly, companies that close a plant are often accused of violating an implicit contract with a community that has provided support. Critics of hostile takeovers have argued that one source of financing for the raid on a target company is the value of the implicit contracts with various constituencies that shareholders are able to capture. Thus, the takeover of a lumber company that has made an implicit contract with environmentalists to limit logging can be financed, in part, by increasing the number of trees felled after the takeover.

The defense against these charges is that the affected groups are still better off with implicit claims that can be violated. Without the freedom to restructure or downsize a work force, for example, corporations would be less able to compete and hence to offer high wages. Employees could gain greater job security only by settling for lower wages, and communities could keep plants only by settling for lesser benefits. Faced with these alternatives, each constituency would negotiate contracts that rely to some extent on vague promises and nonbinding commitments instead of precisely written, legally enforceable contracts.

Still, implicit contracts are a kind of promise, and it seems unfair for shareholders to benefit by, in effect, going back on their word. For this reason, Congress has addressed the plight of communities by requiring prior notification of plant closings,[50] and some states have sought to limit the impact of hostile takeovers by so-called "other constituency" statutes that permit directors to consider the interests of nonshareholder groups.[51] Congress has also imposed a fiduciary duty on corporations to serve the interests of employees in the management of pension funds. The effect of these measures is to limit the freedom of corporate managers to violate various implicit contracts with nonshareholder groups.

Residual Risk. The contractual theory assumes that shareholders bear all residual risk, but other constituencies, most notably employees and suppliers, bear some. In truth, well-diversified individual shareholders bear relatively little risk, but the relevant point is that their claim is on the residual returns of a firm. By the logic of the argument for shareholder control, however, any group that bears some residual risk should have some say in major corporate decisions. It has been argued, for example, that highly skilled employees who develop valuable firm-specific human capital may, in fact, assume considerable residual risk.[52] This is especially true in start-up companies that can attract employees only with promises of higher wages in the future. These promised wages are contingent on the performance of the firm, so that employees, in the words of one writer, "are also 'residual claimants,' who share in the business risk associated with the enterprise."[53] For this reason, many start-up companies offer their employees shares of stock or stock options. When other groups besides shareholders bear residual risk, they are sometimes accorded a seat on the board of directors.

Distribution and Power. Finally, the contractual theory takes no account of the fact that the contracting groups have unequal bargaining power, and this imbalance results in correspondingly unequal distribution of the wealth created by a firm. As in any market, those with the greatest resources will reap the lion's share of goods. If workers, for example, are weak and disempowered, they will not be able to bargain effectively in a nexus-of-contracts firm. Unequal bargaining power is a serious problem in most societies. Some of the inequality in assets comes from accidents of birth, as when one person is more intelligent or more talented than another. The main sources of inequality, however, are social and political in nature. Holders of the contractual theory maintain that all kinds of inequality can be corrected only by social and political change. No change in corporate governance can improve the condition of any corporate constituency without some alteration in its underlying bargaining power.

Stakeholder Theory

The contractual theory generally supports a stockholder-centered conception of the corporation. A much-discussed alternative to this view is *stakeholder theory*. The central claim of the stakeholder approach is that corporations are operated or ought to be operated for the benefit of all those who have a *stake* in the enterprise, including employees, customers, suppliers, and the local community. A stakeholder is variously defined as "those groups who are vital to the survival and success of the corporation"[54] and as "any group or individual who can affect or is affected by the achievement of the organization's objectives."[55] Although the relation of each stakeholder group to the corporation is different, each of these constituencies is integral to the operation of a corporation, and its role must be taken into account by managers.

Serious attempts have been made to develop the stakeholder concept into a full-blown view of the corporation that might replace the stockholder-centered conception. In the standard stockholder view, business is primarily an economic activity in which economic resources are marshaled for the purpose of making a profit. Employees are critical to this enterprise as a source of labor, but they are merely one *input* that can be "bought" in the market. Customers are also critical, and they receive the *output* of a corporation's activity, namely some good or service. But what customers give and receive is also the result of market exchanges. The resulting view of the corporation is the input–output model displayed in Figure 14.1.

The concept of a stakeholder highlights the fact that corporate activity is not solely a series of market transactions but also a cooperative (and competitive)

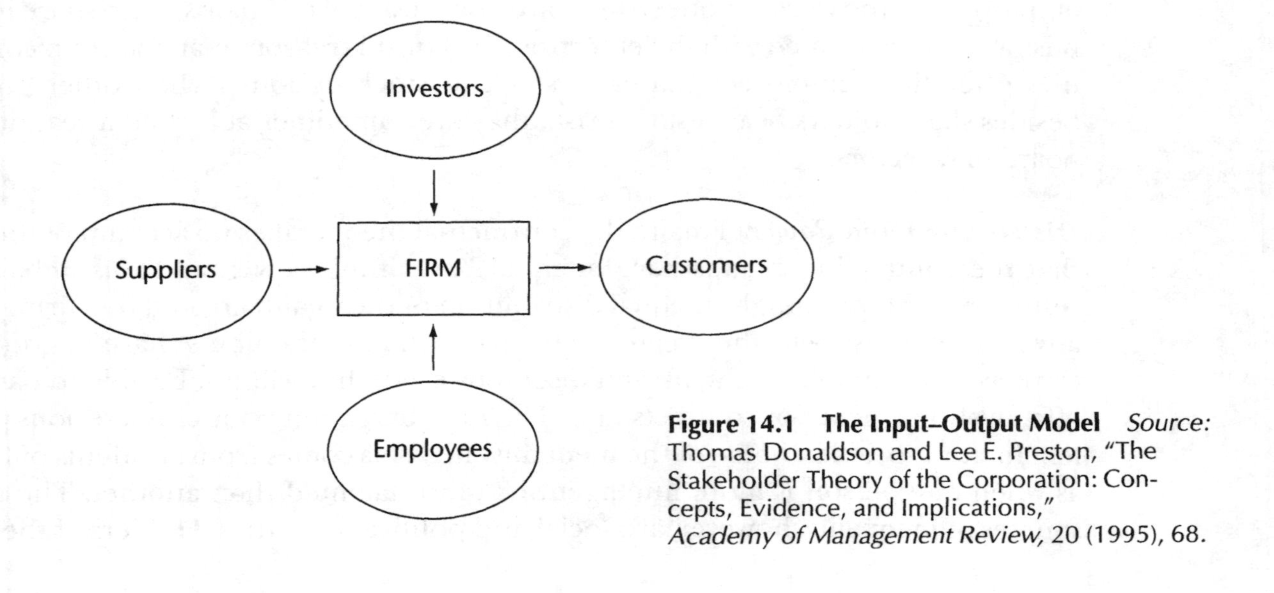

Figure 14.1 The Input–Output Model *Source:* Thomas Donaldson and Lee E. Preston, "The Stakeholder Theory of the Corporation: Concepts, Evidence, and Implications," *Academy of Management Review,* 20 (1995), 68.

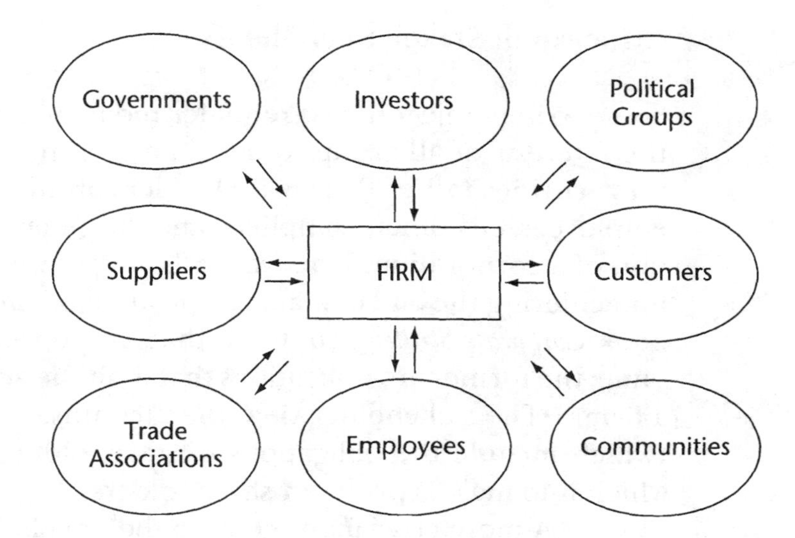

Figure 14.2 The Stakeholder Model *Source:* Thomas Donaldson and Lee E. Preston, "The Stakeholder Theory of the Corporation: Concepts, Evidence, and Implications," *Academy of Management Review,* 20 (1995), 69.

endeavor involving large numbers of people organized in various ways. The corporation or firm is an organizational entity through which many different individuals and groups attempt to achieve their ends. A firm interacts continually with its stakeholder groups, and much of the success of a firm depends on how well all of these stakeholder relations are managed. Managing stakeholder relations, rather than managing inputs and outputs, may provide a more adequate model for understanding what people in corporations actually do as well as what they ought to do. Such a stakeholder model of the corporation is displayed in Figure 14.2.

Thomas Donaldson and Lee E. Preston have distinguished three uses of the stakeholder model: descriptive, instrumental, and normative.[56] First, the model can be used as a *description* of the corporation that can enable us to understand the corporation better. That is, a researcher who believes that the stakeholder model accurately describes corporations can use it to answer questions about how corporations are organized and managed or about how people in corporations think about their roles. The belief that the stakeholder model is an accurate description can be confirmed to the extent that these answers are put to a test and empirically verified.

Second, the stakeholder model can be used *instrumentally* as a tool for managers. Even if making a profit is the ultimate goal of corporate activity, this goal does not provide much help in the daily conduct of business. By contrast, telling managers to handle stakeholder relations well is a more practical action guide that may actually lead to greater profit. Certainly, many companies that care deeply about their employees, customers, suppliers, and other affected groups are also highly profitable.

Third, the stakeholder model can be used as a *normative* account of how corporations *ought* to treat their various stakeholder groups. The descriptive and instrumental uses of the stakeholder model suggest that corporations must deal with their stakeholders as a matter of practical necessity. Used normatively, the stakeholder model would have managers recognize the interests of employees, customers, and others as worth furthering for their own sakes. As Donaldson and Preston explain, "The interests of all stakeholders are of '*intrinsic value.*'"[57]

Criticism of Stakeholder Theory

Some writers reject the stakeholder model in its normative use on the ground that the interests of all groups other than shareholders constitute *constraints* on corporate activities rather than *goals*. Holders of the stockholder view are well aware that employees, customers, suppliers, and the general public are important to the operation of a corporation. However, satisfying these groups is necessary only as a means for achieving the end of making a profit. Igor Ansoff, for example, in his classic 1965 book *Corporate Strategy*, contends that "responsibilities" and "objectives" are not the same; the former are obligations that limit the achievement of the main objectives of a firm.[58] The stakeholder view, then, confuses the responsibilities of a corporation (which include the obligations to stakeholder groups) with its objectives (one of which is to make a profit for shareholders).

A more crucial objection to the stakeholder model is its shortcomings as an action guide for business. Even managers committed to honoring obligations to all stakeholders will find that the stakeholder model leaves many questions unanswered. Many difficult corporate decisions involve trade-offs in which a benefit to one group must be balanced against a loss to another. Thus, increasing the pension benefits of employees might result in higher prices to consumers, or a switch to environmentally safer packaging might lead to the termination of a supplier. A company that protects one community by keeping an unprofitable factory open might become uncompetitive and be forced eventually to close more factories in other communities.

Finally, the implications of stakeholder theory for corporate governance are unclear. In keeping with Berle's concern about the dangers of unrestrained managerial power, a stakeholder corporation would need to be structured so as to ensure the well-being of corporate constituencies. This is no easy task. To date, no stakeholder theorist has offered a detailed proposal for changes in corporate governance that would result in a stakeholder corporation. The systems of corporate governance in some foreign countries provide examples of some possibilities for changes. For example, workers in Germany and Japan have a larger role in strategic decision making than their counterparts in the United States. These systems reflect cultural and historical differences, however, and it is questionable whether they could be adopted in other settings.

Despite these objections, the stakeholder model remains a promising alternative to the stockholder view. The concept of a stakeholder is a valuable device for identifying and organizing the multitude of obligations that corporations have to different groups. At the present time, however, the theory is only a framework to help us get started on this very difficult task.

Case 14.2 Bath Iron Works

On May 17, 1991, a quick decision by CEO William E. Haggett almost destroyed Bath Iron Works, the largest private employer in Maine.[59] Founded in 1884, Bath Iron Works (BIW) is a major shipbuilder for the U.S. Navy with 10,400 employees. As one of two companies with the capability to build Aegis naval destroyers worth $250 million each, BIW was competing fiercely for contracts with its rival, Ingalls Shipbuilding in Mississippi. At 5:30 that morning, a janitor found a 67-page document stamped "Business Sensitive" in a conference room that had been used the previous day for a meeting with Navy officials. Two vice presidents who examined the document realized that it contained a detailed comparison of BIW's and Ingalls's costs for building the Aegis destroyer. They delivered the document to Mr. Haggett at 9:00 A.M. The CEO, who was leaving the office to deliver a luncheon speech, examined it for 15 minutes before making a decision. He ordered the two vice presidents to copy the document, return the original to the conference room, and meet with him late in the afternoon to discuss how they should handle the situation.

During the next few hours, the two executives analyzed the information and did some computer modeling based on it. At 2:15 they decided to notify the president of BIW, Duane D. "Buzz" Fitzgerald, who had a reputation for impeccable integrity. Mr. Fitzgerald immediately recognized that the federal Procurement Integrity Act requires defense contractors to certify that they have not been in unauthorized possession of any propriety information. In addition, Bath Iron Works is a signatory to the Defense Industry Initiative on Business Ethics and Conduct (DII), which was formed in 1986 in response to revelations by the Packard Commission of irregularities in defense industry contracting. The six principles of the DII require not only that signatories adopt a written code of ethics, engage in ethics training, and provide mechanisms for internal reporting of possible misconduct, but also that they take responsibility for any violation of law. Principle 4 states, "Each company has the obligation to self-govern by monitoring compliance with federal procurement laws and adopting procedures for voluntary disclosure of violations of federal procurement laws and corrective actions taken." Mr. Fitzgerald ordered that all copies be shredded and all data erased from the computer. Upon his return, Mr. Haggett agreed with the action taken and admitted that he had made an "inappropriate business-ethics decision." The CEO personally delivered the original document to Navy officials on site. However, Mr. Haggett decided not to reveal that copies had been made but to admit only that "no copies existed."

The Navy launched its own investigation and concluded that the bidding process had not been compromised. An adverse decision could have resulted in suspension or debarment as a government contractor, which would have jeopardized the survival of the firm with devastating consequences for its employees and the surrounding community. As part of the settlement with the Navy, BIW agreed to establish an ethics program headed by an ethics officer, expand ethics training, create a board committee for ensuring compliance, and report to the Navy for three years on the implementation of this agreement. BIW was still competing for contracts to build at least two new Aegis destroyers, and many at the company feared that lingering suspicion about the use of a competitor's information would be an impediment. To allay this concern, the two vice presidents who first handled the discovery of the document were asked to leave the company and William Haggett resigned as CEO. He later severed all connections with BIW, thus ending a 28-year career with a company where his father had worked as a pipe fitter. He lamented that 15 minutes of ethical uncertainty had cost him his job. Buzz Fitzgerald became the new CEO and immediately declared that BIW "must meet the highest ethical standards and avoid even the appearance of impropriety."

CORPORATE ETHICS PROGRAMS

Corporations are increasingly paying attention to ethics in the conduct of employees at all level of the organization. Unlike the emphasis on corporate social responsibility, which focuses on the impact of business activity on society at large, the corporate ethics movement addresses the need to guide individual decision making and to develop an ethical workplace environment. Much of the impetus in the United States has come from a recognition of the dangers posed by individual misconduct. However, unethical business practices are seldom due to a lone rogue employee but usually result from factors in the organization.[60] Ethics programs are designed, therefore, to create an organization that fosters ethical conduct. The case of Bath Iron Works shows that no program can prevent momentary lapses of judgment, much less intentional wrongdoing. The incident occurred in spite of an existing ethics program. The consequences of this incident might have been far worse, though, had the company not implemented the principles of the Defense Industry Initiative. Significantly, the chosen remedy was a strengthening of the program in place in order to prevent a recurrence.

This section examines corporate ethics programs. Specifically, what are the components of an ethics program? What leads corporations to adopt a program, and what do they expect to achieve? Some companies have adopted ethics programs in response to serious scandals, whereas others seek to prevent scandals before they occur. In particular, the corporate ethics movement has been spurred by the Federal Sentencing Guidelines, which offer lenient treatment for convicted organizations with an effective ethics program. These are primarily defensive strategies aimed at legal compliance. However, many corporations strive for a higher level of conduct in the belief that a reputation for integrity provides a strategic advantage. Like all other corporate initiatives, though, ethics programs represent an investment that must be justified, and so we need to take a critical look at their benefits and also at possible objections to them.

The Components of an Ethics Program

Every organization has an ethics program of some kind, although it may not be recognized as such.[61] In the broadest sense, an ethics program consists of the rules and policies of an organization and the procedures and systems for motivating and monitoring ethical performance. Rules and policies include the culture and values of an organization and formal documents, such as mission statements, codes of ethics, policy and personnel manuals, training materials, and management directives. Compliance with rules and policies is secured by various procedures and systems for orientation, training, compensation, promotion, auditing, and investigation. These procedures and systems are essential functions in any business organization. Companies with an identifiable ethics program are distinguished by the emphasis that they place on these functions and the manner in which they address them.

The components of a corporate ethics program generally include a code of ethics, ethics training for employees, means for communicating with employees about matters of ethics, a reporting mechanism for enabling employees to report alleged wrongdoing, an audit system for detecting wrongdoing, and a system for conducting investigations and taking corrective action. In addition, more than 500 U.S. corporations have established the position of ethics officer to oversee all aspects of an ethics program. Many companies without an ethics officer still assign the main responsibilities to one or more high-level executives.

This list of components does not reveal the range of corporate ethics programs. At one end of the spectrum are programs designed merely to secure compliance with the law and with the company's own rules and policies. The goals are to prevent criminal conduct and violation of government regulations on the one hand and to protect the company from self-interested action by employees on the other. Compliance of this kind is essential in any organization, but some corporations take a broader view of ethics. At the other end of the spectrum are ethics programs that communicate the values and vision of the organization, seek to build relations of trust with all stakeholder groups, and emphasize the responsibility of each employee for ethical conduct.

Lynn Sharp Paine describes this latter kind of program as an *integrity strategy* in contrast to the *compliance strategy* that is represented by the former kind.[62] Whereas a compliance approach imposes standards of conduct on employees and attempts to compel acceptable behavior, a program guided by integrity aligns the standards of employees with those of the organization and enables them to act ethically. An integrity strategy seeks to create conditions that foster right action instead of relying on deterrence and detection. These conditions are created by the whole management team rather than being relegated to lawyers or others in compliance, and by employing the whole resources of the organization. In particular, the full range of procedures and policies, the accounting and control systems, and the decision-making structures of the corporation are utilized for the end of fostering right conduct. An integrity strategy also attempts to motivate employees by appealing to their values and ideals, rather than relying solely on material incentives.

The Benefits of an Ethics Program

The main benefit of an ethics program is to prevent ethical misconduct by employees, which is costly to companies not only in direct losses but also in those sustained from a tarnished reputation. The total cost to Sears, Roebuck and Company for settling suits nationwide over allegations that its Sear Auto Center made unnecessary repairs (see Case 14.3) has been estimated to be $60 million. In addition, the trust of consumers that enabled the company to enter the competitive auto repair market was seriously damaged. The falsification of records by defense contractors, for which the companies were fined and forced to make restitution, led to development of the Defense Industry Initiative.

The financial services industry has produced some examples of very costly misconduct. A bond trading scandal at Salomon Brothers in 1991 cost the firm almost $1 billion, and in 1994 Prudential Securities agreed to pay fines and penalties in excess of $700 million for crimes committed in the sale of limited partnerships in the 1980s. A Japanese copper trader hid losses estimated at $2.6 billion from his employer, Sumitomo Corporation; and Nicholas Leeson, a 29-year-old, Singapore-based trader for Barings Bank, destroyed this venerable British firm by losing more than $1 billion in unauthorized trading. In some instances, the main loss from employee misconduct has been the company's reputation. For example, NYNEX adopted an ethics program after learning that between 1984 and 1988, its purchasing unit had hosted an annual convention in Florida for suppliers and company employees featuring strippers and prostitutes. The public exposure of these events—dubbed "pervert conventions" by the press—came at the same time that the struggling company was seeking an unpopular $1.4 billion rate increase from the New York State Public Service Commission.

Second, ethics programs provide a managerial tool for adapting the organization to rapid change. Among the factors that have led corporations to adopt ethics programs are increased competition, the development of new technologies, increased regulation, recent mergers and acquisitions, and the globalization of business. The problems at NYNEX, for example, were not confined to risqué parties. The breakup of AT&T in 1984 had forced NYNEX and all Baby Bells to compete in an unfamiliar environment that required new ways of doing business. NYNEX needed to provide individual guidance to employees during a period in which all the rules were being rewritten. Mergers and acquisitions also disrupt familiar routines and create the need to develop new ones rapidly. Finally, a formerly domestic company that becomes a global enterprise must not only set the rules for its own employees' behavior abroad but also mesh its conduct with that of foreign customers, suppliers, and joint venture partners.

A third benefit of ethics programs is managing relations with external constituencies. An ethics program serves to reassure customers, suppliers, investors, and the general public of the serious intent of a corporation to adhere to high ethical standards. It is no accident that the first ethics programs were developed by defense contractors, which have only one customer, namely the Department of Defense. The Defense Industry Initiative, which commits each signatory to develop an ethics program, was an attempt to assure this all-important customer of its trustworthiness. Problems often develop when a company and its suppliers or vendors operate by different standards, and so a company's ethics program helps make its standards known. For example, some companies notify suppliers of their policy on gift giving and ask them to respect it.

The existence of an ethics program is an assurance not only to socially responsible investors, who look for such indicators, but also to shareholders generally, who want to avoid the cost of major scandals. The shareholders of Caremark International, Inc., a health-care provider, sued the individual members of the board of directors for failing to prevent criminal violations that cost the company $260 million. In deciding this case, the Delaware State Supreme Court held in 1996 that directors have a fiduciary duty to the shareholders to ensure that the corporation's reporting systems are reasonably well designed to provide management with sufficient information to detect violations of law.[63] The *Caremark* decision has been described as a "wake-up call" to directors that they may be personally liable for their failure to ensure that a corporation has an adequate compliance system in place.[64] Of course, an ethics program is only one means for securing compliance. However, the *Caremark* decision, combined with the Federal Sentencing Guidelines, provides a strong incentive for developing one.

The Federal Sentencing Guidelines

In 1984, Congress created the United States Sentencing Commission in order to bring greater uniformity and effectiveness to the sentences that judges impose for federal crimes. In developing new guidelines, the Sentencing Commission departed from prevailing practices by holding organizations responsible for the conduct of individual decision makers and creating incentives for organizations to prevent misconduct by their members. Under the Federal Sentencing Guidelines for Organizations, which took effect in 1991, the sentence for an organization that has been convicted of a federal crime depends, in part, on the effort that has been made to prevent and detect criminal wrongdoing, including the adoption of an effective ethics program.

The Federal Sentencing Guidelines have the dual aim of imposing a just sentence on any convicted organization and influencing the conduct of all organizations. The former aim is achieved by guidelines that base the penalty on the seriousness of the offense and the culpability or blameworthiness of the organization. The guidelines provide not only for fines that punish an organization but also for restitution to the victims, and the fines can be set so as to wipe out any gain for an organization from its criminal activity. In addition, the severity of the fines, which can reach $290 million or the higher of the gain to the organization or the loss to the victims, provides a powerful incentive for organizations to take preventive steps and to cooperate in an investigation.

How the Guidelines Work. The first step in applying the guidelines is determining a base fine. This amount is generally taken from a table that ranks crimes according to their seriousness and assigns a monetary amount to each level. The base fine ranges from $5,000 for a level 6 offense or lower (embezzlement, theft, bribery of a public official) to $72.5 million for a level 38 offense or higher. Commercial bribery, for example, is a level 8 offense with a $10,000 base fine, and money laundering is a level 20 offense with a base fine of $650,000.

The base fine may then be either increased or decreased by a multiplier based on a "culpability score." This score, which ranges from 1 to 10, is determined by starting with five points and by subtracting or adding points for certain factors. Five points are added if high-level personnel were involved in the wrongdoing; three points are added if the organization obstructed the investigation or prosecution of the crime; and two points are added if similar misconduct had occurred before. Up to five points are subtracted for reporting an offense, cooperating with the investigation, and accepting full responsibility. The significant factor for the development of an ethics program is that a sentencing judge subtracts three points if the offense occurred "despite an effective program to prevent and detect violation of the law." (This provision does not apply if high-level personnel were involved or if they delayed reporting the offense after becoming aware of it.)

For each culpability score, there is a range from which a judge can choose a multiplier that either reduces or increases the base fine. The minimum multiplier is 0.05, which reduces the fine imposed to 5 percent of the base fine. The maximum multiplier is 4.00, which quadruples the base fine. Hence, the highest fine is $72.5 million (the highest base fine) multiplied by 4.00 (the highest multiplier), or $290 million. The highest fine imposed so far by using the Federal Sentencing Guidelines is $340 million levied against Daiwa Bank in New York, even though the bank was a victim of unauthorized trading by an employee that cost the bank $1.1 billion.[65] The charge against the bank was that officials had failed to inform U.S. officials within 30 days of the discovery of the loss as required by law. The bank officials engaged in the cover-up in part to avoid a decline in the bank's stock price but also because they felt that they needed time to understand what had happened and because the Japanese Ministry of Finance feared that disclosure would have an adverse impact on markets in Japan. However, if the bank had adopted an adequate compliance program, perhaps the loss would have been detected earlier with less severe consequences.

An Effective Ethics Program. The Federal Sentencing Guidelines define an effective ethics program as one "that has been reasonably designed, implemented, and enforced so that it generally will be effective in preventing and detecting criminal conduct."[66] The program need not prevent or detect every instance of wrongdoing, but the organization must have practiced "due diligence," which involves the following steps.[67]

1. The organization must have established compliance standards and procedures that are reasonably capable of reducing misconduct.
2. Specific high-level personnel must have been assigned responsibility for overseeing compliance with the standards and procedures.
3. The organization must take due care not to assign substantial discretionary authority to individuals with a propensity to engage in illegal behavior.
4. Standards and procedures must have been communicated to all employees and agents through such means as publications and training programs.

5. The organization must have taken reasonable steps to ensure compliance by using monitoring and auditing systems and a reporting system that employees may use without fear of retaliation.
6. The standards must have been consistently enforced through appropriate disciplinary measures, including, as appropriate, the punishment of employees who fail to detect an offense by others.
7. After an offense has been detected, the organization must have taken all reasonable steps to respond appropriately and to prevent further similar offenses.

The specific actions involving these steps will depend on many factors, including the size of the organization, the nature of the industry, and the organization's prior history.

Although the Federal Sentencing Guidelines provide a strong incentive for corporations to establish ethics programs and contain a good definition of an effective ethics programs, questions have been raised about the overall approach of the guidelines and specific features of the definition. First, there is no solid evidence that ethics programs are more effective than other kinds of compliance systems in preventing illegal behavior. Some evidence indicates that misconduct occurs not because of ignorance about the standards for acceptable conduct but because of organizational pressures and the actions of peers.[68] To be effective, therefore, an ethics program must go beyond setting and enforcing rules and include the goal-setting and reward systems of an organization. Second, to the extent that ethics programs are not effective, the guidelines may encourage corporations to create highly visible "window dressing" programs at the expense of more substantive initiatives. Moreover, most large corporations already have compliance programs that would satisfy the guideline's requirements, so that little is to be gained by offering a reduction in any fine. But small firms may be penalized for investing their more limited resources in a formal ethics program when other systems of control might be more effective in preventing misconduct.

Codes of Ethics

The first step in developing an ethics program, and the only step that some companies take, is a code of ethics. Codes of ethics vary widely, falling into three main types. The most common is a statement of specific rules or standards for a variety of situations. These are most often called codes of conduct or statements of business standards or practices. A second type is a statement of core values or the vision of an organization, sometimes called a credo or mission statement. These statements frequently include affirmations of the commitments of a company to key stakeholders, such as customers, employees, and the community. Third are corporate philosophies that describe the beliefs guiding a particular company. Perhaps the best-known of these is Hewlett Packard's "The HP Way". Corporate philosophy statements are generally written by the founders of businesses in emerging industries, such as computers, where new ways of doing business are needed.

Most codes of ethics combine elements of the first two types, but at least one firm, Levi Strauss & Company, has adopted all three kinds of statements. An Aspiration Statement describes what kind of company its members want it to be. A Code of Ethics explains the values and ethical principles that guide action. And finally, Levi Strauss has adopted a document entitled "Global Sourcing and Operating Guidelines," which contains very specific rules on working with business partners and choosing countries for operations. A few weeks before the guidelines were officially adopted, Levi Strauss canceled a contract with a supplier in Saipan (a U.S. territory) after reports of human rights violations. Subsequently, the U.S. Department of Labor charged that the contractor worked the employees, mostly Chinese women, up to 11 hours a day in guarded compounds and paid them well below the Saipan minimum wage. The contractor settled the charges for $9 million. One Levi Strauss manager observed, "If anyone doubted the need for guidelines, this convinced them."

In addition to company codes of ethics, there are many industry codes, generally adopted by a trade organization. These include organizations for the advertising, banking, direct marketing, franchising, insurance, and real estate industries. Because a commitment to high ethical standards and self-regulation is integral to a profession, most professional groups have also developed ethics codes to which their members are generally required to subscribe. Among professions with codes of ethics are physicians, lawyers, accountants and auditors, architects, engineers, financial planners, public administrators, consultants, and journalists. Unlike company and industry codes of ethics, which are of recent origin, some professional codes are as old as the profession, as witness the Hippocratic oath for physicians, which dates from the fourth century B.C.

The development of ethics codes for corporations is a relatively recent phenomenon, with most written since 1970.[69] In many instances, these codes replaced other kinds of documents, such as policy manuals, executive directives, and customary practices. An early prominent code of ethics was "The Penney Idea", a set of seven principles set forth by the merchandizing pioneer J.C. Penney in 1913. A major impetus for the development of corporate ethics codes was provided by the influential National Commission on Fraudulent Financial Reporting (the "Treadway Report"), issued in October 1987. This report recommended:

> Public companies should develop and enforce written codes of corporate conduct. Codes of conduct should foster a strong ethical climate and open channels of communication to help protect against fraudulent financial reporting. As a part of its ongoing oversight of the effectiveness of internal controls, a company's audit committee should review annually the program that management establishes to monitor compliance with the code.[70]

Until recently, codes of ethics have primarily been adopted by American companies. A study in 1987 revealed that more than three-quarters of U.S. respondents had a code of ethics, but less than half of the responding European corporations had one.[71] The number of companies abroad with a code of ethics is increasing, however, in part because of the rise of mergers and joint ventures between American and foreign firms.

The Reasons for Adopting a Code. The reasons for adopting a code of ethics include those that lead companies to develop ethics programs. Even without a program, a code of ethics serves a number of valuable functions. A written document enables an organization to clarify standards that may otherwise be vague expectations left to individual interpretation. Where there is disagreement on the appropriate standards, codes can achieve a measure of consensus, and where standards are lacking or in need of revision, codes enable an organization to create new ones. This is especially true for American corporations with foreign operations and relationships, although a code of ethics may need to be modified when applied abroad. Codes of ethics are an effective means for disseminating standards to all employees in an easily understood form. Finally, an effective code of ethics that is enforced in an organization provides employees with a tool for resisting pressure to perform unethical or illegal actions. A code of ethics may enable employees to do what they believe to be right.

Even well-written codes of ethics have limitations, and badly written ones may have some unintended consequences. An emphasis on rules may create a rigid literalness that discourages judicious discretion. An especially dangerous situation is created when employees conclude that whatever is not prohibited is permitted. Some codes focus primarily on employee misconduct that can harm the company, which may lead to cynicism about the purpose of ethics. Some companies do not adopt a code of ethics because they believe that their way of doing business is best achieved by maintaining a strong culture and leading by example. Other companies believe that a code is inappropriate to their situation because extensive government regulation and internal auditing are sufficient to deter both unethical and illegal behavior.

Studies of which companies adopt codes of ethics reflect these advantages and disadvantages. Codes are more prevalent in large companies, in companies with more complex structures, especially those that have grown rapidly or recently merged, and in companies that have high visibility and depend on their reputation.[72] Codes of ethics are less common among financial firms—investment banks, for example—in part because of the extensive government regulation, but also because of the strong incentive to monitor employee behavior closely.

Writing a Code. There is no blueprint for writing a code of ethics. Both the procedure and content must arise from specific features of the company in question. However, some values, such as respect of the individual, fair treatment, honesty, integrity, responsibility, trust, teamwork, and quality, are included in typical codes, as are such topics as conflict of interest, use of company resources, gifts and entertainment, confidentiality of information, and workplace behavior. A few valuable guidelines for developing a code of ethics are offered by W. Michael Hoffman:

- Be clear about the objectives the code is intended to accomplish.
- Try to get support and ideas for the code from all levels of the organization.
- Be aware of the latest developments in the laws and regulations affecting your industry.

- Write as simply and clearly as possible. Be sure the code is legally defensible, but avoid legal jargon.
- Try to give reasons for the various provisions of the code.
- Devise a concrete program for communicating the code and for educating employees about the code and all programs designed to support it.
- Devise a concrete and responsible program for enforcing the code.
- Select competent persons to administer the code and give them the time and resources to get the job done.
- Make sure to provide for changing the code to meet new situations and challenges.[73]

There is one common trait of all *successful* codes of ethics, namely, that they have the clear support of top-level management. A code is unlikely to be successful, though, if it is imposed from the top down. Ideally, everyone in a company should have "ownership" of the code.

Case 14.3 Sears Auto Centers

On June 11, 1992, the CEO of Sears, Roebuck and Company, Edward A. Brennan, learned that the California Department of Consumer Affairs (DCA) was seeking to shut down the 72 Sears Auto Centers in that state.[74] A year-long undercover investigation by the DCA had found numerous instances in which Sears employees had performed unnecessary repairs and services. Officials in New Jersey quickly announced similar charges against six local Sears Auto Centers, and several other states, including Florida, Illinois, and New York, opened their own probes into possible consumer fraud. In the wake of this adverse publicity, revenues from the auto centers fell 15 percent, and the public's trust in Sears was badly shaken.

Sears Auto Centers, which were generally connected with a Sears department store, concentrated on basic "undercar" services involving tires, brakes, mufflers, shock absorbers, and steering mechanisms. Investigators from the DCA's Bureau of Automotive Repair purchased old vehicles in need of minor repairs and disassembled the brakes and suspension systems. After examining and photographing each part, the investigators towed the automobiles to a shop where they requested a brake inspection. In 34 of 38 instances, Sears employees recommended unnecessary repairs and services, and some auto centers charged for parts that were not installed or work that was not performed. The average overcharge was $235, but in two cases the amount overcharged exceeded $500.

Brennan had been notified in December 1991 of early results from the investigation, and Sears executives negotiated for six months with California officials. The company objected to the state's position that no part should be replaced unless it had failed and claimed that many repairs were legitimate preventive maintenance. For example, there is disagreement in the industry on whether brake calipers should be reconditioned whenever the pads are replaced. In addition, some of the automobiles used in the investigation showed sign of damage from worn parts that had already been replaced, thus leading mechanics to believe that repairs were needed. The DCA moved to revoke the licenses of all Sears Auto Centers in the state after the negotiations broke down over details of the financial settlement.

California officials charged that the problems at the Sears Auto Centers were not confined to a few isolated events but constituted systemic consumer fraud. According to a deputy attorney general, "There was a deliberate decision by Sears management to set up a structure that made it totally inevitable that the consumer would be oversold." Until 1991, service advisers, who make recommendations to customers, were paid a flat salary, but subsequently their compensation included a commission incentive. The service advisers were also required to meet quotas for a certain number of parts and services in a fixed period of time. The new incentive system also affected the mechanics, who perform the work on the customers' automobiles. Instead of an hourly wage, they were now compensated by a lower base hourly figure plus a fixed dollar amount based on the time required to install a part or perform a service. Under this system, a mechanic would receive the former hourly wage only by doing an hour's worth of work, but a mechanic could also earn more by working faster.

Commissions and quotas are commonly used in competitive sales environments to motivate and monitor employees. However, critics of Sears charge that there were not enough safeguards to protect the public. One former auto center manager in Sacramento complained that quotas were not based on realistic activity and were constantly escalating. He said that "sales goals had turned into conditions of employment" and that managers were "so busy with charts and graphs" that they could not properly supervise employees. A mechanic in San Bruno, California, alleged that he was fired for not doing 16 oil changes a day and that his manager urged him to save his job by filling the oil in each car only halfway. This illustrated, he said, the "pressure, pressure, pressure to get the dollar."

The changes in the compensation system at Sears Auto Centers were part of a company wide effort to boost lagging performance. In 1990, net income for all divisions, including Allstate (insurance), Coldwell Banker (real estate), and Dean Witter (brokerage), dropped 40 percent. Net income for the merchandising group, which included the department stores and the auto centers, fell 60 percent. Brennan, CEO since 1985, was under strong pressure to cuts costs and increase revenues. Some dissident shareholders were urging the board of directors to spin off the more profitable insurance, real estate, and brokerage divisions and focus on the ailing merchandising group. Brennan's response was to cut jobs, renovate stores, and motivate people. The overall thrust, according to a story in *Business Week*, was to "make every employee, from the sales floor to the chairman's suite focus on profits." Some critics of Sears attribute the problems at the auto centers to an unrealistic strategic plan that sought to wring more revenue out of the auto repair business than was possible. Robert Monk, who unsuccessfully sought a seat on the company's board, said, "Absent a coherent growth strategy, these sorts of things can happen."

At a press conference on June 22, 1992, Edward Brennan announced that, effective immediately, Sears would eliminate its incentive compensation system for automotive service advisers and all product-specific sales goals. Although he admitted that the company's compensation program "created an environment where mistakes did occur," Brennan continued: "We deny allegations of fraud and systemic problems in our auto centers. Isolated errors? Yes. But a pattern of misconduct? Absolutely not." He reaffirmed his belief that the California investigation was flawed and that Sears was practicing responsible preventive maintenance. He further announced that the company would retain an independent organization to conduct random "shopping audits" to ensure that no overcharging would occur. Sears also paid $8 million to settle claims in California and gave auto center customers $50 coupons that were expected to cost the company another $3 million. The total cost, including legal bills and lost sales, is estimated to be $60 million.

On September 30, 1992, Sears revealed plans to spin off its three nonretail divisions, Allstate, Coldwell Banker, and Dean Witter, and to reorganize the merchandising group. A new CEO, Arthur C. Martinez, succeeded Brennan and began a turnaround of the company. In describing his vision, Martinez said, "I want to revisit and intensify the theme of our customer being the center of our universe." A cornerstone of Martinez's strategy, according to the *New York Times*, was "clean business ethics."

Case 14.4 Campbell Soup Company

In 1985, the Campbell Soup Company faced a challenge from an Ohio-based group that was fighting for increased wages and improved living and working conditions for migrant farmworkers.[75] The group, known as the Farm Labor Organizing Committee (FLOC), was threatening to disrupt the annual shareholders' meeting with a demonstration in support of its cause. Since 1979, the company had been the target of a nationwide boycott of its products instigated by FLOC. Under the dynamic leadership of Baldemar Velasquez, the group gained support for the boycott from the major Protestant and Catholic church organizations in Ohio and from many influential national groups. In July 1983, about one hundred members and supporters of FLOC marched 560 miles from FLOC headquarters in Toledo, Ohio, to the headquarters of the Campbell Soup Company in Camden, New Jersey, to dramatize the boycott and to press their demand for a labor contract.

At the urging of the National Council of Churches, which had been persuaded by FLOC to intervene in the dispute, representatives from the two sides sat down and negotiated an agreement that set up procedures for conducting elections to determine whether the farmworkers wanted to be represented by FLOC. The agreement was signed in May 1985, and the voting took place in September, during the first month of the tomato harvest. The election process broke down, however, amid allegations by FLOC of unfair labor practices, including charges that the growers brought in local laborers on the day of the election and prevented some migrant farmworkers from voting. The possibility now existed that the National Council of Churches would support the boycott, a move that would generate considerable adverse publicity for Campbell Soup. FLOC's plan to stage a demonstration at the upcoming shareholders' meeting would create additional bad press.

The plight of the migrant farmworkers is truly deplorable. Many live in crowded camps, without electricity, fresh drinking water, or adequate toilets. Poor nutrition, communicable diseases, and constant exposure to pesticides result in a high infant mortality rate and a life expectancy 25 years below the average. FLOC claimed that laborers received an average hourly wage of less than $2.00, although Campbell Soup disputed this figure and insisted they were paid at least the minimum wage of $3.35 an hour. In addition, migrant farmworkers generally lack health insurance and the other benefits that most American workers take for granted.

When the National Labor Relations Act was passed in 1935, giving most workers the right to organize and engage in collective bargaining, farm laborers were deliberately excluded. So the company was under no legal obligation to recognize the existence of FLOC. The migrant farmworkers, moreover, were not Campbell employees but were hired by independent growers, who held contracts with the company to devote a specified number of acres to tomatoes that were sold to the company at a fixed rate. Executives of Campbell Soup did not believe that they had a right to negotiate over the heads of the growers or to dictate to the growers how they should treat their employees.

FLOC decided to launch a campaign against Campbell Soup in the belief that the price the company set for tomatoes did not allow enough profit margin for the growers to increase wages and improve working conditions even if they wanted to. FLOC disregarded the claim that Campbell Soup did not employ the migrant farmworkers, because the company provided seedlings to the growers and dictated how they were to be raised and picked. In response to a strike organized by FLOC in 1978, the company ordered the growers to switch to mechanical harvesters. Thus, the control that Campbell Soup exercised over the growers was greater than that normally exercised by a company over suppliers. The high visibility of the company and its carefully cultivated reputation also made it vulnerable to attack and contributed to FLOC's decision to make Campbell Soup the target of its campaign.

The charge of allowing child labor was one that deeply stung company officials. The basis of the accusation was a 1983 ruling by a federal district court that a pickle grower, who employed workers on a piece-rate basis, had no legal obligation to prevent children from working alongside their parents in the fields, because the workers, in the view of the court, are independent, self-employed contractors.[76] Although Campbell Soup also markets pickles through its Vlasic subsidiary, the company contended that the decision did not apply to tomato pickers, who are paid hourly rates because of the different method of harvesting tomatoes. The company denied, moreover, that it approved of children helping their parents in the tomato fields. In fact, Campbell Soup created the post of Ombudsman for Migrant Affairs in part to promote the availability of day-care facilities and to ensure that children of migrant farmworkers attend classes during the school year.

Campbell Soup took other steps to improve the living conditions of the workers who picked tomatoes. After the passage of an Ohio law upgrading the minimum standards for migrant housing, the duties of the ombudsman were expanded to include inspection of facilities on farms with company contracts. The company also offered to finance half the cost of new housing and to provide low-interest loans for the balance. In addition, a pilot health-care project was started.

R. Gordon McGovern, president and CEO of Campbell Soup Company, believed that the company had done all it could reasonably be expected to do. At his urging, Campbell executives refused to budge on FLOC's main demand for union recognition and a labor contract. As the day of the annual meeting approached, however, Mr. McGovern realized that he would soon have to face not only the company's shareholders inside the meeting hall but also the protesters from FLOC on the outside.

NOTES

1. Ellen Joan Pollock, "CEO Takes on a Nun in a Crusade against 'Political Correctness'," *Wall Street Journal*, 15 July 1991, A1.
2. Letter dated May 23, 1996, distributed to all Cypress Semiconductor shareholders.
3. For a comprehensive account of the historical development of the concept of corporate social responsibility, see Morrell Heald, *The Social Responsibilities of Business: Company and Community, 1900–1960* (Cleveland: Case Western Reserve University Press, 1970). Brief accounts are given in Clarence C. Walton, *Corporate Social Responsibilities* (Belmont, CA: Wadsworth, 1967), 21–53; and James W. McKie, "Changing Views," in *Social Responsibility and the Business Predicament*, ed. James McKie (Washington, DC: The Brookings Institution, 1974), 17–40.
4. Milton Friedman, *Capitalism and Freedom* (Chicago: University of Chicago Press, 1962), 133.
5. Ibid., 133. The quotation by Adam Smith is from *The Wealth of Nations*, Book IV, chap. II. This famous paragraph concludes: "It is an affectation, indeed, not very common among merchants, and very few words need be employed in dissuading them from it."
6. Joseph W. McGuire, *Business and Society* (New York: McGraw-Hill, 1963), 144. For the point that the assumption of responsibility must be voluntary, see Henry Manne and Henry C. Wallich, *The Modern Corporation and Social Responsibility* (Washington, DC: American Enterprise Institute for Public Policy Research, 1972), 5.
7. Archie B. Carroll, "A Three-Dimensional Conceptual Model of Corporate Performance," *Academy of Management Review*, 4 (1979), 497–505.
8. Ibid., 500.
9. S. Prakash Sethi, "Dimensions of Corporate Social Performance: An Analytical Framework for Measurement and Analysis," *California Management Review*, 17 (Spring 1975), 62. Emphasis in original omitted.
10. *Social Responsibilities of Business Corporations* (New York: Committee for Economic Development, 1971), 15.
11. The concept of corporate social responsiveness is developed in Robert W. Ackerman and Raymond A. Bauer, *Corporate Social Responsiveness: The Modern Dilemma* (Reston, VA: Reston, 1976).
12. William C. Frederick, "From CSR1 to CSR2: The Maturing of Business-and-Society Thought," *Business & Society Review*, 33 (1994), 150-64.
13. Donna J. Wood, "Corporate Social Performance Revisited," *Academy of Management Review*, 16 (1991), 693.
14. McKie, "Changing Views," 18–19.

15. Edward S. Mason, ed., *The Corporation in Modern Society* (New York: Atheneum, 1974), 5.

16. Theodore Levitt, "The Dangers of Social Responsibility," *Harvard Business Review*, 36 (September–October 1958), 49.

17. John G. Simon, Charles W. Powers, and Jon P. Gunnemann, "The Responsibilities of Corporations and Their Owners," in *The Ethical Investor: Universities and Corporate Responsibility* (New Haven, CT: Yale University Press, 1972), 16–17.

18. Keith Davis, "Five Propositions for Social Responsibility," *Business Horizons*, 18 (June 1975), 20. Italics in the original.

19. Keith Davis and Robert L. Blomstrom, *Business and Society: Environment and Responsibility*, 3d ed. (New York: McGraw-Hill, 1975), 50.

20. This objection is formulated in Kenneth E. Goodpaster and John B. Matthews, Jr., "Can a Corporation Have a Conscience?" *Harvard Business Review*, 60 (January–February 1982), 139–40.

21. Ibid., 140.

22. Simon, Powers, and Gunnemann, "Responsibilities of Corporations and Their Owners."

23. Milton Friedman, "The Social Responsibility of Business Is to Increase Its Profits," *New York Times Magazine*, 13 September 1970, 33.

24. Ibid., 122.

25. See, for example, Richard Musgrave, *The Theory of Public Finance* (New York: McGraw-Hill, 1959), in which the three functions of securing efficiency (which includes considerations of externalities), equity, and stability properly belong to government.

26. Holders of the classical view generally favor market solutions over government action in the belief that many externalities result from a lack, rather than an excess, of free market forces and that regulation is often ineffective. Still, they usually admit the principle that government regulation is appropriate in some instances to deal with externalities.

27. For an explanation and discussion of this concept, see Arthur M. Okun, *Equality and Efficiency: The Big Tradeoff* (Washington, DC: The Brookings Institution, 1975).

28. Marvin A. Chirelstein, "Corporate Law Reform," in *Social Responsibility and the Business Predicament*, 55.

29. The distinction between the property rights and the social institution conceptions of the corporation is due to William T. Allen, "Our Schizophrenic Conception of the Business Corporation," *Cardozo Law Review*, 14 (1992), 261–81. See also, William T. Allen, "Contracts and Communities in Corporate Law," *Washington and Lee Law Review*, 50 (1993), 1395–1407.

30. Because the right to incorporate is alleged to "inhere" in the right to own property and to contract with others, this view is also known as the *inherence theory*.

31. The view that incorporation is a privilege "conceded" by the state in order to achieve some social good is also known as the *concession theory*.

32. *Munn* v. *Illinois*, 94 U.S. 113, 24 L. Ed. 77 (1876).

33. *Dodge* v. *Ford Motor Co.*, 170 N.W. 668, 685 (1919).

34. Adolf A. Berle, Jr., and Gardiner C. Means, *The Modern Corporation and Private Property* (New York: Macmillan, 1932).

35. Ibid., 3.

36. Ibid., 355.

37. E. Merrick Dodd, "For Whom Are Corporate Managers Trustees?" *Harvard Law Review*, 45 (1932), 1148.

38. Ibid., 1161.

39. Ibid., 1162.

40. Adolf A. Berle, Jr., "For Whom Corporate Managers Are Trustees: A Note," *Harvard Law Review*, 45 (1932), 1367.

41. Ibid., 1372.
42. Ibid., 1370.
43. Ibid., 1372.
44. Adolf A. Berle, Jr., *The 20th Century Capitalist Revolution* (New York: Harcourt, Brace & World, 1954), 169.
45. Ronald M. Coase, "The Nature of the Firm," *Economica*, N.S., 4 (1937), 386–405. The contractual theory has been developed by economists using an agency or transaction cost perspective. See Armen A. Alchian and Harold Demsetz, "Production, Information Costs, and Economic Organization," *American Economic Review*, 62 (1972), 777–95; Benjamin Klein, Robert A. Crawford, and Armen A. Alchian, "Vertical Integration, Appropriable Rents, and the Competitive Contracting Process," *Journal of Law and Economics*, 21 (1978), 297–326; Michael C. Jensen and William H. Meckling, "Theory of the Firm: Managerial Behavior, Agency Costs, and Ownership Structure," *Journal of Financial Economics*, 3 (1983), 305–60; Eugene F. Fama and Michael C. Jensen, "Separation of Ownership and Control," *Journal of Law and Economics*, 26 (1983), 301–25; Steven N. S. Cheung, "The Contractual Theory of the Firm," *Journal of Law and Economics*, 26 (1983), 1–22; and Oliver E. Williamson, *The Economic Institutions of Capitalism* (New York: Free Press, 1985). An authoritative development of the theory of the firm in corporate law is Frank H. Easterbrook and Daniel R. Fischel, *The Economic Structure of Corporate Law* (Cambridge, MA: Harvard University Press, 1991). See also William A. Klein, "The Modern Business Organization: Bargaining under Constraints," *Yale Law Journal*, 91 (1982), 1521–64; Oliver Hart, "An Economist's Perspective on the Theory of the Firm," *Columbia Law Review*, 89 (1989), 1757–73; and Henry N. Butler, "The Contractual Theory of the Firm," *George Mason Law Review*, 11 (1989), 99–123.
46. Easterbrook and Fischel, *The Economic Structure of Corporate Law*, 38.
47. Ibid., 38.
48. Ibid., 39.
49. This reasoning follows from the Coase Theorem, which is presented in a highly influential paper by Ronald Coase, "The Problem of Social Cost," *Journal of Law and Economics*, 3 (1960), 1–44.
50. Worker Adjustment and Retraining Notification Act of 1988 (WARN).
51. See Eric W. Orts, "Beyond Shareholders: Interpreting Corporate Constituency Statutes," *George Washington Law Review*, 61 (1992), 14–135.
52. Margaret M. Blair, *Ownership and Control: Rethinking Corporate Governance for the Twenty-first Century* (Washington, DC: The Brookings Institution, 1995).
53. Ibid., 257.
54. William M. Evan and R. Edward Freeman, "A Stakeholder Theory of the Modern Corporation: Kantian Capitalism," in *Ethical Theory and Business*, 4th ed., ed. Tom L. Beauchamp and Norman E. Bowie (Upper Saddle River, NJ: Prentice Hall, 1993), 79. See also R. Edward Freeman and D. Reed, "Stockholders and Stakeholders: A New Perspective on Corporate Governance," in *Corporate Governance: A Definitive Exploration of the Issues*, C. Huizinga, ed., (Los Angeles: UCLA Extension Press, 1983).
55. R. Edward Freeman, *Strategic Management: A Stakeholder Approach* (Boston: Pitman, 1984), 46. This book provides a useful discussion of the history of the stakeholder concept and the literature on it.
56. Thomas Donaldson and Lee E. Preston, "The Stakeholder Theory of the Corporation: Concepts, Evidence, and Implications," *Academy of Management Review*, 20 (1995), 65–91.
57. Ibid., 67.
58. Igor Ansoff, *Corporate Strategy* (New York: McGraw-Hill, 1965), 38.
59. Material for this case is taken from Rushworth M. Kidder, *How Good People Make Tough Choices* (New York: Fireside, 1995), 35–38; Glenn Adams, "Bath Iron Works CEO Admits Ethics

Breach, Steps Down," The Associated Press, 16 September 1991; Jerry Harkavy, "Haggett Severs Ties with Shipyard in Aftermath of Photocopy Scandal," The Associated Press, 25 September 1991; Suzanne Alexander, "Bath Iron Works Says Haggett Quit as Chief," *Wall Street Journal*, 17 September 1991, B9; and Joseph Pereira and Andy Pasztor, "Bath Chairman, 2 Vice Presidents Quit under Navy Pressure over Secret Data," *Wall Street Journal*, 26 September 1991, A4.

60. Lynn Sharp Paine, "Managing for Organizational Integrity," *Harvard Business Review*, 72 (March–April 1994), 106.
61. Steven N. Brenner, "Ethics Programs and Their Dimensions," *Journal of Business Ethics*, 11 (1992), 391.
62. Paine, "Managing for Organizational Integrity."
63. *In re Caremark International Inc.* Derivative Litigation. Civil Action No. 13670 (Del. Ch. 1996).
64. Dominic Bencivenga, "Words of Warning: Ruling Makes Directors Accountable for Compliance," *New York Law Journal*, 13 February 1997, 5.
65. For an explanation, see Jeffrey M. Kaplan, "Why Daiwa Bank Will Pay $340 Million under the Sentencing Guidelines," *Ethikos*, 9 (May–June 1996).
66. United States Sentencing Commission, *Federal Sentencing Guidelines Manual*, §8A1.2, Commentary, Application Note 3(k).
67. Ibid., Application Note 3(k) (1-7).
68. O. C. Farrell, Debbie Thorne LeClair, and Linda Ferrell, "The Federal Sentencing Guidelines for Organizations: A Framework for Ethical Compliance," *Journal of Business Ethics*, 17 (1998), 353-63.
69. *Corporate Ethics*, The Conference Board, Research Report No. 900 (1987), 14.
70. National Commission on Fraudulent Financial Reporting, *Report of National Commission on Fraudulent Financial Reporting*, 1987, p. 35.
71. *Corporate Ethics*, 13.
72. Messod D. Benish and Robert Chatov, "Corporate Codes of Conduct: Economic Determinants and Legal Implications for Independent Auditors," *Journal of Accounting and Public Policy*, 12 (1993), 3-35.
73. W. Michael Hoffman, "A Blueprint for Corporate Ethical Development," in *Business Ethics: Readings and Cases in Corporate Morality*, 3d ed., ed., W. Michael Hoffman and Robert E. Frederick (New York: McGraw-Hill, 1995), 580–81.
74. Material for this case is taken from "Sears Auto Centers (A), Harvard Business School, 1993; Kevin Kelly, "How Did Sears Blow This Gasket?" *Business Week*, 29 June 1992, 38; Julia Flynn, "Did Sears Take Other Customers for a Ride?" *Business Week*, 3 August 1992, 24-25; Judy Quinn, "Repair Job," *Incentive*, October 1992, 40-46; Jennifer Steinhauer, "Time to Call a Sears Repairman," *New York Times*, 15 January 1998, sec. 3, pp. 1, 3; News from Sears, Roebuck and Co. [press release], 22 June 1992.
75. Information on this case is taken from "Campbell Soup Company," in *Cases in Ethics and the Conduct of Business*, ed., John R. Boatright (Upper Saddle River, NJ: Prentice Hall, 1995), 314–30.
76. *Brandel* v. *United States*, U.S. District Court, Western District of Michigan, Southern Division, 83–1228 (1984).

Chapter 13

International Business Ethics

Case 15.1 Nike in Southeast Asia

Nike is a leader in the sports shoe industry, with sales of $9.5 billion in 1998 and a 40 percent share of the American sneaker market. This Oregon-based company has also become a lightening rod for worldwide protests over alleged "sweatshop" conditions in factories across Southeast Asia. In a May 1998 speech, Phil Knight, the founder and CEO, admitted that "the Nike product has become synonymous with slave wages, forced overtime, and arbitrary abuse."[1] How did a prominent company, whose "swoosh" logo is a symbol for the "Just Do It" spirit, come to be associated with deplorable labor practices?

Nike's phenomenal success is due to a visionary strategy which was developed by Phil Knight during his student days at the Stanford Business School. The strategy involves outsourcing all manufacturing to contractors in low-wage countries and pouring the company's resources into high-profile marketing. One Nike vice president observed, "We don't know the first thing about manufacturing. We are marketers and designers."[2] Central to Nike's marketing effort is placing the Nike "swoosh" on the uniforms of collegiate and professional athletes and enlisting such superstars as Michael Jordan and Tiger Woods.

When Nike was founded in 1964, the company contracted with manufacturers in Japan, but as wages in that country rose, Nike transferred production to contractors in Korea and Taiwan. By 1982, more than 80 percent of Nike shoes were made in these two countries, but rising wages there led Nike to urge its contractors to move their plants to Southeast Asia. By 1990, most Nike production was based in Indonesia, Vietnam, and China.

In the early 1990s, young Indonesian women working in Korean-owned plants under contract with Nike started at 15 cents an hour. With mandatory overtime, which was often imposed, more experienced workers might make $2 for a grueling 11-hour day. The Indonesian minimum wage was raised in 1991 from $1.06 for a 7-hour day to $1.24, only slightly above the $1.22 that the government calculated as necessary for "minimum physical needs." The women lived in fear of their brutal Korean managers, who berated them for failing to meet quotas and withheld pay to enforce discipline. Indonesian labor laws, lax to begin with, were flouted with impunity by contractors, since the government was eager to attract foreign investment. Workers often toiled in crowded, poorly ventilated factories, surrounded by machinery and toxic chemicals. There was little effective union activity in Indonesia, and labor strikes were firmly suppressed by the army.

Nike's initial response to growing criticism was to deny any responsibility for the practices of its contractors. These are independent companies from which Nike merely buys shoes. The workers are not Nike employees, and their wages are above the legal minimum and the prevailing market rate. When asked about labor strife in some factories supplying Nike, John Woodman, the company's general manager for Indonesia, said that he did not know the causes and added, "I don't know that I need to know."[3] Mr. Woodman defended Nike by arguing, "Yes, they are low wages. But we've come in here and given jobs to thousands of people who wouldn't be working otherwise."[4] He might have added that the company had also given additional employment to Michael Jordan, whose reported $2 million dollar fee in 1992 was larger than the payroll that year for all Nike production in Indonesia.[5]

INTRODUCTION

Increasingly, business is being conducted across national boundaries. Large Multinational Corporations (MNCs) that have long operated in other countries are being joined by smaller domestic firms going abroad for the first time. Intense competition is forcing companies worldwide to enter the global marketplace, whether they are ready or not.

This development presents a host of ethical problems that managers are often unprepared to address. Some of these problems arise from the diversity of business standards around the world and especially from the lower standards that generally prevail in Less Developed Countries (LDCs). Companies such as Nike (Case 15.1) are able to pay wages and impose working conditions that are shockingly low by U.S. standards, and yet they usually operate well above the standards of local firms. Environmental standards in LDCs are also invariably lower than those of more developed countries. And in countries with pervasive corruption it may be difficult to conduct business without paying bribes.

Additional problems result from the power of multinational corporations to affect the development of LDCs. MNCs often exploit the cheap labor and the natural resources of LDCs without making investments that would advance economic development. These problems are exacerbated when companies sucessfully avoid paying their fair share of taxes. Even though less developed countries invariably benefit to some extent from the activities of MNCs, the distribution of the gains is usually unequal. Critics ask whether it is fair for corporations from developed countries to return so little to the less developed parts of the world from which they derive so much.

Operations in foreign countries also raise questions about the proper role of corporations in political affairs. Most multinationals consider themselves to be guests in host countries and refrain from influencing local governments. However, Shell Oil Company (Case 15.3) was widely criticized for failing to intervene in a case of human rights abuse by the Nigerian government. MNCs have an opportunity to play a constructive role in countries making the transition from a socialist, planned economy to a free market. The high level of corruption in some of these countries, though, presents special challenges.

This chapter begins with the problem of determining the appropriate standards for operations in less developed countries. Applying home country standards in all parts of the world is usually not morally required, but adopting host country standards for wages, working conditions, and other matters may be morally impermissible. What principles can guide us in finding a happy medium? These principles are then applied to the issue of wages and working conditions that are raised in the Nike case. Although bribery is universally recognized as wrong, it, too, is a practice that is viewed differently around the world. Accordingly, a section is devoted to understanding this critical problem in international business. Finally, this chapter examines the difference in the ethical outlook of business people in different parts of the world, especially in Asia, and concludes with developing of codes of ethics that attempt to guide responsible business conduct worldwide.

WHAT TO DO IN ROME

The main charge against multinational corporations is that they adopt a double standard, doing in less developed, Third World countries what would be regarded as wrong if done in the developed First World. However, many criticized practices are legal in the countries in question and are not considered to be unethical by local standards. Should MNCs be bound by the prevailing morality of the home country and, in the case of American corporations, act everywhere as they do in the United States? Should they follow the practices of the host country and adopt the adage "When in Rome, do as the Romans do"? Or are there special ethical standards that apply when business is conducted across national boundaries? If so, what are the appropriate standards for international business?

Unfortunately, there are no easy answers to these questions. In some cases, the standards contained in American law and morality ought to be observed beyond our borders; in other cases, there is no moral obligation to do so. Similarly, it is morally permissible for managers of MNCs to follow local practice and "do as the Romans do" in some situations but not others. Even if there are special ethical standards for international business, these cannot be applied without taking into account differences in cultures and value systems, the levels of economic development, and the social, political, and legal structures of the foreign countries in which MNCs operate.

Absolutism versus Relativism

In answer to the question "When in Rome, do what?" there are two extremes. The absolutist position is that business ought to be conducted in the same way the world over with no double standards. In particular, U.S. corporations ought to observe a single code of conduct in their dealings everywhere. This view might be expressed as "When in Rome or anywhere else, do as you would at home."[6] The opposite extreme is relativism, which may be expressed in the familiar adage, "When in Rome do as the Romans do." That is, the only guide for business conduct abroad is what is legally and morally accepted in any given country where a company operates.

Neither of these positions can be adopted without exception. The generally high level of conduct that follows from "When in Rome, do as you would at home" is not morally required of MNCs in all instances, and they should not be faulted for every departure from home country standards in doing business abroad. However, "When in Rome, do as the Romans do" is not wholly justified either. The mere fact that a country permits bribery, unsafe working conditions, exploitive wages, and violations of human rights does not mean that these practices are morally acceptable, even in that country. The debate over absolutism and relativism revolve around four important points.

Morally Relevant Differences. First, some conditions in other countries, especially those in less developed parts of the world, are different in morally relevant ways. As a result, different standards may be morally permitted, indeed required. If Rome is a significantly different place, then standards that are appropriate at home do not necessarily apply there.

For example, pharmaceutical companies have been criticized for adopting a double standard in promoting drugs in less developed countries with more indications for their use and fewer warnings about side effects. Although such practices may be designed solely to promote sales, some drugs may be medically appropriate in an LDC for a wider range of conditions. With regard to one powerful but dangerous antibiotic, which is prescribed in the United States only for very serious infections, doctors in Bolivia claim that this limited use is a luxury that Americans can afford because of generally better health. "Here," they say, "the people's general health is so poor that one must make an all out attack on illness."[7] Thus, an antibiotic that should be marketed in the United States with one set of indications might be justifiably sold abroad with a more extensive list.

More generally, the relative level of economic development must be taken into account in determining the appropriate standards for different countries. For example, health and safety standards in the developed world are very stringent, reflecting greater affluence and a greater willingness to pay for more safety. The standards of these countries are not always appropriate in poorer, less developed countries with fewer resources and more pressing needs. The United States made different trade-offs between safety and other values at earlier stages of the country's economic development. At the present time, less developed countries might prefer lower safety standards in return for more jobs. On the other hand, exposing people in LDCs to unreasonable dangers may be a violation of basic human rights.

The Variety of Ethical Outlooks. Second, the absolutist position assumes that one country's standards are correct and that they should be imposed on people elsewhere, perhaps in conflict with their own moral values and principles. Acting on these assumptions ignores the wide variety of ethical outlooks in the world. Although some bedrock conceptions of right and wrong exist among people everywhere, many variations occur due to cultural, historical, political, and economic factors.

Cultural differences are important because they may affect the meaning of acts performed. For example, lavish gifts that would be considered bribes or kickbacks in the United States are an accepted and expected part of business in Japan and some other Asian countries. This difference in perception is due, in part, to the role that gift giving plays in building relationships, which are more critical in Asian business. Thus, giving gifts in Japan and China is usually viewed not as an attempt to improperly influence a person's judgment but rather as a means to cement a legitimate relationship.[8] Similarly, whistle-blowing, which is generally viewed favorably in the United States as a moral protest, is regarded unfavorably in Japan as an act of disloyalty. In both cases, culture plays a powerful role in the interpretation of what a person has done in giving a gift or blowing the whistle.

The impact of historical, political, and economic differences can be seen in Russian views of business ethics. The collapse of communism and the chaotic development of free markets in the former Soviet Union have created great uncertainty about ethical business behavior.[9] Although Russians and Americans agree on many matters, such as the importance of keeping one's word, paying debts, competing fairly, and avoiding extortion, they still differ in their ethical assessment of certain other matters. For example, less stigma is attached in Russia to making payments for favors (*blat*), falsifying information, and coordinating prices because of the prevalence of these practices in the previous planned economy. The lack of a workable legal system forces Russian managers to ignore senseless and contradictory regulations. Unfortunately, a certain amount of lawlessness is necessary for operating in the current business environment. On the other hand, Russia's socialist tradition leads them to criticize America's tolerance for exorbitant pay differentials and massive layoffs. As in Japan, whistle-blowing is viewed with suspicion, but for a different reason: It reminds Russians of the informer ethos that existed during the communist era.

The Right of People to Decide. Third, the absolutist position denies the right of the people who are affected to decide on important matters of business conduct. The primary responsibility for setting standards should rest on the government and the people of the country in which business is being conducted. The argument that the people affected have a right to decide is not a form of ethical relativism. Just because people approve of a certain practice does not make it right. The argument is rather an expression of respect for the right of people to govern their own affairs, rightly or wrongly. Imposing the standards of a developed, First World country in the Third World is criticized by some as a form of "ethical imperialism."

Avoiding "ethical imperialism" and allowing the people affected to decide must be approached cautiously. A respect for the right of people to set their own standards does not automatically justify corporations in inflicting grave harm on innocent people, for example, or violating basic human rights. Furthermore, it may be difficult to determine what people have decided. Some countries lack the capacity to regulate effectively the activities of multinational corporations within their own borders. The governments of developing countries are, in many instances, no less committed than those in the United States and Western Europe to protecting their people against harm, but they do not always have the resources—the money, skilled personnel, and institutions—to accomplish the task.

Some countries with the capacity to regulate multinationals lack the necessary will. MNCs, through the exercise of economic power, including bribery, are able to influence regulatory measures. The governments of less developed countries are also careful not to offend the developed countries on which they depend for aid. Furthermore, the absence of laws against unethical business practices is sometimes part of a pattern of oppression that exists within the country itself, so that MNCs are taking advantage of the immorality of others when they follow the law of countries with corrupt governments.

Consequently, we need to ask whether a standard in a host country, if it is lower than that at home, truly represents the considered judgment of the people in question. Does it reflect the decision that they would make if they had the capacity to protect their own interests effectively? A genuine respect for the right of people to determine which standards to apply in their own country requires a careful and sympathetic consideration of what people would do under certain hypothetical conditions rather than what is actually expressed in the law, conventional morality, and commonly accepted practices.

Required Conditions for Doing Business. Fourth, some practices may be justified where local conditions require that corporations engage in them as a condition of doing business. This point may be expressed by saying, "We don't agree with the Romans, but find it necessary to do things their way." American firms with contracts for projects in the Middle East, for example, have complied in many instances with requests not to station women and Jewish employees in those countries. Although discrimination of this kind is morally repugnant, it is (arguably) morally permissible when the alternative is to risk losing business in the Arab world. A more complicated case is posed by the Arab boycott of Israel, which was begun by the countries of the Arab League in 1945. In order to avoid blacklisting that would bar them from doing business with participating Arab countries, many prominent U.S. companies cooperated by avoiding investment in Israel. Other firms, however, refused to cooperate with the boycott for ethical reasons. (Congress addressed this issue in 1977 by amending the Export Administration Act to prohibit American corporations from cooperating with the Arab boycott against Israel.)

As with the other arguments, "There is no other way of doing business" cannot be accepted without some qualifications. The alternative is seldom to cease doing business; rather, the claim that a practice is "necessary" often means merely that it is the most profitable way of doing business. For example, the Arab embargo against Israel greatly complicated the problem of doing business in the Middle East, but some companies were able to avoid cooperating with the boycott and still have business relations in Arab countries. Similarly, during the period of apartheid in South Africa, some American companies defied the government and integrated their work forces. There are some situations, however, in which a company is morally obligated to withdraw if there is no other way to do business. Some companies have refused to do business in certain countries because they believe that involvement in an immoral system cannot be justified. For example, Robert Haas, the CEO of Levi Strauss, made the decision in 1993 to discontinue relations with suppliers in China and to defer any direct investment because of "pervasive violations of basic human rights." (Five years later, in 1998, Levi Strauss decided to resume sourcing in China and to sell clothing there.)

Guidelines for Multinationals

If neither home country nor host country standards provide complete guidance, what principles or rules should multinational corporations follow? Three kinds of guidelines have been offered, based on considerations of human rights, welfare, and fairness or justice. All of these are relevant moral concepts; the challenge is determining exactly how they apply to international business.

Human Rights. Thomas Donaldson has proposed that corporations have an obligation to respect certain rights, namely those that ought to be recognized as fundamental international rights.[10] MNCs are not obligated to extend all the rights of U.S. citizens to people everywhere in the world, but there are certain basic rights that no person or institution, including a corporation, is morally permitted to violate. Fundamental international rights are roughly the same as natural or human rights, discussed in Chapter 3, and some of these are given explicit recognition in such documents as the United Nations Universal Declaration of Human Rights, the International Covenant on Social, Economic and Cultural Rights, and the International Covenant on Civil and Political Rights.

The main problem with a principle to respect fundamental international rights (or fundamental rights, for short) is specifying the rights in question. Even undeniable human rights that create an obligation for some person or institution, such as the government of a country, are not always relevant to a multinational corporation. Moreover, observing a right ranges from merely not depriving people from some protection to ensuring the fulfillment of a right. For example, everyone has a right to subsistence, but a corporation may be under no obligation to feed the hungry in a country where it operates, especially if doing so has no relation to its business activity. It has an obligation, however, not to contribute directly to starvation by, say, destroying farm land. In general, Donaldson claims, a corporation is morally bound only by those minimal duties such that "the persistent failure to observe [them] would deprive the corporation of its moral right to exist" and not by maximal duties whose fulfillment would be "praiseworthy but not absolutely mandatory."[11]

Donaldson suggests the following fundamental rights as a moral minimum:

1. The right to freedom of physical movement
2. The right to ownership of property
3. The right to freedom from torture
4. The right to a fair trial
5. The right to nondiscriminatory treatment
6. The right to physical security
7. The right to freedom of speech and association
8. The right to minimal education
9. The right to political participation
10. The right to subsistence[12]

Sample applications of these rights, according to Donaldson, include failing to provide safety equipment to protect employees from serious hazards (the right to physical security); using coercive tactics to prevent workers from organizing (the right to freedom of speech and association); employing child labor (the right to minimal education); and bribing government officials to violate their duty or seeking to overthrow democratically elected governments (the right to political participation).

Donaldson recognizes that it may be impossible to observe all these rights, especially in less developed countries where human rights violations are routine. However, insofar as the acceptance of a practice in a host country is due to its low level of economic development, we can ask ourselves: Would we, in our home country, regard the practice as morally permissible under conditions of similar economic development? He calls this the *rational empathy test*, which he describes as putting ourselves in the shoes of a foreigner:

> To be more specific, it makes sense to consider ourselves and our own culture at a level of economic development relevantly similar to that of the other country. And, if, having done this, we find that under such *hypothetically altered social circumstances* we ourselves would accept the lower risk standards, then it is permissible to adopt the standards that appear inferior.[13]

Although Donaldson's list of fundamental rights sets some minimal conditions for ethical behavior, it is not a complete guide for managers. First, the bearing of these rights on controversial questions is not wholly clear. For example, no one disputes that causing starvation by destroying farm land is a human rights violation.

But what does the right to subsistence tell us about cases in which multinationals convert land from the production of domestic crops to foods for export? Even though the MNC is acting within its rights within a free market as a property owner, and even though the country may benefit from a more productive use of the land, the ability of local people to feed themselves may be severely curtailed. Has the multinational violated the right of these people to subsistence? To this kind of question, Donaldson's rights-based approach offers little guidance.

Second, many of the most difficult moral questions in international business do not involve rights at all. Although rights violations by corporations receive great public attention, they are relatively infrequent. The critical issues at the forefront of global business today focus more on abuses of power by multinationals and on the failure of MNCs to aid developing countries. For example, the OECD Guidelines for Multinational Enterprises, adopted by the Organization for Economic Cooperation and Development (OECD), covers such matters as competing fairly, disclosing information, paying taxes, considering countries' balance of payment and credit policies, utilizing appropriate technologies, and aiding economic development. In general, the goal of the OEDC guidelines is to achieve a smoothly functioning global economic system that spreads the benefits widely, rather than to protect people's rights.

In sum, guidelines based on human rights provide a bedrock moral minimum. However, the application of rights-based guidelines are uncertain in more controversial situations where we are most in need of guidance, and they are inapplicable to many other pressing matters.

Welfare. Richard DeGeorge offers seven basic guidelines for multinational corporations that cover a variety of moral considerations, including rights. However, several of these rules concern avoiding harm and providing benefits. His guidelines are

1. Multinationals should do no intentional direct harm.
2. Multinationals should produce more good than harm for the host country.
3. Multinationals should contribute by their activity to the host country's development.
4. Multinationals should respect the human rights of their employees.
5. To the extent that local culture does not violate ethical norms, multinationals should respect the local culture and work with and not against it.
6. Multinationals should pay their fair share of taxes.
7. Multinationals should cooperate with the local government in developing and enforcing just background institutions.

The first three of these guidelines express in different ways a duty to consider the welfare of people in a host country. The first, do no intentional direct harm, is vacuous if it excludes all actions with a legitimate business purposes. No company intends to do harm; any harm results rather from its regular business activity. However, a company can engage in such activity knowing that harm will result. In some instances, this harm may be wrong, as when a firm produces oil in such a way that the land is polluted. On the other hand, a firm might open a plant that, because of its efficiency, will drive local competitors out of business. This latter result, unlike the former, is not wrong but is merely the working of market forces. In a well-functioning economy, more efficient producers should replace the less efficient. For the same reason, polluting oil production (Is there any other kind?) may be acceptable if the benefits outweigh the costs. What DeGeorge's first guideline presumably excludes is pollution that results from unjustifiably low standards. What standards ought to be adopted, however, is a question not merely about the harm done but about the benefit gained—and also about how these ought to be distributed.

The same problems afflict DeGeorge's second guideline, do more good than harm. Economic theory tells us that all voluntary exchange results in more good than harm for the reason that no one makes a trade that is not beneficial. Thus, as long as a multinational corporation offers employment in a factory and workers in a developing country are willing to accept, then everyone is better off. Controversial cases like that of Nike in Indonesia (Case 15.1) raise two questions. First, how much more good than harm should a multinational bring to a country like Indonesia? And, second, does it matter that multinationals are often able to use their market power to reap most of the benefit, leaving the host country with a narrow balance of good over harm? The answers to these questions depend not whether more good than harm is produced but on whether the outcome is obtained justly.

Multinationals are criticized primarily in cases where they take more than a fair share by exploiting their superior position in an imperfect market. A developed country, such as the United States, attempts to maintain perfect markets by preventing monopolies and other conditions that reduce fair competition. However, the marketplace in which multinationals encounter less developed countries is highly imperfect. Under such circumstances, some outcomes may be criticized for resulting from unfair competition. As Manuel Velasquez observes, DeGeorge's approach "fails to take seriously the importance of justice in evaluating the activities of multinationals."[14]

Justice. Much of the criticism of multinational corporations rests on considerations of justice. Even when MNCs respect human rights and produce more good than harm, their activities may still be criticized for being unfair or unjust. This is true even for the outcomes of voluntary market exchanges when they occur in imperfect markets, as when a multinational exploits a monopoly position.

One kind of unfairness cited by critics is the often one-sided division of the benefits from foreign investment. Certainly, the gap between rich and poor countries is an urgent moral concern, and multinational corporations have much to offer. Thus, the third of DeGeorge's guidelines is that "[m]ultinationals should contribute by their activity to the host country's development." The main questions, however, are who should act and what should be done? National governments and world organizations are the primary actors, and it is questionable what role multinationals should play. What should they do to aid development other than engage in business activity?

The answer to this question depends, in part, on how we answer the second question about what should be done. What is the most effective strategy for aiding developing countries? The main approach being taken today is to increase foreign investment and export production in an increasingly integrated world economy. If this development—generally called *globalization*—is the most effective strategy, then multinational corporations can contribute best by being efficient—but responsible!—businesses. Indeed, if MNCs are expected to expend resources on development, they may then choose not to invest in poorer countries, thus depriving them of any aid. However, opponents of globalization, such as the protesters at meetings of the World Trade Organization (WTO), propose other strategies for development that would place greater responsibilities on multinational corporations.

Another kind of unfairness is violating the rules of the marketplace, which is to say engaging in unfair competition and otherwise taking unfair advantage. One example is the ability of multinationals to avoid paying taxes by means of *transfer pricing*. Transfer prices are the values assigned to raw materials and unfinished products that one subsidiary of a company sells to another. Because transfer prices are set by the company and not the market, they can be raised or lowered so that most of the profits are recorded in countries with low tax rates. This use of transfer pricing is facilitated by the fact that multinationals are usually able to avoid disclosure of the relevant financial information. As a result, host countries often have little knowledge of a company's true financial situation.

Tax avoidance through transfer pricing is a critical problem for both developed and developing countries. Approximately a third of world trade or $1.6 trillion takes place within firms, so the possible loss of tax revenues is enormous. Consequently, the major countries of the world are trying to tighten accounting standards to prevent abuses. The OECD Guidelines for Multinational Enterprises requires firms to disclose financial statements on a regular basis and provide relevant information requested by taxing authorities. Furthermore, the Guidelines states that an enterprise should "[r]efrain from making use of the particular facilities available to them, such as transfer pricing which does not conform to arm's length standard, for modifying in ways contrary to national laws the tax base on which members of the group are assessed." This arm's-length standard is feasible when a market exists for the good in question, and for other goods a market price can be approximated by calculating the costs of production.[15]

If avoiding taxes by means of transfer pricing violates no laws, why should multinationals not take full advantage of this opportunity? The same question can be asked of paying bribes, offering kickbacks, and similar practices. One answer, offered by Norman E. Bowie, is that these actions violate the rules that are required for markets to operate. The very possibility of market exchanges depends on the general observance of certain rules of honesty, trust, and fair dealing. Because businesses benefit from the marketplace that these rules make possible, they are taking an unfair advantage, being a freeloader so to speak, by simultaneously violating these rules. Bowie writes:

> If activities that are permitted in other countries violate the morality of the marketplace—for example, undermine contracts or involve freeloading on the rules of the market—they nonetheless are morally prohibited to multinationals that operate

there. Such multinationals are obligated to follow the moral norms of the market. Contrary behavior is ultimately inconsistent and self-defeating.[16]

An obvious difficulty is determining the essential rules for markets to operate. That problem aside, is avoiding taxes by means of transfer pricing really a violation of market morality? One might argue that prices, which play a critical role in markets, should be set in ways that have a clear economic purpose. Setting prices for no other purpose than reducing taxes is not a genuine economic activity but a sham transaction. Indeed, whether a transaction serves a reasonable business purpose is a test that United States courts use to determine whether a tax shelter is legal.

WAGES AND WORKING CONDITIONS

Public concern about multinational corporations has focused in recent years on the footwear and apparel industries and their relations with foreign contractors. Virtually all major American shoe and clothing companies have adopted the strategy pioneered by Nike (Case 15.1) and outsourced the actual assembly of their products to contractors in Southeast Asia and Central America. This development benefits consumers everywhere by lowering the cost of goods, and jobs are created in countries that desperately need them. Overall, the manufacture of goods in countries with low labor costs is advantageous to developed and developing countries alike.

To many critics, however, the benefits must be weighed against a long list of wrongs that include very low wages, substandard working condition, the use of child labor, and association with repressive regimes. Some of the factories operated by multinationals and their foreign contractors are alleged to be "sweatshops" of the kind that operated in developed countries until the passage of protective legislation in the early twentieth century. The critics also question the ability of foreign contracting to advance economic development. Instead of improving the lives of people, they charge, the contracting system leads to greater misery for the bulk of the population and to a wider gap between the rich and the poor. Although the jobs that are exported overseas are a boon to workers in less developed countries, they reduce job opportunities in the developed world.

At the heart of this controversy is the question, how should the standards for wages and working conditions be determined? One answer is that these standards should be set by the market. In developed countries, the determination of wages and working conditions results primarily from the competition among employers for desirable workers, which compels them to offer high wages and good working conditions. On this view, there is nothing unjust about jobs with lower pay and poorer working conditions. As long as workers are willing to accept employment on the terms offered, then any arrangement is justified. On this view, no wage can be too low in a free market. However, using the market to determine the standards for wages and working conditions in developing countries encounters two obstacles.

First, developed countries do not rely solely on the market but set certain minimum conditions by law, such as minimum wage laws, fair labor standards, and health and safety regulations. These conditions reflect, in part, the recognition of certain human rights that ought to be observed in all economic activity. Thus, one rationale for minimum wage laws is that it is unjust to pay workers less than a certain amount. That is, some wages are unjustifiably low, even if enough workers would accept them. Although multinational corporations and their foreign contractors generally pay the legal minimum wage in the countries where they operate, this amount often provides only a basic subsistence for one person, if that. Consequently, critics argue that the standard should be a "living wage" that enables a worker to live with dignity and support a family.

The second obstacle to using the market to set wages and working conditions is the possibility that the conditions for a free market are lacking. In particular, the mass of unemployed, desperately poor people in less developed countries constitutes a pool of laborers willing accept bare subsistence wages. The market for labor in any given country may also be artificially low because of political repression that prevents workers from organizing. Although the role of correcting such market failures generally falls to national governments—by enacting minimum wage laws, for example—this form of protection is often uncertain in less developed countries.

Consequently, we need to consider the extent to which market forces should be allowed to operate in the setting of wages and working conditions and the extent to which principles of human rights ought to be applied. Specifically, should multinationals and foreign contractors be guided only by the market as long as they observe local laws? Or should they observe higher standards than either the law or the market dictates, guided perhaps by certain human rights principles? In some instances, workplace abuses—such as degrading punishment, forced overtime, and confinement to company quarters—have little or no economic justification. Although the wrongness of these abuses is not in question, we still need to ask whether a company such as Nike is responsible for the abusive practices of its foreign contractors and, if it is responsible, what steps should a company take to prevent these abuses.

What Is a Justified Wage?

The wages paid by multinationals and their foreign contractors are usually above the minimum wage and the prevailing market rate. As a result, the jobs in these factories generally pay better than work in local enterprises, and regular employment in the formal economy is vastly superior to work in the informal sector, which includes agriculture, domestic service, and small, unregulated manufacture. Even so, the wages paid for factory work are seldom sufficient to provide what the nation's government calculates as the minimum for a decent standard of living or the minimum physical needs for one person, let alone a family. In many poor countries of Southeast Asia and Central America, the minimum wage set by law is below the official poverty level.

Critics observe that the labor cost for a pair of shoes or a shirt is usually a few cents and that paying a few cents more would add little to the ultimate price. However, economists warn that raising the pay scales in a developing country has serious adverse consequences. Well-intentioned efforts to better the condition of factory workers will ultimately reduce the number of jobs and the level of foreign investment. If a government raises the minimum wage or multinationals and foreign contractors are pressured to pay above-market wages, the result will be a reduced incentive to relocate jobs from higher-wage countries. Because higher-wage countries have more productive workers and a better infrastructure for manufacturing, firms will have little reason to move to a less developed country unless it offers significantly lower labor costs.

This economic argument shows, first, why less developed countries should not raise the minimum wage beyond the market value of its labor. In a developed country, raising the minimum wage generally benefits low-wage workers without much effect on others, but the effect in a less developed country is different. Although a relatively small minority of urban workers, who already make above-average wages, may benefit, the vast majority will suffer for lack of jobs, and the economy will not develop for lack of foreign investment. For this reason, the economist Jagdish Bhagwati contends, "Requiring a minimum wage in an overpopulated, developing country... may actually be morally wicked."[17]

Low labor costs constitute a competitive advantage for a poor country, and attracting investment on this basis provides jobs that can lead to greater development. Indeed, formerly low-wage countries, such as Korea, Taiwan, and Malaysia, have successfully employed this strategy for creating higher-paying jobs. The result is the same if multinational corporations and their foreign contractors are required, say by public pressure, to pay above-market wages. If firms do not take advantage of the low-cost labor in a countries like Indonesia and Vietnam, then they are depriving these countries of the opportunity to use their main competitive edge, namely unemployed workers, to begin the process of development.

This argument about wages also applies to working conditions inasmuch as both are matters of cost. According to a World Bank report, "Reducing hazards in the workplace is costly, and typically the greater the reduction the more it costs. . . . As a result, setting standards too high can actually lower workers' welfare."[18] One reason for this outcome is that investment to improve working conditions may come at the expense of wages. More significantly, if higher standards inhibit foreign investment, then fewer jobs are created and more of those available are in local industries with lower pay and working conditions.

The dispute between those who advocate paying the market rate for labor and those favoring a "living wage" is not over the ultimate end which is to improve the welfare of people in developing countries. The difference lies in the appropriate means. Economists argue that requiring higher wages is counterproductive; it harms the very people we are trying to benefit. The only path to prosperity is economic development, and this requires an attractive climate for foreign investment. Proponents of a "living wage" believe, on the other hand, that payment of wages above a certain level is morally required. To offer less than a "living wage" is to exploit an opportunity for cheap labor.

One difficulty with the economists' position is that it fails to consider the possibility of exploitation. It assumes that whatever wages people are willing to accept is just. However, most of the jobs in question are among the best paying, so the case for exploitation is weak. Moreover, the "living wage" position seems to entail that no job at all is preferable to one below the living-wage standard. Although developing countries are forced to keep wages low in their competition with each other to attract foreign investment, they still seem to prefer all the low-wage jobs they can get, regardless of whether they pay a "living wage."

Toward a Solution

In contrast to the issue of wages, which remains controversial, there is general agreement on standards for working conditions. When the television personality Kathy Lee Gifford was confronted in 1996 with evidence that the line of clothes she endorsed was made in Honduras by young girls 13 and 14 years old, working 20-hour days for 31 cents an hour, she resolved to correct these abuses. The same year, *Life* magazine published a photograph of a 12-year-old boy in Pakistan stitching a Nike soccer ball. Phil Knight replied that "Nike has zero tolerance for under-age labor." Reports on contractors for other American companies described women who were confined to factory compounds, berated and beaten for violating rules or failing to meet quotas, forbidden to use toilets, and fired for protesting or attempting to organize. In some instances, young women have been forced to take contraceptive pills or undergo pregnancy tests, and they have been dismissed for becoming pregnant. Many factories lack adequate ventilation, sanitation facilities, medical supplies, and fire safety provisions, and workers often have little protection from machines and toxic chemicals.

For many companies, the first step has been to adopt codes of conduct for their own operations and those of contractors. In 1992, Nike adopted a "Code of Conduct" and a "Memorandum of Understanding" which are included with all contracts. The Nike code forbids hiring anyone under 18 in shoe manufacture and under 16 for producing clothing (unless higher ages are mandated by law). It stipulates that workers be paid the higher of the legal minimum wage or the prevailing wage, with a clear, written accounting of all hours and deductions. Although forced overtime is permitted, provided employees are informed and fully compensated according to local law, the code requires one day off in seven and no more than 60 hours a week. Nike also developed a comprehensive Management of Environment, Safety and Health (MESH) that provides for safety standards, a safety committee in each factory, and free personal protective equipment for at-risk employees.

Although these actions addressed the major areas of concern, critics charged that Nike had not gone far enough in setting high standards. In 1990, Reebok, a Nike competitor, adopted a far-reaching human rights policy and inserted human rights language in its contracts. Reebok also committed itself to auditing its contractors for compliance with the human rights policy. Nike, too, agreed to auditing by hiring the firm Ernst & Young to conduct site visits of its contractors. In 1996, Nike also hired the civil rights leader Andrew Young to investigate factories in Asia and to report his findings. Both efforts were denigrated by critics, who challenged the competence of these parties to conduct thorough audits and questioned their independence inasmuch as Nike was footing the bill. Nike's commitment was further undermined when an internal Ernst & Young report, leaked to the press in 1997, revealed serious health and safety issues in a Vietnamese factory.

The challenges of managing foreign contractors are beyond the capability of any single company. First, any firm that invests resources when their competitors do not is put at a competitive disadvantage. Second, each firm deals with thousands of contractors, which in turn manufacture for many brands. The only solution, therefore, is an industrywide effort. The first initiative occurred in 1997 with the launch of the Apparel Industry Partnership (AIP), which Nike immediately joined. Convened by the White House, a group of industry, labor, consumer, and human rights leaders committed themselves to develop a strong workplace code of ethics with internal monitoring and an independent, external monitoring system. The AIP was succeeded the next year by the Fair Labor Association (FLA), which has preserved the same goals. In response to the concern of college students, the Worker Rights Consortium (WRC) was organized to address specifically the conditions under which collegiate apparel with a school's logo is manufactured.

The experiences of the FLA and the WRC reveal substantial agreement on principles and standards, although the issue of a "living wage" has been divisive. The main stumbling block has been monitoring. The practical difficulties of monitoring tens of thousands of contractors around the globe—not to mention the cost of $3,000 to $6,000 for each factory visit—is daunting enough, but the participants have sharply disagreed on issues of principle. For starters, who should do the monitoring? Accounting firms often lack expertise in local situations, whereas activist groups may not be wholly objective. What qualifications should monitors have? How should audits be conducted? Should audits be unannounced or scheduled in advance? Should all of a firm's contractors be audited or only a sample? Should the reports be made public? What actions should be taken when violations are discovered?

As these questions suggest, the solution to the problem of sweatshops requires a sustained, committed effort by all concerned parties. Considerable progress has been made on working conditions—but not on wages. A *New York Times* article profiled a woman who was fired in 1995 for protesting conditions at a factory in El Salvador. Six year later, the woman returned to the factory where workers enjoy coffee breaks in a terrace cafeteria and work in clean, breezy surroundings, but she earns only 60 cents an hour, 5 cents more than before.[19]

Child labor presents an especially thorny issue. Although an estimated 150 million children under the age of 14 work worldwide, less than 5 percent of these make goods for export. The vast majority are employed in the informal economy which contains the most dangerous jobs. Virtually every country bans child labor, but enforcement is often ineffective. Although multinationals should abide by the law and refrain from employing children, the main challenge is how to deal with existing factories that employ children. A *New York Times* editorial observes, "American consumers are right to insist that the goods we buy are not made with child labor. But these efforts will backfire if children kicked out of these factories drift to more hazardous occupations."[20]

In response to this problem, the International Labour Organization has worked with governments and businesses to establish special schools for approximately 10,000 children who worked in garment factories and to pay their parents for the lost wages. Ultimately, the solution to the problem of child labor is not merely to prohibit the employment of underage workers but also to provide schooling for children and jobs for parents so that child labor is no longer an economic necessity.

FOREIGN BRIBERY

As the experience of Lockheed in Japan illustrates (see Case 2.1), bribery is one of the most common and controversial issues that multinational corporations face. Bribery is universally condemned, and no government in the world legally permits bribery of its own officials. However, corruption exists to some extent in every country and is endemic to more than a few. The main ethical question is whether companies are justified in making payments when they are necessary for doing business in a corrupt environment. Although the demand for a bribe may be unethical, is it unethical to give in to a demand? The defenders of bribery thus appeal to the slogan, "We don't agree with the Romans, but find it necessary to do things their way."

The issue of bribery is far from simple. First, the term *bribe* is vague. It applies to many different kinds of payments with varying interpretations, ranging from gift giving and influence peddling to kickbacks and extortion. There is need, therefore, to develop a definition and make some distinctions. Second, corruption is a fact of life in global business, and so MNCs and their home governments must decide how to confront it. The United States has legally prohibited certain kinds of payments since the passage of the Foreign Corrupt Practices Act (FCPA) in 1977. For the next two decades, few countries followed this approach, however, and American companies have complained that they had been placed at a competitive disadvantage. Both the overall approach and specific provisions of the FCPA have been questioned, and so these must be examined.

What Is Bribery? The FCPA forbids American corporations to offer or make any payment to a foreign official for the purpose of "influencing any act or decision of such foreign official in his official capacity or of inducing such foreign official to do or omit to do any act in violation of the lawful duty of such official" in order to obtain or retain business.[21] (The act also covers payments to political parties and candidates for office in foreign countries.) This legal prohibition accords with standard philosophical definitions of bribery.[22] The key point is that a bribe is a payment made with an intention to corrupt. More specifically, the payment is made with the intention of causing a person to be dishonest or disloyal or to betray a trust in the performance of official duties. The holder of a government office has a duty to make decisions about such matters as the purchase of aircraft, for example, according to certain criteria. A corrupt official is one whose decision about this purchase is influenced by a payment, and an aircraft manufacturer who offers something of value for this purpose has made a corrupt payment.

It follows from this definition that certain kinds of payments are legally permitted and do not constitute bribes. These include "facilitating payments," which are made to expedite the performance of "routine governmental action." Also called "grease payments," these are small sums paid to lower-level officials to lubricate the rusty machinery that provides government services. Facilitating payments do not induce anyone to violate a duty or a trust. Still, they are generally prohibited by the same governments that create the need for them, although the laws on such matters are rarely enforced. Also excluded from the category of bribes are reasonable expenditures for legitimate expenses, such as entertaining a foreign official in the course of doing business. Finally, any payments that are permitted or required by the written laws of the country in question are legal under the FCPA. Although such payments might still be considered bribes, the drafters of the FCPA did not believe that American corporations should be prosecuted in the United States for abiding by local laws. The stipulation that the laws be written is designed to ensure that the payments are really legal and not merely customary.

Can a line be drawn between bribes and other kinds of payments that are generally considered ethical? In some business cultures, gifts are means for cementing relations and are given (and reciprocated) without the intention of influencing an official's decision. Payments to gain influence are often intended merely to gain access to a decision maker in order to be heard. If demands for bribes are viewed as a kind of extortion, then companies can say that they make payments not for the purpose of obtaining a favorable decision but in order to avoid being harmed illegitimately. The difficulty with all of these arguments is that the distinctions are subjective at best and prone to special pleading. It is instructive that the Japanese, who have traditionally exchanged gifts in business, have curtailed the practice with government officials after a rash of scandals. If American companies were permitted to make extortion payments but not to pay bribes, then foreign officials might well become more threatening in their requests.

What's Wrong with Bribery? The immorality of demanding or accepting bribes is implicit in the definition of bribery: A government official is violating a duty or a trust. In addition, inducing such a violation by offering a bribe is commonly recognized as a wrong. Corrupting others is as wrong as being corrupt oneself. However, these points do not explain why it is wrong to pay a bribe that is demanded or why a government should prohibit its own citizens from bribing the officials of a foreign country. Each country is generally charged with the task of enforcing its own laws.

The FCPA was enacted by Congress in part to protect American interests. The widespread use of slush funds to make payments during the 1970s raised fears that U.S. corporations were engaging in false financial reporting that compromised the integrity of securities markets. When the Securities and Exchange Commission encouraged the voluntary disclosure of foreign payments without fear of prosecution, more than 450 companies admitted to paying a total of $400 million that was not fully accounted for in their books. In addition, Congress was concerned that foreign payments by American corporations were undermining the governments of friendly countries around the world and interfering in the conduct of U.S. foreign policy.

The principal ethical objection to foreign bribery is that systematic and widespread corruption inhibits the development of fair and efficient markets. First, an economy based on bribery does not provide open access to all competitors on equal terms. Not only are some competitors unable to enter certain markets because of existing bribe arrangements, but all businesses are unable to compete on the merits of their products or services. Bribery generally takes place in secret, so that price and quality are less important factors in making a sale than access. Second, bribery-prone economies are, for the same reasons, less efficient. The efficient allocation of resources depends on readily available information and rational decision making. When bribery occurs, prices are invariably higher than they would be in a competitive market. Higher prices also create a disincentive for domestic and foreign firms to invest in the further development of a nation's economy. These costs of bribery are generally reflected in a lower standard of living for the people of the countries where bribery is commonplace. Put bluntly, corruption is a major cause of poverty and underdevelopment in much of the world today.

Although corrupt government officials bear chief responsibility for the economic consequences of bribery, major multinational corporations contribute to the problem when they actively participate in corruption and take no steps to combat it. They also undermine their own long-term interests, which lie in free and open markets worldwide. Corruption in Russia, for example, does not affect the Russian people alone; it also makes Russia a less attractive environment for investment by corporations from the United States, Europe, and other developed countries. As the economies of all countries become more closely linked, the consequences of corruption in one country impact many others. For example, the turmoil in Russia in 1998, which was due in large part to corruption, caused large losses for many major American banks.

What Should Be Done about Bribery? If bribery is morally wrong as well as economically undesirable, then corporations and governments should take reasonable steps to reduce the incidence of bribery around the world. Some question, however, whether the FCPA is a sound approach. Should the U.S. government attempt to prohibit foreign bribery by American firms, and can the law, as written, be effective? Bribery can effectively be addressed only by concerted action among the major developed countries, and so what kind of cooperation should be sought?

The FCPA forms a legal approach to problems of bribery. In addition to the prohibition of corrupt payments, the act contains an accounting provision that requires corporations to maintain records that "accurately and fairly reflect the transactions and disposition of the assets" of the firm. This provision was drafted in response to the discovery that some corporations had failed to record payments in their books or else disguised their true purpose. For violations of the FCPA, corporations may be fined up to $2 million and individuals may be fined up to $100,000 and imprisoned for up to five years (and the fine for an individual may not be paid by the corporation).

An especially problematic part of the FCPA addresses the responsibility of corporations for the conduct of their agents. Much business in foreign countries is conducted through intermediaries, who may pay bribes without the knowledge of the American firm. When American firms enter into joint ventures with foreign companies, they may have a similar lack of control over the conduct of their business partners and the maintenance of their books. The standard adopted by Congress is that a corporation is responsible when it pays an agent or other third party "knowing or having reason to know" that the payments will be used by that person to bribe a foreign official. Deliberately avoiding knowledge of an agent's activities is not an adequate defense, and so companies should take precautions to "know their agents." Among the advised precautions are checking out the reputation of the agent and being sure that the agent has some genuine service to provide; paying the agent only an amount commensurate with the services provided and seeking an accounting of all expenses incurred; avoiding suspicious requests, such as depositing the money is a certain bank account; and obtaining a detailed agreement that includes a pledge not to violate the FCPA and the right to terminate the contract for any violation.

The justification for prohibiting foreign bribery is rather straightforward. A double standard is employed if a country permits its companies to do abroad what they are forbidden to do at home. Bribery imposes harms and violates basic rights. The main arguments to the contrary are that bribery is necessary for doing business in some countries and that a country that forbids its own companies from bribing places them at an unfair competitive advantage. Some have argued that the FCPA is a form of "ethical imperialism" that imposes our values on other countries.

These arguments are not very persuasive. First, if foreign bribery is wrong, then the fact that America's competitors around the globe practice it does not provide a justification. Second, American firms have been able to compete in many instances without bribing, in part by developing better products and services and marketing them aggressively. Anecdotal evidence suggests that bribery is involved in many contracts that U.S. firms fail to attain, but it is difficult to determine who would have obtained the award had there been a level playing field. No academic studies to date have documented substantial loss of business due to the FCPA.[23] Even if some loss of business has occurred, it must be weighed against the other benefits that led Congress to enact the FCPA. That is, is the United States as a nation better off for the passage of this act? Third, the FCPA is scarcely an instance of "ethical imperialism" because it applies only to the conduct of American firms. In addition, the immorality of bribery comes close to being a universal norm. Perhaps the best way to counter all of these arguments is for the United States to persuade other countries to follow America's lead.

Fortunately, world attitudes are changing. The proposed code of conduct developed by the United Nations Commission on Multinationals has long contained a prohibition on bribery, although the code has yet to be adopted by the organization's membership. The United States has fought, largely without success, to gain agreement for a ban on bribery through the World Trade Organization. However, in the 1990s, leading financial organizations, including the International Monetary Fund and the World Bank, have stressed the economic consequences of foreign bribery and placed restrictions on aid recipients to limit the practice. A private organization, Transparency International, compiles an annual list that scores countries on the perceived level of corruption. These latter efforts seek to influence the "demand" side of the equation by applying pressure on countries that receive bribes.

The most significant development has been the adoption in April 1996 of a legally binding treaty by the 29-member Organization for Economic Cooperation and Development (OECD) which commits each member country to change its laws to accord roughly with the FCPA. Specifically, OECD members, which include the world's richest nations, have agreed to prohibit bribery of foreign officials, impose criminal penalties on those found guilty, and allow for the seizure of profits gained by bribery. This initiative concentrates on the "supply" side by changing the conduct of corporations that have been paying bribes. Many observers are optimistic that the OECD treaty will significantly reduce the incidence of foreign bribery and produce a more level playing field for all multinational corporations.

CULTURAL DIFFERENCES

As globalization advances, business practices are becoming increasingly uniform. Business education is much the same everywhere, and managers from diverse countries approach business in similar ways. Ethics, however, remains stubbornly local. Unlike business skills, which are the same worldwide, people's conceptions of ethical conduct remain rooted in particular cultures. The importance of cultural differences is not confined to the problem of different standards that underlies the "When in Rome" question. Although what is considered right and wrong varies from one culture to another, this kind of difference is only one of the many ways in which different cultures pose a challenge for global business.

Our thinking about ethical issues involves the use of concepts, such as duty, rights, equality, welfare, freedom, and trust. Although these concepts have their counterparts in other languages, their meaning is often slightly different, reflecting each country's culture and history. Indeed, the meanings of these concepts have changed within our own culture over the course of time. As a result, we cannot assume that our conception of rights, for example, is shared by people everywhere.

Furthermore, different cultures place different emphases on these concepts. Thus, some foreign critics contend that Americans place to much stress on rights and too little on equality. For example, high executive compensation in the United States is considered excessive by many people abroad. In response to American criticism of human rights in China, some defenders argue not only that human rights are understood differently in Asia but also that they are less important than the goal of improving people's welfare.

Cultural differences like these occasionally result in misunderstandings and accusations of misconduct. For example, Japanese companies are sometimes accused of showing favoritism to other Japanese firms, thereby mistreating potential foreign business partners. The Japanese response is that they are showing loyalty to companies in long-established relationships. They criticize non-Japanese firms for not establishing close relationships and for lacking loyalty once a relationship is established. Because of this emphasis on loyalty, whistle-blowing is viewed negatively in Japan in contrast to the United States where it is often considered a mark of integrity and moral courage.

Conducting business globally, then, requires us to understand the ways in which cultural differences are reflected in people's moral outlook. Some appreciation of how European and Asian managers view ethics is critical for successful interaction with them, as is a recognition of how America is distinctive.

Is America Distinctive?

Broad generalizations about the ethics of any culture must be made cautiously. Nevertheless, observers have noted some distinctive characteristics of Americans that stand in contrast to the ethical outlook of Europeans, Asians, and others. For example, David Vogel finds evidence of an "ethics gap." "By any available measure," he claims, "the level of public, business, and academic interest in issues of business ethics in the United States far exceeds that in any other capitalist country."[24] This heightened level of concern results, in part, from the higher expectations for business that Americans generally hold.

Vogel further observes that Americans tend to regard the individual as the arbiter of right conduct. That is, Americans are more likely than people elsewhere to consult their own values in deciding what is right and wrong. By contrast, Europeans and Asians generally seek guidance from the community and their own business organization. European managers, in particular, are not inclined to navigate by their own "personal moral compass" but usually consult widely with others and consider the impact of any decision on the organization.[25] As a result, ethical decisions in Europe are more commonly made by a group, not an individual.

Americans are also more legalistic and rule-oriented. They tend not only to embody business ethics in laws that are rigorously enforced but also to think of ethics as a set of rules to be observed. Europeans by contrast disdain Americans' reliance on the law and voluntary codes and rely more on informal mechanisms for securing ethical behavior. In the United States, errant managers are more likely than their counterparts abroad to face legal sanctions, including fines and imprisonment. Moreover, rules are regarded by Americans as universal prescriptions that apply impartially to everyone, whereas Asians, in particular, view moral obligations as arising from specific relationships.

Ethics East and West

Although cultural differences affect people's ethical outlook the world over, the greatest contrast exists between East and West. Westerners who do business in Japan, China, and the other countries of Asia are aware of the different approaches of these two parts of the world to matters of ethics. To be sure, ethics East and West still have much in common, especially with regard to fundamental values. The differences reveal themselves in more subtle ways. We should also be wary of broad generalizations about either Eastern or Western ethics. Neither is monolithic, and both have changed over time. Nevertheless, the ethical outlook of Asians is different in ways that are important for business managers to understand.

The Primacy of Relationships. The most striking feature of Asian firms, especially those in Japan, is the central role of long-term relationships. These rest on a high level of trust among all the parties and require careful attention to each party's interests so as to maintain harmony. In Japan, this feature extends to the *keiretsu,* which is a group of companies closely linked with each other. (A similar structure in Korea is the *Chaebol.*)

Such close ties produce some admired features of Japanese firms, such as lifetime employment and strong employee loyalty. Companies in a *keiretsu* come to each other's aid in times of difficulty. The primacy of relationships has some negative consequences, however. Employees are usually unable to leave a firm, and the pressures to conform have resulted in cases of *karoshi,* in which people are said to work themselves to death. Outside firms complain that they are excluded from doing business with *keiretsu* members. In China, an established relationship, known as *guanxi,* is often critical for gaining access.

In a society built on relationships, ethical obligations depend on what each party owes the other in the relationship. The treatment that one can expect results not only from whether one is inside or outside of a group but also from the specific nature of the relationship itself. Accordingly, norms in such a society tend to be relative or situational rather than absolute and universal.[26] Instead of known rules that are applied equally to all, moral decisions are made on a case-by-case basis with attention to specifics. Laws and regulations are often vague, with large grey areas that are interpreted by government officials to fit the case at hand. Foreign companies often find themselves unsure of the rules, which they suspect, in any event, are being manipulated to favor Japanese firms.

A system built on relationships places great emphasis on reciprocity. That is, each party must take care to return all favors received so as to preserve a balance. Moreover, conflicts need to be handled by a mutual accommodation that preserves the harmony of the group. Any individual or company that takes more than a fair share is viewed as disruptive and, for that reason, untrustworthy. In addition, commitments in a relationship are viewed as binding. Americans, by contrast, tend to make sincere but overly optimistic commitments that they may not be able keep.[27] This cultural difference over the the meaning of commitments is a ready source of misunderstanding.

Explaining Japanese Practices. The features of Japanese firms just described help explain some distinctively Japanese business practices. Although the practices themselves do not bear directly on ethics, they depend crucially on these ethical features, thus illustrating the interplay of ethics and management practice.

First, *kaizen* or continuous improvement is a broad-ranging concept that includes just in time delivery, total quality control, and waste elimination. Making continuous improvements is a responsibility of everyone in a firm, including management, work groups, and individuals, and it utilizes such means as detailed statistical measures, quality circles, and structured group activities. By continually improving all aspects of production, Japanese firms have managed to produce improved products at lower costs.

The success of *kaizen* depends on a strong group commitment, whereby each person aims to benefit the whole organization, and on a high level of trust that one's efforts will be recognized and rewarded. Attempts by American firms to emulate *kaizen* have faltered for lack of these enabling conditions. For starters, workers without job security have little incentive to suggest changes that might eliminate their positions. Although commitment to a firm in Japan results, to some extent, from a distinctively Japanese notion of self-realization through group activity, Japanese companies also create it through a variety of techniques that includes hiring workers in cohorts that generally advance together and receive similar pay. Commitment is further developed by a strict system of seniority and respect for people with diverse talents and abilities.[28]

Second, the *keiretsu* is a distinctively Japanese form of organization that represents extensive horizontal and vertical integration of firms. A horizontally integrated *keiretsu*, such as Mitsubishi, consists of companies that manufacture a wide variety of goods, plus key banks and other financial service firms. Toyota, which is an example of a vertical *keiretsu*, ties together its key suppliers and dealers. Such concentration of economic power would generally be prohibited in the United States by antitrust law.

Although the *keiretsu* system developed in response to historical conditions, it also reflects both the emphasis on relationships and a certain conception fairness. Relationships are conceived by the Japanese as a set of concentric circles. The innermost circle is the family, which has the tightest bonds, and successive circles entail looser ties. Whereas Western firms tend to have arm's-length market relations with other companies, *keiretsu* members have closer working relationships with each other and market relations only with firms outside the group. This arrangement reflects a preference for cooperation over competition.

Moreover, fairness within the sphere of cooperation is primarily a matter of reciprocity, which is to say fulfilling the obligations owed to others, whereas the concept of fairness in competition is reserved for activity outside the *keiretsu*. These two concept of fairness—which may be characterized as doing one's fair share and competing fairly—are applicable to Western firms as well. The main difference is their range of application. Western standards for fair treatment of a supplier are primarily those of fair competition, whereas the standards for a Japanese firm in a *keiretsu* are those of doing one's fair share. Thus, coming to the aid of a supplier may be considered just by a Japanese firm because such treatment is owed to a partner as a matter of doing one's fair share. At the same time, it may be regarded as unjust by a Western company for showing favoritism inasmuch as fair competition requires that all suppliers be treated equally.

Third, regulation in Japan is achieved, in part, through a process known as *administrative guidance*. In the United States and Europe, business is regulated by means of detailed, precise rules that are known to all and applied uniformly. These rules are promulgated primarily by legislatures and regulatory bodies (which are established by legislatures), and they are enforced mainly through the courts. In short, regulation is achieved in the West largely through legislation and adjudication. In Japan, by contrast, powerful administrative bodies, such as the Ministry of Finance and the Ministry for International Trade and Industry, regulate by making decisions in a case-by-case process. The rules themselves are often vague, with the result that business leaders must go to these agencies to get clarification.

Such a system, which is based on administration rather than legislation and adjudication, reflects two features of Japanese ethics. One is the view that ethical norms are situational and relative, instead of being absolute and universal. The second feature is the Confusion ideal of an elite group that is selected and trained to rule. Both Japan and China have centuries-old traditions of bureaucracies staffed by wise and dedicated career civil servants, separated from the political leaders. Affairs in Japan are often described in terms of the "iron triangle" of business, the bureaucracy, and politics.

Although administrative guidance can be viewed as an alternative form of regulation, no better or worse than that of the United States and Europe, the need to establish close working relations with the various ministries is a barrier to foreign enterprises and a source of confusion and misunderstanding. To Americans accustomed to clear and precise rules, the need to obtain clarifications of vague rules raises suspicions of a "rigged game."

Is Agreement Possible?

Given the diversity of ethical outlooks in the world, is it possible to agree on a set of standards for business worldwide? Such a goal must be achievable if globalization is to succeed. The theologian Hans Küng has observed that "the very phenomenon of globalization makes it clear that there must also be a globalization of ethics."[29] Of course, full agreement is not necessary or even desirable, but globalization requires a commitment to some core standards or at least a willingness to abide by them.

Substantial agreement is being achieved through a number of codes that have been developed by international organizations involving governments, religious bodies, and private individuals. The foundational document for human rights is the 1948 United Nations Universal Declaration on Human Rights. In 1966, the U.N. adopted two agreements which have subsequently been ratified by the major countries of the world: the International Covenant on Social, Economic, and Cultural Rights and the International Covenant on Civil and Political Rights. Since 1972, the United Nations has been developing a code of conduct for multinational corporations, which has yet to be completed or adopted. However, in 1999, the U.N. Secretary-General Kofi Annan challenged world business leaders to "embrace and enact" the Global Compact, which consists of nine principles covering human rights, labor, and the environment.

The International Labour Organization, which dates from 1919 and is now a specialized agency of the United Nations, sets many international standards, including those of the Tripartite Declaration of Principles concerning Multinational Enterprises and Social Policy (1977). More recently, the Organization for Economic Cooperation and Development (OECD), whose members are the more developed countries of the world, has adopted the OECD Guidelines for Multinational Enterprises. Several interfaith religious bodies have developed codes. The most prominent are the Principles for Global Corporate Responsibility, adopted by the U.S.-based Interfaith Center on Corporate Responsibility and similar organizations in Great Britain, Ireland, and Canada, and the Interfaith Declaration on International Business Ethics, which resulted from a dialog among Christians, Jews, and Muslims.[30] A group of world business leaders, meeting in Caux, Switzerland, developed the Caux Roundtable Principles for Business.

These codes have many guidelines in common and cover the areas of employment practices, consumer protection, environmental preservation, involvement in politics, including bribery, and basic human rights. The main guidelines, which represent substantial international agreement, are summarized in Exhibit 15.1.

Exhibit 15.1
International Codes of Ethics

Although international codes of ethics have diverse sources, they cover many of the same topics and make similar prescriptions. The following is a summary of the most common elements of these codes.

Employment Practices and Policies

Multinational corporations should

- Respect host-country labor standards and upgrade the local work force through training
- Promote favorable working conditions with limited hours, holidays with pay, and protection against unemployment.
- Promote job stability and job security, avoiding arbitrary dismissals and providing severance pay for those dismissed.

- Pay a basic living wage to employees.
- Develop nondiscriminatory employment policies and provide equal pay for equal work.
- Adopt adequate health and safety standards and inform workers of job-related hazards.
- Respect the right of employees to join labor unions and to bargain collectively.

Consumer Protection

Multinational corporations should

- Respect host-country laws and policies regarding the protection of consumers.
- Safeguard the health and safety of consumers by appropriate disclosures, safe packaging, proper labeling, and accurate advertising.

Environmental Protection

Multinational corporations should

- Respect host-country laws and policies concerning the protection of the environment.
- Preserve ecological balance, adopt preventive measures to avoid harm to the environment, and correct any damage done to the environment by operations.
- Promote the development of international environmental standards.

Political Payments and Involvement

Multinational corporations should

- Avoid paying bribes and making other improper payments to public officials.
- Avoid improper or illegal involvement or interference in the internal politics of host countries.
- Avoid improper interference in relations between national governments.

Basic Rights and Freedoms

Multinational Corporations should

- Respect the rights of all persons to life, liberty, and security.
- Respect the rights of all person to equal protection of the law, freedom of thought and expression, freedom of assembly and association, freedom of residence and movement, and freedom of religion.
- Promote a standard of living that supports the health and well-being of workers and their families, with special attention given to mothers and children.

Source: William C. Frederick, "The Moral Authority of Transnational Corporate Codes," *Journal of Business Ethics*, 10 (1991), 166-67.

The emerging order has been described as a "policy regime" to distinguish it from conventional regulation.[31] Regulation within a state consists of precise rules for most foreseeable circumstances that are enforced by law. In the absence of international government, the main alternative is the development of mutually accepted norms that serve to coordinate global business activity. A policy regime provides everyone with a reasonable set of expectations about how others will behave. The various codes that make up a policy regime do not have the force of law but still represent publicly declared commitments that have some binding force.

A policy regime is enforced primarily by the advantages of cooperation and the threat of retaliation for not cooperating. Although compliance is voluntary, countries usually find it in their interest to abide by the major codes. However, these codes also draw strength from their ethical force. That is, the widespread recognition that the guidelines represent universal values further contributes to their observance. Consequently, codes for international business are more likely to be effective when they have considerable moral authority. William C. Frederick finds four sources from which codes derive moral authority. These are (1) *national sovereignty*, which underlies strictures against interfering in the political process of a host country and bribing foreign officials; (2) *equality*, which supports nondiscriminatory treatment on the basis of race, sex, nationality; (3) *market integrity*, which requires property rights, contracts, fair competition, and the other conditions for free markets to operate; and (4) *human rights*.[32] Any guidelines not supported by these sources—to aid in a country's development, for example—do not have strong moral force and hence are less effective.

Of course, agreement on international codes of ethics can mask some substantial cultural differences and people's positions on specific issues. For example, in response to criticism of their human rights record, the leaders of China and some other Asian countries argue that the rights of people to economic well-being take precedence over other rights. Although the legal and political rights that are essential to a fair judicial system and free, democratic government are long-term goals, they must be deferred, these leaders say, until sufficient economic progress permits their realization. This emphasis on economic development before political liberalization has been defended in the name of "Asian values." However, questions can be raised about whether some rights that are being deferred really do require economic progress to be realized. Indeed, some legal and political rights may be instrumental in furthering economic development.[33]

Conclusion

Operating abroad, especially in less developed countries, creates dilemmas that lead to charges of serious ethical failings. Multinational corporations generally recognize a social responsibility and attempt to fulfill their responsibilities everywhere they are located. The major cause of occasional failures to act responsibly is not the lack of effort but the diversity of political and legal systems around the world and differences in economic development. Foreign operations give rise to challenges—and also create opportunities for misconduct—that simply do not exist for purely domestic enterprises.

The main quandary facing all MNCs is deciding which standards to follow. We have seen that neither of the two extreme positions is satisfactory. The familiar adage "When in Rome, do as the Romans do" and the opposite, "When in Rome or anywhere else, do as you would at home," are both inadequate guides. Instead, this chapter offers guidelines for developing special standards for the conduct of international business that can be applied to such matters as so-called sweatshops and to foreign bribery. Ultimately, the solution to many of the ethical problems of international business lies in the development of international agreements and codes of ethics. As the guidelines for multinational corporations become more detailed and comprehensive, the need for special standards of international business may diminish, and business conduct may eventually be the same worldwide.

Case 15.2 H. B. Fuller in Honduras

In 1985, journalists began writing about a new social problem in Honduras that created an acute dilemma for H. B. Fuller Company, based in St. Paul, Minnesota.[34] The news stories described the ravaging effects of glue sniffing among the street children of Tegucigalpa, the capital of Honduras, and other Central American cities. The drug of choice for these addicts was Resistol, a glue produced by a Honduran subsidiary of H. B. Fuller, and the victims of this debilitating habit were known, in Spanish, as *resistoleros*. The negative publicity was sullying the company's stellar reputation for corporate social responsibility, and company executives came under great pressure to address the problem quickly.

Poverty in Honduras had forced many families to send their children into the streets to beg or do odd jobs. The earnings of these children were critical to the support of many families, especially those headed by a single mother. Some children lived in the streets in order to avoid abusive homes; others were abandoned or orphaned. Many children, some as young as five or six, sought relief from their misery by sniffing glue containing volatile solvents which produces a temporary elation and sense of power. These chemicals are addictive and lead to irreversible damage to the brain and liver. The victims of solvent abuse generally stagger as they walk and exhibit tense, aggressive behavior.

Resistol is a brand name for a line of adhesives manufactured by a wholly owned subsidiary of H. B. Fuller and marketed throughout Latin America. The solvent-based adhesives favored by glue sniffers were widely used in shoemaking and shoe repair and were readily available on the street. H. B. Fuller had urged the press not to use the term *resistoleros* because other brands of adhesives were used as well and the problem was with the abuse of Resistol, not the product itself. Nevertheless, the name was commonly used in Honduras to describe the street children addicted to solvents. One of H. B. Fuller's most successful brands had thus become synonymous with a major social problem.

Criticism of H. B. Fuller for the company's involvement in this problem came not only from activists and public health officials in Honduras but also from customers and shareholders in the United States. One shareholder asked, "How can a company like H. B. Fuller claim to have a social conscience and continue to sell Resistol, which is 'literally burning out the brains' of children in Latin America?" The company's mission statement placed its commitment to customers first, followed by its responsibilities to employees and shareholders. And the statement affirms: "H. B. Fuller will conduct business legally and ethically... and be a responsible corporate citizen." When the company acquired its subsidiary in Honduras, the CEO at the time said:

> We were convinced that we had something to offer Latin America that the region did not have locally. In our own small way, we also wanted to be of help to that part of the world. We believed that by producing adhesives in Latin America and by employing only local people, we would create new jobs and help elevate the standard of living. We were convinced that the way to aid world peace was to help Latin America become more prosperous.

Company executives faced the dilemma of whether these expressions of H. B. Fuller's aspirations could be reconciled with the continued production of Resistol in Honduras.

Community activists in Honduras proposed the addition of oil of mustard to all solvent-based adhesives. This chemical, allyl isothiocyanate, produces a reaction that has been compared to getting an overdose of horseradish. Adding it to Resistol would effectively deter anyone attempting to inhale the fumes. However, research revealed that oil of mustard has many side effects, including severe irritation of the eyes, nose, throat, and lungs, and it can even be fatal if inhaled, swallowed, or absorbed through the skin. In addition, adhesives with oil of mustard have a shelf life of only six months. H. B. Fuller executives were convinced that the addition of oil of mustard was not an acceptable solution. However, in 1989, the Honduran legislature passed a law requiring oil of mustard, despite the lobbying efforts of H. B. Fuller.

Another alternative was a community relations effort to alert people about the dangers of glue sniffing and to address the underlying social causes. By working with community groups and the government, the company could spread the responsibility and expand its resources. On the other hand, the community groups in Honduras and elsewhere in the region were not well organized, and the government was unstable and unreliable. In 1982, the Gillette Company had faced a similar problem with its solvent-based typewriter correction fluid, Liquid Paper, which was being abused by youngsters in the United States. Gillette also rejected the possibility of adding oil of mustard, but the company's community relations effort was facilitated by the existing network of private and government-sponsored drug education programs. In Honduras, H. B. Fuller did not have the same base of community and government support. A community relations effort would be much more difficult in a less developed country.

H. B. Fuller executives also considered withdrawing all solvent-based adhesives from the market and perhaps substituting water-based products, but these alternatives were not very attractive from a business point of view. Furthermore, they would have no impact on the critical social problem of glue sniffing by street children. The waste of young lives would continue unless conditions were changed. But what could a modest-sized company located in St. Paul, Minnesota, do to address a problem caused by deep cultural, social, political, and economic forces? A failure to act, however, would seriously damage H. B. Fuller's carefully built reputation for corporate social responsibility.

Case 15.3 Shell Oil in Nigeria

On November 2, 1995, the Nigerian writer and activist Ken Saro-Wiwa was found guilty of ordering the murder of several Ogoni chiefs who were suspected of collaborating with the military government of Nigeria.[35] The Nigerian junta, headed at the time by General Sani Abacha, was criticized worldwide for bringing trumped-up charges against Saro-Wiwa and 14 co-defendants in order to suppress a resistance movement that had criticized the operations of Shell Oil Company in the oil-rich Ogoniland region of Nigeria. A specially created tribunal, widely regarded as a kangaroo court, sentenced Saro-Wiwa and six others to death by hanging (eight of the accused were acquitted). Many world leaders and human rights organizations called upon Shell Oil Company to persuade the Nigerian government not to execute Ken Saro-Wiwa, but Shell executives were reluctant to intervene. According to one company official, "It is not for a commercial organization like Shell to interfere in the legal processes of a sovereign state such as Nigeria." Another executive said, "Our responsibility is very clear. We pay taxes and [abide by] regulation. We don't run the government." However, critics charged that Shell had been actively involved all along in the military suppression of the Ogoni people. A *New York Times* editorial described Shell's position as "untenable." "If the company is determined to stay in Nigeria, it must use its considerable influence there to restrain the government."

Royal Dutch/Shell is the world's largest oil company, earning profits of $6.2 billion in 1994 on $94.9 billion in revenue. With headquarters in both London and The Hague, Netherlands, and with operations in more than one hundred countries, this joint Anglo-Dutch enterprise is truly a transnational corporation.[36] When oil was discovered in the Niger River delta in 1956, Royal Dutch/Shell was the first major company to begin production. Today, Nigeria pumps approximately two million barrels of crude oil, which provides about $10 billion a year for the military government or more than 80 percent of total government revenues. Almost half of this amount is produced by Shell Nigeria, in which the Nigerian government has a 55 percent stake and Royal Dutch/Shell a 30 percent stake (the remaining 15 percent is owned by a

French and an Italian company). The Nigerian government mainly sits back and rakes in the profits; for its efforts in Nigeria, Royal Dutch/Shell receives about $312 million in profit each year. Nigeria is, arguably, the most corrupt country in the world and, for the vast majority of its people, one of the poorest. Most Nigerians live on less than $300 a year, while the country's elite maintain lavish lifestyles. A military government that came to power in 1993 annulled that year's election for president, abolished the major democratic institutions, closed many newspapers, and silenced all opposition. The country's infrastructure continued to deteriorate because funds for public works were being siphoned off by government officials and their henchmen into guarded villas, fleets of luxury cars, and foreign bank accounts. General Abacha was rumored to have stashed more than a billion dollars abroad.

Shell's operations are centered in Ogoniland, a 400-square-mile area at the mouth of the Niger River, where approximately one-half million Ogoni live in crowded, squalid conditions among some of the world's worst pollution. Although much of the pollution is due to overpopulation, oil spills and atmospheric discharges foul the environment. The most serious oil-related harm is due to flaring, which is the burning of the natural gas that results from oil production. Flares from tall vents create an eerie orange glow in the sky and emit greenhouse gases along with heat, soot, and noise. Very little of the wealth that comes from the ground in Ogoniland reaches the local population. Between 1958 and 1994, an estimated $30 billion worth of oil was extracted from the area. Under the formula for sharing revenue with the states, the federal government was obligated to return only 1.5 percent to Ogoniland (the percentage was increased to 3 percent in 1992), but much of this revenue was diverted by corruption. Shell Nigeria also returned some profits to the region, contributing $20 million in 1995 for schools, hospitals, and other services. However, some of this money was also used to build roads to oil installations, and a World Bank study concluded that the impact of the oil company's investment on the quality of life in Ogoniland was "minimal."

Ken Saro-Wiwa was a successful Ogoni businessman turned writer and television producer who developed an interest in political activism in his late forties. He was instrumental in drafting an Ogoni Bill of Rights that demanded a "fair proportion" of oil revenues and greater environmental protection, and he helped form the Movement for the Survival of the Ogoni People (MOSOP). Saro-Wiwa traveled widely in the United States and Europe to build support for the new organization, and for his efforts he was nominated for the Nobel Peace Prize. Although MOSOP sought change from the federal government (and, to dramatize its cause, issued a symbolic demand for $10 billion in compensation from Shell), the organization opposed the use of violence and the idea of secession from Nigeria. Despite the calls for nonviolence, gangs of armed youths staged raids on oil installations, looting and vandalizing the facilities and attacking workers. In January 1993, Shell Nigeria abruptly ceased production in Ogoniland and evacuated its employees from the region. Amid growing civil unrest and military crackdowns, the leadership of MOSOP split. Ken Saro-Wiwa rejected a strategy of cooperating with the federal government to reduce violence in return for concessions. In particular, he called for a boycott of elections scheduled for June 1993, while some other leaders urged participation. On May 21, 1993, several hundred young men attacked a house where a group of dissident Ogoni chiefs (known as the "vultures") was meeting and killed most of them before the police could intervene. Although Saro-Wiwa was far away from the scene of the killing—he had been prevented from attending a MOSOP rally and had returned home—he was arrested the next day and imprisoned for eight months before his trial.

After the first attacks on Shell installations in Ogoniland, the company accepted the protection of the Nigerian police and provided some support for their services. Shell admits that the company provided firearms to the police, but human rights organizations charge that Shell-owned vehicles were used to transport police and soldiers and Shell officials participated in the planning of security operations. In an effort to induce Shell to resume operations in Ogoniland, General Abacha formed a special Internal Security Task Force to suppress opposition to the company's operations in the area. In a memo dated May 12, 1994, the commander of the task force proposed "wasting" operations to undermine the support for MOSOP and advised the government to seek prompt regular inputs from the oil companies. Shell denied making any payments for this purpose.

In May and June of 1994, the task force attacked at least 30 towns and villages, assaulting and killing the inhabitants and looting and destroying homes, fields, and livestock. By the time of Ken Saro-Wiwa's trial, Shell had not returned to Ogoniland, but its operations elsewhere in Nigeria were conducted with round-the-clock military protection. Critics generally accept Shell's arguments that withdrawing from Nigeria would harm the Nigerian people, but a *New York Times* editorial concluded that "Shell can no longer pretend that the political life of Nigeria is none of its business." To the argument that the company is merely a guest in the country, the editorial responds, "Shell, surely, has never hesitated to use its influence on matters of Nigerian tax policy, environmental rules, labor laws and trade policies."

Postscript

Eight days after being sentenced to death, Ken Saro-Wiwa was hanged along with eight others. The United States, Canada, South Africa, and many European countries withdrew their ambassadors in protest, and a consumer boycott was organized by several human rights and environmental organizations. A Shell statement expressed "deep regret" over the executions. Although the company admitted that its top official had appealed privately to General Abacha for clemency on "humanitarian grounds," a spokesperson said, "We can't issue a bold statement about human rights because ... it could be considered treasonous by the regime and employees could come under attack. It would only inflame the issues." Within a week of Ken Saro-Wiwa's death, Shell announced plans for a $4 billion liquefied natural gas plant in a partnership with the Nigerian government.

NOTES

1. John H. Cushman, Jr., "Nike to Step Forward on Plant Conditions," *San Diego Union-Tribune*, 13 May 1998, A1.
2. Richard J. Barnet and John Cavanagh, *Global Dreams: Imperial Corporations and the New World Order* (New York: Simon & Schuster, 1994), 326.
3. Adam Schwarz, "Running a Business," *Far Eastern Economic Review*, 20 June 1991, 16.
4. Barnet and Cavanagh, *Global Dreams*, 326.
5. Jeffrey Ballinger, "The New Free Trade Heel," *Harper's Magazine*, August 1992, 64.
6. Norman E. Bowie, "The Moral Obligations of Multinational Corporations," in *Problems of International Justice*, ed. Steven Luper-Foy (Boulder, CO: Westview Press, 1987), 97.
7. Ralph J. Ledogar, *Hungry for Profits: U.S. and Drug Multinationals in Latin American* (New York: IDOC/North America, 1975), 46-47.
8. See Paul Steidlmeier, "Gift Giving, Bribery and Corruption: Management of Business Relationships in China," *Journal of Business Ethics*, 12 (1993), 157-64.
9. Sheila M. Puffer and Daniel J. McCarthy, "Finding Common Ground in Russian and American Business Ethics," *California Management Review*, 37 (Winter 1995), 29-46. The points in this paragraph are drawn from this article.
10. Thomas Donaldson, *The Ethics of International Business* (New York: Oxford University Press, 1989).
11. Ibid., 62.
12. Ibid., 81.
13. Ibid., 124.
14. Manuel Velasquez, "International Business Ethics: The Aluminum Companies in Jamaica," *Business Ethics Quarterly*, 5 (1995), 878.
15. Messaoud Mehafdi, "The Ethics of International Transfer Pricing," *Journal of Business Ethics*, 28 (2000), 367, 374-75.
16. Bowie, "Moral Obligations of Multinational Corporations," 529.
17. Jagdish Bhagwati and Robert E. Hudec, eds., *Fair Trade and Harmonization*, Vol. 1 (Cambridge, MA: MIT Press, 1996), 2.
18. World Bank, *Workers in an Integrating World Economy*, 75.
19. Leslie Kaufman and David Gonzalez, "Labor Standards Clash with Global Reality," *New York Times*, 24 April 2001, A1.
20. "The Invisible Children," *New York Times*, 20 February 2000, sec. 4, p. 12.
21. U.S.C. §78dd-1 (a)(1).
22. Michael Phillips, "Bribery," *Ethics*, 94 (1984), 621-36; Thomas L. Carson, "Bribery, Extortion, and the 'Foreign Corrupt Practices Act,'" *Philosophy and Public Affairs*, 14 (1985) 66-90; John Danley, "Toward a Theory of Bribery," *Business and Professional Ethics Journal*, 2 (1983) 19-39; and Kendall D'Andrade, Jr., "Bribery," *Journal of Business Ethics*, 4 (1985), 239-48.
23. See Kate Gillispie, "Middle East Response to the U.S. Foreign Corrupt Policies Act," *California Management Review*, 29 (1987), 9-30; and Paul J. Beck, Michael W. Maher, and Adrian E Tschoegl, "The Impact of the Foreign Corrupt Policies Act on U.S. Exports," *Managerial and Decision Economics*, 12 (1991), 295-303.
24. David Vogel, "The Globalization of Business Ethics: Why America Remains Distinctive," *California Management Review*, 35 (Fall 1991), 35.
25. Henk van Luijk, "Recent Developments in European Business Ethics," *Journal of Business Ethics*, 9 (1990), 542.

26. Ernest Gundling, "Ethics and Working with the Japanese: The Entrepreneur and the Elite Course," *California Management Review,* 33 (Spring 1991), 27.
27. Ibid., 31.
28. Iwao Taka and Wanda D. Foglia, "Ethical Aspects of 'Japanese Leadership Style,'" *Journal of Business Ethics,* 13 (1994), 135-48.
29. Hans Küng, "A Global Ethics in an Age of Globalization," *Business Ethics Quarterly,* 7 (1997), 18.
30. Simon Webley, "The Interfaith Declaration: Constructing a Code of Ethics for International Business, *Business Ethics: A European Review,* 5 (1996), 52-57.
31. Duane Windsor, "Toward a Transnational Code of Business Conduct," in *Emerging Global Business Ethics,* W. Michael Hoffman et al., eds. (Westport, CT: Quorum Books, 1994), 173.
32. William C. Frederick, "The Moral Authority of Transnational Corporate Codes," *Journal of Business Ethics,* 10 (1991), 165-77.
33. This position is argued in Amartya Sen, *Development as Freedom* (New York: Knopf, 1999). See also, Xiaorong Li, "A Question of Priorities: Human Rights, Development, and 'Asian Values'," *Philosophy and Public Policy,* 18 (1998), 7-12.
34. This case was adapted from "H. B. Fuller in Honduras: Street Children and Substance Abuse," prepared by Norman E. Bowie and Stefanie Ann Lenway. Copyright 1991 by Columbia Graduate School of Business.
35. This case is based on "Shell Oil in Nigeria," by Anne T. Lawrence, in *Case Research Journal,* 17 (Fall–Winter 1997), 1-21; Joshua Hammer, "Nigeria Crude," *Harper's Magazine,* June 1996, 58-68; Paul Lewis, "Rights Groups Say Shell Oil Shares Blame," *New York Times,* 11 November 1995, sec. 1, p. 6; "Shell Game in Nigeria," *New York Times,* 3 December 1995, sec. 4, p. 14; Andy Rowell, "Shell Shocked: Did the Shell Petroleum Company Silence Nigerian Environmentalist Ken Saro-Wiwa?" *The Village Voice,* 21 November 1995, 21; Andy Rowell, "Sleeping with the Enemy: Worldwide Protests Can't Stop Shell Snuggling up to Nigeria's Military," *The Village Voice,* 23 January 1996, 23; Paul Beckett, "Shell Boldly Defends Its Role in Nigeria," *Wall Street Journal,* 27 November 1995, A9.
36. Shell Oil Company U.S. is a wholly owned subsidiary of Royal Dutch/Shell. In 1995, the U.S. company had no direct operations or direct investment in Nigeria.